D1562754

HISTORICAL DICTIONARIES OF
WOMEN IN THE WORLD
Edited by Jon Woronoff

1. *Women in Sub-Saharan Africa*, by Kathleen Sheldon. 2005.

Historical Dictionary of Women in Sub-Saharan Africa

Kathleen Sheldon

Historical Dictionaries of
Women in the World, No. 1

The Scarecrow Press, Inc.
Lanham, Maryland • Toronto • Oxford
2005

SCARECROW PRESS, INC.

Published in the United States of America
by Scarecrow Press, Inc.
A wholly owned subsidiary of The Rowman & Littlefield Publishing Group, Inc.
4501 Forbes Boulevard, Suite 200
Lanham, Maryland 20706
www.scarecrowpress.com

PO Box 317
Oxford
OX2 9RU, UK

British Library Cataloguing in Publication Information Available

Library of Congress Cataloging-in-Publication Data

Sheldon, Kathleen E., 1952–
    Historical dictionary of women in Sub-Saharan Africa / Kathleen Sheldon.
      p. cm. — (Historical dictionaries of women in the world ; no. 1)
    Includes bibliographical references.
    ISBN 0-8108-5331-0 (hardcover : alk. paper)
    1. Women—Africa, Sub-Saharan—History—Dictionaries. 2. Feminism—Africa,
Sub-Saharan—History—Dictionaries. I. Title. II. Series.
HQ1787.S44 2005
305.4'0967'03—dc22
                                                2004026089

∞™ The paper used in this publication meets the minimum requirements of
American National Standard for Information Sciences—Permanence of Paper
for Printed Library Materials, ANSI/NISO Z39.48-1992.
Manufactured in the United States of America.

Contents

Editor's Foreword

The current knowledge on sub-Saharan Africa is, in general, inadequate, and specifically there is an abysmal lack of information about the female half of that region's population. It is hard to find much data of note about significant women and female-oriented events, institutions, and organizations even in our African historical dictionaries, which are making a serious attempt to fill the gap. This dearth of information is hardly the fault of the authors, since women have not been written about very much and have been either ignored or purposely excluded in the political, economic, and even social spheres of the continent. It is not that what women do is of little importance. The origin of this problem stretches back over centuries and is far from being resolved, which makes the *Historical Dictionary of Women in Sub-Saharan Africa* particularly welcome as the first in a promising new series.

Like Scarecrow Press's other historical dictionaries, the core of this book is a dictionary, which digs deep to provide entries for more remote historical periods and expands the liberation struggles and activities of sub-Saharan Africa since independence, to which women have contributed substantially. Entries on the past half century or so are more numerous and encouraging, but the most significant women are still mainly in secondary or support positions. Although they're working hard for improvement and there has been some progress, as can be seen by the entries on feminist and more general organizations, the concrete results are still fairly modest. All this information is all charted in a chronology, which for the earlier period pinpoints truly exceptional women, and for the more recent period demonstrates that women have been able to make headway in many more sectors. In some ways the most encouraging section of the book is the bibliography, which clearly shows the amount of interest in the neglected women's side of African history and the efforts in bringing it to light.

Many historical dictionary authors have to start almost from scratch in hunting for topics, collecting facts, and piecing together the bits and pieces of available information. Few have had to work quite as hard at it as Kathleen Sheldon. Indeed, though she has been compiling this historical dictionary for several years, she has in a sense been preparing it since the mid-1970s, when she began studying African history. She has visited Africa periodically (especially Mozambique) and continues her efforts as a research scholar at the Center for the Study of Women of UCLA. During this time, Dr. Sheldon has lectured frequently and written many articles. She has also helped produce a resource guide to women's studies, edited *Courtyards, Markets, City Streets: Urban Women in Africa*, and more recently written *Pounders of Grain: A History of Women, Work, and Politics in Mozambique*.

Jon Woronoff,
Series Editor

Acknowledgments

I could not have completed this historical dictionary without assistance and advice from many people who gave me suggestions for entries and for sources, sent copies of their own papers and publications, and critiqued drafts of some of the entries, thus helping me avoid egregious errors and omissions. I am also very grateful to the African women who responded to my direct queries with information about their careers and organizational affiliations. Unfortunately, the format of an historical dictionary makes it difficult to mention such assistance in the text of the entries. In addition to subscribers to all of the Africa-related listserves at H-Net (http://www.h-net.msu.edu/), the following people offered information and recommendations (many apologies to anyone I have absentmindedly forgotten to note): David Anthony, Gretchen Bauer, Heike Behrend, Elias Bongmba, Inge Brinkman, Georgette Deballe-Koyt, LaRay Denzer, Robert Edgar, Beti Ellerson, Eva Evers Rosander, David Gordon, Jean Hay, Catherine Higgs, 'Mamphono Khatketla for contact with Caroline Ntseliseng 'Masechele Khaketla, Rose Lake, Benjamin Nicholas Lawrance, Jane Martin, Michelle Moyd, Catharine Newbury, Andre Odendaal, David Owusu-Ansah, Isabel Phiri, Martha Saavedra, Gerhard Seibert for contact with Alda Bandeira, Victoria Sekitoleko, Elizabeth Schmidt, Nancy Schwartz, Eugenia Shanklin, Rhiannon Stephens, Beverly Stoeltje, John Thornton, Aili Mari Tripp, Heather Turcotte, Judith Van Allen, Susanna Wing, Patrick Wurster, and Chris Youé. Thanks also to Steve Tarzynski and Mercie Sheldon-Tarzynski for reading and commenting on portions of the manuscript.

I would like to extend my special appreciation to the National Coalition of Independent Scholars, which awarded me a research grant in

2003 to help with expenses related to researching and producing this historical dictionary. In addition, my affiliation as a research scholar at the Center for the Study of Women at the University of California, Los Angeles, has made this work possible by providing Internet access and library privileges.

Abbreviations and Acronyms

AACC	All Africa Conference of Churches
AAWORD	Association of African Women for Research and Development
AAWS	Association of African Women Scholars
ACFODE	Action for Development (Uganda)
ACGD	African Centre for Gender and Development
AFARD	Association des Femmes Africaines pour la Recherche sur le Développement
AFI	Association des Femmes Ivoiriennes
AFN	Association des Femmes du Niger
AFWE	African Federation of Women Entrepreneurs
AGI	African Gender Institute (Cape Town, South Africa)
AGS	Abeokuta Grammar School
AJM	Association des Juristes Maliennes
AKFM	Antoko'ny Kongresi'ny Fahaleovantenan'i Madagasikara/Congress Party of Independence of Madagascar
ALF	Africa Leadership Forum
AMANITARE	African Partnership for Sexual and Reproductive Health and Rights of Women and Girls
AME	African Methodist Episcopal
ANA	Association of Nigerian Authors
ANC	African National Congress (South Africa)
APROFER	Association pour la Promotion de la Femme Rwandaise
ATRCW	African Training and Research Centre for Women
AWMC	African Women's Media Center
AWPSG	African Women and Peace Support Group
BLP	Better Life Programme for Rural Women
BWL	Bantu Women's League

CAFO	Coordination des Associations et ONGs Féminines du Mali
CAMS	Commission pour l'Abolition des Mutilations Sexuelles
CAR	Central African Republic
CCM	Chama cha Mapinduzi/Party of the Revolution (Tanzania)
CCP	Convention People's Party (Ghana)
CEDAW	Convention on the Elimination of All Forms of Discrimination Against Women
CODESRIA	Council for the Development of Economic and Social Research in Africa
COMUTRA	Comité das Mulheres Trabalhadoras/Working Women's Committee (Mozambique)
CPP	Convention People's Party
CPSA	Communist Party of South Africa
CSF	Commission Sociale des Femmes
CUSO	Canadian University Service Overseas
DP	Democratic Party (Kenya)
DHS	Demographic Health Survey
FAS	Femmes Africa Solidarité
FAWE	Forum of African Women Educationalists
FEMNET	African Women's Development and Communication Network
FGM	Female Genital Mutilation
FNWS	Federation of Nigerian Women's Societies
FOA	Femmes de l'Ouest Africa
FORD	Forum for the Restoration of Democracy (Kenya)
FORWARD	Foundation for Women's Health, Research and Development
FOWODE	Forum for Women in Democracy (Uganda)
FRELIMO	Frente de Libertação de Moçambique/Mozambique Liberation Front
FSAW	Federation of South African Women
GACC	Groupe d'Animation Culturel de Cocody (Côte d'Ivoire)
GAIN	Gender in Africa Information Network (South Africa)
GAWE	Ghana Association of Women Entrepreneurs
GRADO	Grassroots Development Organisation (Nigeria)

HIV/AIDS	Human Immune-deficiency Virus/Acquired Immune Deficiency Syndrome
HSM	Holy Spirit Movement
IAC	Inter-African Committee on Traditional Practices Affecting the Health of Women and Children
ICT	Information and Communication Technology
IPPF	International Planned Parenthood Federation
KANU	Kenya African National Union
KNC	Kameruns National Congress
KNDP	Kameruns National Democratic Party
LIFEMO	Liga Feminina Moçambicana/Mozambican Women's League
LIMA	Liga Independente da Mulher Angolana
LMWA	Lagos Market Women's Association
MAW	Mauritius Alliance of Women
MDR	Mouvement Democratique e Republique/Democratic Republican Movement (Rwanda)
MESAN	Movement pour l'Evolution Sociale de l'Afrique Noire (Central African Republic)
MFSA	Mouvement Feminin de la Solidarité Africaine/Women's Movement of African Solidarity (Congo)
MPLA	Movimento Popular para a Libertação de Angola/People's Movement for the Liberation of Angola
MRND	Mouvement Républicain National pour la Démocratie et le Développement/National Republican Movement for Democracy and Development
MYWO	Maendeleo Ya Wanawake Organisation/Women's Progress Orgranization
NAK	National Party of Kenya (originally National Alliance for Change)
NCWK	National Council of Women of Kenya
NCWS	National Council of Women's Societies (Nigeria)
NCWT	National Council of Women of Tanganyika
NDAWU	Namibia Domestic and Allied Workers' Union
NDWJ	Niger Delta Women for Justice (Nigeria)
NEPU	Northern Elements Progressive Union (Nigeria)
NGO	Non-Governmental Organization
NOW	Natal Organisation of Women (South Africa)

NPC	Northern People's Congress (Nigeria)
NRM	National Resistance Movement (Uganda)
NWP	Nigerian Women's Party
NWU	Nigerian Women's Union
OAU	Organization of African Unity
ODEF	Observatoire des Droits de la Femmes et de l'Enfant (Mali)
OMA	Organização da Mulher Angolana/Organization of Angolan Women
OMM	Organização da Mulher Moçambicana/Organization of Mozambican Women
OMCV	Organização das Mulheres de Cabo Verde/Organization of Women of Cape Verde
PAIGC	Partido Africano de Independência de Guinea-Bissau e Cabo Verde
PATH	Program for Appropriate Technology in Health
PAWLO	Pan African Women Liberation Organization
PDCI	Parti Democratique de Cote d'Ivoire/Democratic Party of the Ivory Coast
PNDC	Provisional National Defense Council
PP	Progressive Party (South Africa)
PSA	Patri Solidaire Africaine
PSP	Parti Soudanais Progressiste
REACH	Reproductive and Community Health (Uganda)
RECIF	Réseau de Communication et d'Information des Femmes/Communication and Information Network for Women (Burkina Faso)
ROSCAS	Rotating Savings and Credit Associations
RBVA	Rhodesian Bantu Voters' Association
RDA	Rassemblement Democratique Africaine
SACCOS	Savings and Credit Cooperatives
SADWA	South African Domestic Workers Association
SAP	Structural Adjustment Program
SASO	South African Students' Organisation
SCP	Sudanese Communist Party
SDP	Social Democratic Party (Kenya)
SERG	Social Economic Research Group (Zambia)
SLMWU	Sierra Leone Market Women's Union

SLWM	Sierra Leone Women's Movement
SPUP	Seychelles People's United Party
SWAA	Society for Women and AIDS in Africa
SWAPO	South West African People's Organization
SWU	Sudanese Women's Union
TAMWA	Tanzania Media Women's Association
TANU	Tanganyika (later Tanzania) African National Union
TBAs	Traditional Birth Attendants
UAWO	Uganda Association of Women's Organizations
UCT	University of Cape Town
UCW	Uganda Council of Women
UDEMU	União Democrática das Mulheres/Democratic Union of Women
UDF	United Democratic Front (South Africa)
UFN	Union des Femmes du Niger/Union of Women of Niger
UFS	Union des Femmes du Soudan/Union of Women of Sudan
UFT	Union des Femmes Travailleuses/Union of Women Workers
UGC	União Geral das Cooperativas/General Union of Cooperatives (Mozambique)
UGCC	United Gold Coast Convention (Ghana)
UMWA	Uganda Media Women's Association
UN	United Nations
UNECA	United Nations Economic Commission for Africa
UNESCO	United Nations Educational, Scientific and Cultural Organization
UNFM	Union Nationale des Femmes du Mali/National Union of Women of Mali
UNFPA	United Nations Population Fund
UNICEF	United Nations Children's Fund
UNIFEM	United Nations Development Fund for Women
UNIP	United National Independence Party (Zambia)
UNITA	União Nacional para a Independência Total de Angola
UP	United Party (South Africa)
UPRONA	Parti de l'Unité pour le Progrès National/Union of National Progress

URFC	Union Révolutionnaire des Femmes Congolaises/ Revolutionary Union of Congolese Women
US-RDA	Union Soudanese-Rassemblement Démocratique Africain/Sudanese Union-African Democratic Assembly
UWESO	Uganda Women's Effort to Save Orphans
UWONET	Ugandan Women's Network
UWT	Umoja wa Wanawake wa Tanzania/Tanzanian Women's Union
WAG	Women's Action Group (Zimbabwe)
WASU	West African Students' Union
WAYL	West African Youth League
WCC	World Council of Churches
WCTU	Women's Christian Temperance Union
WFC	Women for Change (Zambia)
WFS	World Fertility Survey
WFTU	World Federation of Trade Unions
WHO	World Health Organization
WiLDAF	Women in Law and Development in Africa
WLSA	Women and Law in Southern Africa
WIN	Women in Nigeria
WIN	Women's International Network
WOPPA	Women as Partners for Peace in Africa
WORDOC	Women's Research and Documentation Center (Nigeria)
WOUGNET	Women of Uganda Network
YWCA	Young Women's Christian Association
ZANLA	Zimbabwe African national Liberation Army
ZANU	Zimbabwe African National Union
ZARD	Zambia Association for Research and Development
ZUD	Zimbabwe Union of Democrats
ZWRCN	Zimbabwe Women's Resource Centre and Network

© Kathleen Sheldon, 1994, 2004

Chronology

10th century BC Maqeda (Queen of Sheba) was the founding ruler of Ethiopia

300 BC to 200 AD The era of important queens in Meroë, who were known as Candace

12th century Yennenga prominent in ruling family in West Africa (present day Burkina Faso)

1240 Kassi ruled in Mali

1500s Daca ruled in Bunyoro-Kitara, East Africa

1560–1610 Amina ruled the northern Nigerian Hausa state of Zaria

1563–1570 Aisa Kili Ngirmarmma ruled Kanuri Empire of Bornu, Nigeria

1630–1650 Nzinga ruled in Matamba, Kongo (now Angola)

1690s Fatuma ruled Zanzibar

1706 Dona Beatriz Kimpa Vita burned at stake in Kongo (Angola)

c. 1730 Pokou founded Baule people in Côte d'Ivoire

1730–1769 Menetewab ruled in Ethiopia

1760–1787 Akech rose to power in Paroketu, East Africa

1793 Birth of Nana Asma'u, Sokoto, Nigeria

1810 Sara Baartman brought to Europe for display

1828–1861 Ranavalona I ruled the Merina Empire, Madagascar

1837–1841 Ileni Hagos ruled Tigrayan communities as regent, Eritrea

1842–1878 Djoumbe Fatima ruled Mwali in the Comoros Islands

1840s Njembot Mboj ruled the Walo kingdom, Senegal

1847–1854 Ndate Yala Mboj ruled the Walo kingdom, Senegal

1848 Iye Idolorusan briefly ruled the Itsekiri kingdom in Nigeria

1849 Immaculate Conception Sisters arrived in Gabon

1851 Mamochisane ruled the Kololo kingdom in Zambia

1856–1857 Nongqawuse emerged as leader in Xhosa cattle-killing

1868–1883 Ranavalona II ruled the Merina Empire, Madagascar

1869 Inanda Seminary founded, South Africa

1873 Ansantehemaa Afua Kobi made a speech arguing against a war with the British

1878 Madam Yoko ascended to chieftancy of Kpa Mende (Sierra Leone)

1881 Binao came to the throne of the Bemihisatra, Sakalava, Madagascar

1884 Yaa Akyaa became asantehemaa in Asante (Ghana)

1888 Emily Ruete published first autobiography by an African woman, *Memoirs of an Arabian Princess from Zanzibar*

1894 Dahomey soldiers, after fighting for their king for decades, disbanded; Lobotsibeni Gwamile Mdluli came to the throne in Swaziland

1896–1997 First Chimurenga (liberation) war in Zimbabwe (then Rhodesia); Charwe emerged as a leader who was believed to be possessed by the spirit of Nehanda

1898 Ahfad University for Women: precursor first established, Sudan

1899–1902 South African War

1900 Yaa Asantewaa exhorted Asante male rulers to fight British colonialism (Ghana)

1902 Bannabikira, a Catholic sisterhood, was founded in Uganda Wangu wa Makeri named a Kikuyu "headman" in Kenya

1905 Charlotte Maxeke earns B.Sc. at Wilberforce University in Ohio, noted as first black South African woman to earn a college degree

1908 Indian Women's Association founded, South Africa

1912 Omu Okwei named to the Native Court in Onitsha, Nigeria

1913 Anti-pass demonstrations in Orange Free State; South Africa Mekatalili led an anti-colonial revolt among the Giriama in Kenya

1916–1930 Zauditu ruled as empress in Ethiopia

1917 East African Women's League founded, Kenya

1918 Bantu Women's League founded, South Africa

1920s African National Congress Women's League founded, South Africa; African Women's Self-Improvement Association founded, South Africa; Bantu Women's League founded, Zimbabwe; Lagos Market Women's Association founded, Nigeria

1922 Mary Nyanjiru was killed in an anti-colonial demonstration in Nairobi in support of Harry Thuku

1923 Gagoangwe ruled the Kwena in Botswana

1925 Seraphim Society founded by Christianah Abiodun Emmanuel, Ghana

1926 Adelaide Casely Hayford opened the Girls' Vocational and Industrial Training School in Freetown

1928 Siti Binti Saadi was the first East African to record her voice, Zanzibar

1929 Aba Women's War, Nigeria

1930s Abeokuta Ladies' Club founded, Nigeria

1931 Liberia Women's League founded

1933 La Révolte des Femmes, Lomé, Togo

1936 Mary Lokko takes official position in the West African Youth League, becoming perhaps the first African woman in leadership of a modern political organization

1943 Mantse Bo named as regent in Lesotho

1944 Basutoland Homemakers' Association founded, Lesotho; Nigerian Women's Party founded

1945 Constance Cummings-John elected to Freetown Municipal Council, Sierra Leone, the first African woman elected to a colonial governing body

1946 Abeokuta Women's Union founded, Nigeria

1947 Muslim Women's Association founded, Kenya; Uganda Council of Women founded

1949 Women's march on Grand Bassam prison in Côte d'Ivoire; Nigerian Women's Union founded

1950 Annie Jiagge was first female lawyer admitted to the bar in Ghana

1951 Sierra Leone Women's Movement founded; Mabel Dove appointed as editor of the *Accra Evening News*, the first African women to hold such a position

1952 Maendeleo ya Wanawake Organisation founded, Kenya; National Council of Women of Tanganyika founded; Union of Sudanese Women founded

1953 Angie Brooks-Randolph is first female minister in Liberia; Lumpa Church founded by Alice Lenshina, Zambia; Federation of Nigerian Women's Societies founded; National Federation of Gold Coast Women founded

1954 *African Women* began publication, London; Mabel Dove was first woman elected to parliament in Ghana and possibly the first African women parliamentarian on the continent

1955 Women's Defence of the Constitution League, later called Black Sash, was founded, South Africa

1956 Defiance Campaign, anti-pass demonstration in Johannesburg, South Africa; Ghana Market Women Association founded; Jèmangèlèn founded in French West Africa; Pumla Kisosonkole was first woman elected to the Legislative Council of the Protectorate Government,

Uganda; Miriam Makeba first released "Pata Pata"; Senedu Gabru was first women elected to the Ethiopian parliament

1958 Amitié Africaine founded, Burkina Faso; Angie Brooks-Randolph of Liberia is the first African woman to be elected president of the United Nations General Assembly; League of Malawi Women founded; National Council of Women's Societies, Nigeria; Célestine Ouezzin Coulibaly named minister of social affairs, housing and work in Burkina Faso, probably first female minister in francophone West Africa; Union des Femmes du Niger / Union of Women of Niger founded; Union des Femmes du Soudan / Union of Women of Sudan founded

1958–1961 Anlu protest in Cameroon

1959 Femmes de l'Ouest Africa founded, French West Africa; Aoua Kéita was the only woman elected to National Assembly of Mali

1960 Conference of Women of Africa and of African Descent, first meeting in Accra; Gambia Women's Federation founded

1961 Lesotho National Council of Women founded; Lesotho Women's Institute founded

1962 All Africa Women's Conference first meeting, Tanzania; Commission Sociale des Femmes founded, Mali; Helen Joseph is first person banned by apartheid government, South Africa; Organização da Mulher Angolana founded, Angola

1963 Association des Femmes Ivoiriennes founded; *Awa* began publication, Senegal; Natal Women's Revolt, South Africa; National Council of Ghana Women founded

1964 Madeleine Akinkamiye was first female minister in Rwanda; Wuraola Adepeju Esan was first female senator in Nigeria; Mouvement National des Femmes founded, Mauritania; National Council of Women of Kenya founded; Women's Front founded, Sudan

1965 Botswana Council of Women founded; Elizabeth Nyabongo was the first female barrister in East Africa

1966 Association pour la Promotion de la Femme Rwandaise founded; Constance Cummings-John elected mayor of Freetown, Sierra

Leone, the first African woman to be a mayor of an African city; Flora Nwapa published her novel, *Efuru*, noted as the first English-language novel published by an African woman (Grace Ogot published *The Promised Land* in the same year); Uganda Association of Women's Organizations founded; Women's Cameroon National Union founded

1967 Conseil National des Associations de Femmes de Madagascar founded; Union des Femmes Burundaises / Union of Burundi Women founded

1968 Folyegbe Akintunde-Ighodalo was first Nigerian woman appointed as permanent secretary; *Azeb* began publication, Ethiopia; Annie Jiagge was first African woman elected to chair the United Nations Commission on the Status of Women

1969 Assembly of Ghana Women founded; Association des Femmes Voltaiques founded, Burkina Faso; Entraine Féminine Voltaique founded, Burkina Faso; Convention on the Elimination of All Forms of Discrimination Against Women (CEDAW) passed United Nations General Assembly

1970 African Women's Association founded, Ethiopia

1971 Blantyre Women's Art and Handicraft Club founded, Malawi; Margaret Kenyatta elected mayor of Nairobi, Kenya; Wangari Maathai earns Ph.D. in veterinary anatomy from University of Nairobi, becoming perhaps the first African woman to earn a doctorate; Union des Femmes du Parti Démocratique Gabonais / Union of Women of the Democratic Party of Gabon founded

1972 Jeanne Martin-Cissé elected president of United Nations Security Council, the first African woman to hold that position; Organização da Mulher Moçambicana founded

1973 Black Women's Federation founded, South Africa

1974 Federation des Femmes Voltaiques founded, Burkina Faso

1975 United Nations Decade for Women held first meeting in Mexico City; African Training and Research Centre for Women established, Addis Ababa; *Africa Woman* began publication, London; Association Nationale des Femmes Mauriciennes founded; Black Women's Federation founded, South Africa; Elisabeth Domitien named premier of the Central African Republic; Bernadette Olowo named as ambassador from Uganda to Vatican City, the first woman in the Vatican diplomatic corps in over 900 years

1976 Jeanne Gervais named first female minister in Côte d'Ivoire; Muvman Liberasyon Fam founded, Mauritius

1977 Association of African Women for Research and Development / Association des Femmes Africaines pour la Recherche sur le Développement founded; Green Belt Movement founded, Kenya; Groupe d'Animation Culturel de Cocody founded, Côte d'Ivoire

1978 National Council of Women founded, Uganda; *Nuvel Fam* began publication, Mauritius

1979 Mariama Bâ published *Une si longue lettre* (*So Long a Letter*); Buchi Emecheta published *The Joys of Motherhood*; National Union of Eritrean Women founded; Women's World Banking formed by Esther Ocloo and others

1980 United Nations Decade for Women held second meeting in Copenhagen; Commission Internationale pour l'Abolition des Mutilations Sexuelles founded, Dakar; Inkatha Women's Brigade founded, South Africa; Organização da Mulheres de Cabo Verde founded; Women's Movement founded, Ghana (31 December)

1982 Botswana passed a restrictive law that denied citizenship to children born to foreign fathers and Botswanan mothers; Organisation des Femmes Revolutionnaires du Benin founded

1983 Foundation for Women's Health, Research and Development founded; Women in Nigeria founded; Women's Action Group founded, Zimbabwe

1984 *Ahfad Journal: Women and Change* began publication, Sudan; Cissin-Natenga Women's Association founded, Burkina Faso; Zambia Association for Research and Development founded

1985 Action for Development (ACFODE) founded, Uganda; Akina Mama wa Afrika founded, London; Namibian Women's Voice founded; United Nations Decade for Women held third meeting in Nairobi

1986 *Echo* began publication, Senegal; Emang Basadi founded, Botswana; Women's Research and Documentation Center (WORDOC) founded, Nigeria

1987 Better Life Programme for the Rural Woman founded, Nigeria

1988 *Agenda: A Journal about Women and Gender* began publication, South Africa; *Nervous Conditions* published by Tsitsi Dangaremgba; *Jornal da Mulher* began publication, Cape Verde; National Commission for Women founded, Nigeria; Society for Women and AIDS in Africa founded

1989 Sister Namibia founded

1990 Ghana Association of Women Entrepreneurs founded

1991 Nadine Gordimer awarded the Nobel Prize for Literature; *Shoeshoe* began publication, Lesotho; Zambia National Women's Lobby Group founded; Zimbabwe Women Writers founded

1992 Unity Dow wins her citizenship case in Botswana's High Court, the first African woman to sue her government for sex discrimination; Forum of African Women Educationalists founded; Women's National Coalition founded, South Africa

1993 Coordination des Associations et ONG Féminines du Mali founded; *GENDEReview* began publication, Kenya; Kampala Action Plan on Women and Peace called for gender parity in peace negotiations; Silvie Kinigi became prime minister of Burundi; Jean-Marie Ruth-Rolland was first woman to run in an African presidential race, Central African Republic

1994 Apartheid ended in South Africa; Antoineta Rosa Gomes ran for president of Guinea-Bissau and lost; Agathe Uwilingiyimana, prime minister of Rwanda, killed in genocide

1995 Forum for Women in Democracy founded, Uganda; Fourth World Conference on Women, Beijing

1996 Femme Africa Solidarité founded; Ruth Sando Perry named as head of Liberian Council of the State

1997 Isatou Njie-Saidy became vice president of the Gambia; Africa Women's Forum founded, Accra; Gender in Africa Information Network founded, South Africa; Charity Ngilu is first woman candidate for president of Kenya

1998 Africa Women's Committee for Peace and Development founded; African Women's Anti-War Coalition founded; Unity Dow is the first woman named to Botswana's High Court; Speciosa Wandira Kazibwe becomes vice president of Uganda; Niger Delta Women for Justice founded, Nigeria

2001 Mame Madior Boye named prime minister of Senegal

2002 Maria das Neves de Sousa became prime minister of São Tomé and Príncipe; *Feminist Africa* began electronic publication, South Africa; Mosadi Muriel Seboko is first woman to be a paramount chief in Botswana

2003 Protocol on the Rights of African Women passed by the African Union

2004 Gertrude Mongella elected president of the parliament of the African Union; Wangari Maathai awarded Nobel Peace Prize

Introduction

African women's history is a vast topic that embraces a wide variety of societies in over 50 countries with different geographies, social customs, religions, and historical situations. It might appear to be an impractical task to compress such an exciting range of experiences into a single history in a brief introductory essay, but it is possible to discuss some common threads and shared occurrences while identifying important events and individuals. The issues, events, and individuals referred to in the essay that follows are explained in greater detail in the dictionary entries. Sources can be found in the bibliography.

Africa is a predominantly agricultural continent, and a major factor in African agriculture is the central role of women as farmers. It is estimated that between 65 and 80 percent of African women are engaged in cultivating food for their families, and in the past that percentage was likely even higher. Thus, one common thread across much of the continent is women's daily work in their family plot. Women's work in agriculture has not been static, but has evolved over the centuries. It is also not identical in all regions of Africa, as different crops are grown depending on the geography and environment of each locality and there are arid zones and urban centers where women do not cultivate.

Because of the shared and divergent experiences, a study of agriculture might be considered a useful entry point into African women's history. Yet women's agricultural work was so prevalent that it garnered almost no attention in the earliest documents about African women, and was often not given prominence in later studies of African women's history. Research into African prehistory, referring to the centuries prior to 1500, has uncovered some information about early African societies, though frequently such information is not specifically gendered. A study using historical linguistics discovered that early peoples in the lakes region of central Africa grew grains and vegetables such as millet and yams as well as bananas, but it cannot be determined if that was specifically women's or men's work. Archeologists have studied housing, farming techniques, and tool and equipment manufacturing, but again cannot state whether such tasks were considered male or female. Yet social relationships can be discerned in studies of these early societies, as women's roles in families and as religious leaders are found through a close investigation of language and ethnicity. For instance, describing the linguistic history of terms referring to mothers helps historians understand early family formations.

* * *

The centrality of agriculture leads to other central characteristics of most African societies, which is the control of land and of labor by kin groups and clans. In most of Africa, land was not owned by individuals but a social group which held the rights of access to land. Use of specific plots of land was decided by leaders of the group, who were usually but not always senior men. Leadership was intertwined with control over women's labor, and the arrangement of families through marriage was a matter of significant interest to the senior clan leaders. One of the central markers of ethnicity is the method of descent, and that factor is directly related to women through social ideas about marriage and kinship.

Not all communities reckoned descent through the male line. Africa is the world region that is most noted for a high incidence of matrilineal descent systems, found in an extensive belt across the center of the continent, and including peoples in parts of West Africa, central Africa, and extending into southern Africa. Matrilineality refers to a social system that places a woman and her female relations at the center of kinship and family, rather than a woman and her husband, or a man and his wife or wives and offspring. The method of reckoning kinship that centers a man and his spouse and assigns offspring as belonging to the father's clan or family is patrilineality.

Matrilineal societies embodied an idea of social organization that privileged the personal and social power of women. The kinship network focused on the relationship between sisters and between siblings more generally, giving place of honor to mothers and their children rather than fathers and their children. Mothers were revered, and frequently all senior female relations were considered to be "mothers" to the kin group. The role of a woman's brother was often of greater importance to her children than that of her husband (their father). Thus, there were examples of elder sisters holding central positions within the clan, and being considered as local chiefs because of their prominence within the kin group.

Societies in eastern and southern Africa, especially groups that depended to a greater extent on cattle or other livestock husbandry, often were patrilineal. It was common in many of those societies for cattle to be an integral part of marriage, as families normally exchanged bridewealth as part of the marital process. The usual form was for the family of the husband-to-be to make an arrangement with the family of the woman he planned to marry regarding the number of cattle and other goods that would be given to her family. Although western observers later described these transactions as commercial, and considered such exchanges to be the sale of a woman, for African communities it meant a tangible economic connection between clans that strengthened both the marital relationship and the bond between families that were now kin. In southern Africa no new homestead could be established without at least the promise of cattle, and cattle ownership was the basis of wealth and well-being. In most cases livestock was controlled by men, and the amount of cattle a man accumulated reflected the social standing and strength of his household. Even in societies that were heavily dependent on cattle, women's agricultural labor was key, as grains and produce were the mainstay of people's daily diet.

* * *

Despite women's centrality to agricultural production, they generally had only indirect access to power and authority in African societies. But there is evidence of a variety of routes to exercise authority, including through women's organizations. Women advanced to leadership positions through elaborate systems of rank and naming, and women's groups were viewed as complementary to men's within the community. In West Africa there were market women's groups that controlled marketplace activities. In many regions of Africa women had important religious roles, especially as they aged and became senior members of their societies. Among the Yoruba in what is today Nigeria, women's trading networks gained increasing importance in the 15th century. Existing markets in produce and crafts grew into long-distance systems of trade from their own coastal area into the northern hinterlands. Men dominated the trade in luxury items, but women controlled trade in cloth, food, and locally produced crafts such as woven mats. And women organized their own local trading activities under a female authority known as the *iyalode*. Women did not inherit the *iyalode* position, but earned it through a life of prosperous trade and virtuous behavior. An *iyalode* mediated conflicts and determined the location of new markets, and women relied on her to protect their commercial and personal interests.

* * *

Europeans first arrived at coastal communities in Africa at the end of the 15th century. Their written observations offer some of the earliest documentation concerning African women, though such sources should be used with care. Such documents are more likely to include information on elite women such as Queen Nzinga of Kongo, or of women who were in regular contact with the European settlers such as Eva in southern Africa or market women on the West African coast. There are few written sources left by African women discussing those early contacts, so it is impossible to know with any certainty what women thought about their encounters. Nonetheless, a history of African women can begin with the stories of these early women who appear in the documents.

In West Africa Queen Amina of Zazzau, in what is today Nigeria, rose to power as an adolescent when her father was ruler. She regularly participated in military expeditions. In 1576 she came to the throne, following her father's successor. She used her military expertise to extend the boundaries of her realm to the Niger River, incorporating the city-states of Kano and Katsina. She brought wealth to her people by extending the long-distance trade routes, and she is credited with introducing kola nuts, an important trade and social item in many West African communities.

Further south, in the west central region known as Angola today, Queen Nzinga rose from slave origins to rule Kongo society. There were earlier women who had exercised local control, often as representatives of male rulers. The senior wife of a nobleman might control several hundred junior wives and slaves. Women were also included in the king's council, thus wielding power at the highest levels of Kongo society. Nzinga began her rise to power as a palace slave who was chosen in the 1620s to act as an emissary to the Portuguese. She was known for collaborating with Portuguese authorities in order to advance her cause, as well as for leading local people in opposition to Portuguese incursions. She is remembered for the latter activities today in Angola, where many consider her to be an honored foremother of the Angolan nation. Her history was unusual, as women rarely ruled societies in that region, although her reign over a region called Matamba was followed by several other female rulers.

Along the West African coast a number of successful female market traders including Alimotu Pelewura, Madam Tinubu, and Omu Okwei played an important role as arbiters between local societies and European traders. Other women developed relationships with European men and used that connection to further their own control over trade routes. Those women were based in societies that recognized a duality of male and female leadership. In some cases women had complementary control over parts of society that were considered primarily female, including agriculture and market trade. In others women had important roles as queen mothers, serving as essential advisors to male rulers who were usually their sons or other kin, and sometimes serving as co-rulers or regents.

In South Africa, the best-known African woman from the initial years of the European presence came to be called Eva, though her original name was Khoena. From a young age she worked for the household of the Dutch commander, Jan Van Riebeeck, and she later married a Dutch surgeon. Her proximity to the European community resulted in an unusual amount of documentation as compared to most African women of the 17th century.

The experience of slavery is another area that has been documented in written sources, largely because of the involvement of western traders. Slaves within Africa were more likely to be women, a reflection of their productive and reproductive contributions to their communities. Men were more often sold into the international market, or in cases where slaves were war captives, women would be integrated into the new society while men were more likely to be killed as enemies. Women were also slave owners, especially in areas where they had the opportunity to accrue wealth through trading and market work. Not only did they then have the resources for acquiring slaves, but they needed the additional labor. African slavery can be described as a continuum of control over people. Many societies accepted pawning as a way of repaying debts or acknowledging an affiliation or dependent relationship. It could offer a greater opportunity for slaves to move out of their enslaved situation than was common in North and South America. But the complicated issues of male control over women's labor meant that women were more vulnerable to capture, pawning, and enslavement, especially in areas where they were already dependent on men for access to land. It also meant that in some areas there was a group of people already considered marginal who were liable to be traded to Europeans and drawn into the international slave trade.

Women played a central role in the expansion of Islam in West Africa during the 19th century. A major event was the campaign by Usman dan Fodio, as he brought extensive areas into the orbit of Islamic beliefs. His daughter, Nana Asma'u, was a prominent scholar and teacher who wrote many poems and religious tracts. She also organized a series of Koranic schools for women, and devised teaching programs that allowed women to participate in the schools while honoring their seclusion.

* * *

The presence of European settlers and trading companies was gradually augmented by a number of missionaries, traders, and officials throughout the 16th to 19th centuries. Trade in such items as rubber, gold, salt, and cloth had an impact on African societies and on international markets. By the late 19th century the conflicts between European powers (England, France, Portugal, Germany, and Belgium) brought those countries to the negotiating table, where they devised a plan for dividing up spheres of interest on the African continent, with absolutely no African input. The 1884–1885 decision led to a greatly increased presence of Europeans, as they laid claim on the ground to territories they had obtained only on paper. Africans did not passively accept European rule, and their resistance meant an increased role for European military forces who engaged in a series of incursions designed to subdue African populations. By the early 20th century parts of southern and eastern Africa were home to numerous settlers as Europeans arrived to seek their fortune in plantations and mining.

Studies of women's work during the colonial period often showed how they lost power and economic autonomy with the arrival of cash crops and their exclusion from the global marketplace, in contrast to men who were more likely to benefit from these economic changes.

Even further, men and international commerce benefited because they were able to rely to some extent on women's unremunerated labor. The dynamic varied from place to place. In Ghana when cocoa trees were introduced and it became clear that cultivating cocoa for export was a lucrative business, men bought land that they could devote to cocoa trees. In most cases they bought the land on credit using female kin as collateral, so that if the man could not repay the loan the women were pawned, or transferred to the creditor. Women and children made up the major share of the labor force in the cocoa plantations, though when the cocoa was sold the male land (and tree) owner kept the proceeds. Though some women did own land themselves, they were in a minority despite continuing to perform nearly all the agricultural work that fed their families. In Senegal and the Gambia women had long cultivated rice, and when groundnuts (peanuts) were added to the agricultural calendar the result was a shift in land ownership patterns. Once again women continued to grow subsistence food crops while also contributing labor to the rice cultivation. In order to accommodate changes in the agricultural season, new varieties of rice were grown to feed the foreign workers brought in to work in the groundnut fields, and men controlled the sale of that rice that brought in an income.

In other places women typically continued their work growing food for their family's consumption while men entered the colonial economy and earned wages by working on tea and cotton plantations or, in central and southern Africa, by going to work under contract at the gold, diamond, and copper mines. In the mining regions some women did move to the newly developing urban areas with their husbands or on their own in search of new opportunities, though the majority remained in the rural areas. Colonial authorities mistrusted the women who were in urban areas and introduced a series of pass laws to control the movement of women on their own. Passes were documents that were required in many parts of colonial Africa for men and women to move out of their home areas. Usually women were allowed to migrate with male kin, as the colonialists believed women were then controlled by those men. There are instances where African men supported the colonial efforts to monitor women's movements, so that women were under the scrutiny of both local men and European authorities who had ideas about women's proper residence, and wished to restrict their behavior, occupation, and ability to travel.

Analysis of the development of legal systems under colonialism has suggested that women were at a disadvantage as "customary" laws were established based on male testimony that gave men, especially elite men, advantages over women in issues of marriage and divorce. It was not uncommon for African societies to recognize that the variety of people's experiences had to be met by a range of punishments, rules, and fines. For instance, communities generally did not approve of adultery, but the social censure might vary among a series of potential disciplinary actions according to the age and rank of the people involved. Women were not necessarily excluded from participation in the discussion of how to make amends. But when the Europeans came they were interested in introducing legal codes that assigned specific punishments for each crime with less room for flexibility. They wrote down penalties for misdeeds as they interpreted the information they received from older men who often were interested in increasing their own control over women in their society, especially in the face of the changes that appeared with colonialism.

Research on the colonial era exhibits a tension between viewing women as victims or as powerful agents within their communities. Women's formal political activity was generally ignored and denigrated by the colonial authorities, who turned exclusively to men when they established local political offices. The colonial agents, nearly always men, disregarded that reality and gave positions of authority only to men. Although much of the writing about African women under colonialism emphasizes the economic and political losses they suffered, when scholars turned to women's specific experiences they discovered evidence of women who found ways to progress and succeed in the face of blatant discrimination. Sometimes the new forms of oppression spurred women to new kinds of activities. Female agricultural innovations were described as essential to community survival, as when they shared knowledge about crops and cultivation methods. Women became politically active, as seen in Nigeria with the development of three different market women's associations in Lagos that mirrored ethnic and class divisions present in the city. Women also found new ways of working and initiated new family forms as urbanization accelerated. For instance, the development of mining compounds, though designed primarily as male work places, opened opportunities for women to move from their rural homes, establish new marital and kin relationships, and develop new ways of earning an income.

* * *

From the earliest years, Africans resisted the increasing control the Europeans were exerting over their societies. The modern nationalist movement gained strength in the early 20th century, as organizations formed across the continent that pushed for local African political control. Women were involved in activities in every region. The role of women in anti-colonial and nationalist organizations offers further evidence of a vibrant and essential community of women who were central to the eventual success of those movements. While earlier research had focused on men and assumed women's passivity in the face of such changes, women were in fact at the forefront of a wide variety of struggles.

One of the best known political actions was the Aba Women's War in 1929 in south-eastern Nigeria, as Ibo women demonstrated against the extension of taxation to women. The British had enforced their rule by destroying an ancient shrine at Aro, and then instituting a system of indirect rule by appointing men as "warrant chiefs" to represent British interests in local districts. To pay for the new administration, the British began imposing taxes. In 1929, when local chiefs began counting women as part of a census, it was believed that counting would lead to taxing women as well as men. Women had a history of authority through local market organizations and trading networks, and the word spread rapidly throughout the region. Drawing on precolonial forms of protest that used insult and dancing, women destroyed British colonial buildings and attacked local and foreign personnel. The result was not promising for women's future role in politics, as 50 women were killed and the British did not incorporate women into their plans for colonial government.

In other parts of Africa women drew on their position as spirit mediums to lead their communities in anti-colonial activities. Spirit mediums were responsible for guiding people's access to ancestors and for assisting in important decisions concerning social well-being. Because of that responsibility, some women played roles in the new anti-colonial movements. The story of Charwe, a woman possessed by the female spirit of Nehanda who was a pivotal actor during an anti-colonial struggle among the Shona (now in Zimbabwe) in the 1890s, is one example of older practices reemerging with a new purpose in the face of oppression.

In another instance in eastern Africa a female spiritual leader known as Nyabingi became notorious among colonial officials for her role in opposing European rule. The early 20th century was an era of severe economic disruption, as the devastation of rinderpest, a serious cattle disease that spread throughout eastern Africa, resulted in increased cattle raids further in the interior. European interests were also moving inland, as they measured land and provoked boundary disputes. Muhumusa, a woman described as an "extraordinary character," came to prominence in the area that is today southern Uganda and Rwanda, in a region where many communities honored religious leaders who were possessed by spirits. She was possessed by the Nyabingi spirit, and as such she was recognized by local people as the representative of that potent presence. She led raids and protests against the colonial authorities, and she and her followers remained a problem in colonial eyes for many years, with attacks on colonial installations occurring until the 1920s.

In eastern and southern Africa women were also at the forefront of overtly anti-colonial protest activities, writing articles in local newspapers, working in organizations, and often arguing on two fronts as they fought for African political control and simultaneously for the inclusion of women at all levels of government. In South Africa women protested against the extension of pass laws, which already controlled men's employment and freedom of movement into towns. Focusing on the respect women were due because of their status as mothers, one of the earliest anti-pass demonstrations occurred in 1913 in the Orange Free State. The Orange Free State began requiring women to have a permit to live in urban areas, and women sent petitions to authorities including the King of England. Charlotte Maxeke, drawing in part from her experience and education in the United States, took on a leadership role. When over 30 women were jailed for marching and tearing up their passes, other women formed a support organization. They drew inspiration from two divergent sources. Mahatma Gandhi was in South Africa at the time, and was active organizing Indians and Africans while formulating his nonviolent methods of protest. South African women were also familiar with the actions of the British suffragists. That early protest was successful, as passes were not issued to women until decades later.

Discovering the history of Muslim women in Dar es Salaam fundamentally changed the view that the Tanzanian anti-colonial movement was led solely by men who were products of Christian mission education. Researchers had previously argued that the colonial powers brought about their own end by educating the men who formed the anticolonial organizations and then came to power after independence. But the Tanzania story demonstrated that Bibi Titi Mohammed and women she recruited, who were outside the colonial educational system, were involved in the struggle to end colonialism. Women were also important leaders of the anti-colonial movement in West Africa, where Aoua Kéita, Célestine Ouezzin Coulibaly, Funmilayo Ransome-Kuti, Hannah Cudjoe, and others worked to bring independence and simultaneously to build women's organizations within the new political forms that developed.

In Kenya and the southern African nations of Angola, Mozambique, Rhodesia (now Zimbabwe), Namibia, and South Africa, African nationalists encountered recalcitrant white settler populations. In those situations they turned to armed struggle and in some cases protracted efforts to win independence and majority rule. Women were centrally involved in all of those struggles, though generally not as actual combatants. In the 1950s Mau Mau struggle in Kenya the most noted leaders in the Land and Freedom Army were men, though they could not have survived in the forests without women supporting them by supplying food and other necessities, acting as spies and messengers, and performing other tasks. Women also were judges in the forest communities, and at least one woman rose to the rank of field marshal. The British colonial authorities recognized the importance of women to the struggle, and incarcerated 13,000 female sympathizers in camps and holding areas, as well as fortifying villages to keep residents from leaving to join or aid the resistance. The colonial authorities used these locations to expand their training in western-style domesticity, which was initially introduced by colonial women through the women's organization, Maendeleo ya Wanawake, or Women's Progress. In 1954 there were 37,000 members of Maendeleo, which became the official women's organization in independent Kenya as well.

In the 1960s and 1970s, as Portugal refused to relinquish its African territories of Angola, Mozambique, Guinea-Bissau, and Cape Verde, the local people initiated an armed struggle that only belatedly included women, and only after women came forward to raise the issue with the male leaders. Again women were vital to the success of the resistance effort through their work in supplying food, acting as couriers, and building an alternative social order in the liberated zones. Zimbabwe, Namibia (South West Africa), and South Africa also endured grueling armed revolts that eventually brought about majority rule in the face of intransigent white populations. Women were active in all aspects of the struggle, including as fighters, though they faced many more obstacles to full acceptance than did men. Nonetheless, women in these countries are today recognized as national heroines for the sacrifices and contributions they made to the freedom of their countries.

* * *

It sometimes seems that women are stagnating in African societies, continuing as the family members primarily responsible for agricultural labor and facing ongoing hindrances to gaining education and employment equal to African men. Illiteracy levels remain high across the continent despite increased schooling for girls. Women still have serious problems in the areas of polygyny, divorce, inheritance, and widowhood, as stories emerge about the families of deceased husbands arriving to claim the household goods as their own rather than belonging to the widow and her children. Since the 1980s the scourge of HIV/AIDS has inflicted untold hardships on women either through acquiring the disease itself or through the added burdens of caring for ill or orphaned kin and others. And recent decades have been marked by terrible so-called low-intensity wars in over a dozen countries, with women frequently the victims of war-related violence, sexual assault, dislocation, disease, and other traumas.

Yet the last half of the 20th century also brought dramatic positive changes to the lives of many African women, as opportunities for formal education, new job possibilities, increased political involvement, and changing family expectations gained in importance. The United Nations Decade for Women, which included a 1985 meeting in Nairobi, Kenya, was an important catalyst for African women, as it increased international backing for their efforts to obtain legal changes in support of equality for women. The Nairobi meeting in particular drew thousands of African women who were able to meet each other as well as hold discussions with activists from around the world. A follow-up meeting in

1995 in Beijing was chaired by Tanzanian politician Gertrude Mongella, resulting in renewed attention and pressure on African governments to develop policy and introduce legislation that would improve women's situation. In the 1990s, as democratization projects expanded, the numbers of women in national parliaments and in ministerial positions grew. In some countries special quota and electoral systems ensured that a core of female legislators would have seats. Ugandan Vice-president Specioza Kazibwe was one of the highest-ranking women on the continent from 1998 to 2003. Nearly every nation had active women's lobbying organizations that engaged in voter education, trained women to hold office, and did the necessary legislative work to create laws that would benefit women. In the 1980s those public groups were supplemented by the efforts of women's studies programs in universities across Africa. In 2003 women activists celebrated a victory when the African Union adopted a landmark Protocol on the Rights of Women that encouraged African nations to enact an impressive catalog of woman-friendly legislation. As farmers, African women know that it takes time and hard work to achieve a bountiful harvest. They have persisted in the face of the massive problems of war, hunger, corporate globalization, and HIV/AIDS. They can now look back, see measurable progress in recent decades, and know that the advances are the result of their own efforts and initiative.

Dictionary

– A –

ABA WOMEN'S WAR. In 1929 women in Igbo areas in southeastern Nigeria around the market town of Aba protested British colonial activities by using a traditional method of critiquing male authority. The action of "**sitting on a man**" involved singing insulting songs and using other methods of ostracizing men who were not following the proper norms of respecting women and their work. The 1929 action was instigated by British attempts to count animals and women, which was viewed as a prelude to imposing taxes. The initial contact was with a woman preparing palm oil in her own compound, Nwanyeruwa Ojim; when an official asked her how many people and livestock were in her compound, she responded, "Was your mother counted?" In the scuffle that ensued, she was able to call on neighboring women, who began "sitting on" the official to demonstrate their displeasure with his intrusion into women's affairs.

The wider context was that women had held recognized political, reproductive, and economic realms of control in precolonial Igbo society, and they were losing authority in all areas. The widespread protests included attacks on British court buildings. Although no British residents were killed, the official response was to open fire upon the crowds of women, killing 50 of them. Following an inquiry into the events, the British introduced some changes in colonial policy, but did not address any of the women's demands, which had included requests for no tax on women, the removal of corrupt chiefs, the institution of female judges, and more general complaints about British practices cutting into women's trading and fears about declining fertility. The new policies did not result in the restoration of political or economic power to women. Sometimes referred to as the

Aba riots, calling the activity a women's war brings the focus to the women who led the event and to the organized nature of their demonstrations. *See also* ADORO; ANLU; DUAL-SEX SYSTEM; GODDESSES; SHAMING PRACTICES.

ABDALLAH, ANNA. Abdallah has been a long-serving politician in Tanzania. She studied rural sociology and **housing** at Columbia University in Missouri (United States) with a scholarship in 1960, and also did a course in nutrition in London in 1966. Her governmental experience began with her appointment as one of the first female district commissioners in 1973. In 1987 she was named minister of capital development which included oversight of the construction of the new capital at Dodoma. Abdallah subsequently held positions as minister of agriculture, livestock development and cooperatives in 1991, minister of works and labor in 1995 to 2000, and minister of health following elections in 2000.

ABEOKUTA LADIES' CLUB. Founded initially in the 1930s as a group of western-educated women involved in civic work with local youth, in the 1940s they began to include **market women** who were interested in learning to read. Through the presence of the market women, the club learned of the seizure of rice that women were taking to sell in the market, and the club's efforts ended the seizures. The club was transformed into a vibrant political organization that fought for market women's rights, and in 1946 it changed its name to **Abeokuta Women's Union**. *See also* RANSOME-KUTI, FUNMILAYO; TAX REVOLTS.

ABEOKUTA WOMEN'S UNION. It was established in 1946 when the **Abeokuta Ladies' Club** began to get involved in broader political issues related to promoting women's rights and African political independence. In one of its first campaigns, focused on the problem of the taxation of **market women**, members criticized the local government for the misuse of funds and recommended that foreign companies pay more taxes in order to diminish the burden on market women. **Funmilayo Ransome-Kuti** was president of the union from its founding until her death in 1978. There were 20,000 dues-paying members and as many as another 100,000 supporters who could be counted on to turn out when needed. After 1949 it was a chapter of the national organization, the **Nigerian Women's Union**. *See also* TAX REVOLTS.

ABORTION. Abortion is not legal in most African countries, though women have used herbs and instruments to perform abortions on themselves and other women. Historically the practice is difficult if not impossible to quantify, but there is abundant anecdotal evidence for the use of herbs in cases where an out-of-wedlock birth would cause harm to the mother or to the social order. As most women in the majority of African societies desired children, there were few situations that would cause a woman to seek to end a pregnancy.

Reliable rates of abortion are difficult to ascertain, though a few statistics indicate the low rate of abortions for sub-Saharan Africa. As a comparison, the rate of legal abortions per 1,000 women in the United States per 100 known pregnancies was 23 percent in 1996; in South Africa (the only African nation where abortion is available on demand) the rate was 2.7 percent in 1997, and in Zambia it was 0.4 percent. Though abortion is not available on demand in Zambia, women can get an abortion for a wide range of reasons including their own mental health and for socioeconomic reasons, making it currently one of the most supportive legal codes concerning abortion rights. In all other African countries abortion is illegal, though that has not stopped women from obtaining illegal abortions. Women are admitted to hospitals when they have problems with amateur abortions; in Nigeria in 1996 142,200 women were admitted to hospitals in such circumstances. In many countries physicians may use medical discretion in providing abortions to women who are in need.

Abortion is considered unacceptable under **Islamic law** as well as in legal systems influenced by Catholic beliefs. A high rate of maternal death resulting from abortions is causing concern; in Africa that rate is 1 death for every 142 abortions, while in the developed world it is 1 for every 3,700. It is likely that many African countries will introduce less-restrictive laws in the future, as the important **Protocol on the Rights of African Women** that was introduced at the 2003 African Union conference stated clearly that women should have the right to a medical abortion when the pregnancy resulted from rape or incest, or when continuing the pregnancy would endanger the life or health of the mother.

ABOULELA, LEILA (1964–). A Sudanese writer, she was born in Cairo, Egypt, and grew up in Khartoum, Sudan. She studied at the University of Khartoum and later in England at the London School of Economics. Aboulela won the Caine Prize in 2000 for her short story, "The Museum," which appeared in her collection *Coloured Lights* (2001). She has also published a novel, *The Translator* (2000). Her fiction often addresses the situation of Sudanese women living in Europe. She lives in Aberdeen, Scotland, with her husband and three children.

ACTION FOR DEVELOPMENT (ACFODE). A Ugandan organization that was established in 1985 following the **Nairobi Women's Meeting** during the **United Nations Decade for Women**, it was designed to raise awareness among women in Uganda. It was subsequently involved in a series of research projects based in rural areas, and was instrumental in getting a **women's studies** program at Makerere University in 1989. In 2001 it worked with the **Uganda Women's Network (UWONET)** in monitoring the parliamentary elections. ACFODE publishes *Arise*, a periodical that deals with women's issues.

ACTION SOCIALE / SOCIAL ACTION. Action Sociale was a program for women in Burundi that was founded by the **White Sisters** in 1949. In 1957 it had 2,332 members.

ADORO. Igbo of southern Nigeria believe in a pantheon of deities who have a role in governing their towns. Many of the powerful deities are female, and the Adoro goddess is among the most powerful. In the Nsukka area, Adoro was developed at the end of the 19th century as the slave trade was abolished and local rivalries increased. Initially she was a medicine designed to heal rifts between and within towns. As she succeeded, as demonstrated by the advent of peaceful relations, she rose to a powerful position and was honored with shrines and followers who maintained her important status. Adoro became a particular focus of Christian missionaries in the early 20th century, as they worked to demolish her shrines and end what they considered pagan worship.

AFRICA WOMAN. Subtitled "A Magazine for the Modern Woman of Africa," this periodical was published in London beginning in 1975 as a companion to *Africa Magazine*. It featured fashion on the cover and in full-color spreads inside as well as many advertisements for a variety of consumer products. The magazine also included "Women on the Move," which was comprised of profiles of prominent and not-so-prominent women who were making a contribution to their societies. It halted publication in 1982.

AFRICA WOMEN'S FORUM. Initially established by the Africa Leadership Forum (ALF) at a meeting in Accra, Ghana in 1997, the Women's Forum convened in Cape Town, South Africa, in May 1998 under the auspices of the ALF and **Akina Mama wa Afrika.** This **organization** was designed to assess progress made by African women in **politics** and economics and to move forward with a shared set of priorities on improving women's position in Africa. A further focus was on networking among the wide variety of women's organizations across the continent. The 1998 proceedings were published by the ALF. The Forum has continued to meet annually, with some of the later proceedings also available. The 2003 meeting in Abuja, Nigeria, focused on **HIV/AIDS**. The forum website is at http://www.africa leadership.org/AboutUs2.htm.

AFRICAN AMERICAN WOMEN. African American women were a presence in many areas of African life. Some traveled and settled as missionaries, others married African men. One well-known woman, **Madie Hall Xuma**, was very active in South African women's organizations, including establishing local branches of the **Young Women's Christian Association** and holding office as the first president of the **African National Congress Women's League**. Another African American woman, Susie Wiseman Yergan, was credited with starting the first **Zenzele** group in South Africa in 1916. Women were also prominent in the Americo-Liberian settlements in Liberia, which was made up of slaves and free blacks who returned to Africa from America in the 19th century, where they were particularly

involved with **education** and **Christian missionary** work. Much of
that resettlement was supported by the American Colonization Society repatriation scheme that was supported by abolitionists, white
Southerners who did not want free black people living in the states
that continued to have legal slavery, and some people of African descent who wished to return to the continent of their own birth or of
their ancestors. Some repatriated women made an indelible impact
on Liberian history, including **Matilda Newport**. In recent decades
African American women scholars have been at the forefront of doing research related to African women's history and developing networks among women across the African diaspora. *See also* WOM-
ANISM.

AFRICAN CENTRE FOR GENDER AND DEVELOPMENT.
Known as the **African Centre for Women** until 2001, this center is
based at Addis Ababa as part of the United Nations Economic Commission for Africa (UNECA). Its mandate focuses on the following
points: analysis of economic and social policies; **development** management; food security and sustainable development; information for
development; and regional cooperation and integration. It publishes
reports on a variety of legal, social, and economic issues, and a
newsletter, *GenderNet*, all of which (including the text of its mandate) are available online at http://www.uneca.org/fr/acgd/en/
1024x768/acgd.htm. *See also* OUEDRAOGO, JOSEPHINE.

AFRICAN CENTRE FOR WOMEN. Originally called the **African
Training and Research Centre for Women**, this well-established
research center affiliated with the United Nations Economic Com-
mission for Africa (UNECA) changed its name in 1995 to the African
Centre for Women. In 2001 the organization was renamed the
African Centre for Gender and Development.

**AFRICAN FEDERATION OF WOMEN ENTREPRENEURS
(AFWE).** Founded by Lucia Quachey in 1990 and headquartered in
Ghana, AFWE has sponsored international trade fairs and other ac-
tivities designed to foster success among women entrepreneurs. In
the 1990s three regional Entrepreneurial Networks (West Africa, East
Africa, and Southern Africa) developed with AFWE support; the net-

works are for men and women, though their membership is about one-fourth female.

AFRICAN GENDER INSTITUTE, UNIVERSITY OF CAPE TOWN. A **women's studies** center that promotes research designed to improve women's lives. It was founded in 1996 with the support of then-university Vice-Chancellor **Mamphela Ramphele**. As its mission statement explains, its goal is "a continent liberated from the legacies of colonial and patriarchal domination," and its contribution is to build intellectual capacity and advance "the work of intellectuals, researchers, policy-makers and practitioners committed to the attainment of gender equity." It sponsors the **Gender and Women's Studies for Africa's Transformation** project (www.gwsafrica.org), and publishes an online journal, *Feminist Africa*, found at www.feministafrica.org. The home website is web.uct.ac.za/org/agi. *See also* GENDER IN AFRICA INFORMATION NETWORK.

AFRICAN NATIONAL CONGRESS WOMEN'S LEAGUE. The Women's League was formed in the 1918, developing out of the anti-**pass law** demonstrations of 1913. It was initially known as the **Bantu Women's League** (BWL) when founded by **Charlotte Maxeke**, and the BWL was formally acknowledged as part of the African National Congress (ANC) in 1931 though women were still not admitted as members. Women were finally welcomed as members to the ANC in 1943, and the ANC Women's League was then established with **Madie Hall Xuma** as the first president. The organization focused on recruiting women to the ANC and on raising issues of importance to women within the ANC. As was the case with many **political party organizations**, it took direction from the ANC and focused its organizing efforts on ANC priorities. It was periodically banned and then reestablished, most recently in 1990 when **Albertina Sisulu** helped it re-form within South Africa. It was part of the coalition of the **Federation of South African Women** and participated in the **Defiance Campaign**. Other prominent women who served the Women's League included **Frances Baard**, **Dorothy Nyembe**, and **Gertrude Shope**. The official history of the organization is at www.anc.org.za/wl/docs/50years.html, and was published in Johannesburg in 1993 as *The ANC Women's League: Contributing to a Democratic, Non-racist and Non-sexist South Africa*.

**AFRICAN PARTNERSHIP FOR SEXUAL AND REPRODUC-
TIVE HEALTH AND RIGHTS OF WOMEN AND GIRLS
(AMANITARE).** Among other health-related projects, Amanitare
honors Africans whose work promotes the sexual health of girls and
women. In 2002 they honored Edna Adan Ismail for her efforts to
open a private maternity hospital in Somaliland in 1998. Their website is found at www.amanitare.org.

AFRICAN REGIONAL CONFERENCE ON WOMEN. Sometimes
called the Regional Conference on African Women, this is a regular
series of policy-oriented meetings sponsored by the United Nations'
African Centre for Gender and Development. The fifth in a series
of meetings was held in Dakar, Senegal, in 1995, where 3,000 women
met and developed a Plan of Action addressing such crucial issues as
the impact of **structural adjustment programs** on women, girls' **education,** maternal mortality, and the implementation of the 1979
**Convention on the Elimination of All Forms of Discrimination
Against Women (CEDAW).** Further meetings were held in 1999 and
2004 at Addis Ababa, Ethiopia.

**AFRICAN TRAINING AND RESEARCH CENTRE FOR WOMEN
(ATRCW), UNITED NATIONS ECONOMIC COMMISSION
FOR AFRICA (UNECA).** Headquartered in Addis Ababa, Ethiopia,
this research center was established in 1975 by a resolution of the UN-
ECA Conference of Ministers as a way of coordinating a variety of UN
projects that focused on women, including the UNECA Women's Programme. The center has sponsored a variety of publications and conferences on issues related to women in Africa, including annual meetings since 1979 of the Africa Regional Coordinating Committee for the
Integration of Women in Development, which formulates specific policy recommendations concerning women for the UNECA Conference
of Ministers. Publications include a series of bibliographies in the
1980s and reports on women and **development,** as well as *ATRCW
Update* (1978–1993). A 1998 conference on African Women and Economic Development included an online discussion and resulted in a
publication about African women and information and communication
technologies (*Gender and the Information Revolution in Africa*, ed.
Eva M. Rathgeber and Edith Ofwona Adera, 2000). In 1995 the name

was changed to the **African Centre for Women**, and in 2001 the name was again changed to the **African Centre for Gender and Development**. The ATRCW history is told by Margaret Snyder and Mary Tadesse in *African Women and Development: A History, The Story of the African Training and Research Centre for Women of the United Nations Economic Commission for Africa* (1995). Further information is available online at http://www.uneca.org/eca_programmes/african_ center_for_women/index.htm.

AFRICAN UNION. *See* MONGELLA, GERTRUDE; PROTOCOL ON THE RIGHTS OF WOMEN IN AFRICA; TANKEU, ELIZABETH.

AFRICAN WOMEN. Beginning in 1954 the Department of Education in Tropical Areas at the University of London's Institute of Education published a twice-yearly journal that reported on women's **education** and **development** in Africa. Most of the articles were about Commonwealth countries and were written by foreign service officers and development workers, though African women also sent reports about their activities. It was an invaluable source of information on women's **organizations**; for example, the second issue (June 1955) carried reports on corn mill societies in Cameroon, women's groups in Sierra Leone, day nurseries in Ghana, women's clubs in Uganda, and girls' education in Somalia, along with other briefer reports. It gradually added reports from other world areas, adding a subtitle, *A Journal for Women in Changing Societies*, in 1958 and changing the title to *Women Today* in 1963 to reflect that broader coverage. It was forced to end publication in 1965 due to budgetary constraints at the University of London.

AFRICAN WOMEN'S ANTI-WAR COALITION. Following a 1998 meeting in Dakar, Senegal, about women and the aftermath of **war**, participants formed a coalition devoted to building **peace** on the African continent. It issued a declaration calling for women to unite by sharing their experiences and working to increase women's participation in the politics of ending conflict.

AFRICAN WOMEN'S COMMITTEE FOR PEACE AND DEVELOPMENT. This committee was established by the Organization of African Unity (OAU) in 1998 as a way of "bringing women into the mainstream of the Continent's efforts aimed at preventing, managing and resolving conflicts" (from the press release announcing the committee's formation). Initial committee members included government representatives, women leaders of **peace** initiatives such as **Gertrude Mongella** and **Ruth Sando Perry**, and delegates from **non-governmental organizations** including the Federation of African Women for Peace and **Femmes Africa Solidarité**.

AFRICAN WOMEN'S DAY. African Women's Day is celebrated on July 31 to commemorate the founding in 1962 of the **All African Women's Conference**, which was later called the **Pan African Women's Organisation**.

AFRICAN WOMEN'S DEVELOPMENT AND COMMUNICATION NETWORK. Commonly called FEMNET, this international network was founded in 1988 to coordinate African women's efforts in **non-governmental organizations** (NGOs). It worked to improve communication between various NGOs, and simultaneously to expand women's influence in **development** programs. It sponsors training, **education**, and outreach projects on issues such as **domestic violence** and the implementation of new **laws** that support women's rights. A focus of its work in 2004 was the ratification of the **Protocol on the Rights of Women in Africa**. FEMNET has published numerous training manuals on gender mainstreaming and related topics as well as a quarterly electronic newsletter *Femnet News*. With funding from a variety of international organizations, its main office is in Kenya, and it is structured with regional offices in all areas of Africa. For further information, see the website at http://www.femnet.or.ke/.

AFRICAN WOMEN'S FORUM. *See* AFRICA WOMEN'S FORUM.

AFRICAN WOMEN'S MEDIA CENTER (AWMC). Formed in 1997 with the support of the International Media Women's Foundation, the AWMC networked among African women journalists, provided skills training and leadership workshops, and published an electronic quarterly newsletter, *On the Wire/Sur le Fil*. The newsletter and further information can be found on the internet at www.awmc.com. *See also* JOURNALISM.

AFRICAN WOMEN'S SELF-IMPROVEMENT ASSOCIATION. An organization founded by **Christian** women in the Cape Province of South Africa in the 1920s to teach **domestic** skills to rural Xhosa women. There was a rival but similar organization, the Bantu Women's Home Improvement Association. *See also* ZENZELE.

AFUA KOBI (fl. 1834–1884). Afua Kobi was an *asantehemaa* (queen mother) who advised the Asante council to avoid war with the British. In 1873 she made a powerful speech before the military chiefs including her son, Asantehene Kofi Karikari, arguing that such a war would destroy Asante. The chiefs decided to fight; they lost to the British and Kofi Karikari was replaced by Afua Kobi's younger son Mensa Bonsu. She continued as senior counselor, though neither of her sons was notably successful during their reigns. Afua Kobi faced competition from her daughter (and Mensa Bonsu's sister) **Yaa Akyaa** who worked to get her own children named to the Golden Stool, as the ruling seat of the Asantehene was known.

AGENDA: A JOURNAL ABOUT WOMEN AND GENDER. A South African **journal** on women's issues, it was first published in 1988. The editors were originally a collective that publicized only the first names of its members; in 1998 it identified itself as a "project of Agenda Feminist Media Co." and the editors were named. A new subtitle was added in 1994, "Empowering women for gender equity;" the current subtitle was introduced in 1998. The journal covers a wide range of issues concerning women across the continent in articles, opinion pieces, and briefings. It is especially strong on South African women.

AGING. *See* WIDOWHOOD.

AGRICULTURE. Agricultural production is at the base of every African economy, and most of the production relies on women's labor. Women generally are most active in the subsistence sector, where they grow food to feed their families, with occasional surplus for trade or sale in the **market**. Though statistics vary across the continent, it is clear that the majority of subsistence labor is women's work with 70 to 80 percent of women involved in that sector. Their efforts are noted for the low level of technology, as women typically work the earth and weed their cultivated plots with short-handled hoes and carry water on their heads. Women are also very active in commercial agriculture and in cultivating cash crops such as cocoa, tea, coffee, and cotton. Although the stereotype is that they do not have control over the proceeds of that work, many women are in fact active businesswomen who control the results of their labor, travel to markets, and make important decisions about cultivation. Such practices may vary over a woman's life, with older women more likely to be involved in commercial agriculture once their children are grown, or when they can rely on younger co-wives to handle household responsibilities while they (the first wives) expand their market activities. The recent introduction of the cultivation of flowers in Kenya for export to Europe has raised concerns about pesticide use and abuse, which may lead to long-term health problems for the women working on the flower farms. Flower export has brought new income to women farmers.

AHEMAA (SING. *OHEMAA*). The Akan (Ghana) word for female chiefs, more often translated as **queen mothers**, *ahemaa* were considered co-rulers with chiefs, as they had joint responsibility for the affairs of state and when there was no male heir they could rule. An *ohemaa*, as the senior woman in a lineage, could be the actual mother of the chief, though sisters, aunts, and other female kin who had the requisite diplomatic and leadership skills could be *ahemaa*. Ahemaa symbolized **motherhood** though they most often took on this role after their own children were grown. Because women were restricted from many ritual activities and from military action during **menstruation**, *ahemaa* often came to power after reaching menopause. As the chief genealogist for the lineage, she nominated the candidate for chief, confirmed his legitimacy, and had veto power over the council in determining the next male chief. She was obliged to be present at the meetings of the governing council, and she also had her own court with female retinue and councillors. In the court of the king she sat at his side, offered advice, and was the only person allowed to reprimand him. The highest queen mother among the Asante was the *asantehe-maa*. The *ahemaa* could amass great wealth through trade in kola nuts, gold, or rubber, and reports from the early 19th century included descriptions of vast estates farmed by **slave** laborers who were held by the *ahemaa*. Three of the most prominent women in Asante history were *asantehemaa*, **Afua Kobi**, **Yaa Akyaa**, and **Yaa Asantewaa**.

AHFAD JOURNAL: WOMEN AND CHANGE. An academic journal from **Ahfad University for Women** in Omdurman, Sudan, it is published in English with Arabic abstracts. The first issue appeared in 1984, and it is published twice a year.

AHFAD UNIVERSITY FOR WOMEN. Ahfad University for Women had its beginnings in the years following the 1898 defeat of Sudanese nationalist forces by the Anglo-Egyptian army. Babicar Badri, a religious man with 13 daughters and some sons, opened a secular school for boys and petitioned the British colonial authorities for permission to open a school for girls. Concerned that the local community would not support such an endeavor, the British refused permission to Badri in 1904 and 1906 before the school was allowed to open in 1907. That initial private elementary school remained under the control of the Badri family for decades, and in 1966 Babikar's son Yusuf opened the Ahfad University College for Women. In 1995 the name was changed to Ahfad University for Women to reflect an expanded curriculum. Ahfad means "for our grandchildren," and the sentiment that women's **education** was essential for an improved future for all has continued to inform its educational philosophy. The university, which also publishes the ***Ahfad Journal***, is the oldest and largest private university in Sudan, and it may be the only private women's university on the continent of Africa. Further information is available at its website, www.ahfad.org.

AICHE, MARIAM MINT AHMED. A Mauritanian political leader, she was minister of women's affairs from 1992 to 1994, and secretary of women's affairs from 1994 to 1995.

AIDOO, AMA ATA (1942–). Aidoo is one of Ghana's best-known writers, producing novels, short stories, poems, and plays. She attended the

University of Ghana at Legon, and in the early 1960s she won a prize awarded by a Nigerian cultural workshop for one of her first short stories. She earned a fellowship that allowed her to study creative writing at Stanford University in California, returning to Ghana in 1969. Her publications include a play, *Dilemma of a Ghost*, the story collection *No Sweetness Here* (1970), and the novels, *Our Sister Killjoy* (1977) and *Changes* (1991), which won the 1992 Commonwealth Writers Prize (Africa region). She has focused on issues of cultural change and women's position in a modernizing society. She also served as minister of education, 1982 to 1983, but found herself in conflict with Ghanaian political authorities and moved to Harare, Zimbabwe, in 1983.

AIDS. *See* HIV/AIDS.

AISA KILI NGIRMARMMA (fl. 16TH CENTURY). She ruled the Kanuri empire of Bornu (now in northern Nigeria and Niger) as *magira*, during the years 1563 through 1570. As the daughter of Dunama, she was recognized locally though her name has been omitted from some Arabic sources. She may have acted to hold the throne for the male heir, Idris.

AKECH (fl. 1760–1787). Akech was the second wife of Rwoth (King) Nyabongo in the East African lake region chiefdom of Paroketu. Succession to the royal seat had been patrilineal, and in the customary order Nyabongo would have been succeeded by Jobi, the oldest son of his **senior wife**, Akura. But Akech was able to move into a powerful position by drawing on her religious leadership, which augmented the political power she enjoyed as a royal wife. By 1760 she rose to political prominence as a royal wife, a ritual leader, and the mother of the heir to the throne. After her son Roketu came to power, the people of the palace came to be known as the Pa-Akech, the people of Akech, and she was recognized as the founder of a ruling dynasty.

AKINA MAMA WA AFRIKA. Akina Mama is a **non-governmental organization** based in London that promotes women's issues in Africa and abroad. Founded in 1985, it sponsored the Africa Women's Leadership Institute in Uganda in 1996, co-sponsored the

Africa Women's Forum in 1998, and continues to hold frequent conferences and training institutes on gender and **development**, **education**, **human rights**, and related issues. Its main goals are "To influence policies that affect African women at national, regional and international levels; to participate in the construction of a feminist epistemology by African women; to strengthen and promote African women's feminist leadership; and to respond to the leadership needs of African women and African women's organizations," and it is especially concerned with training younger women to move into leadership positions. The website is found at http://www.akinamama.org/index.html.

AKINTUNDE-IGHODALO, FOLAYEGBE MOSUNMOLA (1923–). A Nigerian leader in the movement for women's political rights, in 1968 she was the first Nigerian woman to be appointed as a permanent secretary, the highest position in the civil service. Akintunde-Ighodalo won a scholarship to the elite Queen's College in Lagos, and in the 1950s she earned a degree in economics from the University of London. She was a founding member of the **National Council of Women's Societies** (**NCWS**) and of the Nigerian Association of University Women. After retiring from government service she became a successful businesswoman running a poultry farm.

AKONADI. Akonadi is a **goddess** associated with the area around Accra, Ghana. A story is told that illustrates her role as a goddess of justice and one who protects women and children: Three brothers came to a shrine of Akonadi and asked for advice because there had been several deaths in their family. She told them to go to their grandmother's home, where they would find stolen items, as the grandmother was working with a group of thieves. The brothers duly went to the home where they found a metal box with precious items under their grandmother's bed. They brought the box to the goddess; if the stolen items were no longer in their household there would be no more deaths. Soon after that two men came to the goddess and announced that a box of valuables had been stolen from their mother's estate, and asked if the goddess knew who the thieves were. Her priestess gave her answer, that the box was in the shrine, and though they were welcome to take it, they were advised to leave it so that it could be used for charity for poor women and children. Knowing how much suffering the box of treasure had caused, the men chose to leave it with the goddess for distribution to the needy.

ALAKIJA, ADUKE (1921–). Alakija is a Nigerian lawyer who has served as president of the International Federation of Female Lawyers. She initially studied in Lagos before going to England where she studied social science at the London School of Economics and Cambridge University. Alakija was a founding member of the West African Students' Union (WASU) during the **colonial** period. After working in social welfare in Lagos, she returned to England to study **law** in order to better assist the women and children she was seeing in her work. She was called to the bar in 1953. Alakija was part of the Nigerian delegation to the United Nations from 1961 to 1965, and has participated in many political and charitable organizations. She was also named as a director of Mobil Oil, the first African woman to be appointed to that entity. In 2003 she was given Nigerian National Honours by President Olusegun Obasanjo.

ALCOHOL. African women in many areas were responsible for brewing beer from maize or other local crops, which historically was part of the payment made when neighbors and kin helped in seasonal agricultural tasks. Women produced other fermented and distilled beverages as well, and in the 19th and 20th centuries many women began selling such beverages in urban areas. Although most often noted as brewers and sellers, women also drank alcohol, though seemingly not in the quantities ascribed to men. Women were concerned about the overconsumption of alcohol by men, especially as imported and manufactured alcohol gained in popularity. Such beverages are much higher in alcohol content and some questionable brews are known to include toxic and poisonous ingredients. *See also* BEER BREWERS; TEMPERANCE.

ALINESITOUÉ DIATTA (c. 1920–1943). Alinesitoué was a Dioula prophet in Senegal in the early 1940s, the first woman to claim that the supreme being, Emitai, spoke to her. Her experience appeared to be related to the oppression of French **colonialism**, as her first visions came when the French were pushing for increased rice production and were allowing both **Islamic** and **Christian** incursions into local Dioula communities. Alinesitoué used some methods traditionally associated with male prophets and brought women and young men into the process so that they had increased access to religious authority. She also challenged French development schemes that introduced peanuts as a male crop, leaving all rice cultivation to women, when she argued that peanuts were alien to Dioula ecological beliefs because they resulted in a decreased role for women in **agriculture** while increasing Dioula dependence on the French. As her followers increased in number, the French feared she would instigate a rebellion. They arrested her in 1942, and she died of starvation in exile in Timbuktu. She was followed by over two dozen female prophets who have carried on her work.

ALKALI, ZAYNAB (1950–). Alkali is a novelist from northern Nigeria. She was educated and has taught at Bayero University in Kano. Her first novel, *The Stillborn*, was published in 1984, when it won the prose prize from the Association of Nigerian Authors. She also published *The Virtuous Woman* (1987) and *The Cobwebs and Other Stories* (1997). Her work includes female characters negotiating life in modern Nigeria.

ALL AFRICA WOMEN'S CONFERENCE. This organization was first discussed in Bamako, Mali, and held its first full meeting in Tanzania in 1962, with the goal of bringing together women from the newly independent nations and the liberation movements. Other early groups that eventually joined to form a unified organization included the **Conference of Women of Africa and of African Descent** (formed in Ghana with **Hannah Cudjoe**), and the **Kenya Women's Seminar** (with **Bibi Titi Mohammed**). The **Regional Meeting on the Role of Women in National Development** grew out of the early efforts of the All Africa Women's Conference. After 1974 it was called the **Pan African Women's Organisation** and held observer status within the Organization of African Unity (OAU). **Jeanne Martin-Cissé** was the secretary general from its founding until 1972.

AMANITARE. *See* AFRICAN PARTNERSHIP FOR SEXUAL AND REPRODUCTIVE HEALTH AND RIGHTS OF WOMEN AND GIRLS.

AMATHILA (APPOLUS-AMATHISA), LIBERTINE (1940–).
Amathila is a Namibian politician and medical doctor. She was edu-
cated in Namibia and South Africa, but was forced into exile in 1962
when she became politically active. She won a scholarship to the
Warsaw Medical Academy, and also studied medicine in London and
Sweden, specializing in pediatrics, nutrition, and public health. She
has worked in Dar es Salaam, London, and Bamako as a physician.
She directed the **SWAPO Women's Council** of the South West
African Peoples' Organization in the late 1960s, stepping down in
1976. She is a member of the legislative assembly, and was appointed
minister of local government and housing in 1991 and minister of
health and social services in 1996.

AMAZONS. *See* DAHOMEY SOLDIERS.

AMEDOME, ABRA. A leader in Togo, she was trained as a pharmacist in France and returned to become a highly successful businesswoman and "merchant queen." She was a leader in the ruling party,
and beginning in 1975 she was president of the **Union National des
Femmes Togolaise.** From 1979 to 1983 she was minister of social affairs and women's production.

AMINA (c. 1560–1610). Amina was a queen in the northern Nigerian
Hausa state of Zaria (alternatively known as Zauzau), one of two daughters of a female ruler named Bakwa Turunku. She was a warrior herself
and after the death of her husband, chief Karama, in 1576 she took the
throne and ruled for 30 years. She was renowned for her efforts in expanding the boundaries of her state and for building the earth-works that
surrounded many Hausa city-states including a well-known wall around
Katsina. She was also responsible for expanding Hausa trade along east-
west trade routes. A legendary woman, she reportedly had a lover in
each town under her jurisdiction, and some versions claimed each was
beheaded the next morning. Although she is generally described as ruling in the 16th century, other evidence suggests that she was a contemporary of Sarki Dauda, who was active in the early 15th century (c.
1421–1438), and that her activities are not consonant with a 16th century reign when Songhay already controlled Zaria, Kano, and Katsina,
thus making Amina's dominance in Zaria unlikely.

ANIMIST RELIGIONS. Many societies in Africa have followed religious beliefs based on revering the wisdom of the ancestors and respecting the natural environment; such beliefs can be subsumed under the term animist religions or animism. Women have played important roles in the rites associated with such beliefs, as healers, as teachers for girls in their **initiation rites**, and as practitioners knowledgeable about rituals related to marriage, birth, and death.

ANLU. Anlu was a traditional method of protest used by Kom women in the Cameroon Grassfields to ostracize community members, male or female, who transgressed behavioral norms including those that protected women's near-absolute authority in **agriculture**. It most often refers to a widespread protest in 1958 to 1961, when the British **colonial** authorities tried to introduce agrarian reform, including new methods of farming that undercut women's authority. In November 1958 an all-woman delegation marched to the government offices in Bamenda, where Nawain Mwana, one of the *anlu* leaders, expressed fears about women's loss of control over production of food and fertility. Although it began as an autonomous protest, it was eventually affiliated with the anti-colonial political party, Kameruns National Democratic Party (KNDP), which was in the midst of a dispute about Cameroon's future as part of the British or French colonial sphere. The KNDP favored unity between the French and British sectors of Cameroon; the Kameruns National Congress (KNC) preferred integration into a federal system in Nigeria as part of the British sphere. Initially the uprising focused on women and agriculture but within a few months there were 7,000 members meeting in branches throughout the region, and the demands grew to include broader political issues such as Nigerian migration into Kom areas. The 1958 *anlu* was noted for the disruption of both colonial and traditional authority in the region, as roads were blocked and the women obstructed the rule of the Fon, the traditional male ruler. Its techniques have been since been used by other Grassfields ethnic groups to protest abuses of power; for example, the Babanki, a group neighboring the Kom, turned to what they termed "*anlu*" when their Fon was impregnating most of the young women at a boarding school near his palace. He was willing to marry the women, but their mothers had higher aspirations for them and threatened him with complete loss of authority unless he desisted, which he did. *See also* ABA WOMEN'S WAR; SITTING ON A MAN.

ANOMA, GLADYS (1930–). A leading figure in post-independence Côte d'Ivoire, she was the daughter of Joseph Anoma, a prominent leader in the colonial era. She earned a doctorate in tropical botany. She was a member of the political bureau of the Parti Democratique de Côte d'Ivoire (PDCI)/Democratic Party of the Ivory Coast and served as vice president of the general assembly from 1975 until 1989. Anoma was also the secretary general of the **Association des Femmes Ivoiriennes**/Association of Ivoirien Women, the women's wing of the PDCI. *See also* GERVAIS, JEANNE.

ANTI-COLONIAL STRUGGLES. *See* NATIONALISM.

APARTHEID. Apartheid was the system of stringent racial segregation and discrimination that existed in South Africa until multiparty elections were held in 1994. Although there were many restrictive laws from the early days of white settlement, an election in 1948 brought in a new government that expanded and strengthened earlier codes and vastly increased the suffering of the black African population. Women protested apartheid through a number of organizations, including the **African National Congress Women's League, Bantu Women's League, Black Sash, Black Women's Federation**, and the **Federation of South African Women**. The actions of many individual women, including **Frances Baard, Margaret Ballinger, Cheryl Carolus, Sheena Duncan, Ruth First, Frene Ginwala, Helen Joseph, Winnie Mandela, Fatima Meer, Victoria Mxenge, Lilian Ngoyi, Josie Palmer, Mamphela Ramphele, Gertrude Shope, Albertina Sisulu**, and **Helen Suzman**, were also essential to the demise of apartheid. They demonstrated against the expansion of **pass laws** to women, successfully in 1913 in the Orange Free State, and unsuccessfully though notably in the 1950s in Johannesburg during the **Defiance Campaign**.

ART. Though female artists have not been common in Africa, there have been some significant women who were deeply involved in artistic endeavors. In some cases women have recently begun to work in areas conventionally associated with men, such as the Shona stone carvings from Zimbabwe, or women who are painting in oil in a special group outside of Harare. Other women are working in pottery (such as the internationally known **Magdalene Odundo**), textiles, and other media. **Sokari Douglas Camp**, a sculptor based in London, and **Bertina Lopes**, a painter who has lived in Rome for many years, are among the best-known African women artists.

Items such as pots, jewelry, and other material goods can provide some evidence about women's activities in earlier historical periods. Marla Berns raised the issue of who made the well-known ancient pottery statues in West Africa, noting that it is often assumed that these items were made by men because the statues were put into the category of "art" rather than "craft" and because they were believed to have a spiritual component, both categories generally associated with men. That conventional interpretation actually runs counter to the fact that women are mainly responsible for pottery making in modern times, including manufacturing items used in ritual events as well as pots for everyday use. Thus women may have had the central role in making the widely known 2000-year-old Nok ceramic heads from what is now Nigeria, as well as other figures from Chad. Berns suggests that patterns used in working with clay are repeated in tattoo designs on women's bodies, and that those designs reflect social ideas about womanhood and femininity. She further proposes that if we recognize that women may have made some of these items and designed the emblems decorating the pottery we should accept that "women, through what they make, contribute to the construction of symbolic systems," and thus to the development of culture.

ASANTEHEMAA. In Ghana, the *asantehemaa* is the **queen mother** of Kumasi and advisor to the ruler, the *asantehene*. While the *asantehemaa* was the leading queen mother, other female chiefs were called *ahemaa*. The strength of the *asantehemaa* position reflects women's role in matrilineal Asante society. Notable *asantehemaa* include **Afua Kobi**, **Yaa Akyaa**, and **Yaa Asantewaa**.

ASASE YAA (ALSO CALLED ASASE YA, ASASE EFUE). Asase Yaa is the Asante earth **goddess**, recognized as a source of truth; her followers show her respect with a day of rest from tilling the soil on Thursdays. She is not a divinity with shrines and priestesses, though offerings are left on the ground in her honor.

ASMA'U, NANA (1793–1864). Asma'u was an influential Hausa-Fulani poet and scholar in 19th century Sokoto, Nigeria. She was the daughter of the well-known jihad leader Usman dan Fodio, and she made contributions to politics as well to **education** and intellectual endeavors including establishing a network of schools for rural women. She was an **Islamic** activist who worked as a Sufi of the Qadiriyya order, seeking a proper Muslim life following Sunni precepts, and was a mentor and model for women and men throughout Islamic West Africa. She was fluent in Hausa, Fulfulde, Tamachek, and Arabic, and in those languages she wrote **poetry**, histories of the jihad, information on women, and religious texts. She married and had children; her descendents continued her example of scholarship and leadership. Though she was particularly prolific and active, she was not unique as an educated Muslim woman in 19th century West Africa.

ASSEMBLY OF GHANA WOMEN. This national umbrella organization was founded in 1969 to coordinate work among women in Ghana; in 1978 there were 10,000 members. They published *The Ghanaian Woman*.

ASSOCIAÇÃO DE APOIO À AUTO-PROMOÇÃO DA MULHER NO DESENVOLVIMENTO / ASSOCIATION OF SUPPORT FOR SELF-PROMOTION OF WOMEN IN DEVELOPMENT. *See* MORABI.

ASSOCIATION DES FEMMES DU NIGER (AFN) / ASSOCIATION OF WOMEN OF NIGER. Founded following a coup d'etat in 1974, this group has been the primary women's organization in Niger. It replaced the **Union des Femmes du Niger (UFN).** It continued the struggle to introduce a **family law**, and its membership base was still centered in the urban areas despite a shift to recruiting rural rather than urban women.

ASSOCIATION DES FEMMES IVOIRIENNES (AFI) / ASSO-CIATION OF IVOIRIENNE WOMEN. The association was founded in 1963 by the **first lady** of Côte d'Ivoire, Madame Thérèse Houphouet-Boigny, as a replacement for the Feminine Committee which had been an active women's wing of the main anti-colonial party, the Parti Démocratique de Côte d'Ivoire (PDCI)/Democratic Party of the Ivory Coast. From the beginning it was designed to address women's issues and to leave the "real" politics to male party leaders. It maintained a parallel existence with the party, and in 1977 it was formally affiliated with the party apparatus. **Jeanne Gervais** was the first vice president, and was later president for many years, and **Gladys Anoma** was secretary general. The AFI was most involved in activities deemed appropriate for women, such as supporting orphanages, holding conferences on **marriage** and **divorce**, and sending representatives to international meetings. The program was primarily symbolic rather than directly addressing the possibility of change to improve women's lives.

ASSOCIATION DES FEMMES TRAVAILLEUSES / ASSOCIATION OF WORKING WOMEN. *See* UNION DES FEMMES TRAVAILLEUSES.

ASSOCIATION DES FEMMES VOLTAIQUES / ASSOCIATION OF VOLTAIC WOMEN. Formed in Upper Volta (now Burkina Faso) in 1969 to support women and girls' **education** and improved access to **health**.

ASSOCIATION DES JURISTES MALIENNES (AJM) / THE ASSOCIATION OF WOMEN JURISTS OF MALI (VAR. ASSOCIATION DES FEMMES JURISTES DU MALI). In the 1990s the AJM used funding from international aid agencies to support its outreach to rural women in Mali by means of mobile legal clinics and a radio program, "La Voix des Femmes." The main issues centered on **marriage**, including **divorce**, **inheritance**, and **polygyny**. Leading human rights activist **Fatoumata Dembélé Diarra** is a past president.

ASSOCIATION OF AFRICAN WOMEN FOR RESEARCH AND DEVELOPMENT (AAWORD) / ASSOCIATION DES FEMMES AFRICAINES POUR LA RECHERCHE SUR LE DÉVELOPPE-MENT (AFARD). Following a discussion among women scholars meeting in Lusaka, Zambia, in December 1976, AAWORD/AFARD was established in 1977 by African women researchers who wanted to advance their own ideas about **development** and gender issues. Based in Dakar, Senegal, and under the auspices of the Council for the Development of Economic and Social Research in Africa (CODESRIA), AAWORD sponsors a regular series of conferences and publishes bilingual occasional papers, bibliographic materials, and a quarterly newsletter, *Echo* (beginning in 1986). The monographs have investigated reproduction, mass media, youth leadership, **feminism**, and development. AAWORD's written mission statement calls for building a woman's movement linking **human rights** and development while promoting African women's contributions and developing the abilities and opportunities of African women scholars. It has also been concerned with extending networks across the continent and internationally among scholars interested in African women. It has held general assemblies in 1977, 1983, and 1988 in Dakar, and in 1995 in Pretoria, South Africa. Since 1990 it has maintained a documentation center that holds nearly 2,000 books and reports.

ASSOCIATION OF AFRICAN WOMEN SCHOLARS (AAWS). The AAWS is a network of academic women from Africa and the diaspora; founded by Obioma Nnameka, it is based in the United States and has held conferences in Nigeria in the 1990s and in Madagascar in 2001.

ASSOCIATION OF BUSINESSWOMEN OF TANZANIA. Founded in 1990, this group was initiated by middle-class employed women, but also included poorer women who had **micro-enterprises**. The group agitated for more participation of women in government while documenting the obstacles facing women in economics and politics.

ASSOCIATION POUR LA PROMOTION DE LA FEMME RWANDAISE (APROFER) / ASSOCIATION FOR THE ADVANCEMENT OF THE WOMEN OF RWANDA. Formed in 1966, its main objective was to promote unity among all Rwandan women.

ASSOCIATION POUR LE PROGRÈS ET LA DEFENCE DES DROITS DES FEMMES MALIENNES / ASSOCIATION FOR PROGRESS AND DEFENSE OF THE RIGHTS OF WOMEN IN MALI. Founded in 1991, it was one of the leading women's groups in Mali.

AURA POKU. *See* POKOU.

AWA. An early French-language magazine for African women, it was started in Senegal in 1963 by **Annette M'Baye.**

AZEB. The only women's magazine published in Ethiopia, it was initiated in 1968 by the **Ethiopians' Women's Welfare Association.**

– B –

BÂ, MARIAMA (1929–1981). Bâ was a writer from Senegal best known for her brief novel, *Une si longue lettre* (*So Long a Letter*, Dakar, 1979), which won the first Noma Award for Publishing in Africa in 1980. The theme of the novel is **polygyny**, as it relates the story of the dissolution of a monogamous marriage when the husband decides to marry a second, much younger, wife. Bâ's father, a civil servant, insisted that she attend French school. While at the École Normale in Rufisque she wrote two essays that were published, though she did not return to her writing for many years. Bâ trained as a teacher, and after teaching for 12 years she was appointed to the Senegalese Regional Inspectorate of Teaching. She had nine children, and was married to Obèye Diop, a member of the Senegalese parliament.

BAARD, FRANCES (B. GOITSEMANG) (1908–1997). Frances Baard was a South African **trade union** leader and political activist. She was born in Kimberley, South Africa, to Tswana parents who sent her back to family in Botswana when she was a child. She was later educated in South Africa. Her first job was in **domestic service**, but she eventually found work in a fruit canning factory in Port Elizabeth. In 1948 she was introduced to trade union work by Ray Alexander, and joined the African National Congress (ANC) that same year. As an organizer in the **African National Congress Women's League** and in the **Federation of South African Women** she was deeply involved in the mass protests of the 1950s against the expansion of the **apartheid** system and the extension of **pass laws** to women. Baard was arrested, put under house arrest, and banned multiple times during the 1950s and 1960s, at one time spending a year in solitary confinement. She was memorialized by naming a neighborhood in Kimberley the Frances Baard District Municipality. She published her autobiography, *My Spirit is Not Banned* (as told to Barbie Schreiner) in 1986.

BAARTMAN, SARA (c. 1787–1815) (VAR. SAARTJE OR SAARTJIE, MEANING "LITTLE SARA"). Sara Baartman was a Khoisan woman from southern Africa who was brought to Europe as a household slave around 1810 by her owner, English army surgeon Alexander Dunlop. She had extremely large buttocks, a condition known as steatopygia, and she was soon exhibited in London as an exemplar of African exoticism. She was sometimes referred to as the "Hottentot Venus," thus naming her as being from a group long seen by Europeans as the most bestial of Africans (the term Hottentot is most likely a reference to the click languages spoken by the Khoisan and other southern Africans, which Europeans once believed was not a true language but somewhere between animal grunts and human speech). The display of her thinly veiled body in London and Paris was marketed as part of the existing practice of displaying humans with unusual physical features, often called freaks, but also was one of the first exhibits that claimed a scientific and therefore educational motive. In Britain a group of abolitionists took her case to court in a failed attempt to free her. After her death in Paris her genitals were put on display at the Musée de l'Homme until possibly as late as 1982. Her story became emblematic of the misrepresentation of black sexuality and of the exploitation of African women. After an international outcry her remains were returned to South Africa in 2002, where she was welcomed by Griqua people in a ceremony in Cape Town. Zola Maseko has made two films that document her experiences, *The Life and Times of Sara Baartman—The Hottentot Venus* (1998) and *The Return of Sara Baartman* (2003).

BABA OF KARO (c. 1877–1951). Baba of Karo was an ordinary Hausa woman in northern Nigeria who told her life history to the anthropologist Mary Smith. The book, *Baba of Karo: A Woman of the Muslim Hausa* (1954), related many details of women's lives.

BABANGIDA, MARYAM IBRAHIM. Babangida was a Nigerian **first lady** who founded the development organization **Better Life Programme for the Rural Woman**. She was awarded the Africa Prize from the Hunger Project in 1991.

BALLINGER, (VIOLET) MARGARET (LIVINGSTONE) (1894–1980). Ballinger was a politician in South Africa who was a founding member and first national chairperson of the Liberal Party. An immigrant from Scotland, she was educated at Rhodes and Oxford Universities before taking a teaching position in the history department at Witwatersrand University in 1920. She married trade union activist William Ballinger in 1934. In 1937 Ballinger ran for parliament at the request of the African National Congress (ANC), and she continued to represent African voters from the Eastern Cape in parliament until 1960, when Africans were further disenfranchised and such representation was outlawed. She published an autobiography, *From Union to Apartheid: A Trek to Isolation* (1969).

BANDEIRA, ALDA (1949–). Bandeira is the most prominent woman politician in São Tomé and Príncipe. Her father was a nurse, and she was educated in São Tomé and taught in Mozambique before completing a degree in modern languages and literature in Lisbon. She then taught English in secondary schools in Maputo and in São Tomé, and served in the 1980s as the director of multilateral cooperation in the Ministry of Foreign Affairs. After a change in government, she was named minister of foreign affairs in 1991 and 1992, and served as a member of parliament. Bandeira became the parliamentary leader of the party she helped found, the Partido de Convergência Democrática—Grupo de Reflexão/Party of Democratic Convergence—Group of Reflection, in 1994, and was elected president of the party in 1995, holding that office until 2001. She was a candidate in the 1996 presidential election, running third with 14 percent of the vote. Bandeira also served as vice president of a women's organization, Associação da Mulher Mutende. She was briefly minister of foreign affairs and cooperation in 2002, and in

2004 she was serving her fourth term in parliament. *See also* HEADS OF STATE.

BANGOURA, HADJA MAFORY (?–1968). Mafory Bangoura was a leading activist on women's issues in Guinea. She worked as a tailor before she was involved in a group that supported Sekou Touré during the **nationalist** struggles of the 1950s. She became a leader within the Parti Démocratique de Guinée/Democratic Party of Guinea, and held government positions after independence.

BANNABIKIRA. One of the oldest Catholic sisterhoods in Africa, the name means "Daughters of the Virgin" in Baganda. The **White Sisters** had begun work at Buddu in Uganda in 1902 under the leadership of Mother Mechtilde. Within a year the first group of girls trained as catechists, and their numbers grew rapidly. In 1907, when there were 140 girls living in the mission, wearing distinguishing dress, and working with children, some of them asked to become nuns. Mother Mechtilde established a novitiate in 1908, and in 1910 the first three girls were professed. The order applied rules specific to their community, with no vow of poverty, an annual rather than a lifetime commitment, and the sisters kept their own names. The name Bannabikira was also adopted in 1910. By 1926 the order had a new permanent headquarters in Buddu and the first Ugandan mother superior was named (Mama Cecilia Nalube, who took the name Mother Ursula). At that time the congregation adopted the practices of vowing poverty, accepting new names, and making a lifetime commitment to the order. Their numbers and influence continued to grow, and there were 256 nuns in 1956 accompanied by a growing number of sister congregations in other regions of Uganda which counted over 1,000 Ugandan sisters. Other prominent Ugandan orders included the Franciscan Missionary Sisters of Africa, founded by the dynamic leader from Ireland, Mother Kevin (1875–1957). *See also* CONGREGATION OF THE DAUGHTERS OF THE SACRED HEART OF MARY.

BANTU WOMEN'S LEAGUE (BWL) (SOUTH AFRICA). A precursor of the African Women's League which developed into the **African National Congress Women's League** in South Africa, it was founded by **Charlotte Maxeke** in 1918 following her experience organizing against **pass laws** in 1913. In 1931 the BWL was recognized as a formal organization by the African National Congress (ANC).

BANTU WOMEN'S LEAGUE (ZIMBABWE). An early women's **organization**, the Bantu Women's League was established in Bulawayo, Rhodesia (later Zimbabwe), in the 1920s. The founding members were primarily **market** vendors who were interested in protecting their economic interests.

BAOBAB FOR WOMEN'S HUMAN RIGHTS. A Nigerian women's **organization,** Baobab has been a foremost voice in the struggle to limit the implementation of **Islamic shari'a laws** in the northern states. Ayesha Imam, a leading scholar and activist, has been coordinator of Baobab for many years; in 2002 she was awarded the John Humphrey Freedom Award for her work to end the restrictive laws. Baobab is affiliated with the international network Women Living under Muslim Laws. The organization website is found at http://www.baobabwomen.org/.

BAPPO, SHEILABAI. A political leader in Mauritius, she served as minister of **employment**, industrial relations, women's rights, and family welfare in the 1980s and was a member of the cabinet for many years. She was a teacher prior to entering politics. In 1996 she became the secretary general of the Mouvement Socialiste Mauricien.

BASUTOLAND HOMEMAKERS' ASSOCIATION. The organization was established by Bernice Tlalane Mohapeloa in 1944 in Lesotho (then called Basutoland). She had been involved in similar groups in South Africa, including the Home Improvement Club at Fort Hare University, and she brought her interest in domestic science clubs with her when she returned to her native Botswana. At its high point there were 160 clubs, whose focus was on domesticity with an emphasis on hygiene and home care. In 1947 Mohapeloa was awarded the British Empire Medal for her work.

BATUQUE. *Batuque*, or *batuku*, is a women's dance on the Cape Verde Islands, where a group of women singers perform this style of **music** at weddings and other events. Songs may also commemorate historic events and include advice or humor. Traditionally women would fold their cloth wrapper between their legs and beat on the material to make the rhythm. The dance continues to have adherents in Lisbon and in North America among the diasporic community, and has been revived in the islands by Terrero, a group of younger women who added plastic bags to their wrappers to increase the intensity of their music; their recording, *Xubenga* was released in 2000.

BEATRIZ. *See* DONA BEATRIZ KIMPA VITA.

BEER BREWERS. In most African societies women were responsible for the regular brewing of beer as part of their food preparation tasks more generally. Beer or wine as well as other **alcoholic** beverages could be brewed from a variety of local plants, including bananas, sorghum, maize, millet, sugar cane, and palm sap. It was generally a process that lasted several days as women soaked the grain, dried it and pounded it into flour, steeped it in water, heated it, and left it to ferment. In rural societies beer was shared with kin and neighbors who helped with the harvest or other seasonal agricultural tasks, such as when land was cleared for planting, usually a job done by a male work party. Women were noted as selling beer to porters on 19th century trading caravans in East Africa, and as societies became more urban and market oriented, women continued to brew beer in the cities. During the colonial era this practice was condemned by authorities who decried problems of drunkenness among the workers at mines, factories, and other workplaces. Women who brewed beer could be subject to police raids, but they were seldom deterred by such actions as it was a reliable and steady source of income in urban economies that did not offer many options for women. In South Africa women established bars called **shebeens**, and in many areas prominent businesswomen began their entrepreneurial careers brewing beer for male workers. *See also* TEMPERANCE.

BETTER LIFE PROGRAMME FOR THE RURAL WOMAN (BLP). This Nigerian organization was established in 1987 by

Maryam Babangida, the **first lady** from 1985 to 1993. Funded by the government, it was designed to improve women's lives through organizing income-producing projects in **agriculture**, trade, and small-scale production. The BLP sponsored over 9,000 new **cooperatives**, nearly 1,000 cottage industries, and a variety of shops, **markets**, farms, women's centers, and programs. It became a forum for elite women with little service to the poor peasants who were supposed to benefit, and was eventually integrated into the National Commission for Women.

BEYALA, CALIXTHE (1961–). Beyala is a Cameroonian novelist who has received attention for the provocative and sexual themes in her books. Born in Cameroon, she has lived in Paris as an adult. She published her first novel, *C'est le soleil qui m'a brûlée*, in 1987. Her novels have won major awards, including the Prix du roman de l'Académie Française for *Les honneurs perdus* (1996), though she has also been the center of a scandal in France, where a court found her guilty of plagiarism for that same novel. Her novels present a nonlinear impressionistic view of relationships in which women are the victims of men ("every woman is someone's whore," *Assèze l'Africaine* [Paris, 1994], p. 126), and she also discusses a kind of **feminism** she calls "feminitude," that includes dialogue among all the women of the world.

BIBI TITI. *See* MOHAMED, BIBI TITI.

BIBLEWOMEN. Biblewomen were African women who had converted to **Christianity** and who devoted themselves to proselytizing by traveling to distant rural areas and conducting study sessions with local women. Present especially in South Africa, they performed this work in the first half of the 20th century under the auspices of the Methodist Women's Auxiliaries. *See also* CIRCLE OF CONCERNED AFRICAN WOMEN THEOLOGIANS; GIRLS' BRIGADE; *MANYANO*.

BINAO (1867–1923). Binao was a ruler of the Bemihisatra group of Sakalava in Madagascar, taking the throne in 1881. Her domain included the island of Nosy Be and the mainland just opposite the island.

As the Merina Empire expanded she felt pressure on her rule and turned to the French, assisting them in the Malagasy War of 1883 to 1885. Although the Merina gained control of Nosy Be, she again supported the French in the 1895 war between the French and the Malagasy. The French confirmed her as the ruler of an internal protectorate.

BIRTH CONTROL. African women have used certain herbal remedies to prevent or interrupt conception, but as the desire for many children in Africa is still common, it has not been a common practice. The introduction of modern medical methods of controlling family size has had the greatest impact in urban areas. In many communities men are opposed to their wives using any form of birth control, and people commonly express concerns that women will behave promiscuously if they have access to the birth control pill or some other method that is not regulated by men. A recent study by Carolyn Bledsoe, *Contingent Lives: Fertility, Time, and Aging in West Africa* (2002), found that African women turn to birth control as a way to manage and space births, but do not see contraceptive methods as a route to limiting family size overall. *See also* ABORTION; FERTILITY; INFERTILITY.

BIRTH RATE. Africa as a region has one of the highest birth rates in the world, although nearly every nation has encouraged contraceptive use and promoted the value of smaller families. See Table 1, Birth rate, Births per woman, 1990–1995. *See also* FERTILITY; INFERTILITY.

BLACK CONSCIOUSNESS MOVEMENT. The Black Consciousness Movement developed in **apartheid** South Africa during the early 1970s. The primary focus of the movement's politics was an understanding of racism as the crucial factor in South Africa, which meant that gender issues were often ignored or discounted. Many women were active members, however, including **Mamphela Ramphele** who has written about the ways in which women were involved. She comments that women who became assertive were given an honorary male status that allowed them greater freedom in speaking publicly, but that the continued sidelining of women's issues was a difficulty in the movement. Nonetheless, the affirmation that

Table 1. Birth Rate (average number of births per woman), 1990–1995

Country	Rate	Country	Rate
Angola	7.2	Liberia	6.8
Benin	6.5	Madagascar	6.2
Botswana	3.9	Malawi	7.2
Burkina Faso	7.1	Mali	7
Burundi	6.8	Mauritania	6.1
Cameroon	4.7	Mauritius	2.3
Cape Verde	3.2	Mozambique	6.4
Central African Rep.	5.6	Namibia	5.8
Chad	6.3	Niger	8
Comoros	5.8	Nigeria	6.4
Congo	6.7	Rwanda	6.7
Côte d'Ivoire	5.7	Senegal	6.1
Dem. Rep. of the Congo	6.7	Sierra Leone	6.5
Djibouti	6.3	Somalia	7.3
Equatorial Guinea	5.9	South Africa	3.3
Ethiopia	6.8	Sudan	5.3
Gabon	5.2	Swaziland	5.3
Gambia	5.6	Tanzania	5.9
Guinea	5.4	Togo	6.2
Ghana	5.3	Uganda	7.1
Guinea-Bissau	6	Zambia	6.3
Kenya	5.4	Zimbabwe	5.5
Lesotho	5		

Source: United Nations Department of Economic and Social Affairs.

"Black is Beautiful" was important in the development of African women's appreciation of their own physical appearance and gave many women greater self-confidence.

BLACK SASH. When the South African white-controlled government passed the Senate Act in 1955 to enable the government to remove Coloured citizens (the official term for mixed race residents) from the voter's rolls, a group of white women formed the Women's Defence of the Constitution League, later known as Black Sash, to protest. In the 1950s and 1960s Black Sash members held silent vigils in public locations, where they stood with political posters and wore black sashes diagonally across white dresses as a mourning symbol for the death of constitutional rights under the **apartheid** government. In the

1970s and 1980s they shifted their work to support services for women in urban areas, offering advice about **employment, pass laws, housing**, and pensions. Kathryn Spink has written a history, *Black Sash: The Beginning of a Bridge in South Africa* (1991).

BLACK WOMEN'S FEDERATION. Women in Natal, South Africa, founded the Black Women's Federation in 1973. Beginning with local monthly meetings, the group reached out to women in the Transvaal and Soweto, forming a national organization in 1975 under the leadership of **Winnie Mandela**. Issues addressed at the founding conference included **education, housing**, labor, rural development, and detentions under the **apartheid** government. **Fatima Meer** was the first president, though she was banned in 1976 and the government also blocked a meeting planned to be held in Durban to protest Meer being banned. The entire organization was banned in 1977.

BLANTYRE WOMEN'S ART AND HANDICRAFT CLUB. This organization, founded in Malawi in 1971, worked to promote women's crafts as an income-generating program.

BLIXEN, KAREN. *See* DINESEN, ISAK.

BLOUIN, ANDRÉE (1921–). Blouin was born in the Central African Republic, daughter of a French man and Banziri woman. She told her life story in *My Country, Africa: Autobiography of the Black Pasionaria* (1983), where she outlined her growing awareness of oppression as "a system of evil," drawn from her life "in an orphanage for girls [in Brazzaville, Congo], as a repudiated mistress [of a French man], and most of all, as the mother of a dying child." She later lived in Guinea, where she was impressed by the efforts of the anti-colonial leader and first president, Sekou Touré. In 1960 she was recruited to work with women in Leopoldville, Belgian Congo (now Kinshasa, Democratic Republic of the Congo), in the midst of the independence movement led by Patrice Lumumba, whom she served briefly as chief of protocol. After a few months work in the Kwilu, Kwango, and Kasai areas she had brought 45,000 women into the **Mouvement Féminin de la Solidarité Africaine**, which was affiliated with the Lumumba-aligned Parti Solidaire Africain. She was expelled from the Congo just prior to Lumumba's assassination, and spent many years working for social and economic justice in a number of African countries.

BODY MARKING. Many African societies used scarification of faces and bodies as an important social marker and beautifying procedure. It has been suggested that such scars were introduced to make people less desirable to slave traders, and it is also possible that in some areas certain marks indicated slave status. In other societies, tattoos could show an ethnic affiliation, be used to designate religious or medical experiences, or simply be a beauty mark. Body marking usually involved making small cuts that were then rubbed with special lotions, charcoal, or other material to darken and raise the skin and enhance the appearance of the scarring. While both men and women marked their bodies, there were specific gendered histories and designs that men and women utilized in different ways. Certain designs paralleled patterns found on pottery and in hair-braiding, and all drew inspiration from elements of the natural world such as leaves, animals, flowing water, and flowers. Other tattoos, applied to the abdomen, thighs, and genital region were intended to increase the erotic experience. European missionaries disapproved of such tattooing, and with increased urbanization permanent body marking such as tattoos have been less popular. As research in southern Mozambique has shown, women continued to desire scarification throughout the colonial period, although the marks were often relegated to hidden parts of their bodies to avoid missionary comment.

Other forms of body decoration included filing the front teeth to points among the Makonde, the use of large lip and ear plugs, and wearing metal bands on legs, arms, or necks, that resulted in stretching that part of the body. Women have also long been noted for elaborate hairstyles, including braiding and using mud or other compounds to hold hair in place. All of these procedures involved intimate interactions among community members.

BOER WAR. *See* SOUTH AFRICAN WAR.

BONGO, PASCALINE (1956–). Bongo served as minister of foreign affairs in Gabon from 1991 to 1994, when she moved to head the presidential office. She was the oldest daughter of President Omar Bongo. In response to charges of nepotism, President Bongo said she was the most qualified, as she had the necessary experience. She attended the Ecole nationale d'administration in Paris and pursued studies in business administration at the University of California, Los Angeles, later working briefly for Chase Manhattan Bank and the International Monetary Fund in the 1980s. She also serves on the boards of several oil companies with interests in Gabon. In 2003 one of her aides died mysteriously, and two local publications were suspended when they raised questions about her involvement.

BORI. *Bori* is a **spirit possession** cult practiced among Hausa people in northern Nigeria, similar to *zaar* practices in the Horn of Africa. It is most likely based on pre-**Islamic** practices, though it gained greater prominence during the 19th century following a period of social disruption and community dispersal. Although often associated with Islam, it is not a recognized Muslim custom, and has occasionally been a source of conflict between spirit mediums and Muslim clerics. Women are particularly associated with *bori* spirit possession, and at times their spirit possession has been an avenue to redress economic and social inequalities. *Bori* has also been a healing ritual, with the onset of possession indicating problems that can be resolved through following the directions of the spirits.

BOTSWANA COUNCIL OF WOMEN. Established in 1965 to promote good citizenship and self reliance, there were 250 members in 1978. The organization sponsored seminars, organized **childcare** centers, and encouraged self-help projects as a source of income for women.

BOYE, MAME MADIOR (1940–). Boye was prime minister of Senegal. She was trained as a lawyer, and had previously held positions in the Compagnie Bancaire de l'Afrique de l'Ouest (1990–2000), as assistant to the attorney general, and in other judicial appointments. She was the minister of justice in 2000, and was named prime minister in 2001. She resigned following a government ferry disaster in November 2002 that resulted in the deaths of over one thousand people. *See also* HEADS OF GOVERNMENT.

BRIDE SERVICE. In some areas, particularly **matrilineal** communities in Central Africa, a new husband or husband-to-be would join his wife's family and work on their fields for a period of time as part of the process of formalizing the new marital relationship. It is related to **bridewealth** as an obligation from a man to the family of his new wife.

BRIDEPRICE. A common term for **bridewealth**, "brideprice" is considered less accurate because of the implication that women are sold for a price. The renowned anthropologist E. E. Evans-Pritchard argued against the use of the term in *Man* in 1931, saying it misrepresented the actual transaction and, because it implied that women were a marketable commodity, "It is difficult to exaggerate the harm done to Africans by this ignorance." He discussed and rejected other terms (**dowry**, earnest, indemnity, and settlement), and suggested substituting bridewealth.

BRIDEWEALTH. This was a common form of marital exchange among people throughout Africa. Typically a man who planned to marry would begin giving gifts to the family of his intended wife. In the 19th century such gifts in southern Africa were often cattle, and later hoes. As the economy changed and men began working for wages, cash payments and other valuable items began to enter into the exchange. In West Africa cowrie shells, a form of local currency, were often involved. For example, among the Bamana people of Mali in the early 20th century, a standard payment was 30,000 cowries.

Although western observers sometimes interpreted such exchanges as signifying the sale of the woman by her family, Africans valued bridewealth for formalizing the relationship and for tying families together in an economic and social community. It was rare that there was a one-time payment, as the exchange often continued over a period of time with certain specified gifts given to mark the stages of the relationship such as courtship, moving into the same residence, and the birth of the first child. Families would sometimes use the bridewealth that came into the family through a daughter's marriage in order to send bridewealth to the bride of their son, thus circulating the wealth among a variety of families. In some societies it was a reciprocal arrangement, and the bride's family also contributed substantially to the marital expenses, and sometimes gave a

dowry as well to their daughter, the newly married woman. It was expected that the bridewealth would be returned if a marriage ended, and the need to repay that money when seeking a **divorce** was a motivation for many women to seek wage labor. *See also* BRIDE SERVICE; BRIDEPRICE.

BROOKS-RANDOLPH, ANGIE ELIZABETH (1928–). Brooks-Randolph is a prominent diplomat from Liberia. She was born in Virginia, Montserrado County, Liberia. She earned a B.A. from Shaw University in 1949, an LL.B. and an M.S. from the University of Wisconsin at Madison (1952), and attended London University (1952–1953). She returned to Liberia in 1953 and was selected to be assistant attorney general, the first woman in Liberia to hold a cabinet post. She also represented Liberia at the United Nations (UN) as a member of Liberia's permanent delegation beginning in 1954. During her time there Brooks-Randolph served as vice chair of the General Assembly's Fourth Committee (1956) and later as chair of that committee (1961). She was vice chair of the Committee on Information for Non-Self-Governing Territories during a crucial period of decolonization on the African continent (1961), and chair for Ruanda-Urundi (1962), among other positions. In 1958 she became assistant secretary of state of Liberia. In 1969 she was elected president of the UN General Assembly, the first African woman to hold that position. She was Liberia's permanent representative at the UN from 1975 until 1977 when she was recalled to serve on Liberia's Supreme Court. She was also noted for taking in nearly 50 foster children.

BUSINESS AND PROFESSIONAL WOMEN'S CLUB OF GABORONE. This organization was established in the capital of Botswana in 1972 to support women in professional positions; it is affiliated with the International Federation of Business and Professional Women.

– C –

CAFÉ, MARIA MAMBO. Café was an economist and leading politician in Angola, and was the first woman to be appointed to a cabinet position, as minister of social affairs in 1982. She was briefly recognized as one of three "super ministers" in 1986–1987, when she was minister of state for economic and social affairs. After an internal power struggle in 1987 she was appointed as secretary for youth affairs, and in 1990 Café narrowly retained her position on the Central Committee of the ruling party, the Movimento Popular para a Libertação de Angola (MPLA)/Popular Movement for the Liberation of Angola.

CAMARA, MBALIA (?–1955). Camara was active in the anti-colonial struggle in Guinea, and a member of the Parti Démocratique de Guinée/Democratic Party of Guinea. She was assassinated in 1955, making her a martyr for the cause of independence. The main market in Conakry was named after her, reflecting her representation of female militancy.

CAMEROON ASSOCIATION OF UNIVERSITY WOMEN. This organization of educated women has developed a project to bring schools to girls in Muslim northern Cameroon. With international funding from the Global Fund for Women they bring supplies in a "school in a box" to remote villages, allowing a mobile team of educators to provide **literacy** lessons in homes or community centers. *See also* EDUCATION.

CAMP, SOKARI DOUGLAS (1958–). Camp is a sculptor who was born in Nigeria and raised in England. She was educated in California before returning to the Royal College of Art, and she now lives and works in London. She is known for her large-scale metal works that integrate African imagery and draw attention to the situation of Britons of African descent.

CANDACE. Often considered a proper name, Candace is a title equivalent to queen (probably derived from the word Kentake) in the ancient Kushite kingdom of Meroë, which flourished for 1,250 years until 350 AD (CE) in the region now part of Ethiopia and Sudan. The title appears to have lasted for 500 years (from the 3rd century BC until the 2nd century AD/CE). There are four women most often cited as Candace: Amanerinas, Amanishakhete, Nawidemak, and Maleqereabar, each of them powerful rulers in a kingdom known for strong female leaders. One is considered to have converted to Christianity because her eunuch was baptized by St. Philip (Acts of the Apostles 8:28-39). Another, probably Amanerinas (and perhaps the same Candace as the convert), fought the Romans; after suffering a damaging attack on her capital at Napata by Petronius in 22 BC, she attacked the retreating Romans and succeeded in having a boundary established between Roman and Kushite lands.

CAROLUS, CHERYL (1959–). Carolus is a leading **feminist** activist in South Africa. She was trained as a teacher, and earned degrees in **law** and **education** from the University of the Western Cape. She became active in the United Democratic Front in the 1980s, and served time in jail. She eventually served on the African National Congress (ANC) national executive committee and in 1994 as the deputy general secretary of the ANC. She was acting secretary general of the ANC in 1997, and the following year was named as South African High Commissioner to London. She also held the position of general secretary of the **Federation of South African Women**, and was a member of the Communist Party, **Black Consciousness Movement**, and the South African Students' Organisation. She was a founding member of the **United Women's Organisation** (later United Women's Congress). She was also named to the board of the Institute for Democracy and Electoral Assistance, and in 2001 she was appointed as head of South African Tourism.

CASELY HAYFORD, ADELAIDE SMITH (1868–1960). Born in Sierra Leone of mixed Fanti and English heritage, she worked to unite the Creole and African communities and played a prominent role in developing girls' **education**. Raised in England and educated there and in Germany, she returned to Sierra Leone as an adult in 1897. She married a Ghanaian nationalist, Joseph Ephraim Casely Hayford, when she was 35, and they jointly worked to bring independence to West African British colonies until the marriage ended in 1914 and she returned to Sierra Leone. She was also active in the Universal Negro Improvement Association that was founded by Marcus Garvey. Casely Hayford advocated schooling for girls that included African culture as well as **literacy** and vocational training, making a speech on this topic in 1915 to the **Young Women's Christian Association** (YWCA) and finally opening the Girls' Vocational and Industrial Training School in Freetown in 1926. The school faced ongoing budgetary problems, and closed in 1940 when age combined with other obstacles made it impossible to continue. She was made a Member of the Order of the British Empire in 1949. Casely Hayford's daughter, Gladys (1904–1950), was also a writer, though she died young of blackwater fever. Adelaide's memoirs and her daughter's poems were published in 1983 as *Mother and Daughter: Memoirs and Poems* (edited by Lucilda Hunter), and Adelaide M. Cromwell wrote her biography, *An African Victorian Feminist: The Life and Times of Adelaide Smith Casely Hayford* (1986).

CENTRO DAS MULHERES DE CABO VERDE / WOMEN'S CENTER OF CAPE VERDE. A local organization for women's rights, it published *Jornal da Mulher.*

CHARWE (c. 1862–1898). Charwe was a medium for the Mhondoro spirit **Nehanda**, and while possessed by the Nehanda spirit she was a leader of the Ndebele and Shona resistance to British colonial activity in Zimbabwe (then Southern Rhodesia) in 1896 and 1897. Born to a noble Shona family in the Mazowe valley, she was known to have married and borne two daughters and one son. Charwe possibly was possessed in 1884, though the early examples of possession by Nehanda that were reported in the 1880s might have been other mediums than Charwe. The rebellion began in June 1896, and was a widespread anti-colonial activity that included killing a number of British settlers and colonial officials. Charwe was held responsible for the death of an oppressive British colonial official, H. H. Pollard. She was captured in 1897 and after continuing to resist and refusing to convert to Christianity, she was hanged in 1898. Recent research has indicated that she never claimed to be possessed by Nehanda when she was leading the rebellion, that at the time she was no more important than other local leaders, and that it was likely she had little or nothing to do with Pollard's death. Her reputation grew after she was hanged and she came to be considered a legendary resistance leader in Zimbabwe.

CHERUBIM AND SERAPHIM MOVEMENT. *See* EMMANUEL, CHRISTIANAH ABIODUN.

CHIBAMBO, ROSE ZIBA. Chibambo was active in politics in Malawi in the 1950s, when she was instrumental in organizing the **League of Malawi Women** (also known as the Women's League of the Nyasaland African Congress), which she led in 1959. She was elected to parliament in 1964 after Malawi gained independence, but was suspended from the Malawi Congress Party that same year as a result of a political crisis. She became a businesswoman in Mzuzu, and remained prominent in politics and church activities.

CHIEPE, GAOSITWE KEAGAKWA TIBE (1920–). Chiepe, a leading politician in Botswana, was born in Serowe, and educated at the University of Fort Hare in South Africa and in England at Bristol University. She was the first woman from Botswana to earn a university degree, and the first to gain a higher degree when she earned her M.A. in 1959. Chiepe served as an **education** officer from 1948 to 1970. Her first government post was as director of education in 1968. She was minister of commerce (1974–1977), minister of natural resources and water affairs (1977–1984), minister of external affairs (1984–1994) and minister of education (1994–1999). She retired from politics in 1999.

CHILDCARE. There has been some development of childcare programs in Africa, though most care is given by **mothers** with support from female relatives and neighbors. Some **mission** groups and other development workers began to introduce day nurseries; one report tells how a voluntary day nursery was opened in Cape Coast, Ghana, in 1955 with the assistance of the British colonial social welfare office. Mozambique introduced an ambitious childcare program in the 1970s and 1980s as part of a larger project to integrate women into the socialist development of the nation, though it was difficult to maintain the program in the face of financial difficulties.

CHIRWA, VERA CHIBAMBO (1933–). Chirwa was a founding member of the Malawi Congress Party and a national leader of the **League of Malawi Women.** Trained as a lawyer, she was imprisoned under Hastings Banda's government from 1982 to 1993, including four years in solitary confinement and three years in shackles. Her husband was imprisoned at the same time, and he died in prison in 1992. After her release she became active in **human rights** activities, and in 1999 she was elected to the African Human and People's Rights Commission. In 2004 she ran for president as an independent candidate, though she did not win. *See also* HEADS OF STATE.

CHITEPO, VICTORIA (1927–). A senior woman in Zimbabwean politics, she served as minister of natural resources and tourism (1982), and as minister of information, posts, and telecommunications. Chitepo was born in Natal, South Africa, educated in South Africa and in England, and taught in South Africa before moving to Zimbabwe (then Southern Rhodesia) when she married Herbert Chitepo, a leader in the Zimbabwean African National Union (ZANU). She was a social worker before becoming involved in politics, and was forced to live in exile in Tanzania from 1962 until independence in 1980. While in exile she worked with Zimbabwean **refugees**.

CHITUKULU CHA AMAI MU MALAWI. This Malawian group was a women's **organization** founded in 1984 by **Cecilia Kadzamira** under Hastings Banda. Its main goal was to support women's self-sufficiency, with **agricultural** and crafts projects. It was often confused with the older and more politically respected **League of Malawi Women**.

CHRISTIANITY. Most of the African continent only encountered Christianity with the arrival of Catholic and Protestant **missionaries** from the 16th century onward (*see* **Vita, Dona Beatriz Kimpa**), and particularly in the 19th century. Ethiopia was exceptional as there was an indigenous Christian presence from biblical times. Missionaries were more likely to be men and to be interested in recruiting male Africans in the early years, although women were present as wives and as single women from the beginning. Women missionaries, both nuns (such as the **White Sisters**) and lay women, often worked as teachers and **nurses** as part of their outreach efforts.

By the mid-19th century some African women were seeking refuge in mission stations, and women had become an important part of the

Christianizing project. Many peoples' experiences of Christianity in Africa were historically connected to oppressive aspects of **colonialism**, and there were and still are Africans who reject Christianity as a distinctly non-African expression of spirituality. Others adopted aspects of Christian beliefs and developed new forms of worship that integrated local practices into the Christian liturgy. Missionaries often focused on elements in African societies that they deemed particularly pagan and uncivilized, and these were frequently centered on **marriage** and family concerns that directly involved women, such as mission disapproval of **polygyny**, **bridewealth**, and **initiation rites**.

As African societies suffered the disruptions of colonialism, some Africans turned to Christianity as a source of salvation and relief from the difficulties they faced, gladly embracing monogamous marriage and denouncing bridewealth and initiation rites. Another reaction was to establish independent churches which were outside of missionary control though often based in some form of Christianity; several such churches were founded by women, including **Christianah Abiodun Emmanuel**, **Maame Harris "Grace" Tani**, **Alice Auma Lakwena**, **Alice Mulenga Lenshina**, **Mai Chaza**, and **Nontetha**. Another form of African Christianity can be seen in the Kenyan Legio Maria of African Church Mission that centers the Virgin Mary in its worship, and which recognizes the power of women and especially older women in its community. An important international organization of Christian African women is the **Circle of Concerned African Women Theologians**, and African women have also been involved in local branches of the **Girls' Brigade** and the **Young Women's Christian Association**.

CIRCLE OF CONCERNED AFRICAN WOMEN THEOLOGIANS. Sometimes referred to as the Circle of African Women Theologians, the Circle is a group of Christian African women who wished to develop African approaches to reading and understanding the Bible. The idea of such an **organization** was first put forward by a group of five African women in Geneva, Switzerland, and they began by developing a list of African women theologians from different church backgrounds. By 1980, 30 of those women met in Ibadan, Nigeria, and the number of members has continued to grow. Their 1996 meeting in Nairobi brought in over 120 delegates from a variety of careers and positions who shared a commitment to African religious life. In developing the organization's philosophy, members drew on **womanism**, African identity, and **Christianity** as well as encouraging international networks and aspects of liberation theology such as women's **literacy**. In 1998 it set forth four specific areas of work, including "African biblical and cultural hermeneutics." Its interest in explicating the connections between biblical stories and African folktales as sources of moral instruction resulted in a series of essays that were published in *Other Ways of Reading: African Women and the Bible*, ed., Musa W. Dube (2001). The interest in connections between religions resulted in an expansion of the membership to include women of all religious faiths. A history of the organization and its theology can be found in Carrie Pemberton, *Circle Thinking: African Women Theologians in Dialogue with the West* (2003), as well as in the many publications by Circle members, especially the writings of founding member **Mercy Oduyoye**. The organization's website includes access to its newsletter; see http://www.thecirclecawt.org/. *See also* BIBLEWOMEN; GIRLS' BRIGADE; *MANYANO*.

CIRCUMCISION. Though this term is quite commonly used to refer to cutting girls' genitals when they reach puberty, it is subject to widespread criticism because it implies a false commonality with male circumcision. Most scholars now reject the use of the term or enclose it in quotation marks if they do employ it. *See also* FEMALE GENITAL CUTTING.

CISSÉ, JEANNE MARTIN. *See* MARTIN-CISSÉ, JEANNE.

CISSIN-NATENGA WOMEN'S ASSOCIATION. This is an organization in Burkina Faso that offers **literacy** classes. Begun in 1984 by a group of Catholic women who saw a need to improve women's literacy, it also established income-generating projects including weaving and soap making and in 1992 opened its own center, built with the assistance of the Belgian General Federation of Labour and Socialist Solidarity, a **non-governmental organization**.

CITIZENSHIP. Citizenship has sometimes been a contentious legal issue in African countries, where leaders have become concerned with national identity and the enduring legacy of **colonialism**. In Botswana in 1982 a new citizenship act was introduced that restricted citizenship to those who could claim descent through their father's line, not simply those who were born in the country. Thus women who were married to foreigners were legally denied to the right to pass their own Botswana citizenship to their children, even when those children were born in Botswana. This provision reflected traditional patrilineal ideas about the father's family having a claim on children's allegiance, and was changed only after a legal case brought by **Unity Dow**, who won following a ruling from the High Court in the 1992 that led to a new law being passed by parliament in 1996.

CLITORIDECTOMY. See FEMALE GENITAL CUTTING.

CLOTHING. See DRESS.

COLLECTIF DES FEMMES DU MALI (COFEM) / COLLECTIVE OF WOMEN OF MALI. Founded in 1991, the Collectif is a leading women's organization in Mali. It is involved in a wide range of projects concerned with women's political and economic rights. It is particularly concerned with raising women's knowledge about their opportunities for advancement and with changing the legal conditions that restrict women. COFEM holds regular meetings and is involved in international networking. Its website is found at http://www.h-net.org/~batourer/cofem/.

COLONIALISM. The era of colonialism, when European powers had political authority over African societies, does not coincide neatly with a set of years. Europeans began arriving in Africa in the 15th century, most frequently settling in coastal enclaves while they pursued trade in goods such as ivory and gold, as well as in **slaves**. Although some areas came under European sway from those early years, it was not until the late 19th century that the European nations of England, France, Germany, Belgium, and Portugal met in a famous conference in Berlin in 1884 and 1885 and divided areas of influence among themselves. The years of most intense colonialism then followed, with increased warfare when the Europeans attempted and in most areas succeeded in enforcing their own political control over African communities.

Africans resisted these incursions from the beginning, and the first **nationalist** movements arose in the early 20th century, culminating in successful transfers to independent status for most African nations in the 1950s and early 1960s. The exceptions were white settler communities in Zimbabwe and South Africa, which did not allow majority rule until 1980 and 1994 respectively, and the Portuguese colonies of Angola, Mozambique, Guinea-Bissau, Cape Verde, and São Tomé e Príncipe, which only gained their independence in 1975. South Africa also kept a mandate over Namibia until 1980.

Studies of women's work during the colonial period often showed that they lost power and economic autonomy with the arrival of cash crops and women's exclusion from the global marketplace, in contrast to men who were more likely to benefit from these economic changes. Even further, men and international commerce benefited because they were able to rely to some extent on women's unremunerated labor. The dynamic varied from place to place. In Ghana when cocoa trees were introduced and it became clear that cultivating cocoa for export was a lucrative business, men bought land that they could devote to cocoa trees. In most cases they bought the land on credit, and frequently female kin were used as collateral, so if the man could not repay the loan the women were transferred to the creditor. Women and children made up the major share of the labor force on the cocoa plantations, though when the cocoa was sold the male land (and tree) owner kept the proceeds. Some women did own land themselves, but they were in a minority despite continuing to perform nearly all of the **agricultural** work that fed their families. In Senegal and the Gambia women had long cultivated rice, and when groundnuts (peanuts) were added to the agricultural calendar the result was a shift in land ownership patterns. Once again women continued to grow subsistence food crops while also contributing labor to the rice cultivation. New varieties of rice were grown to feed the foreign workers brought in to work in the groundnut fields, and men controlled the sale of the rice that brought in an income.

In other areas women typically continued their work growing food for their family's consumption while men entered the colonial economy and earned wages by working on tea and cotton plantations or, in central and southern Africa, by going to work under contract at the gold, diamond, and copper mines. In the mining areas some women did move to the newly developing urban communities with their husbands or on their own in search of new opportunities, though the majority remained in the rural areas. Colonial authorities mistrusted the women who were in urban areas and introduced a series of **pass laws** to control the movement of women on their own. Usually women were not restricted from migrating with male kin, and the colonialists believed women were then controlled by those men. There are instances where African men supported the colonial efforts to monitor women's movements, so that women were under the scrutiny of both local men and European authorities.

Analysis of the development of legal systems under colonialism has suggested that women were at a disadvantage as "customary" laws were established based on male testimony that gave men, especially elite men, advantages over women in issues of marriage and divorce. It was not uncommon for African societies to recognize that the variety of people's experiences had to be met by a variety of punishments, rules, and fines. For instance, adultery was generally not approved of, but the social reaction might vary among a series of potential disciplinary actions according to the age and rank of the people involved. Women were not necessarily excluded from participation in the discussion of how to make amends. But when the Europeans came they were interested in introducing legal codes that ascribed set punishments for each crime with little scope for flexibility. They wrote down penalties for misdeeds as they interpreted the information they received from older men who often were interested in increasing their own control over women in their society, especially in the face of the changes that appeared with colonialism.

Women's precolonial political activity was generally disregarded by the colonial authorities, who turned exclusively to men when they established local political offices. In many parts of West Africa women had societies that were run by and for women, where women had the final say in disputes over markets or agriculture, sectors where women were the primary actors. Some societies included elaborate systems of rank and naming, and women's groups were viewed as complementary to men's within the community. The colonial agents, nearly always men, ignored that reality.

COMING-OF-AGE RITES. *See* INITIATION RITES.

COMMISSARIAT À LA PROMOTION DES FEMMES / COMMISSION FOR THE ADVANCEMENT OF WOMEN. The commissariat, a "mini-ministry" in Mali responsible for women's affairs, was established in 1993.

COMMISSION POUR L'ABOLITION DES MUTILATIONS SEXUELLES (CAMS) / COMMISSION FOR THE ABOLITION OF SEXUAL MUTILATION. CAMS is an organization based in Paris and in Dakar, Senegal, that is working to end **female genital cutting.** It was founded in 1982 by **Awa Thiam**, and has been actively publishing materials and educating women about the program to end genital cutting. Its website, including a newsletter and other information about CAMS projects, is at http://www .cams-fgm.org/.

COMMISSION SOCIALE DES FEMMES (CSF) / SOCIAL COMMISSION FOR WOMEN. This was the official Malian women's **political organization** active during the government of Modibo Keita from 1960 to 1968. The ruling party of those years, the Union Soudanese-Rassemblement Démocratique Africain (US-RDA) insisted that all political activity occur under its jurisdiction and did not allow autonomous organizations to form. Thus the CSF, as an umbrella for women's organizations, provided the only legal group that espoused women's causes, especially focusing on the role of women within the household and family. Despite its formal control by the US-RDA, women within constituent groups produced skits, formed **rotating savings and credit associations**, and celebrated women-centered festivities. **Aoua Kéita** was named as general secretary of CSF when it was founded at a US-RDA party congress in 1962.

CONFERENCE OF AFRICAN WOMEN. *See* ALL AFRICA WOMEN'S CONFERENCE.

CONFERENCE OF WOMEN OF AFRICA AND OF AFRICAN DESCENT. This conference was organized in Accra, Ghana, in 1960 by **Hannah Cudjoe**. Along with other regional meetings such as the

Kenya Women's Seminar, they led to the eventual contintent-wide organization, the **All Africa Women's Conference**.

CONGREGATION OF THE DAUGHTERS OF THE SACRED HEART OF MARY. The oldest African order of nuns, it was founded in 1858 in Senegal. It continues to be active in the 21st century. *See also* BANNABIKIRA; MISSIONS.

CONSEIL NATIONAL DES ASSOCIATIONS DE FEMMES DE MADAGASCAR / NATIONAL COUNCIL OF WOMEN'S AS-SOCIATIONS OF MADAGASCAR. Founded in 1967, the council is an umbrella organization for women's groups in Madagascar. It promotes **education** and training.

CONVENTION ON THE ELIMINATION OF ALL FORMS OF DISCRIMINATION AGAINST WOMEN (CEDAW). CEDAW was adopted by the United Nations General Assembly in 1979, with important support by **Annie Jiagge**. Consisting of a preamble and 30 articles, it is considered an international bill of rights for women, as it outlines a specific program for individual nations to implement in order to end discrimination against women. The Convention defines discrimination against women as ". . . any distinction, exclusion or restriction made on the basis of sex which has the effect or purpose of impairing or nullifying the recognition, enjoyment or exercise by women, irrespective of their marital status, on a basis of equality of men and women, of human rights and fundamental freedoms in the political, economic, social, cultural, civil or any other field." Any state that adopts CEDAW commits itself to incorporate the principle of equality of men and women in their legal system, to abolish all discriminatory **laws** and adopt appropriate ones prohibiting discrimination against women. All African governments except Somalia and Sudan had passed the Convention, though further compliance has only been completed by a few. The pursuit of international progress to end discrimination against women was furthered during the **United Nations Decade for Women**. Within Africa, the measures of CEDAW were extended in 2003 when the African Union adopted the **Protocol on the Rights of Women in Africa**. *See also* HUMAN RIGHTS.

COOPERATIVES. Cooperatives are **organizations** that bring together producers who share some common work and goals. Women have found cooperatives a valuable method of coordinating their work and income, for example sharing the expense of milling rice, or working together in **agricultural** fields. Women's cooperative initiatives in Tanzania included projects such as collaborating to buy fish and transport it for resale in the market, and bringing together women who were growing pineapples so they could use their common income to establish a flour mill. In Mozambique the União Geral das Cooperativas (UGC)/General Union of Cooperatives unifies workers in the Green Zones around the periphery of Maputo; its membership is 90 percent female and it developed into an important political force during the 1980s and 1990s.

COORDINATION DES ASSOCIATIONS ET ONGS FÉMININES DU MALI (CAFO) / COORDINATION OF WOMEN'S ASSOCIATIONS AND NGOS IN MALI. Formed in 1993 as an association of **non-governmental organizations**, CAFO coordinates **development** projects focused on women. In 1994 it counted 50 member groups, and was headed by Ms. Traoré Affou Chiero, who was also Mali's attorney general.

CUDJOE, HANNAH (1918–1986). A Ghanaian political activist, she was a dressmaker who was influenced by the political leader Kwame Nkrumah. Born Asi Badu, she was part of a politically prominent family, including her brother E. K. Dadson, who introduced her to Nkrumah. She worked with the United Gold Coast Convention (UGCC) in developing **nationalist** propaganda. In 1948 Cudjoe organized a mass demonstration to protest the arrest of UGCC leaders by the British colonial authorities, using her dressmaking work as a cover for visiting households to spread information about the protest. The women spread clay over their bodies and wore white cloth, possibly the first time women dressed in a nationalist uniform. In the 1950s she was a founding member of the Convention People's Party (CPP), and was elected as the CPP national propaganda secretary. She was also involved in an anti-nudity campaign designed to encourage women in northern Ghana to wear clothing. Cudjoe was instrumental in founding the **Conference of Women of Africa and**

African Descent that met in Accra in 1960 and evolved into the **All African Women's Conference**, and she was general director of the **Ghana Women's League**. She fell out of favor when Nkrumah was ousted by a coup in 1966, and though she returned to public life in the mid-1980s she died soon after making a speech for International Women's Day in 1986.

CUMMINGS-JOHN, CONSTANCE AGATHA (1918–2000). Born to the Horton family, an elite Creole (Krio) family in Sierra Leone, she co-founded the Sierra Leone branch of the West African Youth League (WAYL) in 1938 and was a leader in the **nationalist** movement in West Africa. She was educated at elite private schools in Freetown, and at age 17 went to England where she trained as a teacher at the University of London affiliate Whitelands College. She was first involved in political organizations while in London, participating in the West African Students' Union and the League of Coloured Peoples, both groups whose members actively worked to end **colonialism**. Her experience of racism in the United States, where she attended a six-month course at Cornell University in 1936, focused her politics. After she returned to Sierra Leone in 1937 she worked with the radical nationalist I. T. A. Wallace-Johnson in 1938 to found the WAYL which claimed over 42,000 members within a year. Cummings-John was the first woman elected to office in a colonial governing body when she was elected to the Freetown Municipal Council that same year at the age of 20, and where she served until 1945. She lived in the United States from 1945 to 1951, where she was active in the American Council on African Affairs, and had the opportunity to meet Eleanor Roosevelt. Back in Sierra Leone, Cummings-John worked as a teacher at the African-controlled African Methodist Episcopal (AME) Girls' Vocational School (also called the AME Industrial and Literary School for Girls). She also worked closely with women leaders from the markets, and with them founded the **Sierra Leone Women's Movement** (SLWM) in 1951. Cummings-John was elected to the legislature in 1957, but did not take her seat as a result of internal factionalist conflicts. In 1966 she became the mayor of Freetown, the first woman to be a mayor of an African city, but she was forced to live in exile after a military coup in 1967. She was active in Labour Party politics in London until she returned to Sierra Leone in 1976 and worked for the SLWM until forced to return again to London to as political conditions worsened.

– D –

DACA (fl. 16TH CENTURY). Daca was a powerful ruler in the Lwo area of the East African interlacustrine region also known as Bunyoro-Kitara. It was common in Bunyoro to include women in the administration, especially as regional officers in the non-Bunyoro dependent states. Daca was named by her husband, the Mukama of Bunyoro, as a regional governor in the Madi government, and under her rule it became a substantial and successful state. She maneuvered her kin, marriage, and political associations so that the region developed economically. She also became wealthy as a result of the tributes she collected in her position as governor, and solidified the Lwo power throughout the northern Lakes region. People's memory of her was so compelling that two centuries after her death (ca. 1733–1760) a new Acholi chiefdom adopted her name, the Koch Pa-Daca (the People of Daca).

DAHOMEY SOLDIERS. In precolonial Dahomey (located in the present-day state of Benin), an elite group of **slave** women was trained as soldiers and bodyguards. Many of them had been married to the king and had personal loyalty to him. There were between 5,000 and 8,000 of these *ahosi* who were dependent on the king. They had been recruited from local and more distant communities, and included women who had been captured in raids or purchased in slave markets as well as elite women whom the king married as a way to extend political alliances throughout the region. It was possible for low status women to rise through the ranks of the *ahosi* to a powerful position within the royal household. The **queen mother**, known as the *kpojito*, was at the apex of the hierarchy that governed their activities. The woman soldiers fought in battles against the Nigerian Egba in the 1840s, but their forces were destroyed in the 1880s during the Franco-Dahomean Wars and ceased to exist in any formal way following the deposition of the king by the French in 1894.

DAMBA, FANTA (1923–1987). Damba was a very popular singer in Mali, known for her renditions of traditional songs which she learned from her mother. She was born in Ségou to a well-known **musical** family. Known as "La Grande Vedette Malienne" (The Big Malian Star) she was performing by the age of 16 and, with the help of Radio Mali, was recording in her early 20s. She was awarded the Malian national honor, the Silver Star of National Merit, in 1972. A younger singer who has the same name is known as "Fanta Damba Numéro Deux" (Fanta Damba Number Two, b. 1938). *See also* GRIOTTES; DIABATÉ, SIRA MORI; SANGARÉ, OUMOU; WASSOULOU.

DANCE. Dancing is a central part of African culture, and is a major component of many social, religious, and political rituals and activities including **marriages**, funerals, and baby-naming events. Often performed by a number of dancers in unison, female dance groups in many areas are accompanied by male drummers and singers. Throughout Africa formal associations of women dancers compete as teams and the style of dance has particular names such as *batuque*, *tufo*, and *lelemama*. At times women have faced criticism for the amount of time and money that they invest in their groups. The community of sister dancers can take a central role in women's lives, and research among Muslim women in northern Mozambique demonstrated that women experience greater coherence and longevity in their dance groups than they do in their marriages, as there is a high rate of **divorce** in their coastal societies.

Historically women dancers were censured by male authorities for dancing too suggestively, as experienced by **Wangu wa Makeri** in Kenya. That dances might have overtly sexual characteristics would be expected in certain rites, as with the *likili* fertility dance in west central Africa. An observer of women's dance in urban Senegal noted the role of class differences, as elite women favored more restrained movements while non-elite women may choose to perform more suggestive dances. Other behavioral differences exist between rural and urban women, and between unmarried and married women. **Bibi Titi Mohammed** notably recruited women from the dance societies in Dar es Salaam during her work supporting the **nationalist** movement in Tanzania. In recent times women have been called upon to perform at political rallies and other state occasions in many modern African nations.

DANGAREMGBA, TSITSI (1959–). A writer and filmmaker from Zimbabwe, Dangaremgba explores the situation of women in **colonial** and postcolonial society. She was born in Mutoko, but spent part of her childhood in England before returning to Zimbabwe (then Southern Rhodesia), and finally going back to England for her university years at Cambridge University, where she studied medicine. Back in Zimbabwe again in 1980 she studied psychology at the University of Zimbabwe and joined a theater group, Zambuko. She began writing during that period, and several of her plays were produced by Zambuko. She is best known for her partly autobiographical novel *Nervous Conditions* (1988) which considers the different lives of women in a family: Tambu, the daughter who goes to school; her mother who remains in a rural life focused on **agricultural** production; and Tambu's cousin, who becomes ill with what is recognizably anorexia (though it is never named in the novel). The themes of **education** and family and the intersection of those with race, class, and gender, make Dangarembga's well-written and involving novel popular with young women around the world. The book won the Commonwealth Writers Prize (Africa region). Dangarembga then studied film direction in Germany, and produced *Everyone's Child* (1996) about the experience of **HIV/AIDS** orphans in rural and urban Zimbabwe, making the moral point that everyone is responsible for raising the children who are left behind.

DANQUAH, MABEL DOVE. *See* DOVE DANQUAH, MABEL.

DAVIES, NIKE (c. 1952–). Nike is an internationally known batik artist who sells her striking garments in venues throughout the world. Born to a rural Yoruba family in Nigeria, she fled as a teenager in order to avoid an unwanted arranged **marriage**. As she became interested in **art**, she began working for a male artist and eventually married him as one of numerous co-wives. While she lived with him between 1970 and 1986 the compound had a repution for harmony, and while married Nike learned techniques of batik art which she further developed as an independent artist. Behind the compound walls, however, household relations were marked by maltreatment, and Nike and most of the wives **divorced** their common husband. Nike is best known for original indigo batik designs on cotton cloth, known as *adire*. She later established the Nike Center for Arts and Culture, which expanded to five centers throughout Nigeria where women and men can obtain training in the production and marketing of a range of artistic techniques. Kim Marie Vaz wrote her biography, *The Woman with the Artistic Brush: A Life History of Yoruba Batik Artist Nike Davies* (1995), and further information is available at http://www.nikeart.com/main.htm.

DE SOUSA, MARIA DAS NEVES CEITA BATISTA (1958–). De Sousa became prime minister of São Tomé e Príncipe in 2002. She attempted to resign in 2003 following a coup that ousted her government and was finally asked to leave in 2004 when she was implicated in a financial scandal. She had previously held a variety of ministerial posts, initially working as a civil servant in the Ministry of Finance and with the African Development Bank. She was minister of economics, agriculture, fisheries, commerce and tourism (1999–2001), minister of finance (2001–2002), and minister of industry, commerce, and tourism in 2002. *See also* HEADS OF GOVERNMENT.

DE SOUSA, NOÉMIA (CAROLINA ABRANCHES) (NÉE SOARES) (1926–2002). A Mozambican **poet**, she was born in the capital (then called Lourenço Marques), educated in Brazil, and lived in Portugal for many years. She was active as a **journalist** in the early years of the anti-colonial struggle from 1951 to 1964. De Sousa went into exile in France, where she wrote under the name Vera Micaia. The child of two mixed-race parents, her poems celebrated Mozambican culture and history. Among the most often cited are poems about migrant workers in South Africa's gold mines ("Magaiça"), a celebration of "my mother Africa" (Black Blood), and cries for liberation, as with these closing lines from "The Poem of João," "who can take the multitude and lock it in a cage?"

DE ST. JORRE, DANIELLE (1941–1997). De St. Jorre was a politician in the Seychelles, where she served as minister of foreign affairs, the environment, and tourism (later called the Ministry of Foreign Affairs, Planning and Environment) from 1989 until her untimely death in 1997. As minister of foreign affairs, she frequently represented the Seychelles at such international bodies as the World Bank.

Her **education** was in the Seychelles and England, culminating with a B.Phil in linguistics from the University of York, specializing in the Kreol spoken by most people in the Seychelles. De St. Jorre published three monographs on Kreol linguistics and organized Bann Zil, an international organization devoted to encouraging networking among Kreol speakers. She also lived on a kibbutz in Israel for a time as a student, an experience she described as having a major impact on her interest in politics. She is commemorated with a scholarship.

DEFIANCE CAMPAIGN. Women in South Africa were especially active in the 1950s as they protested the extension of restrictive **pass laws** to women. African men had carried detailed identity cards called passes for decades, and the passes were central to the **apartheid** system of racial oppression and control. After the election of 1948 brought in a government intent on expanding racial segregation, women faced new attempts to force them to carry passes as well, though the government initially called them "reference books" and claimed they were not actual passes. Those affected were primarily urban women who had moved into the cities looking for work as they lost access to rural land for cultivation. Women responded by organizing the **Federation of South African Women** (FSAW), and sponsoring demonstrations throughout the country. After a number of smaller protests, FSAW called for a massive demonstration in 1956 that brought 20,000 women to Pretoria where they handed in petitions opposing the new pass laws. Their struggle focused on three primary objections: that passes would restrict women from easily seeking work, women would be subject to sexual abuse by officials, and the inevitable arrest and detention of women for pass offenses (the most common cause of male arrests) would have a negative effect on their homes and families. Despite a massive response by women, they were obliged to carry passes. *See also* AFRICAN NATIONAL CONGRESS WOMEN'S LEAGUE; INDIAN WOMEN'S ASSOCIATION; JOSEPH, HELEN; MEER, FATIMA; SISULU, ALBERTINA.

DEMOCRATIZATION. In the 1990s the issue of democratization came to prominence in many African nations, often guided by western aid donors' demand for more western-style democracies particularly marked by contested multi-party elections. The advent of many new **political** parties as well as other political lobby groups appeared to offer an opportunity for women to become more involved in electoral politics. In reality most new parties were still male dominated. Women did move into many more positions of power and authority, however, as some nations introduced systems that reserved a percentage of legislative seats for women and more women were named to ministerial positions. For example, women in South Africa held 26 percent of the seats in parliament after the first post-**apartheid** election in 1994, and increased that to nearly 30 percent of the seats in the 1999 election.

DEMOGRAPHY. Although statistics are notoriously unreliable for much of Africa, there is information available that provides a general outline of population on the continent. For all of sub-Saharan Africa there are 102 women for every 100 men; no country counted fewer than 97 women, while the high was Cape Verde, with 112 women for every 100 men, a number which is affected by the high rate of male out-migration in search of work. Other information on population statistics can be found in **employment**, **female-headed households**, **fertility**, and **polygyny**.

DEVELOPMENT. Broadly speaking "development" refers to political, social, and economic efforts to improve the daily lives of people. Over the years there have been a number of debates about the best approaches to achieve that goal. Some of the initial projects emerged in the 1950s and 1960s in relation to the political independence of most African nations in those decades. The first programs tended to take a welfare approach, which tried to provide women with programs on **childcare** and housework, tied to the perception that women's primary social role was as **mothers**. Other practitioners introduced methods that took a different slant, whether through **human rights**, or by training women in crafts with the goal of generating income for themselves. In the 1980s and 1990s "gender" began to replace "women" in development discussions, recognizing that development involved both men and women, but differently. There was also some debate as to whether "women (or gender) *and* development" or "women (or gender) *in* development" better reflected the realities of development efforts. All of the varied approaches made some contributions despite various drawbacks, as women were able to see real improvements in certain areas of their lives.

DIABATE, HENRIETTE (VAR. DAGRI DIABATE, HENRIETTE ROSE) (1935–). A political leader in Côte d'Ivoire, she was minister of culture from 1990 to 1993. After schooling in Côte d'Ivoire and Senegal, she earned a doctorate in history at the Sorbonne in Paris, and was a founding member of the Association of African Historians. She taught at the University of Abidjan from 1968 until her retirement in 1995. She served on the editorial board of *Afrika Zamani*, 1974–1975. Diabate's first book was a study of the women's march on **Grand Bassam** prison in 1949 (*La marche des femmes sur Grand-Bassam*, 1975). In 2003 she was secretary general of the ruling political party, Rassemblement des Républicains, for which she also wrote the official anthem.

DIABATÉ, SIRA MORI (VAR. SIRAMORY JABATÉ) (c. 1933–1989). Sira Mori Diabaté was a popular *griotte* from a prominent family of musicians and praise singers in Mali. She was part of a generation that learned from the traditional *griots* but emerged into a modern urban life. She was best known for "Sara," a song about a woman torn between the arranged **marriage** her parents desired for her and her wish to marry the man she loved. Diabaté was described as "knowing all the Mande," because her songs appealed to many sectors of Mande society. *See also* DAMBA, FANTA; SANGARÉ, OUMOU; WASSOULOU.

DIARRA, FATOUMATA DEMBÉLÉ (1949–). Diarra is a judge from Mali. She was educated through high school in Mali, earned her law degree from the University of Dakar, Senegal, and pursued further legal education in France. She served in a variety of legal positions, including as legislative secretary in Mali's national assembly from 1986 to 1991. She was a founder of the **human rights organization** Observatoire des Droits de la Femmes et de l'Enfant (ODEF) in 1995, and a past president of the **Association des Juristes Maliennes**. In 2003 Diarra was elected to a nine-year term with the International Criminal Court at The Hague along with African women jurists Akua Kuenyehia and **Navanethem Pillay**.

She was awarded the Officier de l'ordre national du Mali/National Order of Mali in 2001.

DIÈNE, ARAME. A Senegalese activist in anti-colonial struggles, she was a member of the Bloc Démocratique Senegalaise and later the Parti Socialiste. In 1983 she was elected to the National Assembly along with two other women (Ramatoulaye Seck and Aida Mbaye) who were noted for their political insights despite not having formal **education**.

DINESEN, ISAK (KAREN BLIXEN) (1885–1962). Born in Denmark and educated in several European schools, she married her cousin Baron Bror Blixen-Finecke in 1914 and traveled to Kenya with him. They settled on a coffee plantation outside of Nairobi, famously remembered in her memoir, *Out of Africa* (1937), with the evocative first line, "I had a farm in Africa, at the foot of the Ngong Hills." Her sanitized version of colonial life in Kenya became a dominant view of that era, even more so after the film *Out of Africa* won the Academy Award for best film of 1985. She left Kenya in 1931 after the failure of her marriage and of the plantation, and lived the rest of her life as a writer in Denmark.

DIOGO, LUISA (1958–). Luisa Diogo was named prime minister of Mozambique in 2004. She was born in the western province of Tete and educated in Mozambique through her undergraduate degree at Universidade Eduardo Mondlane in 1983 before earning her master's degree in finance economics from the University of London in 1992. She began working in the Mozambican finance ministry in 1980, became a department head in 1986, and was national budget director from 1989 to 1992. She worked briefly for the World Bank in Mozambique (1993–1994), but returned to government as deputy finance minister after elections in 1994. She was named minister of finance in 1999, and will continue to hold that position while serving as prime minister. She is married and has three children.

DIOP, AMINATA (1978–). Diop is a woman from Mali who refused to undergo a **female genital cutting** ceremony prior to her **marriage** in 1989. After her family had to refund the **bridewealth**, resulting in her father's throwing her mother out of the home for failing to control their daughter, she feared for her life and fled to France. In a case that set international legal precedent, she was apparently the first woman to seek asylum as a refugee from patriarchy. She was initially refused asylum in 1992 because she was being persecuted by her family rather than by a government, but was allowed to remain in France on humanitarian grounds. The French government feared that granting asylum to Diop would open the way for untold numbers of women seeking refuge in Europe and America. Her case spotlighted the importance of including gender in discussions of **human rights**.

DIOP, SOKHNA MAGAT (c. 1917–2003). Sokhna Magat Diop headed a Muslim religious community in Senegal. Daughter of the well-known **Islamic** leader Serigne Abdalaye Yakhine Diop, she was named by him to head a section of his Mouride community in 1943. He had no male heirs, but he also recognized her abilities and religious devotion. Her history is told by Christian Coulon and Odile Reveyrand in *L'Islam au féminin: Sokhna Magat Diop, Chiekh de la confrérie mouride* (1990). *See also* MAM DIARRA BOUSSO.

DIRECTORATE OF WOMEN'S AFFAIRS, UGANDA. An official part of the National Resistance Movement (NRM), the ruling party, the office actively works to improve women's access to government.

DIRIE, WARIS (c. 1963–). Dirie is a Somali who gained fame as an international fashion model, and then came forward with her childhood experience of **female genital cutting**. She lived the first decade of her life as a nomad in the Somali desert, but ran away to relatives in Mogadishu to escape a **marriage** her father had arranged with an elderly man. She then traveled to London and worked in the home of another relative who was the Somali ambassador to the United Kingdom. Dirie's beauty was recognized on the streets of London by a fashion photographer, and she found success modeling. Her story was made into a BBC documentary, *A Nomad in New York* (1995). She first told the story of her **infibulation** to the magazine *Marie Claire*, which led to a television interview with Barbara Walters in 1997. As a result of that high profile, she was appointed as a special ambassador with the United Nations Population Fund and the World

Health Organization to work to end the practice of female genital cutting. She has written about her experiences in *Desert Flower: The Extraordinary Story of a Desert Nomad* (with Cathleen Miller, 1998).

DISABILITIES. During the 1990s new **organizations** with specific political agendas regarding disabled people were established, and other associations began to direct more attention to the particular problems that disabled women encountered. Thus groups such as the Tanzania Association of the Disabled initiated its Women's Department in 1992, with the goal of improving the situation of women with disabilities. Other African countries with associations providing support to disabled women include Botswana, Mauritania, South Africa, Uganda, and Zimbabwe. Though the projects are often small in scale, they provide a way for women to support themselves. Other programs directed at African women with disabilities include the regional Improved Livelihood for Disabled Women, based in Harare, Zimbabwe, which operates under the auspices of the International Labour Organization. Some groups focus on a specific disability such as blindness or deafness, while others are concerned with those who have been disabled during war or by injury from landmines.

DIVORCE. The **laws** concerning divorce vary widely throughout Africa, both in the specific aspects that they address and the extent of their implementation. As with **marriage** laws, women may be subject to western legal codes, a variety of religious practices, and the continuing influence of customary law. While women traditionally had the right to divorce, especially when their husbands were abusive or absent, they often had to repay the **bridewealth** in order to formally end the marriage; this expense was the motive for many women in southern Africa to seek waged work. While modern legal codes may speak about equality of access to divorce, women often face more obstacles, and may fear losing maintenance or the right to land to cultivate if they go forward with a divorce when their husband does not want one. In nations with a strong **Islamic** or Catholic influence, divorce rights may be limited for everyone. In Sudan, men have a right to a unilateral divorce without any court appearance, while women must prove in a legal proceeding that their husband has abandoned them or show other cause for divorce. Frequently women find that once they have married and divorced they have much greater freedom in choosing a second husband.

DJOUMBE FATIMA (1837–1878). Djoumbe Fatima was queen of Mwali in the Comoros Islands between 1842 and 1878. Both her father and mother were members of the Merina royal family that was based in Madagascar. She ascended to the throne at age five when her father, Ramanataka, died, though her mother and stepfather (who had been a close advisor to her father) ruled as regents for some years. Djoumbe Fatima ruled at a time of contesting powers, as the French tried to gain influence while the Comoron rulers continued to favor the Zanzibari Arabs, and her position on the throne reflected that turbulence. The French provided a governess for her when her mother **divorced**, and they arranged for her coronation in 1849 when she was only 12. In 1851 Djoumbe Fatima expelled the governess and married Saïd Mohammed Nasser M'Kadar, a cousin of the sultan of Zanzibar, who ruled with her as prince consort until the French ousted him in 1860. Djoumbe Fatima remained in power, marrying two sultans in succession, and making commercial agreements with a French trader in 1865 which she rescinded two years later. She renewed her ties with Zanzibar, abdicated in favor of her son, and later was restored to the throne when the French returned in 1871. Subsequently she ruled without further interruption until her death.

DOMESTIC SERVICE. Domestic service includes working as cleaners, cooks, and doing home-based **childcare**. Although domestic service was considered primarily women's work in much of the world, in Africa far more men than women found employment in that sector. South Africa was the exception, though even there paid household work was more often done by men until the early 20th century and there were significant differences between provinces. In general across the continent, and especially in eastern and southern Africa, women were not expected to leave their **agricultural** responsibilities to work for wages, so waged work more often went to men. It has been difficult to bring improvements to working conditions for domestic servants as they are employed as individuals within isolated households, making them particularly subject to maltreatment and poverty-level wages. In some countries domestic workers have begun to organize into **trade unions** to improve their situation, notably in the **South African Domestic Workers Association** and the **Namibia Domestic and Allied Workers' Union.**

DOMESTIC VIOLENCE. Long recognized as a problem, in the 1990s women and women's **organizations** began to publicly address the issue, despite continuing opinion from men and some women that it was a man's right to beat his wife. One such group was the Coalition on Violence Against Women in Nairobi, which was founded in 1995. Groups of women lawyers and **human rights** organizations were involved in many countries with providing **education** to communities, training for police and judicial professionals, and working to introduce **laws** that treat domestic violence as a crime. Observers have noted that with the spread of **HIV/AIDS** women are at risk of being beaten if they try to protect themselves by refusing to have sex with their infected husbands. Kenya's attorney general introduced a law in 2000 (though it apparently was not passed by the legislature) that would send wife-beaters to jail for a year and impose a fine of $1,300. The **Protocol on the Rights of Women in Africa** included freedom from domestic violence, which may encourage more African governments to deal with the problem as a serious crime and not simply a personal or private matter. *See also* KAZIBWE, SPECIOZA WANDIRA; RAPE; SEXUAL HARASSMENT.

DOMITIEN, ELISABETH (1926–1997). Domitien was the first woman to head a modern African government, in the Central African Republic (CAR), though under less than auspicious circumstances. After becoming involved in local politics, in 1972 she moved into the vice presidency of the Mouvement pour l'évolution sociale de l'Afrique noire (MESAN)/Movement for the Social Evolution of Black Africa, the only legal political party. She was vice president of CAR when dictator Jean-Bedel Bokassa, who had been raised in her father's house and was a close family friend, named her to the newly created position of premier in January 1975. She was instrumental in organizing women in his support. Domitien was fired in April 1976 when she criticized Bokassa's plans to make himself monarch of the Central African Empire. She remained active in politics, however, and was jailed in 1980 when Bokassa was overthrown. She was a successful businesswoman until her death in 1997. *See also* HEADS OF GOVERNMENT.

DONGO, MARGARET (1959–). Dongo is a popular Zimbabwean politician. She was a prominent ex-combatant of the liberation war of the 1970s, and closely affiliated with Robert Mugabe's presidency and the Zimbabwe African National Union (ZANU). She joined the liberation movement as a teenager, working as a medical assistant. After independence in 1980 she took business and computer courses, worked for ZANU in its publishing office, and as an operative in the national security agency. She was elected to parliament in 1990 and appointed to the ZANU Central Committee. When she publicly criticized the treatment of ex-combatants in 1994, she was ousted from ZANU. She ran for parliament as an independent in 1995 from her district in Harare south, but lost the primary election following political manipulation and harassment of her supporters. Faced with evidence of election irregularities, the High Court called for a new election, which she won. In parliament she was known for speaking out against corruption and in favor of women's rights. Initially part of the Movement of Independent Candidates, she helped establish an opposition party, the Zimbabwe Union of Democrats (ZUD). Following the defeat of all ZUD members in the election of 2000, she accepted a fellowship to study at Harvard University's John F. Kennedy School of Government.

DOVE DANQUAH, MABEL (1905/1910–1984). Mabel Dove Danquah was a journalist and politician from Ghana, which was then called the Gold Coast. Her family came from Sierra Leone, and she attended primary and secondary school in Freetown and was active in a girls' cricket club and in theater. She went to England for further **education**, but earned her father's anger when she secretly took a secretarial course, as he was educating her for status, not as preparation for a career. He sent her home to Freetown, Sierra Leone, and when she was 21 she moved to Accra, Ghana, where she found work as a typist with the well-known trading firm, Elder Dempster. Dove Danquah wrote letters about current events to the newspaper, and in the early 1930s she was asked to write a regular column for women for the *Times of West Africa*, which she did under the by-line "Marjorie Mensah." She wrote short stories as well, publishing her first, "The Happenings of a Night," in serial form in her column in 1931. She was married in 1933 to the prominent scholar and diplomat Joseph Boakye Danquah, though the marriage ended in **divorce** in the 1940s. Dove Danquah supported Kwame Nkrumah's Convention People's Party by writing articles in the party publication, the *Accra Evening News*. In 1951 she was appointed as editor of the newspaper, the first African woman to hold such a position, though she was dismissed after five months when she disagreed with Nkrumah over editorial methods. Dove Danquah was the first woman elected to the Ghanaian parliament in 1954, before independence, and possibly the first woman elected to an African legislature on the continent.

DOW, UNITY (1959–). An activist from Botswana, she gained international attention when she sued her government for sex discrimination in a case related to unequal **citizenship** rights for men and women. In 1992 the Botswana High Court ruled in favor of Dow's claim that the citizenship **law** was in conflict with women's rights as guaranteed under the constitution. Born in rural Botswana, her parents encouraged education for all of their children. She eventually earned law degrees at the University of Botswana and Swaziland (then a single entity) and at Edinburgh. She worked in the Botswana attorney general's office before opening a private law office with a woman partner. Dow was a co-founder of **Women and Law in Southern Africa**, and also founded the Metlhaetsile Women's Center in Botswana in 1990. She was appointed a judge on the High Court in 1998, the first woman to hold that position in Botswana. In 2000 she published her first book of fiction, *Far and Beyon'*, followed by *The Screaming of the Innocent* (2002) and *Juggling Truths* (2003); in all her novels she addresses social issues concerning women in Botswana.

DOWRY. A form of distributing wealth in which a family gives a gift to a daughter upon her **marriage**. In areas where daughters do not usually **inherit** from their fathers, a dowry can be one way for parents to ensure that some of their wealth is held by the next generation of women as well as men. *See also* BRIDEWEALTH.

DRESS. Women's choice of how to dress often has political implications. In many areas women had worn simple cloths wrapped around their bodies, usually woven from local cotton thread. Such cloth was made by women in some societies, such as the indigo-dyed *adire* cloth of West Africa. Additional adornments such as brass wire bracelets and anklets often indicated noble or royal status. In precolonial Rwanda women of high position wore raffia bracelets called *ubutega* from the knee to the ankle, with hundreds of woven circlets embellishing one woman; the raffia bracelets were also a valuable trade item. When colonialism began to have an impact women sometimes shifted to imported cloth and wore *kangas* or similar wrapped cloths. But there was an emphasis, especially among missionaries, to encourage African women to wear western dresses. Much of the effort to teach sewing skills to girls in **mission** schools was related to this effort, as they sewed their own new dresses. It was assumed that women who converted to **Christianity** would dress in the appropriate modest clothing.

The role of dress in marking women's behavior was again emphasized in the period following independence, as urban women were chastised in a number of countries for wearing mini-skirts. In Tanzania for instance, the ruling party instituted a "Vijana" program, in which young men affiliated with the ruling party maintained a street vigilance that allowed them to confront women who were dressed in what the men regarded as an inappropriate style. Women who were wearing short skirts or tight slacks were labeled as prostitutes. **Laws** outlawing mini-skirts, wigs, skin lighteners, and other fashion accoutrements deemed non-African by the male lawmakers were introduced in Kenya and Malawi among other countries. Men were readily adopting western slacks and shirts, or other non-African clothing such as Nehru jackets or military uniforms, without facing legal censure, making it clear that the issue was not "western" versus "African," but cultural ideas about women's **sexuality**.

Women did find work in garment factories, though more commonly men were viewed as tailors despite women being trained as seamstresses in the mission schools. The issues of women's dress, cultural beliefs, sexuality, and **employment**, are intimately connected and little analyzed. *See also* TEXTILES.

DUAL-SEX SYSTEM. The term "dual sex" has most often been applied to Igbo systems of **political organization** that granted equal and complementary roles to men and women. Women usually had control over certain aspects of their community, including marketing and the cultivation of particular crops, and had authority over male behavior that infringed on women's domains. Both men and women had access to prestigious titles and positions within their respective societies, and men were not assumed to be above women in a hierarchical arrangement of power and authority. Under the flexibility of such systems, women held positions in royal councils, were associated with the establishment of towns and villages, at times were rulers and acted to defend their polities, held diplomatic positions, and were closely involved in the making and unmaking of male kings. Notably they exercised authority in women's courts, as market authorities, and in female-specific secret societies and age-grade associations.

Historically in Nigeria the female Omu ruled in parallel to the male Obi ruler. For instance, in 1884 Omu Nwagboka of Onitsha was a signatory to a treaty with the British, and two years later she led the women in a boycott that compelled the Obi to seek peace negotiations. Her actions made it clear to the Obi that he needed the support of the women in order to rule effectively. Women in dual-sex systems also had a judicial role, as they mediated in cases involving women or women's domains in society. Spiritually the dual-sex societies recognized a parallel set of male and female deities, including Ala, an Earth Goddess, who had a direct connection to people's daily lives and well-being. Many lesser **goddesses** were honored in shrines and ceremonies.

DUARTE, DULCE ALMADA. Duarte, an early **nationalist** leader in Guinea-Bissau and Cape Verde, had trained as a sociologist before joining Partido Africano de Independência de Guinea-Bissau e Cabo Verde (PAIGC)/African Party for the Independence of Guinea-Bissau and Cape Verde. She addressed the United Nations Committee on Decolonization in 1962, presenting the case against continued Portuguese control of her country. In the 1970s she worked with linguistic scholars and helped formulate a standard orthography for the Creole spoken in the islands.

DUNCAN, SHEENA (1932–). Duncan was a leader of the South African women's organization **Black Sash**. She was born in the Transvaal, and after marriage in 1955, lived in Southern Rhodesia (now Zimbabwe) until 1963. She joined Black Sash, which her mother had helped to found, when she returned to South Africa, and held several offices within that organization, including the position of president from 1975 to1978, and again from 1982 to 1986.

DURBAN INDIAN WOMEN'S ASSOCIATION. Originally called the **Indian Women's Association**, it took this name in the 1920s when it was under the leadership of Kunwarani Lady Maharaj Singh, the wife of India's agent-general. The group was later renamed the **Durban Women's Association**.

DURBAN WOMEN'S ASSOCIATION. One of the women's groups that helped plan the massive anti-pass demonstration known as the **Defiance Campaign** held in South Africa in 1956, it was originally founded in 1908 as the **Indian Women's Association** (later the **Durban Indian Women's Association**).

DZIVAGURU. A **goddess** recognized by the Korekore people in what is today Zimbabwe. She was said to be the original great deity, the Earth Goddess who was the oldest of the Korekore deities. She had been a goddess of great wealth and magical power, but was driven away by Nosenga, the son of the sky god Chikara.

– E –

EAST AFRICAN WOMEN'S LEAGUE (SOMETIMES EAST AFRICAN WOMEN'S ASSOCIATION). Based in Kenya, this organization was founded in 1917 by Isabel McGregor Ross who was interested in gaining **suffrage** for women, which was granted to white women in 1919. The League continued its work in **development** projects and fund-raising activities to benefit women and children.

ECHO. Published in Dakar, Senegal, by the **Association of African Women for Research and Development (AAWORD)**, the first issue appeared in 1986. The articles have addressed a wide range of issues concerning women, including the media, **feminism**, religious fundamentalism, **health**, international solidarity among women, and regular overviews of women's situation in various African countries.

EDUCATION. Western style classroom education for girls in Africa was introduced by **missionaries** in the 19th century. They generally wished to train girls to be suitable wives for male converts to **Christianity**, and so they emphasized enough **literacy** to read religious materials, and taught domestic skills including sewing. In many areas the **missions** included boarding schools for girls, in order to facilitate their access to regular classroom attendance. Some of the better known schools included the **Inanda Seminary** in South Africa, founded in 1869, the Gayaza Girls' Boarding School in Uganda, and the Mbereshi Girls' Boarding School in Zambia (then Northern Rhodesia). One issue was the much smaller presence of girls than boys in the mission schools. In many African societies, girls had more daily responsibilities for **agriculture** and they tended to be married while still young, both cutting into the time available for an education that African families believed was useless with regard to the main tasks African women faced. The lack of access at lower levels resulted in low rates of participation in **higher education** as well.

Girls had access to Koranic schools in some Muslim areas, and in the 19th century **Nana Asma'u** was instrumental in developing schooling that could be brought to girls in seclusion. She herself was a highly educated woman who wrote on a number of intellectual topics.

Immediately after independence most new governments made improving access to school a high priority, and rates of attendance rose so that by 1970 the continent-wide statistics indicated that 39 percent of primary students were girls; that percentage continued to rise to 45 percent in 1990. The numbers of girls in higher levels of education also rose, but remained a fraction of boys'. Secondary school rates for girls rose from 29 percent of all students in 1970 to 40 percent in 1990; tertiary enrolment rose from 16 percent female in 1970 to 31 percent in 1990. Expanding and improving girls' educational opportunities remains a key issue for Africa.

EMANG BASADI WOMEN'S ASSOCIATION. Emang Basadi, meaning "Stand Up Women" in Setswana, was founded in Botswana in 1986 initially in response to a **citizenship** law that discriminated against women. The name was probably chosen as a comment on the national anthem which exhorted men to "rise up," and women to "rise up" and "stand behind your men." The women who formed the **organization** were concerned with promoting the "legal, social, cultural and economic status of women in Botswana." It has focused in particular on women and **politics**, doing educational and organizational work to improve the situation of women in governance. Emang Basadi has trained female candidates, held workshops for voters, and worked with the women's sections of political parties. Members have actively networked with other women's organizations both inside Botswana and internationally. It has also published a series of informational pamphlets, including a report on their ongoing Political Education Project. Until 1993 Emang Basadi was run by volunteers; after that date it was able to set up an office and recruit staff to perform the work of the organization. Its website is www.hrdc.unam.na/bw_emangbasadi.htm. *See also* DOW, UNITY.

EMECHETA, BUCHI (1944–). Emecheta is an internationally known novelist who was born near Lagos, Nigeria. She followed her husband to London in 1962, and although they later **divorced** she remained in England where she began her writing career while simultaneously raising five children and studying sociology at the University of London. Emecheta's first novel, *In the Ditch* (1972), described her experiences as an immigrant; her best-known books address issues concerning women's burdens in African society, and are based on her own experiences in Igbo culture and in England; they include *The Joys of Motherhood* (1979), *Double Yoke* (1981), and her autobiography *Head Above Water* (1986, reissued 1994).

EMMA SANDILE (1842–1892). The daughter of Xhosa chief Sandile in Cape Province, South Africa, she was sometimes called Princess Emma. She was one of the first African girls to be **educated** in the western system, and she attended Zonnebloem College (originally the Kafir College, founded in 1858 by **missionaries**) in Cape Town for six years. In 1859, while attending the college, she was granted a farm near Middledrift by Sir George Grey, the British colonial administrator, and was therefore an early example of a woman owning **land**. Letters written by her from 1860 onward may be the earliest known writing in English by a South African black woman. She wrote to Bishop Gray and to her teachers at Zonnebloem about plans for her **marriage** to a Thembu chief, though in the end they did not marry. In 1869 (at the comparatively advanced age of 27) she married Stokwe Ndelea, a local chief of the Mqwati, and lived as the wife of a rural leader until her death. She wrote further letters concerning the ownership of land she acquired during that marriage. That land was the subject of additional legal disputes in the 1980s.

EMMANUEL, CHRISTIANAH ABIODUN (1907–?). Emmanuel was a founder and leader of a **Christian** sect known as the Cherubim and Seraphim Society, which was based in Ghana. It was considered a part of the Aladura movement, from the Yoruba word for "owners of prayer," which referred to several West African sects which grew into churches in their own right. In 1925 Emmanuel reported seeing visions, and claimed that angels had taken her up to heaven. She fell into a coma which lasted for seven days until Moses Orimolade Tunolase arrived; he already had a reputation as a healer and was known as the "Praying Man." She awoke from her coma when he prayed for her, and she described her vision of a heavenly city. Soon people were traveling great distances to visit her and hear about her visions. She and Orimolade began holding regular prayer sessions, and by September 1925 they formed an interdenominational prayer society called the Seraphim Society (Egbe Serafu). During the late 1920s the organization spread throughout southern Ghana and Nigeria, encouraging prayer and fasting, condemning **witchcraft**, and calling on people to end their worship of traditional gods. After a disagreement between Emmanuel and Orimolade in 1929, they formed separate organizations; Emmanuel was leader of the Cherubim and Seraphim Society while Orimolade called his group the Eternal Sacred Order of the Cherubim and Seraphim. Further splits continued into the 1930s. Following Orimolade's death in 1933 Emmanuel tried to assert her leadership but was not successful. Another woman, Christianah Olatunrinle (known as Mama Ondo) emerged as the leader in 1935, and served until her death in 1941. *See also* TANI, MAAME HARRIS 'GRACE.'

EMPLOYMENT. Most African women work in **agriculture**, with an average rate of 75 percent of working women in that sector (compared to 61 percent of men), primarily cultivating food for their own families' use. Beginning in the colonial era, women's lack of **education** relative to men was a major obstacle to their job opportunities. In Nigeria, for example, where there was a highly developed colonial governmental service that employed 65,400 people in 1938, only 270 of those positions were held by women.

The skewed nature of women's limited access to salaried jobs continued into the post-independence era. Across the continent, only 5 percent of working women are found in industry (15 percent of men) and 20 percent in services (23 percent of men). Many women earned an income through **informal sector** activities, especially selling goods in **markets**, work that typically was not counted in formal statistics. It was also common for people with a waged job to perform informal sector work in addition to their formal position, as a supplement to chronically low wages.

The *Women's Indicators and Statistics Database* of the United Nations presents the following breakdown of African women's share within the following professional job categories in 1990 (the latest available statistics): Liberal and technical professions, 36 percent; management and administrative personnel, 15 percent; office clerks and related functions, 37 percent; sales people, 52 percent; and production, transportation, unskilled workers, and operators, 20 percent.

ENVIRONMENT. Research on women and gender as related to environmental issues in Africa developed and increased in the 1980s and 1990s. Some of the issues include the important role women play in **agriculture**, the environmental impact of women's search for clean water and sufficient fuel for cooking fires, and the growth of green belt organizations that emphasize regional ecology. The best known is the Kenyan **Green Belt Movement** founded by **Wangari Maathai**, but many countries have women's organizations that focus on environmental issues, including the Zamiba Alliance of Women (founded in 1978). Acknowledgment of the gender aspects of land use, forestry and agroforestry, animal husbandry, population pressures, and other **development** issues have also brought new perspectives to understanding the environment, as has respect for the extent of rural women's environmental knowledge.

ERITREAN WOMEN'S ASSOCIATION. This group was the mass organization of women that was affiliated with the Eritrean People's Liberation Front. It was later renamed the **National Union of Eritrean Women**.

ESAN, WURAOLA ADEPEJU (NÉE OJO) (1909–1985). Esan was a Nigerian **educator** and **politician** from Ibadan. Her parents were locally prominent, and though they were not formally educated, they encouraged their children to succeed in school. Esan earned her Standard 7 certificate in 1927 from the Idi Aba Baptist Girls' School in Abeokuta, and was admitted to the United Missionary College, the first women's training college in Nigeria. She married Victor Owolabi Esan in 1934. After living in Lagos for a few years they returned to Ibadan where she established the Ibadan People's Girls' School. In 1964 she was the first female senator in Nigeria following independence.

ETHIOPIANS' WOMEN'S WELFARE ASSOCIATION. This association organized **development** programs including adult **literacy**, **childcare**, and the Studies of Women Committee, and published *Azeb*. It was sometimes called the Ethiopian Women's Welfare Work Association.

EVE: THE ESSENCE OF AFRICA'S NEW WOMAN. Eve is a new magazine from Nairobi that focuses on popular culture, relationships, and fashion. The first issue appeared in December 2001–January 2002.

EVORA, CESARIA (1941–). Evora is an evocative singer from Cape Verde who is internationally renowned for her renditions of *morna*, a nostalgic style of ballad. After decades spent singing in local bars and cafés and taking time off in the 1970s to raise her family, she returned to the stage in 1985 when the **Organização das Mulheres de Cabo**

Verde / Organization of Women of Cape Verde selected her to go to Lisbon to record songs for a compilation album. While in Lisbon she met Bana, an established Cape Verdean musician, and he helped her record her first album, *Tchitchi Roti*. From there she went to Paris where she won acclaim and launched a series of recordings and world tours. Her 10th album, *Voz d'Amor* (*The Voice of Love*), was released in 2003. Known for singing while barefoot, she earned the sobriquet the Barefoot Diva. Her songs, sung in Portuguese and the local Creole, often reflect on homesickness and loneliness while being firmly focused on Cape Verde.

EXCISION. *See* FEMALE GENITAL CUTTING.

– F –

FAMILY LAW. A number of African countries have introduced family **laws** as a way of reconciling a diverse set of practices from colonial legal codes, customary law, and various religious preferences regarding **marriage**, **divorce**, **inheritance**, and similar legal concerns that are related to the ways in which families are formed and dissolved. The laws diverge in the ways in which they incorporate women's issues; for instance the family law introduced in Côte d'Ivoire in 1964 acknowledged the husband as "head of the family." In Mozambique the provisions of a family law were debated for decades before finally becoming law in 2004; it benefited from the long debate that included input from **feminist** scholars at the university, and the final provisions named all adults as potential "heads of household," suggesting that a family can be organized in a non-hierarchical way.

FASHION. *See* DRESS.

FASSIE, BRENDA (1964–2004). Brenda Fassie was a popular South African singer who was equally known for her lively *kwaito*-style songs and her scandal-ridden life. Born in Cape Town, she began performing as a small child, and gained fame as a teenager with "Weekend Special." Her albums sold more than any other South African singer, and she won many music awards for her recordings, which included the banned "Black President" in 1990 and her best known song, "Vulindlela" (1998) which the African National Congress (ANC) claimed as its theme song in the 1999 election campaign. She also suffered a recurrent and public battle with cocaine addiction, and a series of ill-starred love affairs with men and women. Her low point came in 1995 when she was found semi-conscious in a hotel room with her lesbian lover, Poppie Sihlahla, who was dying of a drug overdose. Though Fassie rose to success again following rehabilitation, she suffered an asthma attack that led to heart failure and her premature demise at age 39. During her last days in a hospital in Johannesburg she was visited by Nelson Mandela and South African President Thabo Mbeki, and her declining health was front-page news in South Africa.

FATUMA (fl. 1690s; d. 1711–1728). Fatuma was a member of the royal family of Zanzibar in the 17th century. Control of the east coast of Africa was then under dispute as the Portuguese claimed areas over which Arab rulers from Oman had previously held power. Fatuma came to the throne of Zanzibar during that time, and married Abdullah, a ruler on the coast near Mombasa. When all the other Arab rulers along the coast opposed the Portuguese presence she arranged for food to be sent to the Portuguese who were under siege at Fort Jesus near Mombasa. When the Arabs defeated the Portuguese in 1698, she was left on her own in Zanzibar where she was captured by Arabs and exiled to Oman with her son. She returned to Zanzibar in 1709 and died there sometime in the early 18th century.

FAYE, SAFI (1943–). A Senegalese filmmaker, she has produced and directed 14 films that mostly deal with women's concerns. She met the French anthropologist and filmmaker Jean Rouch (1917–2004) in 1966, and he recruited her to act in *Petit à petit: lettres persanes* (*Little by Little: Persian Letters*, 1968). The experience motivated Faye to move to Paris where she studied ethnography and filmmaking. Her first film, *La Passante* (*The Passerby*) appeared in 1972. Her films were unconventional in their non-linear approach to telling a story, and she commonly focused on political and social themes. Faye's 1979 film, *Fad'jal* (*Come and Work*), examined the situation of peasants in her home village and the impact of government policies on their condition, with a particular understanding of the plight of female farmers, and another of her films about rural life, *A Letter from My Village*, was banned by the Senegalese government because of its outspoken criticism of official policies. She has made documentaries, including *Selbe: One Among Many* (1983). Her recent production and third feature film, *Mossane* (1996), which Faye wrote and directed, told the story of a rural adolescent torn between her love for a poor student and her arranged betrothal to a wealthy émigré; it was screened at the Cannes Film Festival, as was the earlier *Fad'jal*.

FEDERATION DES FEMMES VOLTAIQUES / FEDERATION OF WOMEN OF UPPER VOLTA. The federation was formed in 1974 to promote women's welfare through **education** and fundraising. (Upper Volta was later called Burkina Faso.)

FEDERATION OF GOLD COAST WOMEN. *See* NATIONAL FEDERATION OF GOLD COAST WOMEN.

FEDERATION OF NIGERIAN WOMEN'S SOCIETIES (FNWS). The Federation was organized at a 1953 national conference called by the **Nigerian Women's Union.** The resolutions passed at that meeting called for more women to be included on local councils, for universal adult **suffrage**, and asked that the FNWS be consulted about any legislation, so that it could assess the impact on women. The organization also advocated for women's **education**, encouraged women to be active in all sectors of the community, and worked to improve women's economic activities, until it was overshadowed by a rival organization, the **National Council of Women's Societies**. The FNWS continued to exist, but was most active in Abeokuta, where **Funmilayo Ransome-Kuti** continued as the leader of the organization. *See also* ABEOKUTA WOMEN'S UNION.

FEDERATION OF SOUTH AFRICAN WOMEN (FSAW). The Federation was founded as a non-racial organization in 1954 by **Lilian Ngoyi** (who was elected president in 1956), Ray Alexander, Florence Mkhize, **Helen Joseph**, **Fatima Meer** and others. Within months there were over 10,000 members, primarily urban African women, and including such activists as **Frances Baard**. Though active in a variety of venues, the focus was on bringing women into the anti-**apartheid** struggle. The most successful action was a march of 20,000 women on the government buildings in Pretoria in 1956 in the **Defiance Campaign**. As government repression escalated, it became increasingly difficult for the Federation to organize, and the African National Congress (ANC) leadership also placed less emphasis on massive demonstrations. Some observers suggested that the male ANC leaders wanted to keep women from playing a central political role, though it is also true that the ANC did not have the resources to defend thousands of arrested activists, whether male or female. The FSAW ceased to be active after 1963. The United Democratic Front (UDF) worked to revive the FSAW in the 1980s, and in 1987 the UDF Women's Congress was established with the goal of "uniting the broadest range of democratic women under the umbrella of the Federation of South African Women." After the 1994 election that marked the end of apartheid, South African Women's Day was established to commemorate the 9 August date of the 1956 march. *See also* AFRICAN NATIONAL CONGRESS WOMEN'S LEAGUE, UNITED WOMEN'S ORGANISATION, WOMEN'S FRONT.

FEDERATION OF TRANSVAAL WOMEN. This group was one of several regional women's **organizations** affiliated with the United Democratic Front in South Africa in the mid-1980s. **Sister Bernard Ncube** was a founding activist. The federation organized a workshop on the role of women in the anti-**apartheid** struggle.

FEDERATION OF WOMEN'S INSTITUTES OF SOUTHERN RHODESIA. The federation was an umbrella organization of white women's groups in Southern Rhodesia (later Zimbabwe) that was active in the 1920s.

FEMALE GENITAL CUTTING. The practice of cutting or excising portions of girls' or women's genitals as part of initiation ceremonies is practiced in a number of African countries, and is the center of an international campaign to end what is variously called "circumcision," "excision," "clitoridectomy," "**infibulation**," and "**female genital mutilation**" or FGM. It is generally assumed to be related to Islamic practice, though the Koran makes no reference to excision. It is most common in West Africa and in Kenya, Sudan, and the Horn of Africa, and is rare in southern Africa. According to United Nations estimates, 130 million women have already had the procedure performed on them, and every year as many as 2 million more are at risk of undergoing genital cutting. The actual cutting can range from a minor nick just to draw blood, to the removal of the clitoris and the labia minora and majora, with the resulting wound sewn together and requiring recutting in order for intercourse to occur. It usually is done as part of a group coming-of-age process, and can be considered a requirement for a girl to be regarded as a proper adult woman who can marry and have children of her own. Frequently the cutting is done in extremely unsanitary conditions with dull implements and inadequate follow-up care. As described by **Waris Dirie**, her legs were tied together to prevent her from walking while the wound healed over the course of weeks, and she was given no medicines for pain or infection. The rates of infection and death are not known, though clearly that is a reality given the way that the cutting is performed. Likewise it is difficult to find reliable data on continuing health problems related to urination, menstruation, intercourse, and childbirth, as well as discerning the sexual experience of women who have been cut.

Western campaigns to end the procedure have not always been well received by African women, who sometimes saw arrogance and attitudes of cultural superiority rather than concern about women's lives. Beginning with the efforts of Christian **missions** in Kenya in the 1930s, through **feminists** concerned about the well-being of women in the 1980s and 1990s, the impact of non-Africans on ending the practice has been complicated. Prominent in initially bringing the custom to international attention in the 1980s were Fran Hosken and Women's International Network (WIN) News and Efua Dorkenoo who founded the **Foundation for Women's Health, Research and Development (FORWARD)**. **Awa Thiam** founded another early group, **Commission pour l'Abolition des Mutilations Sexuelles (CAMS) / Commission for the Abolition of Sexual Mutilation**. African women began working to transform the rites in order to sanitize the cutting and to introduce non-surgical practices in the 1990s. Local groups and projects include Tostan (an American organization based in Senegal), PATH (Program for Appropriate

Technology in Health) in Kenya and elsewhere, **REACH** in Uganda, and Water for Life in Somalia. Womankind Kenya, a grassroots organization, has initiated discussions with individual women who perform the cutting, convincing them one at a time that the procedure should be stopped.

In 2003 a prominent element in the **Protocol on the Rights of Women in Africa** that was passed by the African Union prohibited excision. Prior to that the only countries that had passed national legislation specifically calling for an end to the practice were Senegal and Tanzania, though other nations were pursuing **education** and some were applying existing **laws** that punished assault to include the practice of genital cutting. The United Nations Population Fund (UNFPA) has a useful site offering background information about female genital cutting at http://www.unfpa.org/gender/faq_fgc.htm.

FEMALE GENITAL MUTILATION (FGM). The use of the word "mutilation" is a term that was introduced by western **feminists** concerned with expanding the international outcry against the rites. Though the procedure does mutilate a girl's body, many consider it an overly negative term which reinforces false non-African ideas about African barbarism. By referring to all variations of the procedures as mutilating, the term limits the possibility for further discussion and modifications in the practice. *See* FEMALE GENITAL CUTTING.

FEMALE GENITAL SURGERY. Although some commentators have suggested this term as a replacement for the inaccurate and overly vague term "female circumcision," others reject the term because it implies a surgical practice related to modern medicine that is not actually part of the experience. *See* FEMALE GENITAL CUTTING.

FEMALE-HEADED HOUSEHOLDS. It appears that rates of female-headed households are increasing, in part as a result of men migrating to find work and women remaining in the community of origin. Another factor is related to **war** and conflict; in Rwanda following the 1994 genocide the population was 56 percent female, and half of those women were **widows** supporting their own households. Although there are regional variations, the rate for female-headed households in sub-Saharan Africa is around 20 percent. Statistics indicate that female-headed households have a significantly higher rate of **poverty** than households with a man participating in bringing in an income.

FEMALE HUSBANDS. *See* WOMAN–WOMAN MARRIAGE.

FEMINISM. Feminism has usually been defined as support for the complete equality of women with men, and has included action to bring about changes in **laws** and society that will permit such equality. Many feminists around the world have defined themselves in more specific terms, such as socialist feminist or ecological feminist; other variations include liberal feminist, radical feminist, and Marxist feminist. The overall concept of feminism has been critiqued for being western in its basis and biases. As Gwendolyn Mikell explains in the introduction to *African Feminism: The Politics of Survival in Sub-Saharan Africa* (1997), African women in the 1990s embraced a feminism that developed out of their anti-colonial struggles combined with an intrinsic appreciation of local customs and history. This approach was necessarily different from the elaboration of western feminism, which was a reaction to the growth of industrial capitalism and individual rights. African women have sometimes adopted new terms, such as *womanism*, Molara Ogundipe-Leslie's stiwanism (for "social transformation including African women"), or **Calixthe Beyala**'s *feminitude* to reflect their concern that western-style feminism was too antagonistic to men and in other ways did not reflect African realities. Obioma Nnaemeka coined the term *nego-feminism* to emphasize the way that African feminists negotiate, collaborate, and compromise in their political work that aims to support women's needs. African feminists also contributed to expanding the general definition of feminism to include broader struggles to end racism and imperialism.

Concerns about defining feminism have also addressed the issue of historical practices that would be considered feminist from a modern perspective, although the women of earlier eras might not have applied the term to their own beliefs and actions. Most theorists routinely refer to *feminisms* in the plural in order to acknowledge the variety of approaches both in theory and in practice that all share the goal of women's equality. It has become a cliché to recognize that western feminists list equal pay and **abortion** rights among their top goals, while African feminists give priority to improving **educational** opportunities and insuring clean accessible water as ways to improve women's lives. There was a continuing tension between the common goal of equality for women and the recognition of very real differences between women in different societies. Most feminists understood that such differences would necessarily draw on a variety of theoretical approaches and practical activities, and recognized that men and patriarchy are not the sole source of women's oppression. Women organized as feminists in **non-governmental organizations** that focused on research, such as the **Association of African Women in Research and Development (AAWORD)**, the **Feminist Studies Centre** in Zimbabwe, and **Women in Nigeria (WIN)**. They also established **women's studies** programs at universities, and published journals including *Agenda: A Journal about Women and Gender*, *SAFERE: Southern African Feminist Review* and the online journal *Feminist Africa* from the **African Gender Institute** at the University of Cape Town.

FEMINIST AFRICA. An online journal of **women's studies** first posted on the web in 2002, it is edited by the **African Gender Institute** at the University of Cape Town, South Africa. It can be accessed at www.feministafrica.org.

FEMINIST STUDIES CENTRE. An independent **women's studies** program in Harare, Zimbabwe, that includes a library, meeting room, and support for **feminist** research.

FEMMES AFRICA SOLIDARITÉ (FAS) / SOLIDARITY OF AFRICAN WOMEN. Organized in 1996 under the auspices of the **non-governmental organization** Synergies Africa, the group was based in Geneva, Switzerland, where it worked to promote women's inclusion in all international efforts to end conflicts and build **peace**. It published the twice-yearly English-language newsletter *FAS Advocacy News*. In 2003 FAS was awarded the United Nations Prize for Human Rights for its work with the Mano River Women's Peace Network that brought together women from Liberia, Sierra Leone, and Guinea. It opened a Gender, Peace, and Development Centre in Dakar, Senegal, in early 2004. Information on their activities and networking can be found at http://www.fasngo.org/. *See also* AFRICAN WOMEN'S COMMITTEE ON PEACE AND DEVELOPMENT.

FEMMES DE L'OUEST AFRICA (FOA) / WOMEN OF WEST AFRICA. Founded in July 1959, this association brought together all of the official women's organizations in French West Africa. Among the goals outlined in the initial statement of purpose was the abolition of **polygyny** by 1960, the recognition of a woman's right to **inherit** from her husband's estate, the establishment of civil **marriage**, increased efforts to end sexual discrimination at the work place, work for equality of civil rights between men and women, and action to end **prostitution**. It also drafted a **family law** that became the basis for Mali's 1962 Code du Mariage et de la Tutelle.

FEMNET. *See* AFRICAN WOMEN'S DEVELOPMENT AND COMMUNICATION NETWORK.

FERTILITY. Africa has one of the world's highest fertility rates, measured at 5.6 births per woman. Overall the rate has fallen, though not as rapidly as in other world areas, from 6.6 children per woman in 1950 to 5.6 for sub-Saharan Africa in 2002. The fertility rate is declining more rapidly in urban areas, with a fertility rate of 4.8 compared with 6.6 in rural areas. The timing of the transition, based on longitudinal studies, appears to have begun in the 1960s and 1970s in urban areas, followed by a decline a decade later in rural areas. Fertility rates also decline as women become more educated. The long-term impact of the **HIV/AIDS** pandemic is not yet known. Population growth was also marked by a decline in death rates, and experts considered that population stability would be achieved with a **birth rate** of 2.7.

The central reason for the high rate is the desire for large families; though women in most of the world state a goal of 2.5 to 4.5 children, African women's responses ranged as high as 8.5 children in Chad and Niger; at the lower end, Kenyan women expressed a desire for 4.1 children. Kenya, which once had one of the highest birth rates, embarked on an **education** campaign in the 1990s with a resultant drop in the fertility rate nationwide from 6.7 children per family in 1989 to 4.7 in 1998. The only exception to the expressed desire for many children was South Africa where 3.3 children were seen as a model family size. *See also* BIRTH CONTROL; INFERTILITY.

FILM. Although little known, there are African women making films, often dealing with issues central to women's lives. More often interesting films have been made by men and non-Africans that address central issues of women's condition; among the most important of those are *Finzan* by Cheikh Oumar Sissoko that deals with **initiation rites**, and *Xala* by Sembene Ousmane that focuses on women and **politics** in Senegal; Med Hondo also directed the historical film *Sarraounia*. One of the earliest films by a woman was a 30-minute documentary by Thérèse Sita-Bella, *Tam Tam à Paris* (1963) about the Paris performances of the National Dance Company of Cameroon. Women have made films for television as well as a number of documentaries, such as Mozambican Fatima Alburquerque's *No meu pais existe uma guerra* (*In my country there is a war*, 1989) about the war of the 1980s; **Safi Faye** of Senegal who has made ethnographic films, filmed Serer religious rites, and documented economic issues; and Anne-Laure Folly of Togo who made *Femmes aux yeux ouverts* (*Women with Open Eyes*, 1994) about West African women organizing around marital rights, reproductive **health**, and other issues. Other notable female filmmakers include Mariama Hima, who has filmed artisans in Niger; Lola Fani-Kayode who produces documentaries for Nigerian television (the best known is *Mirror in the Sun* about modern urban life, 1984); Flora M'mbugu-Schelling, who filmed a documentary in 1992 about Mozambican women refugees working in a rock quarry in Tanzania (*These Hands*); and **Anne Mungai** who has made several documentaries about Kenyan women. Female filmmakers have been less successful in finding support for feature films, though such films have been made by **Tsitsi Dangarembga** and **Sarah Maldoror** among others. Many women regarded as African filmmakers live and work in Europe, though they concentrate on African topics. In 2004 the African Women's Film Festival was held in Johannesburg, South Africa, bringing women together with the theme "film from a woman's perspective." Beti Ellerson has organized a very useful website on "African Women in the Cinema" at http://www.founders.howard.edu/beti_ellerson/.

FIRST, RUTH (1925–1982). Ruth First was a scholar, **journalist**, and anti-**apartheid** leader in South Africa. She was born in Johannesburg to Jewish parents who had emigrated from the Baltic. She was educated at Witwatersrand University where she first began working with the Communist Party of South Africa (CPSA). In 1949 she married Joe Slovo, later a leading figure in the CPSA. First was active in a variety of actions to support black workers, including editing the *Guardian, New Age*, and *Fighting Talk*. Her own political activities resulted in her detention in 1963, which she wrote about in *117 Days* (1965; rep. 1989) and which was later depicted in the film *A World Apart* (1988), written by her daughter Shawn Slovo. Another daughter, Gillian Slovo, also explored the impact on their family life of her parents' very high visibility as political activists in a memoir, *Every Secret Thing: My Family, My Country* (1997). Ruth First was forced into exile, first to England where she taught from 1972 to 1979. After 1979 she moved to Mozambique where she worked at the African Studies Center at Universidade Eduardo Mondlane conducting research on the regional impact of apartheid. She published several books examining the history and politics of Africa, including studies of Libya, Namibia, and migrant labor in Mozambique. She was killed by a parcel bomb sent to her university offices in Maputo by South African agents.

FIRST LADIES. While only a few women have been **heads of state** in Africa, a number of women have taken advantage of their position as first lady to initiate programs and to work to advance women, including **Ruth Khama** of Botswana, Adame Ba Konaré of Mali, **Graça Machel** of Mozambique, and **Sally Mugabe** of Zimbabwe. While these projects sometimes have appealed mainly to elite women (the **Better Life for the Rural Woman Programme** in Nigeria under **Maryam Babangida** was a well-known example, as was Mariam Traoré and the **Union National des Femmes Maliennes / National Union of Malian Women**), other endeavors have been lauded, including Janet Museveni's **Uganda Women's Effort to Save Orphans**. Other examples of first lady activists include Aissa Diori and the **Union des Femmes du Niger / Union of Women of Niger**; and the **31st December Women's Movement**, led by Nana Konadu Rawlings of Ghana.

In an example of how the problems of **polygyny** might affect the presidential office, the New Year's celebrations to mark the arrival of 2004 in Kenya were marred by a toast to one of President Mwai Kibaki's wives, Lucy Kibaki, which referred to her as the "second lady," although as the **senior** wife (they married in the 1960s) she normally was the one present at state functions. The co-wife, Wambui (they married in the 1970s), also was accorded security protection and other rights of a first lady. *See also* ASSOCIATION DES FEMMES IVOIRIENNES; HEADS OF GOVERNMENT; NATIONAL COUNCIL OF WOMEN OF TANGANYIKA.

FORUM DE MULHER SANTOMENSE / FORUM OF WOMEN IN SAÕ TOMÉ. The forum is a national women's organization in São Tomé.

FORUM FOR WOMEN IN DEMOCRACY (FOWODE). Founded in 1995 in Uganda, FOWODE's main activities are based in the parliament, where it has brought together members of underrepresented groups including women, youth, and people with **disabilities**. It has had success in ensuring that women's perspectives are incorporated into legislation on **land** and local government, and in the budget process. FOWODE has also sponsored **education** and training to prepare women for involvement in politics at all levels of government.

FORUM OF AFRICAN WOMEN EDUCATIONALISTS (FAWE). FAWE was created in 1992 and it was registered in Kenya as a pan-African **non-governmental organization** in 1993. Its slogan indicates its focus: "Supporting Women and Girls Acquire **Education** for **Development**." The secretariat is in Nairobi, and the membership quickly grew to include 33 national chapters whose members included women policy-makers; male ministers of education were welcomed as associate members. FAWE sought to ensure that girls had access to school, completed their studies, and performed well at all levels. It introduced a program now functioning in several African countries, called "Speak Out," that aimed at limiting the **sexual harassment** of female students by publicizing the names of teachers who violated their students' rights and by educating male students about proper behavior. The website, http://www.fawe.org/, is very informative about its projects and publications.

FOUNDATION FOR WOMEN'S HEALTH, RESEARCH AND DEVELOPMENT (FORWARD). FORWARD is an international organization focused on education about **female genital cutting** with the goal of ending that practice. It was founded by Efua Dorkenoo in 1983 in London as part of the Minority Rights Group, and has played a central role in bringing the issue to the attention of the World Health Organization and other influential bodies. Dorkenoo, who is the author of *Cutting the Rose: Female Genital Mutilation: The Practice and Its Prevention* (1994), was made an Officer of the Order of the British Empire in 1994. FORWARD has a website at http://www.forward.dircon.co.uk/.

FOYERS SOCIAUX. Founded in 1948 in Burundi, the *foyers sociaux* were homemaking clubs designed to allow European women to teach domestic skills to urban African women. Earlier courses on domesticity had been introduced in 1926 by the Union des Femmes Coloniales in the Congo, and expanded throughout the 1930s with new branches in outlying urban centers. Following World War II the colonial authorities increased their attention to what they perceived as problems with urban women, such as **prostitution, divorce**, and licentious behavior. Although there were **organizations** throughout Africa during **colonialism**, the *foyers sociaux* were unusual in the focus on urbanized and educated women and the attention paid to family relations in addition to cooking and sewing.

FRICHOT, SYLVETTE (1945–). Frichot is a leading politician in the Seychelles. She trained as a teacher, and was dismayed when she discovered that she was paid much less than male teachers. In 1966 she joined the Seychelles People's United Party (SPUP), began doing clerical work for the party, and was appointed as principal coordinator. In 1968 she co-founded the SPUP Women's League and was elected chair of the league from 1970 to 1977. Frichot has also held a variety of leadership positions in the party itself. In 1989 she was named minister of information, culture, and sports; the ministry was later renamed the Ministry of Local Government, Youth and Sports.

She has represented the Seychelles at numerous international conferences on issues related to youth and **sports**.

FUNTUWA, BILKISU. Funtuwa is a novelist from northern Nigeria who writes popular fiction in Hausa. The events depicted in her stories suggest ways that women can take more control over their family and **educational** lives while remaining Muslim. A common theme introduced female protagonists who experienced great success as a result of persevering in attaining an education, within a story of love and romance. Her publications include *Allura Cikin Ruwa* (*Needle in a Haystack*, 1994), *Wa Ya San Gobe* (*Who Knows What Tomorrow Will Bring?*, 1996), and *Ki Yarda da Ni* (*Agree with Me*, 1997). *See also* RAMAT YAKUBU, BALARABA.

– G –

GAGOANGWE (c. 1845–1924). A member of a ruling Kwena family in Botswana, she was the daughter of Sechele I. As a child she once put out the eye of a servant, prompting her father to invoke the injunction of "an eye for an eye," and allowing the servant to blind her in one eye. She was known as the "one-eyed Queen." She was married to a ruler of the Kgosi, Mmanaana Kgatla, and left him to elope with Bathoen, who was heir to the throne among the BaNgwaketse. She converted to **Christianity** and supported the London Missionary Society settlements in Botswana. In 1916 when her son was assassinated she took on a leadership role, and in 1923 she became regent for her grandson Bathoen II.

GAMBIA WOMEN'S FEDERATION. Founded in 1960 with the objective of bringing the women of the Gambia together, it sponsored adult **literacy** classes, vocational training for girls, and worked to improve women's situation in the country. The federation was an umbrella organization for 13 women's groups in the Gambia.

GENDER AND WOMEN'S STUDIES FOR AFRICA'S TRANS-FORMATION. This online resource supporting **women's studies** was sponsored by the **African Gender Institute** at the Univer-

sity of Cape Town in South Africa. Its website is at http://www
.gwsafrica.org/.

GENDER IN AFRICA INFORMATION NETWORK (GAIN).
GAIN is a South African organization dedicated to increasing African
women's access to modern communication technologies. It was established in 1997 following a workshop at the **African Gender Institute, University of Cape Town**. Beginning in 2003 it has posted
an electronic newsletter, *Pula*, which focuses on "promoting and pro-
filing the work and activities of women's information and communication technology (ICT) initiatives in Africa."

GENDEREVIEW. *GENDEReview*, described as "Kenya's Women and
Development Quarterly," was published by the Women and Media
Project beginning in 1993. The articles generally focus on political issues, for example, there was extensive coverage of **Charity Ngilu**'s
presidential candidacy in the late 1990s.

GENITAL MUTILATION. *See* FEMALE GENITAL CUTTING; FE-
MALE GENITAL MUTILATION.

**GERTZE, JOHANNA UERIETA (NÉE KAZAHENDIKE) (c.
1840–c. 1930).** Johanna Gertze was a Namibian woman who worked
as a domestic servant for the missionary Carl Hugo Hahn at
Otjikango. She initially came to the **mission** school and learned
sewing; she became so proficient that she was soon teaching classes.
There is evidence that she was fluent in English, Dutch, and German,
and she was instrumental in translating materials into Herero. Although official records are scarce, it is apparent from scattered references in the materials of Carl and Emma Hahn that Johanna Gertze
was an indispensable member of their household and most likely responsible for the success of Carl Hahn's nine Herero publications
(printed in Germany between 1860 and 1862). Johanna accompanied
the Hahns to Germany where she participated in mission work as an
"example" of a Herero convert, as well as working on the Herero
books, which earned an honorary doctorate for Carl Hahn. She returned to Cape Town in 1862 and in 1864 to her home in Otjikango.
In 1865 she was married to a Herero-German convert, Samuel

Gertze, who was a **widower** with eight children; the couple had nine children of their own during their 15-year marriage (until Samuel's death in 1880). Johanna lived another half century, working as a **midwife** and pharmacist.

GERVAIS, JEANNE (1922–). Gervais served as the first woman minister in Côte d'Ivoire. She was trained as a teacher. She was one of three women elected to the general assembly after independence (along with Hortense Aka Anghui and **Gladys Anoma**), and was named in 1976 to head the Ministry of Women's Affairs, a post she held until 1984. Gervais was also president of the **Association des Femmes Ivoiriennes** for many years.

GHANA ASSOCIATION OF WOMEN ENTREPRENEURS (GAWE). Founded in 1990 by Lucia Quachey, GAWE was concerned with a variety of issues pertinent to women's condition, including **divorce** and **female genital cutting**. It focused particularly on economic issues, especially those of interest to the membership, which consisted mainly of large-scale traders and entrepreneurs active in the formal sector. It was affiliated with the **African Federation of Women Entrepreneurs**, which was also founded by Lucia Quachey; the two organizations share office space in Accra, Ghana.

GHANA FEDERATION OF WOMEN. *See* NATIONAL FEDERATION OF GOLD COAST WOMEN.

GHANA MARKET WOMEN ASSOCIATION. Founded in 1956, the 3,000 members of this group were **market women** who worked to promote **education** and business success among market vendors in Ghana.

GHANA WOMEN'S LEAGUE. The league was founded by **Hannah Cudjoe** in the 1950s. It took a strong political position encouraging improvements in women's social conditions, informed in part by Cudjoe's role as a propaganda secretary for the ruling Convention Peoples' Party (CPP). Members of the league visited outlying areas and demonstrated good practices in nutrition and **childcare**. They were also active on international issues, such as the campaign for nuclear disarmament. The league's activities were parallel to the less political **National Federation of Gold Coast Women**.

GINWALA, FRENE (1932–). Ginwala is a political activist of South Asian descent, born in Johannesburg, South Africa. She studied in the United Kingdom and read for a law degree there. When she returned to South Africa she joined the Indian Congress and then the African National Congress (ANC), where her activities forced her into exile for more than 20 years, returning in 1991. While in exile she developed a strong **feminist** approach, served as the ANC spokesperson in London, and edited the ANC newsletter, the *Spearhead*. As **apartheid** crumbled in the early 1990s, she helped organize the **Women's National Coalition** inside South Africa to bring together women who had been living in exile and those who had remained in South Africa, and to push for a stronger role for women in the new independent government. As a member of the ANC she served as speaker of the National Assembly beginning in 1994, where she pushed for greater attention to women's issues through the formation of the Parliamentary Committee on the Quality of Life and Status of Women.

GIRLS' BRIGADE. The Girls' Brigade is an international **Christian organization** founded in the United Kingdom in 1893; in 2004 there were branches in over a dozen English-speaking African nations. Managed at the local level by church women, members met during regular meetings of groups called "companies" whose goal was to instill self-confidence to help girls grow into responsible Christian adults. The stated aim of the organization was "To help girls to become followers of the Lord Jesus Christ and through self control, reverence and a sense of responsibility to find true enrichment of life." The first African brigade was founded in Cape Town, South Africa, in 1925. In Nigeria, where the first branch was established in 1942, there were nearly 500 companies in both rural and urban areas in 1978. Most of the other African companies began in the 1950s, and the first All-African conference was held in Zambia in 1992. *See also* BIBLEWOMEN; CIRCLE OF CONCERNED AFRICAN WOMEN THEOLOGIANS; *MANYANO*.

GODDESSES. In a number of African local religions there were goddesses in the pantheon of ancestors and spirits from whom people seek support. Goddesses were considered patrons of the earth or water, and thus had special powers over human and agricultural fertility. Some better-known goddesses included **Dzivaguru**, **Mami Wata**, **Osun**, and **Yemoja**. Some were believed to have special authority as a source of justice, such as the **Adoro** goddess, **Akonadi**, and **Asase Yaa**. The **Rain Queen** in southern Africa is embodied in the person of the ruler of the Lovedu. People may leave offerings at local shrines built to honor goddesses who have a history of helping believers in need.

THE GOLD COAST WOMAN. A periodical published by the **National Federation of Gold Coast Women** in the 1950s.

GOMES, ANTONIETA ROSA. As a political activist in Guinea-Bissau, Gomes was president of the Foro Civic da Guiné/Guinean Civil Forum beginning in 1995, and she ran for president in 1994 and 1999. She was minister of justice in 2000–2001 and minister of foreign affairs in 2001 until President Kumba Yala fired her; that action was considered a key event in the increasingly erratic behavior by Yala that resulted in a coup to oust him in 2003. In 2004, Gomes was president of the commission of the Supreme Tribunal of Justice.

GOMES, HENRIQUETA GODINHO. Gomes was a political leader in Guinea-Bissau, where she was active in the Partido Africano para Indepêndencia de Guinea-Bissau e Cabo Verde (PAIGC)/African Party for the Independence of Guinea-Bissau and Cape Verde. She was minister of social affairs and public health (1988–1993) and minister of labor (1993–1994).

GORDIMER, NADINE (1923–). A novelist and essayist from South Africa, Gordimer writes observant fiction about the racial conditions in which she lives. Born to Jewish immigrants (her father was from Lithuania, her mother English) in Springs, a small town in the Transvaal, she began writing when very young and first published when she was 13. She attended Witwatersrand University for a year, and published her first novel, *The Lying Days*, in 1953. She married her second husband, Reinhold Cassirer (1908–2001) in 1954. Subsequent novels addressed the intersection of personal and political events in South Africa during the **apartheid** era, especially in *Burger's Daughter* (1979) and *July's People* (1981), and after the end of apartheid, in *The House Gun* (1998). She also published several short story collections, most recently *Loot* (2003). Gordimer won the Nobel Prize for Literature in 1991. Her novel *The Pick-Up* won the 2002 Commonwealth Writers Prize (Africa region).

GRAND BASSAM. Grand Bassam was a prison outside of Abidjan, Côte d'Ivoire, which was the site of a major anti-colonial demonstration by women in 1949. The male leaders of the Parti Démocratique de Côte d'Ivoire (PDCI)/Democratic Party of Ivory Coast had been jailed by the French colonial authorities, and in December 1949 they began a hunger strike. Five hundred women staged a dramatic march filled with songs and dance, traveling the 30 miles from the city to the prison. The women were attacked by French colonial troops, who injured 40 women and arrested four of them. It was a pivotal event that played a role in the French decision to reach an agreement about African independence. A prominent Ivoirienne historian, **Henriette Diabate**, wrote a book about the events, *La marche des femmes sur Grand-Bassam* (1975). *See also* OUEZZIN COULIBALY, CÉLESTINE.

GRASSROOTS DEVELOPMENT ORGANISATION (GRADO). Founded in Calabar, Nigeria, in 1996, the initial motivation came from Gloria Monn who wished to introduce clean water techniques in response to outbreaks of cholera. GRADO has taught rural women to build platform toilets, and has begun income-generating projects focused on sewing, catering, and mushroom cultivation.

GREEN BELT MOVEMENT. Wangari Maathai founded this organization in Kenya in 1977 in order to combine environmental conservation and women's empowerment. Under the auspices of the **National Council of Women of Kenya** she introduced a project that recruited women to plant trees around the capital city of Nairobi and in rural areas. The Green Belt Movement focused on planting trees as an environmental measure that also brought income to the women involved in the project. By 1992 over 10 million trees had been planted and survived, while 80,000 women were working in the tree nurseries. The organization was also a key factor in a victorious effort to halt the building of a 60-story structure in Uhuru Park; the protests included a 1992 demonstration during which many women bared their lower bodies, an instance of a traditional **shaming practice**. Their informative website is at http://www.greenbeltmovement.org/.

GRIOTTES. The feminine form of the more familiar *griots*, the term refers to a particular group of female singers in West Africa. The origin of the word *griot* itself is obscure, and though it is probably derived from a mixture of African and western sources, it has been feminized as a French word to *griotte*. There are local terms in West African societies, such as the Bamana and Maninke term in Mali, *jelimusow* (sing. *jeliw*, sometimes spelled *dyeli*).

Sometimes described as bards, praise-singers, storytellers, historians, or genealogists, *griottes* sing a variety of songs that might include family lineage information, accounts of historic events, morality tales, and laudatory lyrics about rulers and other prominent people. Their role is much broader in some communities, where they may act as counselors, diplomats, interpreters, teachers, and ritual leaders and participants. Women singers are especially involved in weddings and baptisms, and are not as likely to sing the epics commonly associated with *griots*. Though they are often accompanied by male **musicians** playing stringed instruments and beating on drums, women may play an instrument such as the *fle*, a gourd with attached cowrie shells that rattle rhythmically as it is tossed and shaken during the performance. Recordings of *griottes'* compositions and renditions are very popular in West African cities, and include work by **Fanta Damba**, **Sira Mori Diabaté**, and **Oumou Sangaré**. *See also* WASSOULOU.

GROUPE D'ANIMATION CULTUREL DE COCODY (GACC) / COCODY CULTURAL PROMOTION GROUP. This **organization** was founded in the Cocody neighborhood of Abidjan, Côte d'Ivoire, in 1977 as a method of enabling women to work together. Though the members started meeting with a primary interest in developing local cultural activities for women, they have taken on such tasks as mediating disputes among **market women** and promoting cross-ethnic cooperation, which proved to be steps to greater influence in **urban politics**.

GROUPEMENT DE PROMOTION FÉMININE / GROUP FOR WOMEN'S ADVANCEMENT. In Senegal, this term is applied to a variety of local groups that work to promote women's programs including income-generating projects, **literacy** workshops, **health** issues, and in some cases women in these associations have challenged conventional practices of **polygyny** and **female genital cutting**.

GULAMA, ELLA KOBLO (1921–). Gulama was a political leader in Sierra Leone in the 1950s. The daughter of a popular chief in southern Sierra Leone, she was educated as a teacher. In 1953 she inherited her father's position as paramount chief for the Moyamba Kaiyamba region, home to 30,000 people. She simultaneously rose in national politics, and was elected to the House of Representatives, where she served from 1957 to 1967. She was the only woman member of the house in 1958, where she represented the Sierra Leone People's Party. Gulama was also a minister without portfolio from 1962 until 1967. She had particular responsibility for **educational** issues in the government and in her post on the board of Fourah Bay College. Her biography, *The Life and Times of Paramount Chief Madam Ella Koblo Gulama* by Talabi Lucan, was published in 2003. *See also* YOKO, MADAM.

– H –

HABWE, RUTH (?–1996). A pioneer in raising women's issues in Kenya, she was trained as a teacher and was an early leader of **Maendeleo Ya Wanawake Organisation** (MYWO), serving as chair from 1968 to 1971. During her tenure, MYWO passed resolutions calling for increased positions for women at the University of Nairobi, and for equal employment conditions for women and men. Habwe ran for parliament in 1964.

HEAD, BESSIE (1937–1986). Bessie Head was a South African-born writer of mixed race descent who lived much of her adult life in

Botswana. She was taken from her Scottish mother at birth because her father was a black South African, and she was raised by a foster family. After attending a **mission** school she became a teacher, and in 1964 she accepted a teaching post in Botswana where she lived under "refugee" status for 15 years before becoming a citizen. Head began writing novels and short stories in the 1960s. Her main writings include *When Rain Clouds Gather* (1968), *Maru* (1971), and *A Question of Power* (1973). Her deep sense of insecurity was captured in her prose, which reflected her unsettled life and described oppression and abuse, but which also projected hope for a better future. Her letters have also been published posthumously. Head died when only 49 years old.

HEADS OF GOVERNMENT. Beginning in the 1990s a growing number of women have served as prime ministers, or heads of government, in African nations, though most have served abbreviated terms. One of the briefest was served by **Carmen Pereira**, who was acting head of government in Guinea-Bissau for two days in 1984. Others include **Mame Madior Boye** (Senegal, 2001–2002); **Maria das Neves Ceita Batista de Sousa** (São Tomé e Príncipe, 2002–2004); **Elisabeth Domitien** (Central African Republic, 1975–1976); **Sylvie Kinigi** (Burundi, 1993–1994); and **Agathe Uwilingiyimana** (Rwanda, 1993). *See also* FIRST LADIES; HEADS OF STATE.

HEADS OF STATE. Being elected as a head of state has remained an elusive goal for African women, with **Ruth Sando Perry** the only woman head of state; she served as chair of an interim governing council in Liberia in 1996–1997. There have been royal women who have ruled in Ethiopia (**Empress Zauditu** and **Menetewab**) and Madagascar (**Ranavalona I, II,** and **III**). There have also been a small number of female prime ministers or **heads of government.** In the 1990s the numbers of women announcing themselves as candidates in presidential races increased and drew renewed attention. The presidential race in Nigeria in 1992 was marked by the entry of three women into the race, **Alda Bandeira** ran in São Tomé e Príncipe in 1996, and in 1997 **Charity Ngilu** ran in Kenya and **Ellen Johnson Sirleaf** ran in Liberia. Other notable women who have attempted to gain the presidency include **Antonieta Rosa Gomes** in Guinea-

Bissau in 1994 and 1999, and **Vera Chirwa** in Malawi in 2004. *See also* FIRST LADIES; KAZIBWE, SPECIOZA WANDIRA; NJIE-SAIDY, ISATOU; QUEEN MOTHERS.

HEALTH. Health issues cover a wide range of topics, including physical and mental disease, **disability**, **fertility** and **infertility**, **sexuality**, nutrition, and most centrally since the 1980s, **HIV/AIDS**. Women have a crucial role in all of these sectors as caretakers, educators, mothers, and as people who suffer from ill health. Women's work in the household puts them at the center of prevention, as they usually are responsible for maintaining cleanliness and providing good food and clean water. As in other world areas, women frequently train as **nurses**, a career which was considered one of the few appropriate jobs for women for many years. A source of recent research is the *African Journal of Reproductive Health*, published jointly by the Women's Health and Action Research Centre based in Benin City, Nigeria, and the Harvard School of Public Health since 1997.

HIGHER EDUCATION. Women have continued to be seriously underrepresented in colleges and training institutions, largely as a result of their lack of access to **education** at lower levels. Female participation in higher education varies across the continent, from a low of 11 percent women students in Guinea to over 60 percent in Namibia. See Table 2 for information about female attendance at post-secondary institutions by country.

HISTORIANS. For many years there were very few African women who pursued a career in history. Some African women who were trained in history moved on to other careers, such as Agnes Aidoo of Ghana who worked for the United Nations in Addis Ababa for many years, or Maud Shimaayi Muntemba of Zambia, who was an environmental expert with the World Bank. Historians such as Nigerian author Bolanle Awe, **Nina Mba** (also Nigerian), Christine Obbo of Uganda, and others were pioneers in African women's history, increasing knowledge and incorporating women's experiences into broader historical studies. In the 1980s and 1990s more women historians emerged who are making a renewed impact on

Table 2. Higher Education—Percentage of Female Students Attending Post-Secondary Institutions According to United Nations Statistics for the 1990s (countries with no available information are omitted)

Country	Percentage	Country	Percentage
Benin	19	Madagascar	45
Botswana	47	Malawi	30
Burkina Faso	23	Mauritania	18
Burundi	27	Mauritius	51
Central African Republic	15	Mozambique	25
Chad	13	Namibia	61
Côte d'Ivoire	25	South Africa	48
Djibouti	44	Swaziland	44
Eritrea	13	Tanzania	16
Ethiopia	19	Togo	17
Gambia	26	Uganda	33
Guinea	11	Zambia	30
Lesotho	54	Zimbabwe	37

writing the history of African women while centering the voices of African women. These historians include Odile Ekindi-Chatap of Cameroon and Rokhaya Fall of Senegal who served on the editorial board of the history journal *Afrika Zamani*, Tabitha Kanogo (Kenya), Penda Mbow (who was minister of culture in Senegal), Nakanyike Musisi (Uganda), Kenda Mutongi (Kenya), Benigna Zimba (Mozambique), and many others. *See also* HISTORIOGRAPHY.

HISTORIOGRAPHY. Research into the practice of writing and publishing African women's history has found a profound gender bias, as basic African history texts do not include information on African women. Often when women are present in the narrative they are there in subordinate positions as **slaves**, or in unusually exalted situations such as **queen mothers**. It is very rare when women's activities are well integrated into the story of African history as a whole. Tiyambe Zeleza's 1997 survey of eight commonly used African history texts (both multi-volume and single-volume works) found no women authors and nearly no evidence that women contributed to their societies in myriad ways throughout history. *See also* HISTORIANS; WOMEN'S STUDIES.

HIV/AIDS (HUMAN IMMUNE-DEFICIENCY VIRUS / AC-QUIRED IMMUNE DEFICIENCY SYNDROME). The epidemic of AIDS has had a devastating impact on Africa since it was recognized in the early 1980s. Figures from 2003 estimate that 30 million Africans are infected, amounting to 70 percent of the world total. The United Nations (UN) believes that 60 million Africans are affected, as they are either living with HIV, have died of AIDS, or are AIDS orphans. In 2002 women made up 58 percent of infected Africans, making it a significant **health** issue for women.

In the wake of the increasing death rate, there have been studies of **sexuality**, and some researchers, though later proven false, implicated African women in the spread of the disease. In trying to understand why some countries have had particularly high rates of infection, it has been suggested that girls' **initiation rites** that included **female genital cutting** might have been a factor, as well as **polygyny**, **prostitution**, and widespread illiteracy. Research in Uganda in the 1990s showed that the high rates of infection might be related to the practice of having concurrent (rather than sequential) long-term sexual relationships, not only men in poloygynous marriages, but women who also maintain more than one long-term partner during the same time period. Thus educational programs that warn people about prostitutes do not address the more prevalent web of HIV/AIDS that appears because people believe that their friends and long-term partners are safe sexual companions. Women are also at risk due to their vulnerability to **domestic violence** and **rape**.

It is commonly said that African men refuse to use condoms, the easiest barrier to the virus, and the subordinate position of women in male-female relationships has been described as a component in the spread of the disease. Investigators have shown that **poverty** is a major element, and that particular African sexual practices are not the main factors. The rate of infection is much lower in West Africa, a fact that has usually been ascribed to **Islamic** practices that limit women's sexual freedom. Recent research into regional variations has found that societies that commonly circumcise men have lower rates, and that male circumcision may reduce the risk of acquiring HIV/AIDS by up to 70 percent.

For women there are some specific concerns. One is the rising number of orphans, children whose parents have died from AIDS.

As women most often have responsibility for **childcare**, they may find themselves caring for ever-increasing numbers of orphans as relatives and friends succumb to the disease. This reality was a factor in the work of the **Ugandan Women's Effort to Save Orphans**. The UN calculates that by 2010 there may be 20 million "AIDS orphans" in Africa; in 2002 there were already 14 million. A second phenomenon is the increase in older men, sometimes called "sugar daddies," who enter into relationships with teenage girls. While the men may choose relatively young women because they believe those women are free of HIV, it is frequently the case that the women contract AIDS through relations with the man, who may support them generously with money for school, clothes, and food. Girls in Africa between 15 and 19 years of age have HIV infection rates as much as six times higher than boys of the same age group.

Women have been instrumental in HIV/AIDS organizing, founding the **Society for Women and AIDS in Africa (SWAA)** to facilitate a specifically African female response to the crisis. They have also played a leading role in local community groups such as the **Hlomelikusasa Othandweni Women's Group**, **Lesotho Women's Institute**, **Maendeleo Ya Wanawake Organisation**, **Siyazama**, and the **Women's Action Group**. International organizations such as the **United Nations Development Fund for Women (UNIFEM)** and the **Africa Women's Forum** have made HIV/AIDS work a priority.

A variety of documents and statistics is available at the UNAIDS website, www.unaids.org; or through http://www.thebody.com/whatis/africa_statistics.html.

HLOMELIKUSASA OTHANDWENI WOMEN'S GROUP. This South African group has been involved in **HIV/AIDS** education projects, including sewing panels together for an immense red "ribbon" that circled the Durban City Hall during the international World AIDS Conference in July 2000.

HOMOSEXUALITY. *See* LESBIANISM.

HOTTENTOT VENUS. *See* BAARTMAN, SARA.

HOUSING. In many rural societies women and men built houses jointly, and women made an important contribution to the construction and design of their homes. Among the Basotho of South Africa and Lesotho, women decorated the exterior of their mud and wattle homes, and they developed a range of techniques including incising the damp mud and painting geometric designs in bright colors. The space around and within a homestead was often explicitly gendered, with women having greater responsibility for the interior while men had more control over the courtyard, especially in **pastoral** societies that incorporated cattle enclosures within or adjacent to the homestead. Among the Makonde in northern Mozambique, men used to have a separate community shelter where they would meet and socialize, completely apart from individual family homes.

In **polygynous** households in many societies it was customary for each wife to have her own dwelling. The common husband would allocate his time among his wives, visiting each house in rotation. Colonial authorities imposed "hut taxes" that set the amount of tax according to the number of huts in a settlement, thus accounting for the apparent greater wealth of men with more wives. In some areas this practice led to families housing co-wives in the same house so as to avoid paying more taxes. In colonial and modern times, the trend to building single-family residences reflected western family configurations rather than the extended families of rural Africa. A study of urban housing in Port Harcourt, Nigeria, found that such dwellings did not account for the kind of work women and girls performed within the house, did not provide the necessary space and privacy for family rituals, and led to neighborhoods that did not foster community living.

In modern urban communities women have sometimes had problems because they have not had title to property. Urban housing is marked by sub-standard dwellings often on the periphery of burgeoning urban centers. Residents have used whatever materials they can find to construct homes of cardboard and discarded wood. Most such neighborhoods lack access to potable water and electricity. In some cities only waged workers were allowed access to housing, so that men had an advantage beginning in the colonial era, and women had to prove either employment or marriage to get housing.

Women found themselves in vulnerable conditions as renters, and research has shown that they often have a history of frequent moves from lodging to lodging. Their lack of education and regular employment means they are usually not able to get credit that would help them improve their housing situation. Scholars and policy workers have begun investigating gender and housing issues in greater depth, as with a research network based in Zimbabwe which has sponsored conferences and published work in a volume on *Gender Research on Urbanization, Planning, Housing and Everyday Life (GRUPHEL)*, edited by Syliva Sithole-Fundre and her colleagues (1995).

HUMAN RIGHTS. Human rights arose as a concept following World War II, and by the 1980s and 1990s the issue of human rights for African women had become a hotly debated topic among international legal authorities and human rights activists. It is part of a larger debate about incorporating specific concerns pertaining to women, such as **female genital cutting** and **domestic violence**, into the broader interests of human rights. One difficulty has been determining how to address the universal nature of human rights while trying to respect the particularity of different cultures. Historically human rights advocates focused on state abuses of rights and especially political and civil rights, and relegated abuse of women to the private sphere or considered problems to be individual rather than social in nature. Beginning in the 1980s human rights promoters argued that women's rights should not be divided off as a special case, but deserved attention at the center of human rights. Gender-based violence, whether in the home or an aspect of **war**, was analyzed as part of the broader culture, not more narrowly as a woman's problem. Some writers argued that **polygyny** and the exchange of **bridewealth** also infringed on women's human rights, in part because those customs were intrinsically not equal between men and women and placed women at a disadvantage in their communities. Some of the discussions about gender aspects of human rights incorporated larger philosophical dilemmas about the nature of the individual in society. In 2003 the African Union adopted the **Protocol on the Rights of Women in Africa**. *See also* WOMEN IN LAW AND DEVELOPMENT IN AFRICA.

– I –

IBRAHIM, FATMA AHMED. The best-known women's activist in Sudan, she has been a leader of the Sudanese Communist Party (SCP), a founder of the **Sudanese Women's Union** (SWU), and editor of the SWU publication *Sawt al-Mara* (*Women's Voice*) in the 1950s and 1960s. A popular public speaker, she was the first woman elected to parliament in 1965 as a SCP member. During various periods of anti-communist governments, she was under house arrest in the early 1970s and exiled in 1989. In 1993 she was awarded the United Nations Human Rights Prize in recognition of her decades of activism on behalf of women.

IIVULA-ITHANA, PENDUKENI (NÉE KAULINGE) (1952–). Iivula-Ithana is a prominent politician from Namibia who focuses especially on issues of **sport** and women. She was trained as a lawyer, and was active in the liberation movement, serving as secretary of the **SWAPO Women's Council** (the women's **political party organization** affiliated with the South West African Peoples' Organisation). She was the first female attorney general in Namibia, as well as the first female minister of youth and sports, from 1991. She also was minister of lands, resettlement and rehabilitation. Iivula-Ithana has been a co-chair of the International Working Group on Women and Sport since it was founded in 1994, and she also co-founded the African Women in Sport Association, which she served as president. In 1998 she organized the Second World Conference on Women in Sport, which met in Windhoek, Namibia.

ILENI HAGOS (c. 1805–1851). Ileni Hagos was an important leader among the Tigrayan communities (in what is today Eritrea) in the 19th century. The region was marked by feuds and succession disputes. When her husband died around 1837 she defended her son's right to rule. With the support of an important military leader she ruled as regent for her son, though her ascent was opposed by those who did not want to see a woman in power. She also lost popularity by imposing high taxes and by engaging in quarrels with other regional rulers. Though deposed in 1841 she continued to play an influential role until her torture and murder at the hands of an opponent in 1851. Her sons avenged her death, and the blood feud was ended only when her daughter married the nephew of her main opponent.

IMAN (1955–). Iman is a Somali woman who is internationally known as a model and participant in global cultural events. When she was born her grandfather gave her the name "Iman," which is more commonly considered a male name. Her father was a diplomat, and she was attended boarding school in Egypt. After the 1969 revolution in Somalia she and her family went into exile, living for a time in Kenya. She was a university student when she was discovered walking in downtown Nairobi in 1975. She moved to New York and was photographed by important fashion artists by the end of that year, making a statement as a black model in a genre that was at that time still averse to using black models. She married rock music star David Bowie in 1992. She has continued to have success in the fashion world, more recently with a line of cosmetics launched in 1994 that was designed for women of color. She and her friends told a collective version of her story, complete with many photographs and illustrations, in *I am Iman* (2001).

IMMACULATE CONCEPTION SISTERS. An order of nuns also known as the Blue Sisters, they first came to Gabon in 1849 and later introduced **mission** stations in Senegal as well. The order was established by a noble French family to provide care to poor girls, and members went to Africa when the Holy Ghost Fathers requested nuns to teach African girls. *See also* CHRISTIANITY; WESTERN WOMEN; WHITE SISTERS.

INANDA SEMINARY. Inanda Seminary was a landmark **educational** institution for girls in southern Africa, founded in 1869 by Protestant American Board missionaries. Although girls were admitted to the Lovedale Institute in South Africa, Inanda was the first all-female boarding school for African girls. It was established at an established **mission** station which served a rural population in Natal, South Africa, and initially the teaching was geared toward training girls in middle-class domesticity, enabling them to be "proper" wives to educated mission men. Basic **literacy** was taught along with sewing skills, and the students' lives were closely regulated to ensure their clean upbringing. The American Board Women's Auxiliary funded female missionaries to teach at Inanda, including Mary Kelley Edwards, who was head of the seminary from 1869 until 1892, and who continued to live at the school until her death in 1927 at age 98. By the 1930s the school's reputation was such that elite African girls from all regions of South Africa dominated the student body, marking a shift from the earlier years when Inanda served the local community. The early history of the school is told in an article by Heather Hughes in Cherryl Walker's *Women in South Africa* (1990). *See also* INKATHA WOMEN'S BRIGADE.

INDIAN WOMEN'S ASSOCIATION. An organization of women from the Indian sub-continent who resided in the South African city of Durban, it was founded in 1908 with the assistance of Mohandas Gandhi, who was then editing the *Indian Opinion* in Durban. The group later changed its name to the **Durban Indian Women's Association** and then the **Durban Women's Association**.

INFERTILITY. Internationally between 8 and 12 percent of couples experience problems in conceiving, while the prevalence of infertility in sub-Saharan Africa ranges from 11 to 20 percent in the 27 countries surveyed by the Demographic Health Survey (DHS) and World Fertility Survey (WFS). Infertility can be a major problem for African women, especially so in communities where **motherhood** is the route to a woman's recognition as an adult and to her acceptance in her husband's family. Customarily women have been held solely responsible for a couple's childlessness, though one of the most common causes is infection related to sexually transmitted diseases which obviously implicates men as well. An inability to conceive or carry a fetus to term is a common motive for **divorce** as well as for accusations of **witchcraft**. Women seeking remedies have turned to faith healers such as **Mai Chaza** in Zimbabwe. Zimbabwe has one of the highest infertility rates in the world with one in every four women experiencing some degree of infertility. In 1996 a group of women trying to deal with their own infertility formed the first support group in Zimbabwe, the Chipo Chedu Society, a term for "our own gift." There is also increasing demand for high-technology interventions to ensure conception. It can be difficult to assess rates of infertility, as the common practices of fostering and adopting children may mask actual ability or inability to bear children. *See also* BIRTH CONTROL; BIRTH RATE; FERTILITY.

INFIBULATION. Infibulation is the most severe form of **female genital cutting** that is practiced. Though not widespread, it has been reported in Somalia and Sudan. It involves the removal of the clitoris and much or all of the labia, after which the vaginal opening is sewn shut leaving only a small route for urine and menstrual fluids to leave the body, and necessitating new cutting to re-open the vagina for intercourse and child birth. *See also* DIRIE, WARIS.

INFORMAL SECTOR. The informal sector typically refers to the segment of the economy that is outside of formal businesses and **employment** areas. It includes vendors in street **markets**, and a variety of jobs often performed by women, including crocheting items for sale, hairdressing in the home or on the street, and food preparation for sale along the curbs. Such work usually involves very little investment or overhead and also results in very low income levels. Sometimes called "microentrepreneurs," it is the economic sector with the most women following **agriculture**. The informal sector is also the location of many women's **organizations**, including market groups, **rotating savings and credit organizations**, and similar support gatherings.

INHERITANCE. Inheritance has emerged as an important **human rights** issue, with abuse of women's situation noted across the continent. Women in some countries are considered legal minors who remain subordinate to male kin. In a court case in Zimbabwe in 1999, a woman who had been named as heir of her parents' home lost a dispute to her younger half-brother, who claimed he had the right to the house because he was the son. The Supreme Court ruled that customary **law** was the primary legal standard, meaning that only men could inherit. The chief justice, in writing the majority (unanimous) opinion, stated that "women's status is therefore basically the same as that of a junior male in the family." Similar experiences have been found among women in Nigeria, Kenya, and elsewhere. Inheritance is also often an issue for **widows** in patrilineal societies where they may face the loss of all their household goods, access to land they have cultivated for years, and even rights to their children if the kin of their deceased husbands lay claim to those. *See also* LAND TENURE.

INITIATION RITES. Most African societies held ceremonies for both girls and boys that marked their entry into puberty as the first step toward adulthood. Such rites were central to forming girls into women who could participate in their communities as adults, eventually marrying and bearing children. The actual elements of such rites varied from one society to another, but most often girls began the procedures once they had their first **menstruation**. They could be physically separated from the rest of the community, sometimes with other girls of their age cohort for periods of up to three months. They were then taught adult behavior by responsible women who were ritual specialists or respected elders. Such lessons could include imparting sexual information, teaching girls how to please their husbands but also celebrating the joys of adult female **sexuality**, often through song and **dance**. Further lessons focused on other aspects of women's work, such as their responsibility for **agriculture** and food preparation. In some societies it was important that the girls undergo a painful ritual, ranging from burning the inner thigh to various forms of **female genital cutting**. Among many southern African societies girls pulled on their labia in order to lengthen them. The ritual itself, with its isolation and taboos about eating certain foods or behaving in particular ways, was often described as a liminal state, where the girls were in a transitional phase. Their re-entry into society as recognizable young women rather than children was sometimes akin to a rebirth which affirmed their place in their local society and in the world at large as life-giving human beings.

INKATHA WOMEN'S BRIGADE. Inkatha (Inkatha Yenkululeko Yesizwe/National Cultural Liberation Movement) was the Zulu political **organization** that was formed in 1975 in South Africa under the leadership of Chief Mangosutho Buthelezi. It contested leadership with the African National Congress (ANC), and in the 1990s transformed itself into the political party, Inkatha Political Party. The Women's Brigade was similar to many women's groups that were affiliated with **political party organizations**. It was formed in 1980 when the Inkatha central committee decreed that it should be activated. The Brigade had actually been formed in 1977 at the **Inanda Seminary** with the primary goal of promoting women and **development**. But that progressive tendency to encourage women's inclusion in modern society was undercut by a persistent emphasis on women's responsibilities to their husbands and children and on their commitment to the church.

The inaugural congress in 1977 focused on "The Role of Women in Development," but the following year the congress theme was "Work and Pray." An emphasis on women as **mothers** was a common approach of political organizations, especially conservative groups, around the world, as was the expectation that women would uphold the goals of the parent organization rather than formulate their own policy and agenda for action. Development projects were typically small in scale and focused on already existing rural sewing cooperatives. Membership was difficult to verify, but between 8,000 and 10,000 women attended the annual conferences in the 1980s, while Inkatha claimed over 460,000 members in 1989.

INSTITUTO DA CONDIÇÃO FEMININA / INSTITUTE ON THE FEMININE CONDITION. This government institute was based in Cape Verde within the office of the prime minister. In 1999 it published a study of the condition of women in Cape Verde, *Vencendo Barreiras (Surpassing Obstacles)*. Maria Madalena Tavares, formerly leader of **Organização da Mulheres de Cabo Verde**, was president of the institute.

INTER-AFRICAN COMMMITTEE ON TRADITIONAL PRACTICES AFFECTING THE HEALTH OF WOMEN AND CHILDREN (IAC). Formed as a **non-governmental organization** in 1984, the Inter-African Committee has collaborated with the United Nations Children's Fund (UNICEF), the World Health Organization (WHO), and the United Nations Population Fund (UNFPA). Its primary goal was to end the practice of **female genital cutting**, and to work to reduce the rates of injury and death associated with cutting. With branches in 24 countries, the committee trained local activists and birth attendants and worked to spread information about alternative practices. It began publishing the *IAC Newsletter* in 1985, and it has sponsored a series of local and regional conferences and seminars on the topic of harmful traditional practices. The newsletters are available at its website: http://www.iac-ciaf.ch/.

INTERNATIONAL WOMEN'S YEAR. *See* UNITED NATIONS DECADE FOR WOMEN.

ISLAM. Over 50 percent of Africans are Muslim, with Islam especially prevalent in inland areas of West Africa and along the coast of East Africa. In West Africa, Mauritania counted 100 percent of its population as following Islam, Senegal had 92 percent, Mali had 90 percent, and Niger had 80 percent. Nigeria, where the population in the north is heavily Muslim, regarded 50 percent of its total population as followers of Islam. The percentages for other West African nations ranged from 30 percent in Ghana to 60 percent in Côte d'Ivoire. In East Africa, Somalia claimed 100 percent adherence to Islam; Sudan, 70 percent; Tanzania, 35 percent; and Kenya, only 7 percent.

The first contact of Africans with Islam came in the ninth century, as Muslim merchants settled along the East African coast and also moved along trans-Saharan trade routes into West Africa. There were wide variations in the history and practice of Islam between and within regions, as early converts were more often of noble origin and ordinary Africans continued to practice local religions. In West Africa women played a notable role in expanding the reach of Islam, and during the 18th and 19th centuries they benefited from the expansion of Koranic **education** for women. Beginning with **Nana Asma'u** many women undertook the *hajj*, the pilgrimage to Mecca, and the women who went formed an organization in northern Nigeria when they returned. In Niger and other areas of West Africa that were less affected by the 19th century jihad, women leaders of *bori* **spirit possession** cults have played a role in integrating *bori* into Islamic beliefs. Although not common, women also played leadership roles in the Muslim communities called "brotherhoods," such as the Tijaniyya in Kano, and were active as teachers in Muslim schools; two Senegalese examples were **Mam Diarra Bousso** and **Sokhna Magat Diop.** Although many Muslim women were subject to **seclusion** they also have had an important woman-centered culture. In some areas including the

Horn of Africa and across the Sahel region the practice of **female genital cutting** was said to be related to Muslim beliefs, though that relationship was not proven. *See also* RELIGION; ZAAR.

IYALODE. The *iyalode* was a female leader among the Yoruba in southern Nigeria. The term translates as "mother in charge of external affairs," which indicates her responsibilities for political affairs, especially the concerns of **market women**. Considered the ruler of all women, she commanded her own entourage of servants, drummers, and bell ringers. Women achieved this title by their accomplishments rather than simply by inheritance. *See also* MADAM TINUBU.

IYE IDOLORUSAN (QUEEN DOLA) (fl. 1850). Iye Idolorusan briefly ruled the Itsekiri kingdom in Nigeria. She stepped in during a dispute over succession following the death of her half-brother Akengbuwa in 1848, and set up a council of state, which was short lived as the kingdom broke into smaller trading states.

– J –

JABAVU, NONI (NONTANDO) (c. 1920–). Jabavu is a Xhosa writer from South Africa, who was born in Cape Province. She was the granddaughter of John Tengo Jabavu and the daughter of D. T. T. Jabavu, both renowned activists for racial equality in South Africa. In 1933 at the age of 13 she went to England where she studied music and film. She wrote two autobiographical novels, *Drawn in Colour* (1960) and *The Ochre People: Scenes from a South African Life* (1963, rep. 1982). After her marriage to Michael Cadbury Crosfield, a British film director, she could not return to **apartheid** South Africa where interracial marriages were illegal, though she did visit in 1976. Jabavu settled in Zimbabwe in the 1980s.

JÈMANGÈLÈN. An organization in colonial French Sudan, founded in 1956 by Mme. Audibert and Mme. Thiam Fanta Diallo with the goals of providing women with technical skills and **health education** among other **development**-oriented projects. Though not officially connected with the Parti Soudanais Progressiste (PSP)/Sudanese Progressive Party, most of the women in Bamako were members of the PSP, an affiliation that was not replicated throughout the rest of the region. The members also organized a **rotating savings and credit organization** to assist each other with periodic expenditures such as weddings. In 1958 it joined with **Rencontres Africaines** and **Union des Femmes Travailleuses (UFT) / Union of Women Workers** to form the **Union des Femmes du Soudan (UFS) / Union of Women of Sudan**.

JIAGGE, ANNIE RUTH (1919–1996). Jiagge was the first female lawyer in Ghana where she was admitted to the bar in 1950. Born and educated in Lomé, Togo, she was later appointed as a justice on Ghana's Supreme Court. After Kwame Nkrumah was ousted as Ghana's president in 1966 she led the Jiagge Commission which investigated corruption in his government. In 1968 she was elected to chair the 21st session of the United Nations Commission on the Status of Women, the first African woman to hold that post. She remained active with the UN, helping draft the **Convention on the Elimination of All Forms of Discrimination against Women (CEDAW)** in the 1960s and assisting with plans for the Fourth World Conference on Women which met in Beijing in 1995. *See also* UNITED NATIONS DECADE FOR WOMEN.

JOHNSON SIRLEAF, ELLEN (1939–). A Liberian economist, political leader, and **peace** activist, she was jailed and then forced into exile for her opposition to the government of Samuel Doe. Johnson Sirleaf was born in Monrovia of mixed American-Liberian and Gola parentage. She was trained as an economist and earned a master's degree in public administration from Harvard University. She served both in the public and private sectors, as assistant minister of finance in Liberia and as a senior loan officer in the World Bank before returning to Liberia when she was named minister of finance in 1979. She was also the president of the Liberian Bank for Development and Investment.

Johnson Sirleaf helped found the Liberia Action Party and as a result was jailed for sedition in 1985, though she served only a few months of her 10-year sentence. In 1986 she led 500 women in a protest against the imprisonment of opposition political leaders, which lead to her arrest for treason. After she escaped she lived in exile in the United States where she was on the executive board of Equator Bank (1986–1992) and director of the United Nations Development Programme, Regional Bureau for Africa (1992–1997). During those years she also published reports on the economic situation in Africa, including *From Disaster to Development* (1991). In 1997 she returned to Liberia to represent the Unity Party in the elections. She came in second with only 10 percent of the vote (Charles Taylor won with a 75 percent landslide). Charged with treason once again, she went into exile, though she returned in 2003 following Taylor's ouster. In early 2004 she was appointed to head Liberia's anti-corruption committee, the Commission on Good Governance, and she announced plans to run for president in elections scheduled for 2005. She was a lead author on the UN report *Women, War, and Peace: Progress of the World's Women 2002* (2003).

JORNAL DA MULHER. This publication was produced in Cape Verde by the Centro das Mulheres de Cabo Verde/Women's Center of Cape Verde beginning in 1988.

JOSEPH, HELEN BEATRICE MAY FENNELL (1905–1992). Joseph played a prominent role in South African anti-**apartheid** politics, particularly as a leader of the **Federation of South African Women**. She was born in Sussex, England, and earned a degree in English at King's College, University of London. She taught in India before moving to South Africa in 1931. There she married, got involved in women's issues, took courses in social studies at the University of the Witwatersrand, and went to work for the Garment Workers' Union. In the 1950s she helped found the Congress of Democrats, a primarily white organization that worked to end apartheid, and she was one of the founders of the Federation of South African Women, of which she was national president in 1956, the year she helped organize the **Defiance Campaign**, in which 20,000 women participated in a huge anti-pass march and demonstration.

Joseph was arrested in 1956 and was one of those who stood trial at the Treason Trial. She was acquitted in 1961. In 1962 she was the first person to be placed under house arrest, a method used by the apartheid government to restrict activists' political activities. She was generally banned (meaning she could not speak publicly or publish any of her writings) or under house arrest throughout the 1960s. Joseph was an honorary president of the National Union of South African Students and in 1983 was elected a patron of the United Democratic Front.

During her years of house arrest she completed a degree in theology from the University of London, and wrote *If This Be Treason* (1963) about the treason trial and *Tomorrow's Sun* (1966 and 1968) about her extensive visits with other banned political activists. Her autobiography *Side by Side* was published in 1986. Joseph was awarded the African National Congress's highest award, the Isitwalandwe, for "the one who wears the plumes of the rare bird," traditionally given to brave warriors.

JOURNALISM. Women have been able to use journalism as a method of raising awareness of women's issues across the continent of Africa, and some of the first literate women initially turned to publishing in community newspapers. During the **colonial** era elite educated women in Nigeria used local newspapers to publish articles extolling the need for girls' **education** and women's rights. **Folayegbe Mosunmola Akintunde-Ighodalo** frequently contributed editorials and essays that sometimes generated a great deal of debate in Nigerian society, and **Mabel Dove Danquah** played a similar role in Ghana in the 1930s. **Charlotte Maxeke** in South Africa also made important contributions to political debate with her articles. **Grace Ogot** in Kenya, **Joyce Sikakane** and **Ruth First** in South Africa, **Lina Magaia** in Mozambique, and **Annette M'Baye** in Senegal were among those who first became known as writers through their journalism. In the 1980s several **organizations** of women journalists were formed, including the **Tanzania Women's Media Association**, and women began organizing radio programs and other methods of outreach on women's issues. In 1997 the continent-wide group **African Women's Media Center** was established with the support of the International Women's Media Foundation. *See also* DE SOUSA, NOÉMIA; KIMENYE, BARBARA; PERIODICALS.

JUDITH. *See* ZAUDITU.

– K –

KADZAMIRA, CECILIA THAMANDA (1938–). As the personal secretary to President Hastings Banda (served as president, 1966–1994) in Malawi, she was accorded the title of "Official Hostess" and filled the role of **first lady.** She was trained as a **nurse** and initially was employed by Dr. Banda in his medical practice. Kadzamira exerted enormous influence on political events throughout the three decades of Banda's rule. Banda outlawed the song "Cecilia," by Simon and Garfunkel, which he considered disrespectful. She founded the women's organization **Chitukuku cha amai mu Malawi** in 1984. After Banda died in 1997 she continued to influence the Malawi Congress Party, though she reduced her activism to focus on her business and farming interests.

KAMPALA ACTION PLAN ON WOMEN AND PEACE. The first declaration of its kind, put forward by a continent-wide meeting of women in Kampala, Uganda, in 1993, it demanded that African governments have gender parity in all **peace** negotiations and conflict resolution.

KANE, AISSATA. Kane is a Mauritanian politician. She was a founder of the women's movement in 1963, and in 1969 she became secretary of information of the government-affiliated Mouvement National Féminin/National Movement for Women. She was also responsible for publishing their magazine, *Marienou.* Kane was the first woman appointed as a minister, serving as minister for the protection of the family and social affairs from 1975 until a coup d'etat in 1978. Under the military leadership there were no women in governmental positions until 1987. Kane continued her activism on behalf of women as president of l'Association Internationale des Femmes Francophones/International Association of Francophone Women and as the Mauritanian contact for the **African Women's Development and Communication Network (FEMNET).** *See also* AICHE, MARIAM MINT AHMED.

KANGA. Kanga is the name for a wide rectangular piece of cotton cloth worn by women in Tanzania and Kenya. Similar garments are called *capulanas* in Mozambique. Their use can be traced to the 19th century, when the importation of cotton cloth became a status symbol as it replaced the use of bark cloth. Initially *kangas* were produced by sewing handkerchiefs together, and were called *leso* (Portuguese for handkerchief). By the early 20th century the cloths were printed with sayings and were called *kangas*. A woman may wrap one around her waist, use another as a shawl, and frequently fold one to use as a sling for a baby. *Kangas* are nearly always printed with designs representing a wide range of themes and concerns, and often have proverbs and sayings in Swahili. Women typically chose particular cloths to express their feelings, and on occasion are given cloths that reflect on the relationship with the gift-giver. Among the hundreds of examples collected by researchers was the following from a woman in a **polygynous** household: she wore a *kanga* stating "I am the best," to which her co-wives responded with their own *kangas* claiming "I am the very best." *See also* DRESS; TEXTILES.

KANUNI (?–1971). Kanuni was *hompa* (queen) of the Kwangali in the central region of Namibia from 1923 to 1941, when she was deposed in favor of her brother Sivute by the South African Native Commissioner Harold Eedes and forced into exile in Angola. She returned in 1958 after Eedes died, and ruled until her own death. She was typical of a number of women who ruled regionally in Namibia, including her own ancestors *Hompas* Mate I (c. 1750), Nankali (c. 1750–1775), Simbara (1785–1800), Mate II (1800–1818), and Mpande (1880–1886).

KASSI (1241–?). Kassi was an empress of Mali. When her husband, Suleyman, **divorced** her to marry a commoner, she emerged at the center of a political dispute. Noblewomen of the court supported her and refused to recognize the rule of her successor, and she convinced her cousins to rebel. The conflict was part of a larger struggle over who was the legitimate ruler, and Kassi was charged with treason and banished when her plot with her cousins was discovered. Her son, Kassa, ruled Mali briefly after Suleyman.

KAZIBWE, SPECIOZA WANDIRA (1955–). Specioza Kazibwe was one of the highest ranking female politicians in Africa during her tenure as vice president of Uganda from 1998 to 2003 (**Isatou Njie-Saidy** was vice president of the Gambia during the same period). She was educated in Uganda, including studying medicine at Makerere University and earning a master's degree in surgery in 1987. She worked in hospitals while raising her four children and volunteering with the Mother's Union and the Senior Women Advisory Group on Environment. After the dictator Idi Amin was overthrown and Yoweri Museveni came to power with the National Resistance Movement, Kazibwe became active in politics and in 1988 she was elected as a representative to the Kampala district council. In 1989 Kazibwe was elected to parliament, one of the beneficiaries of Uganda's strong support for women seeking office. In 1991 she became minister for women in development, culture and youth, and in 1994 she added the portfolio of tourism and wildlife.

Kazibwe ran for parliament against six men in 1994 without turning to the affirmative action program for support, and she won. In November 1998 she was named national vice president while simultaneously holding the position of minister of gender and community development. In 1999 while still vice president, she was named minister of agriculture. When she threw her husband, an engineer, out of her home after he beat her, she raised public awareness of the problem of **domestic violence**. Kazibwe told women legislators, "Why should I continue staying with a man who beats me? I told him—how can you beat a vice president?" But the very public nature of her personal trials resulted in her decision to resign in 2003, and to leave Uganda to take up graduate work at Harvard University.

KÉITA, AOUA (1912–1979). Kéita was a leading political activist from Mali. She was born in Bamako and educated there and in Dakar, Senegal, where she trained as a **midwife**. As a midwife she was acutely aware of women's difficulties, and she brought that knowledge to her political work. She and her first husband, Daouda Diawara, were very active in the socialist party, Union Soudanaise-Rassemblement Démocratique Africain (US-RDA)/Sudanese Union-African Democratic Assembly, and they enjoyed a modern egalitarian relationship. Nonetheless, the marriage ended in 1949 when it became clear she could not have children and her mother-in-law pressured them to divorce.

Kéita was exiled to Senegal and later a remote region of Mali near the Mauritanian border, as a result of her political militancy. In 1956 she returned to Bamako and was eventually elected to the US-RDA Central Committee; at independence Kéita was the only woman in the party leadership. Kéita along with Aissata Sow formed an early women's organization, the **Union des Femmes Travailleuses** / Union of Women Workers, of which she was president. She was the only woman elected to Mali's National Assembly in 1960, where she continued her activism for women's rights, and she was named as secretary general of the **Commission Sociale des Femmes** when it was formed in 1962. After a military coup in 1968 she left Mali and lived in Congo (Brazzaville) for most of the 1970s. She returned to Mali prior to her death in 1979. While in exile she wrote an acclaimed autobiography, *Femme d'Afrique: La vie d'Aoua Kéita racontée par elle-même* (1975).

KENYA WOMEN'S SEMINAR. The seminars brought women together in Nairobi in the early 1960s with the support of **Margaret Kenyatta**, who organized these initial discussions about women's concerns. The meetings soon resulted in the expanded East African Women's Seminar, which included women in Tanganyika and Uganda as well. Some of the women involved with the seminars continued to be active with the **All Africa Women's Conference**.

KENYATTA, MARGARET WAMBUI (1928–). Margaret Kenyatta is a political leader in Kenya. The daughter of Kenya's first president, Jomo Kenyatta, she was born in Nairobi. She worked as a teacher, and was arrested along with her father in 1952 during the **Mau Mau** Emergency. She joined the Kenya African National Union (KANU) when it was formed in 1960. She was elected to the Nairobi City Council in 1963, and the council elected her deputy mayor of Nairobi in 1969 and mayor in 1971, which position she held until 1977. Kenyatta worked energetically for women's rights, becoming president of the **National Council of Women of Kenya** in 1964. She presided at the **Nairobi Women's Meeting** in 1985. *See also* UNITED NATIONS DECADE FOR WOMEN.

KHAKETLA, CAROLINE NTSELISENG 'MASECHELE (1918–). One of the first women published in Lesotho, she writes in Sotho and promotes efforts to write and publish in African languages. She was educated in Lesotho, earning a grant to study at Morija Training College and later attending Fort Hare University College in South Africa, where in 1941 she was the first woman from Lesotho to obtain a university degree. She taught in Lesotho, and briefly in South Africa where she lived from 1950 to 1953 when her husband, Bennett Makalo Khaketla (d. 2000), was forced into political exile. With two other women she opened the first private primary school in Lesotho in 1960, and she continued to teach until retiring in 1984. She also was the first woman to be appointed as a high court assessor in Lesotho, and served on several other public boards in government and in the Anglican Church. Khaketla bore six children; her daughter 'Mamphono Khaketla (1960–) was named minister of communications in 2002.

Khaketla's first poem collection, *Mantsopa*, appeared in 1963, and she has published 12 books of poetry, drama, and short stories (*Mosiuoa Masilo*, 1990). Her plays have appeared regularly over the years, from *Mosali eo u 'neileng eena* (1954) to *Khotsoaneng* (1998). She was awarded honorary doctorates in literature from the National University of Lesotho (1984) and the University of Fort Hare (2002).

KHAMA, ELISABETA GOBITSAMANG (1846–1889). A royal leader in southern Africa, she was the first wife of Khama III (c. 1837–1923), and queen (*mohumagadi*) of the BaNgwato, one of the main groups living in what later became Botswana. She converted to **Christianity** a month after her marriage to the king in 1862, and adopted the name of the daughter of missionary Robert Moffat. She was Khama III's favored wife, and her son Sekgoma later ascended to the kingship (assumed *bogosi*).

KHAMA, LADY RUTH WILLIAMS (1923–2002). Born in England, Ruth Williams served in the Women's Auxiliary Air Force and after the war worked at Lloyds Insurance Company. She became a *cause célèbre* in Botswana and England when she married Seretse Khama (1921–1980), an Oxford law student and the heir to the Ngwato chiefship, in 1948. Their inter-racial marriage initially pleased no one, and Seretse Khama was forced to renounce his inheritance before the British allowed him to return to what was then Bechuanaland. Lady

Ruth and Seretse Khama prevailed, however, enjoying an enduring marriage and the birth of four sons, and helping to usher in an era of greater racial tolerance. Seretse entered local politics and was the first president of Botswana (1966–1980). Ruth Khama served as Botswana's **first lady**, and in that position she was also head of the Botswana Red Cross and worked with the Girl Guides and the Botswana Council of Women.

KHAMA, SEMANE SETLHOKO (1881–1937). Fourth and last wife of Khama III, they married in 1900. She was a devout Christian. She actively promoted modern **midwifery** techniques, and was a leading member of the Women's Christian **Temperance** Union (WCTU), bringing in the highest number of recruits in 1933. Her son Tshekedi Khama became a ruler of Botswana.

KIBUKA, KATOLINI ESITA NDAGIRE (KATIE) (1922–1985). Katie Kibuka was a leader of women's **organizations** during the **colonial** era in Uganda. She was born to a **Christian** family which valued **education**, and attended Gayaza High School where she later taught home economics. She was a founding member of the Uganda **Young Women's Christian Association** (YWCA), and was actively involved with the **Mother's Union** and the **Uganda Council of Women**. She and her husband moved to Nangabo when he retired, where she founded the Nangabo Centre as a community meeting place that supported girls' education and provided **childcare** in a pre-school for small children.

KIDJO, ANGELIQUE. Born in Benin, Kidjo is an internationally renowned **musical** star who is now based in Paris and New York. Her first recording was released in 1989, and she has had seven releases since then, with *Black Ivory Soul* appearing in 2003. She is particularly noted for mixing West African and Brazilian tempos and musicians into a vibrant mode of modern popular music. Her website is at http://www.angeliquekidjo.com/.

KIMENYE, BARBARA (1940–). Kimenye is a Ugandan writer who is recognized for her children's stories, beginning with a series of tales about village life published as *Kalasanda* (1965). She has published over two dozen volumes including many in her series of comic adventures featuring Kalasanda and Moses. In 1997 she published *The Modern African Vegetable Cookbook*. Kimenye also worked as a **journalist** and for the Kabaka of Buganda (the traditional ruler), before moving to London.

KINGSLEY, MARY (1862–1900). A British-born traveler and writer, Kingsley is best known for *Travels in West Africa* (1897), a report of an extensive journey she made on her own in the 1890s through Gabon, Nigeria, and Cameroon. In England she worked to change attitudes about African culture and abilities, arguing against official views that Africans were inferior to Europeans. She died as a result of illness contracted while working at a hospital in Cape Town during the **South African War**.

KINIGI, SYLVIE (c. 1952–). Kinigi was briefly prime minister of Burundi from 10 July 1993 to 11 February 1994. She was a moderate member of the Tutsi-dominated Parti de l'Unité pour le Progrès National (UPRONA)/Party of Unity for National Progress, and she held the position of prime minister at a key moment, as she was able to assume power when the democratically elected president Melchior Ndadaye and other Hutu members of the government were killed by Tutsi rebels in October 1993. She found asylum in the French embassy, and from there she brought about a peaceful end to the crisis and led her government to take collective power in order to restore order. She acted as president until February 1994 when President Cyprion Ntaryamira took office. She agreed with other moderate Burundians who believed that democracy had come about too quickly, leading to the formation of ethnically based political parties that exacerbated tensions in society. *See also* HEADS OF GOVERNMENT.

KISOSONKOLE, PUMLA ELLEN NGOZWANA (1911–1997). Pumla Kisosonkole was born in South Africa, but married a Ugandan and was active in women's **organizations** in Uganda as an adult. She was educated at **mission** schools in South Africa before marrying Christopher Kisosonkole in 1939 and moving to Uganda. She studied **education** in London and wrote a pamphlet, "Education as I Saw It in England." As a married woman she was restricted from many educational posts in colonial Uganda, but she was the first African woman on the Legislative Council of the Protectorate Government (1956–1958), and she was the first African to serve as president of the **Uganda Council of Women** (1957–1960). She went on to represent Uganda at international meetings, including as president of the International Council of Women from 1959 to 1962, as Ugandan representative at the United Nations General Assembly in 1963 to 1964, and as a **literacy** expert with the United Nations Educational, Scientific and Cultural Organization (UNESCO) in the 1960s.

KPOJITO. *Kpojito* was the Fon term for a **queen mother** in Dahomey (now Benin). It can be literally translated as "she who gave birth to the leopard," with the leopard representing the king, though she was not necessarily the biological mother of the king. From the 17th century to 1900 the *Kpojito* shared leadership responsibilities equally with the king. *Kpojitos* heard court appeals and could intercede with the king on certain cases. The position brought wealth to the title holder, as she gained her own followers and villages that paid tribute. She had an important role as well in controlling the *ahosi*, the female corps of **Dahomey soldiers** who were sometimes described as Amazons.

KUZWAYO, ELLEN (1914–). Kuzwayo is a South African writer and activist best known for her autobiography, *Call Me Woman* (1985). She earned a degree in social work at the University of Witwatersrand when she was in her sixties, and was employed as a social worker and a teacher before writing her book. She was general secretary of the **Young Women's Christian Association** (YWCA) in Soweto for 12 years (1964–1976) and served on other community boards including the Black Consumer Union of South Africa and the Urban Foundation Committee. Kuzwayo also taught at the University of Witwatersrand. She was named Woman of the Year in 1979 by the *Johannesburg Star*. She served as a member of parliament in the post-apartheid government. Her autobiography addressed the experience of black women in **apartheid** South Africa while recognizing their role as agents for change in their communities. She also published a collection of short stories, *Sit Down and Listen* (1990), and *African Wisdom: A Personal Collection of Setswana Proverbs* (1998).

– L –

LABOTSIBENI. *See* MDLULI, LABOTSIBENI GWAMILE.

LAGEM YAM. Lagem Yam, meaning "Uniting our intelligence" in the Moore language, is an **environmental organization** in Ouagadougou, Burkina Faso. Organized in 1993 with the specific objective of cleaning garbage off the neighborhood streets, it now helps a community of 900 with environmental projects such as composting and using animal traction to accomplish tasks. In 1997 members began to focus on the provision of potable water.

LAGOS MARKET WOMEN'S ASSOCIATION (LMWA). Organized in the 1920s following the suggestion of Nigerian nationalist Herbert Macauley, the LMWA brought together over 8,000 female vendors who played a major role in supporting **nationalist** movements in Nigeria throughout the 20th century. Under the leadership of **Alimotu Pelewura** they backed the efforts of the Nigerian National Democratic Party. The women paid three pence weekly into a common fund used to pay clerks and hire lawyers when needed. **Market women's organizations** had played a political role prior to the formation of the LMWA, with evidence from 1908 of protests against the imposition of a water tax in Lagos. *See also* ABEOKUTA WOMEN'S UNION; TAX REVOLTS.

LAKWENA, ALICE AUMA (1956–). Alice Lakwena is an Acholi woman who became a prophet from northern Uganda. Her father, Severino Lukoya, was active in the Church of Uganda and she was an adherent of the Anglican faith when she was young. She married twice but never had children, and because of that her husbands and their families turned her out. After a spiritual crisis in 1985 she was possessed by a powerful **Christian** spirit called Lakwena, which remained her primary identity though she was possessed by a number of other spirits as well. She founded and led the Holy Spirit Movement (HSM, sometimes called the Holy Spirit Mobile Forces) in a war against the Ugandan central government from 1986 until she was defeated in 1987, after which she went into exile in Kenya. In the early years of HSM activities Lakwena and her followers espoused egalitarianism between men and women and advocated an intense purity of spirit and body, including abstinence from **alcohol**, tobacco, sex, and thievery. She quickly rose to prominence, drawing on the disenfranchised sensibility of many poor Ugandans, and she used magical invocations and concoctions to instill power into her followers. The army Lakwena raised posed a serious threat to the government of Ugandan President Yoweri Museveni, as they marched across Uganda and came within 200 miles of the capital, Kampala, before being decisively defeated by government forces. The total number of casualties attributed to attacks by and on the HSM cannot be ascertained, but was likely in the thousands. Some of her followers continued to fight from northern bases into the 1990s. In 2004 she appealed to the United Nations High Commissioner for Refugees in Kenya, saying she wished to return to Uganda. The history of Lakwena and her movement has been told by Heike Behrend in *Alice Lakwena and the Holy Spirits: War in Northern Uganda, 1985-97* (1999). *See also* NONGQAUSE; NYABINGI; SPIRIT POSSESSION.

LAMECK, LUCY (1934–1993). Lameck was a pioneer in Tanzanian politics. Born to a farming family near Kilimanjaro, she attended the Kilema Catholic Mission School and then trained as a **nurse**, finishing in 1950. Later she earned a scholarship to study economics and politics at Ruskin College at Oxford in England, and pursued further **education** in the United States. She returned to Tanzania when she learned that independence was imminent, and held a number of positions in the government. She was organizing secretary of the women's section of the Tanzania African Nationalist Union (TANU), and was appointed to junior positions in the Ministries of Health, Commerce and Industry, and Cooperatives and Community Development. Lameck, one of the first women elected to the parliament in Tanzania, was a member of parliament for over 20 years. She also was a city council member for Moshi.

LAND TENURE. Conventional wisdom claims that African women have little legal right to the land that they cultivate as the primary **agricultural** producers. This construction is far too general and does not take into account the wide variety of ways in which women have been able to gain control over their land, although it is still common for women to lose access to land. Historically in many areas land was not considered to be private property, but was under the control of a clan or other group. Often male chiefs organized access to land for cultivation; in areas where women married into patrilineal systems they farmed land that ostensibly "belonged" to their husbands, and they could lose that land if they were **widowed** or **divorced**. Sometimes women were able to remain on their land if they had developed other connections with people in the village. In **matrilineal** areas the female kin group more often controlled access while the husbands moved in and women in those societies found it easier to retain control over their land.

When western powers took over during the **colonial** era, ideas and practices about land being owned by an individual person became more prevalent, and that individual person was frequently a man. Yet, even with the changes that were introduced, some women were able to maintain control and sometimes prove ownership of land through a variety of legal and social mechanisms. For instance, a study in rural Kabale district in Uganda found that women called on local concepts of fairness to insist that their agricultural labor brought them rights in the land they cultivated. In Mozambique (and other nations) all land is considered to belong to the state, and laws introduced in the 1990s were designed to protect the land rights of peasants and women who could demonstrate a history of cultivating a plot of land even in the absence of proper documentation. It may be a truism that African women do not own their land, and there are certainly examples of husbands and other men taking control of land their wives have labored on, but there are also many counter-examples of women's ingenuity in gaining and retaining access. *See also* INHERITANCE; LAW.

LARA, ALDA (ALDA PIRES BARRETO DE LARA E ALBUQUERQUE) (1930–1962). Alda Lara was an Angolan poet who wrote in Portuguese. She studied medicine at the University of Coimbra in Portugal, where she began publishing poetry in the journal *Mensagem*, a literary publication for Africans. After living in Portugal for 13 years she returned to Angola, only to die in less than a year. She was married to the Portuguese-Mozambican physician and writer, Orlando de Albuquerque; they had four sons. Collections of her poems and short stories, many of them addressing themes of children and **motherhood**, were published posthumously in *Poemas* (1966) and *Tempo de Chuva* (1973). The government of the city of Sa da Bandeira introduced a poetry prize, the Alda Lara prize, after her death.

LAW. Research on the development of legal codes during the **colonial** period has demonstrated that they were primarily written by European men based on discussions with African men. What had been community-based flexible systems of maintaining order were transformed into fixed written codes with specific punishments for particular acts of wrong-doing. In cases concerned with **marriage, divorce**, and **inheritance**, it appeared that in many instances the African male elders related a code that reflected how they wished cases were determined, not how they were decided in reality. At times when they indicated a variety of options for sanctions, the Europeans wrote down a code that did not show the choices available. Many countries continue to operate under a dual system of customary and western law, which can act to abrogate women's rights, as when the Supreme Court of Zimbabwe ruled that because women are considered to be jural minors under customary law, they could not inherit even when named as the heir by the deceased. Marriage laws in particular are prone to being relegated to the customary sphere, which is rarely favorable to women's rights.

In recent decades African women have become lawyers, and have used their expertise to advance legal issues concerning women, such as **domestic violence**. Female lawyers played a leading role in contesting the sentence handed down to **Amina Lawal**, as well as fighting other infringements of women's rights under Shari'a law in Nigeria. Women actively lobbied for the passage of **family laws** that would provide greater protection for women's rights. Many local lobby organizations focused on legal activism. Two leading groups were the regional **Women and Law in Southern Africa (WLSA)** and **Women in Law and Development in Africa (WiLDAF)**, which played important roles in coordinating efforts to improve women's legal situation in Africa.

Some of the more prominent lawyers include **Aduke Alakija**, who has served as the president of the International Federation of Female

Lawyers; **Mame Madior Boye**, who was briefly prime minister of Senegal; Malawian political activist **Vera Chibambo Chirwa**; **Pendukeni Iivula-Ithana**, the first female attorney general in Namibia; and **Annie Jiagge**, who was admitted to the bar in Ghana in 1950 and had a leading role in international politics. **Fatoumata Dembélé Diarra** and **Navanethem Pillay** have both served on international courts and were named to the initial group of judges on the International Criminal Court in 2003.

LAWAL, AMINA (1972–). Amina Lawal came to international notice in 2002 when she was found guilty of adultery and sentenced to death by stoning under strict **Shari'a laws** in **Islamic** northern Nigeria. Her adultery was discovered because she became pregnant, and her sentence was postponed until her infant daughter was weaned. After a worldwide outcry, her case went forward under appeals until 2003, when the Katsina State Shari'a Court of Appeals revoked the sentence, citing irregularities in the prosecution of her case.

LEAGUE OF MALAWI WOMEN. Organized in 1958 as a wing of the Malawi Congress Party (MCP) by **Rose Chibambo**, **Vera Chibambo Chirwa**, and others, members of this party-affiliated association supported President Hastings Banda throughout his tenure. Sometimes called the Women's League, the group had a monopoly on the sale of millet **beer**, and the proceeds supported its political work. Members were called Banda's *mumba*, meaning they were considered female kin, and as such they had exclusive access to Banda concerning women's issues, and enjoyed privileges including ownership of modern homes built to reward them for their loyalty. Members typically wore League uniforms when they performed for official functions. Although every village had a branch, the League proved ephemeral when the Banda government fell in 1994. Many of the members then left the MCP to join newer parties formed under the **democratization** reforms. *See also* CHITUKULU CHA AMAI MU MALAWI.

LEAKEY, MARY DOUGLAS (1913–1996). Born in London, Mary Leakey gained world renown for her archeological research on early humans in Kenya. She was raised and educated in England, studying at University College and the British Museum. In 1936 she married Louis Leakey and they traveled together to Kenya where they commenced archeological research at several sites in Kenya and famously at Olduvai Gorge in Tanzania where Mary Leakey found a *Zinjanthropus* skull in 1959. After Louis Leakey's death in 1972 Mary moved to a site at Laetoli, where in 1978 she found a series of hominid footprints determined to be 3.6 million years old. She received many honorary degrees and awards in recognition of the importance of her discoveries. She retired to a Nairobi suburb in 1983, where she wrote her autobiography published in two volumes, *Disclosing the Past* (1984) and *Lasting Impressions* (1985).

LELEMAMA. *Lelemama* is the term for **dance** associations in Swahili societies in East Africa. Historically the groups brought together women in urban areas such as Mombasa, sometimes crossing class and racial or ethnic boundaries. The groups participated in competitions that involved extensive dancing and singing while wearing matching wraps or *kangas*, usually accompanied by drummers. They often performed on ritual occasions such as weddings. *Lelemama* and other dance associations were precursors to later **organizations** that had a more political motive, as when **Bibi Titi Mohammed** in Tanzania turned to her dance groups to recruit women to the **nationalist** movement. *See also* TAARAB; TUFO.

LENSHINA, ALICE MULENGA (c. 1924–1978). Lenshina founded the Lumpa Church in Zambia in 1953. Her name, Lenshina, is a corruption of "regina," for queen; "Lumpa" in the church name is Bemba for "better than the rest." She had married a Bemba man who was a convert to the Free Church of Scotland's Lubwa Mission. She claimed that Jesus Christ called her to be a prophet after she had died four times, "rising again" after each death. She said she had been given a true Bible, from which she preached an anti-**witchcraft** doctrine. She quickly gathered a large following, estimated at 50,000 to 100,000 during the peak years in the 1950s. People were initially drawn by the strict moral code of the church, which did not allow drinking, smoking, **dancing**, or adultery in addition to a complete renunciation of magic and witchcraft.

By the early 1960s many of her followers left the church and became involved in party politics, especially in the United National Independence Party (UNIP). There developed a strong animosity between UNIP and the Lumpa church, and many churches were burned in arson attacks blamed on UNIP supporters. After Zambia became independent in 1964, serious battles broke out between government authorities and church members, who refused to pay taxes. Over 500 people died in a three-week time span. On 3 August 1964 the new president, Kenneth Kaunda, outlawed the church, and Alice Lenshina surrendered on 12 August. Some church members continued to fight, though most moved to the Democratic Republic of the Congo where they settled. Lenshina was detained until December 1975, and restricted to Zambia's capital, Lusaka, upon her release. The church continued with a new name, as the Jerusalem Church of Christ. *See also* TAX REVOLTS.

LEROTHOLI, 'MAMOHATAO TABITHA 'MASENTLE (1938–2003). Lerotholi was the **Queen Mother** of Lesotho. She served as regent three times during vacancies in the office of king, first from 5 June to 20 November 1970 after the removal of Moshoeshoe II and the brief assumption of power by Prime Minister Leabua Jonathan, until the re-accession of Moshoeshoe II. Then she served from 6 to 12 November 1990, after the deposition of Moshoeshoe II by a military junta and until the installation of Letsie III. And finally she was regent from 15 January to 7 February 1996 after the death of Moshoeshoe II in a car accident and until the election and re-installation of Letsie III.

LESBIANISM. Lesbian women and homosexuality in general are often portrayed as unknown in African societies, and it is certainly the case that most modern African governments do not recognize the civil rights of gay men and lesbians. Nonetheless, there is a growing body of evidence indicating that lesbians have existed in such diverse locales as women living in **seclusion** in East Africa and in urban centers in South Africa. Nor are lesbians found only among women of European descent. South Africa is exceptional in the inclusion of a clause in its post-apartheid constitution that prohibits discrimination on the basis of sexual orientation. The practice of **woman–woman marriage** has been seen by some as evidence of lesbianism, though that institution did not necessarily include sexual activity between the women involved.

LESOTHO NATIONAL COUNCIL OF WOMEN. Founded in 1961, this national **organization** focused on **education** and training, and offered **literacy** and handicrafts classes as well as organizing self-help activities such as poultry farming. In the 1970s there were 50 clubs in urban areas and 30 clubs in rural areas, with a total of 2,000 members.

LESOTHO WOMEN'S INSTITUTE. The Lesotho Women's Institute was founded in 1961 to provide training for young women school-leavers who did not have the expertise needed to find **employment**. It promoted women's welfare through instruction in sewing, cooking, tie-dyeing, and other skills that could be used in income-generating projects. The institute held seminars on **human rights**, **democratization**, **HIV/AIDS**, and other current topics of interest to women. The institute also ran a **childcare** center in Maseru.

LESSING, DORIS (NÉE TAYLOR) (1919–). Lessing is a renowned novelist who wrote her first important books about her years in Zimbabwe (Southern Rhodesia) and South Africa. She was born in Iran (then Persia), and lived in Southern Rhodesia from 1924–1949. She moved to London in 1950. Her first novel, *The Grass is Singing* (1950) was set in Zimbabwe, and her Martha Quest quintet, *The Children of Violence* (1952–1969) was primarily set in southern Africa. Her books and short stories from that period chronicle the lives of young white women and men trying to practice progressive politics under repressive racist regimes, and often address the oppression of Africans and the complexity of interracial relationships. She published her autobiography in two volumes, *Under My Skin* (1994) and *Walking in the Shade* (1997), and she has also published numerous novels, short stories, and essays that address modern women's condition. In 2001 she published a novel partly set in Africa and critical of international **development** aid agencies, *The Sweetest Dream*.

LEVIRATE. The levirate is the **marriage** practice whereby a **widow** is remarried to her deceased husband's brother. The custom was prevalent in the past in many patrilineal African cultures, though the extent is difficult to ascertain. In some instances the father's family would claim any children from the marriage as part of their clan, and encourage the mother of those children to remarry within the clan as a strategy to maintain that link. Widows in that situation would sometimes prefer to remarry within their deceased husband's family in order to keep contact with their children as well as to retain access to land they had cultivated. In most areas this practice is now seen as a form of forced marriage and is discouraged if not actually illegal.

LIBERIA WOMEN'S LEAGUE. The League was founded in 1931 at Monrovia College as a means to promote the involvement of women in the development of Liberia. In the 1950s the Women Social and Political Movement superseded the League as a women's forum.

LIGA FEMININA MOÇAMBICANA (LIFEMO) / LEAGUE OF MOZAMBICAN WOMEN. LIFEMO was founded in 1962 soon after the establishment of the Frente de Libertação de Moçambique (Frelimo)/Mozambique Liberation Front, with which it was affiliated. It was a typical **political party organization**, with the leadership dominated by the wives of the male Frelimo leaders. After it held its first congress in exile in Tanzania in 1966, it came under increasing criticism from Frelimo for its elitism and lack of political acumen concerning events within Mozambique. It was joined by the Destacamento Feminino/Female Detachment, an armed group of women soldiers, and eventually replaced by **Organização da Mulher Moçambicana (OMM) / Organization of Mozambican Women**.

LIGA INDEPENDENTE DA MULHER ANGOLANA (LIMA) / INDEPENDENT LEAGUE OF ANGOLAN WOMEN. LIMA was affiliated with the União Nacional para a Independência Total de Angola (UNITA)/National Union for the Total Liberation of Angola, the party lead by Jonas Savimbi which fought the ruling party Movimento Popular para a Libertação de Angola (MPLA)/People's Movement for the Liberation of Angola for three decades. See also POLITICAL PARTY ORGANIZATIONS.

LIKIMANI, MUTHONI GACHANJA (1926–). Likimani is a Kenyan fiction writer whose best-known work, *Passbook Number F47927*, told the stories of women involved in the **Mau Mau** struggle in Kenya in the 1950s. She was well known as a producer and actor on the Voice of Kenya (Kenyan Broadcasting Commission), and also published *What Does a Man Want?* (1974) and a series of biographical sketches, *Women of Kenya: In the Decade of Development* (1985). Likimani was also a founding member of the **National Council of Women of Kenya** (NCWK).

LIKING, WEREWERE. *See* WEREWERE LIKING.

LITERACY. In many African countries, girls had less access to western **education**, and a legacy of very low literacy rates persists among women. In Mozambique for instance fewer than 10 percent of women are literate in Portuguese, the official language; in Mali, only 10 percent of women are literate in French. But such extremely low rates are not found for the entire continent, as statistics suggest that overall women's literacy rates are rising, from 40 percent in 1995 to 50 percent in 2000. See Table 3, Literacy, Percentage of women over age 25 who were literate, 1990s.

Table 3. Literacy—Percentage of Women Over Age 25 Who Were Literate in the 1990s.

Country	Percentage	Country	Percentage
Benin	12	Mauritius	69
Botswana	60	Namibia	65
Burundi	18	Niger	3
Cameroon	32	São Tomé e Príncipe	46
Cape Verde	37	Senegal	12
Central African Republic	13	Seychelles	78
Côte d'Ivoire	15	Sudan	26
Djibouti	13	Swaziland	54
Kenya	46	Uganda	33
Malawi	25	Zambia	47
Mali	9	Zimbabwe	67
Mauritania	17		

LITERATURE. Although more women write and publish fiction, both short stories and novels, there continue to be constraints on female authors. Women were less likely to have the time to pursue a writing career, and they faced opposition from male family members have gone so far as burning manuscripts to prevent women from publishing. Some suggested that women were more modest, and therefore hesitated to submit their manuscripts for publication. In Zimbabwe by 1987, as one example, 179 men had been published compared to only 31 women. Women writers have found strength in working together in associations such as the **Zimbabwe Women Writers** group, and by organizing the Women Writers Conference affiliated with the Zimbabwe International Book Fair in 1999. African women writers have also won important awards, including the Commonwealth Writers Prize (Africa region), which has been won by **Tsitsi Dangarembga**, **Nadime Gordimer**, Margaret Ogola, and **Yvonne Vera**.

Among the best known and most widely read authors are **Ama Ata Aidoo**, **Mariama Bâ**, **Buchi Emecheta**, **Bessie Head**, **Flora Nwapa**, and **Miriam Tlali**, who have all addressed women's situation in modern African societies. Other writers of note include **Calixthe Beyala**, **Werewere Liking**, and **Rebeka Njau**. Authors have adopted a variety of techniques, sometimes drawing from **oral traditions**, as with **Barbara Kimenye** and **Grace Ogot**. Autobiography has been an important genre as well, with books from **Jane Creider**, **Noni Jabavu**, **Ellen Kuzwayo**, **Emily Ruete**, **Joyce Sikakane**, and **Charity Waciuma**, while others have found success writing short stories, as with **Leila Aboulela** and **Juliana Makuchi Nfah-Abbenyi**. Yet others have written in local languages for a specific audience, such as Hausa writers **Bilkisu Funtuwa** and **Balaraba Ramat Yakubu** and **Caroline Khaketla** in Lesotho. Other authors of European descent who have gained renown for writing about Africa include **Isak Dinesen** and **Doris Lessing**. *See also* JOURNALISM; POETRY; THEATER.

LOBOLA (VAR. *LOBOLO*). *Lobola* or a variation is the most common term in southern Africa for **bridewealth**.

LOKKO, MARY. An early Ghanaian political activist, Lokko was active in the West African Youth League in the 1930s. She initially became involved with the issue of the Italian-Abyssinian conflict, and drew attention because of the intensity of her beliefs. An editorial in the local paper *Vox Populi* commented that she was a "noble example of sincere racial sympathy," and in January 1936 the political leader I. T. A. Wallace-Johnson suggested to the organization that she be named as his assistant. She was perhaps the first West African woman to hold an official position in a modern political organization. She often spoke up to encourage and support women's involvement in the Youth League. There is little further information about her background or her life after the 1930s.

LOPES, BERTINA (c. 1935–). Lopes, a painter and sculptor admired internationally, was born in Lourenço Marques (now Maputo), Mozambique, to a Portuguese father and an African mother. Her early schooling was in Mozambique, and her later training was in Portugal where she earned a degree in painting and sculpture. In 1953 she returned to Mozambique and taught in a technical school until 1962. She was influenced by **Noémia de Sousa**'s **poetry**, and incorporated social themes into her **art**. She traveled to Portugal to study ceramics with a Gulbenkian Foundation fellowship, and because of the increasing intransigience of Portuguese colonialism in the 1960s she chose to remain in exile, moving to Rome where she has resided ever since. She has actively painted, sculpted, and exhibited her art, winning numerous awards. In 2002 in Rome an exhibition of her art, titled "Fragments of Distant Lands," commemorated the 10th anniversary of the Peace Accord that brought an end to conflict in Mozambique.

LOZIKEYI (VAR. LOZIGEYI) (?–1919). Lozikeyi was the senior queen and one of the favored wives out of 82 wives of the Ndebele ruler Lobengula in Matabeleland (later part of Zimbabwe) until 1893. Though she had only daughters, she played an influential part in championing a co-wife's son in his attempt to succeed his father. Known as an outspoken woman, she retired to an island in the Bembezi River which was known as the "Queen's Location." *See also* POLYGYNY; XWALILE.

LUMPA CHURCH. *See* LENSHINA, ALICE MULENGA.

– M –

MAATHAI, WANGARI (1940–). A Kenyan **environmental** leader who trained in veterinary anatomy, she was awarded the 2004 Nobel Peace Prize. According to some sources she was the first African woman to earn a Ph.D., in 1971 from the University of Nairobi where she later taught; she was certainly the first Kenyan woman to do so. She was instrumental in organizing the **Green Belt Movement** in 1977, in concert with the **National Council of Women in Kenya**, which she chaired from 1981 to 1987. Among her many awards, Maathai received the United Nations Environmental Global 500 Award in 1989, the 1991 Africa Prize, and in 2004 the $100,000 Sophie Prize (named after the 1990s international bestseller "Sophie's World") for her work for the environment, justice and **human rights**.

Maathai has been involved with political movements for grassroots empowerment and increased democracy in Kenya, and incurred the enmity of former President Daniel Arap Moi. Maathai successfully worked to stop the construction of a 60-story building on the outskirts of Nairobi, and was able to keep that area as part of the Green Belt. She participated in a hunger strike for democracy, based at a peaceful camp set up in Nairobi's Uhuru Park in 1992 that was attacked by the police. Maathai was hospitalized as a result, and spent part of 1993 in hiding from government oppression. She helped organize the Forum for the Restoration of Democracy (FORD), and ran unsuccessfully for president in 1997 as the Liberal Party candidate. In 2002 Maathai was elected to the Kenyan parliament and named as deputy minister of environment, natural resources and wildlife under the government of President Mwai Kibaki in January 2003.

MACHEL, GRAÇA SIMBINE (1945–). Machel has been a significant political leader in Mozambique and internationally, as well as holding the rare distinction of being the **first lady** of two countries (the only other woman in history to do that was Eleanor of Aquitane). She was born in Mozambique and educated in modern languages at Lisbon University in Portugal. She joined the Frente de Libertação de Moçambique (FRELIMO)/Mozambique Liberation Front in 1972, and went to Tanzania where she received military training. She married Samora Machel shortly after he became Mozambique's first president after independence. Graça Machel was appointed minister of **education** in 1975, and served until 1990; she was the only female government minister in Mozambique during those years. She was also active in the **Organização da Mulher Moçambicana** (OMM)/ Organization of Mozambican Women and in the FRELIMO Central Committee. Samora Machel was killed in 1986 in a plane crash engineered by the apartheid regime in South Africa. In 1998 she married Nelson Mandela while he was president of South Africa.

Graça Machel has been active in the United Nations, focusing on the problem of child soldiers around the world and drawing from her observations in Mozambique in the 1980s. She heads **a nongovernmental organization** she initiated, the Fundação para o Desenvolvimento da Comunidade/Foundation for Community Development, which supports a variety of child-oriented projects and spearheaded the women's groups who advocated for the **Protocol on the Rights of Women in Africa** in 2003. She was also appointed chancellor of South Africa's University of Cape Town (UCT) in 1999, and added the life presidency of a UCT student community outreach group, Students' Health and Welfare Centres Organization, to her portfolio in 2001. Among her many awards are the 1992 Hunger Project's Africa Prize and the 1998 North-South Prize from the Council of Europe's North-South Centre, both in recognition of her work as president of the National Organization of Children of Mozambique.

MACHEL, JOSINA (1946–1971). A leader in the Mozambican armed struggle to end Portuguese **colonialism**, she was head of the social affairs section of the Frente de Libertação de Moçambique (FRELIMO)/Mozambique Liberation Front, which meant she was responsible for women's activities, including establishing orphanages to care for children whose parents died during the struggle. She was married to Samora Machel, the leader of FRELIMO. Josina Machel became ill and died in Tanzania at the age of 25. The date of her death, April 7, is celebrated as Mozambican Women's Day.

MAENDELEO YA WANAWAKE ORGANISATION (MYWO) / WOMEN'S PROGRESS ORGANIZATION. This national **organization** in Kenya was founded in 1952 with the support of Canadian and

British charity groups, and has a history of involvement in **development** projects, **literacy** programs, and political action for women. It was initially affiliated with the Associated Country Women of the World, and focused on teaching domestic skills. It published a newspaper in the 1950s in Luo, Kikamba, Swahili, and Kikuyu. For the most part, its leaders worked to expand the membership while not angering male leaders of the ruling party, the Kenya African National Union (KANU). An exception was **Ruth Habwe** who introduced more political resolutions in the 1960s. A prominent leader of MYWO was Jane Kiano, who was chair from 1971 to 1984, and was responsible for a huge growth in the numbers of branches and members, to 327,000 members in 1983. Beginning in 1967 it published *Sauti ya Mabibi* (*Voice of Women*), though it apparently ceased publication in the 1970s. In 1986 the government dissolved the executive and integrated Maendeleo's activities into KANU, though it was restored to autonomy in 1991. By 2000 it claimed a membership of 1.5 million women. In 2004 its website, http://www.maendeleo-ya-wanawake.org/, listed projects in maternal and child **health** and family planning, **HIV/AIDS**, **environment** and energy conservation, leadership training, income generation, and traditional practices. Lisa Aubrey published a study of MYWO's history and politics, *The Politics of Development Cooperation: NGOs, Gender and Partnership in Kenya* (1997). *See also* NATIONAL COUNCIL OF WOMEN OF KENYA.

MAGAIA, LINA JÚLIA FRANCISCO (1945–). Magaia is a Mozambican journalist, short story writer, and politician. Educated in the mission school system, in the 1960s she joined the Frente de Libertação de Moçambique (FRELIMO)/Mozambique Liberation Front (later Partido Frelimo/Frelimo Party). She graduated from the University of Lisbon with a B.Sc. in economics in 1975. She publicized the atrocities of the war between the ruling party Frelimo and the anti-government forces of Renamo of the 1980s in *Dumba Nengue: Run for Your Life: Peasant Tales of Tragedy in Mozambique* (1988, orig. pub. in Portuguese, *Dumba Nengue: Histórias trágicas do banditismo*, 1987). Magaia worked in agricultural outreach beginning in 1980 when she was asked by President Samora Machel to become involved in the Green Zones **agricultural cooperative** projects outside of Maputo. In 1994 she won a seat in parliament.

MAGIRA. A Kanuri term that referred to the senior female of the royal household, it is sometimes translated as **queen mother**. A woman who was *magira* could rule in her own right, as did **Aisa Kili Ngirmaramma** in the 16th century.

MAI CHAZA (?–1960). Mai Chaza (Mother Chaza) was a woman who founded a religious movement in colonial Zimbabwe. She had been active in the Wesleyan Methodist Church and its **prayer groups** which were known as *ruwadzano*. In 1948 she was accused of causing a sister-in-law's death and was driven from her home. Mai Chaza was believed to have perished, but she had fallen into a coma from which she recovered and went on to become a healer. She founded the Mai Chaza Church, which was headquartered in a village named Guta ra Jehova, the City of God. Her church was especially popular with women because it accentuated **motherhood** and **fertility**. Barren women who traveled to worship at Guta ra Jehova were touched by Mai Chaza, who claimed they would conceive and have a successful pregnancy.

MAKEBA, MIRIAM (1932–). Makeba is a singer from South Africa who attained international recognition for her interpretation of songs and **music** from southern Africa. Born in Johannesburg, she began singing in school choirs, was asked to join the Manhattan Brothers in 1952, and initially released one of her best known songs, "Pata Pata," in 1956. She played herself in the 1959 semi-documentary "Come Back Africa." In 1960 she left South Africa and was then not allowed to return until 1990. While in exile Makeba became active in the anti-**apartheid** movement, speaking before the United Nations General Assembly. She was briefly married to South African trumpet player, Hugh Masekela, and later to black American activist, Stokely Carmichael (Kwame Ture, 1941–1998). After that marriage made her unwelcome in the United States the couple lived in Guinea and she took Guinean citizenship. She continued recording and performing her unique style of popular African music, releasing nearly three dozen albums and compact discs over the years. *See* also DOROTHY MASUKA.

MAKERI, WANGU WA (c. 1856–1915). Wangu wa Makeri was named "headman" of a Kikuyu community at Weithaga at a time when it was an unusual and notable achievement. She was raised in a traditional Kikuyu household, married, and had six children. By the time she reached a mature age and her children were grown, British **colonial** authorities were in place in Kenya. They established a system of indirect rule, whereby Africans, nearly always men, acted as local authorities regarding tax collection, road maintenance, and other tasks related to keeping order. Wangu was a popular and charismatic woman who was named to the position of "headman" (local authority) in 1902. She played an important role in mediating the early contacts between the Kikuyu and British settlers. Wangu set an example when she sent her own son to the **mission** school in 1903. But she was a controversial figure, in part because of her responsibility for carrying out colonial demands, and sentiment began to turn against her. In 1909 she participated in a *kibaata* **dance**, where her abbreviated traditional dress led to accusations that she had danced naked. Those who wanted to remove her from power used that incident to force her resignation. Her story is told by Mary W. Wanyoike, *Wangu wa Makeri* (2002), in the first contribution about a woman to the "Makers of Kenya's History" series.

MAKUCHI. *See* NFAH-ABBENYI, JULIANA MAKUCHI.

MALDOROR, SARAH (NÉE DUCADOS). Maldoror is a filmmaker, born in France to parents from Guadeloupe, who was active in pan-African organizations in Paris in the 1950s and 1960s. She learned filmmaking in Moscow, and also worked with Gillo Pontecorvo on the landmark film *Battle of Algiers* (1966). She is best known for *Sambizanga*, an Angolan film made in 1972 that was based on the novel *The True Life of Domingos Xavier* by Angolan writer Luandino Vieira. It was filmed in Congo (Brazzaville) using Angolan **nationalists** in exile as actors. The film, about the impact of Portuguese **colonialism** on a rural family, focuses on a young woman searching for her husband who has been jailed; when she finds him he has already died from the torture he suffered in custody. Maldoror was married to Mario Pinto de Andrade, a leader in the Angolan resistance organization and later ruling party Movimento Popular para a Libertação de Angola (MPLA)/People's Movement for the Liberation of Angola. She has made over two dozen films, both documentary and fiction, many of them quite short, since 1970.

MAM DIARRA BOUSSO (1833–1866). Mam Diarra Bousso was regarded as an important and saintly person and is the focus of a growing group of followers, especially women. Her son, Sheik Amadou Bamba (1850–1927), founded the **Islamic** Mouride movement in Senegal. Her parents were very devout and she was raised to be familiar with the Koran. She married and had three children, but died young of illness. Frequently the scholarly literature discusses only the male aspects of Islamic brotherhoods, although women are prominent among the followers of Sheik Bamba and in other Muslim communities. Women have also developed a special devotion for Mam Diarra Bousso, who is remembered as a model mother. Her burial place in the village of Porokhane has become a site of pilgrimage for pious women who revere her generosity and kindness, especially related to women's concerns over **infertility**, **marriage** problems, and economic difficulties. The effort and expense of traveling to Porokhane brings blessings to the women who make the pilgrimage. Eva Evers Rosander has written "Mam Diarra Bousso: La bonne mere de Porokhane, Senegal," *Africa* (2003), and in *Jenda* at www .jendajournal.com (2003). *See also* MAGAT DIOP, SOKHNA.

MAMABENZI. The term *mamabenzi*, sometimes *nana benzi* or *nana benz*, refers to wealthy **market women** in West Africa who drove or were believed to drive Mercedes Benz cars. In Togo they were noted as traders in imported wax-printed fabric.

MAMI WATA (MAMMY WATER). Mami Wata, a popular **goddess** originating in the Niger Delta region of Nigeria and in Ghana, was sometimes considered a river goddess. She was associated with water and its life-giving properties, and was viewed by some as a protector of pregnant women. She was commonly pictured as partially a sea creature such as a mermaid or a snake, and in some areas she was identified with crocodiles. She was associated with wealth, and ideas about reciprocity were central to her adherents who believed there must be a balance between giving and receiving. Her flexible nature, combining power and danger, made her a strong presence in traditional and modern contexts across western Africa, where she was the subject of a 1960s popular song, and was pictured in murals and other public venues. In the 1990s Christian fundamentalists began to portray her as an evil presence, and negative ideas about Mami Wata began to spread throughout the region. Many West African societies had similar water-related deities, including **Osun**, **Yemoja**, Faro among the Bambara, Tano in Ghana, and Bia in Côte d'Ivoire.

MAMOCHISANE (MA-MUCHISANE) (fl. MID-19TH CENTURY). Mamochisane ruled the Kololo kingdom in western Zambia after her father, Sebitwane, died. When her father was expanding Kololo control, she was captured by the Lozi, but was treated well and released. Her father later designated her to govern the central province, one of four Kololo territories, and he named her to succeed him as overall ruler upon his death in 1851. She abdicated to pursue a private life, and her brother Sekeletu, ascended the throne.

MANDELA, WINNIE (FULL NAME NOMZANO NOBANDLA WINIFRED MADIKIZELA-MANDELA) (1936–). For many years Winnie Mandela was a leader of the anti-**apartheid** movement in South Africa, using her status as the wife of imprisoned activist Nelson Mandela to agitate for change. She was born in Pondoland, South Africa, and trained as a medical social worker. She married Nelson Mandela in 1958; his first wife was Evelyn Ntoko Mase (1922–2004) and he later married **Graça Machel**. Nelson Mandela was imprisoned from 1962 to 1990, and Winnie Mandela was herself subjected to repeated banning orders and imprisonment for her activities. She was active in the African National Congress (ANC), and helped found the **Black Women's Federation** and the Black Parents' Association in response to the Soweto uprising of 1976. She later gained notoriety for the involvement of her associates in the beating death of Stompie Seipei, a young member of a soccer team she sponsored. After Nelson Mandela was released from prison in 1990 they were **divorced**. She briefly held office as a deputy minister of arts, culture, science, and technology in the post-apartheid ANC government. Though she lost some stature as a result of her divorce and the soccer club scandal, many believed she was the target of a deliberate campaign by the government to diminish her importance in South African political life.

Mandela remained popular in South Africa, and was reelected chair of the **African National Congress Women's League** in 1997.

She went before the Truth and Reconciliation Commission in 1997 to clear her name, but the testimony indicated her involvement in a series of murders in the 1980s. She subsequently lost an election for deputy president of the ANC. In 2003 Mandela was convicted of fraud and theft along with her broker, and sentenced to four years in prison (although the sentence was suspended in 2004 and she did not go to jail). The fraud involved using her position in the Women's League to secure loans for bogus League employees; the theft charges related to her role in establishing phony funeral insurance programs and then embezzling the funds that were deposited. She maintained that she was innocent and had been tricked by associates; she planned to appeal, but resigned her seat in parliament and her position in the Women's League.

MANTSE BO ('MANTSEBO) (AMELIA 'MATSABA SEEISO GRIFFITH) (1902–1964). The first wife of a paramount chief in Lesotho, she was regent during the **colonial** period. Her husband was Seeiso Griffith who ruled for only 18 months before his death in 1940. She was then named by a council of leading men, the sons of Lesotho's founding king Moshoeshoe, to act as regent for her stepson Bereng, who was only two years old when his father died. The high commissioner accepted her appointment, but it was contested by her husband's brother who took her to court. The high court confirmed her as regent in a special session in 1943, and Mantse Bo ruled until Bereng was installed as paramount chief Moshoeshoe II in 1960. During her 20 years as regent she brought issues concerning women to the forefront, as when she overturned a colonial **law** that harassed female **beer brewers** unfairly, or when she argued in 1962 that women should have equal access to credit and **inheritance**. She was also an early supporter of women chiefs as equal to male chiefs in status and salary, advocating this position in 1950 with the Basutoland [Lesotho] National Council.

MANYANO. *Manyano* is the term for a **prayer group** of women in South Africa (in Lesotho similar groups are called *kopanos*). The name is derived from the Xhosa for "to join" or "unite." The groups were started by African women within **Christian missions** and churches, especially among Methodists. In South Africa the Swiss

Mission reported that groups of women were meeting in the 1870s. Though focused on prayer and religious discussion, the groups offered support for women with problems in their **marriages**, in raising their children as Christians, and with other common issues, and for that reason were sometimes considered mothers' groups. Most followed strict rules for membership and attendance including abstinence from **alcohol**, and members wore matching attire. They were sometimes known as Women's Prayer and Service Unions, or similar designations. In Zimbabwe, where they were first established at the Methodist mission in 1929, they were called *ruwadzano*. *See also* BIBLEWOMEN; MAI CHAZA; MOTHERS' UNIONS; ORGANIZATIONS; RELIGION.

MAQEDA (fl. 10TH CENTURY BC). Often referred to as the Queen of Sheba (Saba), she was the founding ruler of Ethiopia in the 10th century BC. As the story is told in the *Kebre Negest*, she traveled to Jerusalem to learn from Solomon, and returned to Ethiopia to have his child, Menelik I. She abdicated in Menelik's favor when he was 22. In Arabic legends she is known as Bilkis.

MARKET WOMEN. Women throughout Africa have been active in market trading, but especially in West Africa they have been noted for the extent and strength of the markets. From the earliest days of European contact women were involved in the exchange of goods with traders along the coast. For many years women were able to exploit a position between the newcomer Europeans and established coastal communities to regulate trade and limit the expansion of European economic power. In some cases they married or formed other intimate relationships with European men who could provide access to imported goods. Some women became wealthy and renowned as a result of their trade, such as **Alimotu Pelewura, Madam Tinubu**, and **Omu Okwei**.

In many parts of West Africa women have been involved in market **organizations** and have had the responsibility of running the markets. That responsibility meant that market women were at the forefront of such actions as **tax revolts** and they were an organized source of support for various political movements. There were many such formal organizations, including the Association des Femmes Commerçantes du Mali/Association of Female Market Traders of Mali, **Ghana Market Women Association**, **Lagos Market Women's Association**, and the **Sierra Leone Market Women's Union**. In southern and eastern Africa many women began working as market vendors in the 1980s and 1990s as they faced increasing economic constraints that resulted from **structural adjustment**. By the late 1990s in Maputo, Mozambique, it was estimated the between 55 and 75 percent of women were involved in market trading, though many of them simply set up a cloth on a curb and could not afford to rent space in the formal cement markets.

Market women have been the focus of government criticism in many areas, resulting from perceptions of their wealth and political clout as well as from fears that their operations were a source of disease. At times markets were razed in response to official desires to control the female vendors. *See also* INFORMAL SECTOR; *IYALODE*; MAMABENZI.

MARKHAM, BERYL (1902–1986). Born in England, Markham lived in Kenya most of her life where she raised race horses and became a celebrated pilot. She moved to Kenya with her father when she was a child, and remained after he moved on to Peru. Her most notable accomplishment was to complete the first ever solo flight from east to west, flying from England to Nova Scotia, Canada, in 1936 in just under 22 hours. She married and **divorced** three times, and after living in the United States she settled in Kenya where she found success in breeding race horses. She published an autobiography, *West with the Night* (1942, reissued 1986).

MARRIAGE. There were a wide variety of marital forms across the continent of Africa, including traditional unions where families played a major role in choosing or approving of the choice of husband, marriages consecrated with **Christian** or **Islamic** rites, and marriages simply registered with government offices and marriage registries. Many countries have struggled to develop legal supports for women regarding **divorce**, **inheritance**, and other issues related to marital status and marriage experience. The enactment of **family laws** that respect sometimes contentious beliefs and practices concerning marriage have been a divisive issue in some countries.

There are still arranged marriages, as many African parents wish to control their daughters' choice of partner. Because they are interested in having their daughters marry young, Africa has the highest rate of girls between the ages of 15 and 19 already in a marriage, as high as 72 percent of adolescent girls being married in Mali (an unusually high percentage), and over 15 percent in 17 countries (in comparison, the U.S. rate is only 8 percent of teenage girls being married). The high rate for girls is not matched by teenage boys' marriage rates, which is rarely over 5 percent in any African nation. *See also* LAW; POLYGYNY; WOMAN–WOMAN MARRIAGE.

MARTIN-CISSÉ, JEANNE (1926–). Martin-Cissé was Guinea's ambassador to the United Nations. During her tenure she was elected to preside over the UN Security Council in 1972, the first African woman to serve in that position. She had previously served as secretary general of the **Conference of African Women** from 1962 to 1972. She was awarded the Lenin Peace Prize in 1975. After Martin-Cissé returned to Guinea she was appointed minister of social affairs from 1976 to 1984, when there was coup and she was arrested. She continued as an advocate for women's issues and in 2004 was a member of L'Association Internationale des Femmes Francophones/ International Association of Francophone Women.

MASUKA, DOROTHY (DOTTY) (1936–). Masuka was a prominent **musician** and jazz singer who was especially popular in southern African in the 1950s. She was born in Zimbabwe, recorded in South Africa and Zambia, and performed frequently in Malawi as well. She influenced her friend **Miriam Makeba** with her songs in a range of African languages, especially Zulu, Xhosa, and Ndebele. Masuka wrote and was the first to record "Pata Pata," which was made famous by Makeba. Masuka was forced into exile in 1961 when the **apartheid** government deemed her song about Patrice Lumumba, the recently assassinated leader of the Congo (Kinshasa), to be too political. She lived in Zambia where she worked as a flight attendant until she was able to return to Zimbabwe following independence there in 1980. Since 1992 she has been back in South Africa, and has released new recordings that have led to a revival of her career. In 2001 she released *Mzilikazi*, and in 2002 she toured to promote her compilation *The Definitive Collection*.

MATRILINEAL DESCENT. Matrilineal descent systems privilege the mother's family with the mother's brother playing an important role in the lives of his sister's children. Matrilineal societies, as described by Karla Poewe in *Matrilineal Ideology: Male-Female Dynamics in Luapula, Zambia* (1981), embodied an idea of community organization that "favours the personal and social power of women." The kinship network focused on the relationship between sisters and between siblings more generally, giving place of honor to mothers and their children rather than fathers and their children. Mothers were often revered, and frequently all senior female kin were considered to be "mothers" to the kin group. The role of a woman's brother commonly was of greater importance to her children than her husband (their father). All known matrilineal societies were based on agricultural production, and tended to have small-scale political systems. Poewe discussed matrilineality as a system of political economy that allowed women to have greater individual control over their production.

Also integral to the society were assumptions about an abundance of resources and the ability to share communally, which was very different from ideas of scarcity and control over the distribution of resources. When cash crops were introduced, or the society in other ways allowed some members to become wealthier than others, there was a tendency for men who controlled the new resources to leave their property to their sons rather than their nephews, rupturing the basic structure of matrilineal kin relations. Men who desired greater control over their own production wanted to pass their goods on to their own children, not to the uncontrollable children of their sisters.

There are complex issues involved in understanding when a society is "matrilineal" or "patrilineal." Although these are often used as descriptive terms, their application to a society does not always indicate the many varieties of matrilineality, or how a society might include some practices considered matrilineal and others considered patrilineal. Reckoning descent through mothers and aunts, making the mother-child bond the central one, and emphasizing matrilocal residence (where a man typically would move into his wife's village and home) all indicate what has been considered "matrilineality." In peoples' actual lives such a schematic approach to society ignores the existing flexibility of their kin relationships.

MAU MAU. Mau Mau was the name given by the British to a **nationalist** revolt in Kenya in the 1950s which was lead by the Land and Freedom Army. The goal was to end British **colonialism** and reclaim **land** that had been alienated by the colonial government. While women played an important role, they have been neglected in the conventional histories of the movement. A study by Cora Presley (*Kikuyu Women, the Mau Mau Rebellion, and Social Change in Kenya*, 1992) indicated that women contributed in several ways. Women had a history of political activism in Kenya, and their participation in Mau Mau was an extension of that experience. Women were present at the oath-taking ceremonies that marked membership in the Land and Freedom Army, they were recognized as district organizers, they were listed among the prisoners (**Margaret Kenyatta** was one of those arrested), and a small number rose to high positions within the organization. Their work was particularly crucial in the provision of food and supplies to the Mau Mau members who were living in the forests outside the urban areas. Women's roles in the Mau Mau rebellion have been described in fiction by **Muthoni Likimani**, and in memoir by **Wambui Otieno**.

MAURITIUS ALLIANCE OF WOMEN (MAW). Initially formed as the Association of Indian Women in Mauritius in 1971 with a particular interest in encouraging Indian cooking and embroidery skills, it maintained its base in the Indian community after broadening its membership and interests in 1978. It then changed its name to the Mauritius Alliance of Women, and served as an umbrella organization for 25 women's **non-governmental organizations**, including the **Women Self-Help Association** and the Association Nationale des Femmes Mauriciennes/National Association of Mauritian Women, which was founded in 1975 with the primary goal of improving women's status. MAW celebrated its 18th anniversary in 1996 with a national meeting. Its ongoing projects include a series of seminars on issues including **education**, food production, **peace**, and

housing. Through its affiliates it is involved in family planning and has established a **childcare** center.

MAWA (c. 1770s–1848). As a member of the Zulu royal family in South Africa, she served under her nephews Shaka and Dingane as the royal representative to a military settlement (c. 1815–1840). In 1842 the candidate she supported in a succession dispute lost, and she fled with several thousand refugees to Natal, where she was allowed to settle permanently by the British colonial authority.

MAXEKE, CHARLOTTE (NÉE CHARLOTTE MAKGOMO MANYE) (1874–1939). Charlotte Maxeke was a leading figure in South African struggles for justice. She had the opportunity as a young woman in the early 1890s to travel to England and the United States as part of a singing group (billed as the African Native Choir, the group included Charlotte's younger sister, Katie Makanya; Katie's story was told in Margaret McCord's *The Calling of Katie Makanya: A Memoir of South Africa* [1995]). While in the United States Maxeke was offered entrance to Wilberforce University in Ohio, which was under the auspices of the African Methodist Episcopal (AME) Church. She met and married fellow South African Rev. Marshall Maxeke while in the U.S. She earned her B.Sc. degree in 1905, and is recognized as the first African woman from South Africa to earn a college degree. Back in South Africa Maxeke and her husband worked to establish the AME Church, and organized the Wilberforce Institute as an institution of higher learning for Africans. She was later president of the Women's Missionary Society of the AME Church. In 1913 Maxeke organized women's demonstrations against the government's plan to extend to women the requirement that Africans carry identity passes, and she went on to help found the **Bantu Women's League**, later the **African National Congress Women's League**. She also contributed as a **journalist**, and she wrote and spoke frequently on women's condition, notably in a speech in 1930 that criticized the negative impact of the migratory labor system on family life. *See also* DEFIANCE CAMPAIGN; FEDERATION OF SOUTH AFRICAN WOMEN; PASS LAWS.

MBA, NINA EMMA (1944–2002). Mba was a trailblazing **historian** who wrote about Nigerian women. Born in Australia, she moved to

Nigeria in 1966, married Benedict Mba, and completed a Ph.D. in history at the University of Ibadan. Her dissertation was published as *Nigerian Women Mobilized: Women's Political Activity in Southern Nigeria, 1900-1965* (1982). Mba was committed to Nigerian history, teaching at the University of Lagos for many years, serving on the executive board of the Historical Society of Nigeria, and helping found the **Women's Research and Documentation Center (WORDOC)**. She also published a column in the Lagos newspaper *Vanguard* and numerous other historical works. Her contributions were recognized in 2001 when she was conferred with the chieftaincy title of Odu of Umudei in Anambra State.

M'BAYE, ANNETTE D'ERNEVILLE (1926–). A **journalist** and poet, she was program director for Radio Senegal. Born and educated in Senegal, she earned her teaching degree in 1945 and initially was the general superintendent at the École Normal in Rufisque. She studied education in Paris, and returned to Senegal in 1959. In 1963 she began working at the radio station, and also established *Awa*, an early French-language magazine for African women. She published a book of **poetry** in 1965, *Poèmes Africains*.

MBOJ, NDATE YALA (fl. 1840s–1860s). A Senegalese **queen mother** in the 19th century, she ruled the Walo kingdom from 1847 until the French conquered it in 1854, though she continued to exercise some authority into the 1860s. The French tried to incorporate her into their plans as early as 1841 when they favored her marriage to their candidate, Yerim Mbanik, but she consistently opposed their incursion into her territory. She married a second time, to Maroso Tase Jop, and her son from that marriage, Sidia Jop, eventually emerged as the Walo leader. *See also* MBOJ, NJEMBOT.

MBOJ, NJEMBOT (c. 1800–1846). Njembot Mboj was a **queen mother** (locally called *linger*) in Walo in present-day Senegal. She played a key role during a time of civil unrest, as the French withdrawal in 1829 brought about a struggle between the Moorish Trarza and the French. She agreed to a marriage with the Trarza leader, which united the kingdoms on each side of the Senegal River and presented a much stronger opposition to French interests. She was succeeded in office by her younger sister, **Ndate Yala Mboj**.

MDLULI, LABOTSIBENI GWAMILE (1858–1925). Labotsibeni was a key figure in ruling circles in Swaziland during a crucial historic period. She was born into a family with close connections to the ruling Dlamini clan, and was raised within the royal household. She was the **senior wife** of Mbandzeni when he ruled from 1874 to 1889, served as **queen mother** when their son Bhunu was on the throne from 1894 to 1899, and was then queen regent from December 1899 to 1921 for her infant grandson Mona who eventually ruled as Sobhuza II. In the Swazi system of dual leadership Labotsibeni was viewed as a co-ruler and was not subservient to the male kin with whom she ruled. She was an intelligent and forceful personality who played a central role in maintaining the cohesiveness of Swazi political structures in the face of aggressive **colonialism**, and whose desire to negotiate was in opposition to Bhunu's wish to engage in all-out warfare with the encroaching British interests. She was particularly noted for her role in regaining Swazi land that had been signed away to British concession holders, and for introducing an extensive system of **education**. Labotsibeni remarked that European power "lies in money and in books; we too will learn. We too will be rich."

MEER, FATIMA (1929–). A leading activist for women in South Africa, Meer was one of the founders of the **Federation of South African Women** and one of the organizers of the 1956 **Defiance Campaign**. In 1977 she became president of the **Black Women's Federation**. She has published a range of genres, including essays, historical studies, biographies, and fiction. *See also* INDIAN WOMEN'S ASSOCIATION.

MEKATALILI (?–c. 1925). Mekatalili was active among the Giriama, a Kenyan coastal people. She led a revolt beginning in July 1913 against **colonial** labor recruitment and in favor of strengthening Giriama traditional government and reclaiming Giriama for the Giriama people. The success of her campaign was in part because she called women together and drew on the tradition of Mepoho, a female prophet who predicted that the land would deteriorate, youth would not respect their elders, and the Giriama would no longer bear healthy children. Mekatalili argued that the Europeans were causing these forecasts to come true. She was not from a leading family, but she was a **widow** (a stage of life that can allow women some freedom of movement and action) and was noted as a charismatic speaker who commanded respect. She helped call the Giriama together to make sacrifices and take oaths regarding the reinvigoration of Giriama political culture. The result was a halt to British colonial activities, as they could no longer recruit porters or collect taxes. Mekatalili was arrested in October 1913 and exiled to Kisii, 1,000 miles away, where she was sentenced to remain for five years. She escaped from prison and apparently returned to the coast, though she was recaptured and again sent to Kisii before the 1914 war between the British and the Giriama. By 1919 the British were still unable to govern directly, and they wished to reintroduce traditional government. Mekatalili was pardoned and returned to become head of the women's council, a position which had not been part of traditional Giriama government. She died in the mid-1920s.

MENETEWAB (MANTAUB) (1720s–1770s). She ruled Ethiopia from c. 1730 to 1769. Her name at birth was Walata Giorgis, and she was also known as Berhan Mogasa. A descendent on one side from Portuguese settlers, she married the Emperor Bakaffa in the 1720s. On his death in 1730 she became regent on behalf of her infant son, Iyasu II, and continued to rule when it became clear that he preferred to spend his time hunting and collecting rather than dealing with politics. Following his death in 1755 she continued to hold the throne in the name of her grandson Iyoas, who himself died at an early age in 1769. Menetewab lost popularity among the nobility because she favored her relatives for powerful positions. After her candidate for succession in 1769 did not become emperor, she moved to Cusquam where she continued to maneuver to enthrone her own choices. Her life story was recorded by James Bruce, the Scottish traveller. *See also* ZAUDITU; HEADS OF STATE.

MENSTRUATION. African methods of recognizing and dealing with the universal experience of menstruation offer insights into cultural ideas about women and their place in society. Researchers have investigated the relationship between the menses and African ideas about astronomy, social ideas about pollution (when the menses are believed to be unclean and even dangerous), and biological understanding of menstruation and **fertility**. Women in many parts of Africa rely on herbal remedies to control and improve the regularity of their menstrual cycles, including inducing the commencement of menstruation when it is determined to be late. As women sometimes believe that regular menses are necessary for cleansing the female body, herbal interventions are perceived as a way of managing the cycle, and are not seen as a form of **abortion**. In many societies the onset of puberty, marked by the first menstrual period, is the time for girls to undergo **initiation rites**, when they are formally acknowledged as entering into adult womanhood. Some areas seclude women during the days of their period, fearing the taint of menstrual blood as polluting and damaging, and women are sometimes expected to refrain from prayers in the mosque and other ritual activities as well as abstaining from sexual relations during those days each month.

MGQWETHO, NONTSIZI (CIZAMA) (fl. 1920s). An early South African **poet** who wrote in Xhosa, Mgqwetho published over 90 poems during the 1920s in the **nationalist** newspaper *Umteteli wa Bantu*. Her style meshed traditional praise poetry with a more modern sensibility, addressing such themes as her adherence to **Christianity** (she was probably a member of a ***manyano*** prayer group) and the role of women in redressing political inequality. She argued for black unity, and was critical of the African National Congress as she believed it brought dissension to the black community. Very little is known of her personal life, though it is likely that two articles published in 1897 and signed "Cizama" were also by her. That name suggests that she was from Tamara near Mount Coke. Other clues in her poems refer to her political activism, as she participated in a mass anti-**pass law** demonstration in 1919 in Johannesburg, and praised the well-known political leader **Charlotte Maxeke**.

MICRO-ENTERPRISE. Micro-enterprise is the practice of earning an income through establishing a very small business. As African economies deteriorated in the 1980s, many **urban** African women began tatting and selling lace, braiding hair, selling charcoal, preparing and selling snack foods, and similar projects which required little capital outlay and could be accomplished in their homes or on the streets. The increased extent of women's involvement in these businesses marked a change from earlier generations. *See also* INFORMAL SECTOR; MARKET WOMEN.

MIDWIVES. Women have had the primary responsibility for caring for pregnant women and delivering their babies. Midwives are women who have specialized **nursing** training in this field, while women with the necessary skills who have not had the nursing education are usually referred to as "traditional birth attendants (TBAs)." TBAs were sometimes involved in other female health issues, including having a role in girls' **initiation rites**. In Sudan women known as *dayas* were responsible for **female genital cutting** and **infibulation** during the rites as well as for re-opening women who had undergone infibulation so that they could give birth. TBAs without western training were often maligned by physicians as being unhygienic and unsafe. In the 19th century, with the global rise of formal and more technical medical training and care, the work of TBAs came under increasing attack, though in many cases they were the only option rural African women had for care in bringing healthy children into the world.

In many African countries nurse and nurse-midwife training courses developed in the first half of the 20th century under colonial auspices; in Sudan for example, two British women opened the Midwifery Training School in 1921 with the goal of creating a group of trained women who would operate in opposition to the TBAs. In Rhodesia (now Zimbabwe) the initial impetus in the late 19th and early 20th centuries was to provide European midwives to care for western women resident there. By the 1930s more African women were beginning to arrive at rural hospitals, though most continued to rely on the TBAs, known as *ambuyas* or *nyamukutas*. The first training program for African midwives, called maternity assistants, was established in 1945, and the program only offered a certificate in midwifery in 1962. *See also* FERTILITY.

MIGRATION. Migration from rural to urban areas, transnational migration within Africa, and international migration have been predominantly male activities, and it was often assumed that women who migrated were accompanying men, most often husbands or fathers. Recent research has brought women's migration experiences to the fore, highlighting the choices women have made to migrate on their own. While reports during the **colonial** era told of the breakdown of rural life that encouraged women to move to urban areas, women migrants often chose migration as their strategy to solve problems they faced, rather than fleeing those problems. In the late 20th century the numbers of young unmarried women migrating to urban areas to seek **education** or **employment** appeared to increase. Women have also been long-distance traders, often traveling to neighboring countries to buy and sell their goods, and in some more limited instances women from Congo (Kinshasa) have become wealthy through their efforts in traveling to Europe to buy cloth destined to be resold in the Congolese markets. Surveys of women migrants in southern Africa have highlighted their desire to visit family members who live across national borders, and to go shopping in stores in South Africa that carry goods not available in their country of origin. *See also* REFUGEES; URBANIZATION.

MISSIONS. For many African women, their first encounter with European **colonialism** was at a **Christian** mission school. From the 16th century when Catholic missionaries settled in what is now Angola and counseled both **Nzinga** and **Dona Beatriz Kimpa Vita**, missions have played an important role in the provision of girls' **education** through establishing schools, courses, and materials. Missionaries have also played a central role in introducing new ideas about **health** and hygiene, and often focused on **motherhood** as an entrée into African women's lives. Mission ideas about education and health were not always easily accepted and sometimes came into conflict with African preferences, though some women sought assistance for **infertility** and illness from the western missionaries. Missionaries also opposed such African practices as **bridewealth** and **polygyny**, stances which were sometimes opposed and sometimes welcomed by African women. In Kenya in the 1930s missionaries tried to end **initiation rites** and the practice of **female genital cutting**, but their efforts led to some Kikuyu embracing their own culture including the rites.

The reactions of African women to the mission presence varied greatly. Some women joined convents such as **Bannabikira** and the **Congregation of the Daughters of the Sacred Heart of Mary** and lived celibate lives, renouncing motherhood and family life. In 1979 there were over 33,000 women religious in Africa, of whom 12,000 were African women, most of them affiliated with African congregations. Other women taunted the African nuns for making what was perceived as a non-African choice. Women who wished to avoid a forced **marriage** sometimes found refuge in mission stations, and their negative stories about polygyny fed missionary ideas about the oppression experienced by African women. Other women who married monogamously according to Christian expectations found that life was too limiting, as they faced restrictions when wishing to leave an unhappy marriage.

European women came with the **White Sisters**, the **Immaculate Conception** order of nuns, other Catholic orders, and Protestant missionary groups. Many **western women** came as missionaries with the hope of converting Africans through the introduction of "modern" schooling and health care, though too often their starting point was the rejection of most aspects of African society. **Mary Slessor** was a well-known missionary in Nigeria; other European female missionaries came as the wives of male missionaries, or married a male missionary as a path to serving in Africa. Many suffered and died in Africa; one of the best known was Mary Livingstone, wife of the famed missionary-explorer David Livingtone; she is buried on the banks of the Zambezi River. Missionary work was also the task which brought **African American women** such as Susie Wiseman Yergan to Africa.

MMANTHATISI (c. 1780–c. 1836). Mmanthatisi lead the Tlokwa group of Sotho in South Africa and Lesotho during the mass migration known as *Difaqane*. She was born in present-day Orange Free State, and married the Tlokwa chief Mokotjo. When her husband died in 1817 she held the position of regent for her son, Sekonyela, who later became chief. Around 1820 the Zulu wars began to encroach on her territory and forced the Tlokwa to move to the west. Over the next few years she led their military campaigns as they joined in the generalized migration and raiding. It was unusual for a woman to have this position in a patrilineal society, and her activities attracted attention throughout the region. Roaming groups in the Vaal and Orange Rivers region were called *mantatees* in a mispronunciation of her name, and she was blamed for many actions taken by these other groups, though not by her personally. Her son joined her when she settled in northern Lesotho, though she continued to be active in Tlokwa politics after he assumed the chiefship around 1824.

MODJADJI (VAR. MUJAJI). Modjadji is the dynastic name for the women who ruled the Lovedu in South Africa; those rulers are known more popularly as **Rain Queens**.

MOHAMED, BIBI TITI (1926–2000). Bibi Titi Mohamed emerged as a **nationalist** leader in Tanzania, and was responsible for bringing women into the Tanganyika African National Union (TANU) in the 1960s. She was a Muslim woman who did not have a formal **education**, but she was involved in community **dance** groups, where she met women from around the city. Women had not been involved in TANU, and when John Hatch of the British Fabian Society visited in 1955 and asked where the women were, the male leaders turned to Bibi Titi to develop their women's section. Bibi Titi and her husband had two of the earliest TANU membership cards, but prior to 1955 there had not been a women's section. She turned to the dance groups to recruit women in the community to the nationalist cause. She was general secretary of the TANU Women's Section beginning in 1959. In 1962 all women's groups were merged into the **Umoja wa Wanawake wa Tanganyika** (UWT)/Tanzanian Women's Union, and Bibi Titi served as president of the UWT until 1967. She was also involved in the East African Women's Seminars and in organizing the **All African Women's Conference**. Bibi Titi was arrested in 1969 and charged with treason, a result of her friendship with a leading dissident and her own involvement with a constitutional reform campaign. She was convicted and sentenced to life in prison, though she was released through a presidential pardon in 1972. In 1985 she was recognized by Tanzanian President Julius Nyerere for her early nationalist work, and his public actions served as an apology for the time of the treason trial. Bibi Titi tells her story in Susan Geiger's

TANU Women: Gender and Culture in the Making of Tanganyikan Nationalism, 1955-1965 (1997).

MONGELLA, GERTRUDE (1945–). Mongella is an internationally known Tanzanian politician who has been committed to women's issues and has participated in numerous international meetings concerning women's rights, **peace**, and **development**. The daughter of farmers, she earned a degree in **education** from the University of Dar es Salaam, and was active in the ruling party, Chama cha Mapinduzi (CCM)/Party of the Revolution. She served in the Tanzanian parliament from 1980 to 1993, and was a member of the CCM central committee from 1977 to 1992. In 1982 she was the only woman member of the CCM central committee, and that year she was also appointed as minister of state in the Prime Minister's Office, which position she held until 1988. As leader of the Tanzanian delegation to the **Nairobi Women's Meeting** in 1985, she was named as one of the vice chairs of that meeting. Mongella was minister of lands, natural resources and tourism from 1986 to 1987, and after losing her position in the CCM central committee, she was minister without portfolio in the President's Office from 1987 to 1990. She was then named minister of state for women's affairs and served as Tanzanian High Commissioner to India from 1992 until she was named as secretary general of the United Nations Fourth World Conference on Women held in Beijing in 1995, the follow-up meeting of the **United Nations Decade for Women**. In 1996 Mongella was one of the founding members of the **non-governmental organization** Advocacy for Women in Africa. At the March 2004 inaugural meeting of the Pan-African Parliament of the African Union, Mongella was elected by an overwhelmlming majority (166 out of 202 sitting legislators) to serve a five-year term as president of the parliament. This action was considered an important commitment to women's rights, following on the July 2003 approval of the **Protocol on the Rights of Women in Africa**.

MORABI. Based in Cape Verde, this is a **non-governmental organization** formally called the Associação de Apoio à Auto-Promoção da Mulher no Desenvolvimento/Association of Support for Self-Promotion of Women in Development. It works to integrate women into **development** projects. In the 1990s it organized women fish vendors to visit women in Senegal who had learned methods of preserving and selling fish so that their incomes and livelihoods were improved.

MOTHERHOOD. Most African societies assumed that motherhood was a major goal of female adult life, and becoming a mother was a common measure of adulthood. Mothers were frequently treated with respect and even reverence, as they had contributed to the continuation of a lineage and to the ongoing development of the community. Motherhood was an essential step in the ritual life of the society as well, and various stages of pregnancy, child birth, and child-raising were all marked by special events. Mothers were recognized when their children reached puberty, and attention to the mothers of the new initiates was an important part of **initiation rites**.

During the **colonial** period many missionaries were concerned with introducing **health** and hygiene standards that would lower infant mortality rates, and they initiated a variety of courses and training programs designed to teach "mothercraft" to African women. As an important part of the colonial enterprise, such projects did not generally recognize the prior knowledge and experience of African mothers. African mothers faced new challenges when they moved to urban areas and began to enter the modern work force. They were hampered by the lack of **childcare** facilities and had fewer options for leaving their children in the care of kin. Some governments introduced maternity leave and and allowed time for nursing infants, acknowledging the importance of mothers.

In 2003 a conference on "Images of Motherhood" was convened in Dakar. Presentations addressed a range of issues focused on African and Nordic ideas about mothering and how those ideas had changed over time. One concern was the lack of theoretical discussion about motherhood; other papers addressed specific issues related to urban working mothers, the role of images of mothers in **Christianity** and **Islam**, and mothers in the legal system. The proceedings were published in *Jenda: A Journal of Culture and African Women Studies*, issues 4 and 5, available on line at www.jendajournal.com. *See also* INFERTILITY; MARRIAGE; MISSIONS.

MOTHERS' UNIONS. Many **Christian** denominations have sponsored meeting groups of mothers, where they can discuss religious and social issues. Though they are known by many different names, Mothers' Unions are often found affiliated to Catholic churches and were an important part of Anglican Church outreach in South Africa. The organization was originally founded in England in 1876 with the primary goal of encouraging **motherhood** among Christian women. One of the earliest affiliates in Africa was founded in Uganda in 1914. *See also MANYANO*; ORGANIZATIONS; RELIGION.

MOUVEMENT FEMININ DE LA SOLIDARITÉ AFRICAINE (MFSA) / WOMEN'S MOVEMENT OF AFRICAN SOLIDARITY. An association based in the Kwilu region of the then Belgian Congo (now the Democratic Republic of the Congo), it benefited from the organizing efforts of **Andrée Blouin**, who arrived in 1960 and quickly signed up 45,000 women in the Kwilu area. The MFSA was affiliated with the Parti Solidaire Africain (PSA)/African Solidarity Party, which was based in Leopoldville (now Kinshasa) and eventually supported Patrice Lumumba. The PSA publication *Solidarité Africaine* printed a call for an independent women's organization, and pinned its hopes of organizing women on the efforts of the MFSA. Both the PSA and the MFSA were short-lived, as they did not survive the assassination of Lumumba in 1961, and the subsequent ascent to power of Mobutu Sese Seko.

MOUVEMENT NATIONAL DES FEMMES / NATIONAL MOVEMENT OF WOMEN. This party-affiliated women's organization was established in 1964, and affiliated with the ruling Parti du Peuple Mauritaniens/People's Party of Mauritania. It worked to protect women and promote income-generation through handicrafts production. *See also* POLITICAL PARTY ORGANIZATIONS.

MPANGA, JOYCE R. (1934–). Mpanga was one of the first African women to serve on a colonial legislative council in Uganda, as she was appointed in 1960. She was educated at Makerere University and at Indiana University in the United States where she earned a master's degree in education and was the first Uganda women to obtain a master's degree. She remained active in Ugandan politics and was the first minister for women in development in Uganda from 1988 to

1989, having previously been chair of the **Uganda Council of Women** (1986–1988). The ministry works on legal affairs, research, **education** and training, **non-governmental organizations**, project implementation, and communication and information. She was also secretary of state for primary education from 1989 to 1992.

MUGABE, SALLY (1932–1992). The first wife of Zimbabwe's first majority president, Robert Mugabe, Sally Mugabe was an activist in her own right, and was known as mother of her nation. She was born in Ghana, and married Robert in 1961. They met when he was teaching in Ghana in the 1950s while exiled from then Southern Rhodesia. She was jailed in Rhodesia for six weeks in 1961 for demonstrating against a new constitution that disadvantaged blacks, and during the 1960s she organized women to oppose the Unilateral Declaration of Independence and the white minority rule of Ian Smith. As with other **first ladies**, she contributed to women's political **organizations** by serving as secretary of the Women's League of the ruling party the Zimbabwe African National Union (ZANU).

MUGO, MICERE GITHAE (1942–). Mugo is a Kenyan playwright and **poet** who lived in exile in Zimbabwe where she taught at the University of Zimbabwe. She was educated at Makerere University in Uganda, and at the University of Toronto in Canada where she earned a Ph.D. in **literature**. Her activist politics resulted in differences with the Kenyan government while she was teaching at the University of Nairobi, and she left Kenya in 1982, settling in Harare where she taught at the University of Zimbabwe. In addition to her own poetry (*Daughter of My People, Sing!*, 1976), plays (*The Long Illness of Ex-Chief Kiti*, 1976), and essays (*Visions of Africa*, 1981), she collaborated with Ngugi wa Thiong'o on *The Trial of Dedan Kimathi* (1976). *See also* THEATER.

MUHANDO, PENINA (1948–). Muhando, a Tanzanian playwright, has chosen to write only in Swahili for Tanzanian audiences. She earned a Ph.D. in language and linguistics from the University of Dar es Salaam, where she taught in the Department of Theatre Arts. Her plays focus on the themes of **development** and social struggles. *See also* THEATER.

MUHUMUSA (fl. 1890s–1945). Muhumusa (sometimes Muhumuza) was a member of the ruling family of Mwami in Rwanda. When her husband died and her son failed to gain support to take his place, she fled north into what is now Uganda. She called on the power of the recognized spirit **Nyabingi** to build up a center of support and raise opposition to the new Mwami. Her attempts to establish control over settlements in the region drew the attention of the colonial authorities, who were threatened by her activities and her claim to have a connection with ancestral powers. The German colonialists imprisoned her from 1908 to 1910; when released she continued to try and organize a power base for her son. Muhumusa was captured in 1911 by the British, who held her in Kampala until her death.

MUJAWAMARIYA, MONIQUE (1955–). A **human rights** leader from Rwanda, Mujawamariya was the daughter of a Hutu father and a Tutsi mother and worked to quell ethnic animosity in her homeland. She was trained as a social worker. She was married to an abusive man; after she left him she became active on projects to end **domestic violence** and in helping battered women find shelter. From 1990 to 1994 she was the executive secretary of the Rwanda Human Rights League. Mujawamariya was threatened with death and attacked three times for speaking out in the 1990s. During the ethnic violence in 1994 in which 800,000 Tutsis were massacred she narrowly escaped death by hiding in the rafters of her home in Kigali for nearly a week.

MUJURU, JOYCE NHONGO (1955–). Nhongo was a well-known guerrilla fighter in Zimbabwe who was given the honorary name "Teurai Ropa," Spill Blood. She joined the military wing of the liberation struggle in 1973, and rose to command the Women's Detachment of the Zimbabwe African National Liberation Army (ZANLA). In 1977 she joined the central command of the army. After independence in 1980 she was briefly the minister of youth, sports, and recreation, and then in 1981 was named minister of community development and women's affairs. She was later minister of rural resources and water development and in 2004 was named as Zimbabwe's first female vice president.

MUNGAI, ANNE. Mungai is a **film** director from Kenya, one of the very few women in East Africa actively making movies. Because of difficulties in funding her creative work, she has made a number of documentaries, including one on women in the **cooperative** movement (1989), another on women and rural **development**, and on street children for the United Nations Children's Fund (UNICEF). In 1992 she released *Saikati*, a film she wrote, directed, and produced, that tells th story of a young woman whose desire to study medicine is thwarted by her uncle's wish to marry her off for the **bridewealth**.

MUSASA PROJECT. This Zimbabwean **non-governmental organization** was begun in 1988 with a specific focus on ending **domestic violence** and other violence against women and sexual abuse of children. It provides counseling and **educational** resources, and also runs a shelter that can house 14 women in need of escaping their abusers. *See also* WOMEN'S ACTION GROUP; ZIMBABWE WOMEN'S RESOURCE CENTRE AND NETWORK.

MUSIC. Women have been renowned as singers and performers both individually and as part of choral groups, though they have been less often recognized as composers. Songs have recalled historic events and praised rulers, and are composed and sung for a variety of festive occasions, including as a part of **initiation rites**, weddings, and funerals. Singing while performing collective work was also a common practice, for example as women pounded grain in a mortar they would often sing in rhythm with the work. In many areas women play only certain instruments, thus they may not be expected to play stringed instruments or drums in public, though they may have the ability and knowledge. Performances are frequently a group experience, with women singing in a chorus while other members of the community drum and play instruments. **Dance** and song are commonly part of the same performance, whether part of a private ritual or on a stage before an audience.

In the 20th century some women singers and musicians became known through recordings and radio play. Women from Mali, drawing on their experience as *griottes*, had many followers who prized their songs for their beauty and spirituality; well known practitioners included **Fanta Damba**, **Sira Mori Diabaté**, and **Oumou Sangaré**. Other famed singers from West Africa were **Cesaria Evora** and **Angelique Kidjo**. Singers from eastern and southern Africa who gained wide recognition included **Brenda Fassie**, **Miriam Makeba**,

Dorothy Masuka, Princess Constance Magogo kaDinuzulu, and Siti Binti Saadi.

MUSLIM WOMEN'S ASSOCIATION. Several African nations have local Muslim women's associations, and the groups generally focus on improving conditions for women while upholding Islamic tenets. One was founded in Kenya 1947, and in modern times Muslim women's associations have been active in the Central African Republic, Ethiopia, the Gambia, Sierra Leone, South Africa, Tanzania, and Uganda. Nigeria has a Federation of Muslim Women's Associations which has published *The Muslim Woman* (1990–1997). *See also* SHARI'A LAW.

MUVMAN LIBERASYON FAM (MLF) / WOMEN'S LIBERATION FRONT. A women's organization in Mauritius, it was established in 1976 following a student uprising. The group is concerned with protecting women's rights, and has been particularly active on reproductive rights including access to **abortion** and with limiting the introduction of laws that restrict **marriage** and family options. It published *Nuvel Fam*, and maintains a website at www.mlfmauritius.org.

MUYUNDA, MAVIS. Muyunda is a political leader in Zambia, where she has held several government posts. She was minister of state of the National Commission for Development Planning (1983–1988), minister of state for foreign affairs (1988–1990), and minister of water, lands, and natural resources (1990–1992). In 2002 she was named special assistant to the president for political affairs.

MWANA KUPONA (1810–1860). Known for her poem "Utendi wa Mwana Kupona," she was the wife of Bwana Mataka who lived in the Lamu coastal Swahili region of Kenya. "Utendi" are a particular kind of epic Swahili poem, in this case conveying instructions to her daughter about proper behavior in domestic, religious, and social realms. The poem is noted for its plea for a wife's complete obedience to her husband.

MXENGE, VICTORIA NONYAMEZELO (1942–1985). Mxenge was active in South African resistance politics, and served on the executive committee of the United Democratic Front, the most important internal anti-**apartheid** group in the 1980s. She had trained as a **nurse** and **midwife**. She was assassinated outside her home in Durban in 1985; though her murderers later confessed to the Truth and Reconciliation Commission, no one was ever charged with her death. Her husband, Griffiths Mxenge, had previously been assassinated in 1981. A women-directed self-help **housing** development in Cape Town and a residence hall at Rhodes University have been named in her honor. *See also* NATAL ORGANISATION OF WOMEN.

MYTHOLOGY. As with all societies, Africans told stories that explained the origins of their communities, and those tales often had a gender component that explained why women and men had particular roles. Among the Kikuyu in Kenya, for example, the myth of origin told how Gikuyu and Moombi had nine daughters who married men from outside, and the families of those women were the core of the clans that eventually developed in Kikuyu society. Women were the center of authority for many years, but they became domineering and brutal, punishing men for adulterous behavior while they took multiple husbands. The men conspired to seduce the leading women simultaneously; the women are portrayed as weak in their acquiescence to the men, and when they were immobilized at the end of their pregnancies the men staged a coup and Kikuyu society became patriarchal.

The Kran of Liberia related a story of their origin that began with an all-powerful woman, Gonzuole, who had many lovely daughters though she never had a husband or any man. Men who saw the daughters conspired to trap them with special mushrooms; when the girls stopped to taste the treat, the men surrounded them and made a bargain with Gonzuole that resulted in marriages between the men and her daughters. The girls were not happy in their new situation, and their actions led to factions and warfare.

Often myths illustrated the separate but complementary spheres that men and women inhabited, as with the origin story of the Nata in Tanzania, where a farming woman and hunting man met and found that they could help each other. They married and their children were the beginning of Nata society. Myths were also told about **Mami Wata** and a variety of **goddesses** who had roles in the origins and continuation of society, through their support of regular rainfall, the abundance of the earth, and women's fertility.

– N –

NACHITUTI (fl. LATE 18TH CENTURY). Nachituti is the focus of stories among the Luapula (in present day Zambia). After the renowned King Kazembe killed her brother she reputedly "gave" the land and lakes of Luapula to Kazembe. Although the story may be apocryphal, people in eastern Luapula care for her grave which is located at the royal cemetery.

NAIROBI WOMEN'S MEETING. The third meeting of the **United Nations Decade for Women** was held in Nairobi, Kenya, in July 1985. It was designed as the final meeting of the decade (the first was in Mexico City in 1975, the second in Copenhagen in 1980) with the theme of reviewing and appraising the achievements of the Decade. **Margaret Kenyatta** presided over the meeting, which was marked by a massive attendance of 16,000 women, with a notable presence of African women. The primary official document to be issued from the meeting was the "Forward-looking Strategies for the Advancement of Women" that provided a blueprint that individual governments could implement to improve women's rights and status. Concurrent with the official meeting was a non-governmental meeting that was the site of many lively workshops and discussions, and was for many attendees the most important part of the gathering. African women were motivated by the meeting to form activist organizations, including **Action for Development (ACFODE)** in Uganda and the **Tanzania Media Women's Association.** The Nairobi meeting was followed in 1995 by a Fourth World Conference on Women in Beijing.

NAKAFWAYA (fl. LATE 19TH CENTURY). Nakafwaya was known for marrying three Kazembes (Luapula kings, located in present day Zambia) in succession. Her name means "I desire [many men]," and her actions guaranteed the permanence of the state under Kazembe.

NAKATINDI WINA, PRINCESS. Princess Nakatindi, a member of the Barotseland royal family in Zambia, was the first female member of parliament in 1964. She has continued to serve in the government in the decades since, in parliament and in ambassadorial positions. She was minister of state for tourism (1992–1993) and minister of community development and social welfare (1993–1998). In 2000 she was in the news when she commented that women should boycott the African Union parliament because male legislators had suggested that each nation be limited to one female representative (the draft protocol stated that "each member state should be represented by five [5] members, one of whom must be a woman," and several countries did send more than the minimum one woman to the March 2004 inaugural meeting). Though one was not a limit on the number of women, it was not a call for gender parity which many women had hoped for. Nakatindi believed that a boycott would be justified because the male legislators seemed to want women only as "colouring flowers" in the assembly. Until 2002 she was the national chair of the women's affairs committee in the reform organization Movement for Multi-Party Democracy.

NAMIBIA DOMESTIC AND ALLIED WORKERS' UNION (NDAWU). The Namibia Domestic and Allied Workers' Union represented people working in homes, including gardeners and private messengers, though the majority of members and potential members were women doing domestic work. The membership of 4,000 (out of an estimated 12,000 domestic workers in Namibia) was 70 percent female in 1994, mainly women between 40 and 60 years of age who were heads of families with four or five children. The NDAWU was begun in 1987 by a committee affiliated with the National Union of Namibian Workers, a result of their concern over the poor working conditions of women in **domestic service**. It was formally established and held its first national meeting in 1990. Most of the leadership positions are filled by women.

THE NAMIBIAN WOMAN. *The Namibian Woman* was the official publication of the **SWAPO Women's Council**, the women's group affiliated with the South West African People's Organization, which was based in Luanda, Angola, prior to Namibia's independence in 1990. It appeared quarterly in the 1980s, publishing articles focused on political issues including the imminent date of independence.

NAMIBIAN WOMEN'S VOICE. This organization was established in Namibia in 1985 with support from the **Christian** churches, which hoped to provide an independent voice for women inside the country during the struggle for independence. They faced opposition from the group affiliated with the primary nationalist organization, **SWAPO Women's Council**, and only lasted until 1989.

NANA ASMA'U. *See* ASMA'U, NANA.

NANDABUNGA (fl. 19TH CENTURY). Nandabunga was chief of Buyenzi-Bweru in Ngozi, in Burundi. It was not common for women to act as chiefs, and she became famous for her position. She inherited her role from her father, Mwezi Gisabo (Mwezi IV, 1845–1908). *See also* NDIRIKUMUTIMA.

NANDI (c. 1760–1827). Nandi was a key figure in South African Zulu history, daughter of a Langeni chief and most renowned as the mother of legendary ruler Shaka. Because Nandi was considered too closely related to marry Shaka's father, Senzangakona, and her pregnancy began before they were legitimagely wed, she was poorly treated by the Zulu community. She took Shaka back to the Langeni when he was six, but was forced to leave the Langeni during a famine and they then settled among the Mtewa where Shaka rose through the ranks of the army of Dingiswayo. When Senzangakona died in 1815 Shaka claimed his seat and Nandi, as **queen mother**, came to be known as Ndlorukazi, "The Great She Elephant" (in Swazi the term was *Ndlovukazi*). When she died of dysentery Shaka instituted an extreme expression of public mourning; although some attendants might normally have been put to death when a ruler died, Shaka began a massacre that resulted in 7,000 deaths and he placed 12,000 warriors to guard her grave for a year. He also commanded that people pour out their milk and stop cultivating crops. In response to such orders his aunt Mnkabayi (his father's sister and friend of his mother) sponsored a coup that brought another nephew, Dingane, into power.

NATAL ORGANISATION OF WOMEN (NOW). Formed in South Africa in 1983, NOW was part of the United Democratic Front (UDF), an umbrella organization that organized anti-**apartheid** work in the 1980s. The members, who included **Victoria Mxenge**, were concerned that women's rights be included in future laws, and worked to train women to take on leadership roles in **politics**. They were also a source of support for those suffering from internecine fighting between the UDF and the Inkatha Freedom Party. After 1990 when political organizations were legal once again in South Africa, NOW disbanded and members joined the African National Congress (ANC). *See also* AFRICAN NATIONAL CONGRESS WOMEN'S LEAGUE; FEDERATION OF SOUTH AFRICAN WOMEN.

NATAL WOMEN'S REVOLT. A rural rebellion in 1963 during which women in Natal, South Africa, refused to cooperate in filling tanks for dipping cattle, and then destroyed the tanks. **Dorothy Nyembe**, one of the leaders of the revolt, was arrested.

NATIONAL COMMISSION FOR WOMEN. A Nigerian organization founded in 1988, it was sponsored by the government as a means to increase women's involvement in civil society, specifically by developing policies that would advance women. Despite their efforts in getting women involved in politics, very few women in Nigeria have taken high office.

NATIONAL CONGRESS OF SIERRA LEONE WOMEN. The Congress was founded in 1960 as the women's wing of the ruling All People's Party. Nancy Steele (1923–2001), founder and chair during the early years of the Congress, had a strong influence on the internal organization and politics, though her increasing militancy made her a threat to the ruling party and she was not supported when she sought higher office. The organization itself pursued political advances for women, and drew members from **market women** as well as professional women. A description of the first decade of the Congress can be found in Filomina Chioma Steady, *Female Power in African Politics: The National Congress of Sierra Leone* (1975). *See also* POLITICAL PARTY ORGANIZATIONS.

NATIONAL COUNCIL OF GHANA WOMEN. The council was formed from two major organizations, the **Ghana Women's League** and the **National Federation of Gold Coast Women** (later known as the Ghana Federation of Women) in 1963, following an initial meeting in 1960 and with the urging of male leaders who desired women to work together in one large national organization. The male leaders of the Convention Peoples' Party (CPP), including Kwame Nkrumah, played a central role in establishing the council, which replaced the women's wing of the party.

NATIONAL COUNCIL OF WOMEN. The National Council was an umbrella organization that was established in Uganda in 1978 by Idi Amin as a way to control other women's groups; there were more than 40 organizations under its auspices.

NATIONAL COUNCIL OF WOMEN OF KENYA (NCWK). Formed in 1964 as an umbrella organization, **Margaret Kenyatta** was president from 1964 to 1966. It was perceived as being elitist and Kikuyu-centered, and was competitive with **Maendeleo Ya Wanawake Organisation. Muthoni Likimani** was a founding member of the council, and **Wangari Maathai** was chair from 1981 to 1987.

NATIONAL COUNCIL OF WOMEN OF TANGANYIKA (NCWT). The NCWT was founded in 1952, and by 1960 there were 3,000 members under the leadership of **First Lady** Maria Nyerere. The focus of the organization's work was on home care and domestic science issues, and it sponsored lectures and demonstrations on **childcare** as well as running an orphanage for girls.

NATIONAL COUNCIL OF WOMEN'S SOCIETIES (NCWS). Established in 1958 when the Women's Movement of Nigeria, the Women's Improvement Society, and the Ibadan Progressive Union merged, it was a rival to the **Federation of Nigerian Women's Societies (FNWS)** and originally did not have the mass appeal or strong **feminist** presence of the FNWS, but was supported by government funding and was seen by the government as the only legitimate women's organization. It promoted **development** activities such as celebrating Women's Day, pursuing fundraising activities including a craft shop, building a children's village, and offering training in civic responsibilities. The NCWS gradually did replace the Federation, and counted many women's organizations as part of its coalition, including Planned Parenthood, Medical Women's Society, Muslim Mothers Association, and other groups involved in promoting opportunities for women. Sola Ojewusi has written an official report, *Speaking for Nigerian Women: A*

History of the National Council of Women's Societies (1996). *See also* AKINTUNDE-IGHODALO, FOLAYEGBE MOSUNMOLA.

NATIONAL FEDERATION OF GOLD COAST WOMEN. Later called the Ghana Federation of Women, it was founded in the Gold Coast (now Ghana) in 1953. The federation worked to gain recognition for customary **marriages** from the colonial government as a way to improve women's situation. It submitted many petitions arguing for an end to discrimination in the arenas of **employment**, marriage, and **inheritance**, and it published a quarterly called *The Federation* in 1957, later calling it *The Gold Coast Woman*. The group never gained national status, and in 1960 it joined with the **Ghana Women's League** and some smaller women's groups to form the **National Council of Ghana Women**.

NATIONAL UNION OF ERITREAN WOMEN. Originally called the **Eritrean Women's Association**, it was the mass organization that represented women's concerns in Eritrea. Established in 1979, it claimed 100,000 members in 1989. By the end of the 1990s it was no longer associated with the government, but functioned as an independent **non-governmental organization**. It published the quarterly newsletter, *Voice of Eritrean Women*.

NATIONAL WOMEN'S LOBBY GROUP. Formed in 1991 with the goal of improving the participation of women in national politics in Zambia, it functioned primarily as a lobby for women's legal rights and for legislative action. It held open meetings where issues were debated, and it established branches throughout the country, ensuring that they represented women from all regions. The group was involved in the development of a new Constitution in the 1990s. It also focused on the issues of girls' **education** and **human rights**. Its publications included *Woman in Politics* and *Increasing Women's Participation in Local Government* (1998). The lobby group's logo, WIZER, stands for Women in Zambia for Equality and Representation. Its website is available at: http://www.womenslobby.org.zm/index.shtml.

NATIONALISM. Women have played a significant role in nationalist movements across the continent. From the early years of **colonialism**

women protested the extension of **taxes** and agitated to be included in political decision-making. Some histories of nationalism portrayed the organizations as male dominated, but more recent scholarship has demonstrated the integral role of women. For instance, the Tanganyika (later Tanzania) African National Union (TANU) was conventionally seen as an organization of western-educated Christian men, but now it is recognized that their success in ending British rule was equally due to the activism of uneducated Muslim women, led by **Bibi Titi Mohammed**, who had specific grievances against British colonial rule. In Nigeria also important protests were registered by women's organizations such as the **Abeokuta Women's Union**. Kwame Nkrumah in Ghana depended on the crucial support of **market women** who provided food and other material that ensured his ability to lead the Convention Peoples' Party (CPP), and similar patterns were seen with the Rassemblement Démocratique Africain (RDA) in Guinea. Many individual women came to prominence as a result of their nationalist endeavors, including **Hadja Mafory Bangoura** in Guinea, **Mary Muthoni Nyanjiru** in Kenya, **Aoua Kéita** and **Célestine Ouezzin Coulibaly** in Mali, and **Funmilayo Ransome-Kuti** in Nigeria.

NCUBE, SISTER BERNARD NEKIE ZELLIE (1935–). Sister Bernard is a South African political activist and Catholic leader. She was born in Johannesburg, and educated at Roma College in Lesotho. She founded the **Federation of Transvaal Women** in 1984, and has been president since then. Sister Bernard has also been a member of the African National Congress (ANC) and the United Democratic Front (UDF), and for several years worked as an organizer of women's projects for the South African Bishops' Conference. She was elected to parliament in 1994 as an ANC member.

NDIAYE, NDIORO (1946–). Ndiaye is a Senegalese politician. She was trained as a physician in Dakar and Paris, and was the first woman to head the department of odontology and stomatology at the Cheikh Anta Diop University in Dakar. In 1988 she was appointed as minister of social development, where she dealt in depth with issues of **migration** between Senegal and Mauritainia. From 1990 to 1995 she was minister for women's, children's, and family affairs. She returned to the university, but increasingly was active in international activities including the **United Nations Decade for Women** world summits on women in 1990 and 1995. She helped found the Scientific Commission for Women and Development and the Network of African Women Leaders for Peace and Development. In 1999 she became deputy director of the International Organization for Migration. She has won many honors including Chevalier de l'Ordre de la Légion d'Honneur.

NDIRIKUMUTIMA. She ruled as regent for Mwezi Gisabo in Burundi in the 19th century. *See also* NANDABUNGA.

NDLOVUKAZI. This term for **queen mother** in Swaziland means "Cow Elephant," a reference to her importance in ruling the nation. The best known was **Labotsibeni Gwamile Mdluli**; the Zulu queen **Nandi** was called the related term Ndlorukazi.

NEHANDA. Nehanda was a spirit among the Shona of Zimbabwe (then Rhodesia) who came to prominence in the 1890s when the **spirit medium** known as **Charwe** was possessed by her. Though initially Nehanda was a relatively innocuous rainmaking spirit, she came to embody resistance to colonial rule through the actions of Charwe. The image and name of Nehanda have taken root in Zimbabwean society as emblematic of a national spirit of independence, with her name given to streets, hospitals, and other public venues. **Yvonne Vera** wrote a novel, *Nehanda* (1993), which deals with the myth and the woman.

NETWORK: A PAN-AFRICAN WOMEN'S FORUM. Published by the International Resource Network of Women of African Descent, the focus of the journal was on women's struggles, especially in southern Africa, and with a particular interest in improving connections internationally between women of African descent. It was short-lived, first being published in 1988 in Harare, Zimbabwe, before moving to Clark Atlanta University in 1989; the last issue apparently appeared in 1990.

NEWPORT, MATILDA (c. 1795–1837). Newport was American born, but of African descent. She was among those who were resettled in Liberia in the early 19th century, where the new settlers encountered hostility from local communities which did not want the newcomers encroaching on their territory. In 1822 African warriors attacked a settlement of American settlers. Matilda Newport, a free black woman, saw that the new settlement was in danger of losing the battle; she was smoking a pipe, and she took a hot coal from the pipe and dropped it into a cannon causing an explosion that frightened the African fighters and turned the tide of the battle. She later married Ralph Newport (her second husband); he perished in a canoe accident in 1836. Newport died of pleurisy in 1837 in Monrovia. Though her action in rescuing the experimental settlement was not deemed exceptional at first, her bravery was remembered in oral histories, and it gained increasing attention over time. The Liberian legislature in 1916 named 1 December Matilda Newport Day, making the day of the battle nearly a century earlier a regular national holiday. A postage stamp was issued in 1947 to commemorate her actions. By the 1960s the role of Americo-Liberians in ruling Liberia was under greater criticism, culminating in a coup in 1980 that brought in leadership that was not of American descent, and Newport was no longer seen as an admirable heroine. *See also* AFRICAN AMERICAN WOMEN.

NFAH-ABBENYI, JULIANA MAKUCHI (1958–). Nfah-Abbenyi is a scholar and writer from western Cameroon. She was educated at the University of Yaoundé in Cameroon and at McGill University in Canada before teaching English at the University of Southern Mississippi, Hattiesburg. She writes in English, one of the few female writers in English from Cameroon, where most of the national **literature** is in French. Under the name Makuchi she published *Your Madness, Not Mine* (1999), a collection of short stories that depicted evocative details of women's lives as market vendors, wives, and mothers, and that made use of local pidgin to recreate women's conversations. She has also written literary analysis and criticism relating to issues of gender in African women's writing.

NGANO, MARTHA (fl. 1890s–1920s). Ngano was a leading figure in the Rhodesian Bantu Voters' Association (RBVA) in the 1920s. She was a well-educated Fingo who moved from South Africa to Southern Rhodesia (now Zimbabwe) in 1897, and worked tirelessly to expand Africans' ability to vote, critiquing the lack of **education** in

English when literacy in English was required to be eligible to vote. She also expanded the RBVA into the rural areas, establishing branches in outlying districts and addressing rural concerns such as cattle-dipping, destocking, and land shortages, while continuing her earlier emphasis on education.

NGCOBO, LAURETTA (1931–). A South African writer, Ngcobo was born in Natal and educated at Fort Hare University. She went into exile in 1963, and settled in England where she worked as a teacher and began writing. Her novel, *And They Didn't Die* (1990), related the resilience of a young woman who worked in a white household where she was raped by the father of the family and bore his child, and then faced ostracism from her home community when she returned with the baby, born out of wedlock. Ngcobo returned to South Africa in 1993.

NGILU, CHARITY KALUKI (1952–). Ngilu is an influential Kenyan politician who is best known for her presidential candidacy in 1997, when she was the first Kenyan woman to run for that office. She was educated at the Alliance Girls High School in Kenya, trained as a secretary and worked at the Central Bank of Kenya in the 1970s. She continued her **education** and worked briefly for the Chase Manhattan Overseas Corporation before opening a bakery and restaurant. Ngilu developed her business interests into a range of fields, including most recently a plastics factory that produces PVC water pipes. She is married with three children.

Her political career emerged on the national scene when she ran as an opposition candidate in 1992 with the Democratic Party (DP) of Kenya, defeating a former cabinet member who was supported by President Arap Moi and the Kenya African National Union (KANU). She had numerous confrontations with the police, as the authorities repeatedly tried to shut down civic education forums and other events that she organized. While she was in parliament, there were only six women out of 188 members. She garnered support from the National Commission on the Status of Women when she ran for president, though she could not run representing the DP and joined the Social Democratic Party (SDP) for that race. She came in fifth, garnering 7.9 percent of the votes (488,600 votes). She quit the SDP when she had differences with it, and helped form the National Alliance for Change that later became the National Party of Kenya (NAK). During the elections in 2002 Ngilu was the NAK prime minister designate, and she was appointed minister of health in 2003 under President Mwai Kibaki.

NGOYI, LILIAN MASEBIDA (1911–1980). Lilian Ngoyi was an anti-**apartheid** and **trade union** leader in South Africa. The daughter of a clergyman in Pretoria, her family could not afford to keep her in school through high school. Widowed when her daughter was three, she worked at a variety of difficult jobs, including in a garment factory. By 1952 she was deeply involved in the Garment Workers Union, and was later elected to the executive committee of the union. A pivotal experience was a trip to attend the World Congress of Women in Switzerland in 1954, where she visited several European countries. The 1956 **Defiance Campaign**, protesting the expansion of restrictive **pass laws**, brought her into the African National Congress (ANC), where she served as president of the **African National Congress Women's League** in 1953 and then as president of the **Federation of South African Women** in 1956. Known to all as MaNgoyi, this powerful orator was also charged with treason as part of the infamous treason trial of the 1950s, and spent most of the subsequent years under banning orders that restricted her public activities. Dianne Stewart has told her story in *Lilian Ngoyi* (1996).

NIGER DELTA WOMEN FOR JUSTICE (NDWJ). Niger Delta Women for Justice was organized in 1998 in response to the abuses suffered by Nigerian women and communities at the hands of international **oil** companies. It has been involved in **educational** work and has connected with **human rights** efforts internationally. The NDWJ goal is to empower local women through training and to embark on research that will further that goal. The NDWJ website is at www.ndwj.kabissa.org. *See also* SUFFRAGE.

NIGERIAN WOMEN'S PARTY (NWP). Founded under the leadership of Lady Oyinkan Ajas Abayomi in 1944 in Lagos, the members were primarily women in the Christian, westernized elite. The main activities of the NWP focused on girls' **education**, **literacy** for adult women, **employment** of women in the civil service, expanding the rights of girls to trade, and gaining the right to vote for women. It ceased to exist in 1956 when the new coalition, the **National Council of Women's Societies**, was established.

NIGERIAN WOMEN'S UNION (NWU). Formed in 1949 at the instigation of **Funmilayo Ransome-Kuti**, it brought together numerous local organizations including the **Abeokuta Women's Union**. It remained independent of any political party as it worked for women's rights. A two-day conference held in August 1953 resulted in turning the organization into the **Federation of Nigerian Women's Societies**, with the understanding that local groups would retain their independence.

NISA (c. 1921–). The pseudonym of a !Kung woman in Botswana, her story was collected and told by Marjorie Shostack in *Nisa: The Life and Words of a !Kung Woman* (1981). The book is known for the intimate details of life among a group still living a gatherer-hunter lifestyle in the Kalahari Desert of Botswana.

NJAU, REBEKA (1930–). A Kenyan novelist and playwright, Njau has written about women in the post-colonial era. She trained as a teacher, and was the headmistress of the Nairobi Girls' Secondary School. Her first publication, *Ripples in the Pool* (1975), was awarded the East African Writing Committee Prize. She is interested in exploring the richness of traditional beliefs and practices and has written about these concerns in *Kenyan Women and Their Mystical Powers* (1985).

NJIE-SAIDY, ISATOU (1952–). Njie-Saidy is a Gambian politician. She became the vice president of the Gambia in 1997, making her the first women to hold that position in any West African government, and one of the highest ranking female politicians on the continent (**Specioza Wandira Kazibwe** was vice president of Uganda during the same years). She trained as a teacher, and taught in secondary schools until 1976, when she began working with the Indigenous Business Advisory Services, followed by a position as deputy executive secretary of the Women's Bureau (1983–1989). She served as minister of health, social welfare and women's affairs in 1996 before becoming vice president.

NJINGA. *See* NZINGA.

NON-GOVERNMENTAL ORGANIZATIONS (NGOs). NGOs, the common name for non-governmental organizations, have become a major way for women to organize and have an impact on changing policies concerning women. Such groups may have a greater ability to push an agenda for women if they are not dependent on governmental funding and support. At the same time, many such organizations do receive government funding, including from such sources as the United States Agency for International Development. Others rely on charitable support and membership dues. In the 1990s, with the increased focus on **democratization** and developing civil society in Africa, hundreds of NGOs were formed. Some focused on specific problems such as **domestic violence, HIV/AIDS,** or **peace,** while others had a broader concentration on women and **development.** Some of the better known NGOs include **Femmes Africa Solidarité, African Women's Development and Communication Network (FEMNET), Forum of African Women Educationalists (FAWE), Inter-African Commmittee on Traditional Practices Affecting the Health of Women and Children (IAC), Morabi, Uganda Women's Network (UWONET), Women for Change, Women in Law and Development in Africa,** and **Women of Uganda Network (WOUGNET).**

NONGQAWUSE (1841–c. 1898). Nongqawuse was a Xhosa girl in South Africa who was seen as a prophet in the 1850s. She had a vision of strangers who were revealed as Xhosa ancestors who called for the Xhosa to halt cultivating and to kill their cattle, the basis of Xhosa society and economy. Nongqawuse said the ancestors claimed that taking such a drastic action would allow "the dead to arise" and the Xhosa to live free of European rule. The result of this millenarian action was a terrible famine which allowed the British to impose colonial rule as the Xhosa people were weakened by the loss of corn and cattle. Recent analysis has suggested that Nongqawuse, an orphan who was dependent on her uncle, might have been responding to abuse from male kin living in her community and was calling for a communal cleansing. It is not possible to prove her motives after so many years, but Helen Bradford has shown that much of her testimony about bad behavior by unnamed Xhosa men has been systematically ignored by researchers (see her 1996 *Journal of African History* article, "Women, Gender and Colonialism: Rethinking the History of the British Cape Colony and Its Frontier Zones, c. 1806-70"). After the famine passed, resulting in the deaths of many thousands of Xhosa, Nongqawuse lived in the household of Major Gawler, a magistrate in the British colonial administration. In 1858 it was recorded that she sailed to Cape Town and was placed in the Paupers' Lodge, a women's prison. Her name then disappears from the public record, as she was not listed as an inmate in 1859 when the Lodge was disbanded. Oral testimony suggests that she settled near Alexandria where she married and had two daughters and perhaps survived until 1898 or as late as 1910. She has been frequently written about; see J. B. Peires, *The Dead Will Arise: Nongqawuse and the Great Xhosa Cattle-Killing Movement of 1856-57* (1989).

NONTETHA (c. 1875–1935). A South African prophet, she established the Church of the Prophetess Nontetha. She reported that she had a series of dreams in 1918, in the aftermath of the international influenza epidemic that devastated Xhosa areas of South Africa. The dreams told her that the epidemic had been a punishment, and she was chosen to lead reforms in her society. In the wake of official attacks on similar movements (notably the massacre of 200 people in nearby Bulhoek in 1922), she was hospitalized as insane, and was kept in jail or hospitalized until her death in 1935 at the Pretoria Mental Hospital. Though her career was short and her church remained small with a congregation of only several hundred, she was typical of many African prophets, such as **Christianah Emmanuel**, **Alice Lakwena**, and **Alice Lenshina**, who preached from the Bible, advocated abstinence from **alcohol**, and spoke out against **witchcraft**. Nontetha never had any formal

education and spoke no English, but developed religious beliefs that incorporated local practices and an idiosyncratic interpretation of **Christianity**. Her story was told by Robert Edgar and Hilary Sapire in *African Apocalypse* (2000).

NTHATISI, MMA. *See* MMANTHATISI.

NURSING. Nursing was one of the few career opportunities open to African women. Beginning in the **colonial** era women were recruited to nursing training programs and were able to work in government clinics and hospitals. Some countries, such as Southern Rhodesia (now Zimbabwe), only allowed women to study nursing beginning in the late 1950s. Sometimes their work brought them into conflict with social expectations, as when they had to examine men who were senior to them in age or rank, and in many areas male nurses outnumbered female nurses. For example, in Nigeria in 1944 there were 289 African female nurses and 747 males, and men dominated the higher-salary positions. Many women with nursing training specialized as **midwives**. There were a number of African women who had initially trained as nurses who went on to become political leaders; their **education** and work made them particularly aware of the oppression of women. Some of those women were **Aoua Kéita**, **Lucy Lameck**, **Victoria Mxenge**, **Grace Ogot**, **Carmen Pereira**, **Francisca Pereira Gomes**, **Albertina Sisulu**, and **Delphine Tsanga**. *See also* HEALTH.

NUVEL FAM. Published in Mauritius by **Muvman Liberasyon Fam**, the first issue appeared in 1978.

NWAPA, FLORA (1931–1993). Nwapa was one of Nigeria's foremost novelists. She was educated at the University of Ibadan and earned a diploma in **education** from the University of Edinburgh, Scotland, in 1958. When she returned to Nigeria she worked as a "woman education officer," and even after gaining fame as a writer she served as the assistant registrar at the University of Lagos (1962–1976), as minister of health and social welfare for East Central State (1970–1971), and then as minister of lands, survey, and urban development (1971–1974). Her first novel, *Efuru* (1966), portrayed the life of a **prostitute**, and was one of the first English-language novels published by an African woman (**Grace Ogot**'s *The Promised Land* was also published in 1966). In addition to four more novels, she published collections of short stories (*This is Lagos*, 1975; *Wives at War*, 1981; *Women are Different*, 1986) and poems, as well as several books for children. In response to what she felt was poor treatment by her publisher, she established her own publishing house in Nigeria, first Tana Press in 1974, and later Flora Nwapa Books (1977), through which she put out her own publications as well as those of other Nigerian writers. All of her writing sought to present a more realistic portrayal of Nigerian women as strong independent people, to improve women's ideas of their own possibilities, and to better the condition of African women.

NYABINGI. Nyabingi was both the name used to refer to individual healers in the Central Lakes area of Africa including Rwanda, and the name for the type of healer, thus a kind of title. The variety of stories told about Nyabingi makes it difficult to write a straightforward history, though she and her followers were part of an established tradition of **spirit possession** called *kubandwa*. The origins of what is sometimes called the Nyabingi "cult" are obscure; reported as originating in Rwanda, adherents were also noted in Uganda, Tanzania, and the Belgian Congo (now the Democratic Republic of the Congo), where women had a longstanding tradition of spirit mediumship which focused on issues of **fertility**. Nyabingi was first described in written sources in the late 19th century as a queen in Mpororo, though documentation is scarce. Mediums known as Nyabingi, who could be either male or female though women predominated, were also leaders of anti-colonial movements, with a series of notable uprisings from 1914 to the 1920s. The British responded by outlawing all activity by spirit mediums (what they termed "**witchcraft**"). It is likely that there was an individual known as Nyabingi who was famous for her skill, and whose spirit later manifested in other individuals, appearing in various contexts over a lengthy period of time. Thus Nyabingi emerges as the granddaughter of a king, but also as the servant of a king, and as an ordinary woman. *See also* MUHU-MUSA; NEHANDA.

NYABONGO, ELIZABETH (1940–). Elizabeth was the daughter of Mukama George Rukiidi III of Toro in Uganda, and was therefore a princess of Toro, who also had a noted career in Ugandan government. She was educated in Uganda and England, earning a **law** degree. She was called to the bar in 1965, and was the first female barrister in East Africa though she never practiced law. In 1968 when President Milton Obote abolished the traditional kingdoms she went into exile where she found work as a fashion model. When Obote was overthrown by Idi Amin in 1971 she returned to Uganda where she served as roving ambassador and in 1974 was made foreign minister. She rapidly fell into disfavor, and was forced to flee to Kenya and then back to Britain. She married Wilbur Nyabongo in 1981; he died in a plane crash in 1986. After Yoweri Museveni came to power she returned to serve the Ugandan government as Ugandan ambassador to the United States. She published her autobiography in 1983, later revising it as *Elizabeth of Toro: The Odyssey of an African Princess* (1989).

NYANJIRU, MARY MUTHONI (?–1922). Nyanjiru was a political activist in Kenya in the 1920s. She worked with Harry Thuku, a leader of the anti-colonial East African Association. Thuku was imprisoned as being a threat to the British colonial government in 1922, and Nyanjiru was present when he was arrested. He had been outspoken in support of women, and many women came to demonstrate in Nairobi to demand his release. The women expected men to take the lead, but when no men came forward, Mary Nyanjiru went to the front of the crowd, and in a typical **shaming practice**, raised her skirts up and challenged the men to take her dress and give her their trousers, as they were too cowardly to take action. Her behavior and comments brought a rousing response from the women who ululated their agreement and then rushed to the prison door, pushing against the armed guards until the soldiers opened fire. Twenty-eight people including Nyanjiru were killed. Harry Thuku was not released, but her example was important to ensuing generations of anti-colonial activists, who learned the political song "Kanyegenuri," which commemorates the actions of women in Nairobi in 1922. Little is known of Mary Nyanjiru's life before she came to the front of the crowd that day. *See also* ABA WOMEN'S WAR; MAU MAU; NATIONALISM.

NYEMBE, DOROTHY (1930–1998). An activist in South Africa, Nyembe led women from Natal in the 1956 anti-pass demonstrations (**Defiance Campaign**) and in the **Natal Women's Revolt** (1963). She was elected president of the **African National Congress Women's League** in Natal in 1959. Nyembe spent many years under banning orders or imprisoned during the years of the **apartheid** government (she served terms from 1963 to 1966 and from 1968 to 1983), but continued her militancy underground as one of the first to join Umkhonto we Sizwe, the armed wing of the African National Congress (ANC). She was elected to parliament in 1994 in the first post-apartheid election.

NZINGA (QUEEN NJINGA) (c. 1582–1663). Nzinga was a queen in the Kongo, in what is now Angola, in the 17th century. She was apparently born of slave origin, but rose through the ranks of the royal household and continued to maneuver her way to power. She is first seen in the historic records in 1622 when she came to Luanda as an emissary to the Portuguese. She converted to **Christianity** and allied herself with the Portuguese, then seized the Ngola throne when the ruler died mysteriously. She later allied herself with the Imbangala and fought the expansion of Portuguese control. After 1630 she moved to Matamba, and established herself as queen, drawing on precedents of female rulers (which had not been the case in Ngola). After 1650 she was a successful merchant, again embracing Christianity, though simultaneously acting as a powerful local man would by taking multiple husbands. Matamba continued to turn to female leaders after her death. Nzinga is claimed by later anti-colonial struggles as an antecedent and role model, and is often portrayed as a heroine of the modern Angolan nation, though her own history was more contradictory and conflicted than the popular image would suggest.

Her name has appeared variously as Nzinga, Nzingha, Njinga, and other similar spellings. In some of the original texts that refer to her, including letters from her, the name is spelled "Ginga," for instance in full as "Dona Anna de Sousa Raynha Ginga." As the "g" was a soft "g," it was written by some European observers as Nginga or Njinga to accommodate a preceding article, such as "o" for "o Njinga." For those following a strict interpretation of Ovimbundu orthography, Njinga or Jinga would be the most accurate spelling, and it tends to be the most common spelling in Angola today, where there is a street in Luanda called "Rua Rainha Jinga." However, some of the earliest observers also wrote it as Nzinga, and that spelling has become the most common form of her name in English-language materials as well as the form used by Angolan nationalists in the mid-20th century.

– O –

OCLOO, ESTHER AFUA (1919–2002). Ocloo was a Ghanaian **market woman** who pioneered micro-loans in Africa. She was the daughter of poor farmers and she went to high school in Accra on a scholarship from the Cadbury chocolate company. After she finished high school in the 1940s her aunt offered her financing of under one dollar which Ocloo used to purchase the materials to make 12 jars of marmalade. With her earnings she expanded into making juice, won a contract with the military to supply orange juice, and began manufacturing other canned foodstuffs. She used her income to finance further **education** in food technology in Britain, and invested in projects designed to improve women's economic opportunities. In 1975 at the **United Nations Decade for Women** meeting in Mexico City she learned about micro-loan programs, in which poor women were awarded very small loans which have a high rate of repayment due to the support groups formed by the grantees. In 1979 Ocloo and several other women established Women's World Banking as a vehicle to make such loans, and Ocloo was named chairwoman. In 1990 she shared the $100,000 Hunger Project Africa Prize with Nigerian leader Olusegun Obasanjo.

ODUNDO, MAGDALENE (1950–). Odundo is an innovative Kenyan ceramicist and sculptor whose designs have been exhibited around the world. She was trained in graphic arts in England in the 1970s, when she studied at the precursor of the Surrey Institute and in the master's program at the Royal College of Art, finishing her degree in 1982. She also studied pottery techniques with Pueblo and Mexican artists. Her vessels are noted for their elegant and sinuous lines, often executed in glossy burnished shades of ochre and ebony. Odundo has had one-person shows in Hamburg, Germany, in a traveling show in the United States, and elsewhere. Her ceramic art is in the collections of the Smithsonian, the British Museum, the Victoria and Albert Museum, and many other noted institutions. In 2002 she was named a professor at the Surrey Institute of Art and Design in England.

ODUYOYE, MERCY (1934–). Oduyoye is a Ghanaian theologian. The daughter of an Asante Methodist pastor, she was educated in Ghana, studying at Legon University before going to Newnham College, Cambridge, England. After marrying Adedoyia Modupe Oduyoye in 1968, they moved to Nigeria where she was the first woman lecturer in the Department of Religious Studies at the University of Ibadan. She worked for the World Council of Churches (WCC) and the All Africa Conference of Churches (AACC), both positions which brought her into contact with women across the continent and internationally who were committed to keeping religion at the center of their lives. She was the principal founder of the **Circle of Concerned African Women Theologians** and the primary public voice of the Circle for many years. In 1991 she was named deputy general secretary at the WCC in Geneva, where she remained until her retirement in 1996. She has been a visiting lecturer at Princeton, Harvard, and the Union Theological Seminary in New York, and in 1990 she was awarded a doctorate by the Academy of Ecumenical Indian Theology at the Lutheran College in Madras, India. She has published extensively on **religion**, **Christianity**, and African women's philosophies.

OGOT, GRACE EMILY AKINYI (1930–). A Kenyan writer of novels and short stories, she has also served in the Kenyan government. She was born in Kenya, and trained as a **nurse** in Uganda (1949–1953) and England (1955–1958). One of the first African female writers to be published, her first short story appeared in 1962, and her novel *The Promised Land* was printed in 1966 (the same year as **Flora**

Nwapa's *Efuru*). She has published two other novels, *The Graduate* and *The Strange Bride*, and three short story collections, *The Other Woman*, *The Island of Tears*, and *Land Without Thunder*. A prominent theme of her stories is the struggle between men and women, often centering on male brutality toward women. Even though she has raised such issues as **rape** and **domestic violence** in her stories, she has only rarely spoken out on these issues in Kenya. She also uses her fiction to discuss **missions**, hospitals, and modern medicine, often shown in conflict with African **witchcraft**, which she presents as part of African reality without condemning it. Ogot was a founding member of the Writer's Association of Kenya. Although many of her works are available in English, she has written novels in the Luo language, Dholuo.

Grace Ogot's political work has included positions in community development, business, and public relations. She has been employed as a **journalist** with the *East African Standard* and for local radio, as well as owning a Nairobi boutique that carried items for girls and babies. Ogot was a member of parliament from 1983 to 1992, first entering as an appointee of President Arap Moi. She served as the assistant minister of culture and social services (1985–1993), and also was Kenya's representative to the United Nations and the United Nations Educational, Scientific and Cultural Organization (UNESCO). Ogot played a controversial role in the burial case of S. M. Otieno (see **Wambui Otieno**), as she initially spoke in favor of **widows'** rights, but withdrew that support when her photo was used without her permission on posters displayed in Nairobi. Her position as a prominent Luo woman illuminated the conflict between ethnic solidarity and women's position in African society. She is married to the well-known Kenyan historian Bethwell Ogot.

OIL PROTESTS. Women in Nigeria have been involved in a series of resistance activities directed at the international oil producing companies that extract oil along the Nigerian coastline. Nigeria depends on oil exports, which account for over 90 percent of its foreign exchange income. In 1986 women demonstrated to protest their loss of access to land in Ekpan and the burden of increased taxes in Ughelli. They formed **Niger Delta Women for Justice** (online at www.kabissa.org .ndwj). In 2002 women gained international attention when they took over the Escravos export terminal and held hundreds of Chevron workers hostage as they demanded that more local people be employed on the project. They threatened to remove their clothing in a traditional **shaming practice** unless their demands were met, which they were when Chevron promised to hire 25 workers from the local community. Although women had been involved in many protests prior to this one, it was believed that the Escravos takeover was the first action entirely by women. One leader, Anunu Uwawah, commented that "We will no longer take this nonsense, this is the beginning of the trouble they have been looking for." In each of the instances women won some or all of their demands, including the increased **employment** of local people in the oil industry. Ultimately protestors want to see a fifty-fifty division of oil revenue between the local and national governments; the current division gives 87 percent to the national coffers while only 13 percent goes to the state governments in the oil region. *See also* ABA WOMEN'S WAR.

OJIAMBO, JULIA. A Kenyan politician, she was a member of parliament and the first female minister in Kenya, as assistant minister for **housing** and social services (1978–1989). She won the United Nations Food and Agriculture Organization Ceres Medal. She was a presidential candidate in 2002 as a member of the Labour Party of Kenya (which was part of the coalition Rainbow Party of Kenya), and though she did not win that race, she did remain in parliament.

OKWEI, OMU (1872–1943). Okwei was a major trader and Igbo **market woman** in Onitsha, Nigeria. Born to a royal family in Ossomari, she was descended from formidable merchants and apprenticed at the age of nine to a maternal aunt to learn the market business. She built her own trading empire from nothing, as she forfeited her **dowry** by marrying men who were not approved by her parents. She began by trading food and expanded to include tobacco and cotton material. As British control grew in the region, she became an agent of the Niger Company in 1904 and began to market vegetable oil in exchange for gin, lamps, matches, and dishes and pots. She benefited from the inter-city trade, and used her profits to acquire girls and young women who she then placed in arranged **marriages** with prominent businessmen. That system of **slavery** meant that all children and goods accrued to Okwei as the owner of the women, and gave her favorable terms of credit as well as privileged access to men who traded in ivory and gunpowder. She was named to the Native Court in 1912, and played an important role in the social life of her city. In 1935 she was crowned as Omu (Queen) in recognition of her central role in the economy and society of Onitsha. There is a life-sized marble statue of her in Onitsha (unveiled in 1963), and one of the city's main roads bears her name. *See also* PELEWURA, ALIMOTU; TINUBU, MADAM.

OLOWO, BERNADETTE (BERNADETTE OLOWO-FREERS). In 1975 Olowo was appointed to serve as ambassador to the Vatican representing Uganda. She was the first woman in over 900 years to be a diplomat in the Vatican. In the 1990s she became involved with **HIV/AIDS** activism, and has worked with the United Nations Children's Fund (UNICEF) and UNAIDS projects in southern and eastern Africa.

ONWUEME, OSONYE TESS (1955–). Onwueme is a prolific playwright from Nigeria whose plays frequently address women's issues. She studied English at the University of Ife, earning a B.A. in 1979 and an M.A. 1982, going on to obtain a Ph.D. from the University of Benin, Nigeria. One of her first plays condemned arranged **marriages** (*A Hen Too Soon*, 1983); *Tell It To Women* (1992, revised 1997) discusses African perspectives on **feminism**. Three of her plays have won the Drama Prize from the Association of Nigerian Authors (ANA): *The Desert Encroaches* (1985), *Tell It To Women* (1995), and *Shakara: Dance-Hall Queen* (2001). She also served as acting vice-president and president of the ANA from 1987 to 1989. Her play *The Missing Face* was produced off Broadway in New York in 2001, and in 2003 the BBC announced plans to produce *Shakara* as a radio play. Onwueme has also published a novel, *Why the Elephant Has No Butt* (2000) and numerous essays of literary criticism. Since 1989 she she has been teaching in the United States, and since 1994 at the University of Wisconsin, Eau Claire. She is married and has five children.

ONYANGO, GRACE MONICA AKECH (1934–). A politician in Kenya, she was elected mayor of the city of Kisumu in 1965 and was the first African women to serve as a member of parliament serving from 1969 until 1984 and acting as deputy speaker of the national assembly from 1979 to 1984.

ORAL TRADITION. Women in many African societies participated in passing along oral traditions, sometimes in the forms of songs or **poetry**. In West Africa women were sometimes professional *griottes*, with a social responsibility for remembering and re-telling history. In other areas women performed stories and songs. In Somalia women's stories included the history of their maternal line of descent, keeping alive women's contribution while men's stories omitted them. In southern Africa women's songs included laments about the burden of colonial demands. Other songs may outline the expected behavior of a married woman, or her role in the spiritual life of her community. These various sources provide a way to discover women's understanding and interpretation of their own history. Playwrights and authors including **Barbara Kimenye**, **Grace Ogot**, and **Efua Sutherland** have drawn from oral traditions as they developed an African form of literary expression.

ORGANISATION DES FEMMES REVOLUTIONNAIRES DU BENIN / ORGANIZATION OF REVOLUTIONARY WOMEN OF BENIN. This association was established to bring more women into government; it was founded in 1982. It has recruited women to run for public office.

ORGANIZAÇÃO DA MULHER ANGOLANA (OMA) / ORGANIZATION OF ANGOLAN WOMEN. The OMA was established in 1962 as a part of the Movimento Popular de Libertação de Angola (MPLA)/Popular Movement for the Liberation of Angola, one of the leading anti-colonial organizations. The group's primary activity was to recruit more women, and to improve the ability of women to participate in MPLA actions, as was common in **political party organizations**. **Literacy** classes and rural **cooperative** work were among the projects initiated by the OMA. Some women were also involved in combat, and 2 March is Angolan Women's Day in recognition of the death of five female combatants at the hands of a rival organization on that day in 1967. In the early 1980s membership expanded dramatically, from 351,590 in 1979 to 1,014,988 in 1983. In the climate of continuing civil **war** during the 1980s and 1990s, the OMA held a series of national meetings, remained involved in international women's activities, and in 1990 made a special appeal to women in the United States to act to end the war, which was having a particularly harsh impact on women and children. *See also* RODRIGUES, DEOLINDA.

ORGANIZAÇÃO DA MULHER MOÇAMBICANA (OMM) / ORGANIZATION OF MOZAMBICAN WOMEN. OMM was founded in 1972 as a wing of the Frente de Libertação de Moçambique (FRELIMO)/Mozambique Liberation Front. There had been two earlier women's organizations, the **Liga Feminina Moçambicana (LIFEMO) / League of Mozambican Women**, and the Destacamento Feminino/Female Detachment, which was essentially a department in the military. Male FRELIMO leaders felt neither of those groups performed the kind of organizing work that was needed and encouraged OMM's emergence as the primary organization for women. When a new constitution was introduced in 1990, OMM became an autonomous organization, but in 1996 it voted to return to close affiliation with Frelimo (no longer capitalized after becoming the Partido Frelimo/Frelimo Party). OMM is a leading member of the Mozambican umbrella group, Forum Mulher/Women's Forum.

ORGANIZAÇÃO DAS MULHERES DE CABO VERDE (OMCV) / ORGANIZATION OF WOMEN OF CAPE VERDE. Initially called the **União Democrática das Mulheres**, the name was changed in 1981 following a coup that resulted in the separation of Cape Verde and Guinea-Bissau. It was then considered a section of the ruling party, the Partido Africano para a Independência da Cabo Verde (PAICV)/African Party for the Independence of Cape Verde. It organized rural centers for women to provide informal **education**, health information, and other supportive programs. The OMCV continued to be active as a **non-governmental organization** in the 1990s under the leadership of Maria Madalena Tavares, working to improve women's condition. *See also* INSTITUTO DA CONDIÇÃO FEMININA; MORABI.

ORGANIZATIONS. African women have been involved in a wide range of organizations in both rural and urban areas. Often responding to social needs and cultural desires, women have banded together in **dance** societies, **initiation rites** collectivities, **rotating savings and credit associations**, age-based societies, and neighborhood groups. Most have been small, local, and short-lived, and so are not recorded in formal history sources. During the colonial era many organizations were formed that focused on teaching western domesticity to African women; the *foyers sociaux* in the Belgian colonies were a model of this type of group. There is also some evidence of women's ethnic societies, such as the Ewe Women's Association that was founded in 1953 in Ghana. Local organizations have included **political**, rotating credit, and **religious** groups, alumni associations, as well as work-related groups such as **nurses'** societies, **market women**'s groups, **cooperatives**, organizations of women **journalists** or teachers, and **trade unions**. Many international groups have had African branches; for instance, the Young Women's Christian Association (YMCA), the International Federation of Business and Professional Women, Associated Country Women of the World, International Planned Parenthood Federation (IPPF), Girl Guides, and a variety of church groups such as the Women's Fellowship of the United Congregational Church and **Mother's Unions** in the Catholic Church. In the 1980s and 1990s there was a proliferation of autonomous groups as governments across the political spectrum loosened control over public civic life. Many new **non-governmental organizations** appeared, with dozens arising in each country; for instance a 1998 list from Malawi lists 35 women's groups. *See also* POLITICAL PARTY ORGANIZATIONS.

OSUN. Osun is a prominent **goddess** in the Yoruba pantheon of *orisa*, and as such has devoted followers not only in Nigeria (and particularly in her home area of Osogbo which sponsors an annual festival in her name), but in Brazil, Cuba, and elsewhere in the African diaspora. Her name, Osun, means "the source," and she is commonly associated with water, the element that flows and seeps, and which is necessary for life itself. Though Osun is sometimes called a river goddess, that name does not reflect the breadth of her authority. Osun is often appealed to for assistance with **fertility** issues, and she is recognized for her role in matters concerning maternity and **health** though she is not limited to those areas. She is generally paired with Ogun, who can be characterized as a male warrior god associated with iron, while she is associated with cowrie shells (both iron and cowrie being sources of wealth in Yoruba society). *See also* MAMI WATA.

OTIENO, WAMBUI WAIYAKI (1936–). Wambui Otieno is a Kenyan woman active in politics. She came to wider prominence in 1986 when her husband, renowned lawyer Silvano Melea Otieno (always called S. M. Otieno), died without leaving a written will. The events that followed brought modern concerns about ethnicity, gender, **inheritance**, **widowhood**, and power to the forefront of public debate in Kenya and elsewhere. Wambui Otieno was from a prominent Kikuyu family. She was deeply involved in the **Mau Mau** anticolonial struggle in the 1950s, where she was a central figure organizing women as scouts and providers of food. She was detained by the British authorities more than once. After independence she settled in Nairobi where she continued to be active in politics, and she met S. M., a Luo. Their marriage embodied the inter-ethnic ideals of the era when the new leadership promulgated the idea of being Kenyan rather than identifying with a particular ethnicity. When S. M. died, Wambui planned to bury him on land they owned together in Nairobi, where he had requested to be buried. His Luo clan insisted on burying him in his homeland, so Wambui took them to court to protect her rights as his wife. In the court case Wambui's lawyers argued that S. M. had turned away from his Luo roots by marrying a Kikuyu woman, living in Nairobi, and converting to **Christianity**. His clan claimed that S. M.'s birth and childhood as a Luo had primacy, and the courts sided with them. Many observers felt the decision, which resulted in a triumphant "homecoming" burial in the Luo home district, undercut legal gains made by women as well as encouraging ethnic dissension. The details of the complicated burial case, as well as information about Wambui's Mau Mau experiences, can be found in her autobiography *Mau Mau's Daughter: A Life History* (ed. by Cora Ann Presley, 1998).

OUATTARA, GUIMBÉ (c. 1836–1919). Guimbé Ouattara was born to a noble family in the area of West Africa that became Burkina

Faso. She was a military leader who was involved in several campaigns, most notably when she called in the renowned ruler Samory to exact revenge on the rebellious Tiéfo. Guimbé was with Samory when Noumoudara was destroyed by his forces, and she continued as a powerful influence in Bobo Dioulasso in the years that followed. She was also noted because she received the French travelers Louis Gustave Binger, François Crozat, and Parfait Lours Monteil.

OUEDRAOGO, JOSEPHINE. Josephine Ouedraogo is a highly influential voice in African women's **development**, serving since 1997 as head of the United Nations Economic Commission for Africa's gender division (most recently called the **African Centre for Gender and Development**, ACGD). Trained as a sociologist, she had previously served as the minister for family affairs and national solidarity in the government in Burkina Faso (1984–1987) where she was noted for her role in preparing a national **family law** and for working to eradicate **female genital cutting**. She was also a project coordinator for the Pan-African Development Institute in Cameroon from 1989 to 1992. As head of the ACGD Ouedraogo has successfully pushed gender issues to the forefront of a variety of African governmental conferences and task forces, and introduced a new evaluation program, the African Gender Development Index.

OUEZZIN COULIBALY, CÉLESTINE-MARIE-MARTHE (NÉE MAKOUKOU TRAORÉ) (c. 1910–?). An anti-colonial leader in French West Africa in the 1940s, she was from the Côte d'Ivoire. Her father was Balla Traoré, the chief of the canton of Sindou with 21 wives and 39 children among them. Makoukou married Daniel Ouezzin Coulibaly (1909–1958) in 1930, and adopted the name Célestine in 1931 when they both were baptized in the Catholic Church. Célestine Ouezzin Coulibaly helped institute the women's section of the Rassemblement Démocratique Africain (RDA) in Côte d'Ivoire and Upper Volta (now Burkina Faso), and was elected as general secretary of the women's section in 1948. When the RDA leadership was imprisoned she was one of the leaders of a successful women's march to **Grand Bassam** calling for their release. After independence in 1958 she was appointed minister of social affairs, **housing**, and work in the new government of Upper Volta, serving until 1959 when she was elected to represent Upper Volta in the French Community senate (1959–1961). Ouezzin Coulibaly was probably the first female cabinet member of any francophone West African government. *See also* KÉITA, AOUA; NATIONALISM.

OUTRAS VOZES. The English-language newsletter *Outras Vozes* (*Other Voices*) is published by the office of **Woman and Law in Southern Africa** in Mozambique. One representative issue from 2003 published articles on women's legal situation, traditional power and women, and several contributions on the debate on the **family law** in Mozambique.

OWINO WOMEN'S GROUP. The Owino market in Kampala, Uganda, the largest in the city, is estimated to have over 30,000 vendors, two-thirds of them women. The **market women** organized into a group in the 1990s with the goal of improving working conditions for women; they have facilitated access to loans for women and have continued to agitate for a **childcare** center onsite, which was included in the original plans when the market was privatized in 1998 but which was never built.

OYEDEPO, STELLA. Oyedepo is one of Nigeria's foremost playwrights; she has written over 100 plays although fewer than one dozen have been published. Her themes focused on daily life and problems, and often address **marriage**, corruption, **politics**, and family life. Her play *The Greatest Gift* (1988) contrasted two families, one driven to destitution by the father's drinking despite the best efforts of the mother to hold everyone together, the other living an exemplary life of cooperation and success. In 2001 she wrote *Brain has no Gender* for the Kwara State Ministry of Education for Women-in-Science Programme. *See also* THEATER.

– P –

PALMER, JOSIE (1903–1979). Born Josie Mpama, Palmer was a political leader in the Communist Party of South Africa (CPSA) who used the pseudonym Beatrice Henderson when visiting the Soviet

Union. She was considered "Coloured," or mixed race in the **apartheid** racial categories, and she married Edwin Mofutsanyane, an African man also active in the CPSA and the African National Congress (ANC). She first joined the CPSA in 1928 when she became involved in Potchefstroom in a campaign against racially based residential permits, and worked closely with the party throughout the 1920s and 1930s. She wrote for the party journal, *Umsebenzi*, was head of the CPSA Women's Department, and was engaged in the anti-pass campaigns of the 1940s. She helped establish the women's anti-pass conference of 1944, and was briefly head of the Transvaal All-Women's Union, renamed the Union of South African Women in 1949, though it remained a regional organization. Palmer went on to participate in founding the **Federation of South African Women**. In the late 1940s she joined the Anglican Church and was active in church women's groups. She was banned in 1955 and was unable to participate in the anti-pass demonstrations of that decade. She died when a car hit her as she waited in a line to collect her pension. *See also* PASS LAWS.

PAN AFRICAN WOMEN'S LIBERATION ORGANIZATION (PAWLO). PAWLO is based in Uganda, and its main aim is to ensure that women's issues are integrated into the work of the Pan African Movement. It was founded in 1994, just prior to the seventh Pan African Congress. PAWLO met in Kampala with the Global Pan African Movement in April 2003 for a conference focused on world **peace**. PAWLO also published a regular bulletin, *Afrika Mama Yetu*. The PAWLO website can be found at: http://www.wougnet.org/Profiles/pawlo.html.

PAN AFRICAN WOMEN'S ORGANISATION. Founded in 1962, the organization was originally called the **All Africa Women's Conference**; the name was changed in 1974. The group held observer status in the Organization of African Unity (OAU). *See also* MARTIN-CISSÉ, JEANNE.

PASS LAWS. Colonial governments in many areas introduced **laws** that required women to carry passes giving them permission to leave their rural homes and move to urban areas. While men had long been subject to pass laws, women had been exempt until African men and colonial authorities became concerned about the numbers of women moving to urban areas. There were variations in the specifics, but many were similar to the law in Southern Rhodesia (later Zimbabwe) which required women seeking employment in the towns to obtain official approval from the colonial authorities. Such laws were designed to keep women under the control of men as they moved away from the influence of male family members. The most stringent laws were imposed under the **apartheid** government of South Africa, which was also the site of one of the largest protests against such laws, the 1956 **Defiance Campaign**.

PASTORALISM. Pastoralism is a system of production that focuses on herding cattle or other animals such as sheep, goats, or camels, sometimes involving lengthy migration in search of good pasture. In the conventional ethnographies of pastoral communities, men were described as owners of the animals and kinship and descent were characterized as exceptionally patriarchal in their organization. Recent scholarship has questioned this portrayal by investigating women's roles in pastoral societies, which range from the well-known Maasai of Kenya and Tanzania and Somali people, to lesser known and smaller groups such as the Turkana, Nuer, Okiek, and Samburu (all in East Africa), Damara and other Khoekhoen (formerly Khoikhoi and, pejoratively, Hottentot) in southern Africa, and western Saharan groups including the Tuareg and Fulani. Women were previously seen as outside of male-dominated positions of authority, which were described as related to male ownership of cattle and other animals, but now it is recognized that women have played a more central role in both caring for animals and governing their communities. Their position has not been static, but has changed over time, and individual women experience shifts in their social and productive roles as they marry, bear children, grow older, and gain or lose wealth and status.

P'BITEK, OKOT. *See* SONG OF LAWINO.

PEACE. African women have been active in a variety of negotiations for peace and have organized continent-wide groups to work to end conflict. One of the first declarations specifically focusing on peace issues came from the **Kampala Action Plan on Women and Peace** in 1993. A series of associations have been established, including **African Women's Anti-War Coalition**, **African Women's Committee for Peace and Development**, the **Federation of African Women for Peace**, and **Femmes Africa Solidarité**. Local groups have also formed, focusing on such intransigient conflicts as in the Democratic Republic of the Congo, where **Ruth Sando Perry** and others formed a lobbying group, **Women as Partners for Peace in Africa** (WOPPA). WOPPA promoted a negotiated peace settlement among the warring groups and simultaneously argued that women's voices should be included in that process. Women in Rwanda formed **Pro-Femmes Twese Hamwe**. In Sudan women desiring an end to the long conflict there formed the Sudan Women's Voice for Peace; similarly the Sierra Leone Women's Movement for Peace, founded prior to 1995, worked to end the conflict in that country. Women in Sierra Leone intervened directly in the war, sitting outside the doors of rooms where men were holding peace talks until they were allowed to enter and participate.

Women in Liberia followed the Sierra Leone example and played an important role in bringing peace. The Mano River Women Peace Network of Liberia was one of six organizations that was awarded the United Nations Human Rights Prize in 2003 for their efforts; the story of the Liberian activists is told in *Liberian Women Peacemakers* (2004). That book includes information by the African Women and Peace Support Group (AWPSG), an international organization formed in 1997 to document African women's involvement in peace activities. Women's efforts have had an important source of support in the United Nations' Security Council Resolution 1325 on Women, Peace and Security. The resolution was submitted by Namibia in 2000 at the instigation of Netumbo Nandi-Ndaitwah, Namibia's minister of women's affairs, and was passed unanimously by the council.

PELEWURA, ALIMOTU (c. 1865–1951). Pelewura was a prominent leader of the **Lagos Market Women's Association** in Nigeria in the first half of the 20th century. She was a Yoruba woman like most of her fellow vendors, and followed her mother into the fish trade where she was well established by 1900. She married and was **widowed**

while young, never had children and never remarried. Pelewura was appointed to the council of Yoruba authorities in Lagos in 1932, when she represented 84 women's market associations. In the 1930s the colonial officials complained of their difficulties with the powerful women's guilds in the markets. Pelewura led the **market women** in a series of protests, first to stop the threatened government effort to relocate their market in the mid-1930s, then against successive attempts to tax women in the 1930s and 1940s, and to resist the imposition of price controls during World War II. *See also* ABA WOMEN'S WAR; TINUBU, MADAM; OKWEI, OMU.

PEREIRA, CARMEN (1937–). Pereira was a **nationalist** leader in Guinea-Bissau. She was the daughter of a lawyer, and she joined the Partido Africano de Independência de Guiné e Cabo Verde (PAIGC)/African Party for the Independence of Guinea-Bissau and Cape Verde in 1962. In 1964 she was exiled, and she then trained as a **nurse** in the (then) Soviet Union. She was the most important woman in the movement, working as the Political Commissar for the southern region. Pereira was the only woman on the 24-member executive committee of the PAIGC, and was head of the Women's Commission of Guinea-Bissau and Cape Verde from 1975 to 1981. She served as second vice president of the national legislature in Guinea-Bissau, and was one of 15 members of the Council of State. Pereira was appointed minister of state for social affairs, and was acting **head of government** for 2 days in May 1984.

PEREIRA GOMES, FRANCISCA. A political leader in Guinea-Bissau, she joined the armed anti-colonial struggle as a teenager in 1960. She later trained as a **nurse** in the Soviet Union and directed the department of **health** during the liberation war. She later served as mayor of Bolama and as president of the **União Democrática das Mulheres (UDEMU) / Democratic Union of Women**. She has continued to serve in the government, as minister of women's affairs from 1990 to 1994, as vice president of the national assembly from 1994 to 1997, and as minister of the interior from 1997 to 1999. In 2002 she was appointed as minister of state, charged with political affairs and diplomacy. She also worked on peace initiatives as a member of **Femmes Africa Solidarité**.

PERHAM, MARGERY (1895–1982). Perham was a major figure in British **colonial** rule in Africa from the 1930s through the 1960s. Trained in history at Oxford, she was deeply affected by a visit to Somalia in 1921 through 1922 when her sister and brother-in-law were stationed there. She traveled across the continent on a series of investigative journeys in the 1930s, and wrote several books and numerous articles about her observations. She also wrote an influential multi-volume biography of Lord Frederick Lugard, the architect of indirect rule in British Africa. Perham was unusual for her involvement in issues of colonial governance, and though she saw herself as suffering for being neither a scholar nor an administrator, she hoped she had an effect on colonial officers in their work. She was most interested in helping Africans progress, but that was couched in a traditional view of a gulf between the races which was difficult to bridge. Her writings include strikingly paternalistic descriptions, as in her comments about **market women** in Nigeria being "in a frenzy," as they only had a "half-knowledge" of legal forms of protest, in her chapter on the **Aba Women's War** in *Native Administration in Nigeria* (1937). An informative set of articles about Perham's contributions can be found in a special issue of *The Journal of Imperial and Commonwealth History* on "Margery Perham and British Rule in Africa" (1991). *See also* WESTERN WOMEN.

PERIODICALS. Journals and periodicals specifically directed at women have a varied history in Africa. In some cases local **organizations**, from the Catholic **missions** to women's political groups published general interest monthly or quarterly magazines, such as *Rencontre Africaine*. After the 1970s, as women became more politically active and **women's studies** programs were established, **feminist** publications and scholarly journals addressing women's research and **development** issues began to appear. These included *Ahfad Journal* (Sudan) and *Agenda* (South Africa). A list of all periodicals included in this dictionary is in the bibliography.

PERRY, RUTH SANDO (1939–). Perry made history as the first female **head of state** of Liberia (1996–1997), and as one of the first women to lead any African government. She was trained as a teacher, and eventually became involved in her nation's troubled politics, serving as a senator. She was also a supervisor of the Chase Manhattan Bank in Liberia, and worked for many child welfare organizations. In 1996 Perry was named by the Economic Community of West African States (ECOWAS) as Chairperson of the Council of State in Liberia, where she presided over the transitional government until 1997. Perry evoked women's role as mothers in her rule, saying that the children—the warlords—must obey their mother. In that capacity she was responsible for disarming the warring factions as a prelude to democratic government. She went on to establish the Perry Centre for Peace, Stability and Development in Africa, to support others working on **peace**-building efforts across the continent, and she has been involved with **Women as Partners for Peace in Africa**.

PILLAY, NAVANETHEM (1941–). Navanethem Pillay is an internationally renowned judge originally from South Africa. She earned her B.A. and Bachelor of Laws degrees from Natal University, followed by masters and doctoral studies in **law** and juridical science at Harvard University. She was the first woman to open a law practice in Natal Province, South Africa, in 1967, and she worked consistently to support opponents of **apartheid**, including on important cases dealing with solitary confinement and political prisoners' rights. In 1995 Pillay was appointed to the Supreme Court of South Africa, followed by her election by the United Nations General Assembly to serve as a judge on the International Criminal Tribunal for Rwanda. During her eight years on that court, she set precedents with rulings that included **rape** and sexual violence as crimes under international law. In 2003 she was elected as one of 18 judges on the International Criminal Court, along with **Fatoumata Dembélé Diarra** and Ghanaian jurist Akua Kuenyehia. She has been honored with international awards for her legal and humanitarian efforts.

POETRY. African women's poetry has a long history and a wide-ranging set of themes. Many poems have a religious source, as with the writings of **Nana Asma'u**. Others have been more overtly political, such as the Mozambican poems by **Noémia da Sousa**, or resistance poems by women in Somalia. Recently poems that had been preserved in **oral tradition** have been retrieved and written down, and other poets have chosen to write in their native language, such as **Caroline Ntseliseng 'Masechele Khaketla** and **Nontsizi Mgqwetho.** Many authors who are better known for their prose publications also wrote poetry; these include **Ama Ata Aidoo, Flora Nwapa,** and **Micere Githae Mugo.** *See also* CASELY HAY-FORD, ADELAIDE SMITH; LARA, ALDA; LITERATURE; M'BAYE, ANNETTE D'ERNEVILLE; MWANA KUPONA; SANTO, ALDA ESPÍRITO; SONG OF LAWINO.

POKOU (c. 1700–1760) (SOMETIMES ABLA POKOU OR AURA POKOU). Queen Pokou is recognized as the founder of the Baulé people in Côte d'Ivoire, though the details of her story are not clearly recorded. She was born to Asante royalty in the area that is today Ghana, and was the niece of the renowned leader Osei Tutu and sister to his heir. Following a succession dispute, which directly involved her because she had an infant son who would have been in line to accede to the throne, she left Asante with a group of followers and traveled to the west. Some stories relate that Pokou had to sacrifice that son in order to permit the group to cross the Comoé River. The Baule became known as important traders in the 19th century. She is the subject of a novel (*La reine Pokou: fondatrice du royaume baoulé*, by Jean-Noël Loucou, with Françoise Ligier, 1977) and plays.

POLITICAL PARTY ORGANIZATIONS. In many African countries the only sanctioned women's organization was one that was affiliated with, and often established by, the ruling party. Although there were variations, in most cases the nation's **first lady** played a leadership role, and the primary work of the organization was to support the ruling party rather than to focus on women's needs. At the same time the presence of these groups allowed women to raise women's issues in the public arena at the national level, and often to have their concerns taken seriously. As **democratization** spread in the 1990s there was an opening for the party organizations to operate independently and there were greater opportunities for many new issue-focused groups to emerge. Some political party organizations included the **Inkatha Women's Brigade, Liga Independente da Mulher Angolana, Mouvement National des Femmes, National Congress of Sierra Leone Women, Organização da Mulher Angolana, Organização da Mulher Moçambicana, Organização das Mulheres de Cabo Verde,**

Uganda Association of Women's Organizations, Union des Femmes du Niger, Union des Femmes Maliennes, Union Revolutionnaire des Femmes du Congo, and the Women's Cameroon National Union.

POLITICS. Women have been active in political organizations throughout history, though it is best documented for recent decades. In earlier times women held political power as **queen mothers** and as spiritual leaders in communities where political and religious roles intersected. In the late 19th century and into the 20th century, women were noted for their involvement in **nationalist** causes. In the post-independence era, women have faced a variety of obstacles to equality in government, and are particularly noted for their absence from the centers of power.

With the international pressure for **democratization** in the 1990s, women were able to find more opportunities for participating, though the obstacles they faced continued to be daunting. Few women have been **heads of state** or **heads of government** for an African nation, but they have made progress in being appointed to cabinet positions, and in 19 countries they are guaranteed a percentage of seats in the national legislature through either a party or electoral quota system. There have also been advances at the level of local government, and following elections in Uganda in 1998 there were more than 10,000 women holding office in local councils and other low-level positions.

The situation of women in national parliaments is well documented. Tanzania, for example, amended its constitution to reserve 15 percent of the seats in the parliament and 25 percent of local council seats for women. Benin named four women to cabinet positions in 1998, but with no clear policy to bring women into government, there were still only six women in parliament out of 82 total members. The average for sub-Saharan Africa in 2003 was about 15 percent female legislators, nearly matching the international average of 15.1 percent. Following elections in 2003 Rwanda leaped to the number one spot in the world, with 48.8 percent women. Eritrea, Mozambique, Namibia, Seychelles, South Africa, Tanzania, and Uganda have between 20 and 30 percent of women representatives, among the highest rates in the world. But in many other countries, especially many of the Francophone countries, women account for less then 10 percent of legislators (Senegal is exception with nearly 20 percent female parliamentarians, but Niger is among the lowest in the world with only 1.2 percent women in the legislature). It is believed that a critical mass of at least 30 percent is needed before women can have an impact on legislation and policy. Once women gain seats, they have used their positions to support legislation in such areas as **marriage** and **inheritance** and to work for **family laws** and **citizenship** provisions that can benefit women. Current statistics regarding the numbers of women in parliaments around the world can be found at the website of the Inter-Parliamentary Union, www.ipu.org.

POLYGAMY. Polygamy, though commonly used to refer to a marriage in which a man married more than one wife, means "multiple spouses" and is not as accurate a term as **polygyny**, which specifically means "many wives."

POLYGYNY. Most African societies have accepted and even preferred a polygynous marital system in which men are permitted and sometimes expected to marry more than one wife. While statistics are not reliable and do not account for second wives who are not legally married, polygyny rates in West Africa are as high as 40 percent of all marriages, ranging between 20 and 40 percent for much of central and southern Africa, and are under 20 percent in South Africa. Other sources suggest that from one-third to one-half of all African women are in polygynous marriages.

The historical record shows a few elite or royal men who had dozens or even hundreds of wives, usually married as a strategy to build political alliances. In one unusual modern example, King Mswati III of Swaziland came under international scrutiny in 2002 for abducting a teenage girl to be his 10th wife and marrying her in 2004 (his father had reportedly accumulated one hundred wives); his actions were seen as particularly reprehensible in a country with a 33 percent **HIV/AIDS** infection rate. More commonly, men would have two or three wives, and the women were able to share a heavy workload of farming, cooking, and **childcare**. In some areas the second wife was chosen in agreement with the first wife, who could arrange for her younger sister or other kinswoman to join her household. In societies where women's daily labor was the basis of cultivating food, a household with more able-bodied women was more capable of survival. Although polygyny has been portrayed by western **feminists** as inherently oppressive to women, the reality has been a wide range of experiences, from households where the co-wives were close, enjoyed sharing agricultural work and childcare responsibilities, and even were known to band together against the husband, to households where jealousy and acrimony were the prevalent sentiments.

Areas of **Islamic** influence appear to have a greater number of polygynous relationships. Polygyny was one of the main practices that Christian **missionaries** struggled to bring to an end, and it has also been the focus of some governmental campaigns (for example, in Mozambique in the early post-independence years). Although the practice is generally in decline as a result of **urbanization**, higher female **educational** levels, and increased costs of living, there has also been a new adherence to the practice as some men and women have seen polygyny as a particularly African form of marriage that should not be abandoned or eradicated. Men sometimes have an informal second wife, setting up two households which may or may not be aware of each other. In some cases the second wife is denied the legal protections and social status that the first wife has, while in other relationships it is the first wife who is abandoned in favor of a younger woman. Women's views of polygyny have been put forward in important fiction by **Mariama Bâ** (*Une si longue lettre*, translated as *So Long a Letter*) and **Ama Ata Aidoo** (*Changes: A Love Story*), and in songs by Malian singer **Oumou Sangaré**.

POONOOSAMY, RADHA (1923–). A political leader in Mauritius, she was the first woman to hold a cabinet post there. She was born in Durban, South Africa, and educated at Natal University. She became active in anti-**apartheid** politics, and was a leader of the Women's League of the Natal Indian Congress as well as serving on the executive committee of the African National Congress (ANC). In 1952 she moved to Mauritius after marrying a Mauritian physician. There she founded the women's section of the Indo-Mauritian Association, was active in the Mauritius Labour Party, was mayor of Quatre Bornes, and in 1975 was elected to parliament, where she introduced laws against sex discrimination. For 18 months in 1975 through 1976 Poonoosamy was minister of women's affairs, prices, and consumer protection.

POVERTY. As in other parts of the world, the feminization of poverty is a notable factor in African life as women in both rural and urban areas confront increasing obstacles to earning enough to support their families. Although statistics are not reliable (a commonly cited figure that 70 percent of the world's poor are women is not considered realistic), women are more vulnerable because they do not have access to the same jobs as men, they do not earn the same pay when they are employed, in many areas they do not have equal **inheritance** rights, they have notably lower **literacy** rates than men, and they often have sole responsibility for their children. The increasing number of **female-headed households** is also a factor, as men frequently do not contribute to the maintenance of their children following a **divorce** or other breakup of a relationship. *See also* STRUCTURAL ADJUSTMENT PROGRAMS.

PRAYER GROUPS. Women have formed groups for Bible study and prayer within a wide variety of **Christian** churches. In some cases these groups have offered the opportunity to gain leadership skills and have provided an outlet where women can discuss family and social problems. *See also MANYANO*; RELIGIOUS ORGANIZATIONS.

PREHISTORY. The roles and contributions of women in African prehistory are particularly difficult to discern. Researchers using historical linguistics and archeology have developed ideas about **motherhood**, early cultivation, and religious beliefs that present some sense of what women's lives might have been like. The difficulty is that the evidence can show how bananas, for instance, became an important crop in the area now part of Uganda, but it cannot definitively demonstrate the gender division of labor.

Great Zimbabwe was an important urban settlement in southern African that was thriving in the 12th to 15th centuries. It then declined for reasons that are not well understood, though some scholars have suggested that a major factor was the scarcity of nearby firewood for cooking. When women refused to walk great distances to gather wood the people dispersed into smaller less urban settlements. Debates about the development and decay of Great Zimbabwe rely heavily on interpretations of archeological evidence concerning royal wives, their housing, female **initiation rites**, and male and female images.

PRINCESS MAGOGO KADINUZULU (1900–1984). Princess Magogo was a much-loved Zulu woman who was the daughter of King Dinuzulu and mother of political leader Mangosuthu Buthelezi. She was renowned for the three-octave range of her singing voice, and she also played the traditional stringed instrument the *ugubhu* and acted as an archivist of Zulu **music**. She was also the first recognized female Zulu praise singer. In 2002 Mzilikazi Khumalo and Theba Msimang wrote an opera based on her life, combining western operatic and Zulu musical traditions; the opera, called *Princess Magogo kaDinuzulu*, first opened in Durban, South Africa, and had its American premier in Chicago in 2004. *See also* GRIOTTES.

PRO-FEMMES TWESE HAMWE / FOR WOMEN, ALL TO- GETHER. Pro-Femmes is a coalition of women's organizations in Rwanda. It was founded in 1992 in response to fears about escalating ethnic violence, and initially had 13 member groups. After 10 years of activity, there were 40 women's groups affiliated with Pro-Femmes focused especially on organizing for **peace**.

PROSTITUTION. It appears that prostitution, at least in forms which are recognized as the practice of exchanging money for sexual favors, was rarely practiced in precolonial African societies. The few exceptions involved **slave** women who were destitute and usually far from their home communities. One of the earliest references to a specific prostitute is to **Eva van Meerhoff**, the South African woman who turned to prostitution following the death of her Dutch husband in the 17th century.

There were instances where women entered into relationships with men who were not their husbands, and these were sometimes of short duration, but they also could last many years and result in children. There were local terms for women who went from man to man, or who sought sexual relationships outside of marriage, including *adana* and *mgboto* (Igbo), and *malaya* and *watembezi* (Swahili). Those words seldom translate easily to "prostitute," but they often refer to aspects of the prostitute's behavior, such as her ease in undressing, or her habit of walking on the streets.

With the onset of **colonialism** and the development of **urban** centers and market economies, some African women found that prostitution was a way to earn an income. Prostitution in African societies rarely involved the presence of a pimp, or male control, and did not necessarily rely on brothels. More common was the individual woman who accepted money from men whom she provided with sexual activity and often with domestic tasks such as a cooked meal or laundry services. Urban women are sometimes perceived as prostitutes if they **dress** in western styles, especially in revealing or form-fitting clothing, and if they appear to be financially independent. This attitude was seen during the colonial era as well, when authorities subjected African women to hygiene controls including forced physical examinations in an attempt to stem the spread of venereal diseases. Though not practiced everywhere, in Southern Rhodesia (now Zimbabwe) from the mid-1920s to the late 1950s, women were regularly examined in a practice they called *chibheura* (open your legs). With the spread of **HIV/AIDS** from the 1980s onward, prostitutes were extremely vulnerable to that disease and were also held responsible for the unchecked epidemic. More African women have migrated to Europe since the 1990s, where they sometimes worked as prostitutes; studies from 2001 and 2002 suggested that from 20,000 to 30,000 Nigerian women were working as prostitutes in Italy.

PROTOCOL ON THE RIGHTS OF WOMEN IN AFRICA. In 2003 the African Union passed a new protocol on women's rights at their summit meeting in Maputo, Mozambique, as a supplement to the African Charter on Human and Peoples' Rights. For it to come into effect fifteen member nations must ratify it. The major provisions set precedent in international law regarding **abortion** and **female genital cutting**. Abortion was established as a right of women who have been **raped**, subject to incest, or when the mother's life or health is in danger. The document also explicitly called on member states to prohibit the practice of female genital cutting. Further sections addressed the issues of **domestic violence** and supported affirmative action in **politics** and **employment**. The document set forth a series of detailed provisions that would substantially improve African women's legal position in a wide range of issues, from ensuring equal access to **land**, to introducing a variety of funded measures to reduce maternal mortality rates. An important element was the pro-active role taken by a number of women's **organizations** to ensure that the protocol would pass; some of those involved were the **Africa Gender Institute** at the University of Cape Town, **African Women's Development and Communication Network (FEMNET)**, **Femmes Africa Solidarité (FAS)**, and **Women and Law in Southern Africa**. The text can be read in full at the website of the Human Rights Education Association: www.hrea.org. *See also* MONGELLA, GERTRUDE; TANKEU, ELIZABETH.

PURDAH. *See* SECLUSION.

– Q –

QUEEN MOTHERS. Queen mothers were women of real power and authority in their societies. They were most common in **matrilineal** groups where the female line of descent was the central one. They were usually but not always the biological mother of the king, and they often had a much wider role as royal counselor and sometimes co-equal sovereign. Although the political offices were generally held by men, in many instances the men had gained that position because of the activity of their female kin. Some of the best known queen mothers, including **Afua Kobi**, **Yaa Asantewaa**, and **Yaa Akyaa**, were among the Asante in what is now central Ghana, where the local term was *ahema* or more specifically, *asantehemaa*. The Akan proverb that "It is a woman who gave birth to a man, it is a woman who gave birth to a chief" encapsulates the philosophy of queen mothers' authority.

"Queen mother" is the most common English rendering of a wide variety of local expressions for royal or noble women in leadership positions though it is not always the best translation of such terms. The queen mother in the area that is now Rwanda was called *umugabekasi*, and she lived at the court, controlled her own land holdings, owned cattle, and earned the loyalty of people who served her as clients. Further examples of specific terminology for female titles include *magira* for the Kanuri queen mother in Bornu in northern Nigeria, *ndlovukazi* for the Swazi queen mother, *ndlorukazi* in Zulu, *kpojito* among the Fon in Dahomey, and *mafo*, the term for the Bamileke queen mother in Cameroon. Many famous African women were queen mothers, including **'Mamohatao Tabitha 'Masentle Lerotholi, Labotsibeni Gwamile Mdluli, Ndate Yala Mboj, Njembot Mboj**, and **Nandi**. *See also* MOTHERHOOD; RAIN QUEEN.

– R –

RABESAHALA, GISÈLE (1930–). A **nationalist** political leader in Madagascar, she served as secretary general of the Comité de Solidarité Malgache in the 1950s when she also worked closely with the **trade union** movement and was on the editoral board of the nationalist newspaper *Imongo Vaovao*. She helped found the communist Antoko'ny Kongresi'ny Fahaleovantenan'i Madagasikara (AKFM)/Parti du Congrès de l'indépendence de Madagascar/Congress Party of Independence of Madagascar, and from 1959 until 1990 she served as AKFM secretary general. In 1977 Rabesahala was named minister for revolutionary art and culture (later minister of culture, 1989), serving until the ministry was abolished and she left the government in 1991. In the 1990s she was a co-leader of the Congress de l'indépendence du Madagaskar, beginning in 1995, and she returned to government where she was non-permanent counselor of the prime minister (1997–1998). Rabesahala also returned to parliament, where she was vice president of the senate in 2001 through 2002.

RAIN QUEEN. The Lovedu of southern Africa recognize both an actual woman who is referred to as a Rain Queen or **Modjadji**, and a **goddess** who is embodied by those queens. During the 19th century the Lovedu were protected from the Zulu incursions by the actions of the Rain Queen, who struck down enemies as they approached the Lovedu realm. The Lovedu are strongly matrilineal and take special pride in the role of women in their spiritual world and in their physical community. The Rain Queen's renown resulted in Rider Haggard's novel *She*, which was published in 1886 and played a role in spreading the word about the Lovedu. The first queen who represented the Rain Queen goddess was Dzugudini, who came from the north (what is today Zimbabwe) around 1600. *See also* QUEEN MOTHERS.

RAMAT YAKUBU, BALARABA (1958–). Ramat Yakubu writes romance novels in Hausa that are sold in the Kano markets. She states that she is a **feminist**, and she explicitly uses the dramatic events in her novels to raise issues central to Muslim women in northern Nigeria, including forced **marriage**, **polygyny**, pregnancy outside of marriage, and similar concerns. By writing from the woman's viewpoint, she suggests how women could gain greater freedom while still living a devout **Islamic** life. Her novels include *Budurwa Zuciya* (*Young at Heart*, 1987), *Alhaki Kuykuyo Ne* (*Retribution is Inescapable*, 1990), *Wa Zai Auri Jahila?* (*Who Will Marry This Ignorant Woman?*, 1990), and *Ina Son Sa Haka* (*I Love Him all the Same*, 2001). The latter two novels, about forced marriage, are considered to be autobiographical (Abdalla Uba Adamu has a lengthy and explanatory review of the latest novel, on line at www.jendajournal.com). *See also* FUNTUWA, BILKISU.

RAMPHELE, MAMPHELA (1947–). Ramphele is a South African activist and educator. She was initially involved in the South African Students' Organisation (SASO), which she joined when she was a medical student at Natal Medical School in the late 1960s (she earned her medical degree in 1972). She later emerged as a leader in the **Black Consciousness Movement** of the 1970s where she met Steve Biko. She was pregnant with their child and banned to a remote location when he was killed by the South African government security forces in 1977. After the banning order was lifted Ramphele returned to school and earned a doctorate in anthropology. She wrote about legal issues and poverty in South Africa in a series of books that exposed the reality of apartheid, including the Noma Award-winning *Uprooting Poverty: The South African Challenge* (1989, coauthored with Francis Wilson). In 1996 she was named vice chancellor of the University of Cape Town, and in 2000 she joined the World Bank to work in the human development section. She wrote an autobiography, *Across Boundaries: The Journey of a South African Woman*

Leader (1996; title of the 1995 South African edition was *Mamphele Ramphele: A Life*).

RANAVALONA I (1792–1861). Ranavalona ruled the Merina Empire on Madagascar from 1828 to 1861. She had been married to Radama as a child, and was suspected of poisoning him before succeeding him on the throne. She was noted for resisting European influence, as she stopped **missionary** teaching and expelled the missionaries in 1835, though she simultaneously cultivated economic exchanges. Ranavalona I published a code of **laws**, supported work on a Malagasy dictionary, and founded the city of Fianarantsoa. She also installed her lover, Rainitaiarivony, as prime minister; he later also married **Ranavalona II** and **Ranavalona III**. Ranavalona I survived a coup attempt in 1857, but after her death her isolationist policies were abandoned by her son, Radama II.

RANAVALONA II (1829–1883). Ranavalona II ruled the Merina Empire in Madagascar from 1868 to 1883, following **Rasoherina**. She was the niece of **Ranavalona I**, but her policies were nearly opposite to her aunt's, as her rule marked the beginning of the growth of **Christian** influence. She and her husband used the Bible rather than traditional Malagasy items during their coronation ceremony, though when they were baptized in 1869 they turned to a Malagasy minister rather than European missionaries.

RANAVALONA III (1861–1917). Ranavalona III reigned over the Merina Empire in Madagascar from 1883 to 1897, though it is acknowledged that she was a ceremonial rather than an actual leader. After the French conquest in 1895 she remained on the throne, though the French sent her into exile in Algeria after they ended the protectorate following the Revolt of Menalamba (1895–1898). She died in Algiers in 1917, and her remains were repatriated in 1939.

RANSOME-KUTI, FUNMILAYO (NÉE FRANCES ABIGAIL THOMAS) (1900–1978). Ransome-Kuti was a pioneering leader in women's political action and in promoting girls' **education**. She was born in Abeokuta, Nigeria, and though much of her inspiration came from her Egba (a Yoruba sub-group) community she was involved in national and international projects. Her family was well known as **Christian** converts and community leaders from the 19th century, and the prominence of her lineage continued with her children, who included two medical doctors and the musician Fela Kuti. She was the first girl to enter the Abeokuta Grammar School (AGS), and after finishing there she went to England for further education. While in England she began using the Yoruba first name Funmilayo. Her marriage to Rev. Israel Oludotun Ransome-Kuti was a major factor in her development, as he was headmaster of the AGS and she became centrally involved in educational politics. Both of them were charter members in the Nigerian Union of Teachers, founded in 1931, and in numerous other organizations.

In the 1940s Ransome-Kuti invited **market women** to attend **literacy** classes at the **Abeokuta Ladies' Club**, originally a civic organization founded in the 1930s by a group of western-educated women. As the group got involved in politics through the issue of taxation, it changed its name to the **Abeokuta Women's Union**, and Ransome-Kuti served as president from its founding in 1946 until her death. During the colonial period she began wearing Yoruba dress exclusively and made all of her public speeches in Yoruba, demonstrating her outspoken **nationalism**. She was a leader not only for women throughout Nigeria and an advocate of Nigerian culture, but she also had a high profile on the international scene during and after the colonial period, when she attended meetings of the Women's International Democratic Federation and the Women's International League for Peace and Freedom. She also traveled to England in 1947 as the only woman in the delegation of the National Council of Nigeria and the Cameroons political party when they protested a proposed constitution.

She was honored with the Order of the Niger in 1963, the Lenin Peace Prize in 1968, and was awarded an honorary doctor of laws from the University of Ibadan in 1968. In the 1970s, following the example of her son, the well-known musician Fela Kuti, she began using the name Anikulapo-Kuti, as a way of further supporting Yoruba culture. She often stayed at her property in Lagos which had been transformed by Fela into the Kalakuta Republic, a center of anti-government activity. In 1977 she was severely injured when police threw her from a second-story window during a raid that resulted in the complete destruction of the property. That experience was generally believed to have led to her death the following year. Her biography, *For Women and the Nation: Funmilayo Ransome-Kuti of Nigeria* was written by Cheryl Johnson-Odim and **Nina Emma Mba** (1997). *See also* LAGOS MARKET WOMEN'S ASSOCIATION; TAX REVOLTS.

RAPE. The incidence of rape has been documented particularly during **war**, for instance in Mozambique in the 1980s, and in Rwanda and the Democratic Republic of the Congo (DRC) in the 1990s. Women have been especially humiliated by being raped with their children or neighbors as witnesses, and are often subjected to additional torture and mutilation. Women victims are at a much increased risk for **HIV/AIDS** or sexually transmitted diseases; as reported by a physician in the DRC, 30 percent of the raped women treated at a hospital in Bukavu had the HIV virus. Although women who have been subjected to such brutality have often faced problems in reintegrating into their communities, women activists have begun to change attitudes and official practice in dealing with rape victims. Following an uprising in the Central African Republic in 2002 the Organisation des femmes centraficaines/Organization of Central African Republic Women made a public appeal for humanitarian aid for women subjected to sexual attacks during the conflict. In a forward-looking and exceptional case, the post-conflict Truth and Reconciliation Commission in Sierra Leone scheduled a special two-day session devoted to hearing women's testimony about their experiences of sexual violence during the civil war that wracked Sierra Leone in the 1990s. In 2004 the United Nations court in Sierra Leone agreed to prosecute "forced marriage" as a crime against humanity. Judge **Navanethem Pillay** also set precedent in the legal treatment of rape in conflict when she sat on the International Criminal Tribunal for Rwanda.

Rape is also a problem for women in peacetime, though there is little statistical information and almost no rape crisis centers or other programs designed to deal with women who have been the victims of attack. In the 1990s women's groups began to make a public stand to increase awareness of the impact of rape on women. The problem received attention when it became a serious crisis, as in South Africa, where several notorious instances of child rape and even infant rape horrified the nation. It appeared that some men believed that having sex with a virgin would cleanse them of their HIV/AIDS infection, or at least would not expose them to the disease. It has been suggested that as many as one in four girls in South Africa were at risk of being raped before they turned 16, and that a South African girl had a better chance of being raped than of learning to read. Kenya was shocked into recognizing the problem of rape when boys raided a girls' school at St. Kizito in central Kenya in 1991, and raped dozens of the female students, resulting in 19 of the girls' dying. *See also* DOMESTIC VIOLENCE; SEXUAL HARASSMENT.

RASOHERiNA (d. 1868). The queen of Madagascar's Merina Empire from 1863 to 1868, she re-introduced customary practices that had been set aside by the previous administration. She was related to the other Malagasy queens, **Ranavalona I**, **Ranavalona II**, and **Ranavalona III**.

REACH (REPRODUCTIVE AND COMMUNITY HEALTH). This Ugandan group won a United Nations award for its efforts to introduce alternatives to **female genital cutting** in isolated Sabiny communities. In the early 1990s authorities who tried to curtail genital cutting showed a film depicting a bloody circumcision rite, with the unexpected result that community members resented the presentation of their practices as barbaric, and twice as many girls chose to undergo the ritual cutting in 1994 in an effort to reclaim a rite that was felt to be under attack by outsiders. REACH then began introducing alternative ways to mark a girl's entry into adulthood, while showing the negative health impact of genital cutting.

REFUGEES. There have been millions of Africans forced into exile as refugees as a result of violence and **war** in their home countries. In the 1990s alone conflict in Somalia, Rwanda, Burundi, Sierra Leone, Liberia, Zaire, and many other countries forced people to seek asylum in more peaceful neighboring nations. Women have generally made up about half of such refugees, but their situation is not the same as male refugees. Often women are responsible for their children, while men are more likely to seek asylum as individuals; in Rwanda families deliberately split up in order to increase their chances for safe emigration. Women frequently have suffered **rape** and other sexual violence, and often find it difficult to speak about their suffering to strange men who are the gatekeepers at refugee camps. They also are more vulnerable to exploitation in the camps or other new settings where they no longer have protectors. In studies of Mozambican refugees in camps in Malawi in the 1980s it was found that training programs favored male refugees in the kinds of skills that were taught, while women developed their own livelihoods based on prior experience with pottery or other crafts. Women have difficulty being taken seriously as individuals, as many programs for training and for repatriation assume that they will be affiliated with a family unit with a male head of household. Sometimes women are denied access to legal supports if they do not have a husband or other male family member to vouch for them. In addition, resettlement can bring further problems when women cannot adequately prove their legal rights to **land** in either their home area or in a new residence.

REGIONAL CONFERENCE ON AFRICAN WOMEN. *See* AFRICAN REGIONAL CONFERENCE ON WOMEN.

REGIONAL MEETING ON THE ROLE OF WOMEN IN NA-TIONAL DEVELOPMENT. One of the earliest continent-wide meetings on women's issues, this one was held in 1969 in Addis Ababa, Ethiopia, with a follow-up meeting in Rabat, Morocco, in 1971. Building on the work of the **All Africa Women's Conference**, the regional meetings recommended that the United Nations Economic Commission for Africa (UNECA) establish an office focused on women's issues. In 1971 and 1972 Margaret Snyder and Daria Tesha were hired to elaborate a program for the next five years. Their efforts led directly to the establishment of the UNECA's **African Training and Research Centre for Women**.

RELIGION. Many Africans continued to follow local animist religious practices, in which there was frequently an important role for women as spirit mediums, healers, and as the embodiment of **fertility** of both the human community and the earth. The specific practices and beliefs varied widely among the numerous cultures of Africa, but generally they relied on ritual and the recognition of the interconnectedness of living human beings, ancestors, and the surrounding **environment**. Disease and suffering were part of the human condition, but could be controlled through the proper rituals, and frequently a lack of well-being could be traced to some difficulty in the performance of the required ceremonies. The rituals also marked important life stages, including **initiation rites** for girls and boys entering puberty, **marriage**, childbirth, and death.

Women's central role in **agriculture** and in bearing children also informed the role of women in local religions. Many societies paid homage to a variety of local deities including **goddesses** who were responsible for fertility and were associated with water and earth, though there may also have been a belief in a supreme being who created the earth. Women were particularly likely to have an important ritual role in **matrilineal** societies, where the female ancestors were a key element in the continued well-being of the community. Groups that included secret societies for women and men provided a way for women to move into leadership positions, often with religious overtones.

The spread of the so-called world religions in Africa included the expansion of **Islam** throughout West Africa and along the East African coast over a period of many centuries, and the arrival of **Christian missionaries** who had an increasing influence in the 19th century and after. In the 20th century evangelical and Pentecostal churches, sometimes offshoots of the primary Christian establishments, were a particular draw for women who made up the majority of members of such churches. Some women who were leaders of religious groups include, **Christianah Abiodun Emmanuel**, **Alice Auma Lakwena**, **Alice Mulenga Lenshina**, **Mai Chaza**, **Nontetha**, and **Maame Harris "Grace" Tani**.

RELIGIOUS ORGANIZATIONS. There have been a wide range of groups formed in connection with various churches, mosques, and other religious centers. The associational activities included prayer meetings, social activism, and **education**. Women's groups have included **Mother's Unions** and **prayer groups** or *manyano*s, as well as societies begun by missionaries such as **Rencontres Africaines / African Encounters**. An important group connecting women across the continent and addressing spiritual concerns was the **Circle of**

Concerned African Women Theologians. International groups with branches in Africa include the **Girls' Brigades** and the **Young Women's Christian Association (YWCA)**.

RENCONTRES AFRICAINES / AFRICAN ENCOUNTERS. This was an organization that was established in 1956 at Bamako, Mali, by the Catholic missionary **White Sisters**. The primary goals were **educational**, and they published a magazine for women, *Rencontres Africaines*. In 1958 it joined with **Jèmangèlèn** and **Union des Femmes Travailleuses (UFT) / Union of Women Workers** to form the **Union des Femmes du Soudan (UFS) / Union of Women of Sudan**.

RENCONTRES AFRICAINES. This was a monthly women's magazine published in Mali by the **White Sisters** in Bamako beginning in January 1958. The name of the magazine was changed to *Rencontres: Revue féminine mensuelle* in 1960 and continued to be published until 1964 though with markedly decreasing political content.

RÉSEAU DE COMMUNICATION ET D'INFORMATION DES FEMMES (RECIF) / COMMUNICATION AND INFORMATION NETWORK FOR WOMEN. Based in Burkina Faso, this local **non-governmental organization** works to improve women's access to information, and has a resource center as well as offering training and publishing a newsletter.

LA REVOLTE DES FEMMES (LOMÉ, TOGO, 1933). In the early 1930s Togo was suffering from the worldwide Depression and the French governor, Robert de Guise, introduced new taxes as a measure to alleviate the economic problems. African residents of Lomé, the capital of Togo, resisted his efforts in a notable **tax revolt**. While men turned to political organization, women found a base of activity and support in the **market women's** networks. As with the **Aba Women's War** in nearby Nigeria a few years earlier, women came together to protest the imposition of increased taxation, though in Lomé the immediate catalyst was the imprisonment of male political leaders in January 1933. Women's activities were marked by their use of voudun (voodoo) ritual, part of the Ewe cultural experience, and the protest spread beyond the urban center to adjacent rural areas. As a result, the prisoners were released and the women were also successful in postponing the tax increase.

RHODESIAN WOMEN'S LEAGUE. The league was an organization of white women who sought heavier penalties for African men convicted of assaulting white women. It was part of the widespread "black peril" fears in southern African in the early years of the 20th century when white settlers believed that African men posed a sexual threat to white women. As a successor to the **Women's Franchise Society** it was also involved in efforts to expand the **suffrage** to white women.

RODRIGUES, DEOLINDA (?–1967). Rodrigues was a leading Angolan **nationalist**, serving as the only woman on the central committee of the Movimento Popular de Libertação de Angola (MPLA)/ Popular Movement for the Liberation of Angola. She was one of five female combatants assassinated on 2 March 1967; that date is commemorated as Angolan Women's Day, and Rodrigues is remembered with a street named for her in Luanda.

ROTATING SAVINGS AND CREDIT ASSOCIATIONS. Sometimes called ROSCAS or SACCOS (Savings and Credit Co-operatives), these are generally local informal groups that assist people in pooling income and saving for large expenses. Women have found this method of budgeting to be helpful because they can avoid banks (which have excluded women at times) and interest payments, and also keep their own income out of the reach of husbands and other male kin. Rotating credit and savings organizations are often formed among kin, neighbors, and friends. The typical method calls for each member to put a set amount of money into a common pot on a regular basis (usually daily or weekly), and for the members to then take turns withdrawing a lump sum that can be used to capitalize a small business or pay for medical or funeral costs. Such groups are an important component in the economy of the **informal sector**, and have also become a cornerstone of many **development** projects. The associations sometimes have a specific name, such as *stokvel* in South Africa, *tontine* in Cameroon and Senegal, or *upato* in Tanzania where historically they involved sharing clothing or food rather than money.

RUETE, EMILY (NÉE SALME BINTE SAID AL-BISAIDI) (1844–1924). Born in Zanzibar, an island off the coast of Tanzania, she was the daughter of a prominent Muslim leader and trader, Seyyid Said. She became pregnant as the result of a relationship with a German trader, Heinrich Reute, and she then fled to Aden where she married Reute after converting to **Christianity**. They lived together in Germany where she took German citizenship. When Heinrich died in 1870 she briefly returned to Zanzibar where she petitioned for her share of her inheritance; after gaining some compensation she returned to live in Germany with her three children. She wrote about her childhood and her family in *Memoirs of an Arabian Princess from Zanzibar* (1888, republished in 1989) one of the earliest published autobiographies by an African woman.

RUTH-ROLLAND, JEANNE-MARIE (1937–1995). Rolland was a politician in the Central African Republic (CAR), and possibly the first woman to run in an African presidential race, though she lost that election in 1993 after garnering only one percent of the vote. She was the daughter of a French man and worked in education and social work before entering politics. Rolland was employed as a monitor in the national education system in the 1950s, and taught until 1964. She also was employed as a social worker, helped street children, and was president of the CAR Red Cross. Rolland was a founder and president of the Parti Republicain Centrafricain/Central African Republic Party. She was imprisoned from 1986 to 1991 for criticizing the corrupt practices of the government under President André Kolingba and for refusing to make way for the president and his entourage. In 1992 she won a seat as the representative from Bakouma, overcoming attempts by Kolingba to annul the vote. She also served as minister of social affairs and women. She died in Paris after being evacuated to France when she fell ill in 1995.

– S –

SAADI, SITI BINTI (NÉE MTUMWA) (1880s–1950). Siti, as she was commonly known, was a prominent *taarab* singer from Zanzibar who recorded over 250 songs in Swahili between 1928 and 1930. She was the first East African to have her voice recorded onto 78-rpm records, an event that is remembered with pride by Zanzibar residents. Her songs were based on Swahili poems and often referred to local history and politics, as with the song "Kwa Heri Rupia" (Goodbye rupee) which marked the introduction of the British shilling to replace the rupee in local currency, and which is associated with demonstrations opposed to the change. Born in the countryside near Zanzibar town to **slave** parents (her given name, Mtumwa, refers to her slave background), she eventually was known as "Siti," a term of honor for Arab women on the island. Siti was revered for remembering her own humble antecedents as well as for her acceptance in elite sectors of society. She was later the inspiration for a newspaper devoted to women's issues, *Sauti ya Siti* (*The Voice of Siti*). See also MUSIC.

SAFERE: SOUTHERN AFRICAN FEMINIST REVIEW. This feminist journal was published twice a year in Harare, Zimbabwe, under the auspices of the Southern Africa Political and Economic Series (SAPES). The first volume was published in 1995 with a series of articles on the theme of **land** politics. Subsequent issues, all edited by Patricia McFadden, have covered **sexuality**, **feminism**, and **politics** in general, as well as spotlighting women's organizing efforts and associations, especially but not exclusively focusing on Zimbabwe and southern Africa. The last issue appeared in 2001; further information is available online at http://www.inasp.org.uk/ajol/journals/safere/.

SAIDY, ISATOU NJIE. *See* NJIE-SAIDY, ISATOU.

SANDE. Sande was a women's **secret society** in Sierra Leone and Liberia among the Mende, Kpelle, and other related peoples. There was a parallel men's society called Poro, and Poro and Sande acted together to consolidate communities. A primary responsibility was to oversee girls' **initiation rites** and to enforce laws that female ancestors had handed down to regulate society. During the initiation schools women wore ritual masks that were well known as an **art** form. The masks, though fashioned by professional male woodcarvers, were only owned by women. A typical mask was shaped like a helmet, and although there was a great deal of variety, included a woman's face, an elaborate hairstyle, and additional pouches for holding medicines. At least one women leader of Sande, Famata Bendu Sandemani (d. 1892) of the Vai people in Liberia, also ruled more generally; she ascended the throne when her husband, the king, died. *See also* MADAM YOKO.

SANGARÉ, OUMOU (1968–). Sangaré is a singer from Mali who popularized the singing style associated with *griottes*. She was born in Bamako, but learned the musical traditions of her family's home region in southwestern Mali. She left school in the eighth grade to pursue a singing career, and toured Europe in 1986 with the Bamba group Joliba Percussion. Her 1989 recording *Moussolou* (*Women*) reportedly sold over 200,000 copies throughout West Africa, and it was followed by the compilation recording of Sangaré and other Malian women in *The Wassoulou Sound: Women of Mali* (1994). The themes of her songs included such female concerns as arranged **marriage** and **polygyny**. In 2003 she released an anthology of some of her most popular songs. *See also* DAMBA, FANTA; DIABATÉ, SIRA MORI; MUSIC; WASSOULOU.

SANTO, ALDA ESPÍRITO (1926–). A poet and political activist from São Tomé e Príncipe, she went to Lisbon in the 1950s to train as a teacher. While living there she met students and activists from the other Portuguese colonies, joined them in anti-colonial political organizations, and was imprisoned by the Portuguese for her activities. Her collections of **poetry** include *O Jogral das Ilhas* (*The Fool of the Islands*, published privately in 1976), *É Nosso o Solo Sagrado da Terra* (*The Sacred Soil of the Earth is Ours*, 1978), and a new book in 2002, *Mataram o Rio da Minha Cidade* (*They Killed the River of My City*). She is president of the writers' organization, União dos Escritories e Artistas de São Tomé e Príncipe, and has served as a member of parliament, twice holding the office of president of the assembly.

SARRAOUNIA. *Sarauniya* (spelled *Sarraounia* in French) is the Hausa word for queen. A specific woman named "Sarraounia" was the subject of a novel by Abdoulaye Mamani, *Sarraounia: le drame de la* *reine magicienne* (1980). A film based on the novel and also called *Sarraounia* was released in 1986. The novel and the film present her story as factual, claiming a warrior queen led the Anza in resisting attempts by the Fulani of Sokoto to convert her people to Islam, and then led her community against the French incursion, eventually claiming victory in 1899. Nonetheless, there is no reliable evidence that she existed in reality. In the 1990s Sarraounia was resurrected with a popular song about her, a radio station with her name, and greater prominence as a national heroine in Niger. For many Muslim Nigeriens she represents backwardness due to her support of animist African religions.

SAUTI YA SITI (THE VOICE OF SITI). A magazine published in Tanzania in Kiswahili and English by the **Tanzania Media Women's Association** (TAMWA). The first issue in 1988 had a cover photograph of **Siti Binti Saadi**, the renowned singer who was recognized in the name of the magazine. The articles ranged over issues such as **domestic violence**, girls' **education**, **market women**, and **politics**, and included fiction, book reviews, and reports of TAMWA activities.

SAWABA, GAMBO (1933–). Sawaba was an important **nationalist** leader in northern Nigeria in the 1950s through the 1970s. She was a Hausa woman who was born in Zaria, where she attended school for three years as a girl but left when her family encountered difficulties. She founded the women's section of the Northern Elements Progressive Union (NEPU), and spoke publicly on NEPU platforms as well as privately in people's homes to comply with expectations regarding women's **seclusion**. Sawaba was impressed by the story of **Funmilayo Ransome-Kuti**'s success and traveled to Abeokuta where she spent three months studying **politics** with the well-known activist. Sawaba was arrested and imprisoned more than once by the colonial authorities and by the independent government under the rule of the Northern People's Congress (NPC), which viewed women who operated outside acceptable boundaries as **prostitutes**. She was also attacked and beaten on more than one occasion by NPC members who disapproved of women going out in public unveiled. In 1976 she was the first Nigerian Muslim woman elected to public office, when she won a seat on the town council of Sabon

Gari, Zaria. She was married four times, three of the marriages failing because her husbands could not tolerate her active political life. A biography, *The Story of Gambo Sawaba*, by Rima Shawulu (1990), recounts her activities.

SCHMELEN, ZARA (c. 1795–1831). Zara was a Namibian woman married to an early German **missionary** among the Nama. She was largely responsible for the initial translation of the Bible into Nama, the first major publication in that language. Her husband received most of the credit for that work, though he admitted his language ability was limited.

SCHREINER, OLIVE (1855–1920). Born and raised in South Africa, Schreiner was a novelist and political activist for women's rights. Her best-known novel, *The Story of an African Farm* (1883), and her collection of essays, *Women and Labour* (1911), demonstrate her concern for women's situation. She was traveling in Germany when World War I broke out, and she then moved to England where she lived the rest of her life. One useful biography is by **Ruth First** and Ann Scott, *Olive Schreiner* (1980).

SEBOKO, MOSADI MURIEL (1950–). Seboko was the first woman in Botswana to become a paramount chief (*kgosi*), taking that post in 2002. She was the oldest child of the Paramount Kgosi Mokgosi III. Her **education** at Moedin College included completion of an overseas school certificate from Cambridge. She worked for Barclays Bank from 1971 until her retirement in 1995. She believed that she had a right to take the paramount *kgosi* seat because she was the oldest child, and she stated that she had been prepared to rule by the managerial positions she held during her career in banking. Although her appointment to the seat was delayed by opposition from some men among the Balete, she was supported by the women's organization **Emang Basadi** and by Minister of Local Government Dr. Margaret Nasha. Mosadi Seboko was elected to succeed her brother in December 2001, and the minister confirmed the choice that had been made. Seboko was the first female paramount chief to be sworn into the House of Chiefs, setting a precedent for other Botswana communities.

SECLUSION. In some **Islamic** societies, notably among the Hausa of northern Nigeria and in some coastal Swahili communities in East Africa, it was expected that women would remain within the family home after they reached puberty or were married. A study in the 1980s among Hausa women found that 95 percent of married women in Kano, Nigeria, were secluded. In Mombasa and on the Comoros Islands as well as other East African communities, women who ventured into public streets wore a long black garment called a *buibui* that effectively hid them from view. The restrictions on their public mobility did not end their involvement in society, however, as they participated in market trading through the use of intermediaries, and they had a rich social life centered on women's relationships and rituals. In the 19th century **Nana Asma'u** developed an **educational** outreach program that brought rural Hausa women leaders to her home where they learned Muslim songs which they then took back to share with women in their own villages, thus permitting them to gain education without violating their seclusion. *See also* SHARI'A LAW.

SECRET SOCIETIES. In many West African communities it was common for women and men to have separate societies that controlled ritual activities. Women's societies usually supported women's activities such as **agriculture** and marketing, as well as overseeing the **initiation rites** of pubescent girls. Often women members could rise through a hierarchy of titled positions through a combination of personal attributes and wealth. Such societies included the **Sande** in Sierra Leone and the Con in Cameroon.

SEKITOLEKO, VICTORIA (1949–). Sekitoleko was minister of **agriculture** in Uganda from 1988 to 1995, and at one time she was the only female minister of agriculture in Africa, where women do the vast majority of daily agricultural labor. Before her appointment she was a farmer herself in Jinja, and she earned a B.Sc. in agriculture from Makerere University. She then worked with the Uganda Development Bank (1973–1986) and helped develop the Rural Farmers Schemes which provided credit to poor farmers. Sekitoleko was a member of parliament and deputy minister of agriculture from 1986 to 1988, when she became minister. She hoped to reorganize agricultural priorities by giving less attention to cash crops and commercial farming, and more to women's work in growing food for their families. Since 1995 she has worked for the United Nations Food and Agriculture Organization as a director and as the representative for southern and eastern Africa.

SEMPE, 'MANTSEBO AMELIA 'MATSABA. *See* MANTSE BO.

SENEDU GABRU (1915-). Senedu Gabru was the first woman elected to Ethiopia's parliament in 1957, and she was a prominent **educational** leader. She was born to an elite family and educated by **missionaries** in Switzerland. She returned to work as a teacher in Ethiopia, and was politically active in the resistance to Italian incursions in the 1930s. In 1945 Senedu was named assistant director of the first girls' school in Ethiopia, the Empress Menen School that had been founded in 1931 in Addis Ababa by the former empress. In 1949 she became the first Ethiopian headmistress, and through her interest in improving educational opportunities for girls she entered politics.

SENIOR WIFE. In many African societies **polygyny** is a common form of **marriage**. For men in leadership positions it was important to specify which wife was the senior wife—usually the first wife was the senior wife, and her sons had priority in inheriting the father's position as chief. In Lesotho the senior wives were those whom a man married while still living with his parents, while the junior wives were those he married upon establishing his own household, and were subordinate to the senior wife rather than to their parents-in-law.

SEXUAL HARASSMENT. Women and girls have suffered from unwanted attentions and overt sexual harassment in their jobs and classrooms. Often women must agree to some sexual interaction with a male teacher or superior in order to pass a course or get or keep a job. Although the problem is best documented in South Africa, a survey in Kenya in 2004 found that as many as 9 out of 10 women workers had been victims of sexual discrimination, and that most of them tolerated harassment in order to remain employed. Women's organizations, including the **Women's Action Group (WAG)** in Zimbabwe and **Women in Law and Development in Africa (WiLDAF)** have included this issue in their lobbying efforts to improve conditions for women.

Young women are particularly vulnerable. There is abundant evidence of teachers preying on their students, and male teachers who claim sexual favors are seen as responsible at least in part for the high rates of girls failing to finish their schooling as a result of pregnancies, shame, or resulting sexually transmitted diseases including **HIV/AIDS**. Harassment by male students is also a serious issue that has made schools a hostile environment for girls in many areas. Togo passed a law in 1984 that would send teachers who made their students pregnant to prison for up to 10 years, though it has not been regularly enforced. The **Forum of African Women Educationalists (FAWE)** has made it a priority to improve the situation confronted by female students. It is working to empower girls to speak out against teachers who harass them as well educating boys and girls about stopping the rampant verbal and physical assaults by male students.

SEXUALITY. Sexuality is a central aspect of everyday life, and inextricably connected to **health, marriage, fertility, infertility,** and **birth control**, as well as to more contentious issues such as the spread of **HIV/AIDS**, the continuing practices of **initiation rites, female genital cutting,** and **prostitution**. Sexuality in African societies has been little studied in comparison to the research done in the West, though it has become more of a focus as a result of the devastation of HIV/AIDS since the 1980s. Although it is not possible to generalize for the whole continent, it appears that in the past many African societies acknowledged female sexuality as a positive experience. In some communities sexual play was permitted between adolescents as long as it did not involve intercourse. For instance among the Xhosa in South Africa, the practice of *ukumetsha* allowed a young couple who were promised in marriage to enjoy unconsummated intimacy, which relied on the girl keeping her leather apron-like garment between her legs. Girls learned about adult sexual behavior during rites of passage, and marriage and **motherhood** were the common experience for the majority of women.

SHAMING PRACTICES. In many African communities (as well as many other world regions) a traditional shaming practice involved women removing their clothes or lifting their coverings to display their nude bodies, sometimes with such comments as "Do you want to see where you came from?" It was considered a potent way for women to control bad behavior by men, though it was also a method for women to insult other women. Variants of such actions were used by women during the **Aba Women's War** which drew on a practice known as "**sitting on a man**," by **Mary Muthoni Nyanjiru** during the **nationalist** struggle in Kenya, during the **Anlu** demonstrations in Cameroon, by women protesting a white official in South Africa who was attempting to halt their shellfish harvesting in the 1970s, by members of the **Green Belt Movement** in Nairobi in 1992, and in the **oil protests** against exploitative production in the Niger Delta in the 1990s and notably in 2002.

SHARI'A LAW. Following the implementation of a new Constitution in Nigeria in 1999, Muslim-dominated states in northern Nigeria introduced strict **laws** following Shari'a **Islamic** precepts in 2000. Several elements of shari'a law specifically discriminate against women. One is the provision that allows husbands to physically chastise their wives as long as they do not cause "grievous bodily harm," which has been broadly interpreted to permit husbands to beat their wives nearly to the point of death. Another law enforces **seclusion** by restricting women from appearing in public without a male escort, a severe limitation that keeps women from participating in community business and activities. Women are only supposed to be in the presence of male relatives; all other men are off-limits, including physicians and other professionals, and in some areas Muslim women are required to cover their hair and bodies. The implementation of these laws has varied from state to state, but there is some popular male interest in extending the laws that control women. Attempts to apply the laws have drawn international outrage, including **Amina Lawal**'s prosecution for adultery, which carried a sentence of death by stoning, and a similar case in 2001 against Safiya Yakubu Hussaini Tungar Tudu (her story was told in *Eu, Safiya*, by Rafaelle Masto, 2004). Another case concerned Bariya Ibrahima Magazu, a young teenager who received one hundred lashes for being pregnant and unmarried. She told the court that she had been **raped** by three married men, but because the attack was not witnessed she was unable to produce the required four "upstanding" men to vouch for her story. Although the national Nigerian government has not openly opposed the laws, Nigerian women's organizations have been active in their resistance, including **Baobab for Women's Human Rights**, **Niger Delta Women for Justice**, and **Women in Nigeria**.

SHEBA, QUEEN OF. *See* MAQEDA.

SHEBEEN. Shebeens were informal bars in South Africa which were often owned and run by women, as an extension of their **beer brewing** activities. The women who ran such establishments were sometimes called Shebeen Queens. *See also* ALCOHOL; TEMPERANCE.

SHOESHOE: THE MAGAZINE FOR ALL LESOTHO'S WOMEN. *Shoeshoe* is a women-oriented magazine published in Lesotho beginning in 1991 in both English and Basotho, with a mix of news, profiles of prominent and remarkable women, recipes, and other items of interest to women.

SHOPE, GERTRUDE NTITI (1925–). A South African political and **trade union** activist, she lived in exile from 1966 to 1990. She was born in Johannesburg, raised and educated in Zimbabwe, and worked as a teacher before joining the African National Congress (ANC) in 1954. She subsequently was active in the **Federation of South African Women**, and was head of the Central Western Jabavu Branch of the ANC women's section. While in exile she helped start publishing the quarterly newsletter, *Voice of Women*, led the ANC delegation to the **Nairobi Women's Meeting**, and also worked for the World Federation of Trade Unions (WFTU). From 1991 to 1993 she was head of the **African National Congress Women's League**. In the first post-apartheid election she won a seat in parliament.

SIERRA LEONE MARKET WOMEN'S UNION (SLMWU). An organization of **market women** active in the 1940s, it was headed by Mary Martyn and affiliated with the West African Youth League. Along with the Sierra Leone Washer Women's Union, the SLMWU tried to register as a **trade union**, but their claim was denied by the government because it asserted that trade unions were for wage earners, and the market women did not earn a wage but were self-employed. The SLMWU continued to raise issues concerning market conditions, the allotment of spaces for vendors, and control over petty traders who competed with the market women.

SIERRA LEONE WOMEN'S MOVEMENT (SLWM). Founded in 1951 by **Constance Cummings-John** and others, it worked to include women in the early efforts at self-government in Sierra Leone. Based among the **market women**, it counted over 20,000 members, and published a newspaper, held mass meetings, and focused attention on women's issues. In 1960, as Sierra Leone was about to gain its independence, the SLWM published a petition calling on the authorities to recognize the central role of women in Sierra Leone society and demanded that the new constitution protect women's rights especially concerning **marriage**, property rights, and **inheritance**. It was not successful in bringing about legal reforms. The SLWM remained active until the coup d'etat of 1967, and in the 1980s it owned a restaurant and a nursery, but was not involved in political action.

SIKAKANE, JOYCE NOMAFA (1943–). Born in South Africa, she grew up in Soweto and worked as a **journalist**, becoming the first black woman hired by the *Rand Daily Mail*. After falling in love with a Scottish doctor, they planned to emigrate as interracial marriages were illegal. She was arrested for her political activity and spent 17 months in detention until she was acquitted and was able to leave. Moving to Scotland with her husband, she became an anti-**apartheid** activist. She is best known for her autobiography, *A Window on Soweto* (1977), and she also served as a technical advisor on the film about **Ruth First**, *A World Apart*. Sikakane worked in Mozambique and Zimbabwe as a journalist, and returned to South Africa in 1994, where she was employed by the South African Broadcasting Corporation until 2001.

SIRAMORI (SIRA MORY). *See* DIABATÉ, SIRA MORI.

SIRLEAF, ELLEN JOHNSON. *See* JOHNSON SIRLEAF, ELLEN.

SISTER NAMIBIA. A media project established in 1989, it supported research on women that challenged the restrictions women faced in all sectors of Namibian society. The group distributed a newsletter, also called *Sister Namibia*, which appeared six times a year. It was originally published only in English, though by 2003 it included articles in Afrikaans and Oshiwambo as well.

SISULU, ALBERTINA NONTSIKELELO (1918–). Sisulu is a prominent anti-**apartheid** activist in South Africa. She wat trained as a **nurse**. Sisulu joined the African National Congress (ANC) Youth League with her husband Walter Sisulu (1912–2003; they married in 1944), a trade union activist and ANC leader. She later was a top member of the **African National Congress Women's League** and a leader of the **Federation of South African Women**, where she was involved in the anti-pass **Defiance Campaign**. She was restricted by banning orders from 1964 to 1983, including 10 years of house arrest. In 1983 she was elected as Transvaal president of the new opposition organization, the United Democratic Front (UDF). In 1990 she helped the ANC Women's League get reestablished inside South Africa, and she was elected to parliament in 1994. She is patron to a number of civic organizations and has been honored with many awards, including an honorary law degree from the University of the Witwatersrand in 1999. Albertina and Walter's daughter-in-law, Elinor Sisulu, published a joint biography, *Walter and Albertina Sisulu: In Our Lifetime* (2002), which won the 2003 Noma Award for Publishing in Africa.

SITTING ON A MAN. "Sitting on a man" was a type of **shaming practice** among the Igbo of southern Nigeria that became associated with the actions women took against the British authorities in the **Aba Women's War** of 1929. Sitting on a man could include singing vulgar songs outside the home of a man who had violated women's rights and activities. During the 1929 events women burned colonial court buildings and took other measures that were derived from traditional practices used to control local men. In the colonial context the women hoped to curtail British policies that infringed on the arenas where women had previously had control, including markets and other economic activities central to women's lives.

SIYAZAMA. Siyazama is a rural South African project involved in producing crafts as part of their **HIV/AIDS** awareness work. They are based in KwaZulu Natal and were active in 1999.

SLAVERY. Slavery can be a difficult term to define, and can take many forms, though most basically it refers to one person owning or controlling another who is involuntarily servile. Slaves were usually marginal to the society and their identity could linger into subsequent generations, although African slavery was more usually attached to individuals rather than a race or other larger cohort. The history of slavery in Africa was deeply gendered. Most slaves in Africa were female. The reasons this occurred included the valuable agricultural labor women could provide, as well as their ability to bear and raise children. A related factor was the greater demand for male slaves in the international market, as the European export market bought twice as many men as women. Male slaves captured during warfare were more likely to be killed while women were integrated into the society; sometimes wars were waged so that men could have access to a new set of women as potential wives. In the internal slave markets the prices for women were nearly always higher than those for male slaves; in the late 19th century in Cameroon women were sold for twice the price that men could command.

In many areas women were more vulnerable to being captured and enslaved. Women in 19th-century southern and central Africa were dependent on men, whether their fathers or husbands or other male kin, in order to have access to land for cultivation. If they lost such connections through death or other misfortune they were susceptible to being sold to slave traders or to a man who wished to expand his household. The stigma of being enslaved varied from place to place. In some areas people were clearly remembered as being slave descendents. Simultaneously however, slave men and women were often able to work in strikingly independent ways and to rise above their slave status through hard work. Research on the slave holdings of the Fon royal family in 19th-century Dahomey (today the nation of Benin) indicates the ways in which captured women could use their position within the royal household to advance their own status and in some cases rise to great wealth and power. That royal household was estimated to have between 5,000 and 8,000 dependents, including slaves captured during war and women recruited as wives from all the allied lineages. Women were also noted as slave owners, particularly in West Africa where some women gained wealth through their market trading and required labor to help them in that business. The British ended the external slave trade in 1807, though the slave trade continued clandestinely for several decades, and internal slavery was not immediately affected. Even though all trade was to have ended by the late 19th century, at the end of the 20th century there were still reports of slavery in Sudan and elsewhere. Ghana, Benin, Togo, and other West African nations were under investigation for continued child slavery with traffic in hundreds of children intercepted at international borders. The children, nearly all girls, were sold to perform **domestic service** and work in markets among other types of jobs. Investigators speculated that girls were less likely to rebel and run away than boys, and that the high cost of marrying off a daughter was a motivation for poor families to sell their girl children.

SLESSOR, MARY (1848–1915). A missionary from Scotland, she lived in West Africa with the Presbyterian **mission** at Calabar, Nigeria, from 1876 until her death. She also worked as a judge, and her skill in nursing and mediation brought her admiration across a wide area. She was especially known for her work to end human sacrifice, ritual killing including the superstitious killing of twin infants, and the poor treatment of **widows**. She took in twins to raise herself, and may have saved hundreds over the years. Fluent in Efik, she was called "Mother of All the People" by those she lived among. A medical journal, the *Mary Slessor Journal of Medicine* began publication at the University of Calabar Teaching Hospital in 2000; more information is available at http://www.inasp.info/ajol/journals.html.

SOCIETY FOR WOMEN AND AIDS IN AFRICA (SWAA). Following the Fourth International AIDS Conference, this association was founded in 1988 to organize African women and others to deal with the **HIV/AIDS** crisis in Africa. Headquartered in Dakar, Senegal, it had 39 branches across the continent, and worked to spread information about women and AIDS, focusing on the plight of orphans and vulnerable children. In 2002 it held a meeting in Nairobi which

resulted in a strategic plan, available at its website at: http://www
.swaainternational.org/, which also has issues of the twice-yearly
publication, *SWAA Infos Magazine*.

SOFOLA, ZULU (NWAZULU) (1935–1995). An Igbo playwright,
she was born and raised in Nigeria, and traveled to the United States
where she earned a B.A. in English at Virginia Union University and
an M.A. in drama at the Catholic University of America. Sofola returned to Nigeria in 1966 and earned a Ph.D. in drama at the University of Ibadan. She taught at the University of Ilorin where she became head of the Department of Performing Arts. Her plays include
The Wizard of Law (1976) and *Old Wines Are Tasty* (1981). A review
of her contributions can be found in *Zulu Sofola: Her Life and Her
Works*, edited by Mary E. Modupe Kolawole (1999).

SONG OF LAWINO. "Song of Lawino" is a Kenyan poem written in
a woman's voice about her lot in life. The author is Okot p'Bitek
(1931–), an Acholi man. Called a "lament" on the title page, the first
of the linked poems is titled "My Husband's Tongue is Bitter," and it
sets the tone for a series of complaints by Lawino about her treatment
by her husband that evokes the drudgery of African women's daily
round of work and her difficulties with the changes that came with
modern life, from the introduction of **Christianity** and western **education** to new methods of cooking. It was first published in English
(translated from Acholi by p'Bitek) in 1966.

SOUTH AFRICAN COMMISSION ON GENDER EQUALITY.
The South African Commission on Gender Equality is an unusual organization, as it is independent of the government but is entrusted with
monitoring official progress on gender issues. It was created as a hor-
izontal structure made up of appointed (not elected) commissioners
when the new constitution was written and came into effect in 1996.
It has investigated issues ranging from rural women's problems collecting water from crocodile-infested rivers, to **widows'** difficulties in
exercising their right to inheritance, to monitoring the promulgation of
laws to ensure the legislators do not ignore women's rights. In 1999
Joyce Piliso-Seroke was appointed chair of the commission, which
has eight members who work full time on commission business with

the support of 38 staff. The commission has stressed all aspects of gender equality, including the need to redefine masculinity, address **sexuality** and reproductive concerns, and improve women's economic opportunities.

SOUTH AFRICAN DOMESTIC WORKERS ASSOCIATION (SADWA). Sometimes referred to as the South African Domestic Workers Union, it was established in 1986, and had 65,000 members in 1989. It focused on improving the pay and working conditions of the mainly female workers in **domestic service** in South Africa.

SOUTH AFRICAN WAR. The conflict between British and Afrikaner forces, sometimes referred to as the Boer War, took place between 1899 and 1902. Discussion of women's involvement previously had been limited to the internment of Afrikaner women in concentration camps, with a terrible cost as over 26,000 women died from starvation and disease. British social reformer Emily Hobhouse (1860–1926) established the Relief Fund for South African Women and Children and published *The Brunt of War and Where It Fell* (1902) in order to publicize the atrocities she observed. She settled in South Africa after the war and is buried at the National Women's Monument in Bloemfontein, South Africa, which commemorates the Afrikaner deaths. Historians have begun to reassess the role of women of all races in this pivotal event, expanding their analyses to include Afrikaner women as leaders in the nascent **nationalist** movement, British women working for **peace**, women's work as **nurses** (whose ranks included **Mary Kingsley**), and the gendered nature of memories of the conflict.

SOUTHERN AFRICAN FEMINIST REVIEW. See SAFERE: SOUTHERN AFRICAN FEMINIST REVIEW.

SOW, FATOU (1941–). Sow is a leading **feminist** scholar from Senegal. She was educated in Dakar, and obtained a doctorate in sociology at the Sorbonne in Paris in 1969. She has published and consulted widely on issues related to women, work, and **development**. Sow currently divides her time between the Centre National de la Recherche Scientifique in Paris and the l'Institut Fundamental d'Afrique Noire at the Université de Cheik Anta Diop in Dakar. She was awarded an honorary doctorate in 2002 from the University of Ottawa in Canada.

SOW FALL, AMINATA (1941–). Sow Fall is a prize-winning novelist from Senegal. She studied at the Sorbonne, earning her French **literature** degree in 1976. Her first novel, *Le Revenant*, appeared in 1976, her sixth, *Douceurs du bercail* (*Home Sweet Home*), in 1998. She won the 1980 Grand Prix de Littérature de l'Afrique Noire and was short-listed for the Prix Goncourt in France for *La Grève des Bôttu* (1979) which was translated as *The Beggars' Strike: Or the Dregs of Society*. Sow Fall has been active in promoting African and Senegalese culture with the Centre Africain d'Animation et d'Echanges Culturels and the Khoudia publishing house. She was also the director of Centre International d'Etudes, de Recherches et de Réactivation sur la Littérature, les Arts et la Culture/International Center for Study, Research, and Development of Literature, Arts, and Culture which holds conferences in Dakar.

SPEAK OUT-TAURAI-KHULUMANI. This magazine is published by the **Women's Action Group** in Zimbabwe, in English, Shona, and Ndebele. It usually includes short topical articles and letters which required a response advocating women's rights and teaching women how to work to improve their situation. It was first published in 1986.

SPIRIT POSSESSION. In a variety of customary **religions** as well as among some practitioners of **Islam** and break-away **Christian** sects, followers on occasion have been possessed by spirits. The experience is sometimes a step on a path to becoming a spiritual leader or a healer; for others it can be a one-time occurrence. There are cults associated with the practice of accepting possession by spirits, for instance *bori* among the Hausa of northern Nigeria, and *zaar*, especially noted in Sudan and Ethiopia. In Zimbabwe, **Nehanda** was a recognized spirit leader whose spirit medium, **Charwe**, was at the forefront of anti-colonial activities at the end of the 19th century. In the 1990s spirit possession appeared in a new form among Hausa school girls in Kano, Nigeria, as many of them underwent possession in what appeared to be an episode of mass hysteria. Muslim leaders sought Islamic methods of treating the girls, though the incident raised issues of Muslim identity, orthodox Islamic practice, and connections between Nigerian Muslims and other Islamic countries.

Women have frequently become spirit mediums in a range of societies and circumstances. Accounts from 19th-century Uganda and Tanzania tell of spirit possession cults that were primarily female, and which counted nearly all of the women in a community as members. Often women who became healers had special authority over women's responsibilities such as childbirth or **agriculture**. Some researchers have suggested that taking on that role in society offers an outlet for women to exercise authority from which they otherwise would be barred; in a few cases women holding positions of ritual authority were treated as men. While in a trance women would be allowed and even expected to criticize the social order including the dominance of men and of a particular man such as a husband. They would also expect or demand gifts from members of their community. *See also* MUHUMUSA; NYABINGI.

SPORT. At the beginning of the 21st century very few African women had become known as athletes. They were hampered by the lack of resources, sponsorship, and training facilities that affect all Africans, and also by continued gender segregation in sport in general. Nonetheless, there was a developing history of African women's involvement with athletic activities. Some of the earliest sports clubs appear to have been formed in South Africa in the 1880s, when African women who had graduated from **missionary** schools formed croquet and tennis associations. White women in South Africa were also involved in cricket and other sports from the late 19th to early 20th centuries. In Tanzania there were inter-school athletic meets in the Lake Victoria region as early as the 1930s that included girls' track competitions and gymnastics. Nigerian women were encouraged by the British colonial government, which introduced tennis and athletics. The first all-woman athletic meeting was held in Lagos in 1951; that year also marked the founding of the Women's Amateur Athletic Association of Nigeria. By 1955 regional meets were held with female athletes from Ghana.

Track and field, which has seen a number of women become world champions, is one area where women have been able to progress. The first black African woman to win an Olympic gold medal was the Ethiopian runner **Derartu Tulu**. Track includes women marathon runners such as Tegla Loroupe of Kenya, who won the New York City Marathon in 1994 and 1995. Other prominent female athletes include Maria de Lurdes Mutola, the Olympic gold-medalist from Mozambique who won the 800-meter race in Sydney in 2000. Track was also a venue for controversy during the 1984 Olympics in Los Angeles, when the young white South African runner, Zola Budd, defied the international sports boycott of **apartheid** South Africa and ran under a British passport.

In the 1990s women have also begun playing soccer, netball, volleyball, cricket, and other team sports. Across the continent women have been organizing their own clubs, such as the Soweto Ladies soccer team in South Africa. In 1995 the newly formed Women's South African Football Association competed in the All Africa Women's Football Competition. South Africa is also the site of Women and Sport in South Africa, which works to increase girls' and women's participation in athletic activities. Women politicians who have advocated for female athletes include **Sylvette Frichot** and **Pendukeni Iivula-Ithana**.

STRUCTURAL ADJUSTMENT PROGRAMS (SAPs). In the 1980s the World Bank and the International Monetary Fund began introducing a series of economic reforms that were considered mandatory policy changes for poor nations to adopt in order to have access to loans. The economic restructuring programs came to be collectively called "structural adjustment." They generally included an emphasis on privatizing services that governments had paid for such as **health** clinics and **education** programs. While many economists looked at macroeconomic guidelines and felt the reforms were successful in reinvigorating **agriculture** and industry, other researchers believed that the economic changes ignored the social impact, particularly on women. That impact was often negative, as salaries and prices for agricultural goods fell and women found they were working harder and longer hours for a diminished return.

SUDAN NATIONAL COMMITTEE ON TRADITIONAL PRACTICES. This national group focuses its efforts on ending **female**

genital cutting, especially by working with local leaders and people of influence and providing information through seminars and training sessions.

SUDANESE WOMEN'S UNION (SWU). A national mass organization claiming over 1,000,000 members in 1978, it was formed in 1946 as an affiliate of the Sudanese Communist Party. Its early organizing focused on **trade unions** and women's economic opportunities. The Union published *Sawt al-Mara* (*Voice of Women*) and advocated for women's right to vote, which came only after the October Revolution of 1964. The SWU incorporated a regional organization, the Southern Women's League, in 1970, and became increasingly critical of the limited appointments of women from southern Sudan to government posts. The SWU subsequently was banned in 1971. A second organization, also called the Sudanese (or Sudan) Women's Union, was then founded as a branch of the Sudanese Socialist Union; it was closely tied to the government and did not exercise the independence of action of the original SWU. *See also* IBRAHIM, FATIMA AHMAD; SUFFRAGE; WOMEN'S FRONT (SUDAN).

SUFFRAGE. Most African countries permitted only limited or no voting rights for African men and women under **colonialism**. As nations gained independence they most often granted universal suffrage; because women gained the right to vote as their countries became independent, there were not widespread women's suffrage movements agitating for the vote for women.

In South Africa in the early 20th century white women had to fight for the right to vote, which was won when the Women's Enfranchisement Bill of 1930 was passed. They were much influenced by the British women's suffrage struggles and maintained contact with the international movement for the right to vote for women through the Women's Enfranchisement Association of the Union which was established in 1911 when it brought several regional suffrage organizations into a single national association. Racial politics were integral to the South African suffrage movement, as women emphasized their potential as white voters while anti-suffrage men argued that if white women gained the vote, black women would perforce have to be included, thus claiming that no women should be able to vote. Black men in some provinces had been able to vote, but their rights were eroded throughout the 20th century; black women did not gain the vote at the national level until apartheid was ended in 1992. In Southern Rhodesia (now Zimbabwe) white women formed the **Women's Franchise Society**, and they gained the vote in 1919.

In some other countries men and women did not gain the vote simultaneously; for example, in Cameroon the male franchise was introduced in 1955, while women were not enfranchised until January 1959. In northern Nigeria, where Islamic law dominated, women did not gain voting rights until 1977, 17 years after the rest of the country adopted universal suffrage at independence.

Only three nations granted the vote to women in the 1940s: Benin and Liberia in 1946, and Togo in 1947. Women's suffrage spread more rapidly in the following decades, as 1955 brought that right in Ethiopia and Ghana, and 1956 saw Benin, Cameroon, Central African Republic, Chad, Congo (Brazzaville), Gabon, Guinea, Ivory Coast, Madagascar, Mali, Mauritania, Niger, Senegal, and Upper Volta (now Burkina Faso) grant women's right to vote in anticipation of the end of colonial rule. Somalia (1958) and Mauritius (1959) were the next two nations, followed by Gabon, Nigeria, and the Congo (Kinshasa) in 1960; and Burundi, the Gambia, Rwanda, Sierra Leone, and Tanzania in 1961. The rest of the decade brought new additions each year: Uganda (1962), Equatorial Guinea and Kenya (1963), Malawi, Sudan, and Zambia (1964), Botswana (1965), Lesotho (1966), and Swaziland (1968). The final nations to grant women the right to vote were the former Portuguese colonies which gained their independence in the 1970s: Angola, Cape Verde, and Mozambique in 1975, and Guinea-Bissau in 1977. African women only gained the right to vote in white-minority ruled nations when majority rule was won: Zimbabwe (formerly Rhodesia) in 1980, Namibia in 1990, and South Africa in 1994. *See also* NIGERIAN WOMEN'S PARTY; SUDANESE WOMEN'S UNION.

SUTHERLAND, EFUA THEODORA (1924–1996). Sutherland was one of Ghana's foremost dramatists. After attending college in England where she earned a B.A. in **education**, she returned to her home in Ghana in 1951 and in 1958 established the Ghana Experimental Theater and formed the Ghana Society of Writers. Her best known plays are *Edufa* (1967) and *Marriage of Anansewa* (1975), in which she demonstrated her contention that African theater should make use of **oral traditions**, in this instance turning to the common folk stories involving the trickster spider Ananse. Sutherland was also committed to improving conditions for children, and her efforts resulted in the founding of the Ghana National Commission on Children, which she chaired. She was also a research fellow at the University of Ghana, Institute of African Studies, School of Music, Dance, and Drama.

SUZMAN, HELEN (1917–). Suzman was a prominent opposition member of the South African parliament from 1953 until 1989. She was born in the Transvaal, the daughter of Jewish immigrants from Lithuania. She studied commerce at the University of Witwatersrand (Wits), but left before completing her degree and married Mosie Suzman in 1937. After the birth of their daughter Frances in 1939 she went back to university and finished her degree. She had a second daughter, Patricia, and later returned to Wits where she taught economic history from 1945 to 1953. Suzman first joined the United Party (UP) in 1949, just as the **apartheid** system was being strengthened. She was elected to parliament in 1953. In 1959 the UP split, and she remained in the more progressive section that formed the Progressive Party (PP). For 13 years, 1961 to 1974, she was the sole PP Member of Parliament and often the only voice opposing the increasingly stringent racial laws. In 1974 there was an increase of PP members; in 1977 the PP became the Progressive Federal Party, which continued as the official opposition party. Suzman's approach to politics is illustrated by her comment that, "I hate bullies. I stand for simple justice, equal opportunity and human rights. The indispensable elements in a democratic society—and well worth fighting for." She retired from parliament in 1989, and wrote her autobiography, *In No Uncertain Terms: A South African Memoir* (1993). She remained active as a commissioner on the South African Human Rights Commission from 1994 to 1998, and with the Helen Suzman Foundation, whose slogan is "Promoting Liberal Democracy in South Africa and Southern Africa" (the foundation website is at http://www.hsf.org.za/home.html).

SWAPO WOMEN'S COUNCIL. The women's group affiliated with the South West African People's Organization (SWAPO), the **nation-**

alist organization fighting for Namibian independence, it was founded in what was then South West Africa in 1969 or 1970. The first congress was held in 1980 in neighboring Angola, attended by 60 people who were primarily living in exile in Zambia and Angola. Women participated in the armed struggle chiefly as support staff rather than combatants. They published *The Namibian Woman*. The group focused on raising understanding of women's oppression and working to improve women's conditions, within the structures of SWAPO. *See also* NAMIBIAN WOMEN'S VOICE; IIVULA-ITHANA, PENDUKENI.

SY DIALLO, MATA. A political leader in Senegal, she was minister-delegate for immigration (1991–1992), vice president of the national assembly (1995–2001), and in 2003 she was elected president of the Mouvement National des Femmes de l'Espoir et du Progrès/National Movement of Women for Hope and Progress. She has also been a leader of Senegal's socialist party, Parti Socialiste du Senegal.

– T –

TAARAB. Taarab is a style of dance and performance found on Zanzibar, and although it is not exclusively female, women have been among its most renowned performers. Typically a *taarab* group included drummers and musicians playing stringed instruments; the most famous singer, **Siti Binti Saadi**, always was accompanied by musicians playing a violin, an *oud* (a kind of lute), drums, and tambourines. *See also LELEMAMA*; MUSIC; *TUFO*.

TAITU BETUL (c. 1844–1918). Taitu married Menelik, who later became emperor of Ethiopia; she was also known as Empress Taitu. She came from a noble family, had been married four times previously, and as a result had extensive experience and connections in political life. Taitu and Menelik married in 1883, and she worked to support his efforts to become emperor in 1889. She had no children in that marriage, and supported **Zauditu**, Menelik's daughter from an earlier marriage, as heir, though Menelik was reluctant to name a woman. Taitu briefly retired from court politics, but reemerged in 1916 in a failed attempt to be named regent for Zauditu's ascendence. She died of heart failure at her home in the mountains.

TAKUMBENG (SOMETIMES TAKEMBENG). Takumbeng refers to a group of Cameroonian women who gather to exert political influence. They were present at political rallies to keep police and soldiers from misbehaving, drawing on the respect typically given to older women. *See ANLU*; SHAMING PRACTICES.

TANI, MAAME HARRIS "GRACE" (c. 1870s–1958). Maame Tani, born in an Nzima coastal fishing community in what is now Ghana, was the first person converted by Prophet Harris in 1914. She became an adept at **spirit possession** and a leader of the Harris-derived Church of the Twelve Apostles. The Harris movement was one of the earliest independent church movements and included many of the elements common to later churches such as the one started by **Alice Lenshina** in Zambia in the 1950s, and another Ghanaian church, the Cherubim and Seraphim society led by **Christianah Abiodun Emmanuel**. The Harris church leaders denounced traditional practices that were branded as **witchcraft**, but supported **polygyny** as that was seen as a legitimate element of African society. Prophet Harris took Maame Tani, already known as a healer and herbalist, as his third wife, though she remained behind when he returned to Côte d'Ivoire. She later joined Papa Kwesi 'John' Nackabah as one of the primary leaders of the Church of the Twelve Apostles. The popularity of the church derived in part from a unique fusion of **Christian** and local religious practices, such as using water to heal illness, thus integrating Christian baptismal and African healing rites.

TANKEU, ELIZABETH NTAENGA NGATCHOU (1944–). A Cameroonian politician, she was educated in Cameroon before going to France where she completed a degree in econometrics at the University of Paris in 1971. She served in various posts in the Ministry of Planning before becoming minister of planning and regional development from 1988 until 1991 when she was removed from the government. She was on the executive board of the African Capacity Building Foundation before being appointed in 2003 as a commissioner in the African Union responsible for trade and industry, one of five women named by the Executive Council on a 50-50 gender-parity basis to the 10 commissioners' positions. *See also* PROTOCOL ON THE RIGHTS OF WOMEN IN AFRICA.

TANZANIA MEDIA WOMEN'S ASSOCIATION (TAMWA). TAMWA began when a group of women **journalists** met in 1979 to discuss their work and the role of women in the media. Initially TMAWA produced radio programs, beginning with a series on schoolgirl pregnancies that was broadcast in Swahili and English. Despite the popularity of the show, the second series on **domestic violence** was blocked by male authorities. After several years of no activity, the women met again in 1986 following the **Nairobi Women's Meeting** and determined to work together and form an official **organization**. It was an early example of organizing among Arican **urban** professional women; such organizations proliferated in the 1990s. TAMWA began publishing an internal newsletter, *Titbits*, in 1987, which later became the magazine, *Sauti ya Siti*. It also established a reference library on women, with an electronic database to facilitate retrieval of sources. The members continued to produce radio programs, and published monographs that documented the condition of women in Tanzania. In the early 1990s TAMWA returned to the issue of domestic violence, publishing a special issue of *Sauti ya Siti* on the topic and producing radio programs, posters, and other materials to raise public awareness of the problem. It also expanded to provide training for community activists in legal issues, counseling for women victims, and to pursue court cases related to domestic violence. Leila Sheikh, one of the founding members, has written about TAMWA's history ("TAMWA: Levina's Song—Supporting Women in Tanzania," in Chigudu, ed. *Composing a New Song*, 2002).

TATTOOS. *See* BODY MARKING.

TAX REVOLTS. African women have a history of resistance to paying taxes, though it was often the case that defying tax assessments symbolized wider disagreements with authorities. Some of the best known activities by women in the **colonial** era were related to increased taxation—for instance, the **Aba Women's War** in 1929

Nigeria, and the tax revolt by Egba women in Nigeria, led by **Funmilayo Ransome-Kuti** and the **Abeokuta Women's Union**, which resulted in the deposition of the Alake, the male ruler. Judith Byfield's 2003 analysis of the Egba revolt suggests the many motivations that women brought to the uprising, which crystalized into a focus on taxation. After independence women continued to protest their tax burdens, for example in the Democratic Republic of the Congo (then Zaire) in 1982 when market women protested the government collection of taxes on their baskets of cassava.

TEMPERANCE. There have been scattered reports of women acting to end excessive drinking by men, particularly related to hard liquor (rather than beer). In the early 20th century there were several African branches of the Women's Christian Temperance Union (WCTU), including one in Zimbabwe. The WCTU tended to be restricted to white women, although **Semane Setlhoko Khama** was a active recruiter in Botswana. In 2002 women in rural Kenya broke into warehouses and destroyed bottles of illegally brewed **alcohol** called *changaa* which is made from maize, sorghum, or sugar cane. There are many local groups, including the Wangerere Anti-Corruption Group in Muranga District, Kenya. The members were not opposed to all alcoholic beverages, but knowing of hundreds of deaths related to toxic mixtures, they opposed illegal brews could kill those who drank them. *See also* BEER BREWERS.

TEXTILES. The production of textiles has often been at least partly women's responsibility, and the process has been marked by a gender division of labor. For example, indigo cloth produced in 19th-century Mali was a joint production of men and women. Typically, men grew the cotton and women cultivated the indigo plant. Women spun and dyed the cotton to produce the indigo cloth for the luxury market, while **slave** labor did the weaving. Plain white cloth, which men produced, was for household use rather than for sale. The process changed after slave emancipation in 1905, and eventually women lost control over the marketing of the indigo cloth. Also in Mali, women have produced distinctive mud cloth called *bogolan* ("bogo" means river mud), printing repetitive geometrical designs in shades of brown and tan. Historically the cloth was made by mothers and grandmothers for a bride-to-be, and the symbols were reminders of proper behavior and advice from their female kin. In the late 20th century new colors were added and the repertoire of designs also expanded to meet the demands of the export market. In the 19th century Sokoto Caliphate (present-day Nigeria) women were spinners, weavers, and dyers, though men performed the same tasks in different geographic areas. Men were able to build on their textile production to develop large-scale industries, while women faced obstacles that kept them in local production despite the high quality of the cloth they produced.

As the modern clothing and textile industry developed in Africa, women rarely found **employment** in the new factories. In Mozambique the garment factories had an almost entirely male labor force until new government policies promoted hiring women in the 1980s. In Lesotho, in contrast, the rapid growth of a new textile industry in the 1980s called on women, and in 1990 the labor force in the clothing and textile factories was 92 percent female. South Africa has the largest textile industry in sub-Saharan Africa, and it began to develop in the 1920s and 1930s with a primarily white labor force. Only in later decades did black women find employment there as well. Nigeria, which comes after South Africa in the size of its textile industry, has a minority of women in the textile labor force. In many regions the textile industry did have an impact on cloth production, as the cheaper mass-produced cloth replaced the labor-intensive cloth that had previously been made in African communities. Women have rarely owned businesses that produced textiles, though there were women in Nairobi who owned small garment factories. *See also* DRESS; *KANGA*.

THAT ROCKY PLACE: CREATIVE WRITING ON WOMEN. A journal showcasing writing by women in Cameroon, edited by Nalova Lyonga of the University of Buea. Volume two was published in 1997, and included short stories, poems, plays, and personal narratives, as well as short pieces on legal issues pertaining to women in Cameroon.

THEATER. Although women were known as story-tellers and performers in African communities, they have not had equal access to modern theatrical life, either as actors, playwrights, or in positions behind the scenes. Despite the obstacles, however, there have been some notable contributions from women. Female playwrights have often focused on women's issues, and have sought to connect with women in the audience; some notable dramatists include **Ama Ata Aidoo, Tsitsi Dangaremgba, Caroline Ntseliseng Khaketla, Stella Oyedepo, Micere Githae Mugo, Penina Muhando, Rebeka Njau, Tess Onwueme, Zulu Sofola**, and **Efua Theodora Sutherland**. In recent decades development organizations have turned to skits and short dramatic pieces to educate non-literate communities about issues such as **HIV/AIDS**, sanitation and other **health** issues, and women's legal rights. Many plays are written and performed for special occasions, and may only belatedly if ever be published for a wider audience.

THIAM, AWA (1936–). A Senegalese politician and writer, she is best known for *La parole aux négresses* (1978), which was published in English as *Black Sisters, Speak Out: Feminism and Oppression in Black Africa* (1986). She has been active in attempts to end the practice of **female genital cutting**, especially as the founder of the **Commission pour l'Abolition des Mutilations Sexuelles (CAMS) / Commission for the Abolition of Sexual Mutilation** in 1982.

31ST DECEMBER WOMEN'S MOVEMENT. The 31st December Women's Movement was established in Ghana in 1982 under the sponsorship of the **first lady**, Nana Konadu Agyeman Rawlings, who has served as president of the organization since 1984. It operated as the women's wing of the Provisional National Defense Council (PNDC), that is, as a typical **political party organization**. An attempt in the early 1980s to merge with the Federation of Ghanaian Women ended in failure and the demise of the federation; in 1984 the All Women's Association of Ghana tried to establish itself as an alternative organization, but it was not able to extend its reach beyond the Accra **market women**. After the 1990s the 31st December Women's Movement registered as a **non-governmental organization**, though it was also allied with the National Democratic Congress, another political party. The focus of the group's activities is on self-help projects and rural development, including initiating income-generating actions, and encouraging women to become more involved in the public life of their communities. One of its major efforts is running **childcare** centers that were initially established to support market women but have expanded to serve a broader clientele. Its website is www.dec31.org.gh.

TINUBU, MADAM (?–1887). Madam Tinubu was an influential businesswoman in 19th century Nigeria. Born in Abeokuta, she learned **market women**'s work from her mother. She set up her own trade in tobacco and salt near Lagos, where she began dealing with European slave traders. She got involved in local politics in 1846 when King Akintoye of Lagos was deposed and turned to her for support in regaining his throne. Madam Tinubu then settled in Lagos where she continued her earlier trade as a middle-woman between the Europeans on the coast and Nigerian traders inland. In 1855 she was involved in an attempt to end the power of wealthy immigrants to Lagos from Brazil and Sierra Leone, but that resulted in her exile from Lagos. She then reestablished her business in Abeokuta, where her prominence was such that she was named *Iyalode* of Abeokuta in 1864. Tinubu Square in Lagos is named to commemorate her contributions to Nigerian history. *See also* PELEWURA, ALIMOTU; OKWEI, OMU.

TLALI, MIRIAM (1933–). Tlali is a significant novelist from South Africa, sometimes described as the first novelist to emerge from Soweto, the African township adjacent to Johannesburg. South African authorities banned her first novel, *Muriel at Metropolitan* (1975), which chronicled the life of a young woman working for an appliance store in a loosely autobiographical story. It was later reissued under her original title, *Between Two Worlds*. Tlali wished to study medicine, but was blocked by the **apartheid**-era laws. She worked in advertising and **journalism**, contributing a regular column, "Soweto Speaking," to the influential *Staffrider* magazine. She also participated in the International Writing Program in Iowa, and in 1990 she was in residence at Yale University, where her play *Crimen Injuria* was staged.

TRADE UNIONS. Women were a distinct minority among unionized workers across the continent; however, when they found **employment**

in factories and other sites of worker's unions, they joined and agitated for issues important to them. It was usually perceived that women were less likely than men to join trade unions, explained by their heavy load of domestic responsibilities that did not allow them the time and energy needed to be involved in work-related organizations. Often women joined a gender-identified affiliate, such as the Women's Wing of the National Union of Plantation and Agricultural Workers in Uganda, the Nigeria Labour Congress Women's Wing or the Comité das Mulheres Trabalhadoras (COMUTRA)/Working Women's Committee in Mozambique. The international organization, Union Network International-Africa, which was formed in 2000 from a merger of several large unions and which represents 655,485 trade unionists in Africa, has a women's section headed by Madeleine Ouedraogo.

Such affiliates have acted to focus women's organizing, but they also have segregated women's issues from the main work of trade unions, to the detriment of their overall objectives of improving working conditions for women. Issues such as pregnancy leave were relegated to women alone, with no recognition that men and families in general also had a stake in improving women's working conditions. There were also cases of employers preferring to hire women because they believed women would be less apt to be involved in unions or to otherwise contest poor wages and working conditions (this problem was documented at a garment factory in Nigeria, and it exists elsewhere as well). South Africa had one of the strongest records of women's involvement in trade union organizing (as described by Iris Berger in *Threads of Solidarity*, 1992), and included individual activists such as **Frances Baard**, Emma Mashinini, and **Lilian Ngoyi**.

TRADITIONAL BIRTH ATTENDANTS. *See* MIDWIVES.

TSANGA, DELPHINE (1935–). Tsanga is a Cameroonian politician and novelist who was born Delphine Zanga Tsogo. She trained as a **nurse** in France, and returned to Cameroon in 1960. In 1964 she was elected president of the **Women's Cameroon National Union**, the women's wing of the Cameroon National Union which was then the ruling party, and she served in that position until 1985. Tsanga was elected to parliament in 1965, and served as deputy minister for health and public welfare (1970–1975) and minister of social affairs (1975–1984). Using her original name, Delphine Zanga Tsogo, she wrote two works of literature in 1983, *Vies de femmes* (*Women's Lives*) and *L'Oiseau en cage* (*The Bird in a cage*).

TUFO. *Tufo* is a kind of performance incorporating **dance,** choral singing, and drumming performed by Makua coastal women in northern Mozambique. Originally associated with **Islamic** religious practices, *tufo* expanded beyond the Muslim community. The women usually performed while seated on the ground, and they were noted for the rhythmic movement of their arms and torsos. The performers were accompanied by drums, usually played by men, and the name "tufo" may have derived from the Arabic word for a frame-drum (*ad-duff*). Though these types of dance groups have older origins, the first references to *tufo* itself appeared in the 1930s, with conflicting stories of its origins. Women typically dressed in matching costumes for their performance, and traveled great distances to participate in *tufo* competitions. In the 1980s and 1990s lyrics began to include political and secular themes. *See also LELEMAMA; TAARAB.*

TULU, DERARTU (1969–). Derartu Tulu is a leading athlete from Ethiopia who was the first black African woman to collect a gold medal at the Olympics, winning the 10,000 meter race in the 1992 games at Barcelona. *See also* SPORT.

– U –

UGANDA ASSOCIATION OF WOMEN'S ORGANIZATIONS (UAWO). Established in 1966 by women who wanted to work politically to improve women's condition, it concentrated on **development** issues and included urban and rural women. It developed into an umbrella organization and the primary mass organization for women, and it was affiliated with the Uganda People's Congress when that was the ruling party. It was later forced to work under the state-controlled **National Council of Women** which was set up by Idi Amin in 1978, and ceased to exist as a separate organization at that time.

UGANDA COUNCIL OF WOMEN (UCW). This council was founded in 1947, and was active in the 1950s and 1960s. It was noted for the multi-racial character of its membership, which included women of Africa, Indian, and European descent as well as women representing religious and community **organizations**. In the 1960s it focused on reforming **marriage laws**, publishing a pamphlet on "Laws about Marriage in Uganda" (1961), though due to male opposition new legislation was not introduced until 1973. The UCW had difficulty working with the ruling party however, and had ceased to exist by 1972. Some of the women leaders who worked with the UCW included, **Katolini Esita Ndagire Kibuka**, **Pumla Kisosonkole**, and **Joyce Mpanga**.

UGANDA MEDIA WOMEN'S ASSOCIATION (UMWA). The UMWA launched a radio program in 2001 as a way to bring more news about and for women onto the airwaves. It planned to broadcast in seven languages.

UGANDA WOMEN'S CAUCUS. After elections in 1994 brought more women into the parliament in Uganda, the elected women decided to work together to push legislation and to provide support for each other. The law called for a minimum of 15 percent of seats to be reserved for women, meaning that over 50 women were members of parliament. They held workshops and training sessions related to improving their political activism, including such issues as parliamentary procedure, campaign strategy, and speech making. They also have sent members as delegates to international conferences. The group works in coalition with others in parliament, and tries to build a consensus on laws that come before the body.

UGANDA WOMEN'S NETWORK (UWONET). A **nongovernmental organization** working to advance public policy on women's issues, it was founded in the mid-1990s. It sponsors workshops and publishes pamphlets on policy issues such as women's **land** rights, **family law**, and electoral strategies, as well as a directory of professional women in Uganda and a biannual newsletter, *UWONET News*. It monitored the parliamentary elections in 2001, working with **Action for Development (ACFODE)**. Its website, www.uwonet.org, documents the group's current projects, which included a five-year plan (2000–2004) aimed at increasing the number of women involved in politics and improving the understanding and actions of women currently serving in government.

UGANDAN WOMEN'S EFFORT TO SAVE ORPHANS (UWESO). Founded in 1986 with the support of **First Lady** Janet Museveni, wife of President Yoweri Museveni, the group initially focused on caring for war orphans, switching in 1990 to working with the estimated 1.7 million **HIV/AIDS** orphans in Uganda. UWESO, with a United Nations partner organization, provides low-interest loans to women to help them generate an income and support themselves. It has a repayment rate of 90 percent. UWESO also holds AIDS prevention workshops and teaches loan recipients about business management.

UMOJA WA WANAWAKE WA TANZANIA (UWT) / TANZANIAN WOMEN'S UNION. UWT is the Tanzanian women's organization affiliated with the ruling party, the Tanzanian African National Union (TANU), later Chama cha Mapinduzi/Party of the Revolution. Formed in 1962 to promote women's issues at the national level of political activity, in 1978 it had 2,000,000 members. It formed a company, Shirika la Uchumi wa Wanawake Katika Tanzania, that focused on **development** projects in rural areas through training women in business essentials.

UNIÃO DEMOCRÁTICA DAS MULHERES (UDEMU) / DEMOCRATIC UNION OF WOMEN. UDEMU was established in 1960 as part of the Partido Africano de Independência de Guiné-Bissau e Cabo Verde (PAIGC)/African Party for the Independence of Guinea-Bissau and Cape Verde, the party fighting to end Portuguese **colonialism** in those countries (then a single nation), with the mandate of representing women's issues. When Guinea-Bissau and Cape Verde split to struggle independently, UDEMU was replaced by the **Organização das Mulheres de Cabo Verde (OMCV) / Organization of Women of Cape Verde.** It later became the Commissão Feminina/Female Commission and after independence was again renamed the Commissão Organização das Mulheres/ Commission [for the] Organization of Women. *See also* PEREIRA, CARMEN; PEREIRA GOMES, FRANCISCA.

UNIFEM. *See* UNITED NATIONS DEVELOPMENT FUND FOR WOMEN.

UNION DES FEMMES BURUNDAISES / UNION OF BURUNDI WOMEN. Founded in Burundi in 1967, this national organization continued to advocate for women in politics into the 21st century. During its decades of organizing efforts, it established a cultural center for women, held annual meetings, conducted **literacy** campaigns, and worked to improve women's legal situation.

UNION DES FEMMES DE L'EMPIRE CENTRAFRICAINE / UNION OF CENTRAL AFRICAN EMPIRE WOMEN. Founded in 1960 in the Central African Republic (Central African Empire, 1976–1979), there were 10,000 members in 1978. Sponsored by the Ministry of Social Welfare, the organization promoted self-help projects, **education** for girls, and training for women. It disappeared with the fall of Emperor Jean-Bédel Bokassa in 1979.

UNION DES FEMMES DU NIGER / UNION OF WOMEN OF NIGER. This organization was formed in 1958 from an early Association des Femmes/Women's Association, which was an alliance of women in the capital city of Niamey, Niger. It was affiliated with the ruling party Parti Progressiste Nigérien (PPN)/Progressive Party of Niger, which was connected to the regional Rassemblement Démocratique Africaine (RDA). The organization was supported by the **first lady**, Aissa Diori, and promoted women's **education**, improved sanitation, and more jobs for women. It also pushed for legal reforms concerning **marriage** and **bridewealth**, and tried to introduce a **family law**, though they were not successful in these attempts. In 1974, following a coup d'etat, it was replaced by the **Association des Femmes du Niger**.

UNION DES FEMMES DU PARTI DÉMOCRATIQUE GABONAIS / UNION OF WOMEN OF THE DEMOCRATIC PARTY OF GABON. Founded in 1971, this affiliate of the Democratic Party of Gabon promoted **education**, social, economic, cultural, and political advancement for women. In 1978 there were 800 members in branches throughout the country.

UNION DES FEMMES DU SOUDAN (UFS) / UNION OF WOMEN OF SUDAN. An umbrella organization unifying three women's groups, the **Union des Femmes Travailleuses**, **Jèmangèlèn**, and **Rencontres Africaines,** in the French Soudan, later Mali. It was founded in November 1958 and only lasted until 1960. The UFS was strictly non-partisan, and worked for all women. The UFS was also involved with the **Femmes de l'Ouest Africain.** The group experienced difficulties in the complex political period around independence in 1960, as the political party Union Soudanese-Rassemblement Démocratique Africain (US-RDA) preferred that women join the women's arm of the party rather than channel their energy into an autonomous organization. By the end of 1960 independent women's organizations ceased to be active and women activists had moved into party-centered work.

UNION DES FEMMES TRAVAILLEUSES (UFT) / UNION OF WOMEN WORKERS. An organization of women workers in the French Soudan, lead by **Aoua Kéita** and Assitan Coulibaly, the UFT was founded in 1956 to improve the situation of women wage workers. It was affiliated with the Union Soudanaise-Rassemblement Démocratique Africain (US-RDA). It is sometimes referred to as the Association des Femmes Travailleuses. In 1958 it joined with **Jèmangèlèn** and **Rencontres Africaines** to form the **Union des Femmes du Soudan (UFS) / Union of Women of Sudan**.

UNION NATIONALE DES FEMMES DU TOGO / NATIONAL UNION OF WOMEN OF TOGO. This organization was formed in 1972 to promote the national political organization, Rassemblement du Peuple Togolais/Assembly of Togolese People.

UNION NATIONALE DES FEMMES DU MALI (UNFM) / NATIONAL UNION OF WOMEN OF MALI. This national organization came under the Mali Ministry of Social Justice. Originally founded in the 1960s, it was dissolved in 1968 following a military coup d'etat. Revived in 1974, the UNFM's aims were to improve women's participation in society and to expand social services such as **childcare** centers. It was the official women's organization under the government of Moussa Traoré (1974–1991) and was affiliated with the ruling party, the Union Démocratique du Peuple Malien (UDPM)/Democratic Union of the Malian People. The **first lady** Mariam Traoré was president of the UNFM, Fatou Tall was the secretary general, and the executive committee membership primarily consisted of female kin of male government leaders. When that government was overthrown in 1991, the UNFM ceased to exist. It had published a monthly magazine.

UNION OF SUDANESE WOMEN. The union was formed in 1952 in Sudan with the stated goals of raising the level of women's **educational** and economic situation and of defending women's rights. By 1959 it reported 1,800 members of 16 branches throughout the country. Its budget was based on dues and income from fundraising events, and it was careful to maintain its independence from political parties.

UNION OF TANZANIAN WOMEN. *See* UMOJA WA WANAWAKE WA TANZANIA.

UNION RÉVOLUTIONNAIRE DES FEMMES CONGOLAISES (URFC) / REVOLUTIONARY UNION OF CONGOLESE WOMEN. The URFC was founded as a support organization for the Parti congolais du travail/Congolese Workers' Party, the ruling Marxist party in the People's Republic of Congo (now the Republic of the Congo). It had its headquarters in Brazzaville, with branches in many other localities. From the 1970s until the 1990s it published *Bakento ya Congo*, a women's journal. When the government felt membership was declining as professional women gained control, the Union was reorganized according to occupational categories with sections for market women, farmers, and so on.

UNIP WOMEN'S BRIGADE. The Women's Brigade was the **organization** in Zambia that was affiliated with the national political party, the United National Independence Party (UNIP).

UNITED NATIONS DECADE FOR WOMEN. The United Nations sponsored a series of international meetings on women's issues which had important implications for African women. The first was held in Mexico City in 1975; the second in Copenhagen in 1980, the third significantly in Nairobi in 1985, and the fourth in Beijing in 1995. During the first decade, **Annie Jiagge** helped write the **Convention on the Elimination of All Forms of Discrimination against Women (CEDAW)**. At each of the international meetings African women participated as representatives of their governments and of **non-governmental organizations**. **Esther Ocloo** was strongly influenced by her encounter with other businesswomen at the 1975 meeting. The **Nairobi women's meeting** had a major impact on the ability of African women to network across the continent, while the platform of "Forward Looking Strategies for the Advancement of Women" set forth at that meeting was used in many African nations by women working to improve women's conditions. Those strategies were reworked into a Platform for Action at the Beijing meeting, which was chaired by **Gertrude Mongella**.

UNITED NATIONS DEVELOPMENT FUND FOR WOMEN (UNIFEM). The United Nations Development Fund for Women, commonly known as UNIFEM, has focused on a range of issues concerning women, including work in the three major areas of economic **development**, **human rights**, and **peace**; specific projects include ending **domestic violence**, combatting **HIV/AIDS**, improving access to safe water, and numerous other endeavors. It was founded in 1976 following the first international meeting of the **United Nations Decade for Women**. It is guided by the policies put forward in the Beijing Platform for Action at the final meeting of the Decade for Women, and by the **Convention on the Elimination of All Forms of Discrimination Against Women (CEDAW)**. In 2004 UNIFEM supported projects in over 100 countries, and had 13 branch offices including four African bureaus in Kenya, Nigeria, Senegal, and Zimbabwe. A trust fund was set up in 1996 to allow it to finance projects and collect donations; since then it has disbursed over $5 million in over 70 countries. It also regularly represents women's issues within the UN at meetings and conferences. Their website can be found at www.unifem.org.

UNITED WOMEN'S ORGANISATION. There were 19 branches of this Cape Town, South Africa, based organization that affiliated with the anti-**apartheid** coalition the United Democratic Front (UDF) in 1983. It was later called the United Women's Congress. *See also* CAROLUS, CHERYL; WOMEN'S FRONT.

URBANIZATION. Women have played a central role in the development of African cities. In West Africa there was a higher level of urban residence historically, and women were noted as active participants in the markets and other activities. In eastern and southern Africa, cities more often emerged in connection with colonial settlements, and Africans moved into urban areas in response to new work opportunities as well as to escape deteriorating rural conditions. The African neighborhoods of Bulawayo, Southern Rhodesia (now Zimbabwe) were founded in the early 20th century when Lobengula's queens settled in the area where his capital had existed and began operating boarding houses, though most of those women lost control of their real estate in the 1920s and 1930s. Conventional studies have emphasized the male-dominant character of urbanization, as men found **employment** and women remained in rural areas engaged in **agriculture**, but many women also moved to the cities. And although women did migrate with male family members, there were also women who traveled alone or with female kin when they sought a new and different life.

In the urban areas some women were able to find factory employment while others entered new occupations in the **informal sector**, including **market** vending or professional work. Other women continued rural activities such as urban farming and **beer brewing** as a way to support themselves and their families; such work indicated the permeable boundaries between urban and rural life. Family life was under less scrutiny in the more impersonal conditions of urban life, and although most women still married and raised their children, some women remained single, lived in **female-headed households**, and were more likely to use contraceptives and live in monogamous relationships than rural women. Urban residence also brought women into contact with a wide variety of **organizations** that were not available in rural locations, including neighborhood groups, religious affiliations, work-related associations, and political alliances. *See also* HOUSING.

UWILINGIYIMANA, AGATHE (1953–1994). Uwilingiyimana was the prime minister of Rwanda in 1994 when extreme ethnic violence broke out. She was born in a rural area and trained as a teacher. She taught high school science for 10 years, earning a master's degree in chemistry and working in industry before entering politics. She joined the Mouvement Démocratique Républicain (MDR)/Democratic Republican Movement and in 1992 she was named minister of **education**. While serving as minister she tried to end the system of favoritism that governed admissions to secondary schools, by guarding the printing of exams to prevent anyone getting advance copies and by publicly posting the examination results. She was assaulted in a probable intimidation effort, though it was made to look like a robbery rather than a politically motivated attack. Women demonstrated in her support, calling for an end to war.

Uwilingiyimana was a Hutu who was considered a moderate because she worked to diminish ethnic tensions in her country, and was appointed prime minister in July 1993 as a compromise candidate among five contending parties. The MDR was involved in a power-sharing arrangement with the other major opposition parties, confronting the former single-party government of the Mouvement républicain national pour la démocratie et le développement (MRND)/National Republican Movement for Democracy and Development. It was expected that she would step down after a transition period ended in 1994.

She was overtaken by events when the plane carrying the Hutu presidents of Rwanda and Burundi crashed under suspicious circumstances as they returned from discussions about future political directions. Immediately Hutus initiated a genocidal attack on Tutsis as well as on Hutus who were perceived as being too moderate. Uwilingiyimana was planning to broadcast a plea for calm and was at her home under a limited guard of Ghanaian and Belgian troops, when the guards were disarmed and she was assassinated along with her husband. *See also* HEADS OF GOVERNMENT.

– V –

VAN MEERHOF, EVA (NÉE KROTOA) (c. 1642–1674). Known popularly as Eva, she was one of the first African women to marry a European. She encountered Dutch settlers in the 1650s at what became Cape Town, South Africa. She was of Khoi background, and initially she was employed as a domestic worker by Jan Van Riebeeck, the Dutch commander. After learning Dutch and some Portuguese she worked as a translator. In 1664 she converted to **Christianity**, and in 1666 she married Pieter van Meerhoff, who died the following year. She then began drinking excessively and became a **prostitute**. Her unsavory behavior led the colonists to take custody of her children and discouraged other inter-racial marriages. As Julia Wells explained in an article in 1998, Eva has become a contradictory emblem of African women, with some describing her as an example of African savagery which cannot be civilized, others discussing her role as mother of the first "coloureds" or mixed race people in South Africa, and still others seeing her experience as one of African female oppression by European men or as an innovative synthesizer of African and Christian religious beliefs.

VERA, YVONNE (1964–). An acclaimed novelist from Zimbabwe, Vera writes poetically about issues central to Zimbabwean women's experiences. She was born and raised in Bulawayo, later studying at York University in Canada. Her first publication was a collection of short stories, *Why Don't You Carve Other Animals* (1992), followed by novels about the legendary figure **Nehanda** (*Nehanda*, 1993), women during the war for independence (*Without a Name*, 1994, winner of the Zimbabwe Publishers' Literary Award, 1995), incest (*Under the Tongue*, 1996, winner of the 1997 Zimbabwe Publishers' Literary Award and the 1997 Commonwealth Writers Prize, Africa region), and 1940s Bulawayo (*Butterfly Burning*, 1998). In 1999 she won the Swedish literary award, The Voice of Africa. For several years Vera was the director of the Bulawayo branch of the National Gallery of Zimbabwe until she resigned in 2003.

VITA, DONA BEATRIZ KIMPA (c. 1684–1706). Beatriz was a woman from a noble Kongo background who popularized a cult devoted to the Catholic Saint Anthony, in what is today Angola. She claimed that she had died and been resurrected as Saint Anthony, and with that persona she preached for reconciliation and the restoration of the Kongolese monarchy. In the aftermath of three decades of war and disruption her peaceful message attracted many followers, who called themselves Antonians. She also drew the wrath of the local Angolan Catholic hierarchy with her calls for the recognition of black saints and her claim that Jesus Christ was Kongolese. A coalition between two aristocratic households adhering to orthodox Catholic beliefs tried Beatriz for heresy, burning her at the stake in 1706. Her movement continued only until 1709 when her followers were decisively defeated by Pedro IV's army. Her story is told by John Thornton in *The Kongolese Saint Anthony: Dona Beatriz Kimpa Vita and the Antonian Movement, 1684-1706* (1998).

VOICE OF ERITREAN WOMEN. This newsletter was published in New York by the **National Union of Eritrean Women**. It appeared four times a year from 1989 to 1991.

VOICE OF WOMEN. This publication was a quarterly newsletter published in Zambia by the **African National Congress Women's League** from 1976 until 1988 under the editorial leadership of **Gertrude Shope**.

VOTING RIGHTS. *See* SUFFRAGE.

– W –

WACIUMA, CHARITY (c. 1930–). Waciuma is a Kenyan writer who has published many children's books as well as novels for adults, the best known of which is the autobiographical *Daughter of Mumbi* (1969).

WAR. War and conflict have affected women in a variety of historical situations and geographical sites. Although women were not usually considered as combatants or warriors, some early queens such as **Amina** and **Yennenga** were legendary for their skill in combat. In the

19th century women were noted as **Dahomey soldiers** in West Africa. Other women appeared in early anti-colonial conflicts, including **Yaa Asantewaa** in opposition to the British in Asante (now part of Ghana), and **Nehanda** via the person of **Charwe** in Zimbabwe. **Nyabingi** was another leader who was a crucial element in anti-colonial efforts through the **spirit-possessed Muhumusa**. One of the earliest notable **tax revolts** is commonly referred to as a war: the **Aba Women's War** in southeastern Nigeria in 1929. In a different kind of war, recent research has reassessed the role of women in the **South African War** in 1899–1902.

Women were centrally involved in key **nationalist** struggles in Angola, Eritrea, Mozambique, Namibia, South Africa, and Zimbabwe. The **Mau Mau** resistance movement in 1950s Kenya involved women in vital support activities. Though they were only occasionally combatants, women such as **Joyce Nhongo Mujuru** rose to prominence in Zimbabwe with the nom de guerre "Teurai Ropa" or "Spill Blood," and Paulina Mateus, who was a major in the army of Mozambique's Frente de Libertação de Moçambique (FRELIMO)/Mozambique Liberation Front, became secretary general of the **Organização da Mulher Moçambicana (OMM) / Organization of Mozambican Women**. However, most of the women who contributed to the liberation wars were marginalized from their independent governments.

In the post-independence era many African nations encountered internal and low-level conflict. One of the first was the Biafran war in Nigeria in the 1960s; **Flora Nwapa** published short stories about that experience in *Wives at War* (1980). During the 1980s and 1990s internal conflicts and civil wars brought misery to Angola, Liberia, Mozambique, Sierra Leone, Rwanda, Somalia and other nations. **Alice Lakwena** played a central role in the conflict in northern Uganda in the 1980s. Conflicts persisted in Sudan and the Democratic Republic of the Congo into the 21st century, and women's experience of famine, **rape**, and displacement were prominent features in reports from those regions.

Women are most often portrayed as victims of war. The documented evidence of women suffering rape, abduction, forced **migration** as **refugees**, and other forms of violence as the result of war is overwhelming. They have seen their husbands and children killed, faced injury from landmines in their fields, and lost access to their livelihoods. In the 1990s women were instrumental in developing new initiatives for an end to conflict and to actively bring **peace** to Africa.

WASSOULOU. Historically *wassoulou* was a form of Bamana song performed only by men in hunting societies in southern Mali. In the late 20th century women began to appropriate the form for themselves, and some became known internationally for their recordings, especially **Fanta Damba**, **Sira Mori Diabaté**, **Oumou Sangaré**, and others who contributed to *The Wassoulou Sound: Women of Mali* (1994). Women singers incorporated traditional lyrics of proverbs and moral lessons as a way to address women's situation in modern Mali, and younger singers such as Rokia Traore have expanded the themes and musicality of the older traditions. *See also* GRIOTTES.

WEREWERE LIKING (1950–) (SOMETIMES WEREWERE-LIKING). Werewere Liking is a Cameroonian writer and artist who addresses issues of femininity and women's position in society in her works. She has been active with Ki-Yi, a community of artists in Côte d'Ivoire, where she has lived since 1978. Ki-Yi sponsors an important experimental theater. Werewere Liking's most significant works included *La Queue du diable* (*The Devil's Tail*), 1979; *Une nouvelle terre: Théatre rituel* (*A New Earth: Ritual Theatre*), 1980; *Elle sera de jaspe et de corail*, 1983, English translation, *It Shall be of Jasper and Coral,* 2000; *Un Touareg s'est marié à une Pygmé* (*A Touareg Married a Pygmy*), 1992; and *La Veuve dilemme* (*The Widow's Dilemma*), 1994. She received the African Literature Association Fonlon-Nichols Award in 1993 for her contributions to African literature.

WESTERN WOMEN. Women from Europe and North America began traveling to Africa in the 18th century, though the earliest such women were more likely to accompany their husbands, as with Anna Maria Falconbridge who wrote *Two Voyages to Sierra Leone* (1794) based on her travels with her husband when he was posted to Sierra Leone and Florence Baker who traveled with her husband in search of the source of the Nile River in the 1860s. In the 19th century women travelers visited Africa as explorers, such as **Mary Kingsley** and May French Sheldon; as **missionaries** (individuals such as **Mary**

Slessor and Mother Kevin, and religious orders including the **Immaculate Conception** and the **White Sisters**); and as settlers. Some of these women wrote widely read fiction and memoirs, including early 20th-century settlers in Kenya, **Isak Dinesen**, and Elspeth Huxley, who wrote *The Flame Trees of Thika: Memories of an African Childhood* (1959). Others were with the colonial administration or conducted research, including **Margery Perham**, who was closely associated with the British colonial office. In the 1930s and 1940s much of the available research about African women was done by western women scholars including Hilda Kuper, Lucy Mair, Audrey Richards, Monica Wilson, and others. By the end of the 20th century the numbers of western women who traveled to Africa as tourists, researchers, Peace Corps workers, and otherwise had grown enormously. *See also* AFRICAN AMERICAN WOMEN.

WHITE SISTERS. The White Sisters were an order of European nuns who were also known as Soeurs Blanches. Their order, the Soeurs Missionaires de Notre-Dame d'Afrique, was established in Algiers in 1869 under Cardinal Lavigerie to assist the better-known Catholic missionary organization, the White Fathers. In many countries where they initiated **mission** work they organized schools for girls as well as providing **health** care. A number of local convents for African girls and women were established under their auspices. Other orders of European religious women who worked as missionaries in Africa included the Sisters of St. Joseph of Cluny, who arrived in Senegal in 1819, the Sisters of Charity of Ghent who traveled to the Belgian Congo (now the Democratic Republic of the Congo) in 1892, and the Sisters of Notre-Dame de Namur who went to Central Africa in 1894. *See also* BANNABIKIRA; CHRISTIANITY; EDUCATION; *RECONTRES AFRICAINES*; RELIGION.

WIDOWHOOD. Widows are often portrayed as one of the most disadvantaged groups of women, as they may lose access to their children, their **land**, and their homes upon the death of their husband. Yet in some areas older women are able to take on leadership roles and they may enter into a stage of life where they enjoy respect and authority that is not accorded to younger women. Research among Kenyan widows found that their main concern in the 1940s and

1950s was not with **inheritance** and forced remarriage (**levirite**), but with securing a good husband for their daughters. They generally preferred not to remarry, and the choices they made within social constraints indicated their resourcefulness rather than their oppressed condition. Nonetheless the issue of inheritance was a central concern of **human rights** activists, as examples from across the continent suggested that widows were barred from inheriting what was rightfully theirs.

In South Africa, widows of political leaders who were assassinated under the **apartheid** system found that they had a public role to play as they embodied the political loss that accompanied the death, regardless of their own political activity and interests. In 2003 Swaziland introduced a retrograde provision that prohibited women whose husbands had died within the previous two years from running for office in the parliamentary elections. The reason given was that a proper mourning period restricted widows to their homes, which also kept them from casting ballots. The enforcement of the mourning period was the focus of many complaints, as it also limited how widows could earn a living, since the traditional family system that once supported older women was no longer in place. An overview of the situation of widows in 10 African countries can be found at http://www.oneworld.org/empoweringwidows/10countries/index.html.

WIFE-BEATING. *See* DOMESTIC VIOLENCE.

WILLIAMS, EKANEM ESU (1950–). A founder of the **Society for Women and AIDS in Africa**, Williams was educated at the University of Nigeria (1975) and earned a doctorate in immunology at the University of London (1984). She teaches at the University of Calabar in Nigeria.

WINA, PRINCESS NAKATINDI. *See* NAKATINDI WINA, PRINCESS.

WITCHCRAFT. Many African societies included beliefs and practices that were labeled "witchcraft," a potentially negative term for a wide variety of magical and spiritual customs. There existed immense variations in witchcraft, with varying views about the positive or negative role witches played in society. Witches included diviners with the ability to view the future, and sorcerers capable of performing transformative and redemptive acts. The incidence of reported witchcraft sometimes increased when a community was undergoing unusual stress. It was also noted that witchcraft was evident among family, kin, and close neighbors; in patrilineal societies wives who married in from other communities were vulnerable to complaints that they were witches. Conflicts over ordinary issues could have an outcome in witchcraft. For instance, any illness that was not explicable might be blamed on an individual who was labeled a witch, or jealousy over a woman who was unusually successful might bring on complaints that she relied on witchcraft. Rituals were used to identify and condemn accused witches and some rites, such as those that relied on poison ordeals or other physical tests, could result in further illness and death.

European colonial officials regularly tried to end what they considered witchcraft. In 1930s Swaziland, as one example among many, a judge imprisoned four people found guilty of witchcraft. The convicted Swazis included a husband and wife who had been seeking a remedy for their **infertility** as well as two women, a healer who used herbs as a cure, and a diviner (*sangoma*) who tried to find the source of the problem by throwing bones and using other methods. Other people, such as **Muhumusa**, who was possessed by the spirit **Nyabingi**, were also accused of witchcraft by colonial officials. In some cases **colonialism** brought disruption to the moral expectations in African communities by condemning people who were not considered to be problems by their own society. Africans also worked to end witchcraft, often through religious organizations such as those affiliated with **Christianah Abiodun Emmanuel**, **Alice Lenshina**, **Nontetha**, and **Maame Harris "Grace" Tani**.

WOMAN–WOMAN MARRIAGE. In some societies a woman could "marry" another woman by offering **bridewealth** to her family. In many cases the new wife would have a conjugal relationship with a man chosen by the "female husband." Any children born to the wife would be affiliated with the woman who had paid bridewealth. By making such a payment, a woman was recognized as having political and economic power, as she was able to gain control of female labor, a domain that was commonly reserved for men. It was sometimes an option for women who had been unable to have children of their own and had been rejected by their (male) husbands when they seemed to be barren. The "female husband" usually had authority over property rights and **inheritance** as related to the offspring, authority which otherwise devolved to a male husband, but they were not considered to be male themselves. Researchers have also commented on the emotional and social bonds shared by women in such relationships. Observers continue to debate the degree of intimacy experienced between women who married other women, though it seems that these relationships do not parallel western **lesbian** associations.

WOMANISM. Womanism was initially introduced by the African American writer and activist Alice Walker in the 1980s. She commented that a "womanist" was a "feminist of color," thus a womanist did not reject **feminism** but sought to expand it beyond the perceived racial limitations that existed in western feminism. Womanism often reflected a cultural rather than a political sense of putting women at the center of social life and respecting the contributions that women of all races have made to history and culture. Though the term was more commonly used by **African American women**, it gained some currency among activists on the continent of Africa as well.

WOMANPLUS. *WomanPlus* was a magazine that was published three times a year by the **Zimbabwe Women's Resource Centre and Network**. The resource center began issuing a newsletter in 1992 and initiated *WomanPlus* in 1996, publishing it regularly until 2001 when the organization shifted to electronic distribution of news and analysis. Each issue focused on a particular theme such as **land**, **rape**, or **religion**, and offered background information and action advice. The final issue is available on the ZWRCN website, www.zwrcn.org.zw.

WOMEN AND LAW IN SOUTHERN AFRICA (WLSA). This regional organization was headquartered in Harare, Zimbabwe, though it served Botswana, Lesotho, Malawi, Mozambique, Swaziland, Zambia, and Zimbabwe, and maintained an office in each of the member countries. It sponsored research and advocacy related to women and the **law**. Since 1987 it has published over 30 monographs on specific topics such as legal issues, **inheritance**, maintenance rights, family and change, **marriage**, and **widowhood**. Books and substantial working papers usually focused on the situation in individual countries (for instance, *Inheritance in Zambia*, 1994). The newsletter, full-text articles, and further information on WLSA's research projects can be found at the website: http://www.wlsa.co.zw/. *See also* DOW, UNITY; *OUTRAS VOZES*.

WOMEN AS PARTNERS FOR PEACE IN AFRICA (WOPPA). Women have organized to seek **peace** in conflict areas in Africa, including the Democratic Republic of the Congo, where WOPPA, led by Liberian activist **Ruth Sando Perry**, encouraged the Inter-Congolese Dialogue as a way of negotiating a peaceful end to the conflict in 2001. Three hundred women demonstrated in the capital city of Kinshasa in February 2003, blocking traffic to protest continued reports of violence, including stories of cannibalism in Ituri province. *See also* WAR.

WOMEN FOR CHANGE (WFC). Women for Change is a **nongovernmental organization** in Zambia that works closely with women in rural communities to end **poverty** and improve women's social and political status. Originally organized by the Canadian **development** group CUSO (formerly Canadian University Service Overseas) and called the Women's Development Programme, it became independent in 1992 and registered as Women for Change. Many of the initial endeavors were focused on developing new income-generating projects, but after 1992 it expanded into **education**, gender analysis, and **human rights** advocacy. Emily Sikazwe, the executive director from 1992, has written a history and description of the project ("Women for Change: Working with Rural Communities," in Chigudu, ed., *Composing a New Song*, 2002).

WOMEN IN LAW AND DEVELOPMENT IN AFRICA. This multinational **non-governmental organization**, commonly called WiLDAF, was established in 1990. It was initiated by a series of international meetings under the auspices of OEF International (formerly the Overseas Education Fund), a donor agency interested in

law and **development**. The stated purpose of WiLDAF was "to promote the development of strategies that link law and development to empower women." The organizers focused on policy reform and worked to mobilize women to better understand their legal rights and to agitate for the expansion of those rights within each country. They also emphasized that women should have equal access to economic resources, and that all forms of violence against women should be ended. Much of the work was accomplished by individual national offices, though there was a continent-wide structure with headquarters in Harare, Zimbabwe.

The organization published *WiLDAF News*, a newsletter with a focus on women's rights. With funding from a variety of international agencies, it held workshops in Togo and elsewhere to spread awareness of **domestic violence**, challenged laws in Swaziland that relegated women to the status of minors, and worked on a number of issues related to women's claim to equal property rights, **inheritance**, access to **health** care, and other problems that illustrated the important link between women's legal rights and their opportunities to participate fully in development. While it initially framed its work as centered on women's needs, WiLDAF shifted to a **human rights** discourse that allows it to talk about legal rights. Practices that oppressed women were addressed as legal issues subject to changes in the law rather than traditional cultural customs that are difficult to alter. Women's situation in **marriage**, **divorce**, and inheritance were not simply religious or cultural conditions, but reflected legal codes that could be changed to improve women's lives. WiLDAF also pushed for a broader view of development that required more than economic expansion, but relied on improving women's legal position, empowering women on all fronts simultaneously.

WOMEN IN NIGERIA (WIN). This national **organization** was founded in 1983 with an overt **feminist** political position. Much of its activities focused on research and publication in **politics**, reproductive rights, and violence against women. It also emphasized child **marriage**, **education**, and **housing**. In the 1990s WIN refused to join an official national council of women's organizations; in response the government refused to register it as a legal entity and threatened the leaders with imprisonment. By the late 1990s they had chapters in 24 of the 36 Nigerian states.

WOMEN OF UGANDA NETWORK (WOUGNET). WOUGNET was founded in May 2000 in Uganda as a **non-governmental organization** with a special mission to "develop the use of information and communication technologies (ICTs) among women as tools to share information and address issues collectively." It aimed to facilitate women's use of technology in contributing to **development**, and worked to promote networking among women in Uganda and elsewhere through links at its website (www.wougnet.org), and by issuing regular electronic informational bulletins.

WOMEN SELF-HELP ASSOCIATION. A group in Mauritius that was founded in 1969 to promote local handicrafts to support women's advancement in society, it still maintained an office in Port Louis in 2000. It was affiliated with the **Mauritius Alliance of Women**.

WOMEN'S ACTION GROUP (WAG). A Zimbabwean organization involved in improving women's status, it was formed following a controversial 1983 sweep called "Operation Clean-Up" in which over 6,000 women were taken into custody because they were presumed to be working as **prostitutes** if they appeared in public and seemed to be outside of male control. WAG has been active on such issues as **health** care, **HIV/AIDS**, **domestic violence**, **sexual harassment**, and **employment** discrimination. The organization published *Speak Out-Taurai-Khulumani.* To mark its 15th anniversary in 1998 it published *Determined to Act: The First Fifteen Years of the Women's Action Group (WAG) 1983-98*, by Peggy Watson. Further information is available on its website: www.kubatana.net/wag. *See also* MUSASA PROJECT; ZIMBABWE WOMEN'S RESOURCE CENTRE AND NETWORK.

WOMEN'S ASSOCIATION FOR NATIONAL DEVELOPMENT. An organization founded to promote women's role in national politics in Sierra Leone in the 1990s, its leaders were forced into exile after a coup in 1997. Those in the country maintained a project to educate displaced youth.

WOMEN'S CAMEROON NATIONAL UNION. As the women's wing of the national party, Cameroon National Union, its position was to stress the importance of women's role within the family and to approve of decisions made by male politicians. It was founded in 1966 after the East Cameroon Conseil National des Femmes Camerounaises (headed by **Delphine Tsanga**) and the West Cameroon Council of Women's Institutes merged and Tsanga then organized the group's incorporation into the party-affiliated group. The organization claimed 700,000 members in 1978. The many programs it supported included **education** for girls, women's **development** activities, and the end of practices that limited women's advancement in society. *See also* POLITICAL PARTY ORGANIZATIONS.

WOMEN'S CHARTER CAMPAIGN. A program initiated in South Africa in 1993 to ensure that women's issues were integrated into the new constitution and bill of rights being written at that time. The campaign was organized by the **Women's National Coalition**.

WOMEN'S DEFENCE OF THE CONSTITUTION LEAGUE. *See* BLACK SASH.

WOMEN'S FRANCHISE SOCIETY. This group was a white women's organization in Southern Rhodesia (later Zimbabwe) that agitated for women's **suffrage**. Women there were granted the vote in 1919, if they met the conditions of being married monogamously or if they or their husband owned property. These conditions effectively excluded African women. *See also* RHODESIAN WOMEN'S LEAGUE.

WOMEN'S FRONT: SOUTH AFRICA. Based in the Western Cape of South Africa, it was affiliated with the United Democratic Front, a major anti-**apartheid** organization founded in 1983. *See also* UNITED WOMEN'S ORGANISATION.

WOMEN'S FRONT: SUDAN. Founded in 1964 by Muslim women in Sudan, it encouraged political advances and **educational** opportunities for women. As a project of Muslim Sisters, who were members of a sisterhood affiliated with an **Islamic** brotherhood, their intention was to counter the overtly political and communist approach of the **Sudanese Women's Union.**

WOMEN'S LEAGUE, MALAWI CONGRESS PARTY. *See* LEAGUE OF MALAWI WOMEN.

WOMEN'S NATIONAL COALITION. A South African organization of 70 women's groups founded in 1992 that focused on the process of writing the new constitution and bill of rights as South Africa moved toward majority rule in 1994. The member organizations represented the full range of South African political perspectives, from the African National Congress (ANC) to white conservative groups and the Zulu Inkatha Freedom Movement. Its project, known as the **Women's Charter Campaign**, involved implementing a major research survey on property rights, reproductive freedom, **domestic violence**, comparable worth, and other topics of particular importance to women, which tried to solicit the views of every woman in South African about these issues. Its slogan was, "South Africa will not be free until its women are free." *See also* GINWALA, FRENE.

WOMEN'S RESEARCH AND DOCUMENTATION CENTER (WORDOC). Based at the University of Ibadan, WORDOC was founded in 1986. Many of Nigeria's foremost scholars of women were involved, including Bolanle Awe, LaRay Denzer, and **Nina Mba**. It worked to collect materials pertaining to women and developed an important repository. It also conducted training programs and published occasional documents on a range of topics, including **women's studies**, women and food, theory, and history. Beginning in 1987 until at least 1997 it published the *WORDOC Newsletter*.

WOMEN'S RESEARCH COLLECTIVE. A **women's studies** group based at the Institute of Southern African Studies at the National University of Lesotho, it promotes research on women in policy and **development**.

WOMEN'S STUDIES. Beginning in the 1970s many African universities established women's studies programs and centers, a process which accelerated following the 1985 **Nairobi Women's Meeting** of the **United Nations Decade for Women**. By 2004 there were over 30 such centers in Africa, with four formal departments: the Department of Women and Gender Studies at Makerere University, Uganda (established in 1991); the Department of Women's Studies at Cameroon's University of Buea; the Gender Studies Department at the University of Zambia; and the **African Gender Institute at the University of Cape Town** in South Africa. A number of academic conferences were held and important books and journals were published on the continent. In 2002 the trienniel "International Interdisciplinary Congress on Women" was held in Kampala. Some of the other important university centers included the Institute of Development Studies Women Studies Group at the University of Dar es Salaam (founded in 1980); the **Women's Research Collective** at the National University of Lesotho; and the **Women's Research and Documentation Center (WORDOC)** at the University of Ibadan. There were also a number of independent centers not based at universities, including the **African Training and Research Center for Women**, the **Association of African Women for Research and Development**, **Women and Law in Southern Africa**, and the **Zimbabwe Women's Resource Center and Network**.

WOMEN'S UNIONIST ASSOCIATION. A South African group based in Johannesburg in the early years of the 20th century, it petitioned British Prime Minister William Gladstone to introduce the death penalty for rapists. It was part of a complicated history of "black peril" issues in southern Africa, in which African men were seen as threats to the virtue of white settler women. Research has shown that there was little or no factual basis for white women's fears, but local white-run newspapers and white political leaders continued to support the spread of hysteria.

WOMEN'SNET. Women'sNet is an internet group for African women founded in South Africa in 1997. It described itself as "a vibrant and innovative networking support program designed to enable South African women to use the Internet to find the people, issues, resources and tools needed for women's social activism." The website, with numerous useful links to articles and resources about women, is at http://www.womensnet.org.za/.

– X –

XUMA, MADIE HALL (1894–1982). Madie Hall Xuma was a prominent **African American woman** from North Carolina. She met South African leader Dr. Alfred Bitini Xuma, who was one of the founders of the African National Congress (ANC) in 1937 when he was visiting the United States, and married him in Cape Town in 1940. She lived in South Africa from 1940 to 1963, and played an important role in revitalizing South African women's **organizations**. Madie Xuma was the first president of the **African National Congress Women's League** from 1943 to 1948, and helped found the **Zenzele** clubs for women's enrichment, drawing from her experience with black women's clubs in the United States. She was also very involved with the **Young Women's Christian Association (YWCA)**. She moved back to the United States following her husband's death, and though she took an around-the-world trip in 1966 she lived quietly in Winston-Salem, North Carolina and participated in local women's clubs.

XWALILE (fl. 1870–1890s). Xwalile was the daughter of the Gaza king Mzila (in present-day Mozambique); she married the Ndebele ruler Lobengula (in modern Zimbabwe) in 1879 and was his **senior wife**. The marriage was arranged as an exchange of royal wives, and seven other Gaza royal women married Lobengula in the same ceremony. The marriage was troubled by discord over the payment of **bridewealth** and the lack of Ndebele women going to marry Mzila in return. In addition, Xwalile proved to be infertile and eventually returned to her home to live, possibly driven in part by **witchcraft** practiced against her by Lobengula's sister Mncengene Khumali, who was executed for her actions in 1880 during a purge of dissidents. *See also* LOZIKEYI; POLYGYNY.

– Y –

YAA AKYAA (1840–1917). A political leader and **queen mother** in 19th century Asante (Ghana), she was the daughter of **Asantehemaa Afua Kobi**. She became *asantehemaa* herself when her son Kwaku Dua II took the Golden Stool (Asante throne) after she ousted her brother Mensa Bonsu and exiled him and their mother Afua Kobi in 1884. When Kwaku Dua II died after only 44 days in office she succeeded in having another son, Prempe I, named at age 15, and was able to exert a strong influence over him while she remained *asantehemaa*. She was resolutely anti-British, and though astute about royal politics, she was ruthless in removing her enemies. The British focused on removing her when they proceeded to subjugate Asante, and in 1896 she was exiled with her son Prempe I and other Asante chiefs to the Seychelles Islands, where she remained until her death. Yaa Akyaa's reputation for violence against those who opposed her has made her a disputed figure in Ghanaian history. *See also* YAA ASANTEWAA.

YAA ASANTEWAA (c. 1830–1921). Yaa Asantewaa was **queen mother** (*ahemaa*) of Edweso (Ejisu), an Asante sub-group, when she rose to prominence in 1900. Her grandson was among the chiefs exiled in 1896 with Prempe I and **Yaa Akyaa**. Yaa Asantewaa worked to end British rule after that event, and in 1900 she exhorted a group of leaderless Asante chiefs to fight back when the British governor Francis Hodgson demanded the Golden Stool, which was the symbol of the Asante ruling house. She exhorted the chiefs, saying "How can a proud and brave people like the Asante sit back and look while white men take away their king and chiefs . . . If you, the chiefs of Asante, are going to behave like cowards and not fight, you should exchange your loincloths for my undergarments." She followed her comments by taking a gun and firing it into the air, and the chiefs vowed to force the British out of Asante as a result of her example. The struggle, which lasted from 1900 to 1901 and included keeping the British under siege for six months, is sometimes called the Yaa Asantewaa War. She was commander-in-chief of the combined Asante forces and also had her own army. When the British were ultimately victorious in 1901, she and others were exiled to the Seychelles Islands where she died. The centenary of the war was marked by celebrations in Ghana in 2000, and A. Adu Boahen published her story in *Yaa Asantewaa and the Asante-British War of 1900-1* (2003). *See also* ASANTEHEMAA.

YAKUBA, BALARABA. *See* RAMAT YAKUBA, BALARABA.

YEMOJA. Yemoja was a **goddess** associated with water; she was especially worshiped by the Yoruba of Abeokuta, who recognized her as the mother of all rivers, and particularly the Ogun River. She was believed to have special value for barren women, who would keep a jar of Ogun water close by to encourage **fertility**. Cowries symbolized her wealth, and women brought her offerings of yams, goats, maize, and other foods. Other goddesses associated with water in West Africa include **Mami Wata**, **Osun**, and Oya, who is patron of the River Niger.

YENNENGA (fl. 12TH CENTURY). The story of Yennenga has entered into legend, though it may have a core of truth. Yennenga was a princess in the Dagomba Empire of the Mossi people in a region that is today part of northern Ghana. She was renowned for her beauty and her skills as a horsewoman, and she participated with her father's soldiers in defending their lands against attack. Her father forbade her to marry, locking her up to prevent her acting against his will. She escaped, fought heroically in a battle, and rode north until she met a famous elephant hunter named Riale. They fell in love, married, and had a son they named Ouedraogo, meaning "male horse," now a common name in Burkina Faso. A statue of a stallion, called the Yennenga Stallion, was the prize for the best film at the biennial FESPACO film festival held in Burkina Faso.

YOKO, MADAM (c. 1849–1906). Madam Yoko rose to power among the Kpa Mende of Sierra Leone in the late 19th century, establishing a confederacy of splinter Mende groups and confronting British imperial forces. When her husband, Gbanye, died in 1878, she ascended to his seat and was recognized as a paramount chief by the British. Madam Yoko extended the area under her control to regions that had not been controlled by her husband. She began with an advantageous social position, and combined traditional strategies such as her leadership of **Sande**, the women's secret society, and her intellect and diplomatic skills to expand her area of influence.

YOUNG WOMEN'S CHRISTIAN ASSOCIATION (YWCA). There are branches of this international **Christian** organization in many African countries, some established during the colonial period including Botswana (est. 1962), Ethiopia (1961), Ghana (1952), and Uganda (1952). One of the earliest was founded in Cape Town, South Africa in 1886. In 2004 branches operated in 24 African nations. The YWCA was also associated with **zenzele** groups in South Africa. Projects include **literacy** programs, community clinics, **childcare**, and crafts, as well as providing safe and inexpensive lodging for young women. The YWCA in Zambia (founded in 1957) runs a shelter for women escaping **domestic violence**. Initially representatives from the YWCA groups in Europe and the United States played an important role in establishing local branches, but African women quickly assumed leadership roles in their own countries; prominent women who were active in the YWCA included **Adelaide Smith Casely Hayford**, **Katie Kibuka**, and **Ellen Kuzwayo**. Information on the international projects of the YWCA can be found at www.worldywca.org.

– Z –

***ZAAR* (VAR. *ZAR*).** *Zaar* was a form of **spirit possession**, dominated by women adherents and known in Sudan, Somalia, Ethiopia, and parts of the Arab world, and it was similar to *bori* practices in West Africa. It was common in Muslim areas, but was not itself an **Islamic** rite; rather it provided an alternative religious experience. *Zaar* referred to a kind of spirit which could cause illness in human beings, and which could only be managed through rituals organized by spiritual leaders. Commonly, a woman came to *zaar* through being afflicted and the process of learning to live with the *zaar* spirits was also part of the learning arc that trained new adepts. *Zaar* was a complex set of cultural practices that could free women to act in uncharacteristic ways such as making demands on their husbands, and it also provided a profound set of social connections infused with deep spirituality that enabled believers to make sense of the world around them.

ZAMBIA ASSOCIATION FOR RESEARCH AND DEVELOPMENT (ZARD). ZARD was an organization that promoted research to improve the status of women in Zambia. It was founded in 1984 when an organization active in the 1970s, the Social Economic

Research Group (SERG), adopted a new name. Both SERG and ZARD have been affiliated with the **Association of African Women for Research and Development (AAWORD)**. ZARD was involved in a variety of research and advocacy projects designed to improve the position of women in Zambia. More information can be found at their website: http://www.zard.org.zm/.

ZANGA TSOGO, DELPHINE. *See* TSANGA, DELPHINE.

ZAUDITU (ZEWDITU, JUDITH) (1876–1930). Zauditu, the daughter of Ethiopia's monarch Menelik II, ruled as empress from 1916 to 1930. Initially her father had resisted naming her as his heir, though he had no sons, and upon his death his grandson Iyasu V became ruler. When Iyasu was overthrown in 1916 Zauditu was named empress. She was forced to renounce her husband Gugsa Wolie (Wele), whom she had married as her fourth husband in 1902. She was titular head, but real power was simultaneously given to Haile Selassie, a second cousin who was named regent and heir apparent. In 1928, as she saw Haile Selassie taking more power for himself, Zauditu attempted to usurp the throne for herself, prompting Selassie to stage a coup after which she had to crown Haile Selassie as king. Her estranged husband also tried to take power in 1930, but was defeated and killed. She herself died of pneumonia two days after his death. *See also* HEADS OF STATE; MENETEWAB; TAITU.

ZENAB, CATARINA (1848–1921). Zenab was a convert to Catholicism in the Sudan. Born in a Dinka village, she studied at the Holy Cross Mission and traveled to the capital Khartoum with the missionary Daniele Comboni in 1860. She was fluent in Dinka and Arabic, and helped the missionaries develop a Dinka dictionary and grammar. She studied in Verona, Italy, and returned to teach in the **mission** schools in Khartoum.

ZENZELE. Zenzele were South African women's clubs, founded with the goal of improving women's situation, and linked to the international **Young Women's Christian Association** (YWCA) after 1951. The term was derived from the Xhosa for "Help yourself" or "Do it yourself." Some sources suggested that the first such group was established as early at 1916 at the instigation of African American missionary Susie Wiseman Yergan. By the 1920s the rival organizations **African Women's Self-Improvement Association** and Bantu Women's Home Improvement Association were active. As with other women's organizations in Africa in the 1950s (**Maendeleo wa Wanawake** in Kenya and *foyers sociaux* in the Belgian colonies, for example), they emphasized domestic skills, and also trained women in public speaking to prepare them for leadership roles in their community.

ZIMBABWE WOMEN WRITERS. An organization founded in 1991 to support and promote writing by Zimbabwean women, primarily by publishing their work. In its first decade it published over two hundred books by and often about women, and included books in English, Shona, and Ndebele.

ZIMBABWE WOMEN'S BUREAU. The Zimbabwe Women's Bureau was established after independence in 1980 as a branch of the National Farmers Association of Zimbabwe. It sponsored workshops and training sessions for women farmers.

ZIMBABWE WOMEN'S RESOURCE CENTRE AND NETWORK (ZWRCN). The ZWRCN, a gender and **development** organization based in Harare, was concerned with gathering, analyzing, disseminating, and utilizing information for advancing the status of women through research-led lobbying and advocacy. It sponsored debates on relevant issues and training sessions on women and development. It published *WomanPlus*, and collaborated with other women's organizations in the publication of *Zimbabwean Women's Voices* in 1995. *See also* MUSASA PROJECT; WOMEN'S ACTION GROUP.

ZUMA, NKOSAZANA DLAMINI (1949–). Minister of **health** in the first post-**apartheid** cabinet in South Africa, she trained as a pediatrician at the University of Natal and was a long time African National Congress (ANC) organizer. She was a leader in the South African Student Organisation (SASO), resulting in her forced exile to England, where she completed her medical degree at the University of Bristol.

In England she headed the ANC Youth Section for Great Britain, and later chaired the ANC Regional Political Committee based in England. She worked at a hospital in Swaziland for a time and traveled throughout the region. Zuma headed the ANC health committee, and pursued further studies in tropical child health at the University of Liverpool. When she was able to return to South Africa in 1990 she became active in women's political activities as well, arguing for the inclusion of women in every delegation and conference. In 1994 she was named minister of health, a position she held until 1999. She used her standing to promote free health care for pregnant women and children under the age of six. Zuma was succeeded by another woman, Dr. Mantombazana E. Tshabalala-Msimang (b. 1940) who had previously been deputy minister of justice (1996–1999).

Appendix
Dictionary Entries by Country

ANGOLA

Café, Maria Mambo
Lara, Alda
Liga Independente da
   Mulher Angolana (LIMA)
Maldoror, Sarah

Nzinga
Organização da Mulher Angolana
   (OMA)
Rodrigues, Deolinda
Vita, Dona Beatriz Kimpa

BENIN

Dahomey Soldiers
Kidjo, Angelique
Kpojito

Organisation des Femmes
   Revolutionnaires du Benin

BOTSWANA

Botswana Council of Women
Business and Professional
   Women's Club of Gaborone
Chiepe, Gaositwe Keagakwa
   Tibe
Dow, Unity
Emang Basadi Women's
   Association

Gagoangwe
Head, Bessie
Khama, Elisabeta Gobitsamang
Khama, Lady Ruth Williams
Khama, Semane Setlhoko
Nisa
Seboko, Mosadi Muriel

BURKINA FASO

Association des Femmes
   Voltaiques

Cissin-Natenga Women's
   Association

Federation des Femmes
  Voltaiques
Lagem Yam
Ouattara, Guimbé
Ouedraogo, Josephine

Ouezzin Coulibaly, Célestine
Réseau de Communication et
  d'Information des Femmes
  (RECIF)

BURUNDI

Action Sociale
Foyers Sociaux
Kinigi, Sylvie

Nandabunga
Ndirikumutima
Union des Femmes Burundaises

CAMEROON

Anlu
Beyala, Calixthe
Cameroon Association of
  University Women
Nfah-Abbenyi, Juliana Makuchi
Takumbeng
Tankeu, Elizabeth

That Rocky Place: Creative
  Writing on Women
Tsanga, Delphine
Werewere Liking
Women's Cameroon National
  Union

CAPE VERDE

Batuque
Centro das Mulheres de Cabo
  Verde
Duarte, Dulce Almada
Evora, Cesária

Instituto da Condição Feminina
Jornal da Mulher
Morabi
Organização da Mulheres de
  Cabo Verde

CENTRAL AFRICAN REPUBLIC

Blouin, Andrée
Domitien, Elisabeth
Ruth-Rolland, Jean-Marie

Union des Femmes de l'Empire
  Centrafricaine

CHAD
No listings

COMOROS ISLANDS
Djoumbe Fatima

CONGO/BRAZZAVILLE
Union Révolutionnaire des Femmes Congolaise (URFC)

CONGO/KINSHASA
Mouvement Feminin de la Solidarité Africaine (MFSA)

CÔTE D'IVOIRE
Anoma, Gladys
Association des Femmes Ivoiriennes (AFI)
Diabate, Henriette
Gervais, Jeanne

Grand Bassam
Groupe d'Animation Culturel de Cocody (GACC)
Pokou

DJIBOUTI
No listings

ERITREA
Eritrean Women's Association
Ileni Hagos
Menetewab

National Union of Eritrean Women
Voice of Eritrean Women

ETHIOPIA
African Centre for Gender and Development
African Centre for Women

African Training and Research Centre for Women (ATRCW), United Nations Economic Commission for Africa (ECA)

Azeb
Candace
Ethiopians' Women's Welfare
  Association
Maqeda

Senedu Gabru
Taitu Betul
Tulu, Derartu
Zauditu

GABON

Bongo, Pascaline
Immaculate Conception Sisters

Union des Femmes du Parti
  Démocratique Gabonais

GAMBIA

Gambia Women's Federation

Njie-Saidy, Isatou

GHANA

African Federation of Women
  Entrepreneurs (AFWE)
Afua Kobi
Ahemaa
Aidoo, Ama Ata
Akonadi
Asantehemaa
Asase Yaa
Assembly of Ghana Women
Cudjoe, Hannah
Dove Danquah, Mabel
Emmanuel, Christianah Abiodun
Ghana Association of Women
  Entrepreneurs
Ghana Market Women
  Association

Ghana Women's League
The Gold Coast Woman
Jiagge, Annie Ruth
Lokko, Mary
National Council of Ghana
  Women
National Federation of Gold
  Coast Women
Ocloo, Esther Afua
Oduyoye, Mercy
Sutherland, Efua Theodora
Tani, Maame Harris "Grace"
31st December Women's
  Movement
Yaa Akyaa
Yaa Asentewaa

GUINEA

Bangoura, Hadja Mafory
Camara, Mbalia

Martin-Cissé, Jeanne

GUINEA-BISSAU

Gomes, Antonieta Rosa
Gomes, Henriqueta Godinho
Pereira, Carmen

Pereira Gomes, Francisca
União Democrática das Mulheres

KENYA

Dinesen, Isak
East African Women's League
*Eve: The Essence of Africa's
New Woman*
GENDEReview
Green Belt Movement
Habwe, Ruth
Kenya Women's Seminar
Kenyatta, Margaret
Lelemama
Likimani, Muthoni
Maathai, Wangari
Maendeleo Ya Wanawake
Makeri, Wangu Wa
Markham, Beryl
Mau Mau
Mekatalili

Mugo, Micere Githae
Mungai, Anne
Mwana Kupona
Nairobi Women's Meeting
National Council of Women of
Kenya
Ngilu, Charity Kaluki
Njau, Rebeka
Nyanjiru, Mary Muthoni
Odundo, Magdalene
Ogot, Grace
Ojiambo, Julia
Onyango, Grace Monica Akech
Otieno, Wambui Waiyaki
Song of Lawino
Waciuma, Charity

LESOTHO

Basutoland Homemakers'
Association
Khaketla, Caroline Ntseliseng
Lerotholi, 'Mamohatao Tabitha
'Masentle
Lesotho National Council of
Women

Lesotho Women's Institute
Mantse Bo
Mmanthatisi
*Shoeshoe: The Magazine for All
Lesotho's Women*
Women's Research Collective

LIBERIA

Brooks-Randolph, Angie
    Elizabeth
Johnson Sirleaf, Ellen

Liberia Women's League
Newport, Matilda
Perry, Ruth Sando

MADAGASCAR

Binao
Conseil National des Associations
    de Femme de Madagascar
Rabesahala, Gisèle

Ranavalona I
Ranavalona II
Ranavalona III
Rasoherina

MALAWI

Blantyre Women's Art and
    Handicraft Club
Chibambo, Rose Ziba
Chirwa, Vera Chibambo

Chitukulu cha Amai mu Malawi
Kadzamira, Cecilia
League of Malawi Women

MALI

Association des Juristes
    Maliennes (AJM)
Association Pour le Progrès et la
    Defence des Droits des
    Femmes Maliennes
Collectif des Femmes du Mali
    (COFEM)
Commissariat à la Promotion des
    Femmes
Commission Sociale des
    Femmes (CSF)
Coordination des Associations et
    ONG Féminines du Mali
    (CAFO)
Damba, Fanta
Diabate, Siramori

Diarra, Fatoumata Dembele
Diop, Aminata
Kassi
Kéita, Aoua
Rencontres Africaines
Rencontres Africaines
Sangare, Oumou
 Union des Femmes du Soudan
    (UFS)
Union des Femmes Travailleuses
    (UFT)
Union Nationale des Femmes du
    Mali (UMFM)
Wassoulou
Yennenga

MAURITANIA

Aiche, Mariam Mint Ahmed
Kane, Aissata

Mouvement National des
Femmes

MAURITIUS

Bappo, Sheilabai
Mauritius Alliance of Women
Muvman Liberasyon Fam

Nuvel Fam
Poonoosamy, Radha
Women Self-Help Association

MOZAMBIQUE

De Sousa, Noémia
Diogo, Luisa
Liga Feminina Moçambicana
Lopes, Bertina
Machel, Graça
Machel, Josina

Magaia, Lina
Organização da Mulher
 Moçambicana (OMM)
Outras Vozes
Tufo

NAMIBIA

Amathila (Appolus-Amathisa),
 Libertine
Gertze, Johanna Uerieta
Iivula-Ithana, Pendukeni
Kanuni
Namibia Domestic and
 Allied Workers' Union

The Namibian Woman
Namibian Women's Voice
Schmelen, Zara
Sister Namibia
SWAPO Women's Council

NIGER

Association des Femmes du
 Niger (AFN)

Sarraounia
Union des Femmes du Niger

NIGERIA

Aba Women's War
Abeokuta Ladies' Club
Abeokuta Women's Union
Adoro Goddess

Aisa Kili Ngirmarmma
Akintunde-Ighodalo, Folayegbe
 Mosunmola
Alakija, Aduke

Alkali, Zaynab
Amina
Asma'u, Nana
Baba of Karo
Babangida, Maryam Ibrahim
Baobab for Human Rights
Better Life Programme for the
  Rural Woman
Bori
Camp, Sokari Douglas
Davies, Nike
Emecheta, Buchi
Esan, Wuraola Adepeju
Federation of Nigerian Women's
  Societies (FNWS)
Funtuwa, Bilkisu
Grassroots Development
  Organisation (GRADO)
Iyalode
Iye Idolorusan
Lagos Market Women's
  Association
Lawal, Amina
Magira
Mba, Nina Emma
National Commission for Women

National Council of Women's
  Societies (NCWS)
Niger Delta Women for Justice
Nigerian Women's Party (NWP)
Nigerian Women's Union (NWU)
Nwapa, Flora
Oil Production
Okwei, Omu
Onwueme, Osonye Tess
Osun
Oyedepo, Stella
Pelewura, Alimotu
Ramat Yakubu, Balaraba
Ransome-Kuti, Funmilayo
Sawaba, Gambo
Shari'a Law
Sitting on a Man
Slessor, Mary
Sofola, Zulu
Tinubu, Madam
Williams, Ekanem Esu
Women in Nigeria
Women's Research and
  Documentation Center
  (WORDOC)
Yemoja

RWANDA

Association pour la Promotion de
  la Femme Rwandaise
  (APROFER)
Muhumuza

Mujawamariya, Monique
Nyabingi
Pro-Femmes Twese Hamwe
Uwilingiyimana, Agathe

SÃO TOMÉ E PRINCIPÉ

Bandeira, Alda
De Sousa, Maria das Neves Ceita
  Batista

Forum de Mulher Santomense
Santo, Alda Espírito

SENEGAL

Alinesitoué Diatta
Awa
Bâ, Mariama
Boye, Mame Madior
Congregation of the Daughters of
    the Sacred Heart of Mary
Diène, Arame
Diop, Sokhna Magat
Faye, Safi
Groupement de Promotion
    Féminine

Mam Diarra Bousso
M'baye, Annette d'Drneville
Mboj, Ndate Yala
Mboj, Njembot
Ndiaye, Ndioro
Sow, Fatou
Sow Fall, Aminata
Sy Diallo, Mata
Thiam, Awa

SEYCHELLES

De St. Jorre, Danielle

Frichot, Sylvette

SIERRA LEONE

Casely-Hayford, Adelaide
Cummings-John, Constance
    Agatha
Gulama, Ella Koblo
National Congress of Sierra
    Leone Women
Sande

Sierra Leone Market Women's
    Union
Sierra Leone Women's Movement
Women's Association for
    National Development
Yoko, Madam

SOMALIA

Iman

Waris Dirie

SOUTH AFRICA

African Gender Institute,
    University of Cape Town
African National Congress
    Women's League

African Women's Self-
    Improvement Association
*Agenda: A Journal about Women
    and Gender*

Apartheid
Baard, Frances
Baartman, Sara
Ballinger, Margaret
Bantu Women's League
Black Consciousness Movement
Black Sash
Black Women's Federation
Carolus, Cheryl
Defiance Campaign
Duncan, Sheena
Durban Indian Women's
  Association
Durban Women's Association
Emma Sandile
Fassie, Brenda
Federation of South African
  Women (FSAW)
Federation of Transvaal Women
First, Ruth
Ginwala, Frene
Gordimer, Nadine
Hlomelikusasa Othandweni
  Women's Group
Inanda Seminary
Indian Women's Association
Inkatha Women's Brigade
Jabavu, Noni
Joseph, Helen
Kuzwayo, Ellen
Makeba, Miriam
Mandela, Winnie
Manyano
Mawa
Maxeke, Charlotte
Meer, Fatima
Mgqwetho, Nontsizi
Modjadji
Mxenge, Victoria

Nandi
Natal Organisation of Women
  (NOW)
Natal Women's Revolt
Ncube, Sister Bernard
Ngcobo, Lauretta
Ngoyi, Lilian Masebida
Nongqawuse
Nontetha
Nyembe, Dorothy
Palmer, Josie
Pillay, Navanethem
Princess Constance Magogo
  kaDinuzulu
Rain Queen
Ramphele, Mamphela
Schreiner, Olive
Shebeen
Shope, Gertrude
Sikakane, Joyce
Sisulu, Albertina
Siyazama
South African Commission on
  Gender Equality
South African Domestic Workers
  Association (SADWA)
South African War
Suzman, Helen
Tlali, Miriam
United Women's Organisation
Van Meerhof, Eva
Voice of Women
Women's Charter Campaign
Women's Front
Women's National Coalition
Women's Unionist Association
Xuma, Madie Hall
Zenzele
Zuma, Nkosazana Dlamini

SUDAN

Aboulela, Leila
Ahfad Journal: Women and Change
Ahfad University for Women
Ibrahim, Fatma Ahmed
Sudan National Committee on Traditional Practices

Sudanese Women's Union (SWU)
Union of Sudanese Women
Women's Front
Zenab, Catarina

SWAZILAND

Mdluli, Labotsibeni Gwamile

Ndlovukazi

TANZANIA

Abdallah, Anna
Association of Businesswomen of Tanzania
Fatuma
Lameck, Lucy
Mohamed, Bibi Titi
Mongella, Gertrude
Muhando, Penina
National Council of Women of Tanganyika

Ruete, Emily
Saadi, Siti Binti
Sauti Ya Siti
Taarab
Tanzania Media Women's Association (TAMWA)
Umoja wa Wanawake wa Tanzania (UWT)

TOGO

Amedome, Abra
La Revolte des Femmes (Lomé, Togo, 1933)

Union Nationale des Femmes du Togo

UGANDA

Action for Development (ACFODE)
Bannabikira
Daca
Directorate of Women's Affairs, Uganda

Forum for Women in Democracy (FOWODE)
Kazibwe, Speciosa Wandira
Kibuka, Katolini Esita Ndagire
Kimenye, Barbara
Kisosonkole, Pumla

Lakwena, Alice
Mpanga, Joyce
National Council of Women
Nyabongo, Elizabeth
Olowo, Bernadette
Owino Women's Group
Reach (Reproductive and
    Community Health)
Sekitoleko, Victoria
Uganda Association of Women's
    Organizations

Uganda Council of Women
Uganda Media Women's
    Association (UMVA)
Uganda Women's Caucus
Ugandan Women's Effort to Save
    Orphans (UWESO)
Ugandan Women's Network
    (UWONET)
Women of Uganda Network
    (WOUGNET)

ZAMBIA

Lenshina, Alice Mulenga
Mamochisane
Muyunda, Mavis
Nachituti
Nakafwaya
Nakatindi Wina, Princess

National Women's Lobby Group
UNIP Women's Brigade
Women for Change (WFC)
Zambia Association for Research
    and Development (ZARD)

ZIMBABWE

Bantu Women's League
Charwe
Chitepo, Victoria
Dangaremgba, Tsitsi
Dongo, Margaret
Dzivaguru
Federation of Women's Institutes
    of Southern Rhodesia
Lessing, Doris
Lozikeyi
Mai Chaza
Masuka, Dorothy
Mugabe, Sally
Mujuru, Joyce Nhongo
Musasa Project

Nehanda
Ngano, Martha
Rhodesian Women's League
*Safere: Southern African
    Feminist Review*
Speak Out-Taurai-Khulumani
Vera, Yvonne
WomanPlus
Women's Action Group (WAG)
Women's Franchise Society
Xwalile
Zimbabwe Women Writers
Zimbabwe Women's Bureau
Zimbabwe Women's Resource
    Centre and Network (ZWRCN)

Bibliography

CONTENTS

INTRODUCTION

There is a large and growing set of published materials on African women, as can be seen in this bibliography of mostly recent sources. The list of materials below begins with some key general monographs and collections, followed by sources that serve as guides to major historiographical and methodological issues. The next section is generally chronological with subsections on precolonial and early colonial history, 19th century, colonialism in the 20th century, resistance and nationalism, and post-independence politics and democratization. The next section is comprised of subject-oriented lists for important historical topics and events. Lists of bibliographies, periodicals, films, and websites complete the bibliography.

It was necessary to be very selective, and therefore the bibliography omits master's theses and doctoral dissertations, conference presentations, working papers, and articles published in popular magazines, while acknowledging the important contribution such texts have made to furthering African women's history. Also excluded are sources that were published prior to 1975 and individual chapters from collected editions where the collection itself is included, though there are a few exceptions for significant publications or for material referred to in the dictionary. Many articles that appeared later in a book by the author have also been excised, though in some cases the article was an important source in its own right. The items included here are primarily in English, though a few in French and Portuguese also appear. Due to space limitations each item was listed only once, though in many cases a source fit more than one category, and at times the decision about the placement of a citation was quite arbitrary. The size of the bibliography, even with these exclusions, is a testament to the growth in African women's history in recent decades.

* * *

The study of the history of women in sub-Saharan Africa is a recent development, with most publications only appearing in the last half of the 20th century following the growth of African studies and African history in general and the development of the study of women's history in societies around the world. Before the 1970s there was little published research on African women's history, and information on women in Africa was more often found in anthropological and ethnographic studies. One of the first publications that moved beyond those categories was Denise Paulme's edited collection, *Women in Tropical Africa* (1963), which initially appeared in French as *Femmes d'Afrique noir* in 1960 (full citations for all referenced publications appear in the bibliography). Early collections of essays that began to bring some of the new research to public attention included special issues of the *Canadian Journal of African Studies* (1972) and *African Studies Review* (1975), followed by *Women in Africa*, edited by Nancy Hafkin and Edna Bay (1976). Bennetta Jules-Rosette edited an influential collection that highlighted women in *The New Religions of Africa* (1979). Official recognition of African women's history came when Margaret Strobel's study, *Muslim Women in Mombasa, 1890–1975*, won the 1979 Herskovits Award for the best book published in African studies.

By the early 1980s the history of African women had emerged as a vibrant and steadily expanding area of research and study, and Strobel was able to write "African Women: Review Essay" for *Signs: Journal of Women in Culture and Society* (1982), the first overview that showed scholars how much was being done. Historians were motivated, as with women's history in other world areas, by the development of the international feminist movement and from the beginning there was a political component to much of the research and writing in African women's history. By the mid-1980s there were a number of important extended studies, still primarily focusing on women's public lives, including Nina Mba's *Nigerian Women Mobilized: Women's Political Activity in Southern Nigeria, 1900–1965* (1982). Research on family and sexuality was also beginning to be published, as with Kristin Mann's *Marrying Well: Marriage, Status and Social Change among the Educated Elite in Colonial Lagos* (1985), Raqiya Abdalla's *Sisters in Affliction: Circumcision and Infibulation of Women in Africa* (1982), and Carolyn Sargent's *The Cultural Context of Therapeutic Choice: Obstetrical Care Decisions among the Bariba of Benin* (1982). Only in the 1990s did a substantial number of monographs on specific topics appear, although most new research is still found in journal and anthology articles.

Despite these advances in the historiography, many stan.'ard histories of Africa still omit women and ignore the implications of gender. Tiyambe Zeleza provided a very useful overview of the continuing problems resulting from the omission of women and women's history from standard African history texts in "Gender Biases in African Historiography" (1997). His 1993 review of the major books assigned in African history courses, "Gendering African History," showed clearly that very few women authors of any nationality were in evidence, and there were almost no African women writing for widely disseminated texts. Equally concerning, content about African women was scarce and biased, with women appearing either as oppressed victims or as heroic queens. The more complicated reality, which would include women as actors equal to men as political leaders, economic innovators, and persistent supporters of their families and children, was difficult if not impossible to find even in books that appeared at the end of the 20th century.

There are still some areas where the sources concerning women are very limited, particularly when studying earlier historical eras. Many African communities were decentralized and non-literate, so that written materials from before the 19th century, especially from an African woman's perspective, were scarce. Scholars have been able to retrieve some information about African women in the distant past by utilizing historical linguistics and archeology to examine changing patterns in women's roles as wives and mothers within pastoralist and agricultural communities. As David Schoenbrun demonstrated in *A Green Place, A Good Place: Agrarian Change, Gender, and Social Identity in the Great Lakes Region to the 15th Century* (1998), linguistic evidence can help explain the gendered development of banana farming and cattle pastoralism at the end of the first millennium (ca. 1000 AD). Susan Kent in *Gender in African Prehistory* (1998) and Lyn Wadley in her article on the "Use of Space in a Gender Study of Two South African Stone Age Sites" (1997) utilized archeological evidence as a way to understand the division of labor and other gendered aspects of life in early societies. Archeologists have also retrieved information about Great Zimbabwe, an extensive urban settlement that thrived prior to the 15th century in southern Africa; the evidence was presented and debated by David Beach in "Cognitive Archaeology and Imaginary History at Great Zimbabwe" (1998).

In a few cases historians have been able to use unusual archival sources to retrieve the stories of elite women. Thus researchers have found material for Queen Nzinga, a 16th-century ruler in what became Angola (Joseph Miller, "Nzinga of Matamba in a New Perspective" [1975], and John Thornton, "Legitimacy and Political Power: Queen Njinga, 1624–1663" [1991]); Dona Beatriz, a religious leader in the 17th-century Kingdom of Kongo (Thornton, *The Kongolese Saint Anthony: Dona Beatriz Kimpa Vita and the Antonian Movement, 1684–1706* [1998]); and wealthy traders along the West African coast (George E. Brooks, *Eurafricans in Western Africa: Commerce, Social Status, Gender, and Religious Observance from the Sixteenth to the Eighteenth Century* [2003], and E. Frances White, *Sierra Leone's Settler Women Traders: Women on the Afro-European Frontier* [1987]). Lesser-known elite women have been written about by Nakanyike Musisi, in "Women, 'Elite Polygyny,' and Buganda State Formation" (1991), and by R. A. Sargent on Daca in Bunyoro-Kitara, in "Found in the Fog of the Male Myths: Analyzing Female Political Roles in Pre-Colonial Africa" (1991). Their examples provide further evidence of the prominent roles women played in the politics of their societies. In South Africa, Julie Wells discusses the extensive documentation about the Khoena girl who became known as Eva in "Eva's Men: Gender and Power in the Establishment of the Cape of Good Hope, 1652–74" (1998). Though not of elite background, Eva was in contact with the first European settlers, and her proximity to the European community resulted in an unusual collection of written sources as compared to most African women of the 17th century.

In all of these cases our understanding of the options these women faced and their motives for making the choices they did are obscured because the available sources are almost entirely written by European men. For Dona Beatriz, for example, nearly every source was written by

Italian priests who were not only observers and recorders but, as John Thornton notes, instigators of events which involved her. Surviving sources written by Kongolese are rare, and those by women nearly nonexistent. Though there are useful insights in the available sources, historians must acknowledge the sexist and ethnocentric assumptions that are evident as well.

By the 19th century, with the arrival of greater numbers of Europeans who recorded their observations of African women and of an increasing cohort of African women who wrote their own stories, the knowledge about African women's history began to expand. Often those reports continued to present a biased view of the role of such women, who were written about as an exotic part of African life. The women of the royal court at Dahomey, who included the women soldiers who have often been called Amazons, are a well-known example. European observers were fascinated with the idea of a female corps of soldiers, though they made up only one segment of women affiliated with the king. Edna Bay, in *Wives of the Leopard: Gender, Politics, and Culture in the Kingdom of Dahomey* (1998), investigates a more complex reality concerning the important role of those royal women in the 18th and early 19th centuries, and discusses how their status declined by the end of the 19th century. Other women in 19th-century West Africa played an important role in the spread of Islam, and left a written record of their beliefs and teachings. Nana Asma'u was the best known, and her life has been recalled by Jean Boyd in *The Caliph's Sister: Nana Asma'u (1793–1865) Teacher, Poet and Islamic Leader* (1989) and by Beverly Mack and Jean Boyd in *One Woman's Jihad: Nana Asma'u, Scholar and Scribe* (2000). The experience of slavery is another area that has been well documented in written sources (see section below on slavery). Claire Robertson and Martin Klein, in their edited collection, *Women and Slavery in Africa* (1983, reprinted in 1998), demonstrated that slaves within Africa were more likely to be women, a reflection of their productive and reproductive contributions to their communities.

Sources about African women become more abundant when looking at the colonial era, though many of those documents were produced by European men (see section on colonialism). Written sources can be biased by focusing on women outside the norm, such as prostitutes or others who came to official attention due to their illegal or non-traditional activities. Not only were records more likely to be written by European men, they often relied on African men to relate the history, which could distort or reduce women's contributions. Analysis of the development of legal systems under colonialism has suggested that women were placed at a disadvantage as "customary" laws were established based on male testimony that gave men, especially elite men, advantages over women in issues of marriage and divorce (Margaret Jean Hay and Marcia Wright, eds., *African Women and the Law: Historical Perspectives* [1982], and Martin Chanock, *Law, Custom, and Social Order: The Colonial Experience in Malawi and Zambia* [1985, reprinted 1998]).

By the mid-20th century, African women were producing more sources about their own history, and researchers were able to find a greater variety of material to reconstruct that history. The role of women in anticolonial and nationalist organizations offers evidence of a vibrant and essential community of women who were central to the eventual success of those movements (see section on nationalism). In an influential article on the 1929 Aba Women's War, Judith Van Allen, in "'Sitting on a Man': Colonialism and the Lost Political Institutions of Igbo Women" (1972), demonstrated that women drew on precolonial practices to make clear their displeasure with the colonial powers. The story of Charwe was another example of older forms re-emerging with a new purpose in the face of oppression (David Beach, "An Innocent Woman, Unjustly Accused? Charwe, Medium of the Nehanda Mhondoro Spirit, and the 1896–97 Central Shona Rising in Zimbabwe" [1998]). Susan Geiger's *TANU Women: Gender and Culture in the Making of Tanganyikan Nationalism, 1955–1965* (1997), a study of the leadership activities of illiterate Muslim women in Dar es Salaam, fundamentally changed the view that the Tanzanian anti-colonial movement was led solely by men who were products of Christian mission education. Women were also important leaders of the anti-colonial movement in French West Africa, where Aoua Kéita and Célestine Ouezzin Coulibaly worked to bring independence and simultaneously to build women's organizations within the new political forms that developed; their stories are found in Henriette Diabate, *La marche des femmes sur Grand-Bassam* (1975), Aoua Kéita, *Femme d'Afrique: La vie d'Aoua Kéita racontée par elle-même* (1975), and Jane Turrittin, "Aoua Kéita and the Nascent Women's Movement in the French Soudan" (1993).

The quantity and quality of source material has grown exponentially in the post-independence era (see section on post-independence politics and democratization). The various subject categories of this bibliography will provide a guide to a tremendous amount of material. There have been some attempts to provide an overview, in the text by Catherine Coquery-Vidrovitch, *African Women: A Modern History* (1997), and the guide for teachers by Iris Berger and E. Frances White, *Women in Sub-Saharan Africa: Restoring Women to History* (1999), which has a particularly useful bibliography. Anthologies are still the best source for new research in women's history, including the wide-ranging volume edited by Ayesha M. Imam, Amina Mama, and Fatou Sow, *Engendering African Social Sciences* (1997), and two commendable recent collections, *"Wicked" Women and the Reconfiguration of Gender in Africa* edited by Dorothy Hodgson and Sheryl McCurdy (2001), and *Women in African Colonial Histories*, edited by Jean Allman, Susan Geiger, and Nakanyike Musisi (2002). Margaret J. Daymond and her co-editors published *Women Writing Africa: The Southern Region* (2003), a stimulating collection of women's writing and texts, suggesting a variety of routes to recovering women's history. Their book was limited to the English-speaking countries of southern Africa, but other regional volumes are being prepared. Desiree Lewis has written "Feminist Knowledge/Review Essay: African Feminist Studies: 1980–2002" (2002), a comprehensive review of the literature, which can be accessed on the web through the African Gender Institute at the University of Cape Town. Information on current activities by African women in an array of fields from peace campaigns to HIV/AIDS and anti-female genital cutting can be found on websites, which are listed at the end of the bibliography.

The following journal abbreviations are used in the citations:

ARUS	*African Rural and Urban Studies*
ASR	*African Studies Review*
CEA	*Cahiers d'Études Africaines*
CJAS	*Canadian Journal of African Studies*
FS	*Feminist Studies*
HA	*History in Africa*
IJAHS	*International Journal of African Historical Studies*
JAH	*Journal of African History*
JMAS	*Journal of Modern African Studies*
JSAS	*Journal of Southern African Studies*
RAL	*Research in African Literatures*

ROAPE   *Review of African Political Economy*
WSIF   *Women's Studies International Forum*

HISTORY

General Sources

Bay, Edna G., ed. *Women and Work in Africa*. Boulder, Col.: Westview, 1982.

Berger, Iris, and E. Frances White. *Women in Sub-Saharan Africa: Restoring Women to History*. Bloomington: Indiana University Press, 1999.

Coquery-Vidrovitch, Catherine. *African Women: A Modern History*. Trans. Beth Gillian Raps. Boulder, Col.: Westview, 1997. Originally published as *Les Africaines: Histoire des femmes d'Afrique noire du XIX au XX siècle* (Paris: Éditions Desjonquères, 1994).

Daymond, M. J., et al., eds. *Women Writing Africa: The Southern Region*. New York: Feminist Press, 2003.

Dunbar, Roberta Ann. "Muslim Women in African History." In *The History of Islam in Africa*, ed. Nehemia Levtzion and Randall L. Pouwels, 397–417. Athens: Ohio University Press, 2000.

Hafkin, Nancy J., and Edna G. Bay, eds. *Women in Africa: Studies in Social and Economic Change*. Stanford, Calif.: Stanford University Press, 1976.

Hansen, Karen Tranberg, ed. *African Encounters with Domesticity*. New Brunswick, N.J.: Rutgers University Press, 1992.

Hay, Margaret Jean, and Sharon Stichter, ed. *African Women South of the Sahara*. London and New York: Longman, 1984.

Hay, Margaret Jean, and Marcia Wright, ed. *African Women and the Law: Historical Perspectives*. Boston: Boston University Papers on Africa VII, 1982.

Hodgson, Dorothy L., and Sheryl A. McCurdy, eds. *"Wicked" Women and the Reconfiguration of Gender in Africa*. Portsmouth, N.H.: Heinemann, 2001.

Imam, Ayesha M., Amina Mama, and Fatou Sow, ed. *Engendering African Social Sciences*. Dakar: CODESRIA, 1997. Reprinted as *Sexe, genre et société: Engendrer les sciences sociales africaines* (Paris: Karthala, 2004).

Lewis, Desiree. "Feminist Knowledge/Review Essay: African Feminist Studies: 1980–2002." Online at the African Gender Institute, http://www.gwsafrica.org/knowledge/africa%20review/main.html.

Ludwar-Ene, Gudrun, and Mechthild Reh, eds. *Focus on Women in Africa*. Bayreuth, 1993.

Paulme, Denise, ed. *Women in Tropical Africa*. Trans. H. M. Wright. Berkeley: University of California Press, 1963. Originally published as *Femmes d'Afrique noir* (Paris: Mouton, 1960).

Robertson, Claire, and Iris Berger, eds. *Women and Class in Africa*. New York: Holmes & Meier/Africana Publishing, 1986.

Sheldon, Kathleen E. *Pounders of Grain: A History of Women, Work, and Politics in Mozambique*. Portsmouth, N.H.: Heinemann, 2002.

Southern African Research and Documentation Centre, Women in Development Southern Africa Awareness. *Beyond Inequalities: Women in Southern Africa*. Harare: SARDC, 2000. SARDC also published individual volumes in the *Beyond Inequalities* series on Angola, Botswana, Lesotho, Malawi, Mauritius, Mozambique, Namibia, South Africa, Swaziland, Tanzania, Zambia, and Zimbabwe.

Stichter, Sharon B., and Jane L. Parpart, eds. *Patriarchy and Class: African Women in the Home and the Workforce*. Boulder, Col.: Westview, 1988.

Tripp, Aili Mari, ed. *Sub-Saharan Africa: The Greenwood Encyclopedia of Women's Issues Worldwide*. Westport, Conn.: Greenwood, 2003.

Historiography and Methodology

Achebe, Nwando. "Getting to the Source: Nwando Achebe—Daughter, Wife, and Guest—A Researcher at the Crossroads." *Journal of Women's History* 14, 3 (2002): 9–31.

Berger, Iris. "African Women's History: Themes and Perspectives." *Journal of Colonialism and Colonial History* (electronic journal) 4, 1 (2003).

——. "'Beasts of Burden' Revisited: Interpretations of Women and Gender in Southern African Societies." In *Paths Toward the Past: African Historical Essays in Honor of Jan Vansina*, ed. Robert W. Harms, Joseph C. Miller, David S. Newbury, and Michele D. Wagner, 123–41. Atlanta: African Studies Association Press, 1994.

Bradford, Helen. "Women, Gender and Colonialism: Rethinking the History of the British Cape Colony and Its Frontier Zones, c. 1806–70." *JAH* 37 (1996): 351–70.

Declich, Francesca. "'Gendered Narratives,' History, and Identity: Two Centuries along the Juba River among the Zigula and Shanbara." *HA* 22 (1995): 93–122.

Geiger, Susan. "Tanganyikan Nationalism as 'Women's Work': Life Histories, Collective Biography and Changing Historiography," *JAH* 37 (1996): 465–78.

——. "Women's Life Histories: Method and Content." *Signs* 11, 2 (1986): 334–51.

Guyer, Jane I. "Female Farming in Anthropology and African History." In *Gender at the Crossroads of Knowledge: Feminist Anthropology in the Postmodern Era*, ed. Micaela di Leonardo, 257–77. Berkeley: University of California Press, 1991.

Hale, Sondra. "Feminist Method, Process, and Self-Criticism: Interviewing Sudanese Women." In *Women's Words: The Feminist Practice of Oral History*, ed. Sherna Berger Gluck and Daphne Patai, 121–36. New York: Routledge, 1991.

———. "Some Thoughts on Women and Gender in Africa: Listening to the Whispers of African Women," *Journal of African Studies* 16, 1 (1998): 21–30.

Hansen, Karen Tranberg, and Margaret Strobel. "Family History in Africa." *Trends in History* 3, 3/4 (1985): 127–49.

Hassim, Shireen, and Cherryl Walker. "Women's Studies and the Women's Movement in South Africa: Defining a Relationship," *WSIF* 16, 5 (1993): 523–34.

Hay, Margaret Jean. "Queens, Prostitutes, and Peasants: Historical Perspectives on African Women," *CJAS* 22, 3 (1988): 431–47.

Hetherington, Penelope. "Women in South Africa: The Historiography in English," *IJAHS* 26, 2 (1993): 242–69.

Hunt, Nancy Rose. "Placing African Women's History and Locating Gender," *Social History* 14 (1989): 359–79.

Imam, Ayesha Mei-Tie. "The Presentation of African Women in Historical Writing." In *Retrieving Women's History: Changing Perceptions of the Role of Women in Politics and Society*, ed. S. Jay Kleinberg, 30–40. Providence, R.I.: Berg/UNESCO, 1988.

Manicom, Linzi. "Ruling Relations: Rethinking State and Gender in South African History." *JAH* 33 (1992): 441–65.

Meena, Ruth, ed. *Gender in Southern Africa: Conceptual and Theoretical Issues*. Harare: SAPES Books, 1992.

Musisi, Nakanyike B. "A Personal Journey into Custom, Identity, Power, and Politics: Researching and Writing the Life and Times of Buganda's Queen Mother Irene Drusilla Namaganda (1896–1957)." *HA* 23 (1996): 369–85.

Oyewumi, Oyeronke. "Making History, Creating Gender: Some Methodological and Interpretive Questions in the Writing of Oyo Oral Traditions," *HA* 25 (1998): 263–305.

———. *The Invention of Women: Making an African Sense of Western Gender Discourses*. Minneapolis: University of Minnesota Press, 1997.

Reh, Mechthild, and Gudrun Ludwar-Ene, eds. *Gender and Identity in Africa*. Munster: LIT Verlag, 1995.

Robertson, Claire. "Developing Economic Awareness: Changing Perspectives in Studies of African Women, 1976–1985." *FS* 13, 1 (1987): 97–135.

———. "In Pursuit of Life Histories: The Problem of Bias." *Frontiers* 7, 2 (1983): 63–69.

———. "Never Underestimate the Power of Women: The Transforming Vision of African Women's History." *WSIF* 11, 5 (1988): 439–53.

Sheldon, Kathleen. "Writing about Women: Approaches to a Gendered Perspective in African History." In *Writing African History*, ed. John Philips, 461–85. Rochester: N.Y.: Rochester University Press, 2005.

Shetler, Jan Bender. "The Gendered Spaces of Historical Knowledge: Women's Knowledge and Extraordinary Women in the Serengeti District, Tanzania." *IJAHS* 36, 2 (2003): 283–307.

Strobel, Margaret. "African Women: Review Essay." *Signs* 8, 1 (1982): 109–31.

Tadesse, Zenebeworke. "Breaking the Silence and Broadening the Frontiers of History: Recent Studies on African Women." In *Retrieving Women's History: Changing Perceptions of the Role of Women in Politics and Society*, ed. S. Jay Kleinberg, 356–364. Providence, R.I.: Berg/UNESCO, 1988.

Zeleza, Tiyambe. "Gender Biases in African Historiography." In *Engendering African Social Sciences*, ed. Ayesha M. Imam, Amina Mama, and Fatou Sow, 81–116. Dakar: CODESRIA, 1997.

———. "Gendering African History [book review]," *Africa Development* 18, 1 (1993): 99–117.

CHRONOLOGICAL GUIDE TO SOURCES

Precolonial and Early Colonial History

Beach, David. "Cognitive Archaeology and Imaginary History at Great Zimbabwe." *Current Anthropology* 19, 1 (1998): 47–72.

Brooks, George E. *Eurafricans in Western Africa: Commerce, Social Status, Gender, and Religious Observance from the Sixteenth to the Eighteenth Century*. Athens: Ohio University Press, 2003.

Guy, Jeff. "Gender Oppression in Southern Africa's Precapitalist Societies." In *Women and Gender in Southern Africa to 1945*, ed. Cherryl Walker, 33–47. London: James Currey, 1990.

Kent, Susan, ed. *Gender in African Prehistory*. Walnut Creek, Calif.: AltaMira Press, 1998.

Musisi, Nakanyike. "Women, 'Elite Polygyny,' and Buganda State Formation." *Signs* 19, 4 (1991): 757–86.

Nast, Heidi J. "Islam, Gender, and Slavery in West Africa circa 1500: A Spatial Archaeology of the Kano Palace, Northern Nigeria," *Annals of the Association of American Geographers* 86, 1 (1996): 44–77.

Sargent, R. A. "Found in the Fog of the Male Myths: Analyzing Female Political Roles in Pre-Colonial Africa." *Canadian Oral History Association Journal* 11 (1991): 39–44.

Schoenbrun, David Lee. *A Green Place, A Good Place: Agrarian Change, Gender, and Social Identity in the Great Lakes Region to the 15th Century*. Portsmouth, N.H.: Heinemann, 1998.

Wadley, Lyn. "Use of Space in a Gender Study of Two South African Stone Age Sites." In *Gender and Material Culture in Archaeological Perspective*, ed. Moira Donald and Linda Hurcombe. New York: St. Martin's, 2000.

———, ed. *Our Gendered Past: Archaeological Studies of Gender in Southern Africa*. New Brunswick, N.J.: Transaction, 1997.

Wells, Julia C. "Eva's Men: Gender and Power in the Establishment of the Cape of Good Hope, 1652–74." *JAH* 39 (1998): 417–37.

Zimba, Benigna. *Mulheres Invisíveis: O Género e as Políticas Comerciais no Sul de Moçambique, 1720–1830*. Maputo: Promédia, 2003.

19th Century

Abrahams, Yvette. "Images of Sara Bartman: Sexuality, Race, and Gender in Early-Nineteenth-Century Britain." In *Nation, Empire, Colony: Historicizing Gender and Race*, ed. Ruth Roach Pierson and Nupur Chaudhuri, 220–36. Bloomington: Indiana University Press, 1998.

Akyeampong, Emmanual. "Sexuality and Prostitution among the Akan of the Gold Coast c. 1650–1950." *Past and Present*, 156 (1997): 144–73.

Alpers, Edward A. "State, Merchant Capital, and Gender Relations in Southern Mozambique to the End of the Nineteenth Century: Some Tentative Hypotheses." *African Economic History* 13 (1984): 23–55.

Amadiume, Ifi. *Male Daughters, Female Husbands: Gender and Sex in an African Society*. London: Zed, 1987.

Bastian, Misty L. "Young Converts: Christian Missions, Gender and Youth in Onitsha, Nigeria, 1880–1929." *Anthropological Quarterly* 73, 3 (2000): 145–58.

Bay, Edna. *Wives of the Leopard: Gender, Politics, and Culture in the Kingdom of Dahomey*. Charlottesville: University of Virginia Press, 1998.

Boyd, Jean. "Distance Learning from Purdah in Nineteenth-Century Northern Nigeria: The Work of Asma'u Fodiyo." *Journal of African Cultural Studies* 14, 1 (2001): 7–22.

Boyd, Jean, and Murray Last. "The Role of Women as 'Agents Religieux' in Sokoto." *CJAS* 19, 2 (1985): 283–300.

Burman, Sandra. "Fighting a Two-Pronged Attack: The Changing Legal Status of Women in Cape-Ruled Basutoland, 1872–1884." In *Women and Gender in Southern Africa to 1945*, ed. Walker, 48–75.

Carter, Marina. *Lakshmi's Legacy: The Testimonies of Indian Women in 19th Century Mauritius*. Stanley, Rose Hill, Mauritius: Editions de l'océan Indien, 1994.

Clark, Carolyn M. "Land and Food, Women and Power, in Nineteenth Century Kikuyu." *Africa* 50, 4 (1980): 357–70.

Cockerton, Camilla. "Less a Barrier, More a Line: The Migration of Bechuanaland Women to South Africa, 1850–1930." *Journal of Historical Geography* 22, 3 (1996): 291–307.

Day, Lynda. "The Evolution of Female Chiefship during the Late Nineteenth-Century Wars of the Mende." *IJAHS* 27, 3 (1994): 481–503.

Deacon, Harriet. "Midwives and Medical Men in the Cape Colony before 1860." *JAH* 39, 2 (1998): 271–92.

Eldredge, Elizabeth A. "Women in Production: The Economic Role of Women in Nineteenth-Century Lesotho." *Signs* 16, 4 (1991): 707–31.

Erlank, Natasha. "Gendered Reactions to Social Dislocation and Missionary Activity in Xhosaland, 1836–1847." *African Studies* 59, 2 (2000): 205–27.

Freund, Bill. "Indian Women and the Changing Character of the Working Class Indian Household in Natal 1860–1990." *JSAS* 17, 3 (1991): 414–29.

Hanretta, Sean. "Women, Marginality and the Zulu State: Women's Institutions and Power in the Early Nineteenth Century." *JAH* 39, 3 (1998): 309–415.

Kinsman, Margaret. "'Beasts of Burden': The Subordination of Southern Tswana Women, ca. 1800–1840." *JSAS* 10, 1 (1983): 39–54.

Kriger, Colleen. "Textile Production and Gender in the Sokoto Caliphate." *JAH* 34 (1993): 361–401.

Labode, Modupe. "From Heathen Kraal to Christian Home: Anglican Mission Education and African Christian Girls, 1850–1900." In *Women and Missions: Past and Present: Anthropological and Historical Perceptions*, ed. Fiona Bowie, Deborah Kirkwood, and Shirley Ardener. Providence, R.I.: Berg, 1993.

Mandala, Elias. "Capitalism, Kinship, and Gender in the Lower Tchiri (Shire) Valley of Malawi, 1860–1960: An Alternative Theoretical Framework." *African Economic History* 13 (1984): 137–70.

Mann, Kristin. "The Dangers of Dependence: Christian Marriage among Elite Women in Lagos Colony, 1880–1915." *JAH* 24 (1983): 37–57.

Nast, Heidi J. "Engendering 'Space': State Formation and the Restructuring of Northern Nigeria's Kano Palace, 1807–1903." *Historical Geography* 23, 1/2 (1993): 62–75.

Nyhagen Predelli, Line. "Sexual Control and the Remaking of Gender: The Attempt of Nineteenth-Century Protestant Norwegian Women to Export Western Domesticity to Madagascar." *Journal of Women's History* 12, 2 (2000): 81–103.

Perinbam, Marie. "The Salt-Gold Alchemy in the Eighteenth and Nineteenth Century Mande World: If Men Are Its Salt, Women Are Its Gold." *HA* 23 (1996): 257–78.

Rich, Jeremy. "'Une babylone noire': Interracial Unions in Colonial Libreville, c. 1860–1914." *French Colonial History* 4 (2003): 145–69.

Roberts, Richard. "Women's Work and Women's Property: Household Social Relations in the Maraka Textile Industry of the Nineteenth Century." *Comparative Studies in Society and History* 26, 2 (1984): 229–50.

Robertson, Claire C. "Gender and Trade Relations in Central Kenya in the Late Nineteenth Century." *IJAHS* 30, 1 (1997): 23–47.

Rockel, Stephen J. "Enterprising Partners: Caravan Women in Nineteenth Century Tanzania." *CJAS* 34, 3 (2000): 748–78.

Scully, Pamela. "Rape, Race, and Colonial Culture: The Sexual Politics of Identity in the Nineteenth-Century Cape Colony, South Africa." *American Historical Review* 100, 2 (1995): 335–59.

van Heyningen, Elizabeth B. "The Social Evil in the Cape Colony, 1868–1902: Prostitution and the Contagious Diseases Act." *JSAS* 10, 2 (1984): 170–98.

van Onselen, Charles. "Prostitutes and Proletarians, 1886–1914." In *Studies in the Social and Economic History of the Witwatersrand 1886–1914,* vol. 1, *New Babylon*, ed. Charles van Onselen, 103–62. New York: Longman, 1982.

———. "The Witches of Suburbia: Domestic Service on the Witwatersrand, 1890–1914." In *Studies in the Social and Economic History of the Witwatersrand 1886–1914,* vol. 2, *New Nineveh*, ed. Charles van Onselen. New York: Longman, 1982.

Walker, Cherryl. "Gender and the Development of the Migrant Labour System c. 1850–1930." In *Women and Gender in Southern Africa to 1945*, ed. Cherryl Walker, 168–96. London: James Currey, 1990.

Wheeler, Douglas. "Angolan Woman of Means: D. Ana Joaquina Dos Santos e Silva, Mid-Nineteenth Century Luso-African Merchant-Capitalist of Luanda." *Portuguese Studies* 3 (1996): 284–97.

White, E. Frances. *Sierra Leone's Settler Women Traders: Women on the Afro-European Frontier*. Ann Arbor: University of Michigan Press, 1987.

Wright, John. "Control of Women's Labour in the Zulu Kingdom." In *Before and After Shaka*, ed. J. B. Peires, 82–99. Grahamstown: Rhodes University, 1981.

Colonialism in the 20th century

Achebe, Nwando. "Igo Mma Ogo: The Adoro Goddess, Her Wives, and Challengers—Influences on the Reconstruction of Alor-Uno, Northern Igboland, 1890–1994." *Journal of Women's History* 14, 4 (2003): 83–105.

Allman, Jean, Susan Geiger, and Nakanyike Musisi, eds. *Women in African Colonial Histories*. Bloomington: Indiana University Press, 2002.

Allman, Jean, and Victoria Tashjian. *"I Will Not Eat Stone": A Women's History of Colonial Asante*. Portsmouth, N.H.: Heinemann, 2000.

Barnes, Teresa. *"We Women Worked So Hard": Gender, Urbanization and Social Reproduction in Colonial Harare, Zimbabwe 1930–1956*. Portsmouth, N.H.: Heinemann, 1999.

Booth, Alan R. "'European Courts Protect Women and Witches': Colonial Law Courts as Redistributors of Power in Swaziland, 1920–1950." *JSAS* 18, 2 (1992): 253–75.

Brantley, Cynthia. "Colonial Africa: Transforming Families for Their Own Benefit (And Ours)." In *Families of a New World: Gender, Politics, and State Development in a Global Context*, ed. Lynne Haney and Lisa Pollard, 139–55. London: Routledge, 2003.

———. "Through Ngoni Eyes: Margaret Read's Matrilineal Interpretations from Nyasaland." *Critique of Anthropology* 17, 2 (1997): 147–70.

Byfield, Judith. *The Bluest Hands: A Social and Economic History of Women Dyers in Abeokuta (Nigeria), 1890–1940*. Portsmouth, N.H.: Heinemann, 2001.

Callaway, Helen. *Gender, Culture, and Empire: European Women in Colonial Nigeria*. Urbana: University of Illinois Press, 1987.

Chanock, Martin. *Law, Custom, and Social Order: The Colonial Experience in Malawi and Zambia*. 1985. Reprint, Portsmouth, N.H.: Heinemann, 1998.

Chauncey, George, Jr. "The Locus of Reproduction: Women's Labour in the Zambian Copperbelt, 1927–1953." *JSAS* 7, 2 (1981): 135–64.

Cock, Jacklyn. "Domestic Service and Education for Domesticity: The Incorporation of Xhosa Women into Colonial Society." In *Women and Gender in Southern Africa to 1945*, ed. Cherryl Walker, 76–96. London: James Currey, 1990.

Comaroff, Jean. "The Empire's Old Clothes: Fashioning the Colonial Subject." In *Situated Lives: Gender and Culture in Everyday Life*, ed. Louise Lamphere, Helena Ragoné, and Patricia Zavella, 400–19. New York: Routledge, 1997.

Comaroff, Jean, and John L. Comaroff. "Home-Made Hegemony: Modernity, Domesticity, and Colonialism in South Africa." In *African Encounters with Domesticity*, ed. Karen Tranberg Hansen, 37–74. New Brunswick, N.J.: Rutgers University Press, 1992.

Conklin, Alice L. "Redefining 'Frenchness': Citizenship, Race Regeneration, and Imperial Motherhood in France and West Africa, 1914–40." In *Domesticating the Empire: Race, Gender, and Family Life in French and Dutch Colonialism*, ed. Julia Clancy-Smith and Frances Gorda, 65–83. Charlottesville: University Press of Virginia, 1998.

Dagut, Simon. "Gender, Colonial 'Women's History' and the Construction of Social Distance: Middle-Class British Women in Later Nineteenth-Century South Africa." *JSAS* 26, 3 (2000): 555–72.

Debroux, Catherine. "Les activités professionelles de la femme européenne au Congo Belge de 1945 à 1960;" "La situation juridique de la femme europeéne au Congo Belge de 1945 à 1960;" and "La vie quotidienne de la femme européenne au Katanga entre 1945 à 1960." *Enquêtes et Documents d'Histoire Africaine* 7 (1987): 14–55.

Epprecht, Marc. *"This Matter of Women is Getting Very Bad": Gender, Development and Politics in Colonial Lesotho*. Pietermaritzburg: University of Natal Press, 2000.

Gaitskell, Deborah. "Hot Meetings and Hard Kraals: African Biblewomen in Transvaal Methodism, 1924–60." *Journal of Religion in Africa* 30, 3 (2000): 277–309.

Grier, Beverly. "Pawns, Porters, and Petty Traders: Women in the Transition to Cash Crop Agriculture in Colonial Ghana." *Signs* 17, 2 (1992): 304–28.

Hunt, Nancy Rose. *A Colonial Lexicon: Of Birth Ritual, Medicalization, and Mobility in the Congo*. Durham, N.C.: Duke University Press, 2000.

Kaler, Amy. *Running After Pills: Politics, Gender, and Contraception in Colonial Zimbabwe*. Portsmouth, N.H.: Heinemann, 2003.

———. "Visions of Domesticity in the African Women's Homecraft Movement in Rhodesia." *Social Science History* 23, 3 (1999): 269–309.

Kanogo, Tabitha. "Mission Impact on Women in Colonial Kenya." In *Women and Missions: Past and Present: Anthropological and Historical Perceptions*, ed. Fiona Bowie, Deborah Kirkwood, and Shirley Ardener. Providence, R.I.: Berg, 1993.

Larsson, Birgitta. *Conversion to Greater Freedom? Women, Church and Social Change in North-Western Tanzania under Colonial Rule*. Uppsala, Sweden: Historiska Institutionen vid Uppsala Universitet, 1991.

Lindsay, Lisa A. "Domesticity and Difference: Male Breadwinners, Working Women, and Colonial Citizenship in the 1945 Nigerian General Strike." *American Historical Review* 104, 3 (1999): 783–812.

Lydon, Ghislaine. "The Unraveling of a Neglected Source: A Report on Women in Francophone West Africa in the 1930s." *CEA* 37, 3; 147 (1997): 555–84.

Maddox, Gregory H. "Gender and Famine in Central Tanzania: 1916–1961." *ASR* 39, 1 (1996): 83–101.

Mandala, Elias. "Peasant Cotton Agriculture, Gender and Inter-Generational Relationships: The Lower Tchire (Shire) Valley of Malawi, 1906–1940." *ASR* 25, 2/3 (1982): 27–44.

Martin, Susan. "Gender and Innovation: Farming, Cooking and Palm Processing in the Ngwa Region of South Eastern Nigeria, 1900–1930." *JAH* 25 (1984): 411–27.

May, Joan. *Zimbabwean Women in Customary and Colonial Law*. Gweru: Mambo Press, 1983.

Mbilinyi, Marjorie. *Big Slavery: Agribusiness and the Crisis in Women's Employment in Tanzania*. Dar es Salaam: Dar es Salaam University Press, 1991.

McKittrick, Meredith. "Faithful Daughter, Murdering Mother: Transgression and Social Control in Colonial Namibia." *JAH* 40, 4 (1999): 265–84.

Meintjes, Sheila. "Family and Gender in the Christian Community at Edendale, Natal, in Colonial Times." In *Women and Gender in Southern Africa to 1945*, ed. Cherryl Walker, 125–45. London: James Currey, 1990.

Moore, Henrietta L., and Megan Vaughan. *Cutting Down Trees: Gender, Nutrition, and Agricultural Change in the Northern Province of Zambia, 1890–1990*. Portsmouth, N.H.: Heinemann, 1994.

Moss, Barbara A. "Mai Chaza and the Politics of Motherhood in Colonial Zimbabwe." In *Stepping Forward: Black Women in Africa and the Americas*, ed. Catherine Higgs, Barbara A. Moss, and Earline Rae Ferguson, 143–57. Athens: Ohio University Press, 2002.

———. "'And the Bones Come Together': Women's Religious Expectations in Southern Africa, c. 1900–1945." *Journal of Religious History* 23, 1 (1999): 108–27.

Parpart, Jane L. "The Household and the Mineshaft: Gender and Class Struggles on the Zambian Copperbelt, 1924–1966." *JSAS* 13, 1 (1986): 36–56.

Santoru, Marina E. "The Colonial Idea of Women and Direct Intervention: The Mau Mau Case." *African Affairs* 95 (1996): 253–67.

Schmidt, Elizabeth. *Peasants, Traders, and Wives: Shona Women in the History of Zimbabwe, 1870–1939*. Portsmouth, N.H.: Heinemann, 1992.

Shaw, Carolyn Martin. *Colonial Inscriptions: Race, Sex, and Class in Kenya*. Minneapolis: University of Minnesota Press, 1995.

Stichter, Sharon. "The Migration of Women in Colonial Central Africa: Some Notes toward an Approach." In *Demography from Scanty Evidence: Central Africa in the Colonial Era*, ed. Bruce Fetter, 207–18. Boulder, Col.: Lynne Rienner, 1990.

Summers, Carol. "Intimate Colonialism: The Imperial Production of Reproduction in Uganda, 1907–1925." *Signs* 16, 4 (1991): 787–807.

Thomas, Lynn M. "'The Politics of the Womb': Kenyan Debates Over the Affiliation Act." *Africa Today* 47, 3 & 4 (2001): 151–76.

Tsikata, Dzodzi. "Gender, Kinship and the Control of Resources in Colonial Southern Ghana." In *Shifting Circles of Support: Contextualising Gender and Kinship in South Asia and Sub-Saharan Africa*, ed. Rajni Palriwala and Carla Risseeuw, 110–32. New Delhi: Sage, 1996.

Turrittin, Jane. "Aoua Kéita and the Nascent Women's Movement in the French Soudan." *ASR* 36, 1 (1993): 59–89.

Walker, Cherryl, ed. *Women and Gender in Southern Africa to 1945*. London: James Currey, 1990.

Wells, Julia. "The Sabotage of Patriarchy in Colonial Rhodesia: Rural African Women's Living Legacy to Their Daughters." *Feminist Review* 75 (2003): 101–17.

White, Luise. "A Colonial State and an African Petty Bourgeoisie: Prostitution, Property, and Class Struggle in Nairobi, 1936–1940." In *Struggle for the City: Migrant Labor, Capital, and the State in Urban Africa*, ed. Frederick Cooper, 167–94. Beverly Hills, Calif.: Sage, 1983.

Wilson, Monica. *For Men and Elders: Change in the Relations of Generations and of Men and Women among the Nyakusa-Ngonde People, 1875–1971*. London: International African Institute, 1977.

Yates, Barbara A. "Church, State and Education in Belgian Africa: Implications for Contemporary Third World Women." In *Women's Education in the Third World: Comparative Perspectives*, ed. Gail P. Kelly and Carolyn M. Elliott, 127–51. Albany: State University of New York Press, 1982.

Resistance and Nationalism

Allen, Chris. "Gender, Participation, and Radicalism in African Nationalism: Its Contemporary Significance." In *Democracy and Socialism in Africa*, ed. Robin Cohen and Harry Goulbourne. Boulder, Col.: Westview, 1991.

Bernstein, Hilda. *For Their Triumphs and For Their Tears*. 2nd. ed. London: International Defence and Aid Fund, 1985.

Bradford, Helen. "'We Women Will Show Them': Beer Protests in the Natal Countryside, 1929." In *Liquor and Labor in Southern Africa*, ed. Jonathan Crush and Charles Ambler. Athens: Ohio University Press, 1992.

Byfield, Judith. "Taxation, Women, and the Colonial State: Egba Women's Tax Revolt." *Meridians: Feminism, Race, Transnationalism* 3, 2 (2003): 250–77.

Chadya, Joyce M. "Mother Politics: Anti-Colonial Nationalism and the Woman Question in Africa." *Journal of Women's History* 15, 3 (2003): 153–57.

d'Almeida-Ekué, Silivi. *La révolte des Loméennes, 24–25 Janvier 1933*. Lomé: Nouvelles Éditions Africaines, 1992.

Denzer, LaRay. "Women in Freetown Politics, 1914–61: A Preliminary Study." *Africa* 57, 4 (1987): 439–55.

Diabate, Henriette. *La marche des femmes sur Grand-Bassam*. Abidjan: Nouvelles Editions Africaines, 1975.

Diduk, Susan. "Women's Agricultural Production and Political Action in the Cameroon Grassfields." *Africa* 59, 3 (1989): 338–55.

Eales, Kathy. "Patriarchs, Passes and Privilege: Johannesburg's African Middle Classes and the Question of Night Passes for African Women, 1920–1931." In *Holding Their Ground: Class, Locality and Culture in 19th and 20th Century South Africa*, ed. Philip Bonner et al., 105–39. Johannesburg: Witwatersrand University Press and Ravan, 1989.

Eames, Elizabeth A. "Why the Women Went to War: Women and Wealth in Ondo Town, Southwestern Nigeria." In *Traders Versus the State: Anthropological*

Approaches to Unofficial Economies, ed. Gracia Clark, 81–98. Boulder, Col.: Westview, 1988.

Gaidzanwa, Rudo. "Citizenship, Nationality, Gender, and Class in Southern Africa." *Alternatives* 18 (1993): 39–59.

Gaitskell, Deborah, and Elaine Unterhalter. "Mothers of the Nation: A Comparative Analysis of Nation, Race and Motherhood in Afrikaner Nationalism and the African National Congress." In *Woman–Nation–State*, ed. Nira Yuval-Davis and Floya Anthias, 58–78. London: Macmillan, 1989.

Geiger, Susan. *TANU Women: Gender and Culture in the Making of Tanganyikan Nationalism, 1955–1965*. Portsmouth, N.H.: Heinemann, 1997.

———. "Specificities: Citizens and Subjects—Engendering and Gendering African Nationalism: Rethinking the Case of Tanganyika (Tanzania)." *Social Identities* 5, 3 (1999): 332–43.

———. "Women and African Nationalism." *Journal of Women's History* 2, 1 (1990): 227–37.

Isaacman, Allen, and Barbara Isaacman. "The Role of Women in the Liberation of Mozambique." *Ufahamu* 13, 2–3 (1984): 128–85.

Johnson, Cheryl. "Grass Roots Organizing: Women in Anti-Colonial Activity in Southwestern Nigeria." *ASR* 25, 2/3 (1982): 137–57.

Kanogo, Tabitha. "Kikuyu Women and the Politics of Protest: Mau Mau." In *Images of Women in Peace and War: Cross-Cultural and Historical Perspectives*, ed. Sharon Macdonald, Pat Holden, and Shirley Ardener, 78–99. Madison: University of Wisconsin Press, 1988.

Kimble, Judy, and Elaine Unterhalter. "'We Opened the Road for You, You Must Go Forward': ANC Women's Struggles, 1912–1982." *Feminist Review* 12 (1982): 11–36.

Klugman, Barbara. "Women in Politics under Apartheid: A Challenge to the New South Africa." In *Women and Politics Worldwide*, ed. Barbara J. Nelson and Najma Chowdhury, 639–59. New Haven, Conn.: Yale University Press, 1994.

Krikler, Jeremy. "Women, Violence and the Rand Revolt of 1922." *JSAS* 22, 4 (1996): 349–72.

Kumsa, Kuwee. "Oromo Women and the Oromo National Movement: Dilemmas, Problems and Prospects for True Liberation." In *Oromo Nationalism and the Ethiopian Discourse: The Search for Freedom and Democracy*, ed. Asafa Jalata. Lawrenceville, N.J.: Red Sea Press, 1998.

Ladner, Joyce. "Tanzanian Women and Nation Building." In *The Black Woman Cross-Culturally*, ed. Filomina Chioma Steady, 197–17. Cambridge, Mass.: Schenkman, 1981.

Lapchick, Richard E., and Stephanie Urdang. *Oppression and Resistance: The Struggle of Women in Southern Africa*. Westport, Conn.: Greenwood, 1982.

Lawrance, Benjamin N. "*La Révolte des Femmes*: Economic Upheaval and the Gender of Political Authority in Lomé, Togo, 1931–1933." *ASR* 46, 1 (2003): 43–67.

Likimani, Muthoni. *Passbook Number F.47927: Women and Mau Mau in Kenya*. London: Macmillan, 1985.

Lipman, Beata. *We Make Freedom: Women in South Africa*. London: Routledge & Kegan Paul; Pandora, 1984.

Lippert, Anne. "Sahrawi Women in the Liberation Struggle of the Sahrawi People." *Signs* 17, 3 (1992): 636–51.

Lyons, Tanya. *Guns and Guerilla Girls: Women in the Zimbabwean National Liberation Struggle*. Trenton, N.J.: Africa World Press, 2004.

MacKenzie, Fiona. "Political Economy of the Environment, Gender, and Resistance under Colonialism: Murang'a District, Kenya, 1910–1950." *CJAS* 25, 2 (1991): 226–56.

Mager, Anne. "'The People Get Fenced': Gender, Rehabilitation and African Nationalism in the Ciskei and Border Region, 1945–1955." *JSAS* 18, 4 (1992): 761–82.

Mama, Amina. "Sheroes and Villains: Conceptualizing Colonial and Contemporary Violence against Women in Africa." In *Feminist Genealogies, Colonial Legacies, Democratic Futures*, ed. M. Jacqui Alexander and Chandra Talpade Mohanty, 46–62. New York: Routledge, 1997.

Mangaliso, Zengie A. "Gender and Nation-Building in South Africa." In *Feminist Nationalism*, ed. Lois A. West, 130–44. New York: Routledge, 1997.

Mba, Nina. *Nigerian Women Mobilized: Women's Political Activity in Southern Nigeria, 1900–1965*. Berkeley: Institute of International Studies, University of California, 1982.

McClintock, Anne. "'No Longer in a Future Heaven': Women and Nationalism in South Africa." *Transition* 51 (1991): 104–23.

McCurdy, Sheryl. "The 1932 'War' Between Rival Ujiji (Tanganyika) Associations: Understanding Women's Motivations for Inciting Political Unrest." *CJAS* 30, 1 (1996): 10–31.

Meintjes, Sheila. "Gender, Nationalism and Transformation: Difference and Commonality in South Africa's Past and Present." In *Women, Ethnicity and Nationalism: The Politics of Transition*, ed. Rick Wilford and Robert E. Miller, 62–86. New York: Routledge, 1998.

Moran, Mary H. "Uneasy Images: Contested Representations of Gender, Modernity and Nationalism in Pre-War Liberia." In *Gender Ironies of Nationalism: Sexing the Nation*, ed. Tamar Mayer, 113–36. London: Routledge, 2000.

National Union of Eritrean Women. *Eritrea Women and their Tradition of Resistance*. 1985. Reprint, Asmara: NUEW, 1999.

Newbury, M. Catherine. "Ebutumwa Bw'Emiogo: The Tyranny of Cassava: A Women's Tax Revolt in Eastern Zaire." *CJAS* 18, 1 (1984): 35–54.

Nhongo-Simbanegavi, Josephine. *For Better or Worse? Women and ZANLA in Zimbabwe's Liberation Struggle*. Harare: Weaver, 2000.

Nkwi, Paul Nchoji. "Traditional Female Militancy in a Modern Context." In *Femmes du Cameroun: Mères pacifique, femmes rebelles*, ed. Jean-Claude Barbier, 181–91. Paris: Karthala-Orstrom, 1985.

Presley, Cora Ann. "Gender and Political Struggle in Kenya, 1948–1998." In *Stepping Forward: Black Women in Africa and the Americas*, ed. Catherine Higgs, Barbara A. Moss, and Earline Rae Ferguson, 173–88. Athens: Ohio University Press, 2002.

———. *Kikuyu Women, the Mau Mau Rebellion, and Social Change in Kenya*. Boulder, Col.: Westview, 1992.

Ramphele, Mamphela. "The Dynamics of Gender within Black Consciousness Organisations: A Personal View." In *Bounds of Possibility: Steve Biko and the Legacy of Black Consciousness*, ed. N. Barney Pityana et al., 214–27. Cape Town: David Philip, 1991.

Ranchod-Nilsson, Sita. "(Gender) Struggles for the Nation: Power, Agency, and Representation in Zimbabwe." In *Women, States, and Nationalism: At Home in the Nation?* ed. Sita Ranchod-Nilsson and Mary Ann Tétreault, 164–80. New York: Routledge, 2000.

———. "'This, Too, is a Way of Fighting': Rural Women's Participation in Zimbabwe's Liberation War." In *Women and Revolution in Africa, Asia, and the New World*, ed. Mary Ann Tétreault, 62–88. Columbia: University of South Carolina Press, 1994.

Ritzenthaler, Robert E. "Anlu: A Women's Uprising in the British Cameroons." *African Studies* 19, 3 (1960): 151–56.

Scarnecchia, Timothy. "Poor Women and Nationalist Politics: Alliances and Fissures in the Formation of a Nationalist Political Movement in Salisbury, Rhodesia, 1950–6." *JAH* 37 (1996): 283–310.

Scott, Catherine. "'Men in Our Country Behave Like Chiefs': Women and the Angolan Revolution." In *Women and Revolution in Africa, Asia, and the New World*, ed. Mary Ann Tétreault, 89–108. Columbia: University of South Carolina Press, 1994.

Scott, Leda. *Women and the Armed Struggle for Independence in Zimbabwe*. Edinburgh: University of Edinburgh, 1990.

Shanklin, Eugenia. "Anlu Remembered: The Kom Women's Rebellion of 1958–61." *Dialectical Anthropology* 15, 2/3 (1990): 159–81.

Soiri, Iina. *The Radical Motherhood: Namibian Women's Independence Struggle*. Uppsala: Nordiska Afrikainstitutet, 1996.

Tamale, Sylvia. "Taking the Beast by Its Horns: Formal Resistance to Women's Oppression in Africa." *Africa Development* 21, 4 (1996): 5–21.

Urdang, Stephanie. *Fighting Two Colonialisms: Women in Guinea-Bissau*. New York: Monthly Review Press, 1979.

Wells, Julia. "'The Day the Town Stood Still': Women in Resistance in Potchefstroom, 1912–1930." In *Town and Countryside in the Transvaal: Capitalist
Penetration and Popular Response*, ed. Belinda Bozzoli, 269–307. Johannesburg: Ravan, 1983.

———. "The War of Degradation: Black Women's Struggle against Orange Free
State Pass Laws, 1913." In *Banditry, Rebellion and Social Protest in Africa*,
ed. Donald Crummey, 253–70. Portsmouth, N.H.: Heinemann, 1986.

———. "Why Women Rebel: A Comparative Study of South African Women's
Resistance in Bloemfontein (1913) and Johannesburg (1958)." *JSAS* 10, 1
(1983): 55–70.

West, Harry G. "Girls with Guns: Narrating the Experience of War of Frelimo's
'Female Detachment.'" *Anthropological Quarterly* 73, 4 (2000): 180–94.

Wilson, Amrit. *The Challenge Road: Women and the Eritrean Revolution*. Trenton, N.J.: Red Sea Press, 1991.

Wipper, Audrey. "Kikuyu Women and the Harry Thuku Disturbances: Some
Uniformities of Female Militancy." *Africa* 59, 3 (1989): 300–37.

Zimbabwe Women Writers. *Women of Resilience*. Harare: Zimbabwe Women
Writers, 2000.

Post-independence Politics and Democratization

Abwunza, Judith M. *Women's Voices, Women's Power: Dialogues of Resistance
from East Africa*. Ontario, Canada: Broadview Press, 1997.

Adeleye-Fayemi, Bisi, and Algresia Akwi-Ogojo. *Taking the African
Women's Movement into the 21st Century*. Kampala: Akina Mama wa
Afrika, 1997.

African Women and Peace Support Group. *Liberian Women Peacemakers:
Fighting for the Right To Be Seen, Heard and Counted*. Trenton, N.J.: Africa
World Press, 2004.

Ahlberg, Beth Maina. *Women, Sexuality and the Changing Social Order: The
Impact of Government Policies on Reproductive Behavior in Kenya*. London:
Gordon and Breach, 1991.

Amadiume, Ifi. *Daughters of the Goddess, Daughters of Imperialism: African
Women Struggle for Culture, Power and Democracy*. New York: St. Martin's,
2000.

Arnfred, Signe. "Notes on Gender and Modernization: Examples from Mozambique." In *The Language of Development Studies*, ed. Agnete Weis Bentzon,
71–107. Copenhagen: New Social Science Monographs, 1990.

———. "Women in Mozambique: Gender Struggle and Gender Politics." *Review of African Political Economy* 41 (1988): 5–12.

Assie-Lumumba, N'dri Thérèse. *Les Africaines dans la politique: Femmes
Baoulé de Côte d'Ivoire*. Paris: L'Harmattan, 1996.

Bankson, Barbro, and R. W. Niezen. "Women of the Jama'a Ansar al-Sunna: Female Participation in a West African Reform Movement." *CJAS* 29, 3 (1995): 375–402.

Batezat, Elinor, M. Mwalo, and K. Truscott. "Women and Independence: The Heritage and the Struggle." In *Zimbabwe's Prospects: Issues of Race, Class, State and Capital in Southern Africa*, ed. C. Stoneman. Basingstoke: Macmillan, 1988.

Beall, Jo. "Doing Gender from Top to Bottom? The South African Case." *Women: A Cultural Review* 12, 2 (2001): 135–46.

Beall, Jo, Shireen Hassim, and Alison Todes. "A Bit on the Side? Gender Struggles in the Politics of Transformation in South Africa." *Feminist Review* 33 (1989): 32–56.

Beck, Linda J. "Democratization and the Hidden Public: The Impact of Patronage Networks on Senegalese Women." *Comparative Politics* 35, 2 (2003): 147–69.

Becker, Heike. "A Concise History of Gender, 'Tradition' and the State in Namibia." In *State, Society and Democracy: A Reader in Namibian Politics*, ed. Christiaan Keulder, 171–99. Windhoek: Gamsberg Macmillan, 2000.

———. "'We Want Women to Be Given an Equal Chance': Post-Independence Rural Politics in Northern Namibia." In *The Aftermath: Women in Post-Conflict Transformation*, ed. Sheila Meintjes, Anu Pillay, and Meredeth Turshen, 225–42. London: Zed, 2001.

Berhane-Selassie, Tsehai. "Ethiopian Rural Women and the State." In *African Feminism: The Politics of Survival in Sub-Saharan Africa*, ed. Gwendolyn Mikell, 182–205. Philadelphia: University of Pennsylvania Press, 1997.

Bernal, Victoria. "Equality to Die For? Women Guerrilla Fighters and Eritrea's Cultural Revolution." *PoLAR: Political and Legal Anthropology Review* 23, 2 (2000): 61–76.

Bonnin, Debby. "Claiming Spaces, Changing Places: Political Violence and Women's Protests in KwaZulu-Natal." *JSAS* 26, 2 (2000): 301–16.

Boyd, Rosalind. "Empowerment of Women in Contemporary Uganda: Real or Symbolic?" In *Women, Feminism and Development*, ed. Huguette Dagenais and Denise Piché, 305–26. Montreal: McGill-Queen's University Press, 1994.

Britton, Hannah E. "Coalition Building, Election Rules, and Party Politics: South African Women's Path to Parliament." *Africa Today* 49, 4 (2002): 33–67.

Brown, Andrea M. "Democratization and the Tanzanian State: Emerging Opportunities for Achieving Women's Empowerment." *CJAS* 35, 1 (2001): 67–98.

Brydon, Lynne. "Women Chiefs and Power in the Volta Region of Ghana." *Journal of Legal Pluralism* 37–38 (1996): 227–47.

Byanyima, Karagwa W. "Women in Political Struggle in Uganda." In *Women Transforming Politics*, ed. Jill M. Bystydzienski, 129–42. Bloomington: Indiana University Press, 1992.

Cagatay, Nilufer, Caren Grown, and A. Santiago. "The Nairobi Women's Conference: Toward a Global Feminism?" *FS* 12, 2 (1986): 401–12.

Callaway, Barbara, and Lucy Creevey. *The Heritage of Islam: Women, Religion, and Politics in West Africa*. Boulder, Col.: Lynne Rienner, 1994.

Cawthorne, Maya. "The Third Chimurenga." In *Reflections on Gender Issues in Africa*, ed. Patricia McFadden, 55–84. Harare: SAPES Trust, 1999.

Cheater, A. P., and R. B. Gaidzanwa. "Citizenship in Neo-Patrilineal States: Gender and Mobility in Southern Africa." *JSAS* 22, 2 (1996): 189–200.

Chingono, Mark. "Women, Knowledge, and Power in Environmental and Social Change." In *African Women and Children: Crisis and Response*, ed. Apollo Rwomire. Westport, Conn.: Praeger, 2001.

Cock, Jacklyn. "Women in South Africa's Transition to Democracy." In *Transitions Environments Translations: Feminism in International Politics*, ed. Joan W. Scott, Cora Kaplan, and Debra Keates, 310–33. New York: Routledge, 1997.

Connell, Dan. "Strategies for Change: Women and Politics in Eritrea and South Africa." *ROAPE* 25, 76 (1998): 189–206.

Cooper, Allan D. "State Sponsorship of Women's Rights and Implications for Patriarchism in Namibia." *JMAS* 35, 3 (1997): 469–83.

Creevey, Lucy. "Islam, Women, and the Role of the State in Senegal." *Journal of Religion in Africa* 36, 3 (1996): 268–307.

Crehan, Kate. "The Rules of the Game: The Political Location of Women in North-Western Zambia." In *African Democracy in the Era of Globalisation*, ed. Jonathan Hyslop, 139–51. Johannesburg: Witwatersrand University Press, 1999.

Dennis, Carolyne. "Women and the State in Nigeria: The Case of the Federal Military Government, 1984–5." In *Women, State, and Ideology: Studies from Africa and Asia*, ed. Haleh Afshar, 13–27. Albany: State University of New York, 1987.

Donaldson, Shawn Riva. "'Our Women Keep Our Skies from Falling': Women's Networks and Survival Imperatives in Tshunyane, South Africa." In *African Feminism: The Politics of Survival in Sub-Saharan Africa*, ed. Gwendolyn Mikell, 257–75. Philadelphia: University of Pennsylvania Press, 1997.

El-Sanousi, Magda M., and Nafisa Ahmed El-Amin. "The Women's Movement, Displaced Women, and Rural Women in Sudan." In *Women and Politics Worldwide*, ed. Barbara J. Nelson and Najma Chowdhury, 674–89. New Haven, Conn.: Yale University Press, 1994.

Epprecht, Marc. "Women's 'Conservatism' and the Politics of Gender in Lesotho." In *The Politics of Change in Southern Africa; Vol.1*, ed. Dan

O'Meara, 204–40. Montreal: Canadian Research Consortium on Southern Africa, 1995.

Fall, Yassine. "Gender and Social Implications of Globalization: An African Perspective." In *Gender, Globalization, and Democratization*, ed. Rita Mae Kelly et al., 49–74. Lanham, Md.: Rowan and Littlefield, 2001.

Favali, Lyda, and Roy Pateman. *Blood, Land, and Sex: Legal and Political Pluralism in Eritrea*. Bloomington: Indiana University Press, 2003.

Ferguson, Anne E., and Beatrice Liatto Katundu. "Women in Politics in Zambia: What Difference Has Democracy Made?" *ARUS* 1, 2 (1994): 11–30.

Fick, Glenda, Sheila Meintjies, and Mary Simons, eds. *One Woman, One Vote: The Gender Politics of South African Elections*. Johannesburg: EISA, 2002.

Gaidzanwa, Rudo. "Citizenship, Nationality, Gender, and Class in Southern Africa." *Alternatives* 18 (1993): 39–59.

Galloy, Martine Renee. "The Electoral Process and Women Contestants: Identifying the Obstacles in the Congolese Experience." In *Reflections on Gender Issues in Africa*, ed. Patricia McFadden, 19–26. Harare: SAPES Trust, 1999.

Geisler, Gisela. "Troubled Sisterhood: Women and Politics in Southern Africa: Case Studies from Zambia, Zimbabwe and Botswana." *African Affairs* 94 (1995): 545–78.

———. "Women Are Women or How to Please Your Husband: Initiation Ceremonies and the Politics of 'Tradition' in Southern Africa." *African Anthropology* 4, 1 (1997): 92–128.

———. "'Parliament is Another Terrain of Struggle': Women, Men and Politics in South Africa." *JMAS* 38, 4 (2000): 605–30.

Gilman, Lisa. "Purchasing Praise: Women, Dancing, and Patrongage in Malawi Party Politics." *Africa Today* 48, 4 (2001).

Glazer, Ilsa M. "Alcohol and Politics in Urban Zambia: The Intersection of Gender and Class." In *African Feminism: The Politics of Survival in Sub-Saharan Africa*, ed. Gwendolyn Mikell, 142–58. Philadelphia: University of Pennsylvania Press, 1997.

Goetz, Anne Marie, and Shireen Hassim, eds. *No Shortcuts to Power: African Women in Politics and Policy Making*. London: Zed, 2003.

Gordon, April. "Gender, Ethnicity, and Class in Kenya: 'Burying Otieno' Revisited." *Signs* 20, 4 (1995): 883–912.

Gouws, Amanda. "Gender Dimensions." In *Election '99 South Africa: From Mandela to Mbeki*, ed. Andrew S. Reynolds. St. Martin's Press, 1999.

Graybill, Lynn. "The Contribution of the Truth and Reconciliation Commission toward the Promotion of Women's Rights in South Africa." *WSIF* 24, 1 (2001): 1–10.

Hale, Sondra. "Alienation and Belonging: Women's Citizenship and Emancipation Visions for Sudan's Post-Islamist Future." *New Political Science* 23, 1 (2001): 25–43.

——. *Gender Politics in Sudan: Islamism, Socialism, and the State*. Boulder, Col.: Westview, 1996.

——. "The Islamic State and Gendered Citizenship in Sudan." In *Gender and Citizenship in the Middle East*, ed. Suad Joseph, 88–104. Syracuse: Syracuse, N.Y., 2000.

——. "Liberated, but Not Free: Women in Post-War Eritrea." In *The Aftermath: Women in Post-Conflict Transformation*, ed. Sheila Meintjes, Anu Pillay, and Meredeth Turshen, 122–41. London: Zed, 2001.

Hassim, Shireen. "The Gender Pact and Democratic Consolidation: Institutionalizing Gender Equality in the South African State." *FS* 29, 3 (2003): 505–28.

Hirsch, Susan F. "Kadhi's Courts as Complex Sites of Resistance: The State, Islam, and Gender in Postcolonial Kenya." In *Contested States: Law, Hegemony and Resistance*, ed. Mindie Lazarus-Black and Susan F. Hirsch, 207–30. New York: Routledge, 1994.

Hirschmann, David. "The Malawi Case: Enclave Politics, Core Resistance, and 'Nkhoswe No. 1.'" In *Women, International Development, and Politics: The Bureaucratic Mire*, ed. Kathleen Staudt, 163–79. Philadelphia, Pa.: Temple University Press, 1990.

Ibeanu, Okechukwu. "Healing and Changing: The Changing Identity of Women in the Aftermath of the Ogoni Crisis in Nigeria." In *The Aftermath: Women in Post-Conflict Transformation*, ed. Sheila Meintjes, Anu Pillay, and Meredeth Turshen, 189–209. London: Zed, 2001.

Ibrahim, Fatima Ahmed. "Sudanese Women under Repression, and the Shortest Way to Equality." In *Frontline Feminisms: Women, War, and Resistance*, ed. Marguerite R. Waller and Jennifer Rycenga, 129–39. New York: Garland, 2000.

Jacobs, Susie M., and Tracey Howard. "Women in Zimbabwe: Stated Policy and State Action." In *Women, State, and Ideology: Studies from Africa and Asia*, ed. Haleh Afshar, 28–47. Albany: State University of New York Press, 1987.

Jacobson, Ruth. "Women's Political Participation: Mozambique's Democratic Transition." *Gender and Development* 3, 3 (1995): 29–35.

James, Valentine Udoh, and James S. Etim, eds. *The Feminization of Development Processes in Africa: Current and Future Perspectives*. Westport, Conn.: Praeger, 1999.

Jua, Roselyn. "Women's Role in Democratic Change in Cameroon." In *Anglophone Cameroon Writing; Bayereuth African Studies 30; WEKA No. 1*, ed. Nalova Lyonga, Eckhard Breitinger, and Bole Butake, 180–83. Bayreuth: Bayreuth University, 1993.

Kadalie, Rhoda. "Constitutional Equality—The Implications for Women in South Africa." *Social Politics* 2, 2 (1995): 208–24.

Khasiani, Shanyisa Anota. "Enhancing Women's Participation in Governance: The Case of Kakamega and Makueni Districts, Kenya." In *Gender and the Information Revolution in Africa*, ed. Eva M. Rathgeber and Edith Ofwona Adera, 215–37. Ottawa: International Development Research Centre, 2000.

Kruks, Sonia, and Ben Wisner. "Ambiguous Transformations: Women, Politics, and Production in Mozambique." In *Promissory Notes*, ed. Sonia Kruks, Rayna Rapp, and Marilyn B. Young, 148–71. New York: Monthly Review, 1989.

Kuumba, M. Bahati. "'You've Struck a Rock': Comparing Gender, Social Movements, and Transformation in the United States and South Africa." *Gender and Society* 16, 4 (2002).

Leisure, Susan. "Exchanging Participation for Promises: Mobilization of Women in Eritrea." In *Democratization and Women's Grassroots Movements*, ed. Jill M. Bystydzienski and Joti Sekhon, 95–110. Bloomington: Indiana University Press, 1999.

Lewis, Barbara C. "Farming Women, Public Policy, and the Women's Ministry: A Case Study from Cameroon." In *Women, International Development, and Politics: The Bureaucratic Mire*, ed. Kathleen Staudt, 180–200. Philadelphia, Pa.: Temple University Press, 1990.

Liebenberg, Sandra, ed. *The Constitution of South Africa from a Gender Perspective*. Cape Town: David Philip, 1995.

Lippert, Anne. "Sahrawi Women in the Liberation Struggle of the Sahrawi People." *Signs* 17, 3 (1992): 636–51.

Lisk, Franklyn, and Yvette Stevens. "Government Policy and Rural Women's Work in Sierra Leone." In *Sex Roles, Population and Development in West Africa: Policy-Related Studies on Work and Demographic Issues*, ed. Christine Oppong, 182–202. Portsmouth, N.H.: Heinemann, 1987.

Longwe, Sara Hlupekile. "Towards Realistic Strategies for Women's Political Empowerment in Africa." *Gender and Development* 8, 3 (2000): 24–30.

Maathai, Wangari. "Women, Information, and the Future: The Women of Kenya and the Green Belt Movement." In *A Rising Public Voice: Women in Politics Worldwide*, ed. Alida Brill, 241–48. New York: Feminist Press, 1995.

Mabandla, Brigitte. "Women in South Africa and the Constitution-Making Process." In *Women's Rights, Human Rights: International Feminist Perspectives*, ed. Julie Peters and Andrea Wolper, 67–71. New York: Routledge, 1995.

Mama, Amina. "Khaki in the Family: Gender Discourses and Militarism in Nigeria." *ASR* 41, 2 (1998): 1–17.

Manicom, Linzi. "Claiming Our Rights as Women: Issues of Gender and Democracy in the New South Africa." In *Democracy, Globalisation and Transformation in Southern Africa*, ed. Linda Freeman. Montreal: Canadian Research Consortium on Southern Africa, 1996.

Masquelier, Bertrand M. "Women's Constitutional Role in Politics: The Ide of West-Cameroon." In *Femmes du Cameroun: Mères pacifique, femmes rebelles*, ed. Jean-Claude Barbier, 105–18. Paris: Karthala-Orstrom, 1985.

McFadden, Patricia, ed. *Reflections on Gender Issues in Africa*. Harare: Southern African Research and Documentation Centre, 1999.

Meer, Shamim, ed. *Women Speak: Reflections on Our Struggles 1982–1997*. Sterling, Va.: Stylus, 1999.

———, ed. *Women, Land and Authority: Perspectives from South Africa*. Cape Town: David Philip, 1997.

Mikell, Gwendolyn. "Ghanaian Females, Rural Economy and National Stability." *ASR* 29, 3 (1986): 67–88.

Moran, Mary H. "Collective Action and 'Representation' of African Women: A Liberian Case Study." *FS* 15, 3 (1989): 443–60.

Mtintso, Thenjiwe. "Representivity: False Sisterhood or Universal Women's Interests? The South African Experience." *FS* 29, 3 (2003): 569–79.

Njiro, Ester Igandu. "Women's Empowerment and the Anthropology of Participatory Development." In *The Feminization of Development Processes in Africa: Current and Future Perspectives*, ed. Valentine Udoh James and James S. Etim. Westport, Conn.: Greenwood, 1999.

Nzomo, Maria. "Kenyan Women in Politics and Public Decision Making." In *African Feminism: The Politics of Survival in Sub-Saharan Africa*, ed. Gwendolyn Mikell, 232–53. Philadelphia: University of Pennsylvania Press, 1997.

———. "Women, Democracy and Development in Africa." In *Democratic Theory and Practice in Africa*, ed. W. Oyugi et al. Portsmouth, N.H.: Heinemann, 1987.

Nzomo, Maria, and Kathleen Staudt. "Man-Made Political Machinery in Kenya: Political Space for Women?" In *Women and Politics Worldwide*, ed. Barbara J. Nelson and Najma Chowdhury, 415–35. New Haven, Conn.: Yale University Press, 1994.

Ochwada, Hannington. "Politics and Gender Relations in Kenya: A Historical Perspective." *Africa Development* 22, 1 (1997): 123–40.

Odoul, Wilhelmina. "Kenyan Women in Politics: An Analysis of Past and Present Trends." *Transafrican Journal of History* 22 (1993): 166–80.

Ogundipe-Leslie, 'Molara. *Re-Creating Ourselves: African Women and Critical Transformations*. Trenton, N.J.: Africa World Press, 1994.

Okeke, Philomina E. "Reconfiguring Tradition: Women's Rights and Social Status in Contemporary Nigeria." *Africa Today* 47, 1 (2000): 49–64.

Okonjo, Kamene. "Reversing the Marginalization of the Invisible and Silent Majority: Women in Politics in Nigeria." In *Women and Politics Worldwide*, ed. Barbara J. Nelson and Najma Chowdhury, 512–26. New Haven, Conn.: Yale University Press, 1994.

———. "Women and the Evolution of a Ghanaian Political Synthesis." In *Women and Politics Worldwide*, ed. Barbara J. Nelson and Najma Chowdhury, 285–97. New Haven, Conn.: Yale University Press, 1994.

Onah, Roseline C. "Unequal Opportunities and Gender Access to Power in Nigeria." In *African Women and Children: Crisis and Response*, ed. Apollo Rwomire. Westport, Conn.: Praeger, 2001.

Osei-Hwedie, Bertha Z. "Constraints on Women's Participation in Zambian Politics: A Comparative Analysis of the First, Second, and Third Republics." In *African Women and Children: Crisis and Response*, ed. Apollo Rwomire. Westport, Conn.: Praeger, 2001.

Osinulu, Clara, and Nina Mba. *Nigerian Women in Politics 1986–1993*. Nigeria: Malthouse Press, 1996.

Ottemoeller, Dan. "The Politics of Gender in Uganda: Symbolism in the Service of Pragmatism." *ASR* 42, 2 (1999): 87–104.

O'Barr, Jean F. "Reflections on Forum '85 in Nairobi, Kenya: Voices from the International Women's Studies Community." *Signs* 11, 3 (1986): 584–608.

Pankhurst, Helen. *Gender, Development and Identity: An Ethiopian Study*. Atlantic Highlands, N.J.: Zed Books, 1992.

Parpart, Jane L. "Gender, Patriarchy and Development in Africa: The Zimbabwean Case." In *Patriarchy and Economic Development: Women's Positions at the End of the Twentieth Century*, ed. Valentine Moghadam. Oxford: Clarendon, 1996.

Parpart, Jane L., and Kathleen A. Staudt, eds. *Women and the State in Africa*. Boulder, Col.: Lynne Rienner, 1989.

Patterson, Amy. "The Impact of Senegal's Decentralization on Women in Local Governance." *CJAS* 36, 3 (2002): 490–529.

Phiri, Isabel A. "Marching, Suspended and Stoned: Christian Women in Malawi 1995." In *God, People and Power in Malawi: Democratization in Theological Perspective*, ed. K. R. Ross. Blantyre: CLAIM, 1996.

Poluha, Eva. "Beyond the Silence of Women in Ethiopian Politics." In *Multiparty Elections in Africa*, ed. Michael Cowen and Liisa Laakso. James Currey, 2001.

Potgieter, P. J. J. S. "Namibia: The Last African Colony's First Election." In *Electoral Systems in Comparative Perspective: Their Impact on Women and Minorities*, ed. Wilma Rule and Joseph F. Zimmerman. Westport, Conn.: Greenwood, 1994.

Ranchod-Nilsson, Sita. "Zimbabwe: Women, Cultural Crisis, and the Reconfiguration of the One-Party State." In *The African State at a Critical Juncture: Between Disintegration and Reconfiguration*, ed. Leonardo Villalón and Phillip Huxtable. Boulder, Col.: Lynne Rienner, 1997.

———. "Zimbabwe: Women's Rights and African Custom." In *Women's Rights: A Global View*, ed. Lynn Walker, 199–211. Westport, Conn.: Greenwood, 2001.

Reynolds, Jonathan T. "Islam, Politics and Women's Rights." *Comparative Studies of South Asia, Africa and the Middle East* 18, 1 (1998): 64–72.

Roberts, Pepe, and Gavin Williams. "Democracy and the Agrarian Question in Africa: Reflections on the Politics of States and the Representation of Peasants' and Women's Interests." In *Democracy and Socialism in Africa*, ed. Robin Cohen and Harry Goulbourne. Boulder, Col.: Westview, 1991.

Robinson, Pearl T. "Women in Rural Africa: The Political and Policy Imperatives." *Sage* 7, 1 (1990): 2–3.

Rosenthal, Michelle. "Danger Talk: Race and Feminist Empowerment in the New South Africa." In *Feminism and Antiracism: International Struggles for Justice*, ed. France Winndance Twine and Kathleen M. Blee. New York: New York University Press, 2001.

Schoepf, Brooke Grundfest. "Gender Relations and Development: Political Economy and Culture." In *Twenty-First Century: Toward a New Vision of Self-Sustainable Development*, ed. Ann Seidman and Frederick Anang, 203–41. Trenton, N.J.: Africa World Press, 1992.

Schroeder, Richard A. *Shady Practices: Agroforestry and Gender Politics in the Gambia*. Berkeley: University of California Press, 1999.

Schuster, Ilsa. "Political Women: The Zambian Experience." In *Women's Worlds: From the New Scholarship*, ed. Marilyn Safir et al., 189–98. New York: Praeger, 1985.

Seidman, Gay W. "Gendered Citizenship: South Africa's Democratic Transition and the Construction of a Gendered State." *Gender and Society* 13, 3 (1999): 287–307.

——. "Institutional Dilemmas: Representation versus Mobilization in the South African Gender Commission." *FS* 29, 3 (2003): 541–63.

——. "'Strategic' Challenges to Gender Inequality: The South African Gender Commission." *Ethnography* 2, 2 (2001): 219–41.

——. "Women in Zimbabwe: Postindependence Struggles." *FS* 10 (1984): 419–40.

Sekitoleko, Victoria. "The African Woman on the Continent: Her Present State, Prospects and Strategy." In *Pan Africanism: Politics, Economy and Social Change in the Twenty-First Century*, ed. Tajudeen Abdul-Raheem. New York: New York University Press, 1996.

Semu, Linda. "Kamuzu's Mbumba: Malawi Women's Embeddedness to Culture in the Face of International Political Pressure and Internal Legal Change." *Africa Today* 49, 2 (2002): 77–99.

Sheldon, Kathleen. "Women and Revolution in Mozambique: *A Luta Continua*." In *Women and Revolution in Africa, Asia, and the New World*, ed. Mary Ann Tétreault. Columbia: University of South Carolina Press, 1994.

Stamp, Patricia. "Burying Otieno: The Politics of Gender and Ethnicity in Kenya." *Signs* 16, 4 (1991): 808–45.

———. "Mothers of Invention: Women's Agency in the Kenyan State." In *Provoking Agents: Gender and Theory in Practice*, ed. J. K. Gardiner, 69–92. Urbana: University of Illinois Press, 1995.

Staudt, Kathleen A. "Uncaptured or Unmotivated? Women and the Food Crisis in Africa." *Rural Sociology* 52, 1 (1987): 37–55.

Stewart, Ann. "Should Women Give Up on the State? The African Experience." In *Women and the State: International Perspectives*, ed. Shirin M. Rai and Geraldine Lievesley. Bristol, Penn.: Taylor & Francis, 1996.

Tamale, Sylvia. "Between a Rock and a Hard Place: Women's Self-Mobilization to Overcome Poverty in Uganda." In *Women Resist Globalization: Mobilizing for Livelihood and Rights*, ed. Sheila Rowbotham and Stephanie Linkogle, 70–85. London: Zed, 2001.

———. *When Hens Begin to Crow: Gender and Parliamentary Politics in Contemporary Uganda*. Boulder, Col.: Westview, 1998.

———. "'Point of Order, Mr. Speaker': African Women Claiming Their Space in Parliament." *Gender and Development* 8, 3 (2000): 8–15.

Tashjian, Victoria B. "Nigeria: Women Building on the Past." In *Women's Rights: A Global View*, ed. Lynn Walker, 155–68. Westport, Conn.: Greenwood, 2001.

Tenga, Nakazael, and Chris Maina Peter. "The Right to Organise as Mother of All Rights: The Experience of Women in Tanzania." *JMAS* 34, 1 (1996): 143–62.

Thomas, Lynn M. *Politics of the Womb: Women, Reproduction, and the State in Kenya*. Berkeley: University of California Press, 2003.

Tjihero, Kapena L., Doufi Namalambo, and Dianne Hubbard. *Affirmative Action for Women in Local Government in Namibia: The 1998 Local Government Elections*. Windhoek: Legal Assistance Centre, 1998.

Tripp, Aili Mari. "Gender and the Transformation of Civil Society in Tanzania." In *Civil Society and the State in Africa*, ed. John W. Harbeson, Donald Rothchild, and Naomi Chazan. Boulder, Col.: Lynne Rienner, 1994.

———. "The New Political Activism in Africa: Women and Democracy." *Journal of Democracy* 12, 3 (2001): 141–55.

———. "Rethinking Difference: Comparative Perspectives from Africa." *Signs* 32, 3 (2000): 649–75.

———. *Women and Politics in Uganda*. Madison: University of Wisconsin Press, 2000.

Tsikata, Dzodzi. "Gender Equality and the State in Ghana: Some Issues of Policy and Practice." In *Engendering African Social Sciences*, ed. Ayesha M. Imam, Amina Mama, and Fatou Sow, 381–412. Dakar: Codesria, 1997.

Turshen, Meredeth. "Africa: Women in the Aftermath of Civil War." *Race and Class* 41, 4 (2000).

Turshen, Meredeth, and Clotilde Twagiramariya, ed. *What Women Do in Wartime: Gender and Conflict in Africa*. London: Zed, 1998.

Uganda Department of Women in Development. *Kampala Action Plan on Women and Peace*. Kampala: Uganda Ministry of Women in Development, Culture, and Youth, 1993.

Umerah-Udezulu, Ifeyinwa E. "The State and Feminization of Developmental Processes in West Africa." In *The Feminization of Development Processes in Africa: Current and Future Perspectives*, ed. Valentine Udoh James and James S. Etim. Westport, Conn.: Greenwood, 1999.

———. "The State and Integration of Women in Ibo: Patriarchy and Gender Advancement." In *The Feminization of Development Processes in Africa: Current and Future Perspectives*, ed. Valentine Udoh James and James S. Etim. Westport, Conn.: Greenwood, 1999.

———. "The State and Interplay of Gender and Class on the Emergence of Women as Political Leaders in Developing Countries." In *Capacity Building in Developing Countries: Human and Environmental Dimensions*, ed. Valentine Udoh James. Westport, Conn.: Praeger, 1998.

Unterhalter, Elaine. "Class, Race and Gender." In *South Africa in Question?* ed. John Lonsdale. Portsmouth, N.H.: Heinemann, 1989.

———. "Constructing Race, Class, Gender and Ethnicity: State and Opposition Strategies in South Africa." In *Unsettling Settler Societies: Articulations of Gender, Race, Ethnicity and Class*, ed. Daiva Stasiulis and Nira Yuval-Davis, 207–40. London: Sage, 1995.

Urdang, Stephanie. *And Still They Dance: Women, War, and the Struggle for Change in Mozambique*. New York: Monthly Review Press, 1989.

van Allen, Judith. "'Bad Future Things' and Liberatory Moments: Capitalism, Gender and the State in Botswana." *Radical History Review* 76 (2000): 136–68.

———. "Women's Rights Movements as a Measure of African Democracy." *Journal of Asian and African Studies* 36, 1 (2001).

van der Spuy, Patricia. "Silencing Race and Gender?" *South African Historical Journal* 36 (1997).

Vijfhuizen, C. "Rainmaking, Political Conflicts and Gender Images: A Case from Mutema Cheiftaincy in Zimbabwe." *Zambezia* 24, 1 (1997): 31–50.

Vijfhuizen, Carin, and Locadia Makora. "More Than One Paramount Chief in One Chieftaincy? The Gender of Maintaining Worlds." *Zambezia* 25, 1 (1998): 59–81.

Wakoko, Florence, and Linda Labao. "Reconceptualizing Gender and Reconstructing Social Life: Ugandan Women and the Path to National Development." *Africa Today* 43, 3 (1996).

Weinrich, A. K. H. "Changes in the Political and Economic Roles of Women in Zimbabwe since Independence." In *Women—From Witch-Hunt to Politics*, ed. UNESCO, 49–68. Paris: UNESCO, 1985.

Welch, Gita Honwana, and Albie Sachs. "The Bride Price, Revolution, and the Liberation of Women." *International Journal of the Sociology of Law* 15 (1987): 369–92.

Williams, Pat. "The State, Women and Democratisation in Africa: The Nigerian Experience (1987–1993)." *Africa Development* 22, 1 (1997): 141–82.

Yusuf, Bilkisu. "Hausa-Fulani Women: The State of the Struggle." In *Hausa Women in the Twentieth Century*, ed. Catherine Coles and Beverly Mack, 90–106. Madison: University of Wisconsin Press, 1991.

SPECIAL TOPICS

Aba Women's War

Abaraonye, Felicia Ihuoma. "The Women's War of 1929 in South-Eastern Nigeria." In *Women and Revolution: Global Expressions*, ed. M. J. Diamond, 109–32. Dordrecht, Netherlands: Kluwer Academic Publishing, 1998.

Afigbo, A. E. "Revolution and Reaction in Eastern Nigeria: 1900–1929 (The Background to the Women's Riot of 1929)." *Journal of the Historical Society of Nigeria* 3, 3 (1966): 539–57.

Akpan, Ekwere Otu, and Violetta I. Ekpo. *The Women's War of 1929: Preliminary Study*. Calabar: Nigeria Government Printer, 1988.

Ardener, Shirley. "Sexual Insult and Female Militancy." *Man* 8 (1973): 422–40.

Dike, Chike, ed. *The Women's Revolt of 1929: Proceedings of a National Symposium to Mark the 60th Anniversary of the Women's Uprising in South-Eastern Nigeria*. Lagos: Nelag, 1995.

Hanna, Judith Lynne. "Dance, Protest, and Women's Wars: Cases from Nigeria and the United States." In *Women and Social Protest*, ed. Guida West and Rhoda Lois Blumberg, 333–45. New York: Oxford University Press, 1990.

Ifeka-Moller, Caroline. "Female Militancy and Colonial Revolt: The Women's War of 1929." In *Perceiving Women*, ed. Shirley Ardener, 127–57. New York: John Wiley, 1975.

Teboh, Bridget. "West African Women: Some Considerations." *Ufahamu* 22, 3 (1994): 50–62.

Umoren, U. E. "The Symbolism of the Nigerian Women's War of 1929: An Anthropological Study of an Anti-Colonial Struggle." *African Study Monographs (Kyoto)* 16, 2 (1995): 16–72.

van Allen, Judith. "'Aba Riots' or Igbo 'Women's War'? Ideology, Stratification, and the Invisibility of Women." In *Women in Africa: Studies in Social and Economic Change*, ed. Nancy J. Hafkin and Edna G. Bay, 59–85. Stanford, Calif.: Stanford University Press, 1976.

———. "'Sitting on a Man': Colonialism and the Lost Political Institutions of Igbo Women." *CJAS* 6, 2 (1972): 165–81.

Ward, Kathryn B. "Female Resistance to Marginalization: The Igbo Women's War of 1929." In *Racism, Sexism, and the World System*, ed. Joan Smith. Greenwood, 1988.

Art

Adams, Monni. "Women and Masks Among the Western We of Ivory Coast." *African Arts* 19, 2 (1986): 46–55, 90.

Arnold, Marion. *Women and Art in South Africa*. New York: St. Martin's Press, 1997.

Ben-Amos, Paula. "Artistic Creativity in Benin Kingdom." *African Arts* 19, 3 (1986): 60–63, 83–84.

Berns, Marla C. "Art, History, and Gender: Women and Clay in West Africa," *African Archaeological Review* 11 (1993): 129–48.

———. *Ceramic Gestures: New Vessels by Magdalene Odundo*. Los Angeles: Fowler Museum, 1995.

Boone, Sylvia Ardyn. *Radiance from the Waters: Ideals of Feminine Beauty in Mende Art*. New Haven, Conn.: Yale University Press, 1986.

Brett-Smith, Sarah C. *The Making of Bamana Sculpture: Creativity and Gender*. Cambridge: Cambridge University Press, 1994.

Burman, Pauline. "The Thread of the Story: Two South African Women Artists Talk about Their Work." *RAL* 31, 4 (2000): 155–65.

Coombes, Annie E., and Penny Siopis. "Gender, 'Race,' Ethnicity in Art Practice in Post-Apartheid South Africa." *Feminist Review* 55 (1997): 110–29.

Courtney-Clarke, Margaret. *African Canvas: The Art of West African Women*. New York: Rizzoli International, 1990.

Daly, M. Catherine, Joanne B. Eicher, and Tonye V. Erekosima. "Male and Female Artistry in Kalabari Dress." *African Arts* 19, 3 (1986): 48–51, 83.

Dewey, William J. "Shona Male and Female Artistry." *African Arts* 19, 3 (1986): 64–67, 84.

Drewal, Henry John, and Margaret Thompson Drewal. *Gelede: Art and Female Power among the Yoruba*. Bloomington: Indiana University Press, 1983.

Gerdes, Paulus. *Women, Art and Geometry in Southern Africa*. Trenton, N.J.: Africa World Press, 1998.

Glazer, Anita. "Dialectics of Gender in Senufo Masquerades." *African Arts* 19, 3 (1986): 30–39, 82.

Gunner, Liz. "A Royal Woman, an Artist, and the Ambiguities of National Belonging: The Case of Princess Constance Magogo." *Kunapipi: Journal of Postcolonial Studies* 24, 1&2 (2002).

Hassan, Salah, and Dorothy Desir Davis, eds. *Gendered Visions: The Art of Contemporary Africana Women Artists.* Trenton, N.J.: Africa World Press, 1997.

LaDuke, Betty. *Africa through the Eyes of Women Artists.* Trenton, N.J.: Africa World Press, 1991.

———. *Africa: Women's Art, Women's Lives.* Trenton, N.J.: Africa World Press, 1997.

Lagoutte, Christine. "L'artisanat feminine dans la region du fleuve Senegal." *CJAS* 22, 3 (1999): 448–71.

Liddell, Marlane A. "Fine Artists Who Paint Their Lives on a Canvas of Mud." *Smithsonian* 21, 2 (1990): 128–35.

Meurant, Georges, and Robert Farris Thompson. *Mbuti Design: Paintings by Pygmy Women of the Ituri Forest.* New York: Thames and Hudson, 1995.

Miller, Kimberly. "The Philani Printing Project: Women's Art and Activism in Crossroads, South Africa." *FS* 29, 3 (2003): 619–37.

Niger-Thomas, Margaret. "Women and the Arts of Smuggling in Western Cameroon." *CODESRIA Bulletin* 2–4 (2000): 45–60.

Nnabuko, Justie O. "The Place of Women in Communication, Information, and Art." In *Gender Issues in Development and Environment*, ed. Ifeyinwa U. Ofong. Enugu, Nigeria: B-Teks, 1998.

Noy, Ilse. *The Art of the Weya Women.* Harare: Baobab Books, 1992.

Omari-Obayemi, Mikelle S. "An Indigenous Anatomy of Power and Art: A New Look at Yoruba Women in Society and Religion." *Dialectical Anthropology* 21, 1 (1996): 89–98.

Opondo, Patricia Achieng. "Strategies for Survival by Luo Female Artists in the Rural Environment in Kenya." In *Stepping Forward: Black Women in Africa and the Americas*, ed. Catherine Higgs, Barbara A. Moss, and Earline Rae Ferguson, 205–26. Athens: Ohio University Press, 2002.

Picton, John. "Women's Weaving: The Manufacture and Use of Textiles among the Igbirra People of Nigeria." In *Textiles of Africa*, ed. Dale Idiens and K. G. Ponting. Bath: Pasold Research Fund, 1980.

Ragland-Njau, Phillda. "Rhoda Muchoki: Social Commentary from a Young Woman's Brush." *Sage* 7, 1 (1990): 46–48.

Roy, Christopher D. *Women's Art in Africa: Woodfired Pottery from Iowa Collections.* Gallery Guide and Exhibition Checklist, October 23, 1991 to June 28, 1992. University of Iowa Museum of Art, 1991.

Russell, Margo. *The Production and Marketing of Women's Handicrafts in Swaziland.* Geneva: ILO Rural Employment Policies Branch, 1983

Schmahmann, Brenda, ed. *Material Matters: Appliqués by the Weya Women of Zimbabwe and Needlecraft by South African Collectives.* Johannesburg: Witwatersrand University Press, 2000.

Smith, Fred T. "Compound Entryway Decoration: Male Space and Female Creativity." *African Arts* 19, 3 (1986): 52–58, 83.

——. "Male and Female Artistry in Africa." *African Arts* 19, 3 (1986): 28–29, 82.

Tesfagiorgis, Freida High W. "The Search of a Discourse and Critique/s that Center the Art of Black Women Artists." In *Theorizing Black Feminisms: The Visionary Pragmatism of Black Women*, ed. Stanlie M. James and Abena P. A. Busia, 228–66. London: Routledge, 1993.

van Wyk, Gary N. *African Painted Houses: Basotho Dwellings of Southern Africa*. New York: Harry N. Abrams, 1998.

Vaz, Kim Marie. *The Woman with the Artistic Brush: A Life History of Yoruba Batik Artist Nike Davies*. Armonk, N.Y.: M. E. Sharpe, 1995.

Wagner, Ulla. *Catching the Tourist: Women Handcraft Traders in the Gambia*. Stockholm: Stockholm Studies in Social Anthropology, 1982.

Warin, François. "Le sexe de l'artiste: Le devenir femme du sculpteur Bamana." *CEA* 36, 1–2 (1996).

Wolff, Norma. "A Hausa Aluminum Spoon Industry." *African Arts* 19, 3 (1986): 40–44, 82.

Autobiography and Biography

Abrahams, Cecil. *The Tragic Life: Bessie Head and Literature in South Africa*. Trenton, N.J.: Africa World Press, 1990.

Akello, Grace. *Self Twice Removed: Ugandan Women*. London: Calvert's North Star Press, 1982.

Albuquerque, Orlando de. *Alda Lara: A Mulher e a Poetisa*. Lubango, Angola: Imbondeiro, 1966.

Alexander, Caroline. *One Dry Season: In the Footsteps of Mary Kingsley*. New York, Alfred A. Knopf, 1990.

Aman. *The Story of a Somali Girl*. Ed. Virginia Lee Barnes and Janice Boddy. New York: Pantheon, 1994.

Andreski, Iris. *Old Wives' Tales: Life-Stories of African Women*. London: Routledge & Kegan Paul, 1970.

Awe, Bolanle, ed. *Nigerian Women in Historical Perspective*. Lagos: Sankore, 1992.

Ba Konaré, Adame. *Dictionnaire des femmes cèlébres du Mali*. Bamako: Ed. Jamana, 1993.

Baard, Frances, as told to Barbie Schreiner. *My Spirit is Not Banned*. Harare: Zimbabwe Publishing House, 1986.

Bair, Barbara. "Pan-Africanism as Process: Adelaide Casely Hayford, Garveyism, and the Cultural Roots of Nationalism." In *Imagining Home: Race,*

Class, Nationalism, ed. Sidney Lemelle and Robin Kelley. London: Verso, 1994.

Ballinger, Margaret. *From Union to Apartheid; A Trek to Isolation.* Cape Town: Juta, 1969.

Behrend, Heike. *Alice Lakwena and the Holy Spirits: War in Northern Uganda, 1985–97.* Athens: Ohio University Press, 1999.

Berger, Iris. "An African American 'Mother of the Nation': Madie Hall Xuma in South Africa, 1940–1963," *JSAS* 27, 3 (2001): 547–66.

Berrian, Brenda. "Interview with Micere Githae-Mugo." *World Literature Written in English* 22, 3 (1982): 521–30.

Biobaku, Saburi. "Madame Tinubu." In *Eminent Nigerians of the Nineteenth Century*, ed. Nigerian Broadcasting Corporation, 33–41. Cambridge: Cambridge University Press, 1960.

Blouin, Andrée, with Jean MacKellar. *My Country, Africa: Autobiography of the Black Pasionaria.* New York: Praeger, 1983.

Blunt, Alison. *Travel, Gender, and Imperialism: Mary Kingsley and West Africa.* New York: Guilford, 1994.

Blyden, Nemata. "The Search for Anna Erskine: African American Women in Nineteenth-Century Liberia." In *Stepping Forward: Black Women in Africa and the Americas*, ed. Catherine Higgs, Barbara A. Moss, and Earline Rae Ferguson, 31–43. Athens: Ohio University Press, 2002.

Boahen, A. Adu. *Yaa Asantewaa and the Asante–British War of 1900–1.* Oxford: James Currey, 2003.

Boyd, Jean. *The Caliph's Sister: Nana Asma'u (1793–1865) Teacher, Poet and Islamic Leader.* London: Frank Cass, 1989.

Brantley, Cynthia. "Mekatalili and the Role of Women in Giriama Resistance." In *Banditry, Rebellion and Social Protest in Africa*, ed. Donald Crummey, 333–50. Portsmouth, N.H.: Heinemann, 1986.

Chawner, Ingrid Løkken. *Nkosazana: The King's Daughter.* Chicago: Philadelphia Publishing House, 1936.

Coulon, Christian, and Odile Reveyrand. *L'Islam au féminin: Sokhna Magat Diop, Cheikh de la confrérie mouride.* Bordeaux: CEAN, 1990.

Crane, Louise. *Ms. Africa: Profiles of Modern African Women.* New York: Lippincott, 1973.

Creider, Jane Tapsubei. *Two Lives: My Spirit and I.* London: Women's Press, 1986.

Cromwell, Adelaide M. *An Afro-Victorian Feminist: The Life and Times of Adelaide Smith Casely Hayford.* London: Frank Cass, 1984.

Cummings-John, Constance Agatha. *Memoirs of a Krio Leader.* Edited with introduction and notes by LaRay Denzer. Ibadan, Nigeria: Sam Bookman, 1995.

Davies, Carole Boyce. "Private Lives and Public Spaces: Autobiography and the African Woman Writer." In *Crisscrossing Boundaries*, ed. Kenneth Harrow, Jonathan Ngaté, and Clarisse Zimra, 109–27. Washington, D.C.: Three Continents Press, 1990.

Daymond, Margaret J. "Class in the Discourses of Sindiwe Magona's Autobiography and Fiction." *JSAS* 21, 4 (1995): 561–72.

——. "Complementary Oral and Written Narrative Conventions: Sindiwe Magona's Autobiography and Short Story Sequence, 'Women at Work.'" *JSAS* 28, 2 (2002): 331–46.

Denzer, LaRay. "Constance A. Cummings-John of Sierra Leone: Her Early Political Career." *Tarikh* 7, 1 (1981): 20–32.

——. *Folayegbe Akintunde-Ighodalo: A Biography* (Ibadan: Sam Bookman, 2001).

——. "Gender and Decolonisation: A Study of Three Women in West African Public Life." In *People and Empires in African History: Essays in Memory of Michael Crowder*, ed. J. F. Ade Ajayi and J. D. Y. Peel, 217–36. London: Longman, 1992.

——. "The Influence of Pan-Africanism in the Political Career of Constance A. Cummings-John." In *Pan-African Biography*, ed., Robert A. Hill. Los Angeles: Crossroads, 1987.

Dolphyne, Florence Abena, ed. *Ten Women Achievers from the Ashanti Region of Ghana*. Kumasi: CEDEP Women's Forum, 2000.

Drew, Allison. "Andrée Blouin and Pan-African Nationalism in Guinea and the Congo." In *Pan-African Biography*, ed. Robert A. Hill, 209–17. Los Angeles: Crossroads Press, 1987.

Edgar, Robert R., and Hilary Sapire. *African Apocalypse: The Story of Nontetha Nkwenkwe, a Twentieth-Century South African Prophet*. Athens: Ohio University Press, 2000.

Eilersen, Gillian Stead. *Bessie Head: 'Thunder Behind My Ears': A Biography*. Portsmouth, N.H.: Heinemann, 1996.

Emecheta, Buchi. *Head Above Water: An Autobiography*. London: Fontana, 1986.

Evers Rosander, Eva. "Mam Diarra Bousso—The Mourid Mother of Porokhane, Senegal." *Jenda: A Journal of Culture and African Women Studies* 4 (2003), online at www.jendajournal.com.

——. "Mam Diarra Bousso: La bonne mère de Porokhane, Senegal." *Africa* (Rome) 58, 3–4 (2003): 296–317.

Fair, Laura. "Voice, Authority, and Memory: The Kiswahili Recordings of Siti Binti Saadi." In *African Words, African Voices: Critical Practices in Oral History*, ed. Luise White, Stephan F. Miescher, and David William Cohen, 246–63. Bloomington: Indiana University Press, 2001.

Fairbairn, Jean. *Flashes in Her Soul: The Life of Jabu Ndlovu*. Cape Town: Buchu, for Natal Worker History Porject, 1991.

Fall, Babacar. "Senegalese Women in Politics: A Portrait of Two Female Leaders, Arame Diène and Thioumbé Samb, 1945–1996." In *African Words,*

African Voices: Critical Practices in Oral History, ed. Luise White, Stephan F. Miescher, and David William Cohen, 214–23. Bloomington: Indiana University Press, 2001.

First, Ruth. *117 Days*. New York: Monthly Review Press, 1989 [1965].

First, Ruth, and Ann Scott. *Olive Schreiner*. London: Deutsch, 1980.

Freeman, Sharon T. *Conversations with Powerful African Women Leaders: Inspiration, Motivation, and Strategy*. Washington, D.C.: All American Small Business Exporters Association, 2002.

Gastrow, Shelagh. *Who's Who in South African Politics*. Johannesburg: Ravan Press, 1985.

Gollock, G. A. *Daughters of Africa*. London: Longmans, Green, 1932; rep. New York, Negro University Press, 1969.

Henderson, Michael. "These Terrible Times [Profile of Abeba Tesfagiorgis]." In *All Her Paths Are Peace: Women Pioneers in Peacemaking*, ed. Michael Henderson, 43–53. West Hartford, Conn.: Kumarian Press, 1994.

Hill, Kevin A. "Agathe Uwilingiyimana." In *Women and the Law, a Bio-Bibliographical Sourcebook*, ed. Rebecca Mae Salokar and Mary L. Volcansek, 323–28. Westport, Conn.: Greenwood Press, 1996.

Hodgson, Janet. *Princess Emma*. Cape Town: AD. Donker, 1987.

Hoffer, Carol P. "Madam Yoko: Ruler of the Kpa Mende Confederacy." In *Women, Culture, and Society*, ed. Michelle Zimbalist Rosaldo and Louise Lamphere, 173–87. Stanford, Calif.: Stanford University Press, 1974.

Hunter, Lucilda. *Mother and Daughter Memoirs and Poems, by Adelaide and Gladys Caseley-Hayford*. Sierra Leone University Press, 1983.

Hunter, Monica. "The Story of Nosente, the Mother of Compassion of the Xhosa Tribe, South Africa." In *Ten Africans*, ed. Margery Perham. London: Faber and Faber, 1963.

Iman and others. *I Am Iman*, ed. by Dean Kuipers. New York: Universe Publishing, 2001.

Jabavu, Noni. *The Ochre People*. Johanessburg: Ravan Press, 1982 [1963].

Johnson, Cheryl. "Madam Alimotu Pelewura and the Lagos Market Women." *Tarikh* 7, 1 (1981): 1–10.

Johnson-Odim, Cheryl, and Nina Emma Mba. *For Women and the Nation: Funmilayo Ransome-Kuti of Nigeria*. Urbana: University of Illinois Press, 1997.

Joseph, Helen. *Side by Side: The Autobiography of Helen Joseph*. New York: William Morrow, 1986.

Kanduza, Ackson. "'You Are Tearing My Skirt': Labotsibeni Gwamili LaMdluli." In *Agency and Action in Colonial Africa: Essays for John E. Flint*, ed. Chris Youé and Tim Stapleton, 83–99. New York: Palgrave, 2001.

Kaunda, Betty. *Betty Kaunda: Wife of the President of the Republic of Zamiba*. Lusaka: Longmans of Zambia, c. 1969.

Kéita, Aoua. *Femme d'Afrique: La vie d'Aoua Kéita racontée par elle-même.* Paris: Ed. Présence Africaine, 1975.

Kolawole, Mary E. Modupe, ed. *Zulu Sofola: Her Life and her Works.* Ibadan: Caltop Publications, 1999.

Lau, Brigitte. "Johanna Uerieta Gertze and Emma Hahn: Some Thoughts on the Silence of Historical Records, with Reference to Carl Hugo Hahn." *Logos* (Windhoek) 6, 2 (1986): 62–71.

Lessing, Doris. *Under My Skin: Volume One of My Autobiography, to 1949.* New York: HarperCollins, 1994.

———. *Walking in the Shade: Volume Two of My Autobiography, 1949–1962.* New York: HarperCollins, 1997.

Lucan, Talabi. *The Life and Times of Madam Ella Koblo Gulama.* Freetown: Reffo Printing, 2003.

Mack, Beverly B., and Jean Boyd. *One Woman's Jihad: Nana Asma'u, Scholar and Scribe.* Bloomington: Indiana University Press, 2000.

Makeba, Miriam, with James Hall. *Makeba: My Story.* New York: New American Library, 1987.

Mandela, Winnie. *Part of My Soul Went with Him.* Ed. Anne Benjamin. New York: W. W. Norton, 1985.

Mashinini, Emma. *Strikes Have Followed Me All My Life: A South African Autobiography.* New York: Routledge, 1991.

Matembe, Miria R. K. *Miria Matembe: Gender, Politics, and Constitution Making in Uganda.* Kampala: Fountain, 2002.

McCord, Margaret. *The Calling of Katie Makanya.* New York: John Wiley, 1995.

McNee, Lisa. *Selfish Gifts: Senegalese Women's Autobiographical Discourses.* Albany: State University of New York Press, 2000.

Michaelson, Marc. "Wangari Maathai and Kenya's Green Belt Movement: Exploring the Evolution and Potentialities of Consensus Movement Mobilization." *Social Problems* 41, 4 (1994): 540–61.

Miller, Joseph. "Nzinga of Matamba in a New Perspective." *JAH* 16, 2 (1975): 201–16.

Mirza, Sarah, and Margaret Strobel. *Three Swahili Women: Life Histories from Mombasa, Kenya.* Bloomington: Indiana University Press, 1989.

Molvaer, Reidulf K. "Siniddu Gebru: Pioneer Woman Writer, Feminist, Patriot, Educator, and Politician." *Northeast African Studies* 4, 3 (1997): 61–75.

Moretti, Cecilia. "Black South African Women and the Autobiographical Text: A Contextual Reading of Emma Mashinini's *Strikes Have Followed Me All My Life.*" *AFSAAP Review and Newsletter* 18, 2 (1996): 4–9.

Mukurasi, Laeticia. *Post Abolished: One Woman's Struggle for Employment Rights in Tanzania.* Ithaca, N.Y.: ILR Press, 1991.

Mumba, Norah M. *A Song in the Night: A Personal Account of Widowhood in Zambia*. Multimedia, 1992.

Mutunhu, Tendai. "Nehanda of Zimbabwe (Rhodesia): The Story of a Woman Liberation Leader and Fighter." *Ufahamu* 7, 1 (1976): 59–70.

Ntantala, Phyllis. *A Life's Mosaic: The Autobiography of Phyllis Ntantala*. Berkeley: University of California Press, 1993.

Nthunya, Mpho 'M'atsepo. *Singing Away the Hunger: The Autobiography of an African Woman*. Bloomington: Indiana University Press, 1997.

Nyabongo, Elizabeth. *Elizabeth of Toro: The Odyssey of an African Princess*. New York: Simon and Schuster, 1989.

Osaki, Lilian Temu. "Siti Binti Saad: Herald of Women's Liberation." *Sage* 7, 1 (1990): 49–54.

Otieno, Wambui Waiyaki, with Cora Ann Presley. *Mau Mau's Daughter: A Life History*. Boulder, Col.: Lynne Rienner, 1998.

Pankhurst, Rita. "Senedu Gabru: A Role Model for Ethiopian Women?" In *Gender Issues in Ethiopia*, ed. Tsehai Berhane-Selassie. Addis Ababa: Institute of Ethiopian Studies, Addis Ababa University, 1991.

Peires, J. B. *The Dead Will Arise: Nongqawuse and the Great Xhosa Cattle-Killing Movement of 1856–57*. Bloomington: Indiana University Press, 1989.

Pohlandt-McCormick, Helena. "Controlling Woman: Winnie Mandela and the 1976 Soweto Uprising." *IJAHS* 33, 3 (2000): 585–614.

Prouty, Chris. *Empress Taytu and Menilek II, Ethiopia 1883–1910*. Trenton, N.J.: Red Sea Press, 1986.

Ramphele, Mamphela. *Across Boundaries: The Journey of a South African Woman Leader*. New York: Feminist Press, 1996; published in South Africa as *Mamphela Ramphele: A Life,* Cape Town: David Philip, 1995.

Resha, Maggie. *"Mangoana o Tsoara Thipa Ka Bohaleng": My Life in the Struggle*. London: Robert Vicat, 1990.

Reyher, Rebecca Hourwich. *Zulu Woman: The Life Story of Christina Sibiya*. New York: Feminist Press, 1999 [1948].

Roberts, Andrew D. "The Lumpa Church of Alice Lenshina." In *Protest and Power in Black Africa*, ed., Robert I. Rotberg and Ali A. Mazrui, 513–68. New York: Oxford University Press, 1970.

Romero, Patricia, ed. *Life Histories of African Women*. London: Ashfield Press, 1988.

Ruete, Emily. *Memoirs of an Arabian Princess from Zanzibar*, ed. Patricia Romero. 2nd ed.; Princeton, N.J.: Markus Wiener, 1989 [1888].

Scheub, Harold. "'And So I Grew Up': The Autobiography of Nongenile Masithathu Zenani." In *Life Histories of African Women*, ed., Romero, 7–46.

Schildkrout, Enid. "Hajiya Husaina: Notes on the Life History of a Hausa Woman." In *Life Histories of African Women*, ed., Romero, 78–98.

Shostak, Marjorie. *Nisa: The Life and Words of a !Kung Woman*. Cambridge, Mass.: Harvard University Press, 1981.

———. *Return to Nisa*. Cambridge, Mass.: Harvard University Press, 2000.

Sicard, Grace Mesopirr. *A Tale of a Maasai Girl*. Sussex, England: Book Guild, 1998.

Sikakane, Joyce. *A Window on Soweto*. London: International Defence and Aid Fund, 1977.

Sisulu, Elinor. *Walter & Albertina Sisulu: In Our Lifetime*. Cape Town: David Philip, 2002.

Smith, Alison, and Mary Bull. *Margery Perham and British Rule in Africa*. London: Frank Cass, 1991.

Smith, Mary F. *Baba of Karo: A Woman of the Muslim Hausa*. New Haven, Conn.: Yale University Press, 1981 [1954].

Staunton, Irene. *Mothers of the Revolution: The War Experiences of Thirty Zimbabwean Women*. Bloomington: Indiana University Press, 1991.

Stewart, Dianne. *Lilian Ngoyi*. Cape Town: Maskew Miller Longman, 1996.

Strangwayes-Booth, Joanna. *A Cricket in the Thorn Tree: Helen Suzman and the Progressive Party of South Africa*. London: Hutchinson, 1976.

Strother, Z. S. "Display of the Body Hottentot [Sara Baartman]." In *Africans on Stage: Studies in Ethnological Show Business*, ed. Bernth Lindfors, 1–61. Bloomington: Indiana University Press, 1999.

Suzman, Helen. *In No Uncertain Terms: A South African Memoir*. New York: Alfred A. Knopf, 1993.

Thompson. Nora B. *Africa to Me: Some Women Leaders of Tropical Africa*. Dexter, Mo.: Candor Press, 1963.

Thornton, John. "Legitimacy and Political Power: Queen Njinga, 1624–1663." *JAH* 32, 1 (1991): 25–40.

Thornton, John K. *The Kongolese Saint Anthony: Dona Beatriz Kimpa Vita and the Antonian Movement, 1684–1706*. Cambridge: Cambridge University Press, 1998.

Thurman, Judith. *Isak Dinesen: The Life of a Storyteller*. New York: St. Martin's Press, 1982.

Turrittin, Jane. "Aoua Kéita and the Nascent Women's Movement in the French Soudan." *ASR* 36, 1 (1993): 59–89.

Vigne, Raymond, ed. *A Gesture of Belonging: Letters from Bessie Head, 1965–1979*. Portsmouth, N.H.: Heinemann, 1991.

Wanyoike, Mary W. *Wangu wa Makeri*. Makers of Kenya's History No. 12. Nairobi: East African Educational Publishers, 2002.

Wilks, Ivor. "She Who Blazed a Trail: Akyaawa Yikwan of Asante." In *Life Histories of African Women*, ed., Romero, 113–39.

Yattara, Almamy Maliki, and Bernard Salvaing. *Almamy: Une jeunesse sur les rives du fleuve Niger*. Binon-sur-Sauldre: Grandvaux, 2000.

Education

Adomako Ampofo, A. "Does Women's Education Matter in Childbearing Decision Making? A Case Study from Urban Ghana." *Ghana Studies* 5 (2002).

Agesa, Jacqueline, and Richard U. Agesa. "Gender Differences in Public and Private University Enrollment in Kenya: What Do They Mask?" *Review of Black Political Economy* 30, 1 (2002): 29–55.

Akuffo, Felix Odei. "Teenage Pregnancies and School Drop-Outs: The Relevance of Family Life Education." In *Sex Roles, Population and Development in West Africa: Policy-Related Studies on Work and Demographic Issues*, ed. Christine Oppong, 154–64. Portsmouth, N.H.: Heinemann, 1987.

Ankrah, E. Maxine, and Peninah D. Bizimana. "Women's Studies Program for Uganda." *Signs* 16, 4 (1991): 864–69.

Assie-Lumumba, N'dri Thérèse. "Educating Africa's Girls and Women: A Conceptual and Historical Analysis of Gender Inequality." In *Engendering African Social Sciences*, ed. Ayesha M. Imam, Amina Mama, and Fatou Sow, 297–316. Dakar: Codesria, 1997.

Aumeerruddy-Cziffra, Shirin. "Mauritius: Women, Legal Education and Legal Reform." In *Empowerment and the Law: Strategies for Third World Women*, ed. Margaret Schuler, 283–87. New York: Columbia University Press, 1986.

Awosika, Keziah. "Women's Education and Participation in the Labour Force: The Case of Nigeria." In *Women, Power and Political Systems*, ed. Margherita Rendel, 81–93. London: Croom Helm, 1981.

Barng'etuny, Marylene. *Women's Education and Career Opportunities in Kenya*. Nairobi: Creative Publishing, 1999.

Barthel, Diane. "Women's Educational Experience under Colonialism: Toward a Diachronic Model." *Signs* 11, 1 (1985): 137–54.

Bendera, S. J., and M. W. Mboya. *Gender Education in Tanzanian Schools*. Dar es Salaam: Dar es Salaam University Press, 1999.

Biraimah, Karen. "Class, Gender, and Life Chances: A Nigerian University Case Study." *Comparative Education Review* 31, 4 (1987).

———. "The Impact of Western Schools on Girls' Expectations: A Togolese Case." *Comparative Education Review* 24, 2, part 2 (1980): S196–208.

Bledsoe, Caroline. "School Fees and the Marriage Process for Mende Girls in Sierra Leone." In *Beyond the Second Sex: New Directions in the Anthropology of Gender*, ed. Peggy Reeves Sanday and Ruth Gallagher Goodenough. Philadephia: University of Pennsylvania Press, 1990.

Bloch, Marianne N., Josephine A. Beoku-Betts, and B. Robert Tabachnick, eds. *Women and Education in Sub-Saharan Africa: Power, Opportunities, and Constraints*, Boulder, Col.: Lynne Rienner, 1998.

Bunwaree, Sheila. "Gender Inequality: The Mauritian Experience." In *Gender, Education and Development: Beyond Access to Empowerment*, ed. Christine Heward and Sheila Bunwaree, 135–54. London: Zed Books, 1999.

Chisholm, Linda. "Gender and Deviance in South African Industrial Schools and Reformatories for Girls, 1911–1934." In *Women and Gender in Southern Africa to 1945*, ed. Cherryl Walker, 293–312. London: James Currey, 1990.

———. "Gender and Leadership in South African Educational Administration." *Gender and Education* 13, 4 (2001): 387–99.

Cock, Jacklyn. "Domestic Service and Education for Domesticity: The Incorporation of Xhosa Women into Colonial Society." In *Women and Gender in Southern Africa to 1945*, ed. Cherryl Walker, 76–96. London: James Currey, 1990.

Commeyras, Michelle, and Mercy Montsi. "What If I Woke Up as the Other Sex? Batswana Youth Perspectives on Gender." *Gender and Education* 12, 3 (2000): 327–46.

Conway, Jill Ker, and Susan C. Bourque, ed. *The Politics of Women's Education: Perspectives from Asia, Africa, and Latin America*. Ann Arbor: University of Michigan Press, 1993.

Dangana, Muhammad. "The Intellectual Contribution of Nana Asmau to Women's Education in Nineteenth-Century Nigeria." *Journal of Muslim Minority Affairs* 19, 2 (1999).

Davison, J., and M. Kanyuka. "Girls Participation in Basic Education in Southern Malawi." *Comparative Education Review* 36, 4 (1992): 446–66.

Denzer, LaRay. "Domestic Science Training in Colonial Yorubaland, Nigeria." In *African Encounters with Domesticity*, ed. Karen Tranberg Hansen, 116–39. New Brunswick, N.J.: Rutgers University Press, 1992.

Etim, James S. "Women's Education in Nigeria: Improving Trends." In *The Feminization of Development Processes in Africa: Current and Future Perspectives*, ed. Valentine Udoh James and James S. Etim. Westport, Conn.: Greenwood, 1999.

Evenson, R. E., and Michele Siegel. "Gender and Agricultural Extension in Burkina Faso." *Africa Today* 46, 1 (1999): 75–92.

Fallon, Kathleen M. "Education and Perceptions of Social Status and Power among Women in Larteh, Ghana." *Africa Today* 46, 2 (1999): 67–91.

Gaidzanwa, Rudo B. "Gender Analysis in the Field of Education: A Zimbabwean Example." In *Engendering African Social Sciences*, ed. Ayesha M. Imam, Amina Mama, and Fatou Sow, 271–95. Dakar: Codesria, 1997.

Gaitskell, Deborah. "Ploughs and Needles: State and Mission Approaches to African Girls' Education in South Africa." In *Christian Missionaries and the State in the Third World*, ed. Holger Bernt Hansen and Michael Twaddle, 98–120. Athens: Ohio University Press, 2002.

Glick, Paul, and David E. Salin. "Gender and Education Impacts on Employment and Earnings in West Africa: Evidence from Guinea." *Economic Development and Cultural Change* 45, 4 (1997): 793–824.

Hollos, Marida. "Migration, Education, and the Status of Women in Southern Nigeria." *American Anthropologist* 93, 4 (1991): 852–70.

Hughes, Heather. "'A Lighthouse for African Womanhood': Inanda Seminary, 1869–1945." In *Women and Gender in Southern Africa to 1945*, ed. Cherryl Walker, 197–220. London: James Currey, 1990.

Human Rights Watch. *Scared at School: Sexual Violence Against Girls in South African Schools*. New York: Human Rights Watch, 2001.

Johnson, Vivian R. "Rural African Women: The Struggle for Literacy." *Sage* 7, 1 (1990): 38–42.

Kapungwe, Augustus K. "Traditional Cultural Practices of Imparting Sex Education and the Fight Against HIV/AIDS: The Case of Initiation Ceremonies for Girls in Zambia." *African Sociological Review* 7, 1 (2003): 35–52.

Karelse, Cathy-Mae, and Fatimata Seye Sylla. "Rethinking Education for the Production, Use, and Management of ICTs." In *Gender and the Information Revolution in Africa*, ed. Eva M. Rathgeber and Edith Ofwona Adera, 125–67. Ottawa: International Development Research Centre, 2000.

Kiluva-Ndunda, Mutindi Mumbua. *Women's Agency and Educational Policy: The Experiences of the Women of Kilome, Kenya*. Albany: State University of New York Press, 2000.

Koenig, Dolores B. "Education and Fertility among Cameroonian Working Women." In *Women, Education and Modernization of the Family in West Africa*, ed. Helen Ware, 134–53. Canberra: Australian National University Press, 1981.

Kwesiga, Joy C. *Women's Access to Higher Education in Africa: Uganda's Experience*. Kampala: Fountain, 2002.

Lamba, Isaac C. "African Women's Education in Malawi, 1875–1952." *Journal of Education Administration and History* 14, 1 (1982): 46–54.

Logan, B. I., and J. A. Beoku-Betts. "Women and Education in Africa: An Analysis of Economic and Sociocultural Factors Influencing Observed Trends." *Journal of Asian and African Studies* 31, 3–4 (1996): 217–39.

Mabokela, Reitumetse Obakeng. "'Hear Our Voices!': Women and the Transformation of South African Higher Education." *Journal of Negro History* 70, 3 (2001): 204–18.

Maduewesi, Ebele J. "The Girl Child: Education and Training." In *Gender Issues in Development and Environment*, ed. Ifeyinwa U. Ofong. Enugu, Nigeria: B-Teks, 1998.

Mahlase, Shirley. *The Careers of Women Teachers under Apartheid*. Southern African Printing and Publishing House, 1998.

Maloba-Caines, Kathini. "Workers' Education for Women Members of Rural Workers' Organizations in Africa." In *Women in Trade Unions: Organizing the Unorganized*, ed. Margaret Hosmer Martens and Swasti Mitter, 99–106. Geneva: International Labour Office, 1994.

Mariro, Augustin, ed. *Access of Girls and Women to Scientific, Technical and Vocational Education in Africa*. Dakar: Regional Office for Education in Africa, 1999.

McSweeney, Brenda Gael, and Marion Freedman. "Lack of Time as an Obstacle to Women's Education: The Case of Upper Volta." *Comparative Education Review* 24, 2, part 2 (1980): S124–39.

Meekers, Dominique, and Ghyasuddin Ahmed. "Pregnancy-Related School Dropouts in Botswana." *Population Studies: A Journal of Demography* 53, 2 (1999): 195–209.

Mensch, Barbara S., et al. "Premarital Sex, Schoolgirl Pregnancy, and School Quality in Rural Kenya." *Studies in Family Planning* 32, 4 (2001): 285–301.

Mirembe, Ronina, and Lynn Davies. "Is Schooling a Risk? Gender, Power Relations, and School Culture in Uganda." *Gender and Education* 13, 4 (2001): 401–16.

Musisi, Nakanyike B. "Colonial and Missionary Education: Women and Domesticity in Uganda, 1900–1945." In *African Encounters with Domesticity*, ed. Karen Tranberg Hansen, 172–94. New Brunswick, N.J.: Rutgers University Press, 1992.

Naré, C. Zoe. "Etre une femme intellectuelle en Afrique: De la persistance des stéréotypes culturels sexistes." *Africa Development* 22, 1 (1997): 65–78.

Ngware, Moses Waithanji. "Gender Participation in the Technical Training Institutions: An Assessment of the Kenyan Case." *Eastern Africa Social Science Research Review* 18, 1 (2002).

Nnaemeka, Obioma. "Bringing African Women into the Classroom: Rethinking Pedagogy and Epistemology." In *Borderwork: Feminist Engagements with Comparative Literature*, ed. Margaret R. Higonnet, 301–18. Ithaca, N.Y.: Cornell University Press, 1994.

Obbo, Christine. "Bitu: Facilitator of Women's Educational Opportunities." In *Life Histories of African Women*, ed. Patricia W. Romero, 99–112. Atlantic Highlands, N.J.: Ashfield Press, 1988.

Oduaran, A. B., and L. A. Okukpon. "Building Women's Capacity for National Development in Nigeria." *Convergence: International Journal of Adult Education* 30, 1 (1997): 60–69.

Ogunsulire, Olayinka. "Gender Issues in Environmental Education." In *Gender Issues in Development and Environment*, ed. Ifeyinwa U. Ofong. Enugu, Nigeria: B-Teks, 1998.

Omale, Juliana. "Tested to Their Limit: Sexual Harassment in Schools and Educational Institutions in Kenya." In *No Paradise Yet: The World's Women Face the New Century*, ed. Judith Mirsky and Marty Radlett, 19–38. London: PANOS/Zed, 2000.

Orubuloye, Israel O. "Education and Socio-Demographic Change in Nigeria: The Western Nigerian Experience." In *Women, Education and Modernization of the Family in West Africa*, ed. Helen Ware, 22–41. Canberra: Australian National University Press, 1981.

Otunga, Ruth N. "School Participation by Gender: Implications for Occupational Activities in Kenya." *Africa Development* 22, 1 (1997): 39–64.

Porter, Mary A. "Resisting Uniformity at Mwana Kupona Girls' School: Cultural Productions in an Educational Setting." *Signs* 23, 1 (1998): 619–43.

Prah, M. "Gender Issues in Ghanaian Tertiary Institutions: Women Academics and Administrators at Cape Coast University." *Ghana Studies* 5 (2002).

Puchner, Laurel. "Researching Women's Literacy in Mali: A Case Study of Dialogue among Researchers, Practitioners, and Policy Makers." *Comparative Education Review* 45, 2 (2001): 242–56.

Rajuili, Khanya, and Ione Burke. "Democratization through Adult Popular Education: A Reflection on the Resilience of Women from Kwa-Ndebele, South Africa." In *Democratization and Women's Grassroots Movements*, ed. Jill M. Bystydzienski and Joti Sekhon, 111–28. Bloomington: Indiana University Press, 1999.

Rose, Pauline, and Mercy Tembon. "Girls and Schooling in Ethiopia." In *Gender, Education and Development: Beyond Access to Empowerment*, ed. Christine Heward and Sheila Bunwaree, 85–100. London: Zed Books, 1999.

Sall, Ebrima. *Women in Academia: Gender and Academic Freedom in Africa*. Dakar: CODESRIA, 2000.

Shapiro, David, and B. Oleke Tambashe. "Education, Employment, and Fertility in Kinshasa and Prospects for Changes in Reproductive Behavior." *Population Research and Policy Review* 16, 3 (1997): 259–87.

Sharp, Lesley A. "Girls, Sex, and the Dangers of Urban Schooling in Coastal Madagascar." In *Contested Terrains and Constructed Categories: Contemporary Africa in Focus*, ed. George Clement Bond and Nigel C. Gibson, 321–44. Boulder, Col.: Westview, 2002.

Sheldon, Kathleen. "'I Studied with the Nuns, Learning to Make Blouses': Gender Ideology and Colonial Education in Mozambique." *IJAHS* 31, 3 (1998): 595–625.

Sicherman, Carol. "Drama and AIDS Education in Uganda: An Interview with Rose Mbowa." In *History and Theatre in Africa*, ed. Yvette Hutchinson and Eckhard Bretiinger. Stellenbosch: University of Stellenbosch, 2000.

Sperandio, Jill. "Leadership for Adolescent Girls: The Role of Secondary Schools in Uganda." *Gender and Development* 8, 3 (2000): 57–64.

Steeves, H. Leslie. *Gender Violence and the Press: The St. Kizito Story*. Athens: Ohio University Press, 1997.

Sudarkasa, Niara. "Sex Roles, Education, and Development in Africa." *Anthropology and Education Quarterly* 13, 3 (1982): 279–89.

Summers, Carol. "'If You Can Educate the Native Woman . . .': Debates Over the Schooling and Education of Girls and Women in Southern Rhodesia, 1900–1934." *History of Education Quarterly* 36, 4 (1996): 449–71.

Tamale, S., and J. Oloka-Onyango. "Bitches at the Academy: Gender and Academic Freedom at the African University." *Africa Development* 22, 1 (1997): 13–38.

Tansel, Aysit. "Schooling Attainment, Parental Education and Gender in Côte d'Ivoire and Ghana." *Economic Development and Cultural Change* 45, 4 (1997): 825–56.

Thomas, Samuel S. "Transforming the Gospel of Domesticity: Luhya Girls and the Friends Africa Mission, 1917–1926." *ASR* 43, 2 (2000): 1–27.

Tibenderana, Peter Kazenga. "The Beginning of Girls' Education in the Native Administration Schools in Northern Nigeria, 1930–1945." *JAH* 26 (1985): 93–109.

Uchendu, Patrick K. *Education and the Changing Economic Role of Nigerian Women*. Enugu, Nigeria: Fourth Dimension Publishers, 1995.

Unterhalter, Elaine. "Remembering and Forgetting: Constructions of Education Gender Reform in Autobiography and Policy Texts of the South African Transition." *History of Education* 29, 5 (2000): 457–72.

———. "The Schooling of South African Girls." In *Gender, Education and Development: Beyond Access to Empowerment*, ed. Christine Heward and Sheila Bunwaree, 49–64. London: Zed Books, 1999.

Urban-Mead, Wendy. "'Girls of the Gate': Questions of Purity and Piety at the Mtshabezi Girls' Primary Boarding School in Colonial Zimbabwe, 1908–1940." *Le Fait Missionaire* 11 (2001): 75–99.

Vavrus, Frances. "Uncoupling the Articulation between Girls' Education and Tradition in Tanzania." *Gender and Education* 14, 4 (2002): 367–90.

Vavrus, Frances, and Ulla Larsen. "Girls' Education and Fertility Transitions: An Analysis of Recent Trends in Tanzania and Uganda." *Economic Development and Cultural Change* 51, 4 (2003): 945–75.

Vijverbert, Wim P. M. "Education Investments and Returns for Women and Men in Côte d'Ivoire." In *Investment in Women's Human Capital*, ed. T. Paul Schultz, 304–42. Chicago: University of Chicago Press, 1995.

Ware, Helen, ed. *Women, Education and Modernization of the Family in West Africa*. Canberra, 1981.

Werthmann, Katja. "'Seek for Knowledge, Even If It is in China!' Muslim Women and Secular Education in Northern Nigeria." In *Africa, Islam and Development*, ed. Thomas Salter and Kenneth King. Edinburgh: University of Edinburgh Centre of African Studies.

Westaway, M., and M. Skuy. "Self-Esteem and the Educational and Vocational Aspirations of Adolescent Girls in South Africa." *South African Journal of Psychology* 14, 4 (1984): 113–17.

Wynd, Shona. "Education, Schooling and Fertility in Niger." In *Gender, Education and Development: Beyond Access to Empowerment*, ed. Christine Heward and Sheila Bunwaree, 101–16. London: Zed Books, 1999.

Yates, Barbara A. "Church, State and Education in Belgian Africa: Implications for Contemporary Third World Women." In *Women's Education in the Third World: Comparative Perspectives*, ed. Gail P. Kelly and Carolyn M. Elliott, 127–51. Albany: State University of New York Press, 1982.

Zewdie, Gennet. "Women in Primary and Secondary Education." In *Gender Issues in Ethiopia*, ed. Tsehai Berhane-Selassie. Addis Ababa: Institute of Ethiopian Studies, Addis Ababa University, 1991.

Female Genital Cutting (FGM and Circumcision)

Abdalla, Raqiya Haji Dualeh. *Sisters in Affliction: Circumcision and Infibulation of Women in Africa*. London: Zed, 1982.

Amiak, Almaz G. "Le Point sur l'excision dans la Corne de l'Afrique." *Présence Africaine* 160 (1999): 100–08.

Assaad, Fawzia. "The Sexual Mutilation of Women." *World Health Journal* 3, 4 (1982): 391–94.

A'Haleem, Asma M. "Claiming Our Bodies and Our Rights: Exploring Female Circumcision as an Act of Violence." In *Freedom from Violence: Women's Strategies from around the World*, ed. Margaret Schuler, 141–56. UNIFEM, 1992.

Babatunde, Emmanuel. *Women's Rites Versus Women's Rights: A Study of Circumcision Among the Ketu Yoruba of South Western Nigeria*. Trenton, N.J.: Africa World Press, 1997.

Bashir, Layli Miller. "Female Genital Mutilation: Balancing Intolerance of the Practice with Tolerance of Culture." *Journal of Women's Health* 6 (1997).

Baum, Rob. "Transformative Geographies in West African Female Initiation Ceremonies." *Journal of Research Methodology and African Studies* 1, 1 (1996): 35–89.

Bell, Heather. "Midwifery Training and Female Circumcision in the Inter-War Anglo-Egyptian Sudan." *JAH* 39, 2 (1998): 293–312.

Boddy, Janice. "Body Politics: Continuing the Anti-Circumcision Crusade." *Medical Anthropology Quarterly* 5, 1 (1991): 15–17.

———. "Womb as Oasis: The Symbolic Context of Pharaonic Circumcision in Northern Sudan." *American Ethnologist* 9, 4 (1982): 682–98.

Boyle, Elizabeth Heger. *Female Genital Cutting: Cultural Conflict in the Global Community.* Baltimore: Johns Hopkins University Press, 2002.

Boyle, Elizabeth Heger, and Sharon E. Preves. "National Politics as International Process: The Case of Anti-Female-Genital-Cutting Laws." *Law and Society Review* 34, 3 (2000): 703–37.

Chugulu, Juliet, and Rachael Dixey. "Female Genital Mutilation in Moshi Rural District, Tanzania." *International Quarterly of Community Health Education* 19, 2 (1999–2000): 103–18.

Davison, Jean. *Voices from Mutira: Change in the Lives of Rural Gikuyu Women, 1910–1995.* 2nd. ed. Boulder, Col.: Lynne Rienner, 1996.

Dawit, Seble. *Female Genital Mutilation: Violence and Women's Human Rights.* London: Zed, 1993.

DeLuca, Laura, and Shadrack Kamenya. "Representation of Female Circumcision in Finzan, A Dance for the Heroes." *RAL* 26, 3 (1995).

Dirie, Waris. *Desert Flower.* New York: William Morrow, 1999.

Dorkenoo, Efua. "Combating Female Genital Mutilation: An Agenda for the Next Decade." *Women's Studies Quarterly* 27, 1/2 (1999): 87–97.

———. *Cutting the Rose: Female Genital Mutilation, The Practice and Its Prevention.* London: Minority Rights Group, 1994.

Dorkenoo, Efua, and Scilla Elworthy. "Female Genital Mutilation." In *Woman and Violence: Realities and Responses Worldwide*, ed. Miranda Davies. London: Zed, 1994.

Droz, Yvan. "Circoncision féminine et masculine en pays Kikuyu: Rite d'institution, division sociale et droits de l'homme." *CEA* 40, 2; 158 (2000): 215–40.

d'Alvarenga, Henriette Kouyate Carvalho. "L'excision." *Présence Africaine* 160 (1999): 117–26.

El Dareer, Asma. *Woman, Why Do You Weep? Circumcision and Its Consequences.* London: Zed, 1982.

El-Tom, Abdullahi Osman. "Female Circumcision and Ethnic Identification in Sudan with Special Reference to the Berti of Darfur." *GeoJournal* 46, 2 (1998): 163–70.

Gosselin, Claudie. "Feminism, Anthropology and the Politics of Excision in Mali: Global and Local Debates in a Postcolonial World." *Anthropologica* 42, 1 (2000): 43–60.

Gruenbaum, Ellen. *The Female Circumcision Controversy: An Anthropological Perspective*. Philadelphia: University of Pennsylvania Press, 2001.

———. "The Movement against Clitoridectomy and Infibulation in Sudan: Public Health Policy and the Women's Movement." *Medical Anthropology Newsletter* 13, 2 (1982): 4–12.

———. "Reproductive Ritual and Social Reproduction: Female Circumcision and the Subordination of Women in the Sudan." In *Economy and Class in the Sudan*, ed. N. O'Neil and J. O'Brien. Aldershot: Avebury, 1988.

Gunning, Isabelle. "Women and Traditional Practices: Female Genital Surgery." In *Women and International Human Rights Law, vol. 1*, ed. Kelly D. Askin and Dorean Koenig. Ardsley, N.Y.: Transnational Publishers, 1998.

———. "Arrogant Perception, World-Travelling and Multicultural Feminism: The Case of Female Genital Surgeries." *Columbia Human Rights Law Review* 23 (1992): 189–248.

———. "Female Genital Surgeries and Multicultural Feminism: The Ties That Bind; The Differences That Distance." *Third World Legal Studies* (1994–95): 17–48.

Hale, Sondra. "A Question of Subjects: The 'Female Circumcision' Controversy and the Politics of Knowledge." *Ufahamu* 22, 3 (1994): 26–35.

Hetherington, Penelope. "The Politics of Female Circumcision in the Central Province of Colonial Kenya, 1920–30." *Journal of Imperial and Commonwealth History* 26, 1 (1998): 93–126.

Hicks, Esther K. *Infibulation: Female Mutilation in Islamic Northeastern Africa*. New Brunswick, N.J.: Transaction, 1993.

Hosken, Fran. *The Hosken Report: Genital and Sexual Mutilation of Females*. Lexington: Women's International Network News, 1982.

James, Stanlie M. "Shades of Othering: Reflections on Female Circumcision/Genital Mutilation." *Signs* 23, 4 (1998): 1031–48.

James, Stanlie M., and Claire C. Robertson, Eds. *Genital Cutting and Transnational Sisterhood: Disputing U.S. Polemics*. Urbana: University of Illinois Press, 2002.

Jones, Heidi, et al. "Female Genital Cutting Practice in Burkina Faso and Mali and their Negative Health Outcomes." *Studies in Family Planning* 30, 3 (1999): 193–211.

Kandji, Saliou. "L'excision: De la circoncision négro-pharaonique a la clitoridectomie semito-orientale, des sources traditionelles islamiques." *Présence Africaine* 160 (1999): 42–54.

Kassamali, Noor J. "When Modernity Confronts Traditional Practices: Female Genital Cutting in Northeast Africa." In *Women in Muslim Societies: Diversity Within Unity*, ed. Herbert L. Bodman and Nayereh E. Tohidi, 39–61. Boulder: Lynne Rienner, 1998.

Kassindja, Fauziya, and Layli Miller Bashir. *Do They Hear You When You Cry.* New York: Delacorte, 1997.

Knudsen, Christiana Oware. *The Falling Dawadawa Tree: Female Circumcision in Developing Ghana.* Højbjerg, Denmark: Intervention Press, 1994.

Koso-Thomas, Olayinka. *The Circumcision of Women: A Strategy for Eradication.* London: Zed, 1987.

Kouba, Leonard J., and Judith Muasher. "Female Circumcision in Africa: An Overview." *ASR* 28, 1 (1985): 95–110.

Kratz, Corinne A. "Teaching about Female Circumcision." In *Great Ideas for Teaching About Africa*, ed. Misty L. Bastian and Jane L. Parpart. Boulder, Col.: Lynne Rienner, 1999.

Leakey, L. S. B. "The Kikuyu Problem of the Initiation of Girls." *Journal of the Royal Anthropological Institute* 61 (1931): 277–85.

Levin, Tobe. "Abolition Efforts in the African Diaspora: Two Conferences on Female Genital Mutilation in Europe." *Women's Studies Quarterly* 27, 1/2 (1999).

Lewis, Hope. "Between 'Irua' and 'Female Genital Mutilation': Feminist Human Rights Discourse and the Cultural Divide." *Harvard Human Rights Journal* 8 (1995).

Lightfoot-Klein, Hanny. *Prisoners of Ritual: An Odyssey into Female Genital Circumcision in Africa.* New York: Haworth/Harrington Park, 1989.

Lockhat, Haseena. *Female Genital Mutilation: Treating the Tears.* Middlesex, Eng.: Middlesex University Press, 2004.

Mandara, Mairo Usman. "Female Genital Cutting in Nigeria: Views of Nigerian Doctors on the Medicalization Debate." In *Female "Circumcision" in Africa: Culture, Controversy, and Change*, ed. Bettina Shell-Duncan and Ylva Hernlund, 95–107. Boulder: Lynne Rienner, 2000.

Mansaray, Khadijatu. "Female Circumcision, Fertility Control, Women's Roles, and the Patrilineage in Modern Sierra Leone: A Functional Analysis." *International Journal of Sierra Leone Studies* 1 (1988): 114–30.

Mbow, Penda. "Pénaliser un fait culturel: quelle solution à l'excision?" *Présence Africaine* 160 (1999): 67–77.

McLean, Scilla. *Female Circumcision, Excision and Infibulation: The Facts and Proposals for Change.* London: Minority Rights Group, 1980.

Mottin Sylla, Marie-Hélène. "De quelques faux débats autour de l'excision. Incidences sur toute tentative d'action en la matière." *Psychopathologie africaine* 25, 3 (1993): 347–61.

——. *Excision au Sénégal.* Dakar: ENDA-Tiers Monde, 1990.

Murray, Jocelyn. "The Church Missionary Society and the 'Female Circumcision' Issue in Kenya 1929–1932." *Journal of Religion in Africa* 8, 2 (1976): 92–104.

Natsoulas, Theodore. "The Politicization of the Ban on Female Circumcision and the Rise of the Independent School Movement in Kenya: The KCA, the

Missions and the Government, 1929–1932." *Journal of Asian and African Studies* 33, 2 (1998): 137–58.

Nypan, Astrid. "Revival of Female Circumcision: A Case of Neo-Traditionalism." In *Gender and Change in Developing Countries*, ed. Kristi Anne Stølen and Mariken Vaa, 39–65. Oslo: Norwegian University Press, 1991.

Okwubanego, John Tochukwu. "Female Circumcision and the Girl Child in Africa and the Middle East: The Eyes of the World Are Blind to the Conquered." *International Lawyer* 33, 1 (1999): 159–87.

Rahman, Anika, and Nahid Toubia, ed. *Female Genital Mutilation: A Guide to Laws and Policies Worldwide*. London: Zed, 2000.

Robertson, Claire. "Grassroots in Kenya: Women, Genital Mutilation, and Collective Action, 1920–1990." *Signs* 21, 3 (1996): 615–42.

Sanderson, Lilian Passmore. *Against the Mutilation of Women: The Struggle against Unnecessary Suffering*. London: Ithaca Press, 1981.

Sarr, Fatou. "De la survivance d'un mode de pensée archaique au contrôle de la sexualité féminine: La question de l'excision." *Présence Africaine* 160 (1999): 78–88.

Shell-Duncan, Bettina, and Ylva Hernlund, ed. *Female 'Circumcision' in Africa: Culture, Controversy, and Change*. Boulder, Col.: Lynne Rienner, 2000.

Sidibe, Amasatou Sow. "Les mutilations genitales féminines au Sénégal." *Présence Africaine* 160 (1999): 55–66.

Skinner, Elliot P. "Female Circumcision in Africa: The Dialectics of Equality." In *Dialectics and Gender: Anthropological Approaches*, ed. Richard R. Randolph, David M. Schneider, and May N. Diaz, 195–210. Boulder, Col.: Westview, 1988.

Slack, Alison. "Female Circumcision: A Critical Appraisal." *Human Rights Quarterly* 10 (1988).

Talle, Aud. "Transforming Women into Pure Agnates: Aspects of Female Infibulation in Somalia." In *Carved Flesh/Cast Selves: Gendered Symbols and Social Practices*, ed. Tone Bleie, Vigdis Broch-Due, and Ingrid Rudie. Providence, R.I.: Berg, 1993.

Thomas, Lynn M. "Imperial Concerns and 'Women's Affairs': State Efforts to Regulate Clitoridectomy and Eradicate Abortion in Meru, Kenya, c. 1910–1950." *JAH* 39, 1 (1998): 121–45.

———. "'Ngiatana (I Will Circumcise Myself)': The Gender and Generational Politics of the 1956 Ban on Clitoridectomy in Meru, Kenya." *Gender and History* 3 (1996): 338–63.

Toubia, Nahid. "Female Genital Mutilation." In *Women's Rights, Human Rights: International Feminist Perspectives*, ed. Julie Peters and Andrea Wolper, 224–36. New York: Routledge, 1995.

van der Kwaak, Anke. "Female Circumcision and Gender Identity: A Questionable Alliance." *Social Science and Medicine* 35 (1992): 777–87.

BIBLIOGRAPHY • 343

Walley, Christine J. "Searching for 'Voices': Feminism, Anthropology and the Global Debate over Female Genital Operations." *Cultural Anthropology* 12, 3 (1997): 405–38.

Wembonyaama, S. O., and Marianne Bukwe Bubi. "Considerations médicales des mutilations genitales feminines." *Présence Africaine* 160 (1999): 31–41.

Feminism

Abdullah, Hussaina. "Wifeism and Activism: The Nigerian Women's Movement." In *The Challenge of Local Feminisms: Women's Movements in Global Perspective*, ed. Amrita Basu, 209–25. Boulder, Col.: Westview, 1995.

Acholonu, Catherine Obianuju. *Motherism: The Afrocentric Alternative to Feminism*. Owerri: AFA Publications, 1995.

Aidoo, Ama Ata. "To Be a Woman." In *Sisterhood Is Global*, ed. Robin Morgan, 258–65. New York: Anchor Doubleday, 1985.

Allen, Tuzyline Jita. *Womanist and Feminist Aesthetics: A Comparative Review*. Athens: Ohio University Press, 1996.

Arndt, Susan. "African Gender Trouble and African Womanism: An Interview with Chikwenye Ogunyemi and Wanjira Muthoni." *Signs* 25, 3 (2000): 709–26.

Azodo, Ada Uzoamaka. "Issues in African Feminism." *Women's Studies Quarterly* 25, 3/4 (1997): 201–07.

Barnes, Teresa. "Owning What We Know: Racial Controversies in South African Feminism, 1991–1998." In *Stepping Forward: Black Women in Africa and the Americas*, ed. Catherine Higgs, Barbara A. Moss, and Earline Rae Ferguson, 245–56. Athens: Ohio University Press, 2002.

Daymond, M. J., ed. *South African Feminisms: Writing, Theory, and Criticism, 1990–1994*. New York: Garland, 1996.

Dove, Nah. "Defining African Womanist Theory." In *The Afrocentric Paradigm*, ed, Ama Mazama, 165–83. Trenton, N.J.: African World Press, 2003.

Drew, Allison. "Female Consciousness and Feminism in Africa." *Theory and Society* 24 (1995): 1–33.

Hassim, Shireen. "Gender, Social Location and Feminist Politics in South Africa." *Transformation* 15 (1991): 65–82.

———. "The Limits of Popular Democracy: Women's Organisations, Feminism and the UDF." *Transformation* 51 (2003).

Hudson-Weems, Clenora. "Africana Womanism." In *The Afrocentric Paradigm*, ed. Ama Mazama, 153–63. Trenton, N.J.: African World Press, 2003.

Jagne, Siga Fatima. "Introduction on African Feminisms." In *Postcolonial African Writers: A Bio-Bibliographical Critical Sourcebook*, ed. Pushpa Naidu Parekh and Siga Fatima Jagne. Westport, Conn.: Greenwood Press, 1998.

Johnson-Odim, Cheryl. "Actions Louder Than Words: The Historical Task of Defining Feminist Consciousness in Colonial West Africa." In *Nation, Empire, Colony: Historicizing Gender and Race*, ed. Ruth Roach Pierson and Nupur Chaudhuri, 77–93. Bloomington: Indiana University Press, 1998.

Kemp, Amanda, et al. "The Dawn of a New Day: Redefining South African Feminism." In *The Challenge of Local Feminisms: Women's Movements in Global Perspective*, ed. Amrita Basu, 131–62. Boulder: Westview, 1995.

Kolawole, Mary E. Modupe. *Womanism and African Consciousness*. Trenton, N.J.: Africa World Press, 1997.

Mianda, Gertrude. "Feminisme africain: Divergences ou convergences de discours." *Présence Africaine* 155 (1997): 87–99.

Mikell, Gwendolyn, ed. *African Feminism: The Politics of Survival in Sub-Saharan Africa*. Philadelphia: University of Pennsylvania Press, 1997.

———. "African Feminism: Toward a New Politics of Representation." *FS* 21, 2 (1995): 405–24.

Nnaemeka, Obioma. "Nego-Feminism: Theorizing, Practicing, and Pruning Africa's Way." *Signs* 29, 2 (2004): 357–85.

———, ed. *Sisterhood, Feminisms and Power from Africa to the Diaspora*. Trenton, N.J.: Africa World Press, 1998.

Nzenza, Sekai. "Women in Postcolonial Africa: Between African Men and Western Feminists." In *At the Edge of International Relations: Postcolonialism, Gender and Dependency*, ed. Phillip Darby, 214–35. London: Pinter, 1997.

Ogundipe-Leslie, 'Molara. "Stiwanism: Feminism in an African Context." In *Women Imagine Change: A Global Anthology of Women's Resistance from 600 B.C.E. to the Present*, ed. Eugenia C. Delamotte, Natania Meeker, and Jean F. O'Barr. New York: Routledge, 1997.

Okeke, Philomina E. "Postmodern Feminism and Knowledge Production: The African Context." *Africa Today* 43, 3 (1996).

Oloka-Onyango, J., and Sylvia Tamale. "'The Personal is Political,' or Why Women's Rights are Indeed Human Rights: An African Perspective on International Feminism." *Human Rights Quarterly* 17, 4 (1995): 691–731.

Oyewumi, Oyeronke, ed. *African Women and Feminism*. Trenton, N.J.: Africa World Press, 1997.

Ramphele, Mamphela. "Whither Feminism?" In *Transitions Environments Translations: Feminism in International Politics*, ed. Joan W. Scott, Cora Kaplan, and Debra Keates, 334–38. New York: Routledge, 1997.

Roberts, Pepe. "Feminism in Africa, Feminism and Africa." *ROAPE* 27/28 (1984): 175–84.

Shaw, Carolyn Martin. "Working with Feminists in Zimbabwe: A Black American's Experience of Transnational Alliances." In *Feminism and Antiracism: International Struggles for Justice*, ed. France Winndance Twine and Kathleen M. Blee. New York: New York University Press, 2001.

Steady, Filomina Chioma. "African Feminism: A Worldwide Perspective." In *Women in Africa and the African Diaspora*, ed. Rosalyn Terborg-Penn, Sharon Harley, and Andrea Benton Rushing, 3–24. Washington, D.C.: Howard University Press, 1989.

Steyn, Melissa. "A New Agenda: Restructuring Feminism in South Africa." *WSIF* 21, 1 (1998): 41–52.

Straker, Gill. "Some Aspects of Feminism in the South African Context." In *Women's Worlds: From the New Scholarship*, ed. Marilyn Safir et al., 127–34. New York: Praeger, 1985.

Sylvester, Christine. "African and Western Feminisms: World-Traveling the Tendencies and Possibilities." *Signs* 20, 4 (1995): 941–69.

Terborg-Penn, Rosalyn. "African Feminism: A Theoretical Approach to the History of Women in the African Diaspora." In *Women in Africa and the African Diaspora*, ed. Rosalyn Terborg-Penn, Sharon Harley, and Andrea Benton Rushing, 43–63. Washington, D.C.: Howard University Press, 1989.

Thiam, Awa. *Black Sisters, Speak Out: Feminism and Oppression in Black Africa*. London: Pluto Press, 1986 [1978].

Thompson, Lisa. "Feminist Theory and Security Studies in Southern Africa: Yet another Faddish Trend?" In *Theory, Change and Southern Africa's Future*, ed. Peter Vale, Larry A. Swatuk, and Bertil Oden, 237–65. New York: Palgrave, 2001.

Tickner, J. A. "Feminist Perspectives." In *Globalization, Human Security, and the African Experience*, ed. Caroline Thomas and Peter Wilkin. Boulder, Col.: Lynne Rienner, 1998.

Health: Fertility, HIV/AIDS, Nursing, and Nutrition

Agadjanian, Victor. "Economic Security, Informational Resources, and Women's Reproductive Choices in Urban Mozambique." *Social Biology* 45, 1–2 (1998): 60–79.

———. "Women's Choice between Indigenous and Western Contraception in Urban Mozambique." *Women and Health* 28, 2 (1998): 1–17.

Agyei-Mensah, Samuel, and John B. Casterline, eds. *Reproduction and Social Context in Sub-Saharan Africa: A Collection of Micro-Demographic Studies*. Westport, Conn.: Greenwood Press, 2003.

Albertyn, Catherine. "Contesting Democracy: HIV/AIDS and the Achievement of Gender Equality in South Africa." *FS* 29, 3 (2003): 595–615.

Allison, Caroline. "Health and Education for Development: African Women's Status and Prospects." In *Crisis and Recovery in Sub-Saharan Africa*, ed. Tore Rose, 111–23. Washington, D.C.: OECD, 1985.

Anarfi, John K. "The Role of Local Herbs in the Recent Fertility Decline in Ghana: Contraceptives or Abortifacients?" In *The Sociocultural and Political*

Aspects of Abortion: Global Perspectives, ed. Alaka Malwade Basu, 139–51. Westport, Conn.: Praeger, 2003.

Avotri, Joyce Yaa, and Vivienne Walters. "'We Women Worry a Lot about Our Husbands': Ghanaian Women Talking About Their Health and Their Relationships with Men." *Journal of Gender Studies* 10, 2 (2001): 197–211.

Baylies, Carolyn, and Janet Bujra. *AIDS, Sexuality and Gender in Africa: Collective Strategies and Struggles in Tanzania and Zambia.* New York: Routledge, 2000.

Biesele, Megan. "An Ideal of Unassisted Birth: Hunting, Healing, and Transformation among the Kalahari Ju/'Hoansi." In *Childbirth and Authoritative Knowledge: Cross-Cultural Perspectives*, ed. Robbie E. Davis-Floyd and Carolyn F. Sargent, 474–92. Berkeley: University of California Press, 1997.

Bishaw, Mekonnen. "The Role and Status of Women in Traditional Health Care Services in Ethiopia." In *Gender Issues in Ethiopia*, ed. Tsehai Berhane-Selassie. Addis Ababa: Institute of Ethiopian Studies, Addis Ababa University, 1991.

Boelaert, Marleen, et al. "The Relevance of Gendered Approaches to Refugee Health: A Case Study of Hagadera, Kenya." In *Engendering Forced Migration: Theory and Practice*, ed. Doreen Indra, 165–76. New York: Bergahn Books, 1999.

Boerma, J. T., and Z. Mgalla, eds. *Women and Infertility in Africa: A Multidisciplinary Perspective.* Netherlands, 1999.

Booth, Karen M. *Local Women, Global Science: Fighting AIDS in Kenya.* Bloomington: Indiana University Press, 2004.

Bradford, Helen. "Herbs, Knives and Plastic: 150 Years of Abortion in South Africa." In *Science, Medicine and Cultural Imperialism*, ed. Teresa Meade and Mark Walker. New York: St. Martin's, 1991.

Burns, Cathy. "Louisa Mvemve: A Woman's Advice to the Public on the Cure for Various Diseases." *Kronos: Journal of Cape History* 23 (1996): 108–34.

Center for Reproductive Law and Policy. *Women of the World: Laws and Policies Affecting Their Reproductive Lives: Anglophone Africa.* New York: Center for Reproductive Law and Policy, 1997.

Cook, Rebecca J., and Bernard M. Dickens. "Abortion Laws in African Commonwealth Countries." *Journal of African Law* 25, 2 (1981): 60–79.

Cossa, H. A., et al. "Sylphilis and HIV Infection among Displaced Pregnant Women in Rural Mozambique." *International Journal of STD & AIDS* 5 (1994): 117–23.

Dada, John Olusegun, Isaac Oladayo Olaseha, and Ademosla Johnson Ajuwon. "Sexual Behavior and Knowledge of AIDS among Female Trade Apprentices in a Yoruba Town in South-Western Nigeria." *International Quarterly of Community Health Education* 17, 3 (1997–1998): 255–70.

Devisch, René. *Weaving the Threads of Life: The Khita Gyn-Eco-Logical Healing Cult Among the Yaka*. Chicago: University of Chicago Press, 1993.

du Toit, Brian. *Aging and Menopause among Indian South African Women*. Albany: State University of New York Press, 1990.

du Toit, Marijke. "'Dangerous Motherhood': Maternity Care and the Gendered Construction of Afrikaner Identity, 1904–1939." In *Women and Children First: International Maternal and Infant Welfare, 1870–1945*, ed. Valerie Fildes, Lara Marks, and Hilary Marland. London: Routledge, 1992.

Dupré, Marie-Claude. "Mothers, Healers and Farmers in Congo." In *Women Wielding the Hoe: Lessons from Rural Africa for Feminist Theory and Development Practice*, ed. Deborah Fahy Bryceson, 151–64. Oxford: Berg, 1995.

Friday, Arglenda. "Health Issues in Africa: The Role of Women." In *Health Communication in Africa: Contexts, Constraints and Lessons*, ed. Andy O. Alali and B. A. Jinadu, 118–35. Lanham, Md.: University Press of America, 2002.

Gaitskell, Debby. "'Getting Close to the Hearts of Mothers': Medical Missionaries among African Women and Children in Johannesburg Between the Wars." In *Women and Children First: International Maternal and Infant Welfare, 1870–1945*, ed. Valerie Fildes, Lara Marks, and Hilary Marland, 178–202. London: Routledge, 1992.

Garenne, Michel, and Veronique Joseph. "The Timing of the Fertility Transition in Sub-Saharan Africa." *World Development* 30, 10 (2002): 1835–43.

Gelfand, Michael. *Midwifery in Tropical Africa: The Growth of Maternity Services in Rhodesia*. Supplement to Zambezia. Salisbury: University of Rhodesia, 1978.

Geurts, Kathryn. "Childbirth and Pragmatic Midwifery in Rural Ghana." *Medical Anthropology* 20, 4 (2001): 379–408.

Goosen, Margaretha, and Barbara Klugman, eds. *The South African Women's Health Book*. Cape Town: Oxford University Press, 1996.

Gottlieb, Alma. "Menstrual Cosmology among the Beng of Ivory Coast." In *Blood Magic: The Anthropology of Menstruation*, ed. Thomas Buckley and Alma Gottlieb, 55–74. Berkeley: University of California Press, 1988.

Gruenbaum, Ellen. "The Islamic Movement, Development, and Health Education: Recent Changes in the Health of Rural Women in Central Sudan." *Social Science and Medicine* 33, 6 (1991): 637–45.

Harrison, Abigail, and Elizabeth Montgomery. "Life Histories, Reproductive Histories: Rural South African Women's Narratives of Fertility, Reproductive Health and Illness." *JSAS* 27, 2 (2001): 311–28.

Hassoun, Judith. *Femmes d'Abidjan face au SIDA*. Paris: Karthala, 1997.

Hunt, Charles W. "Africa and AIDS: Dependent Development—Sexism and Racism." *Monthly Review* 39, 8 (1988): 10–22.

International Labour Organization. *No Application Form: Poems and Stories by Women with Disabilities from Southern Africa*. Geneva: ILO, 1993.

Jacobson, Jodi L. *Challenge of Survival: Safe Motherhood in the SADCC Region*. New York: Family Care International, 1991.

Jambai, Amara, and Carol MacCormack. "Maternal Health, War, and Religious Tradition: Authoritative Knowledge in Pujehun District, Sierra Leone." In *Childbirth and Authoritative Knowledge: Cross-Cultural Perspectives*, ed. Robbie E. Davis-Floyd and Carolyn F. Sargent, 421–40. Berkeley: University of California Press, 1997.

Juk, Jok Madut. *Militarization, Gender and Reproductive Health in South Sudan*. Lewiston, N.Y.: Edwin Mellen, 1998.

Kabira, W. M., E. W. Gachukia, and F. O. Matiangi. "The Effect of Women's Role on Health: The Paradox." *International Journal of Gynecology and Obstetrics* 58, 1 (1997): 23–34.

Kidanemariam, Adanech, and Azeb Tamirat. "Gender Influence on Women's Health." In *Gender Issues in Ethiopia*, ed. Tsehai Berhane-Selassie. Addis Ababa: Institute of Ethiopian Studies, Addis Ababa University, 1991.

Klausen, Susanne. "'For the Sake of the Race': Eugenic Discourses of Feeble-mindedness and Motherhood in the South African Medical Record, 1903–1926." *JSAS* 23, 1 (1997): 27–50.

Koster, Winny. *Secret Strategies: Women and Abortion in Yoruba Society, Nigeria*. Amsterdam: Aksant Academic Publishers, 2003.

Kwagala, Betty. "Integrating Women's Reproductive Roles with Productive Activities in Commerce: The Case of Businesswomen in Kampala, Uganda." *Urban Studies* 36, 9 (1999): 1535–50.

Lamp, Frederick. "Heavenly Bodies: Menses, Moon, and Rituals of License Among the Temne of Sierra Leone." In *Blood Magic: The Anthropology of Menstruation*, ed. Thomas Buckley and Alma Gottlieb, 210–31. Berkeley: University of California Press, 1988.

Lesthaeghe, Ron J., ed. *Reproduction and Social Organization in Sub-Saharan Africa*. Berkeley and Los Angeles: University of California Press, 1989.

Levin, Elise. "Cleaning the Belly: Managing Menstrual Health in Guinea, West Africa." In *The Sociocultural and Political Aspects of Abortion: Global Perspectives*, ed. Alaka Malwade Basu, 103–18. Westport, Conn.: Praeger, 2003.

Livingston, Julie. "Reconfiguring Old Age: Elderly Women and Concerns over Care in Southeastern Botswana." *Medical Anthropology* 22, 2 (2003): 205–31.

MacCormack, Carol P. "Health, Fertility and Birth in Moyamba District, Sierra Leone." In *Ethnography of Fertility and Birth*, ed. Carol P. MacCormack, 115–39. New York: Academic Press, 1982.

Machungo, Fernanda, Giovanni Zanconato, and Staffan Bergström. "Reproductive Characteristics and Post-Abortion Health Consequences in Women

Undergoing Illegal and Legal Abortion in Maputo." *Social Science and Medicine* 45, 11 (1997): 1607–13.

Maclean, Una. "Folk Medicine and Fertility: Aspects of Yoruba Medical Practice Affecting Women." In *Ethnography of Fertility and Birth*, ed. Carol P. MacCormack, 161–79. New York: Academic Press, 1982.

Magadi, Monica Akinyi, Eliya Msiyaphazi Zulu, and Martin Brockerhoff. "The Inequality of Maternal Health Care in Urban Sub-Saharan Africa in the 1990s." *Population Studies* 57, 3 (2003): 347–66.

Maman, Suzanne, et al. "HIV-Positive Women Report More Lifetime Partner Violence: Findings from a Voluntary Counseling and Testing Clinic in Dar es Salaam, Tanzania." *American Journal of Public Health* 92, 8 (2002): 1331–37.

Marks, Shula. "British Nursing and the South African War." In *Writing a Wider War: Rethinking Gender, Race, and Identity in the South African War, 1899–1902*, ed. Greg Cuthbertson, Albert Grundlingh, and Mary-Lynn Suttie, 159–85. Athens: Ohio University Press, 2002.

Marks, Shula, and Neil Andersson. "Women and Health in South Africa." *Canadian Woman Studies* 7, 1&2 (1986): 93–97.

Matokot-Mianzenza, Sidonie. *Viol des femmes dans les conflits armés et therapies familiales: Cas du Congo Brazzaville*. Paris: L'Harmattan, 2003.

McGrath, Janet W., et al. "Anthropology and AIDS: The Cultural Context of Sexual Risk Behavior among Urban Baganda Women in Kampala, Uganda." *Social Science and Medicine* 36, 4 (1993): 429–38.

Meda, N., S. Cousens, and B. Kanki. "Anaemia among Women of Reproductive Age in Burkina Faso." *World Health Forum* 17, 4 (1996): 369–72.

Moultrie, Tome A., and Ian M. Timaeus. "The South African Fertility Decline: Evidence from Two Censuses and a Demographic and Health Survey." *Population Studies* 57, 3 (2003): 265–83.

Mpangile, G. S., M. T. Leshabari, and D. J. Kihwele. "Induced Abortion in Dar es Salaam, Tanzania: The Plight of Adolescents." In *Abortion in the Developing World*, ed. Axel I. Mundigo and Cynthia Indriso, 387–403. London: Zed, 1999.

Munyakho, Dorothy. "Less Than Human Treatment: Maternity Protection in Kenya." In *No Paradise Yet: The World's Women Face the New Century*, ed. Judith Mirsky and Marty Radlett, 175–92. London: PANOS/Zed, 2000.

Nwana, Olu C. "Introduction and Rationale for Improvement of Women's Health." In *Gender Issues in Development and Environment*, ed. Ifeyinwa U. Ofong. Enugu, Nigeria: B-Teks, 1998.

Nxumalo, Mamane. "On Women and Health in Swaziland." In *Swaziland: Contemporary Social and Economic Issues*, ed. Peter G. Forster and Bongani J. Nsibande. Aldershot: Ashgate, 2000.

Obianyo, Nene. "The Girl Child: Health and Protection." In *Gender Issues in Development and Environment*, ed. Ifeyinwa U. Ofong. Enugu, Nigeria: B-Teks, 1998.

Ogbuago, S. "Depo Provera—A Choice or an Imposition on the African Woman: A Case Study of Depo Provera Usage in Maiduguri." *African Review* 10, 2 (1983): 39–51.

Ogbuago, Stella. "Women and Depo-Provera Usage in Nigeria: Chosen or Imposed Forms of Birth Control?" *Rural Africana* 21 (1985): 81–90.

Oppong, Christine. "The Crumbling of High Fertility Support: Data from a Study of Ghanian Primary School Teachers." In *The Persistence of High Fertility*, ed. John C. Caldwell. Canberra: Australia National University, 1977.

Orubuloye, I. O., John C. Caldwell, and Pat Caldwell. "African Women's Control over Their Sexuality in an Era of AIDS: A Study of the Yoruba of Nigeria." *Social Science and Medicine* 37 (1993): 859–72.

Page, Hilary J., and Ron Lesthaeghe, eds. *Child-Spacing in Tropical Africa: Traditions and Change*. New York: Harcourt Brace Jovanovich, 1981.

Renne, Elisha P. "Changing Assessments of Abortion in a Northern Nigerian Town." In *The Sociocultural and Political Aspects of Abortion: Global Perspectives*, ed. Alaka Malwade Basu, 119–38. Westport, Conn.: Praeger, 2003.

Richey, Lisa Ann. "Women's Reproductive Health and Population Policy: Tanzania." *ROAPE* 30, 96 (2003): 273–92.

Rothblum, Esther D., and Ellen Cole, eds. *Women's Mental Health in Africa*. Binghamton, N.Y.: Haworth, 1990.

Rowley, Chishamiso. "Challenges to Effective Maternal Health Care Delivery: The Case of Traditional and Certified Nurse Midwives in Zimbabwe." *Journal of Asian and African Studies* 35, 2 (2000): 251–64.

Russell, Diana E. H. "AIDS as Mass Femicide: Focus on South Africa." In *Femicide in Global Perspective*, ed. Diana E. H. Russell and Roberta A. Harmes. New York: Teachers College Press, 2001.

Sargent, Carolyn Fishel. *The Cultural Context of Therapeutic Choice: Obstetrical Care Decisions among the Bariba of Benin*. Dordrecht: D. Reidel, 1982.

——. *Maternity, Medicine, and Power: Reproductive Decisions in Urban Benin*. Berkeley and Los Angeles: University of California Press, 1989.

Schoepf, Brooke Grundfest. "AIDS Action–Research with Women in Kinshasa, Zaire." *Social Science and Medicine* (1993).

——. "Sex, Gender, and Society in Zaire." In *Sexual Behaviour and Networking: Anthropological and Sociocultural Studies on the Transmission of HIV*, ed. Tim Dyson, 353–75. Liege: Editions DeRousux-Ordina, 1992.

——. "Social Structure, Women's Status and Sex Differential Nutrition in the Zairan Copperbelt." *Urban Anthropology* 16, 1 (1987): 73–102.

———. "Women, AIDS, and Economic Crisis in Central Africa." *CJAS* 22, 3 (1988): 625–44.

Searle, C. *History of the Development of Nursing in South Africa, 1652–1960.* Pretoria: South African Nursing Association, 1970.

Shapiro, David, with B. Oleke Tambashe. *Kinshasa in Transition: Women's Education, Employment, and Fertility.* Chicago: University of Chicago Press, 2003.

Stambach, Amy. "Kutoa Mimba: Debates about Schoolgirl Abortion in Machame, Tanzania." In *The Sociocultural and Political Aspects of Abortion: Global Perspectives*, ed. Alaka Malwade Basu, 79–102. Westport, Conn.: Praeger, 2003.

Turshen, Meredeth, ed. "The Impact of Economic Reforms on Women's Health and Health Care in Sub-Saharan Africa." In *Women in the Age of Economic Transformation: Gender Impact of Reforms in Post-Socialist and Developing Countries*, ed. Nahid Aslanbeigui, Steven Pressman, and Gale Summerfield, 77–94. New York: Routledge, 1994.

———. *African Women's Health.* Trenton, N.J.: Africa World Press, 2000.

———, ed. *Women and Health in Africa.* Trenton, N.J.: Africa World Press, 1991.

Upton, Rebecca. "'Infertility Makes You Invisible': Gender, Health and the Negotiation of Fertility in Northern Botswana." *JSAS* 27, 2 (2001): 349–62.

Usman, Hajara. "Reproductive Health and Rights: The Case of Northern Nigerian Hausa Women." *Africa Development* 22, 1 (1997): 79–94.

van Heyningen, Elizabeth. "Women and Disease: The Clash of Medical Cultures in the Concentration Camps of the South African War." In *Writing a Wider War: Rethinking Gender, Race, and Identity in the South African War, 1899–1902*, ed. Greg Cuthbertson, Albert Grundlingh, and Mary-Lynn Suttie, 186–212. Athens: Ohio University Press, 2002.

Varga, Christine A. "How Gender Roles Influence Sexual and Reproductive Health among South African Adolescents." *Studies in Family Planning* 34, 3 (2003): 106–72.

Vuorela, Ulla. *The Women's Question and the Modes of Human Reproduction: An Analysis of a Tanzanian Village.* Uppsala: Scandinavian Institute of African Studies, 1987.

Walker, Liz. "'They Heal in the Spirit of the Mother': Gender, Race and Professionalisation of South African Medical Women." *African Studies* 62, 1 (2003): 99–124.

Wood, K., R. Jewkes, and N. Abrahams. "'Cleaning the Womb': Constructions of Cervical Screening and Womb Cancer among Rural Black Women in South Africa." *Social Science and Medicine* 45, 2 (1997): 283–94.

Human Rights

Askin Kelly D., and Dorean Koenig, eds. *Women and International Human Rights Law,* Ardsley, N.Y.: Transnational Publishers, 1998.

Berat, Lynn. "Issues Affecting African Women." In *Women and International Human Rights Law*, Vol. 4, ed. Askin and Koenig.

Beyani, Chaloka. "Toward a More Effective Guarantee of Women's Rights in the African Human Rights System." In *Human Rights of Women*, ed. Cook, 285–306.

Butegwa, Florence. "The Challenge of Promoting Women's Rights in African Countries." In *Ours by Right: Women's Rights as Human Rights*, ed. Joanna Kerr, 40–42. Atlantic Highlands, N.J.: Zed, 1993.

Center for Women's Global Leadership. *Gender Violence and Women's Human Rights in Africa*. Center for Women's Global Leadership, 1994.

Coker-Appiah, Dorcas, and Kathy Cusack, eds. *Violence against Women and Children in Ghana*. Accra: Gender Studies and Human Rights Documentation Centre, 1999.

Cook, Rebecca J., ed. *Human Rights and Women: National and International Perspectives*. Philadelphia: University of Pennsylvania Press, 1994.

Danka, Evo. "The Organization of African Unity and Women." In *Women and International Human Rights Law*, Vol. 2, ed. Askin and Koenig.

Diagne, Seny. "Defending Women's Rights: Facts and Challenges in Francophone Africa." In *Ours by Right: Women's Rights as Human Rights*, ed. Joanna Kerr, 43–51. Atlantic Highlands, N.J.: Zed, 1993.

Fox, Diana J. "Women's Human Rights in Africa: Beyond the Debate Over the Universality or Relativity of Human Rights." *African Studies Quarterly* 2, 3 (1998): [online].

Fox, Diana J., and Naima Hasci, eds. *Challenges of Women's Activism and Human Rights in Africa*. Lewiston, N.Y.: Edwin Mellen, 2000.

Halim, Asma Mohamed Abdel. "Challenges to the Application of International Women's Human Rights in the Sudan." In *Human Rights of Women*, ed. Cook, 397–421.

Harrington, Julia. "African Commission on Human and Peoples' Rights." In *Women and International Human Rights Law*, Vol. 2, ed. Askin and Koenig.

Howard, Rhoda. "Human Rights and Personal Law: Women in Sub-Saharan Africa." In *Human Rights and Development in Africa*, ed. Claude E. Welch and Ronald I. Meltzer. Albany: State University of New York Press, 1984.

———. "Women's Rights and the Right to Development." In *Women's Rights, Human Rights: International Feminist Perspectives*, ed. Julie Peters and Andrea Wolper, 301–15. New York: Routledge, 1995.

Ilumoka, Adeowun O. "African Women's Economic, Social, and Cultural Rights—Toward a Relevant Theory and Practice." In *Human Rights of Women*, ed. Cook, 307–25.

Johnson, Paula C., and Leslye Amede Obiora. "How Does the Universal Declaration of Human Rights Protect African Women?" *Syracuse Journal of International Law and Commerce* 26 (1999): 195–214.

Kerr, Joanna, ed. *Ours by Right: Women's Rights as Human Rights*. London: Zed, 1993.

Mugo, Micere Githae, Peter Takirambudde, Horace Campbell, and Louis Kriesberg. "How Does the Universal Declaration of Human Rights Guarantee Social and Economic Rights for African Men and Women?" *Syracuse Journal of International Law and Commerce* 26 (1999): 215–37.

Muli, Koki. "'Help Me Balance the Load': Gender Discrimination in Kenya." In *Women's Rights, Human Rights: International Feminist Perspectives*, ed. Julie Peters and Andrea Wolper, 78–81. New York: Routledge, 1995.

Sa'ad, Abdul-Mumin. "Traditional Institutions and the Violation of Women's Human Rights in Africa: The Nigerian Case." In *African Women and Children: Crisis and Response*, ed. Apollo Rwomire. Westport, Conn.: Praeger, 2001.

Wing, Susanna D. "Women Activists in Mali: The Global Discourse on Human Rights." In *Women's Activism and Globalization: Linking Local Struggles and Transnational Politics*, ed. Nancy A. Naples and Manisha Desai, 172–85. New York: Routledge, 2002.

Land

Akeroyd, Anne V. "Gender, Food Production and Property Rights: Constraints on Women Farmers in Southern Africa." In *Women, Development and Survival in the Third World*, ed. Haleh Afshar, 139–71. London: Longman, 1991.

Badri, Balghis. "Women, Land Ownership and Development in the Sudan." *Canadian Woman Studies* 7, 1&2 (1986): 89–92.

Butegwa, Florence. "Mediating Culture and Human Rights in Favour of Land Rights for Women in Africa: A Framework for Community-Level Action." In *Cultural Transformation and Human Rights in Africa*, ed. Abdullahi A. An-Na'im, 108–25. London: Zed, 2002.

———. "Using the African Charter on Human and Peoples' Rights to Secure Women's Access to Land in Africa." In *Human Rights of Women: National and International Perspectives*, ed. Rebecca J. Cook, 495–516. Philadelphia: University of Pennsylvania Press, 1994.

Carney, Judith, and Michael Watts. "Disciplining Women? Rice, Mechanization, and the Evolution of Mandinka Gender Relations in Senegambia." *Signs* 16, 4 (1991): 651–81.

Carr, Marilyn, ed. *Women and Food Security: The Experience of the SADCC Countries*. London: IT Publications, 1991.

Crummey, Donald. "Women and Landed Property in Gondarine Ethiopia." *IJAHS* 14, 3 (1981): 444–65.

Davison, Jean, ed. *Agriculture, Women, and Land: The African Experience*. Boulder, Col.: Westview, 1988.

Gaidzanwa, Rudo. "Land and the Economic Empowerment of Women: A Gendered Analysis." *Safere: Southern African Feminist Review* 1, 1 (1995): 1–12.

Gengenbach, Heidi. "Naming the Past in a 'Scattered' Land: Memory and the Powers of Women's Naming Practices in Southern Mozambique." *IJAHS* 33, 3 (2001): 523–42.

Goebel, Allison. "'Here It is Our Land, the Two of Us': Women, Men and Land in a Zimbabwean Resettlement Area." *Journal of Contemporary African Studies* 17, 1 (1999): 75–96.

Goheen, Miriam. *Men Own the Fields, Women Own the Crops: Gender and Power in the Cameroon Grassfields*. Madison: University of Wisconsin Press, 1996.

Gray, Leslie, and Michael Kevane. "Diminished Access, Diverted Exclusion: Women and Land Tenure in Sub-Saharan Africa." *ASR* 42, 2 (1999): 15–39.

Hilhorst, Thea. "Women's Land Rights." In *Evolving Land Rights, Policy and Tenure in Africa*, ed. Camilla Toulmin and Julian Quan. London: IIED and DfID, 2000.

Jacobs, Susan. "Land Resettlement and Gender in Zimbabwe: Some Findings." *JMAS* 29, 3 (1991).

Kajoba, Gear M. "Women and Land in Zambia: A Case Study of Small-Scale Farmers in Chenena Village, Chibombo District, Central Zambia." *Eastern Africa Social Science Research Review* 18, 1 (2002).

Khadiagala, Lynn S. "Justice and Power in the Adjudication of Women's Property Rights in Uganda." *Africa Today* 49, 2 (2002): 101–21.

Kishindo, Paul. *Women, Land and Agriculture in Lesotho*. Roma: National University of Lesotho, 1993.

Lado, Cleophas. "Informal Urban Agriculture in Nairobi: Problem or Resource in Development and Land Use Planning?" *Land Use Policy* 7, 3 (1990): 257–66.

Lastarria-Cornhiel, Susana. "Impact of Privatization on Gender and Property Rights in Africa." *World Development* 25, 8 (1997): 1317–33.

Lesetedi, Gwen N. "The Feminization of Poverty: Effects of the Arable Lands Development Program on Women in Botswana." In *African Women and Children: Crisis and Response*, ed. Apollo Rwomire. Westport, Conn.: Praeger, 2001.

MacKenzie, Fiona. "Gender and Land Rights in Murang'a District, Kenya." *Journal of Peasant Studies* 17, 4 (1990): 609–43.

———. "'Without a Woman There is No Land': Marriage and Land Rights in Smallholder Agriculture, Kenya." *Resources for Feminist Research* 19, 3/4 (1990): 68–74.

Made, Pat. "A Field of Her Own: Women and Land Rights in Zimbabwe." In *No Paradise Yet: The World's Women Face the New Century*, ed. Judith Mirsky and Marty Radlett, 81–100. London: PANOS/Zed, 2000.

Mamashela, Mothokoa. "Women's Property Rights in Lesotho: A Basic Human Right or a Privilege?" In *Women in Development: Gender and Development in Southern Africa, Problems and Prospects*, ed. R. C. Leduka, K. Matlosa, and T. Petlane, 168–82. Maseru: National University of Lesotho, 1993.

Manji, Ambreena. "Gender and the Politics of the Land Reform Process in Tanzania." *JMAS* 36, 4 (1998): 645–67.

Meer, Shamim, ed. *Women, Land and Authority: Perspectives from South Africa*. Cape Town: David Philip, 1997.

Moyo, Sam. "A Gendered Perspective of the Land Question." *Safere: Southern African Feminist Review* 1, 1 (1995): 13–31.

Muigai, G. "Women and Property Rights in Kenya." In *Women and Law in Kenya*, ed. M. A. Mbeo and O. Ooko-Ombaka. Nairobi: Public Law Institute, 1989.

Mwagiru, Makumi. *Women's Land and Property Rights in Conflict Situations*. Nairobi: Women and Law in East Africa, 1999.

Nasimiyu, Ruth. "Changing Women's Rights over Property in Western Kenya." In *African Families and the Crisis of Social Change*, ed. Thomas S. Weisner, Candice Bradley, and Philip L. Kilbride. Westport, Conn.: Greenwood, 1997.

Ngwafor. "Cameroon: Property Rights for Women." *Journal of Family Law* 29, 2 (1991): 297–302.

Nyamu-Musembi, Celestine. "Are Local Norms and Practices Fences or Pathways? The Example of Women's Property Rights." In *Cultural Transformation and Human Rights in Africa*, ed. Abdullahi A. An-Na'im, 126–50. London: Zed, 2002.

Nzioki, Akinyi. "The Effects of Land Tenure on Women's Access and Control of Land in Kenya." In *Cultural Transformation and Human Rights in Africa*, ed. Abdullahi A. An-Na'im, 218–60. London: Zed, 2002.

Pala, Achola O. "Women's Access to Land and Their Role in Agriculture and Decision-Making on the Farm: Experiences of the Joluo of Kenya." *Journal of Eastern African Research and Development* 13 (1983): 69–87.

Pala Okeyo, Achola. "Daughters of the Lakes and Rivers: Colonization and the Land Rights of Luo Women." In *Women and Colonization: Anthropological Perspectives*, ed. Mona Etienne and Eleanor Leacock, 186–213. New York: Praeger, 1980.

Peters, Pauline E. "Against the Odds: Matriliny, Land and Gender in the Shire Highlands of Malawi." *Critique of Anthropology* 17, 2 (1997): 189–210.

Potts, Deborah. "Worker–Peasants and Farmer–Housewives in Africa: The Debate About 'Committed' Farmers, Access to Land and Agricultural Production." *JSAS* 26, 4 (2000): 807–32.

Quisumbing, Agnes R., et al. "Women's Land Rights in the Transition to Individualized Ownership: Implications for Tree-Resource Management in Western Ghana." *Economic Development and Cultural Change* 50, 1 (2001): 157–81.

Rose, Laurel. *The Politics of Harmony: Land Dispute Strategies in Swaziland.* New York: Cambridge University Press, 1991.

——— . "Women's Strategies for Customary Land Access in Sw‹ ziland and Malawi: A Comparative Study." *Africa Today* 49, 2 (2002): 123–49.

Tadesse, Zenebeworke. "The Impact of Land Reform on Women: The Case of Ethiopia." In *Women and Development: The Sexual Division of Labor in Rural Societies*, ed. Lourdes Beneria, 203–22. New York: Praeger, 1982.

Valentine, Theodore R. "Female-Headed Households, Private Transfer Entitlements, and Drought Relief in Rural Botswana." In *Population Growth and Environmental Degradation in Southern Africa*, ed. Ezekiel Kalipeni. Boulder, Col.: Lynne Rienner, 1994.

van den Berg, Adri. *Land Right, Marriage Left: Women's Management of Insecurity in North Cameroon.* Leiden: CNWS Publications, 1997.

Walker, Cherryl. "Land Reform and the Empowerment of Rural Women in Postapartheid South Africa." In *Shifting Burdens: Gender and Agrarian Change under Neoliberalism*, ed. Shahra Razavi. Bloomfield, Conn.: Kumarian Press, 2002.

Wanyeki, L. Muthoni, ed. *Women and Land in Africa: Culture, Religion and Realizing Women's Rights.* London: Zed Books, 2003.

Women and Law in Southern Africa Research and Educational Trust. *A Critical Analysis of Women's Access to Land in the WLSA Countries.* Harare: Women and Law in Southern Africa Research Trust, 2001.

Zimbabwe Women's Resource Centre and Network. *Women and Land.* Harare: Zimbabwe Women's Resource Centre and Network, 1994.

Literature and Literary Criticism

Abraham, Keshia Nicole. "Resistance Innovations in African Feminist Literary Discourses: African Women Negotiating Cultures of Resistance." In *Reflections on Gender Issues in Africa*, ed. Patricia McFadden, 1–18. Harare: SAPES Trust, 1999.

Adamu, Abdalla Uba. "Parallel Worlds: Reflective Womanism in Balaraba Ramat Yakubu's *Ina Son Sa Haka*." *Jenda: A Journal of Culture and African Women Studies* 4 (2003), online at www.jendajournal.com.

Afolabi, Niyi. "New Mozambican Women Writers." In *Seasons of Harvest: Essays on the Literatures of Lusophone Africa*, ed. Niyi Afolabi and Donald Burness, 197–228. Trenton, N.J.: Africa World Press, 2003.

Aidoo, Ama Ata. "To Be an African Woman Writer—An Overview and a Detail." In *Criticism and Ideology*, ed. Kirsten Holst Petersen, 155–72. Uppsala: Scandinavian Institute of African Studies, 1988.

Ajayi-Soyinka, Omofolabo. "From His Symbol to Her Icon, A Semiotic Analysis of Women in African Literature." *American Journal of Semiotics* 8, 3 (1991): 31–52.

Arndt, Susan. *African Women's Literature: Orality and Intertexuality*. Bayreuth, Germany: Eckhard Breitinger, 1998.

———. *The Dynamics of African Feminism: Defining and Classifying African Feminist Literatures*. Trenton, N.J.: Africa World Press, 2002.

Azodo, Ada Uzoamaka, ed. *Emerging Perspectives on Mariama Bâ: Postcolonialism, Feminism and Postmodernism*. Trenton, N.J.: Africa World Press, 2003.

Azodo, Ada Uzoamaka, and Gay Wilentz, eds. *Emerging Perspectives on Ama Ata Aidoo*. Trenton, N.J.: Africa World Press, 1999.

Backström, Carita. "In Search of Psychological Worlds—On Yvonne Vera's and Chenjerai Hove's Portrayal of Women." In *Same and Other: Negotiating African Identity in Cultural Production*, ed. Maria Eriksson Baaz and Mai Palmberg, 79–93. Stockholm: Nordiska Afrikainstitutet, 2001.

Bayi, Omofolabo. "Negritude, Feminism, and the Quest for Identity: Re-Reading Mariama Ba's 'So Long a Letter.'" *Women's Studies Quarterly* 25, 3/4 (1997): 35–52.

Bazin, Nancy Topping. "Southern Africa and the Theme of Madness: Novels by Doris Lessing, Bessie Head, and Nadine Gordimer." In *International Women's Writing: New Landscapes of Identity*, ed. Anne E. Brown and Marjanne E. Gooze, 137–49. Westport, Conn.: Greenwood, 1995.

Boswell, Barbara. "WEAVEing Identities [Women's Education and Artistic Voice Expression, a writer's collective in Cape Town, South Africa]." *FS* 29, 3 (2003): 581–91.

Boyd, Jean, and Beverly B. Mack. *The Collected Works of Nana Asma'u, 1793–1864*. Ann Arbor: Michigan State University Press, 1997.

Brahimi, Denise, and Anne Trevarthen. *Les femmes dans la littérature africaine: portraits*. Paris: Karthala, 1998.

Brinkman, Inge. *Kikuyu Gender Norms and Narratives*. Leiden: Leiden University Research School, 1996.

Brown, Lloyd W. *Women Writers in Black Africa*. Westport, Conn.: Greenwood, 1981.

Bruner, Charlotte H., ed. *Unwinding Threads: Writing by Women in Africa*. Portsmouth, N.H.: Heinemann, 1983.

Burness, Donald. "Children in the Poetry and Short Stories of Alda Lara." In *Seasons of Harvest: Essays on the Literatures of Lusophone Africa*, ed. Niyi Afolabi and Donald Burness, 45–54. Trenton, N.J.: Africa World Press, 2003.

Busby, Margaret, ed. *Daughters of Africa: An International Anthology of Words and Writings by Women of African Descent from the Ancient Egyptian to the Present*. New York: Pantheon, 1992.

Cazenave, Odile. *Rebellious Women: The New Generation of Female African Novelists*. Boulder, Col.: Lynne Rienner, 2000 (originally published as *Femmes rebelles: Naissance d'un nouveau roman africain au féminin*. Paris: L'Harmattan, 1996).

Chennels, Anthony. "Tsitsi Dangarembga's *Nervous Conditions*." In *New Writing from Southern Africa: Authors Who Have Become Prominent Since 1980*, ed. Emmanuel Ngara. Portsmouth, N.H.: Heinemann, 1995.

Chukukere, Gloria Chineze. *Gender Voices and Choices: Redefining Women in Contemporary African Fiction*. Enugu, Nigeria: Fourth Dimension Publishing, 1995.

Chukwuma, Helen. "Positivism and the Female Crisis: The Novels of Buchi Emecheta." In *Nigerian Female Writers: A Critical Perspective*, ed. Henrietta C. Otokunefor and Obiageli C. Nwodo, 2–18. Malthouse Press, 1989.

Coundouriotis, Eleni. "Authority and Invention in the Fiction of Bessie Head." *RAL* 27, 2 (1996): 17–32.

d'Almeida, Irène Assiba. *Francophone African Women Writers: Destroying the Emptiness of Silence*. Gainesville: University Press of Florida, 1995.

Darlington, Sonja. "Calixthe Beyala's Manifesto and Fictional Theory." *RAL* 34, 2 (2003): 41–52.

Davies, Carole Boyce, and Anne Adams Graves, eds. *Ngambika: Studies of Women in African Literature*. Trenton, N.J.: Africa World Press, 1986.

Egejuru, Phanuel Akubueze, and Ketu H. Katrak, eds. *Nwanyibu: Womanbeing and African Literature*. Trenton, N.J.: Africa World Press, 1997.

Elder, Arlene A. "'Who Can Take the Multitude and Lock It In a Cage?': Noemia de Sousa, Micere Mugo, Ellen Kuzwayo: Three African Women's Voices of Resistance." In *Moving beyond Boundaries: Volume 2: Black Women's Diasporas*, ed. Carole Boyce Davies, 255–71. London: Pluto, 1995.

Emenyonu, Ernest. "Technique and Language in Buchi Emecheta's *The Bride Price*, *The Slave Girl* and *The Joys of Motherhood*." *Journal of Commonwealth Literature* 22, 1 (1988): 130–41.

Emenyonu, Ernest, ed. *New Women's Writing in African Literature*. Trenton, N.J.: Africa World Press, 2004.

Fishburn, Katherine. *Reading Buchi Emecheta: Cross-Cultural Conversations*. Westport, Conn.: Greenwood, 1995.

Gagiano, Annie. *Achebe, Head, Marechera: On Power and Change in Africa*. Boulder, Col.: Lynne Rienner, 2000.

Gairola, Rahul Krishna. "Western Experiences: Education and 'Third World Women' in the Fictions of Tsitsi Dangarembga and Meena Alexander." *Jouvert* 4, 2 (2000).

Harrow, Kenneth W. *Less Than One and Double: A Feminist Reading of African Women's Writing*. Portsmouth, N.H.: Heinemann, 2002.

———. "'I'm Not a Western Feminist But . . .': A Review of Recent Critical Writings on African Women's Literature." *RAL* 29, 3 (1998): 171–90.

Henderson, Heather. "Beyond Streetwalking: The Woman of the City as Urban Pioneer." In *Beyond Survival: African Literature and the Search for New Life*, ed. Kofi Anyidoho, Abena P. A. Busia, and Anne V. Adams, 225–32. Trenton, N.J.: Africa World Press, 1999.

Hitchcott, Nicki. *Women Writers in Francophone Africa*. New York: Berg, 2000.

Horton, Susan R. *Difficult Women, Artful Lives: Olive Schreiner and Isak Dinesen, In and Out of Africa*. Baltimore: Johns Hopkins University Press, 1995.

Hunter, Eva. "Zimbabwean Nationalism and Motherhood in Yvonne Vera's *Butterfly Burning*." *African Studies* 59, 2 (2000): 229–43.

Ibrahim, Huma. *Bessie Head: Subversive Identities in Exile*. Charlottesville: University of Virginia Press, 1996.

James, Adeola. *In Their Own Voices: African Women Writers Talk*. Portsmouth, N.H.: Heinemann, 1990.

James, Valentine Udoh, et al., eds. *Black Women Writers across Cultures: An Analysis of Their Contributions*. Lanham, Md.: University Press of America, 2000.

Japtok, Martin, ed. *Postcolonial Perspectives on Women Writers from Africa, the Caribbean, and the U.S.* Trenton, N.J.: Africa World Press, 2003.

Jones, Eldred Durosimi, Eustace Palmer, and Marjorie Jones, eds. *Women in African Literature Today*. Trenton, N.J.: Africa World Press, 1987.

Kalu, Anthonia C. "Those Left Out in the Rain: African Literary Theory and the Re-Invention of the African Woman." *ASR* 37, 2 (1994): 77–95.

———. *Women, Literature and Development in Africa*. Trenton, N.J.: Africa World Press, 2001.

Kamara, Gibreel M. "The Feminist Struggle in the Senegalese Novel: Mariama Bâ and Sembene Ousmane." *Journal of Black Studies* 32, 2 (2001): 212–28.

Katrak, Ketu H. "Womanhood/Motherhood: Variations on a Theme in Selected Novels of Buchi Emecheta." *Journal of Commonwealth Literature* 23, 1 (1988): 159–70.

Kemp, Yakini B. "Romantic Love and the Individual in Novels by Mariama Bâ, Buchi Emecheta, and Bessie Head." In *Arms Akimbo: Africana Women in Contemporary Literature*, ed. Janice Lee Liddell and Yakini Belinda Kemp. Gainesville: University Press of Florida, 1999.

Killam, Douglas, and Ruth Rowe, eds. *The Companion to African Literatures*. Bloomington: Indiana University Press, 2000.

Kumah, Carolyn. "African Women and Literature." *West Africa Review* 2, 1 (2000).

Kuria, Mike, ed. *Talking Gender: Conversations with Kenyan Women Writers.* Nairobi: PJ Kenya, 2003.

Kusunose, Keiko. "Bessie Head and Pan-Africanism." In *Migrating Words and Worlds: Pan-Africanism Updated*, ed. E. Anthony Hurley, Renée Larrier, and Joseph McLaren, 233–46. Trenton, N.J.: African World Press, 1999.

McWilliams, Sally. "Tsitsi Dangarembga's *Nervous Conditions*: At the Crossroads of Feminism and Post-Colonialism." *World Literature Written in English* 31, 1 (1991): 103–12.

Meyer, Stephan. "Interview with Sindiwe Magona." *Current Writing: Text and Reception in Southern Africa* 11, 1 (1999): 79–90.

Mitifu, Faida M. "Zairian Novelists and Their Female Characters." *Women's Studies Quarterly* 25, 3/4 (1997): 97–108.

Mogan, Elizabeth. "Writing Our Way Out: The Cross-Cultural Dynamics of African Women's Novels." *World Literature Written in English* 37, 1–2 (1998): 102–17.

Monsman, Gerald. *Olive Schreiner's Fiction: Landscape and Power.* New Brunswick, N.J.: Rutgers University Press, 1991.

Muhlebach, Andrea. "Between the Fires: Gender and Post-Apartheid Reasoning in Two South African Novels: Nadine Gordimer's *Burger's Daughter* and Miriam Tlali's *Muriel at Metropolitan*." *World Literature Written in English* 36, 1 (1997).

Muponde, Robert, and Mandivavarira Maodzwa-Taruvinga, ed. *Sign and Taboo: Perspectives on the Poetic Fiction of Yvonne Vera.* Oxford: James Currey, 2003.

Myambo, Mmashikwane. "'Sometimes Reading Can Be Your Friend': Black Professional South African Women Readers." *African Research and Documentation* 83 (2000).

Nasta, Susheila, ed. *Motherlands: Black Women's Writings from Africa, the Caribbean, and South Asia.* New Brunswick, N.J.: Rutgers University Press, 1992.

Nelson, N. "Representations of Men and Women, City and Town in Kenyan Novels of the 1970s and 1980s." *African Languages and Cultures* 9, 2 (1996): 145–68.

Newell, Stephanie. *Ghanaian Popular Fiction: "Thrilling Discoveries in Conjugal Life" and Other Tales.* Athens: Ohio University Press, 2000.

———, ed. *Writing African Women: Gender, Popular Culture and Literature in West Africa.* London: Zed Books, 1997.

Ngcobo, Lauretta. "The African Woman Writer; My Life and My Writing." In *A Double Colonization: Colonial and Post-Colonial Women's Writing*, ed. Kirsten Holst Petersen and Anna Rutherford, 81–86. Mundelstrup, Denmark: Dangaroo Press, 1986.

Nfah-Abbenyi, Juliana Makuchi. *Gender in African Women's Writing: Identity, Sexuality, and Difference.* Bloomington: Indiana University Press, 1997.

Nnaemeka, Obioma. "Black Women Writers." *Women's Studies Quarterly* 25, 3/4 (1997): 208–24.

———. "Feminism, Rebellious Women, and Cultural Boundaries: Rereading Flora Nwapa and Her Compatriots." *RAL* 26, 2 (1995): 80–113.

———. "Urban Spaces, Women's Places: Polygamy as Sign in Mariama Bâ's Novels." In *The Politics of (M)Othering: Womanhood, Identity, and Resistance in African Literature*, ed. Obioma Nnaemeka, 162–91. London: Routledge, 1997.

Nuttall, Sarah. "Reading in the Lives and Writing of Black South African Women." *JSAS* 20, 1 (1994): 85–98.

O'Brien, Louise. "Buchi Emecheta and the 'African Dilemma.'" *Journal of Commonwealth Literature* 36, 2 (2001): 95–106.

Odamtten, Vincent O. *The Art of Ama Ata Aidoo: Polylectics and Reading against Neocolonialism.* Gainesville: University Press of Florida, 1994.

Ogundipe-Leslie, Molara. *Re-Creating Ourselves: African Women and Critical Transformations.* Trenton, N.J.: Africa World Press, 1994.

Ogunyemi, Chikwenye Okonjo. *Africa Wo/Man Palava: The Nigerian Novel by Women.* Chicago: University of Chicago Press, 1995.

———. "Womanism: The Dynamics of the Contemporary Black Female Novel in English." *Signs* 11, 1 (1985): 63–80.

Ogwude, Sophia Obiajulu. "Protest and Commitment in Bessie Head's *Utopia.*" *RAL* 29, 3 (1998): 70–81.

Okonkwo, Christopher. "Space Matters: Form and Narrative in Tsitsi Dangaremgba's *Nervous Conditions.*" *RAL* 34, 2 (2003): 53–74.

Olaussen, Maria. "'About Lovers in Accra': Urban Intimacy in Ama Ata Aidoo's *Changes: A Love Story.*" *RAL* 33, 2 (2002).

———. "'Imagined Families' in South African Women's Autobiographies." In *Same and Other: Negotiating African Identity in Cultural Production*, ed. Maria Eriksson Baaz and Mai Palmberg, 159–80. Stockholm: Nordiska Afrikainstitutet, 2001.

Opoku-Agyemang, Naana Jane. "Reading Love Stories by Women from Ghana." *African Research and Documentation* 83 (2000).

Otokunefor, Henrietta C., and Obiageli C. Nwodo, eds. *Nigerian Female Writers: A Critical Perspective.* Malthouse Press, 1989.

p'Bitek, Okot. *Song of Lawino.* Nairobi: East African Publishing House, 1966.

Petersen, Kirsten Holst. "First Things First: Problems of a Feminist Approach to African Literature." *Kunapipi* 6, 3 (1985): 35–47.

———. "Unpopular Opinions: Some African Women Writers." In *A Double Colonization: Colonial and Post-Colonial Women's Writing*, ed. Kirsten Holst Petersen and Anna Rutherford, 107–20. Mundelstrup, Denmark: Dangaroo Press, 1986.

Prabhu, Anjali. "Mariama Bâ's *So Long a Letter*: Women, Culture and Development from a Francophone / Post-Colonial Perspective." In *Feminist Futures: Re-Imagining Women, Culture and Development*, ed. Kum-Kum Bhavnani, John Foran, and Priya A. Kurian, 239–55. London: Zed, 2003.

Primorac, Ranka. "Crossing Into the Space-Time of Memory: Borderline Identities in Novels by Yvonne Vera." *Journal of Commonwealth Literature* 36, 2 (2001): 77–93.

Reyes, Angelita. "The Epistolary Voice and Voices of Indigenous Feminism in Mariama Bâ's *Une Si Longue Lettre*." In *Moving Beyond Boundaries: Volume 2: Black Women's Diasporas*, ed. Carole Boyce Davies, 195–217. London: Pluto, 1995.

Rueschmann, Eva. "Female Self-Definition and the African Community in Mariama Bâ's Epistolary Novel *So Long a Letter*." In *International Women's Writing: New Landscapes of Identity*, ed. Anne E. Brown and Marjanne E. Gooze, 3–18. Westport, Conn.: Greenwood, 1995.

Salvodon, Marjorie. "Contested Crossings: Identities, Gender, and Exile in *Le Baobab Fou*." In *Spoils of War: Women of Color, Culture, and Revolution*, ed. T. Denean Sharpley-Whiting and Renee T. White. Lanham, Md.: Rowman and Littlefield, 1998.

Schipper, Mineke, ed. *Unheard Words: Women and Literature in Africa, the Arab World, Asia, the Caribean and Latin America*. London: Allison & Busby, 1984.

Scott, Joyce Hope. "Daughters of Yennenga: 'Le Mal de Peau' and Feminine Voice in the Literature of Burkina Faso." *Women's Studies Quarterly* 25, 3/4 (1997): 83–96.

Sougou, Omar. *Writing across Cultures: Gender Politics and Difference in the Fiction of Buchi Emecheta*. Amsterdam: Rodopi, 2002.

Schatteman, Renee. "Fanon and Beyond: The 'Nervous Condition' of the Colonized Woman." In *Beyond Survival: African Literature and the Search for New Life*, ed. Kofi Anyidoho, Abena P. A. Busia, and Anne V. Adams, 207–16. Trenton, N.J.: Africa World Press, 1999.

Schreiner, Barbara. *A Snake with Ice Water: Prison Writings by South African Women*. Fordsburg, S.A.: COSAW, 1991.

Stratton, Florence. *Contemporary African Literature and the Politics of Gender*. New York: Routledge, 1994.

Stringer, Susan. *The Senegalese Novel by Women: Through Their Own Eyes*. New York: Peter Lang, 1996.

Taiwo, Oladele. *Female Novelists of Modern Africa*. New York: St. Martin's Press, 1985.

Tsikang, Seageng, and Dinah Lefakane, eds. *Women in South Africa: From the Heart: An Anthology of Stories by a New Generation of Writers*. Johannesburg: Seriti sa Sechaba, 1988.

Umeh, Marie, ed. *Emerging Perspectives on Buchi Emecheta*. Trenton, N.J.: Africa World Press, 1996.

——, ed. *Emerging Perspectives on Flora Nwapa*. Trenton, N.J.: Africa World Press, 1998.

Uraizee, Joya. *This is No Place for a Woman: Nadine Gordimer, Buchi Emecheta, Nayantara Sahgal, and the Politics of Gender*. Trenton, N.J.: Africa World Press, 2000.

Volet, Jean-Marie. "Francophone Women Writing in 1998–99 and Beyond: A Literary Feast in a Violent World." *RAL* 32, 4 (2001): 187–200.

Wallace, Karen Smyley. "The Black Female Presence in Black Francophone Literature." In *Women in Africa and the African Diaspora*, ed. Rosalyn Terborg-Penn, Sharon Harley, and Andrea Benton Rushing, 181–86. Washington, D.C.: Howard University Press, 1989.

Wehrs, Donald R. *African Feminist Fiction and Indigenous Values*. Gainesville: University Press of Florida, 2001.

Whitsitt, Novian. "Islamic-Hausa Feminism and Kano Market Literature: Qur'anic Reinterpretation in the Novels of Balaraba Yakubu." *RAL* 33, 2 (2002): 119–38.

——. "Islamic-Hausa Feminism Meets Northern Nigerian Romance: The Cautious Rebellion of Bilkisu Funtuwa." *ASR* 46, 1 (2003): 137–53.

Wilentz, Gay. "The Politics of Exile: Ama Ata Aidoo's *Our Sister Killjoy*." In *Arms Akimbo: Africana Women in Contemporary Literature*, ed. Janice Lee Liddell and Yakini Belinda Kemp. Gainesville: University Press of Florida, 1999.

——, ed. *Binding Cultures: Black Women Writers in Africa and the Diaspora*. Bloomington: Indiana University Press, 1992.

Zabus, Chantal. "Writing Women's Rites: Excision in Experiential African Literature." *WSIF* 24, 3/4 (2001): 335–45.

Marriage, Bridewealth, Divorce, and Polygyny

Ankomah, Augustine. "Premarital Relationships and Livelihoods in Ghana." *Gender and Development* 4, 3 (1996): 39–47.

Arowolo, Oladele. "Plural Marriage, Fertility and the Problem of Multiple Causation." In *Women, Education and Modernization of the Family in West Africa*, ed. Helen Ware, 112–33. Canberra: Australian National University Press, 1981.

Bledsoe, Caroline. *Contingent Lives: Fertility, Time, and Aging in West Africa*. Chicago: University of Chicago Press, 2002.

——. "Transformations in Sub-Saharan African Marriage and Fertility." *Annals of the American Academy of Political and Social Science* 510 (1990): 115–25.

——. *Women and Marriage in Kpelle Society*. Stanford, Calif.: Stanford University Press, 1980.

Bledsoe, Caroline, and Gilles Pison, ed. *Nuptiality in Sub-Saharan Africa*. Oxford: Clarendon Press, 1994.

Brydon, Lynne. "The Dimensions of Subordination: A Case Study from Avatime, Ghana." In *Women, Work, and Ideology in the Third World*, ed. Haleh Afshar, 109–27. London: Tavistock, 1985.

Byfield, Judith. "Women, Marriage, Divorce and the Emerging Colonial State in Abeokuta (Nigeria) 1892–1904." *CJAS* 30, 1 (1996): 32–51.

Carrier, Joseph M., and Stephen O. Murray. "Woman–Woman Marriage in Africa." In *Boy–Wives and Female Husbands: Studies of African Homosexualities*, ed. Stephen O. Murray and Will Roscoe, 255–66. New York: St. Martin's, 1998.

Clignet, Remi. *Many Wives, Many Powers*. Evanston: Northwestern University Press, 1972.

Comaroff, John, ed. *The Meaning of Marriage Payments*. New York: Academic Press, 1980.

Cooper, Barbara M. *Marriage in Maradi: Gender and Culture in a Hausa Society in Niger, 1900–1989*. Portsmouth, N.H.: Heinemann, 1997.

Cornwall, Andrea. "Spending Power: Love, Money, and the Reconfiguration of Gender Relations in Ado-Odo, Southwestern Nigeria." *American Anthropologist* 29, 4 (2002): 963–80.

Curtin, Patricia Romero. "Weddings in Lamu: An Example of Social and Economic Change." *CEA* 94 (1984): 131–56.

Dalton, George. "Bridewealth vs. Brideprice." *American Anthropologist* (1966): 732–38.

David, Soniia. "'You Become One in Marriage': Domestic Budgeting Among the Kpelle of Liberia." *CJAS* 31, 1 (1997): 144–69.

de Smedt, Johan. "Child Marriages in Rwandan Refugee Camps." *Africa* 68, 2 (1998): 211–37.

Douglas, Mary. "Is Matrilyny Doomed in Africa?" In *Man in Africa*, ed. Mary Douglas and Phyllis Kaberry. London: Tavistock, 1969.

Evans-Pritchard, E. E. "An Alternative Term for 'Bride-Price.'" *Man* 41–42 (1931): 36–39.

Fall, Wendy Wilson. "The Upward Mobility of Wives: Gender, Class and Ethnicity." *African Philosophy* 12, 2 (1999): 175–96.

Feldman-Savelsberg, Pamela. "Cooking Inside: Kinship and Gender in Bangangte, Idioms of Marriage and Procreation." *American Ethnologist* 22, 3 (1995): 483–501.

Fiedler, Klaus. "For the Sake of Christian Marriage: Abolish Church Weddings." In *Rites of Passage in Contemporary Africa: Interaction Between*

Christian and African Traditional Religions, ed. James L. Cox, 46–60. Cardiff: Cardiff Academic Press, 1998.

Goebel, Allison. "'Men These Days, They Are a Problem': Husband-Taming Herbs and Gender Wars in Rural Zimbabwe." *CJAS* 36, 3 (2002): 460–89.

Greene, Beth. "The Institution of Woman-Marriage in Africa: A Cross-Cultural Analysis." *Ethnology* 37, 4 (1998): 395–413.

Griffiths, Anne M. O. *In the Shadow of Marriage: Gender and Justice in an African Community*. Chicago: University of Chicago Press, 1997.

Grosz-Ngaté, Maria. "Monetization of Bridewealth and the Abandonment of 'Kin Roads' to Marriage in Sana, Mali." *American Ethnologist* 15, 3 (1988): 501–14.

Gulbrandsen, O. "To Marry or Not to Marry? Marital Strategies and Sexual Relations in a Tswana Society." *Ethnos* 51 (1986): 7–21.

Guyer, Jane I. "The Economic Position of Beti Widows, Past and Present." In *Femmes du Cameroun: Mères pacifique, femmes rebelles*, ed. Jean-Claude Barbier, 313–25. Paris: Karthala-Orstrom, 1985.

———. "The Value of Beti Bridewealth." In *Money Matters: Instability, Values, and Social Payments in the Modern History of West African Communities*, ed. Jane I. Guyer. Portsmouth, N.H.: Heinemann, 1995.

Hale, Sondra. "Gender and Economics: Islam and Polygamy—A Question of Causality." *Feminist Economics* 1, 2 (1995).

Hanak, I. "Language, Gender and the Law: Divorce in the Context of Muslim Family Law in Zanzibar." *African Languages and Cultures* 9, 1 (1996): 27–42.

Hansen, Karen Tranberg. "Planning Productive Work for Married Women in a Low-Income Settlement in Lusaka." *African Social Research* 33 (1982): 211–23.

———. "When Sex Becomes a Critical Variable: Married Women and Extra-Domestic Work in Lusaka, Zambia." *African Social Research* 30 (1980): 831–49.

Jeater, Diana. *Marriage, Perversion and Power: The Construction of Moral Discourse in Southern Rhodesia, 1890–1930*. Oxford: Oxford University Press, 1993.

Jensen, An-Magritt. "Economic Change, Marriage Relations and Fertility in a Rural Area of Kenya." In *Gender and Change in Developing Countries*, ed. Kristi Anne Stølen and Mariken Vaa, 68–89. Oslo: Norwegian University Press, 1991.

Krige, Eileen Jensen. "Woman-Marriage, with Special Reference to the Lovedu—Its Significance for the Definition of Marriage." *Africa* 44, 1 (1974): 11–37.

Krige, Eileen Jensen, and John Comaroff, eds. *Essays on African Marriage in Southern Africa*. Cape Town: Juta, 1981.

Kuenyehia, Akua. "Women and Family Law in Ghana: An Appraisal of Property Rights of Married Women." *University of Ghana Law Journal* 17 (1986–1990): 72–99.

Kuper, Adam. *Wives for Cattle: Bridewealth and Marriage in Southern Africa.* London: Routledge and Kegan Paul, 1982.

Le Vine, Sarah. *Mothers and Wives: Gusii Women of East Africa.* Chicago: University of Chicago Press, 1979.

Lesthaeghe, Ron J., ed. *Reproduction and Social Organization in Sub-Saharan Africa.* Berkeley and Los Angeles: University of California Press, 1989.

Lewis, Barbara C. "Economic Activity and Marriage among Ivoiran Urban Women." In *Sexual Stratification: A Cross-Cultural View*, ed. Alice Schlegel, 161–91. New York: Columbia University Press, 1977.

Liebenberg, Alida. "Dealing with Relations of Inequality: Married Women in a Transkei Village." *African Studies* (1997): 349–73.

Linares, Olga F. "Kuseek and Kuriimen: Wives and Kinswomen in Jola Society." *CJAS* 22, 3 (1988): 472–90.

Lovett, Margot. "From Sisters to Wives and 'Slaves': Redefining Matriliny and the Lives of Lakeside Tonga Women, 1885–1955." *Critique of Anthropology* 17, 2 (1997): 171–87.

———. "On Power and Powerlessness: Marriage and Political Metaphor in Colonial Western Tanzania." *IJAHS* 27, 2 (1994): 273–301.

———. "'She Thinks She's Like a Man': Marriage and (De)Constructing Gender Identity in Colonial Buha, Western Tanzania, 1943–1960." *CJAS* 30, 1 (1996): 52–68.

Mack, Beverly. "Royal Wives in Kano." In *Hausa Women in the Twentieth Century*, ed. Catherine Coles and Beverly Mack, 109–29. Madison: University of Wisconsin Press, 1991.

Madhavan, Sangeetha. "Best of Friends and Worst of Enemies: Competition and Collaboration in Polygyny." *Ethnology* 41, 1 (2002): 69–84.

Magaisa, Ishmael. "Prostitution, Patriarchy, and Marriage: A Zimbabwean Case Study." In *African Women and Children: Crisis and Response*, ed. Apollo Rwomire. Westport, Conn.: Praeger, 2001.

Mason, Kathryn F. "Co-Wife Relationships Can Be Amicable as Well as Conflictual: The Case of the Moose of Burkina Faso." *CJAS* 22, 3 (1988): 615–24.

Mbilinyi, Marjorie. "Runaway Wives in Colonial Tanganyika: Forced Labour and Forced Marriage in Rungwe District 1919–1961." *International Journal of the Sociology of Law* 16 (1988): 1–29.

McKinney, Carol V. "Wives and Sisters: Bajju Marital Patterns." *Ethnology* 31, 1 (1992): 75–87.

Meekers, Dominique, and Nadra Franklin. "Women's Views of Polygyny among the Kaguru of Tanzania." *Ethnology* 34, 4 (1995): 315–29.

Molokomme, Athaliah. "Marriage—What Every Woman Wants or 'Civil Death?' The Status of Married Women in Botswana." In *Women and Law in Southern Africa*, ed. A. Armstrong and Welshman Ncube, 181–92. Harare: Zimbabwe Publishing House, 1987.

Mope Simo, J. A. "Royal Wives in the Ndop Plains." *CJAS* 25, 3 (1991): 418–30.

Mulder, Monique Borgerhoff. "Marital Status and Reproductive Performance in Kipsigis Women: Re-Evaluating the Polygyny–Fertility Hypotheses." *Population Studies* 43 (1989): 285–304.

Munachonga, Monica. "Income Allocation and Marriage Options in Urban Zambia." In *A Home Divided: Women and Income in the Third World*, ed. Daisy Dwyer and Judith Bruce, 173–94. Stanford, Calif.: Stanford University Press, 1988.

Murray, Colin. *Families Divided: The Impact of Migrant Labour in Lesotho*. Cambridge: Cambridge University Press, 1981.

Mushanga, Tibamanya mwene. "Wife Victimization in East and Central Africa." In *International Perspectives on Family Violence*, ed. Richard J. Gelles and Claire Pedrick Cornell, 139–45. Lexington Books, 1983.

Mutongi, Kenda. "'Worries of the Heart': Widowed Mothers, Daughters and Masculinities in Maragoli, Western Kenya, 1940–60." *JAH* 40 (1999): 67–86.

Nagar, Richa. "Communal Discourses, Marriage, and the Politics of Gendered Social Boundaries among South Asian Immigrants in Tanzania." *Gender, Place and Culture* 5, 2 (1998): 117–40.

Njambi, Wairimu Ngaruiya, and William E. O'Brien. "Revisiting 'Woman–Woman Marriage': Notes on Gikuyu Women." *NWSA Journal* 12, 1 (2000): 1–23.

Notermans, Catrien. "Polygyny and Christianity: Local Interpretations in Cameroon." In *Anthropologists and the Missionary Endeavour: Experiences and Reflections*, ed. Ad Borsboom and Jean Dommers, 182–97. Nijmegen: Verlag fur Entwicklungspolitik Saarbrucken, 2000.

Oboler, Regina. "Is the Female Husband a Man: Woman/Woman Marriage Among the Nandi of Kenya." *Ethnology* 14, 1 (1980): 69–88.

Okereke, Grace Eche. "The Birth Song as a Medium for Communicating Woman's Maternal Destiny in the Traditional Community." *RAL* 25, 3 (1994).

Oppong, Christine. *Middle Class African Marriage*. London: George Allen & Unwin, 1982.

———, ed. *Female and Male in West Africa*. London: Allen & Unwin, 1983.

O'Laughlin, Bridget. "Missing Men? The Debate over Rural Poverty and Women-Headed Households in Southern Africa." *Journal of Peasant Studies* 25, 2 (1998): 1–48.

Parkin, David, and David Nyamwaya, ed. *Transformations of African Marriage*. New York: St. Martin's Press, 1987.

Poewe, Karla O. *Matrilineal Ideology: Male–Female Dynamics in Luapula, Zambia.* New York: Academic Press, 1981.

Potash, Betty. "Gender Relations in Sub-Saharan Africa." In *Gender and Anthropology: Critical Reviews for Teaching and Research*, ed. Sandra Morgen, 189–227. Washington, D.C.: American Anthropological Association, 1989.

——, ed. *Widows in African Societies: Choices and Constraints.* Stanford, Calif.: Stanford University Press, 1986.

Renne, Elisha P. "'If Men Are Talking, They Blame It on Women': A Nigerian Woman's Comments on Divorce and Child Custody." *Feminist Issues* 10, 1 (1990): 37–49.

Roberts, Penelope A. "The State and the Regulation of Marriage: Sefwi Wiawso (Ghana) 1900–1940." In *Women, State, and Ideology: Studies from Africa and Asia*, ed. Haleh Afshar, 48–69. Albany: State University of New York Press, 1987.

Roberts, Richard. "Representation, Structure and Agency: Divorce in the French Soudan during the Early Twentieth Century." *JAH* 40, 3 (1999): 389–410.

Sacks, Karen. *Sisters and Wives: The Past and Future of Sexual Equality.* 1979, rep., Urbana: University of Illinois Press, 1982.

Schaefer, Rita. "Variations in Traditional Marriage and Family Forms: Responses to the Changing Patterns of Family-Based Social Security Systems in Sierra Leone and Kenya." *History of the Family: An International Quarterly* 2, 2 (1997).

Schnier, David, and Brooke Hintmann. "An Analysis of Polygyny in Ghana." *Georgetown Journal of Gender and the Law* 2 (2001): 795–839.

Shadle, Brett L. "Bridewealth and Female Consent: Marriage Disputes in African Courts, Gusiiland, Kenya." *JAH* 44 (2003): 241–62.

Solway, Jacqueline S. "Affines and Spouses, Friends or Lovers: The Passing of Polygyny in Botswana." *Journal of Anthropological Research* 46, 1 (1994): 41–66.

Spiegel, Andrew D. "Polygyny as Myth: Towards Understanding Extramarital Relations in Lesotho." In *Tradition and Transition in Southern Africa: Festschrift for Philip and Iona Mayer*, ed. A. D. Spiegel and P. A. McAllister, 145–66. Johannesburg: Witwatersrand University Press, 1991.

Ssennyonga, Joseph W. "Resource Allocation and Polygyny in the Lake Victoria Basin." In *African Families and the Crisis of Social Change*, ed. Thomas S. Weisner, Candice Bradley, and Philip L. Kilbride. Westport, Conn.: Greenwood, 1997.

Stephens, Connie. "Marriage in the Hausa Tatsuniya Tradition: A Cultural and Cosmic Balance." In *Hausa Women in the Twentieth Century*, ed. Catherine

Coles and Beverly Mack, 221–31. Madison: University of Wisconsin Press, 1991.

Timaeus, Ian M., and Angela Reynar. "Polygynists and Their Wives in Sub-Saharan Africa: An Analysis of Five Demographic and Health Surveys." *Population Studies* 52, 2 (1998): 145–62.

Toungara, Jeanne Maddox. "Changing the Meaning of Marriage: Women and Family Law in Côte d'Ivoire." In *African Feminism: The Politics of Survival in Sub-Saharan Africa*, ed. Gwendolyn Mikell, 53–76. Philadelphia: University of Pennsylvania Press, 1997.

van den Berg, Adri. *Land Right, Marriage Left: Women's Engagement of Insecurity in North Cameroon*. Leiden: CNWS Publications, 1997.

van der Vliet, Virginia. "Traditional Husbands, Modern Wives? Constructing Marriages in a South African Township." In *Tradition and Transition in Southern Africa: Festschrift for Philip and Iona Mayer*, ed. A. D. Spiegel and P. A. McAllister, 219–42. Johannesburg: Witwatersrand University Press, 1991.

van Driel, Francien. "Marriage—From Rule to Rarity? Changing Gender Relations in Botswana." In *Shifting Circles of Support: Contextualising Gender and Kinship in South Asia and Sub-Saharan Africa*, ed. Rajni Palriwala and Carla Risseeuw, 51–78. New Delhi: Sage, 1996.

Wanitzek, Ulrike. "Bulsa Marriage Law and Practice: Women as Social Actors in a Patriarchal Society." In *Sovereignty, Legitimacy, and Power in West African Societies: Perspectives from Legal Anthropology*, ed. E. Adriaan B. van Rouveroy van Nieuwaal and Werner Zips, 119–71. Hamburg: Lit. Verlag, 1998.

Ware, Helen, ed. *Women, Education and Modernization of the Family in West Africa*. Canberra, 1981.

Watts, Susan J. "Marriage Migration, a Neglected Form of Long-Term Mobility: A Case Study from Ilorin, Nigeria." *International Migration Review* 17, 4 (1983): 682–98.

White, Burton. "Causes of Polygyny: Ecology, Economy, Kinship, and Warfare." *American Anthropologist* 90 (1988): 871–87.

Whitehead, Ann. "Wives and Mothers: Female Farmers in Africa." In *Gender, Work and Population in Sub-Saharan Africa*, ed. Aderanti Adepoju and Christine Oppong, 35–53. Portsmouth, N.H.: Heinemann, 1994.

Women and Law in Southern Africa Research Trust. *Lobola: Its Implications for Women's Reproductive Rights in Botswana, Lesotho, Malawi, Mozambique, Swaziland, Zambia and Zimbabwe*. Harare: Weaver Press, 2002.

Marcia Wright. "Technology, Marriage and Women's Work in the History of Maize-Growers in Mazabuka, Zambia: A Reconnaissance." *JSAS* 10, 1 (1983): 71–85.

Organizations

Adeleye-Fayemi, Bisi, and Algresia Akwi-Ogojo. *Taking the African Womens' Movement into the 21st Century*. Kampala: Akina Mama wa Afrika, 1997.

African Training and Research Centre for Women. *Directory of African Women's Organizations*. Addis Ababa: United Nations, Economic Commission for Africa, 1978.

Aguilar, Mario I., and Laurel Birch de Aguilar. *Women's Organizing Abilities: Two Case Studies of Kenya and Malawi*. Washington, D.C.: Organizing for Development International Institute, 1993.

Alloo, Fatma. "Using Information Technology as a Mobilizing Force: The Case of the Tanzania Media Women's Association (TAMWA)." In *Women Encounter Technology: Changing Patterns of Employment in the Third World*, ed. Swasti Mitter and Sheila Rowbotham, 303–13. New York: Routledge, 1995.

ANC Women's League. *The ANC Women's League: Contributing to a Democratic, Non-racist and Non-sexist South Africa*. Johannesburg: ANC Women's League, 1993.

Aubrey, Lisa. *Politics of Development Co-Operation: NGO's, Gender and Partnership in Kenya*. New York: Routledge, 1997.

———. "Gender, Development, and Democratization in Africa." *Journal of Asian and African Studies* 36, 1 (2001): 87–111.

Awe, Bolanle. "Women's Research and Documentation Centre (Nigeria)." *Signs* 16, 4 (1991): 859–64.

Barrett, Minna. "Women's Income-Generating Initiatives in Kenya: A Self-Report, Perceptions of Need for Value and Women's Groups." *African Urban Quarterly* 2, 4 (1987): 365–77.

Berger, Iris. *Threads of Solidarity: Women in South African Industry, 1900–1980*. Bloomington: Indiana University Press, 1992.

Buelow, George. "Eve's Rib: Association Membership and Mental Health among Kru Women." *Liberian Studies* 9, 1 (1980–1981): 23–33.

Burman, Sandra, and Nozipho Lembete. "Building New Realities: African Women and ROSCAs in Urban South Africa." In *Money-Go-Rounds: The Importance of Rotating Savings and Credit Associations for Women*, ed. Shirley Ardener and Sandra Burman, 23–47. Washington, D.C.: Berg, 1995.

Chigudu, Hope. "Establishing a Feminist Culture: The Experience of Zimbabwe Women's Resource Centre and Network." *Gender and Development* 5, 1 (1997): 35–42.

Chitere, Preston O. "The Women's Self-Help Movement in Kenya: A Historical Perspective, 1940–80." *Transafrican Journal of History* 17 (1988): 50–68.

Cochran, Augustus B., III, and Catherine V. Scott. "Class, State, and Popular Organizations in Mozambique and Nicaragua." *Latin American Perspectives* 19, 2; 73 (1992): 105–24.

Cooper, Barbara M. "The Politics of Difference and Women's Associations in Niger: Of 'Prostitutes,' the Public and Politics." *Signs* 20, 4 (1995): 851–82.

Danka, Evo. "The Organization of African Unity and Women." In *Women and International Human Rights Law*, vol. 2, ed. Kelly D. Askin and Dorean Koenig. Ardsley, N.Y.: Transnational Publishers, 1998.

de Jongh, Michael. "The Ciskei Zenzele Women's Association: A Study in Selective Cultural Adaptation to Change." In *Culture Change in Contemporary Africa*, ed. Brian M. du Toit, 13–2. Gainesville: University of Florida Center for African Studies, 1970.

Dolphyne, Florence Abena. "The Ghana National Council on Women and Development: An Example of Concerted Action." In *Sex Roles, Population and Development in West Africa: Policy-Related Studies on Work and Demographic Issues*, ed. Christine Oppong, 213–18. Portsmouth, N.H.: Heinemann, 1987.

El Bakri, Zeinab Bashir. "The Crisis in the Sudanese Women's Movement." In *Subversive Women: Historical Experiences of Gender and Resistance*, ed. Saskia Wieringa, 199–212. London: Zed Books, 1995.

Emang Basadi. "A Summary of Botswana Women's Issues and Demands." *Safere: Southern African Feminist Review* 1, 1 (1995): 99–111.

Epprecht, Marc. "Domesticity and Piety in Colonial Lesotho: The Private Politics of Basotho Women's Pious Associations." *JSAS* 19, 2 (1993): 202–24.

Everett, Elizabeth. "Women's Rights, the Family, and Organisational Culture: A Lesotho Case Study." *Gender and Development* 5, 1 (1997): 54–59.

Evers Rosander, Eva, ed. *Transforming Female Identities: Women's Organizational Forms in West Africa*. Uppsala: Nordiska Afrikainstitutet, 1997.

Fester, Gertrude. "Despite Diversity: Women's Unity in Western Cape, South Africa (1980–94)." In *Global Feminist Politics*, ed. Suki Ali, Kelly Coate, and Wangui wa Goro, 11–27. New York: Routledge, 2000.

Geiger, Susan. "Umoja wa Wanawake wa Tanzania and the Needs of the Rural Poor." *ASR* 25, 2/3 (1982): 45–65.

Hale, Sondra. "Transforming Culture or Fostering Second-Hand Consciousness? Women's Front Organizations and Revolutionary Parties—the Sudan Case." In *Arab Women: Old Boundaries, New Frontiers*, ed. Judith E. Tucker. Bloomington: Indiana University Press, 1993.

Harrington, Julia. "African Commission on Human and Peoples' Rights." In *Women and International Human Rights Law*, vol. 2, ed. Kelly D. Askin and Dorean Koenig. Ardsley, N.Y.: Transnational Publishers, 1998.

Hassim, Shireen. "'A Conspiracy of Women': The Women's Movement in South Africa's Transition to Democracy." *Social Research* 69, 3 (2002).

——. "Family, Motherhood, and Zulu Nationalism: The Politics of the Inkatha Movement's Brigade." *Feminist Review* 43 (1993): 1–77.

Hubbard, Dianne, and Collette Solomon. "The Many Faces of Feminism in Namibia." In *The Challenge of Local Feminisms: Women's Movements in Global Perspective*, ed. Amrita Basu, 163–86. Boulder, Col.: Westview, 1995.

Hunt, Nancy Rose. "Domesticity and Colonialism in Belgian Africa: Usumbura's *Foyer Social*, 1946–1960." *Signs* 15, 3 (1990): 447–74.

Hutson, Alaine S. "The Development of Women's Authority in the Kano Tijaniyya, 1894–1963." *Africa Today* 46, 3/4 (1999).

Imam, Ayesha M. "The Dynamics of WINing: An Analysis of Women in Nigeria (WIN)." In *Feminist Genealogies, Colonial Legacies, Democratic Futures*, ed. M. Jacqui Alexander and Chandra Talpade Mohanty, 280–307. New York: Routledge, 1997.

Jules-Rosette, Bennetta. *The New Religions of Africa*. Norwood, N.J.: Ablex, 1979.

Kappers, Sophieke. "Sitani—Let's Help Each Other: Women and Informal Saving, Credit, and Funeral Organisations in Swaziland." In *Scenes of Change: Visions on Developments in Swaziland*, ed. Henk J. Tieleman, 163–90. Leiden: African Studies Centre, 1988.

Keirn, Susan Middleton. "Voluntary Associations among Urban African Women." In *Culture Change in Contemporary Africa*, ed. Brian M. du Toit, 25–40. Gainesville: University of Florida Center for African Studies, 1970.

Khalid, Tomadur Ahmed. "The State and the Sudanese Women's Union, 1971–1983: A Case Study." In *Subversive Women: Historical Experiences of Gender and Resistance*, ed. Saskia Wieringa, 183–98. London: Zed Books, 1995.

Kinuthia, Cecilia. "Women's Groups in Kenya with Special Reference to Housing and Community Development." In *The Women's Movement in Kenya*, ed. S. A. Khasiani and E. I. Njiro, 39–58. Nairobi: AAWORD, 1993.

Komon, Jean Paul. "Women Peasants Organisations in Cameroon." In *Peasant Organisations and the Democratisation Process in Africa*, ed. Mahmud Ben Romdhane and Sam Moyo. Dakar: Council for the Development of Social Science Research in Africa, 2002.

Labour Resource and Research Institute. *Still Fighting for Social Justice: A Survey of Trade Unions, Women's Organisations, Communal Farmers' and Service Organisations in Namibia*. Windhoek: Labour Resource and Research Institute, 1998.

Ladipo, Patricia. "Women in a Maize Storage Co-Operative in Nigeria: Family Planning, Credit and Technological Change." In *Sex Roles, Population and Development in West Africa: Policy-Related Studies on Work and Demographic Issues*, ed. Christine Oppong, 101–17. Portsmouth, N.H.: Heinemann, 1987.

Leisure, Susan. "Exchanging Participation for Promises: Mobilization of Women in Eritrea." In *Democratization and Women's Grassroots Move-*

ments, ed. Jill M. Bystydzienski and Joti Sekhon, 95–110. Bloomington: Indiana University Press, 1999.

Manuh, Takyiwaa. "Women and Their Organizations in the Period of CPP Rule in Ghana." In *The Life and Work of Kwame Nkrumah*, ed. Kwame Arhin, 101–28. Trenton, N.J.: Africa World Press, 1993.

Matobe, Thope. "An Analysis of the Proliferation of Voluntary Associations Among Basotho Women." In *Women in Development: Gender and Development in Southern Africa, Problems and Prospects*, ed. R. C. Leduka, K. Matlosa, and T. Petlane, 140–49. Maseru: National University of Lesotho, 1993.

Meena, Ruth, and Marjorie Mbilinyi. "Women's Research and Documentation Project (Tanzania)." *Signs* 16, 4 (1991): 852–59.

Miles, Miranda. "Women's Groups and Urban Poverty: The Swaziland Experience." In *Associational Life in African Cities: Popular Responses to the Urban Crisis*, ed. Arne Tostensen, Inge Tvedten, and Mariken Vaa, 64–73. Uppsala: Nordiska Afrikainstitutet, 2001.

Mindry, Deborah. "Nongovernmental Organizations, 'Grassroots,' and the Politics of Virtue." *Signs* 26, 4 (2001): 1187–211.

Modic, Kate. "Negotiating Power: A Study of the Ben Ka Di Women's Association in Bamako, Mali." *Africa Today* 41, 2 (1994): 25–37.

Molokomme, Athaliah. "Emang Basadi (Botswana)." *Signs* 16, 4 (1991): 848–51.

Mulder, Anneke. "The Participation of Women in the Agricultural Cooperatives in Maputo, Mozambique." In *All Are Not Equal: African Women in Cooperatives*, ed. Linda Mayoux, 57–60. London: Institute for African Alternatives, 1988.

Nelson, Nici. "The Kiambu Group: A Successful Women's ROSCA in Mathare Valley, Nairobi (1971 to 1990)." In *Money-Go-Rounds: The Importance of Rotating Savings and Credit Associations for Women*, ed. Shirley Ardener and Sandra Burman, 49–69. Washington, D.C.: Berg, 1995.

———. "Mobilizing Village Women: Some Organizational and Management Considerations." In *African Women in the Development Process*, ed. Nici Nelson, 47–58. London: Frank Cass, 1981.

Nzegwu, Nkiru. "Recovering Igbo Traditions: A Case for Indigenous Women's Organizations in Development." In *Women, Culture, and Development: A Study of Human Capabilities*, ed. Martha C. Nussbaum and Jonathan Glover, 444–65. Oxford: Oxford University Press, 1995.

Nzomo, M. "Kenya: Women's Movements and the Democratic Agenda." In *The African State at a Critical Juncture: Between Disintegration and Reconfiguration*, ed. Leonardo Villalón and Phillip Huxtable. Boulder, Col.: Lynne Rienner, 1997.

Odoul, Wilhelmina, and Wanjiku Mukabi Kabira. "The Mothers of Warriors and Her Daughters: The Women's Movement in Kenya." In *The Challenge of Local Feminisms: Women's Movements in Global Perspective*, ed. Amrita Basu, 187–207. Boulder, Col.: Westview, 1995.

Ojewusi, Sola. *Speaking for Nigerian Women: A History of the National Council of Women's Societies.* Abuja: All State Publishing, 1996.

Osirim, Mary J. "Vehicles for Change and Empowerment: Urban Women's Organisations in Nigeria and Zimbabwe." *Scandinavian Journal of Development Alternatives and Area Studies* (1998): 145–64.

Ottenberg, Simon. "Male and Female Secret Societies among the Bafodea Limba of Northern Sierra Leone." In *Religion in Africa: Experience and Expression*, ed. Thomas D. Blakeley, Walter E.A. van Beek, and Dennis L. Thomson, 363–87. Portsmouth, N.H.: Heinemann, 1994.

Petzer, Shane A., and Gordon M. Issacs. "SWEAT: The Development and Implementation of a Sex Worker Advocacy and Intervention Program in Post-Apartheid South Africa (with Special Reference to the Western City of Cape Town)." In *Global Sex Workers: Rights, Resistance, and Redefinition*, ed. Kamala Kempadoo and Jo Doezema, 192–99. New York: Routledge, 1998.

Pickering, Helen, and others. "Women's Groups and Individual Entrepreneurs: A Ugandan Case Study." *Gender and Development* 4, 3 (1996): 54–60.

Rajuili, Khanya, and Ione Burke. "Democratization through Adult Popular Education: A Reflection on the Resilience of Women from Kwa-Ndebele, South Africa." In *Democratization and Women's Grassroots Movements*, ed. Jill M. Bystydzienski and Joti Sekhon, 111–28. Bloomington: Indiana University Press, 1999.

Ranchod-Nilsson, Sita. "'Educating Eve': The Women's Club Movement and Political Consciousness among Rural African Women in Southern Rhodesia, 1950–1980." In *African Encounters with Domesticity*, ed. Karen Tranberg Hansen, 195–217. New Brunswick, N.J.: Rutgers University Press, 1992.

Roy-Campbell, Makini. "Empowerment of African Women across Geographical Boundaries: Formation of a Pan-African Women's Liberation Organisation." *Safere: Southern African Feminist Review* 1, 1 (1995): 87–89.

Sandberg, Eve. "Multilateral Women's Conferences: The Domestic Political Organization of Zambian Women." *Contemporary Politics* 4, 3 (1998).

Sikazwe, Emily. "Women for Change: Working with Rural Communities." In *Composing a New Song: Stories of Empowerment from Africa*, ed., Hope Chigudu, 129–59. London: Commonwealth Foundation, 2002.

Sheikh, Leila. "TAMWA: Levina's Song—Supporting Women in Tanzania." In *Composing a New Song: Stories of Empowerment from Africa*, ed. Hope Chigudu, 95–127. London: Commonwealth Foundation, 2002.

Spink, Kathryn. *Black Sash: The Beginning of a Bridge in South Africa.* London: Methuen, 1991.

Staudt, Kathleen A. "The Umoja Federation: Women's Cooptation into a Local Power Structure." *Western Political Quarterly* 33, 2 (1980): 278–90.

Staudt, Kathleen, and Jane Jaquette. "Women's Programs, Bureaucratic Resistance and Feminist Organization." In *Women Power and Policy*, ed. Ellen Boneparth and Emily Stoper. New York: Pergamon, 1988.

Tarfa, Sintiki. "Why Rural Technologies Fail to Meet the Needs of Nigerian Women: Evidence from Hausa Women's Groups in Kano State." In *Women, Globalization and Fragmentation in the Developing World*, ed. Haleh Afshar and Stephanie Barrientos, 215–25. London: Macmillan, 1999.

Tripp, Aili Mari. "Deindustrialisation and the Growth of Women's Economic Association and Networks in Urban Tanzania." In *Dignity and Daily Bread: New Forms of Economic Organising Among Poor Women in the Third World and the First*, ed. Sheila Rowbotham and Swasti Mitter, 139–57. New York: Routledge, 1994.

———. "Gender, Political Participation and the Transformation of Associational Life in Uganda and Tanzania." *ASR* 37, 1 (1994): 107–31.

———. "The Politics of Autonomy and Cooptation in Africa: The Case of the Ugandan Women's Movement." *JMAS* 39, 1 (2001): 101–28.

Tripp, Ail Mari, and Joy C. Kwesiga, eds. *The Women's Movement in Uganda: History, Challenges and Prospects*. Kampala: Fountain, 2002.

Tsikata, Edzodzinam. "Women's Political Organizations 1951–1987." In *The State, Development and Politics in Ghana*, ed. Emmanuel Hansen and Kwame A. Ninsin, 73–93. London: CODESRIA, 1989.

Turner, Terisa E. "Oil Workers and Oil Communities in Africa: Nigerian Women and Grassroots Environmentalism." *Labour Capital and Society* 30, 1 (1997): 66–89.

Udvardy, Monica L. "Theorizing Past and Present Women's Organizations in Kenya." *World Development* 26, 9 (1998): 1749–61.

———. "Women's Groups near the Kenyan Coast: Patron-Clientship in the Development Arena." In *Anthropology of Development and Change in East Africa*, ed. David W. Brokensha and Peter D. Little, 217–35. Boulder, Col.: Westview, 1988.

Vuorela, Ulla. "No Sugar—No Tea! A Women's Cooperative in a Crisis, Experiences from Manyoni." In *Tanzania: Crisis and Struggle for Survival*, ed. Jannik Boesen, Kjell J. Havnevik, Juhani Koponen, and Rie Odgaard, 253–68. Uppsala: Scandinavian Institute of African Studies, 1986.

Wipper, Audrey. "The Maendeleo ya Wanawake Organization: The Co-Optation of Leadership." *ASR* 18, 3 (1975): 99–120.

Pastoralism

Blystad, Astrid. "'Dealing with Men's Spears': Datooga Pastoralists Combating Male Intrusion on Female Fertility." In *Those Who Play with Fire: Gender,*

Fertility and Transformation in East and Southern Africa, ed. Henrietta L. Moore, Todd Sanders, and Bwire Kaare, 187–223. London: Athlone, 1999.

Broch-Due, Vigdis. "Creation and the Multiple Female Body: Turkana Perspectives on Gender and Cosmos." In *Those Who Play with Fire: Gender, Fertility and Transformation in East and Southern Africa*, ed. Henrietta L. Moore, Todd Sanders, and Bwire Kaare, 153–84. London: Athlone, 1999.

Hodgson, Dorothy L. *Once Intrepid Warriors: Gender, Ethnicity, and the Cultural Politics of Maasai Development*. Bloomington: Indiana University Press, 2001.

———. ed. *Rethinking Pastoralism in Africa: Gender, Culture and the Myth of the Patriarchal Pastoralist*. Oxford: James Currey, and Athens: Ohio University Press, 2000.

Holtzman, Jon. "Politics and Gastropolitics: Gender and the Power of Food in Two African Pastoralist Societies." *Journal of the Royal Anthropological Institute* 8, 2 (2002): 259–78.

Hutchinson, Sharon. "The Cattle of Money and the Cattle of Girls among the Nuer." *American Ethnologist* 19, 2 (1992): 294–316.

Kapteijns, Lidwien, and Maryan Omar Ali. *Women's Voices in a Man's World: Women and the Pastoral Tradition in Northern Somali Orature, c. 1899–1980*. Portsmouth, N.H.: Heinemann, 1999.

Little, P. D. "Maidens and Milk Markets: The Sociology of Dairy Marketing in Southern Somalia." In *African Pastoralist Systems: An Integrated Approach*, ed. Elliot Fratkin, Kathleen A. Galvin, and Eric Abella Roth. Boulder, Col.: Lynne Rienner, 1994.

Llewelyn-Davies, Melissa. "Two Contexts of Solidarity among Pastoral Maasai Women." In *Women United, Women Divided: Comparative Studies of Ten Contemporary Cultures*, ed. Patricia Caplan and Janet Bujra, 206–37. Bloomington: Indiana University Press, 1979.

Oboler, Regina Smith. "The House-Property Complex and African Social Organization." *Africa* 64, 3 (1994): 342–58.

Shehu, D. J., and W. A. Hassan. "Women in Dairying in the African Savanna: Their Contribution to Agro-Pastoral Household Income in the Dry Northwest of Nigeria." *Nomadic Peoples* 36/37 (1995): 53–63.

Talle, Aud. "Ways of Milk and Meat among the Maasai: Gender Identity and Food Resources in a Pastoral Economy." In *From Water to World-Making*, ed. Gisli Palsson. Uppsala: Scandinavian Institute of African Studies, 1991.

VerEecke, Catherine. "From Pasture to Purdah: The Transformation of Women's Roles and Identity among the Adamawa Fulbe." *Ethnology* 28, 1 (1989): 53–73.

Virtanen, Tea. "Ambiguous Followings: Tracing Autonomy in Pastoral Fulbe Society." In *Shifting Ground and Cultured Bodies: Postcolonial Gender Relations in Africa and India*, ed. Karen Armstrong, 41–46. Lanham, Md.: University Press of America, 1999.

Worley, Barbara A. "Bed Posts and Broad Swords: Twareg Women's Work Parties and the Dialectics of Sexual Conflict." In *Dialectics and Gender: Anthropological Approaches*, ed. Richard R. Randolph, David M. Schneider, and May N. Diaz, 273–87. Boulder, Col.: Westview, 1988.

———. "Property and Gender Relations among Twareg Nomads." *Nomadic Peoples* 23 (1987): 31–36.

Poetry

Adan, Amina H. "Women and Words [Somalia]." *Ufahamu* 10, 3 (1981): 115–42.

Anyidoho, Akosua. "Techniques of Akan Praise Poetry in Christian Worship: Madam Afua Kuma." In *Multiculturalism and Hybridity in African Literatures*, ed. Hal Wylie and Bernth Lindfors, 71–86. Trenton, N.J.: African World Press, 2000.

Barber, Karin. *I Could Speak Until Tomorrow: Oriki, Women and the Past in a Yoruba Town*. Washington, D.C.: Smithsonian Institution Press, 1992.

Biersteker, Ann. "Language, Poetry, and Power: A Reconsideration of 'Utendi wa Mwana Kupona.'" In *Faces of Islam in African Literature*, ed. Kenneth W. Harrow, 59–77. Portsmouth, N.H.: Heinemann, 1991.

Bond-Stewart, Kathy. *Young Women in the Liberation Struggle: Stories and Poems from Zimbabwe*. Harare: Zimbabwe Publishing House, 1984.

Boyd, Jean. "The Fulani Woman Poets." In *Pastoralists of the West African Savannah*, ed. Mahdi Adamu and A. H. M. Kirk-Green. Manchester: Manchester University Press, 1986.

Burness, Donald. "The Poetry of Alda Espirito Santo: Convergence toward Liberation." In *Seasons of Harvest: Essays on the Literatures of Lusophone Africa*, ed. Niyi Afolabi and Donald Burness, 97–113. Trenton, N.J.: Africa World Press, 2003.

Chipasula, Stella, and Frank Chipasula, ed. *The Heinemann Book of African Women's Poetry*. Portsmouth, N.H.: Heinemann, 1995.

Hassan, Dahabo Farah, Amina H. Adan, and Amina Mohamoud Warsame. "Somalia: Poetry as Resistance against Colonialism and Patriarch." In *Subversive Women: Historical Experiences of Gender and Resistance*, ed. Saskia Wieringa, 165–82. London: Zed, 1995.

Hurst, Christopher. "Izimbongi, Images and Identity: Interpreting Two of the Later Praise Poems of Elizabeth Ncube." *Current Writing: Text and Reception in Southern Africa* 11, 1 (1999): 1–19.

Mack, Beverly B. "'Waka Daya Ba Ta Kare Nika': One Song Will Not Finish the Grinding: Hausa Women's Oral Literature." In *Contemporary African Literature*, ed. Hal Wylie, 15–46. Washington, D.C.: Three Continents Press, 1983.

Mbele, J. L. "Wimbo wa Miti: An Example of Swahili Women's Poetry." *African Languages and Cultures* 9, 1 (1996): 71–82.

Oha, Obododimma. "Culture and Gender Semantics in Flora Nwapa's Poetry." In *Writing African Women: Gender, Popular Culture and Literature in West Africa*, ed. Stephanie Newell. London: Zed, 1997.

O'Brien, Colleen. "The Search for Mother Africa: Poetry Revises Women's Struggle for Freedom." *ASR* 37, 2 (1994): 147–55.

Queen Mothers

Aidoo, Agnes Akosua. "Asante Queen Mothers in Government and Politics in the Nineteenth Century." In *The Black Woman Cross-Culturally*, ed. Filomina Chioma Steady, 65–77. Cambridge, Mass.: Schenkman, 1981.

Awe, Bolanle. "The Iyalode in the Traditional Yoruba Political System." In *Sexual Stratification*, ed. Alice Schlegel, 144–61. New York, Columbia University Press, 1977.

Bay, Edna G. "Belief, Legitimacy and the Kpojito: An Institutional History of the 'Queen Mother' in Precolonial Dahomey." *JAH* 36, 1 (1995): 1–27.

Blier, Suzanne Preston. "The Path of the Leopard: Motherhood and Majesty in Early Danhomè." *JAH* 36 (1995): 391–417.

Day, Lynda R. "Long Live the Queen!: The Yaa Asantewaa Centenary and the Politics of History." *Jenda: A Journal of Culture and African Women Studies* 1, 2 (2001), online at www.jendajournal.com.

Feeley-Harnik, Gillian. "Dying Gods and Queen Mothers: The International Politics of Social Reproduction in Africa and Europe." In *Gendered Encounters: Challenging Cultural Boundaries and Social Hierarchies in Africa*, ed. Maria Grosz-Ngaté and Omari H. Kokole, 153–81. New York: Routledge, 1997.

Ifeka, Caroline. "The Mystical and Political Powers of Queen Mothers, Kings and Commoners in Nso, Cameroon." In *Persons and Powers of Women in Diverse Cultures: Essays in Commemoration of Audrey I. Richards, Phyllis Kaberry and Barbara E. Ward*, ed. Shirley Ardener. Providence, R.I.: Berg, 1992.

Kaplan, Flora Edouwaye S., ed. *Queens, Queen Mothers, Priestesses, and Power: Case Studies in African Gender*. New York: New York Academy of Sciences, 1997.

Slavery

Bastian, Misty L. "'The Daughter She Will Eat Agousie in the World of the Spirits': Witchcraft Confessions in Missionized Onitsha, Nigeria." *Africa* 72, 1 (2002): 84–111.

Beall, Jo. "Women under Indentured Labour in Colonial Natal, 1860–1911." In *Women and Gender in Southern Africa to 1945*, ed. Cherryl Walker. London: James Currey, 1990.

Boaten, Abayie B. "The Trokosi System in Ghana: Discrimination against Women and Children." In *African Women and Children: Crisis and Response*, ed. Apollo Rwomire. Westport, Conn.: Praeger, 2001.

Cooper, Barbara M. "Reflections on Slavery, Seclusion, and Female Labor in the Maradi Region of Niger in the 19th and 20th Centuries." *JAH* 35, 1 (1994): 61–79.

Diawara, Mamadou. "Women, Servitude and History: The Oral Historical Tradition of Women of Servile Condition in the Kingdom of Jaara (Mali) from the Fifteenth to the Mid-Nineteenth Century." In *Discourse and Its Disguises: The Interpretation of African Oral Texts*, ed. Karin Barber and P. F. de Moraes Farias, 109–37. Birmingham: University of Birmingham Centre of West African Studies, 1989. Originally published in French in *HA* 16 (1989).

Eastman, Carol. "Women, Slaves and Foreigners: African Cultural Influences and Group Processes in the Formation of Northern Swahili Coastal Society." *IJAHS* 21, 1 (1987): 1–20.

Goodridge, Richard. "Restrictions and Freedoms for Women in Northern Cameroons to 1961: An Examination of the Liberating Influences." In *Working Slavery, Pricing Freedom: Perspectives from the Caribbean, Africa and the African Diaspora*, ed. Verene A. Shepherd. New York: Palgrave, 2002.

Greene, Sandra E. "Crossing Boundaries/Changing Identities: Female Slaves, Male Strangers, and their Descendants in Nineteenth- and Twentieth-Century Anlo." In *Gendered Encounters: Challenging Cultural Boundaries and Social Hierarchies in Africa*, ed. Maria Grosz-Ngaté and Omari H. Kokole, 23–41. New York: Routledge, 1997.

Lovejoy, Paul E. "Concubinage and the Status of Women Slaves in Early Colonial Northern Nigeria." *JAH* 29 (1988): 245–66.

Mack, Beverly B. "Service and Status: Slaves and Concubines in Kano, Nigeria." In *At Work in Homes: Household Workers in World Perspective*, ed. Roger Sanjek and Shellee Colen, 14–34. Washington, D.C.: American Anthropological Association, 1990.

Martin, Susan. "On Slavery, Igbo Women, Palm Oil." In *From Slave Trade to 'Legitimate' Commerce: The Commercial Transition in Nineteenth Century West Africa*, ed. Robin Law. Cambridge: Cambridge University Press, 1995.

McDougall, E. Ann. "A Sense of Self: The Life of Fatma Barku." *CJAS* 32, 2 (1998).

Morton-Williams, Peter. "A Yoruba Woman Remembers Servitude in a Palace of Dahomey, in the Reigns of Kings Glele and Behanzin." *Africa* 63, 1 (1993): 102–17.

Nast, Heidi J. "The Impact of British Imperialism on the Landscape of Female Slavery in the Kano Palace, Northern Nigeria." *Africa* 64, 1 (1994): 34–73.

———. "Islam, Gender, and Slavery in West Africa circa 1500: A Spatial Archaeology of the Kano Palace, Northern Nigeria." *Annals of the Association of American Geographers* 86, 1 (1996): 44–77.

Robertson, Claire C., and Martin A. Klein, ed. *Women and Slavery in Africa.* Portsmouth, N.H.: Heinemann, 1998 [Madison: University of Wisconsin Press, 1983].

Ruf, Urs Peter. *Ending Slavery: Hierarchy, Dependency and Gender in Central Mauritania.* Bielefeld: Transcript Verlag, 1999.

Scully, Pamela. *Liberating the Family? Gender and British Slave Emancipation in the Rural Western Cape, South Africa, 1823–1853.* Portsmouth, N.H.: Heinemann, 1997.

Sikainga, Ahmad A. "Shari'a Courts and the Manumission of Female Slaves in the Sudan." *IJAHS* 28, 1 (1995): 1–24.

Turrell, Rob. "The 'Singular Case' of Mietje Bontnaal, the Bushmanland Murderess." *JSAS* 29, 1 (2003): 83–103.

Vanderspuy, Patricia. "Gender and Slavery: Towards a Feminist Revision." *South African Historical Journal* 25 (1991): 184–95.

Woodward, Wendy. "Contradictory Tongues: Torture and the Testimony of Two Slave Women in the Eastern Cape Courts in 1833 and 1834." In *Deep hiStories: Gender and Colonialism in Southern Africa*, ed. Wendy Woodward, Patricia Hayes, and Gary Minkley, 55–83. Amsterdam: Rodopi, 2002.

Wright, Marcia. *Strategies of Slaves and Women: Life-Stories from East/Central Africa.* New York: Lilian Barber Press, 1993.

———. "Women in Peril: A Commentary on the Life Stories of Captives in Nineteenth-Century East-Central Africa." *African Social Research* 20 (1975): 800–19.

Spirit Possession and Spirit Mediums

Alpers, Edward A. "'Ordinary Household Chores': Ritual and Power in a 19th-Century Swahili Women's Spirit Possession Cult." *IJAHS* 17, 4 (1984): 677–702.

Beach, D. N. "An Innocent Woman, Unjustly Accused? Charwe, Medium of the Nehanda Mhondoro Spirit, and the 1896–97 Central Shona Rising in Zimbabwe." *HA* 25 (1998): 27–54.

Ben-Amos, Paula Girshick. "The Promise of Greatness: Women and Power in an Edo Spirit Possession Cult." In *Religion in Africa: Experience and Expression*, ed. Thomas D. Blakeley, Walter E. A. van Beek, and Dennis L. Thomson, 118–34. Portsmouth, N.H.: Heinemann, 1994.

Berger, Iris. "Fertility as Power: Spirit Mediums, Priestesses and the Precolonial State in Interlacustrine East Africa." In *Revealing Prophets: Prophecy in*

East African History, ed. David M. Anderson and Douglas H. Johnson, 65–82. London: James Currey, 1995.

Boddy, Janice. *Wombs and Alien Spirits: Women, Men, and the Zar Cult in Northern Sudan*. Madison: University of Wisconsin Press, 1989.

Buckner, Margaret. "Modern Zande Prophetesses." In *Revealing Prophets: Prophecy in East African History*, ed. David M. Anderson and Douglas H. Johnson, 102–21. London: James Currey, 1995.

Constantinides, Pamela. "Women's Spirit Possession and Urban Adaptation in the Muslim Northern Sudan." In *Women United, Women Divided: Comparative Studies of Ten Contemporary Cultures*, ed. Patricia Caplan and Janet Bujra, 185–205. Bloomington: Indiana University Press, 1979.

de Sousa, Alexandra O. "Defunct Women: Possession Among the Bijagós Islanders." In *Spirit Possession: Modernity and Power in Africa*, ed. Heike Behrend and Ute Luig, 81–88. Madison: University of Wisconsin Press, 1999.

Echard, Nicole. "Gender Relationships and Religion: Women in the Hausa Bori of Ader, Niger." In *Hausa Women in the Twentieth Century*, ed. Catherine Coles and Beverly Mack, 207–20. Madison: University of Wisconsin Press, 1991.

El-Nagar, Samia El-Hadi. "Zaar Practitioners and Their Assistants and Followers in Omdurman." In *Urbanization and Urban Life in the Sudan*, ed. Valdo Pons. University of Hull, Department of Sociology and Social Anthropology, 1980.

Hodgson, Dorothy. "Embodying the Contradictions of Modernity: Gender and Spirit Possession among Maasai in Tanzania." In *Gendered Encounters: Challenging Cultural Boundaries and Social Hierarchies in Africa*, ed. Maria Grosz-Ngaté and Omari H. Kokole, 111–29. New York: Routledge, 1997.

Hopkins, Elizabeth. "The Nyabingi Cult of Southwestern Uganda." In *Rebellion in Black Africa*, ed. Robert I. Rotberg, 60–132. Oxford: Oxford University Press, 1971.

Kenyon, Susan M. "The Case of the Butcher's Wife: Illness, Possession and Power in Central Sudan." In *Spirit Possession: Modernity and Power in Africa*, ed. Heike Behrend and Ute Luig, 89–108. Madison: University of Wisconsin Press, 1999.

Kilson, Marion. "Ritual Portrait of a Ga Medium." In *The New Religions of Africa*, ed. Bennetta Jules-Rosette, 67–79. Norwood, N.J.: Ablex, 1979.

Lewis, I. M., Ahmed Al-Safi, and Sayyid Hurreiz, eds. *Women's Medicine: The Zar-Bori Cult in Africa and Beyond*. Edinburgh: Edinburgh University Press, 1991.

Masquelier, Adeline. "Mediating Threads: Clothing and the Texture of Spirit/Medium Relations in Bori (Southern Niger)." In *Clothing and Difference: Embodied Identities in Colonial and Post-Colonial Africa*, ed. Hildi Hendrickson, 66–93. Durham, N.C.: Duke University Press, 1996.

Middleton-Keirn, Susan. "Convivial Sisterhood: Spirit Mediumship and Client-Core Network among Black South African Women." In *Women in Ritual and Symbolic Roles*, ed. Judith Hoch-Smith and Anita Spring, 191–205. New York: Plenum, 1978.

Nisula, Tapio. "'The Woman in the Body': Spirits and Spouses in Zanzibar Town." In *Shifting Ground and Cultured Bodies: Postcolonial Gender Relations in Africa and India*, ed. Karen Armstrong, 67–102. Lanham, Md.: University Press of America, 1999.

O'Brien, Susan M. "Spirit Discipline: Gender, Islam, and Hierarchies of Treatment in Postcolonial Northern Nigeria." *Interventions: International Journal of Postcolonial Studies* 3, 2 (2001): 222–41.

Prince, Rugh, and P. Wenzel Geissler. "Becoming 'One Who Treats': A Case Study of a Luo Healer and Her Grandson in Western Kenya." *Anthropology and Education Quarterly* 32, 4 (2001): 447–71.

Rasmussen, Susan J. "The 'Head Dance,' Contested Self, and Art as a Balancing Act in Tuareg Spirit Possession." *Africa* 64, 1 (1994): 74–98.

Sibisi, Harriet. "How African Women Cope with Migrant Labor in South Africa." *Signs* 3, 1 (1977): 167–77.

Spring, Anita. "Epidemiology of Spirit Possession among the Luvale of Zambia." In *Women in Ritual and Symbolic Roles*, ed. Judith Hoch-Smith and Anita Spring, 165–90. New York: Plenum, 1978.

Vail, Leroy, and Landeg White. "The Possession of the Dispossessed: Songs as History among Tumbuka Women." In *Power and the Praise Poem: Southern African Voices in History*, ed. Leroy Vail and Landeg White, 231–77. Charlottesville: University Press of Virginia, 1991.

Structural Adjustment Programs

Brand, V., R. Mupedziswa, and P. Gumbo. "Structural Adjustment, Women and Informal Trade in Harare." In *Structural Adjustment in Zimbabwe*, ed. P. Gibbon. Uppsala: Nordiska Afrikainstitutet, 1995.

Creevey, Lucy. "Structural Adjustment and the Empowerment (Disempowerment) of Women in Niger and Senegal." In *Women in Developing Countries: Assessing Strategies for Empowerment*, ed. Rekha Datta and Judith Kornberg. Boulder, Col.: Lynne Rienner, 2002.

Dennis, Carolyne. "The Christian Churches and Women's Experience of Structural Adjustment in Nigeria." In *Women and Adjustment Policies in the Third World*, ed. Haleh Afshar and Carolyne Dennis, 179–204. New York: St. Martin's Press, 1992.

———. "The Limits to Women's Independent Careers: Gender in the Formal and Informal Sectors in Nigeria." In *Male Bias in the Development*

Process, ed. Diane Elson, 83–104. Manchester: Manchester University Press, 1991.

Elabor-Idemudia, Patience. "Nigeria: Agricultural Exports and Compensatory Schemes—Rural Women's Productive Resources." In *Mortgaging Women's Lives: Feminist Critiques of Structural Adjustment*, ed. Pamela Sparr, 134–64. London: Zed, 1994.

Feldman, Rayah. *Women for a Change!: The Impact of Structural Adjustment on Women in Zambia, Tanzania, and Mozambique*. London: War on Want, 1989.

Geisler, Gisela, and Karen Tranberg Hansen. "Structural Adjustment, the Rural–Urban Interface and Gender Relations in Zambia." In *Women in the Age of Economic Transformation: Gender Impact of Reforms in Post-Socialist and Developing Countries*, ed. Nahid Aslanbeigui, Steven Pressman, and Gale Summerfield, 95–112. New York: Routledge, 1994.

Gladwin, Christina H., ed. *Structural Adjustment and African Women Farmers*. Gainesville: University of Florida Press, 1991.

Horn, Nancy E. "Market Women, Development, and Structural Adjustment in Harare, Zimbabwe." *ARUS* 2, 1 (1995): 17–42.

Kanji, Nazneen, and Niki Jazdowska. "Structural Adjustment and Women in Zimbabwe." *ROAPE* 56 (1993): 11–26.

Kuenyehia, Akua. "The Impact of Structural Adjustment Programs on Women's International Human Rights: The Example of Ghana." In *Human Rights of Women: National and International Perspectives*, ed. Rebecca J. Cook, 422–36. Philadelphia: University of Pennsylvania Press, 1994.

Manuh, Takyiwaa. "Ghana: Women in the Public and Informal Sectors Under the Economic Recovery Program." In *Mortgaging Women's Lives: Feminist Critiques of Structural Adjustment*, ed. Pamela Sparr, 61–77. London: Zed, 1994.

Mbilinyi, Marjorie. "'Structural Adjustment,' Agribusiness and Rural Women in Tanzania." In *The Food Question: Profits Versus People*, ed. Henry Bernstein, et al., 111–24. New York: Monthly Review Press, 1990.

Mupedziswa, Rodrick, and Perpetua Gumbo. *Structural Adjustment and Women: Informal Sector Traders in Harare, Zimbabwe*. Uppsala: Nordiska Afrikainstitutet, 1998.

Mwansa, Lengwe-Katembula J. "Structural Adjustment and the Question of Poor Urban Women in Zambia." In *Women in Development: Gender and Development in Southern Africa, Problems and Prospects*, ed. R. C. Leduka, K. Matlosa, and T. Petlane, 60–76. Maseru: National University of Lesotho, 1993.

Ongile, Grace Atieno. *Gender and Agricultural Supply Responses to Structural Adjustment Programmes*. Uppsala: Nordiska Afrikainstitutet, 1999.

Osirim, Mary J. "The Dilemmas of Modern Development: Structural Adjustment and Women Microentrepreneurs in Nigeria and Zimbabwe." In *The Gendered New World Order: Militarism, Development, and the Environment*, ed. Jennifer Turpin and Lois Ann Lorentzen, 127–46. New York: Routledge, 1996.

———. "Negotiating Identities during Adjustment Programs: Women Microentrepreneurs in Urban Zimbabwe." In *African Entrepreneurship: Theory and Reality*, ed. Anita Spring and Barbara E. McDade. Gainesville: University Press of Florida, 1998.

Palmer, Ingrid. *Gender and Population in the Adjustment of African Economies: Planning for Change*. Geneva: International Labor Office, 1991.

Riphenburg, Carol J. "Changing Gender Relations and Structural Adjustment in Zimbabwe." *Africa (Rome)* 52, 2 (1997): 237–60.

Shehu, D. J. "Technology and the Fuel Crisis: Adjustment among Women in Northern Nigeria." In *African Feminism: The Politics of Survival in Sub-Saharan Africa*, ed. Gwendolyn Mikell, 276–97. Philadelphia: University of Pennsylvania Press, 1997.

Stromquist, Nelly P. "The Impact of Structural Adjustment Programmes on Africa and Latin America." In *Gender, Education and Development: Beyond Access to Empowerment*, ed. Christine Heward and Sheila Bunwaree, 17–32. London: Zed, 1999.

Thomas-Emeagwali, Gloria, ed. *Women Pay the Price: Structural Adjustment in Africa and the Caribbean*. Trenton, N.J.: Africa World Press, 1995.

Tsikata, Dzodzi, and Joanna Kerr, eds. *Demanding Dignity: Women Confronting Economic Reforms in Africa*. Ottawa: North-South Institute, 2000.

Wangari, Esther, Barbara Thomas-Slayter, and Dianne Rocheleau. "Gendered Visions for Survival: Semi-Arid Regions in Kenya." In *Feminist Political Ecology: Global Issues and Local Experiences*, ed. Dianne Rocheleau, Barbara Thomas-Slayter, and Esther Wangari, 127–54. New York: Routledge, 1996.

Weekes-Vagliani, Winifred. "Structural Adjustment and Gender in Côte d'Ivoire." In *Women and Adjustment Policies in the Third World*, ed. Haleh Afshar and Carolyne Dennis, 117–49. New York: St. Martin's Press, 1992.

Theater, Film, and Performance

Beik, Janet. "Women's Roles in the Contemporary Hausa Theater of Niger." In *Hausa Women in the Twentieth Century*, ed. Catherine Coles and Beverly Mack, 232–43. Madison: University of Wisconsin Press, 1991.

Bjorkman, Ingrid. *Mother, Sing for Me: People's Theatre in Kenya*. London: Zed, 1989.

Cham, Mbye. "African Women and Cinema: A Conversation with Anne Mungai." *RAL* 25, 3 (1994).

Ellerson, Beti. "The Female Body as Symbol of Change and Dichotomy: Conflicting Paradigms in the Representation of Women in African Film." *Matatu* 19 (1997): 31–41.

———. *Sisters of the Screen: Women of Africa on Film, Video and Television.* Trenton, N.J.: Africa World Press, 1999.

Glazer, Anita. "Dialectics of Gender in Senufo Masquerades." *African Arts* 19, 3 (1986): 30–39, 82.

Harrow, Kenneth, ed. *African Cinema: Postcolonial and Feminist Readings.* Trenton, N.J.: Africa World Press, 1999.

Hoch-Smith, Judith. "Radical Yoruba Female Sexuality: The Witch and the Prostitute." In *Women in Ritual and Symbolic Roles*, ed. Judith Hoch-Smith and Anita Spring, 245–68. New York: Plenum, 1978.

James, Deborah. *Songs of the Women Migrants: Performance and Identity in South Africa.* Witwatersrand: Witwatersrand University Press, 1999.

Kratz, Corinne A. *Affecting Performance: Meaning, Movement, and Experience in Okiek Women's Initiation.* Washington, D.C.: Smithsonian, 1993.

MacRae, Suzanne H. "The Mature and Older Women of African Film." *Matatu* 19 (1997).

Maldoror, Sarah. "To Make a Film Means to Take a Position." In *African Experience of Cinema*, ed. Imruh Bakari and Mbye Cham, 45–47. London: BFI, 1966.

Moorman, Marissa. "Of Westerns, Women, and War: Re-Situating Angolan Cinema and the Nation." *RAL* 32, 3 (2001): 103–23.

Muller, Carol Ann. *Rituals of Fertility and the Sacrifice of Desire: Nazarite Women's Performance in South Africa.* Chicago: University of Chicago Press, 1999.

Murphy, David. "Mothers, Daughters and Prostitutes: The Representations of Women in Sembene's Work." In *Sembene: Imagining Alternatives in Film and Fiction*, ed. David Murphy. Trenton, N.J.: Africa World Press, 2000.

Nwachukwu-Agbada, J. O. J. "Women in Igbo-Language Videos: The Virtuous and the Villainous." *Matatu* 19 (1997).

Onwueme, Osonye Tess. "Drumbeats in Black Women's Drama." *Obsidian* 111 (1999): 160–67.

Outa, George Odera. "Lysistrata in Nairobi: Performing the Power of Womanhood in the Post-Colony." *African Studies* 58, 2 (1999).

Perkins, Kathy A., ed. *Black South African Women: An Anthology of Plays.* New York: Routledge, 1998.

Petty, Sheila J. "'How an African Woman Can Be': African Women Filmmakers Construct Women." *Discourse* 18, 3 (1996): 72–88.

——. "(Re)Presenting the Self: Identity and Consciousness in the Feature Films of Safi Faye." In *International Women's Writing: New Landscapes of Identity*, ed. Anne E. Brown and Marjanne E. Gooze, 19–28. Westport, Conn.: Greenwood, 1995.

Plastow, Jane, ed. *African Theatre: Women*. Oxford: James Currey, 2002.

Power, Camilla, and Ian Watts. "The Woman with the Zebra's Penis: Gender, Mutability and Performance." *Journal of the Royal Anthropological Institute* 3, 3 (1997): 537–60.

Radhakrishnan, Smitha. "'African Dream': The Imaginary of Nation, Race, and Gender in South African Intercultural Dance." *FS* 29, 3 (2003): 529–37.

Rasmussen, Susan J. "The 'Head Dance,' Contested Self, and Art as a Balancing Act in Tuareg Spirit Possession." *Africa* 64, 1 (1994): 74–98.

Schmidt, Nancy. "Sub-Saharan African Women Filmmakers: Agendas for Research with a Filmography." *Matatu* 19 (1997).

Twiggs, Laura, and Kgafela oa Magogodi. "Jump the Gun: Departing from a Racist/Feminist Nexus in Postapartheid Cinema." In *To Change Reels: Film and Culture in South Africa*, ed., Isabel Balseiro and Ntongela Masilela. Detroit, Mich.: Wayne State University Press, 2003.

Ukadike, N. Frank. "Reclaiming Images of Women in Films from Africa and the Black Diaspora." *Frontiers* 15, 1 (1994): 102–22.

Urbanization: Housing, Employment, and Markets

Abwunza, Judith. "'Mulugulu Avakali': City Women in Nairobi." *Journal of Contemporary African Studies* 14, 1 (1996): 105–18.

Adepoju, Aderanti. "Migration and Female Employment in Southwestern Nigeria." *African Urban Studies* 18 (1984): 59–75.

Agadjanian, Victor. "Trapped on the Margins: Social Characteristics, Economic Conditions, and Reproductive Behaviour of Internally Displaced Women in Urban Mozambique." *Journal of Refugee Studies* 11, 3 (1998): 285–303.

Antoine, Philippe, and Jeanne Nanitelamio. "More Single Women in African Cities: Pikine, Abidjan and Brazzaville." *Population, English Selection* 3 (1992): 149–69.

——. "Nouveaux statuts feminins et urbanisation en Afrique." *Genus* 46, 3–4 (1990): 17–30.

Asiama, Seth Opuni. "Crossing the Barrier of Time: The Asante Woman in Urban Land Development." *Africa (Rome)* 52, 2 (1997): 212–35.

Bakwesegha, Christopher J. *Profiles of Urban Prostitution: A Case Study from Uganda*. Nairobi: Kenya Literature Bureau, 1982.

Bardouille, Raj. "The Sexual Division of Labour in the Urban Informal Sector: The Case of Some Townships in Lusaka." *African Social Research* 32 (1981): 29–54.

Baylies, Carolyn, and Caroline Wright. "Female Labour in the Textile and Clothing Industry of Lesotho." *African Affairs* 92 (1993): 577–91.

Beavon, K. S. O., and C. M. Rogerson. "The Changing Role of Women in the Urban Informal Sector of Johannesburg." In *Urbanization in the Developing World*, ed. D. Drakakis-Smith. London: Croom Helm, 1986.

Biaya, Tshikala Kayembe. "Les plaisirs de la ville: masculinité, sexualité et féminité à Dakar (1997–2000)." *ASR* 44, 2 (2001): 71–86.

Bjeren, Gunilla. *Migration to Shashemene: Ethnicity, Gender and Occupation in Urban Ethiopia*. Uppsala: Scandinavian Institute of African Studies, 1985.

Brand, V., R. Mupedziswa, and P. Gumbo. "Structural Adjustment, Women and Informal Trade in Harare." In *Structural Adjustment in Zimbabwe*, ed. P. Gibbon. Uppsala: Nordiska Afrikainstitutet, 1995.

Brockerhoff, Martin, and Hongsook Eu. "Demographic and Socioeconomic Determinants of Female Rural to Urban Migration in Sub-Saharan Africa." *International Migration Review* 27, 3 (1993): 557–77.

Callaway, Barbara J. "The Role of Women in Kano City Politics." In *Hausa Women in the Twentieth Century*, ed. Catherine Coles and Beverly Mack, 145–59. Madison: University of Wisconsin Press, 1991.

Campbell, Catherine. "The Township Family and Women's Struggles." *Agenda* 6 (1990): 1–22.

Chamlee-Wright, Emily. *Cultural Foundations of Economic Development: Urban Female Entrepreneurship in Ghana*. New York: Routledge, 1997.

Chimanikire, Donald P. "Women in Industry: Legal and Social Attitudes." *Africa Development* 12, 4 (1987): 27–38.

Chiré, A. S. "Djibouti: Migrations de populations et insertion urbaine des femmes." *L'Afrique Politique: Femmes d'Afrique* (1998): 121–46.

Clark, Gracia. "Market Association Leaders' Strategic Use of Language and Narrative in Market Disputes and Negotiations in Kumasi, Ghana." *Africa Today* 49, 1 (2002): 43–58.

———. "Mothering, Work, and Gender in Urban Asante Ideology and Practice." *American Anthropologist* 101, 4 (1999): 717–29.

———. "'Nursing-Mother Work' in Ghana: Power and Frustration in Akan Market Women's Lives." In *Women Traders in Cross-Cultural Perspective*, ed. Linda Seligmann. Stanford, Calif.: Stanford University Press, 2001.

Cohen, Barney, and William J. House. "Women's Urban Labour Market Status in Developing Countries: How Well Do They Fare in Khartoum, Sudan?" *Journal of Development Studies* 29, 3 (1993): 461–83.

Coles, Catherine. "Hausa Women's Work in a Declining Urban Economy: Kaduna, Nigeria, 1980–1985." In *Hausa Women in the Twentieth Century*, ed. Catherine Coles and Beverly Mack, 163–91. Madison: University of Wisconsin Press, 1991.

——. "The Older Woman in Hausa Society: Power and Authority in Urban Nigeria." In *The Cultural Context of Aging: Worldwide Perspectives*, ed. Jay Sokolovsky, 57–81. New York: Bergin & Garvey, 1990.

Comhaire-Sylvain, Suzanne. *Femmes de Lomé*. Bandundu: CEEBA, 1982.

Date-Bah, Eugenia. "Sex Segregation and Discrimination in Accra-Tema: Causes and Consequences." In *Sex Inequalities in Urban Employment in the Third World*, ed. Richard Anker and Catherine Hein, 235–76. New York: ILO/St. Martin's Press, 1986.

Dauda, Carol L. "Preparing the Ground for a New Local Politics: The Case of Women in Two African Municipalities." *CJAS* 35, 2 (2001): 246‑81.

Davis, Paula Jean. "On the Sexuality of 'Town Women' in Kampala." *Africa Today* 47, 3 & 4 (2001): 29–60.

de Herdt, Tom, and Stefaan Marysse. "The Reinvention of the Market from Below: The End of the Women's Money Changing Monopoly in Kinshasa." *ROAPE* 26, 80 (1999): 239–54.

Dei, Carlene H. "Women and Grassroots Politics in Abidjan, Côte d'Ivoire." In *African Feminism: The Politics of Survival in Sub-Saharan Africa*, ed. Gwendolyn Mikell, 206–31. Philadelphia: University of Pennsylvania Press, 1997.

Deniel, Raymond. *Femmes des villes africaines*. Abidjan: Inades Edition, 1985.

Dennis, Carolyne. "The Limits to Women's Independent Careers: Gender in the Formal and Informal Sectors in Nigeria." In *Male Bias in the Development Process*, ed. Diane Elson, 83–104. Manchester: Manchester University Press, 1991.

Di Domenico, Catherine. "Urban Yoruba Mothers: At Home and at Work." In *Sex Roles, Population and Development in West Africa: Policy-Related Studies on Work and Demographic Issues*, ed. Christine Oppong, 118–32. Portsmouth, N.H.: Heinemann, 1987.

Dickerman, Carol. "City Women and the Colonial Regime: Usumbura, 1939–1962." *African Urban Studies* 18 (1984): 33–48.

Drakakis-Smith, D. W. "The Changing Economic Role of Women in the Urbanization Process: A Preliminary Report from Zimbabwe." *International Migration Review* 18, 4 (1984): 1278–92.

Edwards, Iain. "Cato Manor: Men, Women, Crowds, Violence, and Politics." In *The People's City: African Life in 20th-Century Durban*, ed. Paul Maylam and Iain Edwards. Portsmouth, N.H.: Heinemann, 1996.

——. "Shebeen Queens: Illicit Liquor and the Social Structure of Drinking Dens in Cato Manor." *Agenda* 3 (1988): 75–97.

Egziabher, Axumite G. "Urban Farming, Cooperatives, and the Urban Poor in Addis Ababa." In *Cities Feeding People: An Examination of Urban Agriculture in East Africa*, ed. Axumite G. Egziabher et al., 85–104. Ottawa: IDRC, 1994.

El Bakri, Zeinab B., and El-Wathig M. Kameir. "Women's Participation in Eco-
nomic, Social and Political Life in Sudanese Urban and Rural Communities:
The Case of Saganna in Khartoum and Wad al-'Asha Village in the Gezira
Area." In *Women in Arab Society: Work Patterns and Gender Relations in
Egypt, Jordan and Sudan*, ed. Seteney Shami et al., 160–98. Providence, R.I.:
Berg/UNESCO, 1990.

Ellovich, Risa S. "Dioula Women in Town: A View of Intra-Ethnic Variation
(Ivory Coast)." In *A World of Women: Anthropological Studies of Women in
the Societies of the World*, ed. Erika Bourguignon, 87–103. New York:
Praeger, 1980.

Fapohunda, Eleanor R. "Urban Women's Roles and Nigerian Government Development Strategies." In *Sex Roles, Population and Development in West
Africa: Policy-Related Studies on Work and Demographic Issues*, ed. Christine Oppong, 203–12. Portsmouth, N.H.: Heinemann, 1987.

Findley, Sally E. "Les migrations féminines dans les villes africaines: Une revue de leurs motivations et experiences." In *L'Insertion Urbaine des Migrants en Afrique*, ed. Philippe Antoine and Sidiki Coulibaly, 55–70. Paris:
L'Orstom, 1989.

Flynn, Karen Coen. "Urban Agriculture in Mwanza, Tanzania." *Africa* 71, 4
(2001).

Freeman, Donald B. *A City of Farmers: Informal Urban Agriculture in the
Open Spaces of Nairobi, Kenya*. Montreal: McGill-Queen's University Press,
1991.

———. "Survival Strategy or Business Training Ground? The Significance of
Urban Agriculture for the Advancement of Women in African Cities." *ASR*
36, 3 (1993): 1–22.

Freidberg, Susanne. "To Garden, To Market: Gendered Meanings of Work
on an African Urban Periphery." *Gender, Place and Culture* 8, 1 (2001):
5–24.

Friedman, Michelle, and Maria Hambridge. "The Informal Sector, Gender, and
Development." In *South Africa's Informal Sector*, ed. Eleanor Preston-
Whyte and Christian Rogerson, 161–80. Cape Town: Oxford University
Press, 1991.

Frishman, Alan. "Hausa Women in the Urban Economy of Kano." In *Hausa
Women in the Twentieth Century*, ed. Catherine Coles and Beverly Mack,
192–203. Madison: University of Wisconsin Press, 1991.

Gaitskell, Deborah. "Housewives, Maids or Mothers: Some Contradictions of
Domesticity for Christian Women in Johannesburg, 1903–39." *JAH* 24, 2
(1983): 241–56.

———. "'Christian Compounds for Girls': Church Hostels for African Women
in Johannesburg, 1907–1970." *JSAS* 6, 1 (1979): 44–69.

Glazer, Ilsa M. "Alcohol and Politics in Urban Zambia: The Intersection of Gender and Class." In *African Feminism: The Politics of Survival in Sub-Saharan Africa*, ed. Gwendolyn Mikell, 142–58. Philadelphia: University of Pennsylvania Press, 1997.

Gondola, Ch. Didier. "Popular Music, Urban Society, and Changing Gender Relations in Kinshasa, Zaire (1950–1990)." In *Gendered Encounters: Challenging Cultural Boundaries and Social Hierarchies in Africa*, ed. Maria Grosz-Ngaté and Omari H. Kokole, 65–84. New York: Routledge, 1997.

Gugler, Josef. "Women Stay on the Farm No More: Changing Patterns of Rural–Urban Migration in Sub-Saharan Africa." *JMAS* 27, 2 (1989): 347–52.

Gugler, Josef, and Gudrun Ludwar-Ene. "Gender and Migration in Africa South of the Sahara." In *The Migration Experience in Africa*, ed. Jonathan Baker and Tade Akin Aina, 257–68. Uppsala: Nordiska Afrikainstitutet, 1995.

Hainard, François, and Christine Verschuur. *Femmes dans les crises urbaines: Relations de genre et environnements précaires*. Paris: Karthala, 2002.

Hansen, Karen Tranberg. *Keeping House in Lusaka*. Irvington, N.Y.: Columbia University Press, 1996.

———. "Negotiating Sex and Gender in Urban Zambia." *JSAS* 10, 2 (1984): 219–38.

Hirschmann, David. "Urban Women, Civil Society, and Social Transition in the Eastern Cape, South Africa." *ARUS* 1, 2 (1994): 31–48.

Horn, Nancy E. *Cultivating Customers: Market Women in Harare, Zimbabwe*. Boulder, Col.: Lynne Rienner, 1994.

———. "Market Women, Development, and Structural Adjustment in Harare, Zimbabwe." *ARUS* 2, 1 (1995): 17–42.

———. "Overcoming Challenges: Women Mircroentrepreneurs in Harare, Zimbabwe." In *African Entrepreneurship: Theory and Reality*, ed. Anita Spring and Barbara E. McDade. Gainesville: University Press of Florida, 1998.

House-Midamba, Bessie, and Felix K. Ekechi, eds. *African Market Women and Economic Power: The Role of Women in African Economic Development*. Westport, Conn.: Greenwood, 1995.

Imam, Ayesha M. "Politics, Islam, and Women in Kano, Northern Nigeria." In *Identity Politics and Women: Cultural Reassertions and Feminisms in International Perspective*, ed. Valentine M. Moghadam, 123–44. Boulder, Col.: Westview, 1994.

Ishani, Zarina, and Davinder Lamba, eds. *Emerging African Perspectives on Gender in Urbanisation: African Research on Gender, Urbanisation and Environment*. Nairobi: Mazingira Institute, 2001.

Ivaska, Andrew M. "'Anti-Mini Militants Meet Modern Misses': Urban Style, Gender and the Politics of 'National Culture' in 1960s Dar es Salaam, Tanzania." *Gender and History* 14, 3 (2002): 584–607.

Iyun, B. Folasade, and E. A. Oke. "The Impact of Contraceptive Use among Urban Traders in Nigeria: Ibadan Traders and Modernization." In *Different Places, Different Voice: Gender and Development in Africa, Asia and Larin America*, ed. Janet Henshall Momsen and Vivian Kinnaird, 63–73. London and New York: Routledge, 1993.

Jackson, Lynette. "'Stray Women' and 'Girls on the Move': Gender, Space, and Disease in Colonial and Post-Colonial Zimbabwe." In *Sacred Spaces and Public Quarrels: African Cultural and Economic Landscapes*, ed. Paul Tiyambe Zeleza and Ezekiel Kalipeni, 147–67. Trenton, N.J.: Africa World Press, 1999.

Jeater, Diana. "No Place for a Woman: Gwelo Town, Southern Rhodesia, 1894–1920." *JSAS* 26, 1 (2000): 29–42.

Johnson, Willene A. "Women and Self-Employment in Urban Tanzania." In *Slipping Through the Cracks: The Status of Black Women*, ed. Margaret C. Simms and Julianne Malveaux, 245–57. New Brunswick, N.J.: Transaction, 1986.

Jules-Rosette, Bennetta. "Women and Technological Change in the Informal Urban Economy: A Zambian Case Study." In *Women's Worlds: From the New Scholarship*, ed. Marilyn Safir et al., 58–70. New York: Praeger, 1985.

———. "The Women Potters of Lusaka: Urban Migration and Socioeconomic Adjustment." In *African Migration and National Development*, ed. Beverly Lindsay, 82–112. University Park: Pennsylvania State University Press, 1985.

Larsson, Anita, Matseliso Mapetla, and Ann Schlyter, eds. *Changing Gender Relations in Southern Africa: Issues of Urban Life*. Roma: National University of Lesotho, 1998.

Lee-Smith, Diana, ed. *Women Managing Resources: African Research on Gender, Urbanisation and Environment*. Nairobi: Mazingira Institute, 1999.

Mann, Kristin. *Marrying Well: Marriage, Status and Social Change among the Educated Elite in Colonial Lagos*. New York: Cambridge University Press, 1985.

———. "Women, Landed Property, and the Accumulation of Wealth in Early Colonial Lagos." *Signs* 16, 4 (1991): 682–706.

Mashiri, Pedzisai. "Street Remarks, Address Rights and the Urban Female: Socio-Linguistic Politics of Gender in Harare." *Zambezia* 27, 1 (2000): 55–70.

May, Joan. *African Women in Urban Employment: Factors Influencing Their Employment in Zimbabwe*. Gweru: Mambo Press, 1979.

McAdoo, Harriette, and Miriam Were. "Extended Family Involvement of Urban Kenyan Professional Women." In *Women in Africa and the African Diaspora*, ed. Rosalyn Terborg-Penn, Sharon Harley, and Andrea Benton Rushing, 133–64. Washington, D.C.: Howard University Press, 1989.

Mianda, Gertrude. "Women and Garden Produce of Kinshasa: The Difficult Quest for Autonomy." In *Women, Work, and Gender Relations in Developing Countries: A Global Perspective*, ed. Parvin Ghorayshi and Claire Bélanger, 91–101. Westport, Conn.: Greenwood, 1996.

Mikell, Gwendolyn. "Using the Courts to Obtain Relief: Akan Women and Family Courts in Ghana." In *Poverty in the 1990s: The Responses of Urban Women*, ed. Fatima Meer, 1994.

Minkley, Catherine. "'I Shall Die Married to the Beer': Gender, 'Family,' and Space in the East London Locations, c. 1923–1952." *Kronos: Journal of Cape History* 23 (1996): 135–57.

Mitullah, Winnie. "Hawking as a Survival Strategy for the Urban Poor in Nairobi: The Case of Women." *Environment and Urbanization* 3, 2 (1991): 13–22.

Moodie, T. Dunbar, and Vivienne Ndatshe. "Town Women and Country Wives: Migrant Labour, Family Politics and Housing Preferences at Vaal Reefs Mine." *Labour Capital and Society* 25, 1 (1992): 116–32.

Muchena, Olivia N. *Women in Town*. Harare: University of Zimbabwe, 1980.

Mudimu, Godfrey D. "Urban Agricultural Activities and Women's Strategies in Sustaining Family Livelihoods in Harare, Zimbabwe." *Singapore Journal of Tropical Geography* 17, 2 (1996): 179–94.

Mupedziswa, Rodrick, and Perpetua Gumbo. *Women Informal Traders in Harare and the Struggle for Survival in an Environment of Economic Reforms*. Uppsala: Nordiska Afrikainstitutet, 2000.

———. *Structural Adjustment and Women: Informal Sector Traders in Harare, Zimbabwe*. Uppsala: Nordiska Afrikainstitutet, 1998.

Nelson, Nici. "How Women and Men Get By: The Sexual Division of Labour in the Informal Sector of a Nairobi Squatter Settlement." In *Casual Work and Poverty in Third World Cities*, ed. Ray Bromley and Chris Gerry, 283–302. New York: John Wiley and Sons, 1979.

———. "'Women Must Help Each Other': The Operation of Personal Networks among Buzaa Beer Brewers in Mathare Valley, Kenya." In *Women United, Women Divided: Comparative Studies of Ten Contemporary Cultures*, ed. Patricia Caplan and Janet Bujra, 77–98. Bloomington: Indiana University Press, 1979.

Niehaus, Isak A. "Domestic Dynamics and Wage Labour: A Case Study among Urban Residents in Qwaqwa." *African Studies* 47, 2 (1988): 121–43.

Nimpuno-Parente, Paula. "The Struggle for Shelter: Women in a Site and Service Project in Nairobi, Kenya." In *Women, Human Settlements, and Housing*, ed. Caroline O. N. Moser and Linda Peake. London: Tavistock, 1987.

Njeru, Enos H. N., and John M. Njoka. "Women Entrepreneurs in Nairobi: The Socio-Cultural Factors Influencing Their Investment Patterns." In *Negotiating Social Space: East African Microenterprises*, ed. Patrick O. Alila and Paul Ove Pedersen, 141–74. Trenton, N.J.: Africa World Press, 2001.

Njoh, Ambe J. "Gender-Based Discrimination in Housing and Urban Development Policies in Cameroon." In *The Feminization of Development Processes in Africa: Current and Future Perspectives*, ed. Valentine Udoh James and James S. Etim. Westport, Conn.: Greenwood, 1999.

Ntege, Hilda. "Women and Urban Housing Crisis: Impact of Public Policies and Practices in Uganda." *Economic and Political Weekly* 28, 44 (30 October 1993): 46–62.

Obbo, Christine. *African Women: Their Struggle for Economic Independence.* London: Zed Press, 1980.

Okojie, Christiana E. E. "Female Migrants in the Urban Labour Market: Benin City, Nigeria." *CJAS* 18, 3 (1984): 547–62.

Okpala, Amon O. "Female Employment and Family Size among Urban Nigerian Women." *Journal of Developing Areas* 23, 3 (1989): 439–56.

Olurode, Lai. "Women in Rural–Urban Migration in the Town of Iwo in Nigeria." In *The Migration Experience in Africa*, ed. Jonathan Baker and Tade Akin Aina, 289–302. Uppsala: Nordiska Afrikainstitutet, 1995.

Onibokun, Adepoju, and Adetoye Faniran, ed. *Women in Urban Land Development in Africa: Case Studies from Nigeria, Ghana and Tanzania.* Ibadan: Centre for African Settlement Studies and Development, 1995.

Oruwari, Yomi. "The Changing Role of Women in Families and Their Housing Needs: A Case Study of Port Harcourt, Nigeria." *Environment and Urbanization* 3, 2 (1991): 6–12.

———. "New Generation Churches and the Provision of Welfare: A Gender Study from Port Harcourt, Nigeria." In *Associational Life in African Cities: Popular Responses to the Urban Crisis*, ed. Arne Tostensen, Inge Tvedten, and Mariken Vaa, 64–73. Uppsala: Nordiska Afrikainstitutet, 2001.

———. "Planners, Officials, and Low Income Women and Children in Nigerian Cities: Divergent Perspectives over Housing and Neighborhoods." *CJAS* 37, 2–3 (2003): 396–410.

Otunga, Ruth Nabwala, Grephus Opata, and Fred Nafukho Muyia. "Women Entrepreneurs in Eldoret Town: Their Socio-Economic Background and Business Performance." In *Negotiating Social Space: East African Microenterprises*, ed. Patrick O. Alila and Paul Ove Pedersen, 121–40. Trenton, N.J.: Africa World Press, 2001.

Parpart, Jane L. "'Where is Your Mother?': Gender, Urban Marriage, and Colonial Discourse on the Zambian Copperbelt, 1924–1945." *IJAHS* 27, 2 (1994): 241–71.

Pearce, Tola Olu, Olufemi O. Kujore, and V. Aina Agboh-Bankole. "Generating an Income in the Urban Environment: The Experience of Street Food Vendors in Ile-Ife, Nigeria." *Africa* 58, 4 (1988): 385–400.

Pellow, Deborah. "From Accra to Kano: One Woman's Experience." In *Hausa Women in the Twentieth Century*, ed. Catherine Coles and Beverly Mack, 50–68. Madison: University of Wisconsin Press, 1991.

Penvenne, Jeanne. "Seeking the Factory for Women: Mozambican Urbanization in the Late Colonial Era." *Journal of Urban History* 23, 3 (1997): 342–79.

Pine, Frances. "Family Structure and the Division of Labor: Female Roles in Urban Ghana." In *Introduction to the Sociology of 'Developing Societies,'* ed. Hamza Alavi and Teodor Shanin, 387–405. London: Macmillan, 1982.

Pittin, Renée. *Women and Work in Northern Nigeria: Transcending Boundaries.* Hampshire, England: Palgrave Macmillan, 2002.

Power, Joey. "'Eating the Property': Gender Roles and Economic Change in Urban Malawi, Blantyre-Limbe, 1907–1953." *CJAS* 29, 1 (1996): 78–106.

Preston-Whyte, Eleanor. "'Invisible Workers': Domestic Service and the Informal Economy." In *South Africa's Informal Sector*, ed. Eleanor Preston-Whyte and Christian Rogerson, 34–53. Cape Town: Oxford University Press, 1991.

Rakodi, Carole. "Self-Reliance or Survival? Food Production in African Cities, with Particular Reference to Zambia." *African Urban Studies* 21 (1985): 53–63.

———. "Urban Agriculture: Research Questions and Zambian Evidence." *JMAS* 26, 3 (1988): 495–515.

Rasing, Thera. *The Bush Burnt, the Stones Remain: Female Initiation Rites in Urban Zambia.* New Brunswick, N.J.: Transaction, 2002.

Renaud, Michelle Lewis. *Women at the Crossroads: A Prostitute Community's Response to AIDS in Urban Senegal.* Newark, N.J.: Gordon and Breach, 1997.

Ridd, Rosemary. "Where Women Must Dominate: Response to Oppression in a South African Urban Community." In *Women and Space: Ground Rules and Social Maps*, ed. Shirley Ardener, 187–204. Providence, R.I.: Berg, 1993.

Robertson, Claire. *Sharing the Same Bowl: A Socioeconomic History of Women and Class in Accra, Ghana.* Bloomington: Indiana University Press, 1984.

———. *Trouble Showed the Way: Women, Men, and Trade in the Nairobi Area, 1890–1990.* Bloomington: Indiana University Press, 1997.

Rogerson, Christian. "Home-Based Enterprises of the Urban Poor: The Case of Spazas." In *South Africa's Informal Economy*, ed. Eleanor Preston-Whyte and Christian Rogerson, 336–44. Cape Town: Oxford University Press, 1991.

Rorich, Mary. "Shebeens, Slumyards and Sophiatown: Black Women, Music and Cultural Change in Urban South Africa c. 1920–1960." *World of Music* 3, 1 (1989): 78–101.

Salih, Alawiya Osman M. "Women in Trade: Vendors in Khartoum Area Markets." *Ahfad Journal* 3, 2 (1986): 37–40.

Sanjek, Roger. "The Organization of Household in Adabraka: Toward a Wider Comparative." *Comparative Studies in Society and History* 24, 1 (1982): 57–103.

Saunders, Margaret O. "Women's Role in a Muslim Hausa Town (Mirria, Republic of Niger)." In *A World of Women: Anthropological Studies of Women in the Societies of the World*, ed. Erika Bourguignon, 57–86. New York: Praeger, 1980.

Scarnecchia, Timothy. "Mai Chaza's Guta Re Jehova (City of God): Gender, Healing and Urban Identity in an Independent Church." *JSAS* 23, 1 (1997): 87–105.

Schildkrout, Enid. "Women's Work and Children's Work: Variations among Moslems in Kano." In *Social Anthropology of Work*, ed. Sandra Wallman, 69–85. New York: Academic Press, 1979.

Schlyter, Ann. *Women Householders and Housing Strategies: The Case of George, Lusaka*. Gavle: National Swedish Institute for Building Research, 1988.

———. *Women Householders and Housing Strategies: The Case of Harare, Zimbabwe*. Gavle: National Swedish Institute for Building Research, 1989.

———. "Women in Harare: Gender Aspects of Urban–Rural Interaction." In *Small Town Africa: Studies in Rural–Urban Interaction*, ed. Jonathan Baker, 182–91. Uppsala: Scandinavian Institute of African Studies, 1990.

Schoepf, Brooke Grundfest, and Walu Engundu. "Women's Trade and Contributions to Household Budgets in Kinshasa." In *The Real Economy of Zaire: The Contribution of Smuggling and Other Unofficial Activities to National Wealth*, ed. Janet MacGaffey, 124–51. Philadelphia: University of Pennsylvania Press, 1991.

Schulz, Dorothea E. "The World is Made by Talk: Female Youth Culture, Pop Music Consumption, and Mass-Mediated Forms of Sociality in Urban Mali." *CEA* 42, 168 (2002).

Schuster, Ilsa. *New Women of Lusaka*. Palo Alto, Calif.: Mayfield Publishing, 1979.

Sheldon, Kathleen. "*Machambas* in the City: Urban Women and Agricultural Work in Mozambique." *Lusotopie* (1999): 121–40.

———. "Markets and Gardens: Placing Women in the History of Urban Mozambique." *CJAS* 37, 2/3 (2003): 358–95.

———. "Sewing Clothes and Sorting Cashew Nuts: Factories, Families, and Women in Beira, Mozambique." *WSIF* 14, 1/2 (1991): 27–35.

———, ed. *Courtyards, Markets, City Streets: Urban Women in Africa*. Boulder, Col.: Westview, 1996.

Shephard, Gill. "Rank, Gender, and Homosexuality: Mombasa as a Key to Understanding Sexual Options." In *The Cultural Construction of Sexuality*, ed. Pat Caplan, 240–70. London: Tavistock, 1987.

Simard, Gisèle. "The Case of Mauritania: Women's Productive Activities in Urban Areas—A Process of Empowerment." In *Women, Work, and Gender Relations in Developing Countries: A Global Perspective*, ed. Parvin Ghorayshi and Claire Bélanger, 152–66. Westport, Conn.: Greenwood, 1996.

Simon, D. "Responding to Third World Urban Poverty: Women and Men in the Informal Sector in Windhoek, Namibia." In *Women's Role in Changing the Face of the Developing World*, ed. Janet Henshall Momsen and Janet Townsend. Durham: Institute of British Geographers, 1984.

Sithole-Fundire, Sylvia et al., ed. *Gender Research on Urbanization, Planning, Housing and Everyday Life: GRUPHEL, Phase One*. Harare: Zimbabwe Women's Resource Centre and Network, 1995.

Slater, Rachel J. "Urban Agriculture, Gender and Empowerment: An Alternative View." *Development Southern Africa* 18, 5 (2001): 635–50.

Strobel, Margaret. *Muslim Women in Mombasa, 1890–1975*. New Haven: Yale University Press, 1979.

Sule, Balaraba B. M., and Priscilla E. Starratt. "Islamic Leadership Positions for Women in Contemporary Kano Society." In *Hausa Women in the Twentieth Century*, ed. Catherine Coles and Beverly Mack, 29–49. Madison: University of Wisconsin Press, 1991.

Togunde, Oladimeji. "Determinants of Women's Employment in Urban Nigeria: The Impact of Socio-Cultural Factors." *Journal of Asian and African Studies* 34, 3 (1999): 279–97.

———. "A Social Structural Analysis of the Effects of Women's Employment on Fertility in Urban Nigeria." *Journal of Developing Societies* 15, 2 (1999): 172–88.

Trager, Lillian. "From Yams to Beer in a Nigerian City: Expansion and Change in Informal Sector Trade Activity." In *Markets and Marketing*, ed. Stuart Plattner, 259–85. Lanham, Md.: University Press of America, 1985.

———. "Women Migrants and Rural–Urban Linkages in South-Western Nigeria." In *The Migration Experience in Africa*, ed. Jonathan Baker and Tade Akin Aina, 269–88. Uppsala: Nordiska Afrikainstitutet, 1995.

Tripp, Aili Mari. "The Impact of Crisis and Economic Reform on Women in Urban Tanzania." In *Unequal Burden: Economic Crises, Persistent Poverty, and Women's Work*, ed. Lourdes Beneria and Shelley Feldman, 159–80. Boulder, Col.: Westview, 1992.

Vaa, Mariken. "Paths to the City: Migration Histories of Poor Women in Bamako." In *Small Town Africa: Studies in Urban–Rural Interaction*, ed. Jonathan Baker, 172–81. Uppsala: Scandinavian Institute of African Studies, 1990.

———. "Self-Employed Urban Women: Case Studies from Bamako." *African Population Studies* 3 (1990): 72–84.

———. "Work, Livelihoods and Family Responsibilities in Urban Poverty." In *Gender and Change in Developing Countries*, ed. Kristi Anne Stølen and Mariken Vaa, 121–46. Oslo: Norwegian University Press, 1991.

Vaa, Mariken, Sally Findley, and Assitan Diallo. "The Gift Economy: A Study of Women Migrants' Survival Strategies in a Low-Income Bamako Neighbourhood." *Labour Capital and Society* 22, 2 (1989): 234–60.

van Santeen, José C.M. "Islam, Gender and Urbanisation Among the Mafa of North Cameroon: The Differing Commitment to 'Home' Among Muslims and Non-Muslims." *Africa* 68, 3 (1998): 403–24.

Verhaegen, Benoit. "La famille urbaine face à la polygamie et à la prostitution, le cas de Kisangani au Zaire." In *Processus d'urbanisation en Afrique, Tome II*, ed. Catherine Coquery-Vidrovitch, 124–30. Paris: L'Harmattan, 1988.

———. *Femmes zairoises de Kisangani: Combat pour la survie*. Paris: L'Harmattan, 1990.

wa Karanja, Wambui. "Women and Work: A Study of Female and Male Attitudes in the Modern Sector of an African Metropolis." In *Women, Education and Modernization of the Family in West Africa*, ed. Helen Ware, 42–66. Canberra: Australian National University Press, 1981.

Wallman, Sandra. *Kampala Women Getting By: Wellbeing in the Time of AIDS*. Athens: Ohio University Press, 1996.

Wan, Mimi Y. "Secrets of Success: Uncertainty, Profits and Prosperity in the Gari Economy of Ibadan, 1992–94." *Africa* 71, 2 (2001): 225–52.

Warkentin, Raija. "Rural and Urban Bira Women: An Anthropological Case Study from Central Africa." *Anthropos* 94, 4–6 (1999): 369–79.

Werthmann, Katja. "Matan Bariki, 'Women of the Barracks': Muslim Hausa Women in an Urban Neighbourhood in Northern Nigeria." *Africa* 72, 1 (2002): 112–30.

Wery, Rene. "Women in Bamako: Activities and Relations." In *Sex Roles, Population and Development in West Africa: Policy-Related Studies on Work and Demographic Issus*, ed. Christine Oppong, 45–62. Portsmouth, N.H.: Heinemann, 1987.

White, Luise. *The Comforts of Home: Prostitution in Colonial Nairobi*. Chicago: University of Chicago Press, 1990.

Yacoob, May. "Ahmadiyya and Urbanization: Easing the Integration of Rural Women in Abidjan." In *Rural and Urban Islam in West Africa*, ed. Nehemia Levtzion and Humphrey J. Fisher. Boulder, Col.: Lynne Rienner, 1987.

OTHER SOURCES

Bibliographies

African Academy of Sciences and the Association of African Women for Research and Development. *Infobank of Gender and Gender-Related Institutions in Kenya*. Academy Science Publ., 1998.

Ardayfio-Schandorf, Elizabeth, and Kate Kwafo-Akoto. *Women in Ghana: An Annotated Bibliography*. Accra: Woeli Publishing Services, 1990.

Azikiwe, Uche. *Women in Nigeria: An Annotated Bibliography.* Westport, Conn.: Greenwood, 1996.

Berrian, Brenda F. *Bibliography of African Women Writers and Journalists (Ancient Egypt to 1984).* Washington, D.C.: Three Continents Press, 1985.

Buchholz, Irmela, Marianne C. Gei-khoibes, and Fred Onyango. *Education and Gender in Namibia 1980–1997: An Annotated Bibliography.* Windhoek: University of Namibia Library, 1998.

Bullwinkle, Davis A. *Women of Eastern and Southern Africa: A Bibliography, 1976–1985.* New York: Greenwood, 1989.

——. *Women of Northern, Western and Central Africa: A Bibliography, 1976–1985.* New York: Greenwood, 1989.

Chadzingwa, M. M. *Women in Development in Southern Africa (Botswana, Lesotho, Malawi, and Zambia): An Annotated Bibliography, Vol. 2: Lesotho.* Wageningen, Netherlands: CTA Technical Centre for Agricultural and Rural Cooperation, 1991.

Coles, Catherine, and Barbara Entwisle. *Nigerian Women in Development: A Research Bibliography.* Los Angeles: African Studies Association, 1985.

Desta, Alem. *Women in Development: An Annotated Bibliography on Women and Development in Africa.* The Hague: Institute of Social Studies, 1983.

Duesterhoeft, Diane M. "Special Periodical Issues about African Women, 1972–1991." *A Current Bibliography on African Affairs* 24, 1 (1992–93): 1–52.

Durban Women's Bibliography Group. *South African Women: A Select Bibliography.* 3rd ed. Johannesburg: South Africa Institute of International Affairs, 1996.

Erickson, Christine. *Women in Botswana: An Annotated Bibliography.* Gaborone: Women and Law in Southern Africa Research Project, 1993.

Giorgis, Belkis Wolde. *A Selected and Annotated Bibliography on Women and Health in Africa.* Dakar: Association of African Women for Research and Development, 1986.

Hafkin, Nancy J. *Women and Development in Africa: An Annotated Bibliography.* UN/ECA Bibl. Series No. 1. Addis Ababa: United Nations, Economic Commission on Africa, African Training and Research Center for Women, 1977. This general bibliography was followed by individual monographs on various countries that were published throughout the 1980s by UN/ECA/ATRCW.

Mascarenhas, Ophelia, and Marjorie Mbilinyi. *Women in Tanzania: An Analytical Bibliography.* Uppsala: Scandinavian Institute of African Studies, 1983.

Moshoeshoe-Chadzingwa, Matšeliso, and Matšeliso Mapetla. *Women in Lesotho: an Annotated Bibliography.* 3rd ed. Roma: Institute of Southern African Studies, National University of Lesotho, 1996.

Mugwaneza, Annie. *Recueil des études et ouvrages ayant trait á la femme rwandaise: Bibliographie analytique*. Kigali: Reseau des femmes oeuvrant pour le developpement rural, 1989.

Mukangara, Fenella. *Women and Gender Studies in Tanzania: An Annotated Bibliography (1982–1994)*. Dar es Salaam: Dar es Salaam University Press, 1995.

Oheneba-Sakyi, Yaw. *Family Planning and Reproductive Health Services in Ghana: An Annotated Bibliography*. Westport, Conn.: Greenwood, 1994.

Zanzig, Heike, and Marianne Weiss. *The Role of Women in Africa: A Selected Bibliography*. Hamburg: Institut für Africa, 1984.

Journals and Periodicals from Africa

Note: This list of publications is limited to those included in the dictionary; see entries in dictionary for further information.

Africa Woman
African Women
Agenda: A Journal about Women and Gender
Ahfad Journal: Women and Change
Awa
Azeb
Echo
Eve: The Essence of Africa's New Woman
Outras Vozes
Rencontres Africaines
Safere: Southern African Feminist Review
Sauti Ya Siti (The Voice of Siti)
Shoeshoe: The Magazine for All Lesotho's Women

Feminist Africa
GENDEReview: Kenya's Women and Development Quarterly
The Gold Coast Woman
Jenda: A Journal of Culture and African Women Studies
Jornal da Mulher
Namibian Woman
Nuvel Fam
Speak Out-Taurai-Khulumani
That Rocky Place: Creative Writing on Women
Voice of Eritrean Women
Voice of Women
WomanPlus
WORDOC Newsletter

Journals: Special Issues on Women and Gender

Africa 50, 4 (1980), "The Interdependence of Women and Men."
Africa Report 22, 1 (1977), "Women in Africa."
Africa Report 26, 2 (1981), "Women and Africa."
Africa Report 28, 2 (1983), "Women in Southern Africa."

Africa Report 30, 2 (1985), "The End of the UN Decade: What Advances for African Women?"

Africa Today 37, 1 (1990), Stanlie M. James, ed., "After the Women's Decade: The Task Ahead for Africa."

Africa Today 47, 3/4 (2001), Elisha P. Renne, ed., "Sexuality and Generational Identitites in Sub-Saharan Africa."

Africa Today 49, 1 (2002), Beverly J. Stoeltje, Kathryn Firmin-Sellers, and Okello Ogwang, eds., "Women, Language, and Law in Africa I."

Africa Today 49, 2 (2002), Beverly J. Stoeltje, ed., "Women, Language, and Law in Africa II."

African Arts 19, 3 (1986).

African Literature Today 15 (1987), Eldred Durosimi Jones, Eustace Palmer, and Marjorie Jones, eds., "Women in African Literature Today."

African Review (Dar es Salaam) 11, 1 (1984), "The Women's Question."

African Studies Review 18, 3 (1975), Edna Bay and Nancy Hafkin, eds., "Women in Africa."

African Urban Notes 2, 2 and 2, 3 (1976–1977), "Women in Urban Africa" in two parts.

African Theatre (2002), Jane Plastow, ed., "African Theatre: Women."

Africana Research Bulletin 6, 4 (1976), "Women of Sierra Leone."

L'Afrique Politique (1998), "Femmes Afriques."

Cahiers d'Etudes Africaines 71, 1 (1977), "Des femmes sur l'Afrique des femmes."

Cahiers d'Etudes Africaines 19, 1–4 (1979), "Gens et paroles d'Afrique."

CJAS 6, 2 (1972), "The Roles of African Women: Past, Present, Future."

Canadian Journal of African History 22, 3 (1988), Audrey Wipper and Harriet Lyons, eds., "Current Research on African Women."

CJAS 30, 1 (1996), Dorothy L. Hodgson and Sheryl McCurdy, ed., "Wayward Wives, Misfit Mothers, and Disobedient Daughters: 'Wicked' Women and the Reconfiguration of Gender in Africa."

Critique of Anthropology 17, 2 (1997), Pauline Peters, ed., "Revisiting the Puzzle of Matriliny in South-Central Africa."

Feminist Studies 29, 3 (2003), women in democratic South Africa.

Gender & History 8, 3 (1996), Nancy Rose Hunt, Tessie R. Liu, and Jean Quataert, eds., "Gendered Colonialisms in African History."

Issue 17, 2 (1989), "Beyond Nairobi: Women's Politics and Policies in Africa, Revisited."

Issue 25, 2 (1997), "African Women in the Age of Transformation: Women's Voices from the Continent."

Journal of Development Studies 17, 3 (1981), "African Women in the Development Process."

Journal of Eastern African Research and Development 15 (1985), Gideon Were, ed., "Women and Development in Africa."

JSAS 10, 1 (1983).

Matutu 19 (1997), "Women and Cinema."

ROAPE 27–28 (1984), "Women, Oppression, and Liberation."

Rural Africana (1975–1976).

Rural Africana 21 (1985).

Signs: Journal of Women in Society and Culture 16, 4 (1991), Bolanle Awe, Susan Geiger, Nina Mba, Marjorie Mbilinyi, Ruth Meena, and Margaret Strobel, eds., "Women, Family, State, and Economy in Africa."

Third World Legal Studies (1994–1995), "Women's Rights and Traditional Law: A Conflict."

Ufahamu 22, 3 (1994), "Gender in Africa."

Women's Studies Quarterly 25, 3/4 (1997), "Teaching African Literatures in a Global Literary Economy."

Films

Note: Further information on these films can be found at the distributors' websites: California Newsreel, www.newsreel.org; Filmakers Library, www.filmakers.com; First Run/Icarus Films, www.frif.com; Women Make Movies, www.wmm.com.

!Nai, The Story of a Kung Woman, by John Marshall and Adrienne Miesman. PBS, 1980.

Asante Market Women, Granda Television. Filmakers Library.

Asylum: Fleeing Genital Mutilation, by Sandy McLeod and Fini Reticker. Filmakers Library, 2003.

Chronicle of a Savanna Marriage, by Stig Holmqvist. Filmakers Library, 1997.

Finzan: A Dance for the Heroes, by Cheick Oumar Sissoko. California Newsreel, 1990.

Fire Eyes: Female Circumcision, by Soraya Mire. Filmakers Library, 1994.

Flame, by Ingrid Sinclair. California Newsreel, 1996.

Goldwidows: Women in Lesotho, by Don Edkins, Ute Hall, and Mike Schlomer. First Run/Icarus Films, 1990.

I Have a Problem, Madam, by Maarten Schmidt and Thomas Doebele. First Run/Icarus Films, 1995.

In the Name of God: Changing Attitudes towards Mutilation. Cadmos Film. Filmakers Library, 1996.

The Life and Times of Sara Baartman—The Hottentot Venus, by Zola Maseko. First Run/Icarus Films, 1998.

Mama Awethu!, by Bethany Yarrow. First Run/Icarus Films, 1993.

Mama Benz. Filmakers Library, 1994.

Ndebele Women: The Rituals of Rebellion, by Shelagh Lubbock. Filmakers Library, 1997.

The Return of Sara Baartman, by Zola Maseko. First Run/Icarus Films, 2003.

Rites, by Penny Dedman. Filmakers Library, 1992.

Selbe: One Among Many, by Safi Faye. Women Make Movies, 1983.

Sisters of the Screen: African Women in the Cinema, by Beti Ellerson. 2002.

These Girls Are Missing: The Gender Gap in Africa's Schools, by Shari Robertson and Michael Camerini. Filmakers Library, 1996.

Women of the Sahel, by Paolo Quaregna and Maharmane Souleymane. First Run/Icarus Films, 1995.

You Have Struck a Rock, by Deborah May. California Newsreel, 1981.

Websites

Africa Action, which has links to many sources on women and women's issues: www.africaaction.org

Africa Women's Forum: http://www.africaleadership.org/AboutUs2.htm.

Africabib.org, an online bibliographic resource on African women: http://www.africabib.org/women.html

African Gender Institute, University of Cape Town: web.uct.ac.za/org/agi

African Partnership for Sexual and Reproductive Health and Rights of Women and Girls (Amanitare): www.amanitare.org

African Women in the Cinema: http://www.founders.howard.edu/beti_ellerson/.

African Women's Development and Communication Network (FEMNET): http://www.femnet.or.ke/.

African Women's Media Center: http://www.awmc.com.

Ahfad University for Women and *Ahfad Journal:* www.ahfad.org

Anglophone and Lusophone African Women Writers: http://www.ex.ac.uk/~ajsimoes/aflit/index.html

Association for Progressive Communication–Africa–Women: http://www.enda.sn/synfev/apcfemafr/indexapc.html

Association of African Women Scholars: http://www.iupui.edu/~aaws/

Baobab for Women's Human Rights: http://www.baobabwomen.org/

Circle of Concerned African Women Theologians: http://www.thecirclecawt.org/

Colletif des femmes du Mali: http://www.h-net.org/~batourer/cofem/

Commission pour l'Abolition des Mutilations Sexuelles (CAMS): http://www.cams-fgm.org

Emang Basadi (Botswana): www.hrdc.unam.na/bw_emangbasadi.htm

Empowering Widows in Development: http://www.oneworld.org/empowering-widows/10countries/index.html

Federation of African Women Educationalists (FAWE): http://www.fawe.org/
Feminist Africa: www.feministafrica.org
Femmes Africa Solidarité: http://www.fasngo.org/
Flame: African Sisters Online: http://www.flamme.org
Foundation for Women's Health, Research, and Development (FORWARD): http://www.forward.dircon.co.uk/
Francophone African Women Writers: http://www.arts.uwa.edu.au/AFLIT/FEMEChome.html
Gender and Women's Studies for Africa's Transformation Project: www.gwsafrica.org
Green Belt Movement: http://www.greenbeltmovement.org/.
Inter-African Committee on Traditional Practices Affecting the Health of Women and Children: http://www.iac-ciaf.ch/
Jenda: A Journal of Culture and African Women Studies: www.jendajournal.com
Maendeleo ya Wanawake: http://www.maendeleo-ya-wanawake.org
Muvman Liberasyon Fam: www.mlfmauritius.org
Niger Delta Women for Justice: www.ndwj.kabissa.org
Pan African Women Liberation Organization: http://www.wougnet.org/Profiles/pawlo.html
Reading Women Writers and African Literatures (Francophone African Women's Writing): http://www.arts.uwa.edu.au/aflit/FEMEChome.html
Safere: Southern African Feminist Review: http://www.inasp.org.uk/ajol/journals/safere
Society for Women and AIDS in Africa: http://www.swaainternational.org/
31st December Women's Movement: www.dec31.org.gh
UNIFEM (United Nations Development Fund for Women): www.unifem.org
United Nations Population Fund (UNFPA): http://www.unfpa.org/gender/faq_fgc.htm
Viva, at the International Institute of Social History: http://www.iisg.nl/~womhist/vivahome.html (includes African history as special subsection of women's history bibliography).
Women and Law in Southern Africa (WLSA): http://www.wlsa.co.zw/
Women of Uganda Network: www.wougnet.org
Women'sNet: www.womensnet.org.za
Women's Action Group, Zimbabwe: http://www.kubatana.net/wag/
Zambia Association for Research and Development: http://www.zard.org.zm/
Zambia National Women's Lobby Group: http://www.womenslobby.org.zm/
Zimbabwe Women's Resource Centre and Network: http://www.zwrcn.org.zw/

About the Author

Kathleen Sheldon is an independent historian who is affiliated as a research scholar with the Center for the Study of Women at the University of California, Los Angeles (UCLA). She has taught African women's history at UCLA and Occidental College, and she served as treasurer of the Women's Caucus of the African Studies Association (U.S.). Her contributions have been recognized with the Catherine Prelinger Scholarship Award from the Coordinating Council of Women in History and smaller awards from the Ford Foundation, the National Women's Studies Association, and the American Council of Learned Societies. She has published widely on African women's history, especially on women in Mozambique, and has contributed entries on African women's history to reference works on historical writing, African history, and the history of ideas. Her articles have been published in edited collections and in *History in Africa*, *International Journal of African Historical Studies*, *Lusotopie*, *Signs*, and *Canadian Journal of African Studies*. Her books include the edited collection *Courtyards, Markets, City Streets: Urban Women in Africa* (Boulder, Col.: Westview, 1996) and *Pounders of Grain: A History of Women, Work, and Politics in Mozambique* (Portsmouth, N.H.: Heinemann, 2002).